Police and Policing Law

The International Library of Essays in Law and Society
Series Editor: Austin Sarat

Titles in the Series:

Police and Policing Law

Edited by

Jeannine Bell

Indiana University, Bloomington, USA

ASHGATE

Published by
Ashgate Publishing Limited
Gower House
Croft Road
Aldershot
Hampshire GU11 3HR
England

Ashgate Publishing Company
Suite 420
101 Cherry Street
Burlington, VT 05401-4405
USA

Ashgate website: http://www.ashgate.com

British Library Cataloguing in Publication Data
  Police and policing law. -- (The international library of
  essays in law and society)
  1. Law enforcement 2. Law enforcement -- United States
  3. Police -- Attitudes 4.Police -- United States -- Attitudes
  I. Bell, Jeannine, 1969--
  363.2'3

Library of Congress Cataloging-in-Publication Data
Police and policing law / edited by Jeannine Bell.
      p.cm. -- (The international library of essays in law and society)
  Includes bibliographical references.
  ISBN 0--7546--2578--8 (alk paper)
    1. Police discretion. 2. Police. 3. Law enforcement. I. Bell, Jeannine, 1969-- II. Series

HV7936.D54P65 2006
363.2--dc22

                                                                    2006044039

ISBN-10: 07546 2578 8
ISBN-13: 978 0 7546 2578 0

Printed in Great Britain by TJ International Ltd, Padstow, Cornwall

Contents

PART IV DISCRETION, RACE AND GENDER

Acknowledgements

The editor and publishers wish to thank the following for permission to use copyright material.

American Society of Criminology for the essays: Stephen D. Mastrofski, Jeffrey B. Snipes, Roger B. Parks and Christopher D. Maxwell (2000), 'The Helping Hand of the Law: Police Control of Citizens on Request', *Criminology*, **38**, pp. 307–42; Richard J. Lundman (1994), 'Demeanor or Crime? The Midwest City Police–Citizen Encounters Study', *Criminology*, **32**, pp. 631–56; James J. Fyfe, David A. Klinger and Jeanne M. Flavin (1997), 'Differential Police Treatment of Male-On-Female Spousal Violence', *Criminology*, **35**, pp. 455–73.

Blackwell Publishing for the essays: John P. Crank (1994), 'Watchman and Community: Myth and Institutionalization in Policing', *Law and Society Review*, **28**, pp. 325–51. Copyright © 1994 Law and Society Association; Steve Herbert (1996), 'Morality in Law Enforcement: Chasing "Bad Guys" with the Los Angeles Police Department', *Law and Society Review*, **30**, pp. 799–818. Copyright © 1996 Law and Society Review; Loretta J. Stalans and Mary A. Finn (1995), 'How Novice and Experienced Officers Interpret Wife Assaults: Normative and Efficiency Frames', *Law and Society Review*, **29**, pp. 287–321; Trish Oberweis and Michael Musheno (1999), 'Policing Identities: Cop Decision Making and the Constitution of Citizens', *Law and Social Inquiry – Journal of the American Bar Foundation*, **24**, pp. 897–923. Copyright © 1999 American Bar Foundation.

Canadian Journal of Economics for the essay: E. Nick Larsen (1996), 'The Effect of Different Police Enforcement Policies on the Control of Prostitution', *Canadian Public Policy – Analyse de Politiques*, **22**, pp. 40–55.

Fordham Urban Law Journal for the essay: Jeffrey Fagan and Garth Davies (2000), 'Street Stops and Broken Windows: *Terry*, Race, and Disorder in New York City', *Fordham Urban Law Journal*, **23**, pp. 457–504.

Northwestern University School of Law for the essays: Richard A. Leo (1996), 'Inside the Interrogation Room', *Journal of Criminal Law and Criminology*, **86**, pp. 266–303. Copyright © 1996 Northwestern University School of Law; Craig D. Uchida and Timothy S. Bynum (1991), 'Search Warrants, Motions to Suppress and "Lost Cases:" The Effects of the Exclusionary Rule in Seven Jurisdictions', *Journal of Criminal Law and Criminology*, **81**, pp. 1034–66. Copyright © 1991 Northwestern University School of Law.

Oxford University Press for the essay: Susan J. Lea, Ursula Lanvers and Steve Shaw (2003), 'Attrition in Rape Cases: Developing a Profile and Identifying Relevant Factors', *British Journal of Criminology*, **43**, pp. 583–99. Copyright © 2003 Centre for Crime and Justices Studies.

Sage Publications, Inc. for the essays: Wesley G. Skogan and Tracey L. Meares (2004), 'Lawful Policing', *Annals of the American Academy of Political and Social Science*, **593**, pp. 66–83; Kenneth J. Novak, James Frank, Brad W. Smith and Robin Shepard Engel (2002), 'Revisiting the Decision to Arrest: Comparing Beat and Community Officers', *Crime amd Delinquency*, **48**, pp. 70–98. Copyright © 2002 Sage Publications.

Taylor & Francis for the essay: Robin Shepard Engel and Jennifer M. Calnon (2004), 'Examining the Influence of Drivers' Characteristics during Traffic Stops with Police: Results from a National Survey', *Justice Quarterly*, **21**, pp. 49–90. Copyright © 2004 Academy of Criminal Justice Sciences. http://www.tandf.co.uk/journals

University of Chicago Press for the essay: David Jacobs and Robert M. O'Brien (1998), 'The Determinants of Deadly Force: A Structural Analysis of Police Violence', *American Journal of Sociology*, **103**, pp. 837–62. Copyright © 1998 University of Chicago.

Every effort has been made to trace all the copyright holders, but if any have been inadvertently overlooked the publishers will be pleased to make the necessary arrangement at the first opportunity.

Series Preface

The International Library of Essays in Law and Society is designed to provide a broad overview of this important field of interdisciplinary inquiry. Titles in the series will provide access to the best existing scholarship on a wide variety of subjects integral to the understanding of how legal institutions work in and through social arrangements. They collect and synthesize research published in the leading journals of the law and society field. Taken together, these volumes show the richness and complexity of inquiry into law's social life.

Each volume is edited by a recognized expert who has selected a range of scholarship designed to illustrate the most important questions, theoretical approaches, and methods in her/his area of expertise. Each has written an introductory essay which both outlines those questions, approaches, and methods and provides a distinctive analysis of the scholarship presented in the book. Each was asked to identify approximately 20 pieces of work for inclusion in their volume. This has necessitated hard choices since law and society inquiry is vibrant and flourishing.

The International Library of Essays in Law and Society brings together scholars representing different disciplinary traditions and working in different cultural contexts. Since law and society is itself an international field of inquiry it is appropriate that the editors of the volumes in this series come from many different nations and academic contexts. The work of the editors both charts a tradition and opens up new questions. It is my hope that this work will provide a valuable resource for longtime practitioners of law and society scholarship and newcomers to the field.

AUSTIN SARAT
William Nelson Cromwell Professor of Jurisprudence and Political Science
Amherst College

Introduction

Around the world, the police are distinctive as an institution and can be identified by the fact that they are given the authority by the state to use force to maintain order (Bayley, 1985). Although the police may not always need to use physical force to control behaviour, the threat of force constitutes a crucial mechanism in the system of social control. In societies governed by the rule of law, in addition to the duty to maintain order – 'order maintenance' – police are also required to enforce the law. This means that the police are charged with apprehending suspects who appear to have violated the law's dictates, but they must do so in a manner that is lawful. Allegiance to order maintenance while respecting the law has been one of the central struggles of the police and perhaps best illustrates the delicate balance that the police are required to maintain in democratic societies. The difficulty that the police face is complicated by task-oriented ambiguity – vagueness in what the law dictates. This collection of essays explores the ways in which public police manage the job put to them and the extent to which the law figures in what they do.

In addition to a focus on the ways in which police officers approach the law, many of the essays in this collection fall squarely into the law and society or sociolegal tradition as empirical explorations of the ways in which law works 'on the ground'. In several essays in this book (see, for example, Leo, Chapter 4; LaFave, Chapter 7; Herbert, Chapter 11; Oberweis and Musheno, Chapter 10; Larsen, Chapter 13, Bell, Chapter 16; Lea *et al.*, Chapter 18), the authors' conclusions are based on data they have collected from police officers working in the field. In some cases, this involved observing and/or interviewing the police. In other cases, the data on which the scholarship is based was originally compiled by the police themselves – arrest records, for example – and is analysed to distill the police approach to real-world situations and to legal categories.

Police Research and the Socio-legal Tradition

There is a long tradition of sociolegal studies on the police. A prominent example includes a study conducted in the late 1950s by the American Bar Foundation (ABF) on the administration of justice. In a one oft-cited essay generated from the ABF data, Joseph Goldstein investigated police power to decide not to invoke the criminal process, even in cases when violation had occurred. Goldstein examined three police decisions: (1) not to enforce narcotic laws; (2) not to enforce felony assault laws when the victim does not sign a complaint; and (3) not to enforce gambling laws. One enduring lesson of this early work was that police decisions not to invoke the criminal process are very rarely publicized yet 'largely determine the outer limits of law enforcement' (Goldstein, 1960, p. 543).

Goldstein's work highlighted an issue that has been a theme in much of the police scholarship since its publication – the frequency with which and the myriad circumstances in which the criminal law is *not* followed. In other words, the very fact that the police are given the ability to decide whether the criminal law will be enforced means that we will not have full enforcement of the law – the investigation of every violation of the law. In democratic societies, some measure of police discretion is a byproduct of the rule of law. For instance, the police are not required to enforce the substantive law unless they can conform to its procedural requirements. Ambiguities in the law itself, limitations of time, personnel and investigative duties also restrict them. Finally, the fact that the police have individualized discretion means that they may decide for their own reasons not to enforce the law. Such reasons may or may not be supported by the state's legislature. For instance, Goldstein found that narcotics officers adopted a policy of trading full enforcement of the narcotics laws for information regarding future drug deals – in other words, if the suspect becomes an informant then charges against him or her may be dismissed or reduced. This is not a harmless use of discretion. Ignoring particular types of behaviour, Goldstein suggests, has the potential to undermine legislative objectives in passing particular laws in the first place (Goldstein, 1960).

Jerome Skolnick's *Justice Without Trial*, appearing soon after Goldstein's essay, was another prominent early sociolegal work that analysed the ways in which the police use the law. Skolnick posited that there is an ideological conflict between norms which govern the maintenance of order and those which mandate accountability to the rule of law. This conflict forces the police to serve at various points as rule enforcer, father, friend, social servant, moralist, street fighter, marksman and an officer of the law (Skolnick, 1967, p. 17). Skolnick found that a number of features – the sociology of police work, officers' stake in maintaining their authority, their socialization, the pressure to produce, as well as the invisibility of the work – had the effect of weakening their ability to adhere to the rule of law (ibid., p. 231).

This collection contains one selection of this early group of foundational sociolegal scholarship on police officers' interaction with the law. Wayne LaFave's essay, 'The Police and the Nonenforcement of the Law – Part II' (Chapter 7), addresses some normative issues that arise when police are given discretion. The essay focuses on whether police officers should ever be entitled to exercise discretion in a way that leads them not to invoke the law. In it, LaFave finds that police officers use a variety of reasons to justify not invoking the law: because the criminal process would be inappropriate or ineffective; because doing so would prevent loss of public respect; and because not invoking the law provides more benefits than invoking the law. LaFave calls for greater recognition of the broad scope of police discretion and for legal principles on which it may be governed (p. 259).

In several studies over the last four decades, sociolegal scholars have tackled the question whether the race of either the officer or of the citizen involved affects the invocation of law. Sociolegal research conducted during the 1950s and 1960s found police officers, the vast majority of whom were white, to hold racial biases (see, for example, Westley, 1953; Skolnick, 1967; Wilson, 1973) While some researchers during this period found officers to invoke the law using objective criteria (Skolnick, 1967, p. 89), others, evaluating the impact of citizens' race on officers' behaviour found that officers applied the law differently in black and white communities (Wilson, 1973; Goldstein, 1960). In some cases this involved a greater tendency to enforce the law when racial and ethnic minorities were involved (Wilson, 1973). Contemporary explorations of the role of police officers' treatment of the law is further explored in Part IV of this volume on 'Discretion, Race and Gender'.

Police and the Law: Patrol, Arrest and Extralegal Decision-making

Police interaction with the law and their approach to following legal dictates are heavily bound to the circumstances in which police officers find themselves. Enforcing the law and maintaining order thrust police officers into several different roles – watchman, investigator, crime fighter, guardians of public safety, therapist and judge. Many of these roles offer different opportunities to interact with the law. It is important to acknowledge the difficulty inherent in fully compartmentalizing police officers' behaviour, since in the course of a single afternoon they may be called upon to fill a variety of different roles. In recognition of the complexity of officers' roles, Parts I, II and III of this volume focus primarily on some of the research that explores how police officers respond to the law in three different contexts – on patrol, as investigators and as law enforcers charged with the duty to arrest.

Maintaining Order versus Enforcing the Law

Police officers' work on patrol has been understood to be entirely different from that performed in their roles as law enforcers. On patrol, police officers' very presence may deter crime, with their actions as 'watchmen' or 'peace officers' consisting of surveillance, assistance to citizens and warning potential criminals. As long as they do not invoke the law, officers' behaviour in this order maintenance role has exceedingly low visibility. Thus, while they are functioning as peacekeepers, officers' behaviour is neither under judicial control nor regulated by executive or legislative mandates (Bittner, 1967). Egon Bittner's study of peacekeeping on 'skid row' found that patrol officers coped with the difficulty of maintaining order not by invoking the law, but rather by relying on a richly particularized knowledge of the people in the area and using an aggressively personal approach in scrutinizing individuals (Bittner, 1967, p. 708). At times, such behaviour may have conflicted with legal mandates – especially those imposed by civil liberties – but officers maintained that their behaviour was appropriate given the norms of skid row society (ibid.).

In police departments organized around reactive policing – which require police officers to spend most of their time in centralized stations waiting to respond to emergencies – patrolling by officers was relatively rare. Few areas were patrolled by the police working in watchman or peace officer modes. The development of community policing was designed to combat crime at least in part by using community-based police officers. This implementation of community policing has led to a reorientation of activities to emphasize the provision of services and also to involve citizens in the local community (Skolnick and Bayley, 1988).

Community policing was intended to be a return to the watchman ideal in which police officers and citizens become co-producers in the project of law enforcement. In reality, however, in some jurisdictions its implementation may have fallen short of the mark. In Chapter 2 John Crank identifies the myth inherent in the idea of the watchman. According to Crank, the myth was transformed with the publication of 'Broken Windows'. Published in the early 1980s, this much-cited essay by James Q. Wilson and George L. Kelling called for increasing neighbourhood safety with the return of police foot patrols in order to bolster residents' feelings of security, maintain order and decrease the number of low-level crimes – 'broken windows' (Wilson and Kelling, 1982). Crank suggests that the broken windows style of policing turned the watchman on its head. Rather than being hesitant to invoke the law, police became aggressive 'superenforcers' of the law (p. 38). Crank points to organizational innovations in the Denver Police Department which, though appearing to manifest some of the qualities of community policing, in the end led to aggressive order maintenance – officers searching for minor violations (p. 40).

The Fourth and Fifth Amendments 'on the Ground' – Search, Seizure and Interrogation

In both proactive situations aimed at uncovering crime previously unknown to the police and reactive situations where the police officers find themselves responding to a crime, police must commence an investigation (LaFave *et al.*, 2000). The US Constitution provides explicit procedural protections that police officers engaging in criminal investigations are required to respect. The Fourth Amendment allows individuals the right to be secure 'in their persons, papers, and effects against unreasonable searches and seizures.' The Supreme Court has interpreted this to mean that, in most cases, prior to commencing a search or seizure police officers must have the requisite level of suspicion – either reasonable suspicion or probable cause, depending on the circumstances. The Supreme Court has also said that, in some cases, the Fourth Amendment requires police officers to have a warrant before commencing a search. As Wesley Skogan and Tracey Meares detail in Chapter 1, the cost of the police ignoring the law is high. In *Mapp* v. *Ohio*[1] the Supreme Court held that evidence obtained by the police in violation of the Fourth Amendment could not be used in a state court. In other words, any evidence obtained in violation of the Fourth Amendment was to be suppressed (p. 8).

In their essays in the book, Jeffrey Fagan and Garth Davies (Chapter 3), Craig Uchida and Timothy Bynum (Chapter 5) and Skogan and Meares (Chapter 1) describe how police officers have wrestled with the law in the Fourth Amendment context. Skogan and Meares describe several empirical studies which investigate how police officers conduct searches. In Chapter 5 Uchida and Bynum deal with a related issue, the cost of the Fourth Amendment exclusionary rule – how often evidence gets excluded from trial proceedings as a result of an illegal search or seizure. Their analysis of motions to suppress in several different cities suggests the exclusionary rule has a very slight cost. In other words, their results indicate that, at least in the contexts they studied, police officers tend to follow the limits imposed by the law.

When police investigation has progressed to the point that they begin interrogation, the Fifth Amendment is implicated, providing that individuals cannot be compelled testify against themselves. In *Miranda* v. *Arizona*[2] the Supreme Court considered what the privilege against self-incrimination meant for police interrogation. In making its decision, the Court looked to a variety of police practices outlined in interrogation manuals and decided that, since custodial interrogation was inherently compulsory, prophylactic measures were needed to ensure that confessions obtained during custodial interrogation were truly voluntary. The Court designed a set of warnings, including warnings of the right to silence and the right to counsel, which had to be given prior to interrogation in order to safeguard the privilege.

The Supreme Court's decision requiring warnings only matters if they are administered prior to interrogation. Richard Leo's groundbreaking essay (Chapter 4), based on observations of

---

[1]   377 US 643 (1961).
[2]   384 US 436 (1966).

interrogation in two jurisdictions, explicitly addresses the issue of whether the police actually administer the warning. Leo finds that the warning is given to suspects prior to interrogation in the vast majority of cases but also that the police have developed a variety of techniques which encourage suspects to speak despite having been warned that they have the right to remain silent.

Discretion in the Decision to Arrest

The law on the books provides limited control of police behaviour in the area of arrest. Police officers' ability to decline to arrest violators has routinely been considered part and parcel of police discretion. Studies have shown that police officers tend to use their discretion frequently, often declining to arrest for everyday violations (Bittner, 1967; Lafave, Chapter 7; Goldstein, 1960; Mastrofski *et al.*, Chapter 9).

A significant category of sociolegal scholarship on arrest has concentrated on the situations in which the police are most likely to make arrests. Early sociolegal scholarship on arrest, based on research conducted in the 1960s, suggested that most arrest situations are reactive – they arise through citizen, rather than police, initiative (Black, 1971). In other words, police officers' invocation of the law arose as a rule of ordinary citizens' desires to wield legal power. Essays published during the last 20 years confirm the reactive nature of arrest and have investigated the extent to which police officers respond to citizens' requests to invoke the law, especially at the high level of arrest. For instance, Mastrofski and his co-authors (Chapter 9) describe the cases in which citizens are able to mobilize the police to administer high level sanctions such as arrest. In contrast to earlier studies, their results show that the law has a strong effect. For instance, citizens who have evidence on their side are most likely to be able to get police officers to make an arrest.

Particular attention has been paid to the effect of extralegal variables on arrest (see, for example, Worden, 1989; Smith and Vischer, 1981) Richard Lundman's essay (Chapter 12) investigates the impact of demeanour – in particular, whether the suspect's hostility is likely to increase the chances that he or she will be arrested. Several of the essays in this volume consider other situational and community-level variables in officers' decisions to arrest. Politics is a situational variable that is briefly explored in Larsen's essay (Chapter 13). He reveals a class bias in the police approach to controlling prostitution in three Canadian cities. The police were much more responsive to middle-class concerns about prostitution than complaints voiced by poorer residents (Larsen, p. 407). In Chapter 8 Kenneth Novak and his co-authors consider whether officers' assignment as either community police officers or patrol officers affects their decisions to arrest. Fagan and Davies (Chapter 3) evaluate order maintenance policing under the 'broken windows' rationale, demonstrating that it has led to an increased number of low-level arrests, many of which are eventually dismissed.

Sociolegal scholarship has also explored police officers' own justifications for their behaviour. In the area of arrest, this has focused on how police officers' norms may lead them to justify making an arrest. In Chapter 10 Trish Oberweis and Michael Musheno explore officers' norms with respect to their identity as police officers. Similarly examining how ideological approaches may mediate officers' approaches to their task, Steve Herbert's essay on norms of officers in the Los Angeles Police Department concentrates on the interrelationship between legality and morality and officers' construction of their work. He finds that in particular circumstances – such as those involving spousal abusers – morality may be used to justify officers' decisions to arrest a suspect.

Discretion, Race and Gender

Situational explanations of police behaviour posit that the likelihood of formal action is influenced by structural characteristics such as the characteristics of the suspect – that is, his or her sex, race, age, demeanour and social class (cf. Lundman, Chapter 12). With respect to gender, scholars have investigated police officers' behaviour in cases in which women are victims – particularly spousal abuse and rape cases. A number of studies in the area of male-on-female spousal violence have focused on evaluating the leniency thesis: police officers are reluctant to arrest men who batter their female partners (see Fyfe, Klinger and Flavin, Chapter 15; Hirschel and Hutchinson, 1992). Research has shown that officers may not wish to enforce the law in this context because they do not consider incidents of domestic violence to be serious violations of law (Hirschel and Hutchinson, 1992).

The essays in Part IV of this volume, evaluating officers' approaches to situations involving female domestic violence and rape victims, provide a nuanced picture of the ways in which gender interacts with the law. In Chapter 14 Loretta Stalans and Mary Finn analyse the differing normative frames used by novice and experienced officers responding to domestic violence cases and the ways in which experience affects their interaction with victims and their decision to arrest. In Chapter 15 James Fyfe and his co-authors provide a compelling re-evaluation of the leniency thesis. Their data compares police officers' responses to domestic violence assaults with officers' responses to other types of violence. In Chapter 18 Susan Lea, Ursula Lanvers and Steve Shaw turn their attention to police officers' approaches to rape cases, evaluating the role of police officers and the rest of the system in the disappearance of such cases from the system as a whole.

Contemporary research on the interaction of the police with minorities has concerned their approach to stopping vehicles, particularly in the context of traffic enforcement, arrest procedures and the use of force. The research has investigated whether police officers are engaging in racial profiling – targeting individuals for either investigation or ill-treatment because the officer concerned believes that persons of their race are more likely to commit crimes. The frequency with which officers have been said to stop African-American drivers has even led researchers to coin the term 'DWB' (driving while black) (Harris, 1999). Focusing on all the myriad behaviours that can occur during a traffic stop, Robin Shepard Engel and Jennifer Calnon (Chapter 17) investigate the contention that minority males are at the highest risk for citations, searches, arrests and use of force during traffic stops.

Two of the essays in the volume evaluate police use of the law when dealing with minorities outside of the context of traffic stops. David Jacobs' and Robert O'Brien's essay (Chapter 6) explores the police use of force and the extent to which theories of racial inequality can explain police killings of civilians. Jeannine Bell's essay (Chapter 16) explores police behaviour in the area of hate crimes – crimes motivated by prejudice on the basis of race, religion or sexual orientation. The police investigation of hate crime is a noteworthy context for two reasons. First, this context assesses police behaviour in cases in which studies have shown minorities to predominate as victims (Bell, 2002). Second, it deals with police officers' approach to higher or constitutional law – in this case the First Amendment.

Conclusion

Much of the recent scholarship on policing expresses broad scepticism regarding the ability of the police to obey the rule of law. The majority of essays in this volume reflect that general trend. In documenting how the law works 'on the ground', sociolegal scholars have documented a significant failure on the part of the police to obey the law. Sometimes the lack of obedience to the rule of law stems from the difficulty of the task – for example, the law's ambiguity (Goldstein, 1960) At other times, police violate the law's procedural constraints to pursue their own investigatory ends (Leo, Chapter 4) In the latter case, police may see such violations of the rule of law as minor given the importance of what they view as their primary task, catching criminals. The work of socio-legal scholars like David Bayley suggests otherwise (Bayley, 2002). There may be significant costs to violating the rule of law: one of these costs may be the law's very effectiveness.

References

Bayley, David H. (1985), *Patterns of Policing: A Comparative International Analysis*, New Brunswick, NJ: Rutgers University Press.

Bayley, David H. (2002), 'Law Enforcement and the Rule of Law: Is There a Tradeoff?', *Criminology and Public Policy*, **2**(1), pp. 133–54.

Black, Donald J. (1971), 'The Social Organization of Arrest', *Stanford Law Review*, **23**, pp. 1087–1111.

Bittner, Egon (1967), 'The Police on Skid Row: A Study of Peacekeeping', *American Sociological Review*, **32**(5), pp. 699–715.

Bell, Jeannine (2002), *Policing Hatred: Law Enforcement, Civil Rights and Hate Crime*, New York: New York University Press.

Goldstein, Joseph (1960), 'Police Discretion not to Invoke the Criminal Process: Low Visibility Decisions in the Administration of Justice', *The Yale Law Journal*, **69**, pp. 543–94.

Harris, David A. (1999), 'The Stories, the Statistics, and the Law: Why 'Driving while Black' matters', *Minnesota Law Review*, **84**, pp. 265–326.

Hirschel, J. David and Hutchinson, Ira W. III (1992), 'Female Spouse Abuse and the Police Response: The Charlotte, North Carolina Experiment', *Journal of Criminal Law and Criminology*, **83**, pp. 73–119.

LaFave, Wayne R., Israel, Jerold H. and King, Nancy J. (2000), *Criminal Procedure* (4th edn), St Paul, MN: West Publishing.

Skolnick, Jerome (1967), *Justice Without Trial*, New York: John Wiley & Sons.

Skolnick, Jerome H. and Bayley, David H. (1988), *Community Policing: Issues and Practices Around the World*, Washington, DC: National Institute of Justice.

Smith, Douglas A. and Visher, Christy A. (1981), 'Street-level Justice: Situational Determinants of Police Arrest Decisions', *Social Problems*, **29**, pp. 167–77.

Westley, William (1953), 'Violence and the Police', *American Journal of Sociology*, **59**, pp. 34–41.

Wilson, James Q. (1973), *Varieties of Police Behavior: The Management of Law and Order in Eight Communities*, New York: Atheneum.

Wilson, James Q. and Kelling, George L. (1982), 'Broken Windows: The Police and Neighborhood Safety', *The Atlantic Monthly*, March, pp. 29–38.

Worden, Robert E. (1989), 'Situational and Attitudinal Explanations of Police Behaviors: A Theoretical Reappraisal and Empirical Assessment', *Law & Society Review*, **23**, pp. 667–711.

Part I
Maintaining Order
versus
Enforcing the Law

[1]

Lawful Policing

By
WESLEY G. SKOGAN
and
TRACEY L. MEARES

Police compliance with the law is one of the most important aspects of a democratic society. Americans expect the police to enforce laws to promote safety and to reduce crime, victimization, and fear, but no one believes that the police should have unlimited power to do so. We expect police to enforce laws fairly according to law and rules that circumscribe their enforcement powers. The existence of these rules justify the claim that police are a rule-bound institution engaged in the pursuit of justice and the protection of individual liberties, as well as the battle against crime. This article reviews research on the extent to which police follow laws and rules, especially constitutional criminal procedure rules, addressing seizures, searches, interrogations, and deadly force. Also reviewed is research pertaining to police adherence to rules governing excessive force, corruption, and racial profiling.

Keywords: constitutionality; interrogation; search and seizure; excessive force; corruption

As the National Research Council's report *Fairness and Effectiveness in Policing: The Evidence* (hereafter referred to as the "committee's report") points out, police compliance with the law is one of the most important aspects of a democratic society. The committee reviewed research on police compliance with the U.S.

Wesley G. Skogan has been a faculty member at Northwestern University since 1971 and holds joint appointments with the political science department and the Institute for Policy Research. His research focuses on the interface between the public and the legal system. Much of this research has examined public encounters with institutions of justice, in the form of crime prevention projects and community-oriented policing. His most recent books on policing are On the Beat: Police and Community Problem Solving *(Westview, 1999) and* Community Policing, Chicago Style *(Oxford University Press, 1997). They are both empirical studies of Chicago's community policing initiative. His 1990 book* Disorder and Decline *examined public involvement in these programs, their efficacy, and the issues involved in police-citizen cooperation in order maintenance. This book won a prize from the American Sociological Association. He is also the author of two lengthy reports in the* Home Office Research Series *examining citizen contact*

Constitution, state laws, and the policies and standards of their own organizations. The existence of these rules justify the claim that police are a rule-bound institution engaged in the pursuit of justice and the protection of individual liberties, as well as the battle against crime. Although the authority of the state granted to police to enforce the laws is circumscribed by the various types of laws we review here, it is also the case that the exercise of police power in the United States takes place largely at the discretion of individual officers. The decision to make a traffic stop or issue a ticket, to make an arrest or issue a stern warning, or to use force to accomplish any of these things is in the hands of officers on the street.

Everything about policing makes this exercise of discretion hard to monitor and control. The organization under which officers work struggles to keep control of its field force. Most police officers work alone or with a partner—not under the constant gaze of an assembly-line foreman. Police officers go out into the night heavily armed, and we know little about what they do there except what they report on pieces of paper that they sometimes fill out to document their activities. Many of the encounters police officers have occur under potentially troublesome circumstances. The individuals whom officers meet during these encounters include alleged offenders, drunks, the homeless, and prostitutes—those with "spoiled" identities. The complaints these individuals may have about their treatment by officers may not be taken very seriously. Because police work outside the public eye, they routinely have opportunities to engage in a laundry list of corrupt activities. Moreover, it is difficult to punish such misbehavior due to the civil service protections afforded police as public employees. In many regions of the country, policing is unionized, and provisions of the labor agreement can further bind the hands of top management when it comes to supervising, rewarding, disciplining, and firing employees.

---

and satisfaction with policing in Britain. Other articles on police-citizen issues include "The Impact of Community Policing on Neighborhood Residents: A Cross-Site Analysis" in Rosenbaum's The Challenge of Community Policing. *He chaired the National Research Council's Committee to Review Research on Police Policies and Practices.*

Tracey L. Meares graduated from the University of Illinois with a B.S. in general engineering in 1988. She then obtained her J.D. with honors from The Law School at The University of Chicago in 1991. After clerking for the Honorable Harlington Wood Jr. of the U.S. Court of Appeals for the Seventh Circuit, she was an Honors Program Trial Attorney for the U.S. Department of Justice in the Antitrust Division. In 1994, she joined the law faculty of The University of Chicago as an assistant professor. In 1999, she accepted a joint appointment as a research fellow at the American Bar Foundation. Her research brings insights from sociological theory and contemporary poverty research to the analysis of criminal law policy. A related group of writings explores the impact of the evolution of law enforcement policy on constitutional criminal procedure, of which "The Coming Crisis of Criminal Procedure," 86 Georgetown Law Journal 1153 (1998) (with Dan Kahan), is a notable example. She is also involved in a large empirical study funded by the Catherine T. and John D. MacArthur Foundation of cooperation between churches (predominantly black) and the police on Chicago's West Side. In "Place and Crime," 73 Chicago-Kent Law Review 669 (1998), she offers a foundational framework for exploring the questions posed by this research, but the work, both theoretical and empirical, is ongoing. She was a member of the National Research Council's Committee to Review Research on Police Policies and Practices.

In addition to this long list of factors, many of the recent innovations reviewed in the committee's report recognize, celebrate, and extend this operational independence. The foundational premise underlying both problem-solving policing and community policing is that community and crime-related problems vary tremendously from place to place and that their causes and solutions are highly contextual. In such contexts, we expect police to use good judgment rather than enforce the letter of the law in order to produce good results. Decentralizing, reducing hierarchy, granting officers more independence, and trusting in their professionalism are the organizational reforms of choice today, not tightening up the management screws to further constrain officer discretion. This is especially true when "we," the segment of the public that has not traditionally had antagonistic relationship with the police, are the ones demanding better outcomes from policing.

> *Most police officers are honest and stay out of serious trouble for their entire careers. Most citizens who come into contact with the police are satisfied with the experience, even when they were on the receiving end of an investigation.*

Somehow, this witches' brew of authority and autonomy usually works out. Most police officers are honest and stay out of serious trouble for their entire careers. Most citizens who come into contact with the police are satisfied with the experience, even when they were on the receiving end of an investigation. There is evidence that it has been working out better and better over time. In a paper reviewing trends in American policing over the course of the twentieth century, historian Samuel Walker (2001a) concludes that police at century's end are better trained, more professional, less likely to use excessive or fatal force, and more effective than they were in previous decades.

But, inevitably, it sometimes does not work out. Police are what the British call "the sharp end of the stick" when it comes to regulating the social and economic relationships in society. Their capacity to use force authoritatively and take lives lawfully in the course of regulating our lives uniquely defines *the police*. We are then led to the task of constructing legal and organizational mechanisms for hemming in the exercise of police discretion and ensuring that it is exercised in accordance with law and public policy. Just how to construct and enforce such rules can be a difficult puzzle. It is not easy to impose these rules, and it is not easy to make them work. This article presents an overview of what is known about the nature and extent of police lawfulness and about the effectiveness of mechanisms to control it. The evidence that it summarizes is documented in detail in the committee's report. Here, we present our main conclusions about this research and our judgments about its implications for policies aimed at ensuring police lawfulness.

How Police Get in Trouble

Since 1934, the Supreme Court has regularly reviewed the practices of local police. Like many early cases, *Brown v. Mississippi* (297 U.S. 278, 1935) evoked the Court's twin concern with racial discrimination—Brown was a black man—and egregious police conduct, in this instance the extraction of a confession through torture. Later cases erected a dense network of rules delimiting police power to stop people on the street, conduct searches, question them in custody, and listen in on their conversations. Taken together, these cases establish what we now recognize as modern constitutional criminal procedure: rules that provide the link between constitutional principles and the daily actions of the police. On their face, these rules greatly constrain the authority of the police. Social scientists know, of course, that pronouncing a rule does not automatically make it so. They are not self-enforcing, and individual officers have to learn and actually follow them. Where they do not, police can get in trouble, and this section reviews what we know about the lawfulness of police activities in the line of duty in several key areas. Neither are the more mundane laws that govern police corruption automatically effective, and corruption is another way that police get in trouble.

Interrogations

Brown involved the lawfulness of an interrogation. It was followed by a line of cases reviewing under the due process clause of the Constitution the appropriate and voluntary nature of police questioning of suspects and taking of confessions. *Miranda v. Arizona* (372 US. 436, 1966), one of the best-known and most thoroughly researched Supreme Court decisions, represents a break in this sort of decision making. Rather than reviewing the voluntarism of Miranda's confession under due process principles, the Court imposed on police via the Fifth Amendment responsibility for delivering the famous four-part warning, which is familiar to any regular viewer of television drama, to any suspect during a custodial interrogation. In fact, *Miranda's* four-part warning may be the best-known element of criminal procedure. Initially, the *Miranda* decision was criticized for "hamstringing" police in the pursuit of criminals, but in *Dickerson v. United States* (120 S. Ct. 2326, 2000), even a Supreme Court that might have threatened the ruling decided instead that it "has become embedded in routine police practice to the point where the warnings have become part of our national culture (p. 2336)."

Miranda presented a natural case for social research. It involves a clearly observable requirement (the four warnings) that might be followed or ignored, and its critics posed a hypothesis to be tested (it would hamstring the police). The studies that followed paint an ironic picture of *Miranda* in action: it seems that the police follow the rule, and it does not have much effect.

The first big study of *Miranda* did not actually come to that complete conclusion. Donald Black and Albert Reiss Jr. had a large field study of police operations under way when the decision was announced. They added the warning to the checklist of things their observers were looking for as they rode along with officers. They found that the required warnings were frequently not given when police arrested suspects, but they also found that for felonies, there was typically alternate physical evidence and eyewitness testimony that police could rely on (Black and Reiss 1967). Subsequent studies have almost universally found high levels of verbal compliance with this constitutional requirement, so it is likely that the low compliance rate they observed was an artifact of the timing of the Black and Reiss project. For example, Leo (1996) observed detectives at work and found essentially 100 percent compliance with the letter of the law.

Other studies have confirmed the other Black and Reiss conclusion: in routine cases, confessions are rarely the only evidence available for submission to the prosecutor. This is one of the factors that has mitigated the impact of *Miranda*, belying the early charge that it would severely undercut the crime-fighting effectiveness of the police. The reason that the existence of nonconfessional evidence can undercut the sting of *Miranda*'s exclusionary rule in situations in which police do follow *Miranda*'s prescriptions is that *Miranda*'s exclusionary rule requires that only a tainted confession be excluded from trial, not other evidence. Another mitigating influence on *Miranda*'s bite is the strategic manner in which police deliver the message. Leo noted how police presented the four warnings in ways that encouraged suspects to waive their rights. Terms like *perfunctory* and *superficial* are used by researchers to describe police delivery. Cassell and Hayman (1996) also observed a number of "noncustodial" interviews that took place (technically, legally) without warnings, presumably in an attempt to skirt the requirement. In a summary, Meares and Harcourt (2000) concluded that in practice, *Miranda* may reduce the number of confessions between 4 and 16 percent, but the availability of other evidence means that its real impact is considerably lower than that range.

Searches and seizures

Seizing people and searching them and their properties are basic law enforcement tools. Searches and seizures are vital to removing weapons and contraband from the street, building criminal cases, and potentially preventing crime. But searches and seizures can also be extremely problematic for police. While Americans recognize that searches and seizures are necessary tools for police to do their jobs of maintaining order and responding to criminal events, Americans have always feared the misuse of these intrusions by the state into their lives. The Fourth Amendment speaks directly to "the right of the people to be secure in their persons, houses, papers and effects, against unreasonable searches." Through its interpretation of the Fourth Amendment, the Supreme Court has established concepts such as "probable cause" and "reasonable suspicion" in criminal procedure cases as the standard for justifying different types of searches and seizures.

The principal tool for enforcing judicially imposed injunctions against unreasonable police conduct is the exclusionary rule, which applies both to state and federal prosecutions. A deterrence model underlies the logic of the decision: the rule that a demonstrably bad guy can earn a "get out of jail free card" if the evidence required to convict him (perhaps a seized gun or trunk load of drugs) was obtained improperly is supposed to keep police and prosecutors in line.

Research in this area attempts to document the extent of police propriety and the factors associated with rule bending versus rule minding. Much of it has been reactive to changes in legal standards. A large body of research was stimulated by the Supreme Court's decision in *Mapp v. Ohio* (367 U.S. 643, 1961) to extend the Fourth Amendment exclusionary rule to the states. More appeared in the wake of follow-up search-and-seizure cases. These include *Terry v. Ohio* (392 U.S. 1, 1968), which justifies pat-down searches under the rubric of Fourth Amendment reasonableness by sanctioning them so long as police could demonstrate reasonable suspicion; *United States v. Calandra* (414 U.S. 338, 1974), which balances the exclusion of evidence against its deterrent effect; and *United States v. Leon* (486 U.S. 897, 1984), which permits the use of evidence obtained faultily but in good faith. Because they have been reactive, there are few before-and-after studies assessing the impact of these new rules for police conduct, even though many of them read as if that were their goal.

Search-and-seizure actions by individual officers have been examined in a variety of ways. Researchers have ridden with detectives or interviewed them in the stationhouse, passed out questionnaires to uniformed officers, and observed encounters between the police and the public in the field. Collectively, these studies indicate that police mostly follow the rules, but sometimes, they do not. Officers know the rules, but they sometimes skirt constitutional standards because they want to deter crime by incarcerating the truly guilty. Or if deterrence is not their immediate goal, officers sometimes bend rules because they simply want an individual that they have identified as a lawbreaker to get his or her "due" in a sort of retributive justice sense. Officers can be quite strategic in pursuing these goals, including risking a bit of censure when they have other forms of evidence to fall back on if their actions are challenged. Several studies found that officers intent on seizing contraband, disrupting illicit networks, or asserting their authority on the street freely violated the rules because their goal was not principally to secure an individual conviction.

One of the most recent of these studies involved observations of what happens when police confront citizens in the field. The study (Gould and Mastrofski forthcoming) documents that field searches are fairly uncommon. Trained observers in two cities spent in total more than 2,800 hours in the field observing 12,000 police-citizen encounters. During this period, they observed just 115 searches. About 30 percent were judged to be unconstitutional, but only 10 percent of those (and just 3 percent of all searches) involved what they classified as egregious police miscon-duct. About 7 percent of suspects who were arrested or cited were searched improperly. Most improper searches occurred when officers were looking for drugs, a finding that is consistent with earlier work on detective practices. Most of the observed violations involved frisking suspect's outer clothing and were not par-ticularly invasive. The authors describe the officers involved as "respectful, even solicitous," and not distinguishable by their attitudes or other behaviors. Most of the rule violations arose during encounters that did not ultimately lead to an arrest or citation, so no record of them was left behind.

Another large study examined the lawfulness of street encounters in New York City. The New York Office of the Attorney General (1999) analyzed forms that are supposed to be completed by officers when they conduct a stop and frisk. On their face, the stops described there were judged to violate *Terry* standards 14 percent of the time (Fagan and Davies 2000). Two measures were also used to test whether there was racial bias in the stops themselves. One compared stops by race with the race of the neighborhood in which they occurred, while the other made a similar adjustment for the racial makeup of arrests in the area as a proxy for who the trou-blemakers there were. Both analyses suggested that African Americans were disproportionately stopped.

Researchers have used case files to assess the magnitude of search-and-seizure issues and their aggregate consequences at the system level. To assess the cost of excluding evidence of guilt, studies have counted lost convictions and concluded that they are not particularly frequent. Sutton's (1986) study tracked a large sample of cases in seven cities. He found that search warrants were rarely used, judges gave only perfunctory review of warrant applications, and the participants sub-verted the process by fabricating evidence when necessary. Other researchers have done pre-post studies of the impact of *Leon* and found no impact on police practices (Uchida and Bynum 1991).

Excessive and lethal force

The use of force is so integral to the police role that a common definition of the term *police* is the body that is lawfully authorized to exercise deadly force against citizens. As a price for holding a virtual monopoly over this power, there are stan-dards for the use of force, standards that are too often violated. In the United States, use of deadly force has been a major source of conflict between minority groups and the police. Numerous studies have demonstrated large discrepancies between the rate at which African Americans are shot and killed by the police and the comparable rate for whites. One found that between 1950 and 1960, African Americans were killed by Chicago police at a rate of 16.1 per 100,000, compared with a rate of 2.1 per 100,000 for whites (Robin 1963).

The constitutional rule adopted by the Court to circumscribe the use of deadly force by police officers is found in *Tennessee v. Garner* (471 U.S. 1, 1985). In this case, the Supreme Court overturned a permissive fleeing-felon rule that allowed police officers to use "all the means necessary to effect an arrest" of even an unarmed fleeing felon. The case arose from the killing of a fifteen-year-old African American male in suburban Memphis, and it was imbued with racial tensions. Interestingly, few of the states whose statutes on this matter did not comply with the Court's ruling were willing to change them; the states relied instead on departments to change their policies and procedures. Generally, police are now authorized to use force in self-defense or when a life is in danger, when certain forcible felons flee, or when other means have been exhausted. Both deadly force and excessive force claims are also grounds for civil suits under state tort law and federal civil rights laws.

Officers know the rules, but they sometimes skirt constitutional standards because they want to deter crime by incarcerating the truly guilty.

This is a difficult research area. There is no national repository of data on police use of force, and access to local records is difficult. Virtually every study has been based on the records of one or a small number of local police departments. Official case files inevitably present a situation in which every incentive exists for the organization to present a favorable version of events. Studies conducted in agencies that voluntarily open their records to researchers probably represent those that are most confident of their professionalism. Studies of agencies that are forced to open their records because of suits alleging use of excessive force, or through freedom of information suits by media organizations, tend to find more racial disparity in the use of force, great deals of disparity in the use of deadly force, and higher rates of shootings of racial minorities that appear to be questionable (Fyfe 2002). For example, Meyer (1980) found that African Americans in Los Angeles were more often unarmed when they were shot, and Fyfe (1982) found that African Americans in Memphis were more often shot in circumstances that were not as threatening to the officer.

One firm conclusion that can be drawn from this research is that rates of police use of force and deadly force are highly variable. In a recent study, Fyfe (2002) analyzed the results of a project conducted by the *Washington Post*. Using freedom of information requests and suits, they assembled data on fatal police shootings in fifty-one large municipal and county police and sheriff's departments during 1990 to 2000. Fatal shootings rates for county police departments varied by a factor of 14, while for city departments, the ratio of shootings from top to bottom was 8:1

and among sheriff's departments it was almost 6:1. In a seven-city study by Milton et al. (1977), the top to bottom ratio was also 6:1. Another general conclusion is that most police use of force is nonfatal. In one six-agency study, only 17 percent of "potentially volatile encounters" (a high-risk sample of incidents) led to the use of force, and most of the force was confined to threats, use of restraints, weaponless tactics, and control holds (Garner and Maxwell 1999). A final conclusion is that there is usually considerable racial disparity in the use of force and often in the use of fatal force. Many see such disparities in the exercise of force lying at the core of challenges to the legitimacy of American policing in the twenty-first century.

There is also evidence of the positive effects of legal and administrative efforts to control police use of force. Many before-and-after studies of changes in department rules or leadership find evidence that management makes a difference. In a study of the use of force by the New York Police Department, Fyfe (1979) found that a policy change by the agency led to a precipitous drop in shootings by officers there. He also found that New York City police rarely shot unarmed people. Sparger and Giacopassi (1992) conducted a follow-up study in Memphis, the jurisdiction in which the *Garner* decision originated, and found a dramatic reduction in racial disparities in police shootings in the post-*Garner* period. Tennenbaum (1994) concluded that *Garner* reduced fatal police shootings by about sixty per year.

Corruption

The previous sections reviewed research in which the disjuncture between police activity and legal standards ostensibly and typically were grounded in the officers' desire to pursue public ends. However, police also deviate from the law for personal gain. Corruption is to a certain extent endemic in police departments because of the attractive opportunities officers can face when deciding when and how to enforce the law. The range of what constitutes corruption is a wide one and, at the lower end, depends on department policies. "Police discounts" for meals and haircuts fall at one end of the continuum, which widens to include the sale of inside information, accepting bribes not to enforce the law or to testify falsely, and even payoffs to secure advancement within the department. Corruption may be proactive, as when officers seek out and rob street drug dealers, or reactive to offers large and small from community members. Some researchers include so-called noble-cause corruption in their inventories. This includes investigating, arresting, and "testi-lying" people who are "deserving" of punishment, whatever the "legal niceties." It is not clear, however, whether including these practices increases our ability to understand the scope and frequency of corruption for gain or if it just muddies the concept. Other important distinctions are whether corruption is organized or freelance work, if it is widespread or found only in isolated pockets, if it permeates management ranks or is confined to street officers, and if it is linked to more widespread political corruption or is largely confined to police ranks.

Corruption is not only hard to control but also hard to study systematically. Much of what we know in any detailed fashion flows from investigations and testimony collected by commissions set up in response to public uproar over revelations of corruption. New York City provides a treasure trove of these reports, including those of the Knapp Commission (City of New York 1973) and the Mollen Commission (City of New York 1994). Sherman (1978) used media reports and investigatory material like these commission reports to develop comparative case studies of corruption and reform efforts in four cities. He concluded that corruption was highly organized before it surfaced in public view. Another approach is to survey officers. While self-report surveys are unlikely to uncover revelations of any but the smallest scale side benefits of serving the public, Klockars et al. (2000) and others have demonstrated that it is quite fruitful to ask police about the practices of others in their agency, the "climate of opinion" among their peers concerning corruption, their awareness of the rules concerning misconduct, their support for imposing discipline, and their (hypothetical) willingness to report various kinds of misconduct internally. For example, Klockars et al. (2000) surveyed officers in thirty American police departments and found that, overall, a majority would not report a colleague who engaged in the least serious misbehavior (e.g., accepting free meals and discounts) but that they would report someone who engaged in behaviors judged to be at intermediate or high levels of seriousness (e.g., accepting kickbacks from an auto repair shop for referrals, turning in a lost wallet while keeping the cash from that wallet). Their study also found that police departments varied considerably in the climate of integrity.

Surveys have also asked the general public whether they had been required to bribe public officials, including the police, and these open an alternative window into the extent of that problem. Some of these, conducted in a number of countries, lend a comparative aspect to experiences with police corruption. Unfortunately, no studies have compared police with any other occupation's corruption rate, for this would provide a useful avenue for testing hypotheses involving some of the reputedly unique features of police work.

What seems to lead to corruption? As noted above, many of the most important explanations are systemic in character. History provides evidence of the importance of very broad social and regulatory factors, for probably no event had a greater corrupting effect on police and the American political system generally than did the passage of a constitutional amendment prohibiting the manufacture and sale of alcoholic beverages in the 1920s. Today's equivalent is drugs. Police work combines high discretion with low-visibility decision making in an environment that can be awash with tempting opportunities and an ample supply of "regular" citizens willing to offer up even more. The drug dealers, prostitutes, and others that officers routinely deal with can be robbed or abused with relative impunity. Narcotics units are especially prone to problems because of the very large sums of money and drugs that come their way, the willingness of both buyers and sellers in the marketplace to pay bribes to avoid regulation, and the very low visibility of the many discretionary decisions that are made on a daily basis by investigators and their supervisors (U.S. General Accounting Office 1998; Manning and Redlinger 1977). Officers whose opportunities for career advancement have come to an end may be more prone to being on the take. Corruption is very much facilitated by tolerance—or at least passive unresponsiveness—by peer officers in the organization. Integrity, on the other hand, can be measured by officers' support for the rules, their belief that internal complaints will be investigated fully and fairly, and their willingness to report misconduct (Klockars et al. 2000). The public's standards concerning what constitutes intolerable corruption may set an upper boundary on how out of hand corruption may get, and the views of the politicians who represent them are probably even more directly important. The aggressiveness of local and federal prosecutors, and the intrusiveness of the media, also determine how much can go on before heads start to roll.

Racial profiling

No controversy in law enforcement today has received more attention than racial profiling. There is no ready agreement on what the term means, however. While the law enforcement community has defined *racial profiling* as the practice of stopping citizens solely or exclusively because of their race, many others use the term to refer to police using race in any way in deciding whom to stop or search, except in the instance when race is part of a specific description of a wanted offender. Police have defended the legitimacy of considering race along with other factors with respect to their decision to stop, search, or otherwise engage citizens, arguing that consideration of race in decision making is justified by statistics demonstrating that racial minorities make up a disproportionate number of suspects arrested, convicted, and sentenced nationwide. This stance was quickly challenged by the observation that this proved only that the criminal justice system targeted black male offenders. While this debate continues, there can be little doubt that the term *racial profiling* and the offense known as *driving while black* have become a part of the nation's lexicon. And it seems that the threat of global terrorism will keep the debate alive.

The problem of racial profiling is inextricably intertwined with the fact that police officers have a great deal of discretion in performing their job. Key Supreme Court decisions have further increased the range of police discretion in ways that are relevant to the racial profiling controversy. *Ohio v. Robinette* (519 U.S. 33, 1996) made it easier for police to talk suspects into consenting to a search of their person or vehicle. *Whren v. United States* (517 U.S. 806, 1996) holds that police can make traffic stops to investigate suspicions that have nothing to do with the traffic offense for which the stop was made—so long as there is an offense. These are known as "pretextual traffic stops."

Given that police must make determinations as to how to perform their job, it is not surprising that their judgments could be influenced by racial, ethnic, or gender stereotypes. At some point, this becomes a lawfulness issue, although debate over where the boundary begins and the appropriate penalties continues. For example, a bill introduced (but not passed) during the 107th Congress (*Racial Profiling Pro-*

hibition Act of 2001, HR 1907, 107th Cong., 2nd sess.) defined racial profiling as the consideration of race "to any degree or in any fashion" by an officer when deciding whom to stop or search, except when race is part of a specific description of an offender who committed a crime. The penalties that have been considered include losing federal highway funds and other federal grants. On various hit lists are the Edward Byrne Memorial State and Local Law Enforcement Assistance Programs; the "Cops on the Beat" program under part Q of title I of the Omnibus Crime Control and Safe Streets; and the Local Law Enforcement Block Grant program of the Department of Justice.

The road to police reform is largely an internal one, featuring training, supervision, internal inspections, performance measures, and policy making.

The legal handle for judicial intervention to restrict racial profiling is the constitutional injunction against depriving persons of their rights, privileges, or immunities because of their race, a "legally protected" social category. In the federal system, the Justice Department is authorized to investigate allegations of a pattern or practice of discrimination, and it can file civil litigation against police agencies found not to be in compliance with the Constitution.

However, there is just as much controversy over the extent of racial profiling as there is over its definition or any other part of this issue. The lack of definitional clarity, combined with serious flaws in methods for assessing profiling, make it difficult to identify with any confidence how much of it there is, who is doing it, or whether it is increasing or decreasing in the face of new policies. A large number of agencies are now engaged in new data collection documenting their activities; some of this is voluntary, while many are doing so in the face of municipal or state requirements. But detecting a "pattern of profiling" (whatever that is defined to be) presents difficult data and analytic issues. Studies of the accuracy with which officers complete the forms they are supposed to use to record stops, and the accuracy with which they guess citizens' races, do not point in a hopeful direction. Furthermore, the racial distribution of stops, citations, and even searches does not in itself demonstrate much. Profiling can be identified only by comparing the frequency of encounters to some baseline, a denominator that yields an interpretable stop rate. Some have compared traffic stops by race to the population composition of the neighborhoods in which they were made. This has little to do with the population at risk of being stopped, or even better, the offending population at risk of being apprehended. There have been attempts to standardize stop counts by the racial distribution of drivers, in the expectation that everyone speeds. Traffic offending is not randomly distributed, however, and not all police-initiated encounters involve only traffic offenses. Studies have used the racial distribution of arrests in the area, and even counts of the racial distribution of drivers timed to be actually exceeding the speed limit, to estimate the relative size of offending populations. However, it is clear that the cheap and simple denominators do not adequately represent the population at risk of being stopped and that the effort and expense required to generate more focused and localized measures is far beyond the scope of policing agencies. It is not even clear that the population at risk is the most appropriate baseline measure. To develop policies to address the problem, it is not enough simply to gather information about those stopped; therefore, another way to measure profiling activity might be to focus on the group doing the stopping—police. Common sense suggests that the problem of racial profiling, however defined, is different if a small isolated number of officers are stopping individuals as opposed to a large dispersed group (Walker 2001c). Other strategies that have been proposed for eliminating racial profiling, including in-car video cameras, have not been evaluated.

How Police Can Get Out of Trouble

In the view of the committee, the road to police reform is largely an internal one, featuring training, supervision, internal inspections, performance measures, and policy making. At this level, controlling police behavior is a management problem. For example, a department's use of force policy includes the types of weapons that are made available to officers, the rules for their use, training in weapon safety, reporting requirements when they are employed, procedures for reviewing the appropriateness of their use in an "after-action" report, and the kinds of sanctions that can be imposed for their misuse.

To date, however, little research has examined the effectiveness of managerial strategies to secure officer compliance with department policies. As noted earlier, some the best evidence comes from studies of the use of lethal force, which has shown that administrative changes and determined leadership can reduce shootings by police. Changes in policies governing high-speed pursuits can reduce their number and save lives. Randomized experiments in responding to domestic violence have demonstrated along the way that careful training and supervision can change how officers handle those cases, whatever the eventual findings regarding their effectiveness. Research on corruption points to the importance of leadership, internal accountability, training, internal inspections, and a willingness to challenge informal practices and peer tolerance.

Otherwise, there is not much research on internal police control processes. In particular, virtually no research has studied police internal inspection bureaus, which are increasingly called professional standards units. They are recognized by police leaders to play a critical role in keeping their organizations in line, but little is known about the organization, management, and staffing of these units. Nor is much known about the investigative procedures used or patterns of discipline. Interestingly, unlike the private sector, virtually no research has focused on systems for rewarding good officer performance, through pay or perquisites. Traditionally, police management consists of overseeing subordinates until they break a rule in the book and then punishing them. It is essentially negative, with little in their management kitbag but sanctions for noncompliance; hence, the emphasis on internal inspections to ensure compliance with rules.

If internal processes could be effective at controlling police misconduct, why are so many departments demonstrably lacking effective internal controls? One problem is that there are contrary political and organizational pressures. Calls to get tough on crime can drown out concern about excessive police zeal. In fact, one controversial feature of the committee report itself is that it tried to attend to research on police lawfulness as well as their crime-fighting effectiveness. Public-sector workers, including police and firefighters, are usually well organized on the political front, with independent links to powerful local politicians, state legislators, and the governor's office. Attempts to reform their organizations thus can lead to a tough political fight. In many cities, police departments operate with a significant degree of autonomy, protected by law and order rhetoric, labor agreements, and the political clout of their employees. Calls for administrative reform can seem to fall on deaf ears, when they do not have to listen. Instead, we tend to get individualized, short-term responses to widespread, systemic problems.

In reaction to the perceived inability of departments to manage themselves, external pressure can be mounted in an attempt to reign in police. We have emphasized internal management efforts because ultimately processes have to be put into motion inside the organization to make those changes. In the end, these processes make up the "transmission belt" by which external pressures translate into internal change, and in our judgment, they should be the central focus of reform efforts. Without engaging these, most externally imposed solutions to lawfulness problems will not be very effective.

For example, prosecutors can bring criminal charges against individual police officers accused of using excessive force or engaging in acts of corruption. In addition to exacting justice in that case, we can hope that the message that initiating a prosecution sends sets in motion deterrent processes leading to general changes in behavior within the organization. However, the committee concluded that this is an extremely limited vehicle for changing police organizations. Few cases are brought forward by internal inspectors, prosecutors are wary of indicting the police officers on whom they depend, intent is difficult to document in excessive force cases, it is difficult to convince judges and juries to convict, and the best evidence is that the few sentences that are actually imposed in these cases are light.

The odds of effecting organizational change through civil suits are only a little better. In most states, individual victims can sue police for damages, and federal rules are in place that allow similar cases to be brought. To a certain extent, civil rights and civil liberties groups have begun to use the civil process, again to both

right individual wrongs and force organizational reform. Although they can be difficult to win, these cases can elicit fairly substantial individual payments. Their
deterrent impact is muted, however, because legal fees and judgments are paid
by the city's taxpayers not by individual officers or even (typically) out of the
department's own budget. The limited research on this point also suggests that
departments often do not take meaningful disciplinary action against the officers

---

*Calls to get tough on crime
can drown out concern about
excessive police zeal.*

---

involved, even when they are found at fault in civil court. There is also little evidence of structural changes in big-city police organizations as a result of damage
payments, despite the public lamentations of mayors and city council members
over their cost. It is a cost of doing business, and in actuality, the cost amounts to
only a small fraction of municipal budgets. Patton (1993, 767) concluded that in
Los Angeles, the cost of civil suits is considered "a reasonable price for the presumed deterrent effect of the department's most violent responses to
lawbreaking."

A very limited number of agencies have been swept up in federal "pattern-and-
practice" suits initiated by the civil rights division of the Department of Justice.
Congress empowers the department to conduct investigations and to bring suits
against departments that routinely deprive persons of rights, privileges, or immunities secured or protected by the Constitution. Three features of these cases
promise that they may have more impact than the usual criminal and civil suits.
First, the pattern-and-practice language of the act enables litigation against the
general practices of a police department, as opposed to identifying and holding a
single officer culpable for unlawful actions. Second, the settlement agreements
that arise from these cases include implementing agreed-upon best practices in
new training, internal investigations, use of potentially lethal equipment, and incident reporting. These are the mechanisms for making change in police organizations. Third, there is continued supervision of the settlement agreements. In every
case, a court-appointed monitor watches over its implementation, and in some cities (including Pittsburgh and Cincinnati), universities or nonprofit research groups
monitor the effectiveness of the decrees in resolving the problems that led to them
in the first place. Often, consent decrees require the collection of systematic data

on departmental practices, increasing their transparency. Most have focused on police use of force, but the federal settlement with the New Jersey State Police required the collection of data on traffic stops, and these have been used to monitor for racial disparities. In other words, although they are not numerous, pattern-and-practice settlements are designed to activate the internal organizational mechanisms that we identified at the outset as crucial for sustaining true organizational change.

Citizen-complaint review agencies provide another form of external control of the police. There has been a steady growth in the number of citizen-complaint review agencies in the United States over the past twenty years. By 2001, there were slightly more than a hundred such agencies (Walker 2001b). Virtually all of them are created by local ordinances. They take a variety of forms, and this count used a broad definition that included any procedure where there is some input, however limited, by persons who are not sworn officers in the review of citizen complaints against police officers. Some of these agencies have original jurisdiction for receiving and investigating citizen complaints. Others play an auditing or monitoring function, generally overseeing the internal investigatory actions of departments. They take so many forms and responsibilities that it is difficult to say much in general about them, and the committee's review indicated that so little systematic research on these agencies has taken place that their impact is unknown. Their appearance reflects a widely enough held belief that police internal affairs units, in varying degrees, discourage complaints, fail to investigate complaints thoroughly and fairly, and fail to discipline officers who are found to have committed misconduct. Police and their supporters in turn deny that excessive force is a problem and argue that police departments are better equipped to investigate complaints internally, for no one outside the organization can really understand police work.

Conclusion

The National Research Council's report on policing, *Fairness and Effectiveness in Policing: The Evidence*, emphasizes fairness for a reason. People expect the police to enforce laws to promote safety; to reduce crime, victimization, and fear; and to redress wrongs, but no one believes that the police should have unlimited power to prevent, reduce, or deter crime. In a democratic society, fundamental principles of liberty and justice require the circumscription of the authority of the state to enforce laws. It is police adherence to the rules that limit their power that informs at least one notion of the legitimacy of police operation. The research reviewed here goes some way to demonstrating—at least according to available research—that police tend to obey the law. The more important, and perhaps deeper, question is whether adherence to these rules is enough to establish the legitimacy of a key government institution.

References

Black, Donald, and Albert J. Reiss Jr. 1967. Interrogation and the criminal process. *The Annals of the American Academy of Political and Social Science* 374:47-57.

Cassell, Paul G., and Bret S. Hayman. 1996. Dialog on *Miranda*-police interrogation in the 1990s: An empirical study of the effects of *Miranda*. *UCLA Law Review* 43:840-929.

City of New York, Commission to Investigate Allegations of Police Corruption. 1973. *The Knapp Commission report on police corruption*. New York: George Braziller.

City of New York, Commission to Investigate Allegations of Police Corruption and the Anti-Corruption Procedures of the Police Department. 1994. *Mollen Commission report*. New York: Mollen Commission.

Fagan, Jeffrey, and Garth Davies. 2000. Street stops and broken windows: Terry, race and disorder in New York City. *Fordham Urban Law Journal* 28:457-82.

Fyfe, James J. 1979. Administrative interventions on police shooting discretion: An empirical examination. *Journal of Criminal Justice* 7:309-23.

———. 1982. Blind justice: Police shootings in Memphis. *Journal of Criminal Law and Criminology* 73:702-22.

———. 2002. Too many missing cases: Holes in our knowledge about police use of force. *Justice Research and Policy* 4:87-102.

Garner, Joel H., and Christopher D. Maxwell. 1999. Measuring the amount of force used by and against the police in six jurisdictions. In *Use of force by police: Overview of national and local data*, edited by Jeremy Travis, Jan M. Chaiken, and Robert J. Kaminski, 25-44. Washington, DC: National Institute of Justice and Bureau of Justice Statistics.

Gould, Jon B., and Stephen D. Mastrofski. Forthcoming. Suspect searches: Assessing police behavior under the U.S. Constitution. *Criminology and Public Policy*.

Klockars, Carl B., Sanja Kutnjak Ivkovich, William E. Harver, and Maria R. Haberfeld. 2000. *The measurement of police integrity*. Washington, DC: National Institute of Justice.

Leo, Richard. 1996. The impact of *Miranda* revisited. *Journal of Criminal Law and Criminology* 86:621-93

Manning, Peter K., and Lawrence J. Redlinger. 1977. Invitational edges of corruption: Some consequences of narcotics law enforcement. In *Drugs and politics*, edited by Paul Rock, 279-310. Rutgers, NJ: Transaction Books.

Meares, Tracey L., and Bernard E. Harcourt. 2000. Transparent adjudication and social science research in constitutional criminal procedure. *Journal of Criminal Law and Criminology* 90:733-69.

Meyer, Marshall W. 1980. Police shootings of minorities: The case of Los Angeles. *The Annals of the American Academy of Political and Social Science* 452:98-110.

Milton, Catherine H., Jeanne W. Halleck, James Lardner, and Gary Albrecht. 1977. *Police use of deadly force*. Washington, DC: Police Foundation.

New York Office of the Attorney General. 1999. *The New York City Police Department's "stop & frisk" practice: A report from the Office of the Attorney General*. New York: Author.

Patton, Alison L. 1993. The endless cycle of abuse: Why 42 U.S.C. § 1983 is ineffective in deterring police brutality. *Hastings Law Journal* 44:753-68.

Robin, Gerald. 1963. Justifiable homicide by police officers. *Journal of Criminal Law, Criminology, and Police Science* 54:225-54.

Sherman, Lawrence W. 1978. *Scandal and reform: Controlling police corruption*. Berkeley: University of California Press.

Sutton, Peter. 1986. Fourth Amendment in action: An empirical view of the search warrant process. *Criminal Law Bulletin* 22:405-29.

Sparger, Jerry R., and David J. Giacopassi. 1992. Memphis revisited: A reexamination of police shootings after the *Garner* decision. *Police Quarterly* 9:211-25.

Tennenbaum, Abraham N. 1994. The influence of the *Garner* decision on police use of lethal force. *Journal of Criminal Law and Criminology* 85:241-60.

Uchida, Craig D., and Timothy S. Bynum. 1991. Search warrants, motions to suppress, and "lost cases": The effects of the exclusionary rule in seven jurisdictions. *Journal of Criminal Law and Criminology* 81:1034-66.

U.S. General Accounting Office. 1998. *Law enforcement: Information on drug-related police corruption.*
     Washington, DC: Author.
Walker, Samuel. 2001a. The trees and the forest: Reflections on whether American policing has improved
     over time. Unpublished manuscript, University of Nebraska–Omaha.
———. 2001b. *Police accountability: The role of citizen oversight.* Belmont, CA: Wadsworth.
———. 2001c. Problems with traffic stop data and an early warning system solution. *Justice Research and
     Policy* 3:63-95.

[2]

Watchman and Community:
Myth and Institutionalization in Policing

John P. Crank

The author uses a conceptual framework grounded in theory of institutional process to assess developments in the theory of community-based policing. He suggests that two contemporary myths in policing—the myth of the police watchman and the myth of community—provide core elements the theory. Both liberal and conservative advocates for reform have drawn on these myths to support reinstitutionalizing police as community protectors with broad authority, including authority to arrest, unconstrained by law enforcement or due process considerations. He also discusses fundamental differences in the ways in which liberal and conservative reform advocates perceive the relationship between the myths.

[C]ertain ideas burst upon the intellectual landscape with a tremendous force. They solve so many fundamental problems at once that they seem also to promise that they will resolve all fundamental problems, clarify all obscure issues.

—Clifford Geertz 1973:3

Clifford Geertz thus described the force with which the idea of culture energized the development of the field of anthropology. It is with such dynamic vigor that the idea of community-based policing currently envelops police work (Manning 1984; Trojanowicz & Bucqueroux 1990; Walker 1992b). Community-based policing has emerged as the articulation of a police reform movement that addressed a central problem confronting police in the 1960s—the problem of legitimacy (Mastrofski 1991). By invoking two powerful myths—the myth of the 18th-century morally invested "small-town" American community and the myth of police officers as community watchmen—community-based policing provided a source of legitimation for police activity in terms of community protection when legitimacy in terms of police professionalization had been lost (Klockars 1991).

Address correspondence to John P. Crank, Department of Criminal Justice, 4505 Maryland Parkway, Box 455009, Las Vegas, NV 89154-5009.

326   Myth and Institutionalizing in Policing

The police had failed by many accounts to do much in the way of controlling sharply increasing crime; moreover, they were implicated by the 1967 Kerner and 1968 Crime Commissions in the devastating urban riots of the 1960s.[1] Police practice following the reports of these commissions began to change from structures and activities associated with the police professionalism movement and toward the adoption of structures and policies that would forge relationships between police and communities. This change coalesced under the rubric of community policing by the 1980s.

Community policing involved the adoption of elements of structure, activity, and policy designed to make the police look like an organization should look that was responding to problems associated with police professionalism (among them, abrasive enforcement practices that alienated minority communities and police inability to do much about crime). By the 1980s community-based policing was rapidly being institutionalized. Its popularity stemmed from its seeming potential to alleviate a broad range of social and moral dilemmas overwhelming contemporary urban society (Mastrofski 1991).

I argue that the diffusion of the philosophy and programmatic elements of community-based policing across the political landscape of the United States from the early 1970s to the present was an institutional process aimed at restoring legitimacy to the police (Crank & Langworthy 1992). In this essay on institutionalization in the policing sector, I adopt the perspective that institutionalization is a process guided by myth construction, and I hold that the community policing movement is guided by powerful myths of community and watchman (Klockars 1991). By looking at how these two myths developed, we gain insight into how community-based policing is becoming institutionalized as the way police organizations should organize and accomplish their work, independent of the efficiency or effectiveness of community-based strategies and tactics to accomplish the prevention of crime and the production of arrests.

Integral to the process of institutionalization is the entrepreneurial activity of individuals with broad influence within the institutional field (DiMaggio 1988:15). Consequently, the assessment of the process of institutionalization of community-based policing takes into consideration how particular institutional entrepreneurs have influenced the development of the myths of watchman and community.

Finally, I suggest that, because the process of institutionalization for the police occurs within a broad political environment,

---

[1] Throughout, the report of the National Advisory Commission on Civil Disorders (1967) is cited as "Kerner Commission"; the report of the U.S. President's Commission on Law Enforcement & Administration of Justice (1967) is cited as "Crime Commission." The References include cross-references from the informal names to the official reports.

elements of community policing can and should be described in terms of conservative and liberal crime-control conceptions (Walker 1989a). The implementation of particular strategies under the rubric of community policing in specific police organizations does not indicate how efficient or effective they are in dealing with crime; instead, such implementation reveals the dominant crime-control theology at that place and at that time.

Legitimacy and Community Policing

Legitimacy Lost

Within highly institutionalized environments, particular organizational structures, policies, and behaviors take the form they do because of prevailing values and beliefs that have become institutionalized (Hall 1982:313). Random preventive patrol, rapid police response systems, the importance of technology in the investigation of criminal suspects, organizational elaboration in crime-fighting areas, and a militaristic system of rank are aspects of policing that, under the banner of the police professionalism movement, have been institutionalized (Crank & Langworthy 1992).

Prevailing values and beliefs, however, may have their legitimacy challenged. Legitimacy crises may emerge of such severity that they bring into question the fundamental purpose of the organization itself (Meyer & Scott 1983). Such a crisis occurred for policing in the late 1960s. This crisis was precipitated by several factors. The presidential elections of 1964 and 1968 elevated street crime to national attention for the first time. In part, this stemmed from the public perception that crime was sharply increasing (Walker 1980). However, regardless of how crime was measured, police were unable to improve on their performance (Kelling & Moore 1989). Widespread protests against the Vietnam War and the violent urban riots of 1963–67 fostered a public image of police forces ill prepared to accomplish their primary mandate—preserving and protecting the citizenry (Walker 1985).[2] The assassinations of President John Kennedy, his brother Robert Kennedy, and Martin Luther King and the emergence of crime as a topic of national political interest contributed to a broad-based concern over lawlessness and a sharp increase in fear of crime (Michalowski 1985).

This era also witnessed an increasing public mistrust of the police, brought about by such events as the killings of Black Panther leaders by the Chicago police and the Knapp Commission

---

2 Walker (1985:356) describes the "challenge of the 1960's" as the growing momentum of the civil rights movement, problems of police behavior in black neighborhoods, the dramatic increases in crime between 1963 and 1973 resulting in heightened public fear, and urban riots and militant protests against the Vietnam war.

findings of pervasive police corruption in New York City (Manning 1977). A series of Supreme Court decisions, such as *Miranda v. Arizona* (1966), contributed to a public climate of concern over the tendency of the police to engage in illegal behavior (Walker 1980). The reports of the 1950s American Bar Foundation (ABF) Survey of the Administration of Criminal Justice published in the 1960s had a far-reaching impact throughout the criminal justice system (Walker 1992a). The ABF survey reports brought an end to the idea that the police performed their task in a nondiscretionary, ministerial fashion and documented the absence of controls over discretionary police behavior. These events coalesced in the 1967 Kerner and Crime Commissions' reports.

Crank and Langworthy (1992) state that loss of legitimacy is a ceremonial process marked by rituals of public degradation and absolution through the adoption of a new legitimating mandate. Their research focused on police organizations only, but I suggest that a similar ceremonial process also occurred for policing at the national level. For the police, public degradation and revocation of legitimacy occurred ceremonially through two blue-ribbon panels of prominent citizens, acting in the name of elected leadership, and convened to investigate crime control in the United States—the Kerner Commission and the Crime Commission, both issuing reports in 1967—sharply questioned then-current police strategies and related structures. Not only did these commissions cite problems of lawlessness unresolved by current police practices, but they implicated the police in the riots of the late 1960s.

Both commissions called for police reform, to be accomplished through operational strategies and organizational structures that addressed what were described as profound problems of police-community relations. The Kerner Commission noted that in 40% of the riots, police actions triggered the riot (Greene 1989). Institutionalized racism was seen as the underlying problem, but aggressive and violent police behavior was identified as the direct cause. The commission commented on the atmosphere of hostility and cynicism, reinforced by a widespread belief among minorities in rampant police brutality and in a double standard of justice for blacks and whites. This reservoir of grievances, they contended, created an explosive atmosphere where an incident, often involving the police, would spark a riot. Moreover, the commission noted that the most severe disorders were in communities with highly professionalized police agencies.[3] Recommendations included the elimination of abrasive police practices, the establishment of contacts with minority communi-

---

[3] The Kerner Commission (1967:158) noted: "many of the [most] serious disturbances took place in cities whose police are among the best led, best organized, best trained and most professional in the country."

ties, increased hiring of minority members, effective grievance mechanisms, and the creation of the position of community service officer.

The Crime Commission (1967) focused more heavily on the sharp increase in crime through the 1960s. Their criticism struck at the heart of the professionalism movement: The police, in spite of adopting a law enforcement mandate, had failed to stem a rising tide of crime. This commission's recommendations were much like those of the Kerner Commission. It encouraged the creation of police community relations units, the recruitment and promotion of more minority members, experimentation with team policing (a precursor of community policing), and the creation of a new police position, the community service officer, who would be drawn from members of the local community and would provide community liaison work.

Professionalism Reconsidered

Central to the findings of both commission reports were the citation and discussion of profound problems with police-community relations. Following the reports, many observers of the police noted that traditional sources of police legitimacy, grounded in law enforcement activity and described by an aloof and legalistic "professional" police, should be reconsidered (Moore & Kelling 1983; Fogelson 1977). The police professionalism movement, with its narrow view of police legitimacy in terms of law enforcement, had failed by all accounts to accomplish its self-chosen mandate—victory in the war on crime (Walker 1992b; Skolnick & Bayley 1986). Moreover, the quasi-military and bureaucratic organizational structure advocated by crime-control-oriented reformers at the beginning of the 20th century was itself an impediment to the production of law enforcement activity. It was even a source of enduring problems such as a "you cover my ass and I'll cover yours" line-officer mentality (Klockars 1985), line-level discontent (Brown 1981), and police officer corruption (Manning & Redlinger 1977).

The police professionalism movement was admonished for its failure to adapt to a changing urban milieu, particularly changes that involved minority emigration (Walker 1977). That the police professionalism movement advocated forms of police organization and behavior that alienated minority populations has been widely noted (Walker 1992b). Founded in the conflict between political machines and urban progressives at the end of the 19th century (Fogelson 1977), the movement, encouraged by police executives and supported in 1893 by the fledgling International Association of Chiefs of Police, represented the interests of the progressives. Structures associated with the movement—for example, a militaristic rank structure, civil service personnel system, and centralization of authority—provided police organizations with autonomy from local political machines.

The latent consequences of such "professionalized" organizational structures, critics argued, was a fundamental separation of police from community—civil service conflicted with efforts to hire minorities from within the service community, a militaristic rank structure contributed to a "we-them" siege mentality in which the "them" became the local community, and centralization of authority was inconsistent with the need to tailor police delivery of service to the needs of particular neighborhoods.

Following the commission reports, reform advocates promulgated a new police mission, a mission that legitimized police work in terms of protecting neighborhoods and communities (Kelling & Moore 1989; Alpert & Dunham 1988). Yet, whether reform efforts would have coalesced into the community-based policing movement of the 1980s without the support of the federal government by way of the Law Enforcement Assistance Administration (LEAA) is questionable. The history of the LEAA is a widely told story (Duffee 1980; Michalowski 1985). LEAA's contribution to the process of police relegitimation lay in its investment in police experimentation. As Feeley and Sarat (1980) noted, the federal government provided, even required, block grants for program and policy innovation in the Omnibus Safe Streets and Crime Control Act of 1968. As they said, "The message of the act was . . . simple—money would be given, innovation produced" (p. 92).

The LEAA supported widespread experimentation in the delivery of police services.[4] Team policing experiments, popular during the late 1960s and early 1970s, involved a "team" of officers assigned to a permanent geographical location and given the discretionary authority to develop their own solutions to crime problems. Team police were expected to identify with the local community, which would make them more sensitive to developing local crime problems. As many as 40 departments adopted some form of team policing in this period (Walker 1992b).

A second strategy was to reorganize the police into a less militaristic rank structure. For example, the city of Longmont, Colorado, abandoned traditional militaristic rank and insignia for civilian dress and less threatening titles and changed its name to

---

4 This is not to imply that the LEAA was an advocate of community-oriented policing in favor of more traditional police practices. Only a relatively small percentage of the LEAA money was spent for community-oriented experimentation. Michalowski (1985:182) notes that the bulk of LEAA funds for policing went for crime control by supporting strategies for apprehension of criminals and deterrence. In 1973, for example, 29.4% of the monies that went to policing were provided for "soft" crime prevention or community relations programs. What was fortunate for the evolving community-based policing movement was that *any* federal money was being spent for experimentation into crime prevention or community-based programs.

the Longmont Department of Public Safety (Guyot 1979). Third, traditional ideas of police patrol were reconsidered. In what has been called the most significant experiment in policing in the 1970s, the Kansas City Police Department evaluated the efficacy of random preventive patrol, a cornerstone of traditional police patrol practices, and concluded that variations in the level of patrol had no effect on crime (Kelling et al. 1974).

Fourth, a function of police patrol was shifted from the gathering of incident-based statistics to the identification and analysis of problem areas, as proposed by Herman Goldstein (1979). Traditional ideas of random preventive patrol overlooked the fact that crime events were not distinct incidents but tended to be grouped together in problem areas. The proper focus of police patrol, said Goldstein, should not be on providing a broad deterrent by dispersing patrol across the community but rather on identifiable problem areas. Other strategies included "storefront" police stations—small, typically one-person offices scattered around a community providing a restricted range of services—and expanded foot patrol. Both these strategies were aimed at elevating the quality of police-community interaction and lowering citizens' fear of crime (Eck & Spelman 1987).

The 1970s thus witnessed the development of organizational structures and strategies aimed at reinvolving the police in the life of the community. It is against the backdrop of these organizational innovations that the mythos of community and watchman took root. The notions that cities were made up of moral communities, and that police could act as watchmen to protect these communities, were consistent with both the recommendations of both commissions and many of the structural and operational innovations in policing following the commission reports (Eck & Spelman 1987). The myths of watchman and community were to emerge as the foundational myths of the movement to institutionalize community-based policing.

Before examining the specific characteristics of the myths of the watchman and community, I will review the concept of myth and its foundational relationship to institutions and to the process of institutional development.

The Concept of Myth

That myth may take diverse forms in the service of a broad array of social and ceremonial purposes has been noted (Kirk 1974; Day 1984). One of these purposes, the functional role of myth, provides the foundation for institutional analysis of myth as it is used here. Functional perspectives of myth are grounded in the perspective that social customs and institutions are validated by myths. In a word, myths legitimate social institutions and imbue them with meaning (Kirk 1974).

The idea that myth provides a function for society may be traced to the writings of Durkheim (1955). Myth, Durkheim argued, establishes, maintains, and expresses social solidarity. The ritual acting out of myth is in its essence a ceremonial validation of social institutions (Day 1984:249). Durkheim's influence was evident in the work of Malinowski, who extended the functional analysis of myth. Myth, according to Malinowski, was not a reflection of cosmic events or of mysterious impulses in the human soul but acted as a *charter* for social institutions and actions. As a charter, myths validated traditional customs, attitudes, and beliefs (Kirk 1974:32).[5] Thus, myth imbued social institutions with legitimacy. The idea that myth performed important ceremonial functions for particular social groups was extended to police work by Manning (1977).[6]

Myth and Institutional Change

The idea that myth can be an agent of institutional change can be traced to the writings of Georges Sorel (1916), who wrote that myths were ideas carried by particular groups seeking social change. Myths, according to Sorel, had the following properties. They were social, that is, they were held by participants in some collective action. They were political in that they aimed at achieving a change in human affairs. They were intentional, acting on social structure rather than reflecting it. Finally, they were magical, that is, they were beyond the realm of rational choice and consequently could not be evaluated and falsified (Strenski 1987:164).[7]

Contemporary investigation into the function of myth for social institutions is typically traced to the work of Meyer and Rowan (1977). These authors contended that for organizations in highly institutionalized environments, organizational struc-

---

[5] Malinowski (1954:73) described the myth as a "vital ingredient of human civilization" that fulfills "an indispensable function: it expresses, enhances, and codifies belief; it safeguards and enforces morality."

[6] Myth, Manning suggested, served six purposes for the police. The first was to reinterpret events into integrated and holistic units, where police-citizen encounters are transformed into a confrontation between forces of good and evil. Second, police myths removed police activity from the realm of special interest. Third, myth provided an explanation of otherwise inextricable events (e.g., the myth that police enforce the law equally to all obscures the underlying reality that the probability of arrest for violent crime is actually very low). Fourth, mythical actors are provided with human attributes, placed in dramatic events, and given predictable outcomes. Fifth, myths drew public attention to the stability of the police, even in times of change. Sixth, police myths gave the police a symbolic and heightened authority over that which they oppose.

[7] Similar ideas have been used to describe the ideology as a political device. Swidler (1986) noted that highly charged beliefs may emerge in competition with existing cultural frameworks. Systems of such beliefs are ideologies, in which ideology is conceptualized as a highly articulated and organized systems of ideas carried by individuals who aim at fundamental institutional change (Drucker 1974). Crank, Payn, and Jackson (1993) referred to the police professionalism movement in its early days as such a system of highly charged and articulated beliefs.

tures, and formal activities did not serve purposes of efficiency or effectiveness. Instead, forms of organizational structure and activity were highly institutionalized and conformed to widely held ideas about the way organizations should act and work—ideas that were mythic in that they were perceived to be beyond the ability of any particular actor to change.

Organizations that conformed to institutional myths of structure and activity received legitimacy from other institutional actors, thereby facilitating access to resources and improving the prospects of organizational survival (Meyer & Rowan 1977:345). The influence of the institutional environment over organizational structure and behavior was particularly important for public sector organizations that tended to be low on technological development and high on institutional development (Dobbin et al. 1988; Meyer & Scott 1983).

Ritti and Silver (1986) extended Meyer and Scott's ideas to the process of institutionalization. They examined the ways in which a new organization, the Bureau of Consumer Services (BCS) in Pennsylvania, attained legitimacy in a highly institutionalized organizational environment. If, they argued, organizations embodied in their structure and policies prevailing institutional myths in the organizational environment, then "myth making must be a first step in the process of institutionalization" (p. 27). In their analysis, the BCS had to demonstrate that it was a legitimate public representative of consumer concerns, while at the same time insuring a fair return to the industry. Structural innovations, described in their research as formal organizational ties and ceremonial interactions with the electricity, gas, and telephone companies, allowed the BCS to acquire legitimacy in its institutional environment while demonstrating to the public and legislature that it was indeed acting as a legitimate protector of the public interest. Thus, Ritti and Silver suggested, for highly institutionalized sectors such as the one in which BCS was participating, the process of organizational innovation was an institutional solution to the need to attain organizational legitimacy.

Crank and Langworthy (1992) looked at myth and institutionalized environments among police organizations.[8] These authors presented a discussion of three powerful myth-building processes: coercive legitimacy stemming from rules, law, and licensing; the elaboration of relations networks in their organizational and institutional environment; and organizational-institutional reactivity, in which the organization or powerful individuals representing it were recognized as powerful actors in

---

[8] Applying the Meyer & Rowan (1977) perspective of institutionalized organizations to police agencies, the authors argued that police organizations were not "mere engines" of bureaucratic efficiency (Selznick 1957:15) but embodied in their formal structures and activities "widespread understandings of social reality," called myths (Meyer & Rowan 1977:343).

their environments. The incorporation of widely held myths into structure and activity, they suggested, demonstrated to other powerful actors within the institutional sector that a police organization looked and behaved appropriately. When organizations conformed to institutional expectations, they received organizational legitimacy and thus were provided with continuing accesses to resources.

The Properties of Institutional Myths

Four elements common to myths can be drawn from the previous discussion. First, myths, as institutional elements, have *power*. This means two things. On the one hand, they convey a sense of permanence and importance above and beyond the influence of particular actors (DiMaggio 1988; Meyer & Rowan 1977). On the other, myths that invoke history do not derive their power from the historical accuracy of their premises but from the way metaphorical images conjured by myth enables an organization to provide a satisfactory public account of its behavior (Klockars 1991).

Second, a myth contains within it implications regarding features of the environment affected by the myth (Trice & Beyer 1984; Ritti & Silver 1986).[9] That is, the myth is contextualized by a social or physical geography. For the police, this refers to their beat area and the dangers that inhere in that area. Third, contained within a myth is the emergence or transformation of something. For the police, this transformation is from danger to safety (Manning 1977). For example, ideas of community are set against ideas of urban society, with its seeming absence of morality and host of social ills.

The fourth component is specific to the process of institutionalization—the idea that foundational myths are tied to particular powerful individuals or political interest groups within the institutional environment. Traditionally, institutional theorists have looked at how a coercive institutional presence obstructs individual goal-directed behavior (DiMaggio & Powell 1983). The influence of individual actors over particular institutional processes is being increasingly recognized (Powell 1991; Crank & Langworthy 1992). The myth-building process itself may stem from individual goal-directed behavior and may reflect the political influence of "institutional entrepreneurs" (DiMaggio 1988: 13).[10] Because institutionalized myths become "part of the stock

---

9 Ritti and Silver (p. 26) note that myths convey "unquestioned beliefs not only about the origins, functions, and technical efficacy of the innovation, but also about the features of the environment that require adoption of the innovation."

10 In DiMaggio's words, while the *product* of institutionalized environments may place "organizational structures and practices beyond the reach of interest and politics," the *process* of institutionalization "is profoundly political and reflects the relative power of organized interests and the actors who mobilize around them."

of 'things taken for granted' within the prevailing organizational culture" (Ritti & Silver 1986:26), the influence of moral entrepreneurs over the myth-building process may be both powerful and long term, affecting both organizational structure and activity.[11] Thus, elements of police procedure and structure introduced in the current era may extend well into the future, independent of their efficiency or effectiveness in terms of law enforcement or crime prevention.

This review of myth and institutional process provides the framework for discussing the myths of watchman and community and for understanding how those myths contribute to the process of institutionalization of the community policing movement. I argue that community policing as a new legitimating mandate worked because it evoked powerful metaphors of democracy, small-town morality, and local autonomy (Manning 1984). The strength of the metaphorical image of policing as a community-based enterprise derived from its evocation of two powerful myths—the myth of the watchman and of community (Mastrofski 1991; Walker 1989a).

The Mythos of Community Policing

The myth of the watchman is as follows. The primary tasks of the police who do community-based policing are the maintenance of the public order and protection of the community from criminal invasion. To accomplish these tasks, the police mandate is to reinforce the informal social control mechanisms already present in communities (Wilson & Kelling 1982). By adopting strategies and tactics appropriate to the specific needs of particular communities, by dealing with underlying problems rather than incidents, and by generally becoming involved in the life of the community, police can do something about both crime and fear of crime and thus enhance the overall quality of community life (Skolnick & Bayley 1986; Goldstein 1979).

The police officer who does this work is not occupying a police role new to American cities but is a contemporary version of the friendly night watchman who served, in his walking beat, the immigrant masses and urban poor in the 19th century (Moore & Kelling 1983). Thus, there was already in place a historical model, called the "watchman," for the type of policing appropri-

---

[11] An example of the influence of an institutional entrepreneur is revealed in the works of August Vollmer, often cited as the patriarch of the police professionalism movement. One of his contributions to policing was the establishment of the Uniform Crime Reports (UCR) in 1929 (Carte 1986). Vollmer initially proposed the Uniform Crime Reports as a method to track crime in the United States. Today, the ritual of data collection for the UCR is accomplished by tens of thousands of reporting districts across the country, all of which use similar offense classifications for the labeling of crime.

ate for contemporary crime control problems (Wilson 1968; Wilson & Kelling 1982).[12]

The second myth, the myth of community, is a myth about what it is that the watchman protects. The community myth is that there is now, or ever has been, a "community" in the sense of groups of like-minded individuals, living in urban areas, who share a common heritage, have similar values and norms, and share a common perception of social order (see Mastrofski 1991). This image of moral community was presented by Tocqueville (1945:71) in his discussion of the relationship between a New England native and his community, and is used in Kelling's (1987) article advocating order-maintenance policing:

> [The community's] welfare is the aim of his ambition and of his future expectations . . . . [H]e acquires a taste for order, comprehends the balance of powers, and collects clear practical notions on the nature of his duties and the extent of his rights.

The relationship between the watchman and the community has provided the foundation for a mythos of community-based policing. The watchman was responsible for the preservation and protection of a conception of community that celebrated the traditions and values of traditional American society (Klockars 1991; Walker 1989a). Community-based policing "taps a nostalgia for the U.S. democratic grass-roots tradition of citizen initiative" (Mastrofski 1991:515). Thus, the watchman and his work reaffirmed an image of community morality of 19th-century America and provided a blanket of myth to shroud that powerful image in nostalgic imagery.

These myths are consistent with the previous discussion of foundational myths. First, they have power. On the one hand, they convey a sense of durability and permanence to ideas of communities and watchmen. On the other, their power derives not from their historical accuracy (Walker 1989b) but from recognition by the public and police alike that watchman and community are valid metaphors from which to model the organization and activity of police agencies.

Second, these myths provide a transformative image from dangerous urban environments into safe and orderly "communities." Communities destroyed by poverty and criminal predation are transformed by community police into moral communities with like-minded citizens preserving a common heritage. It is the watchman who enables this transformation to occur.

Third, the idea of community contains many implications of the environment encompassed by the myth. Geographically and ethnically identifiable groups become "neighborhoods," or

---

[12] The recurring reference to the watchman in male gender is used instead of a gender-neutral phraseology to indicate the paternalistic quality of the watchman image implicit in early discussions of the watchman. Also, the use of the male gender specification in the word "watchman" is historically accurate.

moral entities characterized by a sense of belonging, a sense of common goals, involvement in community affairs, and a sense of wholeness (Poplin 1979).

Fourth, these myths are linked to particular individuals or political groups in the institutional environment of policing. The development of ideas regarding community-based policing can be traced to the writings of individuals who act as institutional entrepreneurs. The remainder of this article traces the development of the ideas of community policing and the particular influence of institutional entrepreneurs on the process of institutionalization of community-based policing.

The Watchman and the Law Enforcer: The Emergence of the Myth

The idea that police work contains watchman elements can be traced to Wilson's (1968) seminal study of police style in eight communities. His presentation of watchman-style departments provided a perspective for thinking about police work in terms of community protection. By contrasting watchmen and legalistic departments, Wilson provided an alternative to the idea that all police work is characterized by the police professionalism model.

The influence of Wilson's conception of police style stemmed not only from the content of his message but from its timeliness. That Wilson's writing coincided with the broad legitimation crisis that was occurring to the police nationally increased the likelihood that his cogent way of thinking about police would achieve recognition. In the 1960s, the field of criminal justice was undergoing a profound change, described by Walker (1992a) as a shift from a *progressive era* to a *systems* paradigm. An aspect of this new paradigm was a recognition of the wide discretion that police employ in the performance of their work. Although others (e.g., Goldstein 1963) had noted police use of discretion, Wilson (1968) provided a case affirming the centrality of discretion to the task of line-level police. Wilson's recognition of the discretionary quality of police work coincided with and complemented the paradigmatic shift across the field of criminal justice in the 1960s.

Breaking from the idea that police work simply amounted to efforts to maximize law enforcement activity, Wilson argued that there were different styles of police work. Integral to Wilson's presentation of styles of policing was a distinction between policing as a profession and policing as a craft. A craftsmanship style of policing was indicated by departments that displayed a "watchman" style of policing—one in which police activity was directed more toward maintaining the public order than enforcing the law. The watchman Wilson described was a metaphor for the traditions of the department, of the "good old days" when a police officer could, with skills learned through street sense and ap-

prenticeship, solve problems without invoking the formal process
of law. The watchman controlled his beat by relying on personal
authority to solve problems on the street and used his practical
knowledge of local culture as a *tool kit* to provide seemingly intuitive solutions to everyday problems of the citizenry.[13]

Philosophically opposed to craftsmanship was police professionalism, the guiding ideology of police reform from the end of
the 19th century through the 1960s (Brown 1981; Berman 1987).
Professionalism, as an explicit and articulated set of strategies for
police occupational reform, emerged as an ideological challenge
by police reformers to the big-city machine control of the police
organization (Fogelson 1977). However, Wilson argued that order maintenance was central to the police role, and for that reason, professionalizing chiefs would always exist in an uneasy relationship with the rank and file. In sum, Wilson presented an
image of police work that was by its nature dominated by highly
discretionary order-maintenance interventions and an ethic of
craftsmanship that infused this type of work with commonsense
meaning. This image of police work provided the basis for the
later development of the watchman myth.

Myth Transformation in the 1980s: From Description to Prescription

The 1980s witnessed a reconsideration of the federalization
of the crime effort that marked crime-control strategy from the
issuance of the Kerner and Crime Commission reports. This was
an era of a "new federalism" in which fiscal responsibility for
crime control was shifted onto the states. It was an era of crime
control in which ideas of community were increasingly invoked
in conjunction with crime-control strategy. The use of community-based alternative efforts to resolve disputes, for example,
were given impetus by the Dispute Resolution Act of 1980. Alternative dispute resolution (ADR) sought to move disputes out of
the decisionmaking apparatus of the criminal justice system and
into community participation and neighborhood self-governance
(Duffee 1980:230). Intermediate sanctions that placed offenders
within the community became the centerpiece of the community
corrections movement. Much of this movement was aimed at creating the appearance of a more severe criminal justice system
while at the same time allowing offenders to be released from
incarceration.[14]

---

[13] A cultural "tool kit" may be described as a set of cultural skills that direct and
influence behavior. The notion of culture as a tool kit provides a perspective on the differential abilities of individuals to employ particular social actions or behaviors in the
pursuit of similar goals (Swidler 1986).

[14] See Gordon (1991:92–144) for a discussion of community as prison. Duffee
(1980:230) notes: "In corrections, intermediate punishments such as home incarceration,
electronic monitoring, and intensive probation supervision have become the buzzwords
in community programming."

In police work, the 1980s witnessed the coalescence of program innovations, structures, and policies into a full-fledged
community-based policing movement. Skolnick and Bayley
(1986) described how police departments in six major cities reor-
ganized elements of organizational structure and patrol strategy
in line with ideas of community-based policing. Trojanowicz and
Bucqueroux (1990) provide an overview of community efforts in
several communities and describe briefly community-police efforts in 9 cities. And Rosenbaum (1986) provides a detailed description of 11 community-policing evaluations in 14 U.S. cities.

If the 1980s were marked by a shift in police to an enterprise
conceived in terms of ideas of community, they were also marked
by a maturing of the philosophy of the police as community protectors. A broad dialogue on community-based reform was conducted among practitioners and academicians alike (Hartmann
1988; Sykes 1986; Moore & Kelling 1983). Perhaps the most influential of the new conceptualizations of police work was an article
entitled "Broken Windows" (Wilson & Kelling 1982).

In 1982, the publication of "Broken Windows" marked a fundamental transformation in the watchman myth. The transformation was moral: The myth of the watchman shifted from a description of police style in particular types of urban departments
to a prescription describing how police work should generally be.
The watchman image evolved from that of a blue-collar craftsman who displayed an idiosyncratic, street-wise policing style to a
standardbearer for the protection of urban communities in late
20th-century America.

The broken windows idea was a simple metaphor: If a broken
window in an untended building was left unrepaired, the remainder of the windows would soon be broken. Similarly, untended
behavior leads to the breakdown of community controls. The
broken window was an analogy for untended behavior. Wilson
and Kelling linked the broken-window analogy to what they perceived to be a contemporary cycle of urban decay that began with
the presence of untended property (and by implication, "untended" behavior) and ended with the breakdown of community
controls and the moral and economic destruction of neighborhoods via criminal invasion. The police could disrupt the process
of urban decay by reinforcing the informal control mechanisms
of the community itself. The responsibility of the police was to
protect the rights of the community, even if sacrifices to individual liberties were incurred.

The police had only to look to their past to find a model for
the watchman. Wilson and Kelling argued that a community protection style of policing was present prior to the end of the 19th
century. This style, described by a community-oriented order-
maintenance mandate, was present in the activity of the watchman in large urban departments through the latter half of the

19th century. Wilson and Kelling (ibid., p. 38) concluded: "Above all, we must return to our long-abandoned view that the police ought to protect communities as well as individuals." This article thrust Wilson and Kelling into the role of institutional entrepreneurs, providing contemporary police reform with a model of police style constructed from a powerful mythos derived from a historical era of policing and imbued with a "moral rightness" of the police role as community protector derived from that mythos.[15]

The Linkage to Community-based Policing

The linkage of the watchman to ideas of police reform had an inevitability that only retrospect can reveal. The idea of community invoked by proponents of community-based policing provided an appropriate environment for the work of the watchman (Klockars 1991). Simply put, community-based policing, with its emphasis on the maintenance of public order (as opposed to enforcing the law) was precisely the kind of work the watchman did. Mastrofski (1991:515) provided a clear statement of this linkage in his analysis of the community policing reform movement:

> [C]ommunity policing advocates propose a significant departure from the ways in which issues of role, control, and legitimacy are addressed. Order maintenance replaces law enforcement as the police mission; legalistic constraints on officer discretion are reduced, while direct linkages to the community are increased; and policies and actions are justified . . . in terms of the sense of peace, order, and security they impart to the public.

The myth of the watchman was thus joined to an image of community. Like the watchman myth, the community protected by the watchman was also mythic. The community-based policing movement capitalized on a "nostalgia for the U.S. democratic grass-roots tradition of citizen initiative" (ibid.) where "[c]ommunity relationships are based on status not contract, manners not morals, norms not laws, and understandings not regulations" (Klockars 1991:535). In the mythic reconstruction of the past, the image of community that emerged as corollary to the watchman was 19th-century small-town America, with citizenry of moral fiber, of common purpose, and value (Alpert & Dunham 1988). The watchman symbolized protection of small-town America from the profound social and economic dislocations that washed across the American municipal landscape in the 20th century. As a myth of police reform, the watchman promised a rebirth of the spirit of 19th-century small-town morality in

---

[15] See DiMaggio (1988:15) for a discussion of morality and institutional entrepreneurship.

the 21st-century urban metropolis. Thus, the conjoined myths of community and watchman became valid and powerful representations of what community-based policing should be and provided a powerful morality of police behavior that justified legal and extralegal tactics in the name of community preservation.

Watchmen and Arrest Authority

The emergent mythos of community-based policing proved adaptable to the new federalism of the 1980s, a period in which executive federal leadership sought to divest the government of fiscal responsibility for state and municipal problems. A conundrum of the new federalism was to balance the expensive, punishment-oriented crime-control policies characteristic of the 1970s and 1980s with a strategy in which the federal government played a sharply reduced role (Duffee 1980). On the one hand, all segments of the criminal justice system were abandoning rehabilitation in favor of punitive strategies emphasizing incapacitation, deterrence, and retribution (Gordon 1991; Walker 1980). On the other, the federal government was relinquishing its role as bankroller for local crime-control efforts. These trends created a crime-control dilemma at the local level: Legislators at all levels were seeking increasingly punitive crime legislation, while local municipalities were increasingly expected to pick up the cost (Feeley & Sarat 1980). For corrections, this problem has been phrased as a question: How can criminals be sentenced to probation or parole and at the same time the appearance be created that the criminal justice system is being more punitive toward them? The answer was to increase the use of intensive supervision and to stack the sheer number of programs required for probationers and parolees. Communities were thus made to look like prison in concept and in degree of control over offenders (Gordon 1991). But the urban police asked: How could reforms favorable to community-based policing be sustained while preserving politically popular law-and-order ideas of tough-minded, arrest-producing police work?

The answer was a sharp reversal in the conceptualization of the watchman style in the early 1980s, from a police officer who would infrequently invoke formal processes of law, even in the presence of law breaking, to one who would arrest to maintain community order, even in the absence of law breaking. A component of the style of the craftsman, as articulated by Wilson (1977; 1968), was the police tendency to underenforce the law. Arrest was invoked only as a last resort, when all other strategies for restoring order had failed.

By the mid-1980s, the paternalistic image of the police as tough and street-wise but fair underenforcers of the law had evolved into an image of the watchman as a no-holds-barred aggressive order-maintenance superenforcer who would arrest, even in legally ambiguous situations, in the name of protecting the community (Kelling 1985; Sykes 1986). Kelling (1987), citing civic responsibility, advocated police intervention in the public roller-skating activities of juveniles in Chicago. Aggressive order maintenance, including the use of arrest, was needed to provide the public with order and safety from threatening behavior. As Kelling (p. 91) asked, "Do we want police officers to develop a 'What the hell' attitude toward disorderly or dangerous behavior, even if it is not *technically* illegal?" (emphasis added). Wilson and Kelling (1982) similarly argued for the priority of community protection over individual due process protections. This aggressive police response to order-maintenance problems was often cited in the literature (Sykes 1989, Kelling 1985; Moore & Kelling 1983: Wycoff & Manning 1983). Thus, by the mid-1980s, the policing style associated with the watchman had shifted from infrequent intervention and underenforcement of the law, in the name of community preservation and protection, to frequent intervention and arrest even in legally ambiguous situations, again in the name of community preservation and protection.

The Political Dimensions of Institutional Myth Making

> Nostalgia, we must make no mistake, is good politics.
> —Robert Nisbet 1988:110

As a reform agenda, community-based policing has been tractable to both conservative and liberal ideas of crime control. Central elements of community-based policing—an emphasis on problem-oriented tactics, police-community partnership in crime prevention activities, geographical and command decentralization of authority to the line level, and an elevation of the importance of order maintenance and crime prevention activity (Skolnick & Bayley 1986; Kelling & Moore 1989)—are present in both conservative and liberal perspectives of police reform. By considering these two perspectives, we can begin to understand the power and mutability that sustains community-based policing as a reform movement.[16]

Institutional entrepreneurs representing the conservative political view advocate an aggressive order-maintenance style of policing in which due process considerations of individual liberties are less important than community protection (Wilson & Kelling 1982).[17] Aggressive order maintenance is an effective deter-

---

[16] I am not suggesting that the individuals mentioned in this paragraph are either politically conservative or liberal. I am suggesting that the ideas mentioned in conjunction with their work are consistent with either conservative or liberal crime-control ideas (see Walker 1989a:10–17).

[17] Walker (1989a) notes that in practice, the differences between liberal and conservative perspectives tend to become "muddy." The value of the liberal-conservative dis-

rent for crime (Kelling 1985). Community breakdown occurs not from underlying social or structural problems in those communities but from criminal invasion into those communities. The watchman, as the moral representative of the community, is provided with substantial discretion to deal with problems on the street, and may even use arrest when no law has been broken. The issue of discretion, according to this perspective, is about whether to observe an individual's due process protections when observing threats to "community rights" (Alpert & Dunham 1988). Appropriate police strategies to achieve these ends include vigorous enforcement of nuisance and order-maintenance laws, arresting people for violation of order-maintenance statutes, and field interrogations (Mastrofski 1991).

The liberal agenda describes a strikingly different view of community-based policing. The watchman is a community organizer (Skolnick & Bayley 1986) whose task is not aggressive order maintenance but crime prevention through community service. The watchman engages in the shoring up of community institutions through community and neighborhood organization. The watchman approaches crime not through aggressive patrol strategies—these are believed to alienate citizens—but by sponsoring community-based programs that aim at crime prevention and community service (Alpert & Dunham 1988). Consequently, the watchman constructs ties to the local community and develops local strategies that assist the community to repair itself (Guyot 1991). Strategies include newsletters, block watch, nonenforcement police-citizen encounters, and victim follow-up (Mastrofski 1991). Thus, from the liberal perspective, the watchman assists the community in self-repair, while from the conservative perspective, the watchman protects the community from the destructive influence of criminal invasion (Skolnick & Bayley 1986; Wilson & Kelling 1982).

Two examples, drawn from Skolnick and Bayley's (1986) research on contemporary police innovation, illuminate the distinction between the liberal and conservative organizational elements of community-based policing. The first, Detroit, developed innovative structures consistent with what I have described as the liberal conception of community policing. Mayor Coleman Young implemented the program to deemphasize traditional, reactive policing in favor of "intensive community mobilization for self-defense." This was accomplished through the implementation of two organizational units that did only crime prevention activity, a crime prevention section, and a mini-station command. The crime prevention section organized neighborhood watches, apartment watches, and business watches. Special attention was

tinction is that it enables policymakers to assess the assumptions that provide the basis of much current crime-control policy.

given to the needs of elderly citizens, including the maintenance of a senior citizen roster and transportation for personal needs. A mini-station command operating in 52 mini-stations scattered around the city was devoted exclusively to community mobilization. Officers assigned to these beats spent half their time in patrol and half their time in community organization. These officers also would organize citizen band patrols and would maintain regular ongoing contact with community leaders. A great deal of patrol time was devoted by both sections to the organization of and participation in citizen crime-prevention meetings, described as the lifeblood of crime prevention. Meetings were held at the neighborhood level, and each precinct had a police-community relations council. Officers in both sections did what Skolnick and Bayley described as creative, customized fieldwork; their responsibility was to tailor crime prevention efforts to the particular needs of local areas.

Organizational innovations in the Denver Police Department are consistent with conservative ideas of community-based policing. The approach to reducing fear of crime in Denver was in terms of improving patrol effectiveness, accomplished by specialized, proactive field units. This directed patrol strategy involved four elements: intensified coverage, delegation of command responsibility, team activity, and operational crime analysis. The assumption by the Denver command was that some types of crimes were "patrol preventable," where crime prevention was achieved through high patrol visibility. Through the use of crime analysis techniques, specialized squads were engaged in problem-solving activity.

One organizational innovation was the development of a Special Crime Attack Team that attacked the problem of burglary through saturation patrol. A Special Services Unit was also established that required skills in the specialized application of force, such as hostage situations. Another program, called ESCORT (Eliminate Street Crime on Residential Thoroughfares), was described as aggressive order-maintenance. As one officer described the program, their job was to "find a rock and kick it," to look for minor violations and seek out individuals with known reputations. ESCORT was, as Skolnick and Bayley (1986:139) noted, "deterrent policing with a vengeance."

The areas of innovation adopted by Denver represented not so much a change in the role of police as modifications and extensions of traditional patrol strategy. Denver, though adopting programmatic innovations aimed at decentralizing command authority, increasing emphasis on order-maintenance activity, and doing proactive, problem-oriented policing, continued to be wedded to traditional ideas of the centrality of police patrol for police work. Storefront police organizations and a crime-prevention-oriented community services bureau were initiated but were perceived as ineffective; they were not integrated into the ongoing field operations of the department. Thus, Denver implemented types of organizational innovation consistent with three of the ideas of community-based policing stated at the opening of this section—decentralization of authority for specialized patrol activities, an elevation of order-maintenance activity through the use of aggressive order-maintenance street tactics, and the implementation of problem-oriented evaluational strategies. But in operational strategy and organizational development, these innovations matched what I have described as the conservative branch of the community policing movement.

These two examples reveal the flexibility of the foundational myths of watchman and community. Given the right "spin," ideas of community-based policing are acceptable organizational theory for both conservative and liberal advocates of police change. Because legitimacy can be obtained from both conservative and liberal proponents of police change, community-based policing appears to be sufficiently adaptable to survive a changing and somewhat unpredictable political electorate. In other words, even given the mutable tides of American electoral politics, community policing continues to be a healthy and vigorous movement that is becoming institutionalized.

Institutional Change in the Occupation of Policing

The rapidity with which elements of community-based policing are currently diffusing across the municipal landscape is remarkable. By 1985, more than 300 police departments had adopted some form of community policing program (Walker 1992b). The state of Washington is currently exploring a strategy to convert over 50 municipal and county police agencies in the state to a community-based policing model. Support for community-based policing has been provided by the National Institute of Justice, with its allocation of a special grants category for research and experimentation on community-based policing. Textbooks and readers on policing in the United States today all contain sections on community-based policing. Experiments with community-based elements have been conducted in many major U.S. cities (Trojanowicz & Bucqueroux 1990; Skolnick & Bayley 1986). The chiefs of police of 10 major metropolitan police organizations in 1991 issued a position paper in support of community policing (Christopher Commission 1991:104).[18] The past commissioner of New York City, Lee Brown, developed a program to convert the entire New York City Police Department to a community-based model, a program that continues today. In

---

[18] The report of the Independent Commission on the Los Angeles Police Department (1991) is also referred to as "the Christopher Commission." The References include cross-references from the Christopher Commission to the Independent Commission.

short, community-based policing, with its core myths of community and watchman, is being institutionalized.

With the institutionalization of elements of community-based policing, legitimacy lost in the late 1960s becomes legitimacy restored in the current era. A new legitimating mandate, infused with powerful myths of community and watchman, appears to be steadily displacing the previous mandate of police professionalism. That this process is proceeding with fervor is illustrated by the Christopher Commission report (ibid.). That report, an investigation into police conduct in Los Angeles, called for sweeping changes in structure and procedure to refocus department resources in the direction of community-based policing (ibid., pp. 95–106). In microcosm, the Christopher Commission report enacted the drama laid out by the Kerner and Crime Commissions at the national level and affirmed the continuing vitality of the myths of community and police as community watchmen.

Conclusions

By the late 1980s, many scholars had raised important questions regarding community-based policing (Walker 1992b). Walker (1989b) cited problems of historical accuracy in Wilson and Kelling's (1982) discussion of watchman-style 19th-century patrol practices. Klockars (1985) challenged Kelling's (1985) linkage between aggressive order-maintenance patrol practices and the quality of urban life. Bohm (1984) questioned whether community-based institutions could represent the breadth of interests of a diverse citizenry or provide informal systems of control. Crank (1990) suggested that police are more likely to have a professional than a crafts-like view of their occupational activity. Positive, rather than negative, relationships were noted between aggressive order-maintenance behavior and victimization (Sherman 1986). Mastrofski (1991) provided a broad-ranging discussion of misconceptions of the concept of community and implications of those misconceptions for police activity. Klockars (1991) charged that the community-policing movement was a circumlocution whose purpose was to obscure the principal role of police as a mechanism for the distribution of nonnegotiable coercive force (Bittner 1970). Bayley (1988) cited a host of theoretical and practical issues seldom addressed by advocates of community-based policing. Thus, a large body of literature emerged to challenge many facets of the community policing movement.

These challenges to community-based policing, though thoughtful and important, have overlooked an important point regarding community-based policing (but see Klockars 1991). Although it is, of course, important to ask whether community-based structures and policies are efficient or effective in the achievement of crime control, it is also important to note that community-based policing provides police organizations with an organizational theory that is acceptable to other institutional actors, in Meyer and Scott's (1983) terms, whose opinions count. By adopting elements of community and watchman into their structures and formalized activities, police organizations ceremonially regain the legitimacy that was ceremonially withdrawn in the 1960s.

The rapid spread of elements of community-based reform across the institutional sector of policing suggests that the invocation of community is providing an acceptable legitimating theory for police organizations. Furthermore, images of watchman and community do not derive their power from historical accuracy and thus are not vulnerable to inaccuracies in historical reporting. They derive their power to mobilize sentiment from the mythic images of watchmen as community protectors and communities as enclaves of traditional American values. I have argued here that institutional entrepreneurs have latched onto these myths and have modified them in an effort to affect the direction of policing at the outset of the 21st century. This is evident in Wilson and Kelling's 1982 "Broken Windows" piece, in which the authors cast the mythos of the watchman in terms of conservative theology.

There are institutional entrepreneurs on both sides of the conservative-liberal debate, and at present neither side is recognized as the authoritative expression of community-based policing philosophy, policy, and strategy. This can be seen in the widespread popularity of community-based policing and the virtual absence of consensus over the definition of the term or the appropriate role of community-based police officers. Nevertheless, given the current spirit of change in policing, particular community-based strategies will undoubtedly diffuse across the urban vista. The types of organizational structures, policies, and operational strategies that emerge under the banner of community-based policing will, I suspect, depend on the advocacy of institutional entrepreneurs, whose efficacy will in turn reflect the relative prominence of conservative or liberal crime-control agendas in the wider sphere of American politics. However, community-based policing, guided by a powerful and surprisingly mutable mythos of police and community, will probably be with us in one form or another for many years to come.

References

Alpert, Geoffrey P., & Roger G. Dunham (1988) *Policing Multi-ethnic Neighborhoods*. New York: Greenwood Press.

Bayley, David H. (1988) "Community Policing: A Report from the Devil's Advocate," in J. R. Greene & S. D. Mastrofski, eds., *Community Policing: Rhetoric or Reality?* New York: Praeger.

348   **Myth and Institutionalizing in Policing**

Berman, Jay Stuart (1987) *Police Administration and Progressive Reform: Theodore Roosevelt as Police Commissioner of New York.* New York: Greenwood Press.

Bittner, Egon (1970) *The Functions of Police in Modern Society.* Chevy Chase, MD: National Institute of Mental Health.

Bohm, Robert (1984) Book Review, 1 *Justice Q.* 449.

Brown, Michael K. (1981) *Working the Street: Police Discretion and the Dilemmas of Reform.* New York: Russell Sage Foundation.

Carte, Gene Edward (1986) "August Vollmer and the Origin of Police Professionalism," in M. R. Pogrebin & R. M. Regoli, eds., *Police Administrative Issues: Techniques and Functions,* Millwood, NY: Associated Faculty Press.

Christopher Commission (1991) See Independent Commission on the Los Angeles Police Department (1991).

Crank, John P. (1990) "Police: Professionals or Craftsmen? An Empirical Assessment of Professionalism and Craftsmanship among Eight Municipal Police Agencies," 18 *J. Criminal Justice* 333.

Crank, John P., & Robert Langworthy (1992) "An Institutional Perspective of Policing," 83 *J. of Criminal Law & Criminology* 338.

Crank, John P., Betsy Payn, & Stanley Jackson (1993) "The Relationship between Police Belief Systems and Attitude toward Police Practices," 20 *Criminal Justice & Behavior* 199.

Crime Commission (1967) See U.S. President's Commission on Law Enforcement and Administration of Justice (1967).

Day, Martin S. (1984) *The Many Meanings of Myth.* Lanham, MD: Univ. Press of America.

DiMaggio, Paul (1988) "Interest and Agency in Institutional Theory," in Zucker 1988.

DiMaggio, Paul, & Walter Powell (1983) "The Iron Cage Revisited: Institutional Isomorphism and Collective Rationality in Organizational Fields," 48 *American Sociological Rev.* 147.

Dobbin, Frank R., Lauren Edelmen, John W. Meyer, W. Richard Scott, & Ann Swidler (1988) "The Expansion of Due Process in Organizations," in Zucker 1988.

Drucker, H. M. (1974) *The Political Uses of Ideology.* London: Macmillan, for the London School of Economics and Political Science.

Duffee, David (1980) *Explaining Criminal Justice: Community Theory and Criminal Justice Reform.* Cambridge, MA: Oelgeschlager, Gunn & Hain.

Dunham, Roger G., & Geoffrey P. Alpert, eds. (1989) *Critical Issues in Policing.* Prospect Heights, IL: Waveland Press.

Durkheim, Emile (1955) *The Elementary Forms of the Religious Life,* trans. J. W. Swain. New York: Free Press.

Eck, John E., & William Spelman (1987) "Who Ya Gonna Call? The Police as Problem-Busters," 33 *Crime & Delinquency* 31.

Feeley, Malcolm M., & Austin D. Sarat (1980) *The Policy Dilemma: Federal Crime Policy and the Law Enforcement Assistance Administration.* Minneapolis: Univ. of Minnesota Press.

Fogelson, Robert (1977) *Big-City Police.* Cambridge: Harvard Univ. Press.

Geertz, Clifford (1973) "Thick Description: Toward an Interpretive Theory of Culture," in C. Geertz, ed., *The Interpretation of Cultures.* New York: Basic Books.

Geller, William A., ed. (1985) *Police Leadership in America: Crisis and Opportunity.* New York: Praeger.

Goldstein, Herman (1963) "Police Discretion: The Ideal versus the Real," 23 *Public Administration Rev.* 140.

—— (1979) "Improving Policing: A Problem-oriented Approach," 25 *Crime & Delinquency* 25: 236-58.

Gordon, Diana R. (1991) *The Justice Juggernaut: Fighting Street Crime, Controlling Citizens.* New Brunswick, NJ: Rutgers Univ. Press.

Greene, Jack R. (1989) "Police and Community Relations: Where Have We Been and Where Are We Going?" in Dunham & Alpert 1989.

Guyot, Dorothy (1979) "Bending Granite: Attempts to Change the Rank Structure of American Police Departments," 7 *J. of Police Science & Administration* 253.

—— (1991) *Policing as Though People Matter.* Philadelphia: Temple Univ. Press.

Hall, Richard H. (1982) *Organizations: Structures, Processes, and Outcomes.* 3d ed. Englewood Cliffs, NJ: Prentice-Hall.

Hartmann, Francis X. (1988) *Debating the Evolution of American Policing.* Perspectives on the Police #5. Washington: National Institute of Justice.

Independent Commission on the Los Angeles Police Department (1991) *Report of the Independent Commission on the Los Angeles Police Department* ("Christopher Commission"). Los Angeles: The Independent Commission.

Kelling, George L. (1985) "Order Maintenance, the Quality of Urban Life, and Police: A Line of Argument," in Geller 1985.

—— (1987) "Acquiring a Taste for Order: The Community and the Police," 33 *Crime & Delinquency* 90.

Kelling, George, Tony Pate, Duane Dieckman, & Charles E. Brown (1974) *The Kansas City Preventive Patrol Experiment: A Technical Report.* Washington: Police Foundation.

Kelling, George, & Mark H. Moore (1989) *The Evolving Strategy of Policing.* Perspectives on Policing #4. Washington: National Institute on Justice & Harvard Univ.

Kerner Commission (1967) See National Advisory Commission on Civil Disorders (1967).

Kirk, G. S. (1974) *The Nature of Greek Myths.* New York: Penguin Books.

Klockars, Carl B. (1985) "Order and Maintenance, the Quality of Urban Life, and Police: A Different Line of Argument," in Geller 1985.

—— (1991) "The Rhetoric of Community Policing," in Klockars & Mastrofski 1991.

Klockars, Carl B., & Stephen D. Mastrofski, eds. (1991) *Thinking about Policing.* 2d ed. New York: McGraw-Hill.

Malinowski, Bronislaw (1954) *Magic, Science and Religion.* New York: Doubleday.

Manning, Peter K. (1977) *Police Work: The Social Organization of Policing.* Cambridge: MIT Press.

—— (1984) "Community Policing," 3 *American J. of Police* 205.

Manning, Peter, & Lawrence John Redlinger (1977) "Invitational Edges of Corruption: Some Consequences of Narcotic Law Enforcement," in P. E. Rock, ed., *Drugs and Politics.* New Brunswick, NJ: Transaction Books.

Mastrofski, Stephen D. (1991) "Community Policing as Reform: A Cautionary Tale," in Klockars & Mastrofski 1991.

Meyer, John W., & Brian Rowan (1977) "Institutionalized Organizations: Formal Structure as Myth and Ceremony," 83 *American J. of Sociology* 340.

Meyer, John W., & W. Richard Scott (1983) "Centralization and the Legitimacy Problems of Local Government," in J. W. Meyer & W. R. Scott, eds., *Organizational Environments: Ritual and Rationality.* Beverly Hills, CA: Sage Publications.

Michalowski, Raymond J. (1985) *Order, Law, and Crime.* New York: Random House.

Moore, Mark H., & George L. Kelling (1983) "'To Serve and Protect': Learning from Police History," 70 *Public Interest* 49.

National Advisory Commission on Civil Disorders (1967) *Report of the National Advisory Commission on Civil Disorder* ("Kerner Commission"). Washington: GPO.

Nisbet, Robert (1988) *The Present Age: Progress and Anarchy in Modern America.* New York: Harper & Row.

Poplin, Dennis E. (1979) *Communities: A Survey of Theories and Methods of Research*. New York: Macmillan

Powell, Walter (1991) "Expanding the Scope of Institutional Analysis," in W. W. Powell & P. J. DiMaggio, eds., *The New Institutionalism in Organizational Analysis*. Chicago: Univ. of Chicago Press.

Ritti, R. Richard, & Jonathan H. Silver (1986) "Early Processes of Institutionalization: The Dramaturgy of Exchange in Interorganizational Relations," 31 *Administrative Science Q.* 25.

Rosenbaum, Dennis P., ed. (1986). *Community Crime Prevention: Does It Work?* Beverly Hills, CA: Sage Publications.

Selznick, Philip (1957) *Leadership in Administration*. New York: Harper & Row.

Sherman, Lawrence (1986) "Policing Communities: What Really Works?" in A. Reiss & M. Tonry, eds., *Community and Crisis*. Chicago: Univ. of Chicago Press.

Skolnick, Jerome M., & David H. Bayley (1986) *The New Blue Line: Police Innovation in Six American Cities*. New York: Free Press.

Sorel, Georges (1916) *Reflections of Violence*, trans. by T. E. Hulme. London: Allen & Unwin.

Strenski, Ivan (1987) *Four Theories of Myth in Twentieth-Century History*. Iowa City: Univ. of Iowa Press.

Swidler, Ann (1986) "Culture in Action: Symbols and Strategies," 51 *American Sociological Rev.* 273.

Sykes, Gary W. (1986) "Street Justice: A Moral Defense of Order Maintenance Policing," 3 *Justice Q.* 497.

—— (1989) "The Functional Nature of Police Reform: The 'Myth' of Controlling the Police," in Dunham & Alpert 1989.

Tocqueville, Alexis de (1945) 1 *Democracy in America*. New York: Vintage.

Trice, Harrison M., & Janice M. Beyer (1984) "Studying Organizational Cultures through Rites and Ceremonials," 9 *Academy of Management Rev.* 653.

Trojanowicz, Robert, & Bonnie Bucqueroux (1990) *Community Policing: A Contemporary Perspective*. Cincinnati: Anderson Publishing Co.

U.S. President's Commission on Law Enforcement & Administration of Justice (1967) *The Challenge of Crime in a Free Society* ("Crime Commission"). Washington: GPO.

Vernon, Richard (1978) *Commitment and Change: Georges Sorel and the Idea of Revolution*. Toronto: Univ. of Toronto Press.

Walker, Samuel (1977) *A Critical History of Police Reform: The Emergence of Professionalism*. Lexington, MA: Lexington Books.

—— (1980) *Popular Justice: A History of American Criminal Justice*. New York: Oxford Univ. Press.

—— (1985) "Setting the Standards: The Efforts and Impact of Blue-Ribbon Commissions on the Police," in Geller 1985.

—— (1989a) *Sense and Nonsense about Crime: A Policy Guide*. 2d ed. Belmont, CA: Brooks/Cole.

—— (1989b) "'Broken Windows' and Fractured History: The Use and Misuse of History in Recent Police Patrol Analysis," in Dunham & Alpert 1989.

—— (1992a) "Origins of the Contemporary Criminal Justice Paradigm: The American Bar Foundation Survey, 1953–1969," 9 (1) *Justice Q.* 47.

—— (1992b) *Police In America*. 2d ed. New York: McGraw-Hill.

Wilson, James Q. (1968) *Varieties of Police Behavior: The Management of Law and Order in Eight Communities*. Cambridge: Harvard Univ. Press.

—— (1977) "Two Police Departments: The Influence of Structure on Operation," in D. B. Kenny, ed., *The Dysfunctional Alliance: Emotion and Reason in Justice Administration*. Cincinnati: Anderson Publishing.

Wilson, James Q., & George L. Kelling (1982) "Broken Windows," *Atlantic Monthly*, pp. 29-38 (March).

Wycoff, Mary Ann, & Peter K. Manning (1983) "The Police and Crime Control," in G. Whitaker & C. Phillips, eds., *Evaluating Performance in Police Agencies.* Beverly Hills, CA: Sage Publications.

Zucker, Lynne, ed. (1988) *Institutional Patterns and Organizations: Culture and Environment.* Cambridge, MA: Ballinger Publishing Co.

Case Cited

Miranda v. Arizona, 384 U.S. 436 (1966).

Part II
The Fourth and Fifth Amendments
'On the Ground' – Search,
Seizure and Interrogation

[3]

STREET STOPS AND BROKEN WINDOWS: *TERRY*, RACE, AND DISORDER IN NEW YORK CITY

Jeffrey Fagan and Garth Davies*

Patterns of "stop and frisk" activity by police across New York City neighborhoods reflect competing theories of aggressive policing. "Broken Windows" theory[1] suggest that neighborhoods with greater concentration of physical and social disorder should evidence higher stop and frisk activity, especially for "quality of life" crimes.[2] However, although disorder theory informs quality of life policing strategies, patterns of stop and frisk activity suggest that neighborhood characteristics such as racial composition, poverty levels, and extent of social disorganization are stronger predictors of race- and crime-specific stops. Accordingly, neighborhood "street stop" activity reflects competing assumptions and meanings of policing strategy. Furthermore, looking at the rate at which street stops meet Terry *standards of reasonable suspicion[3] in various neighborhoods provides additional perspective on the social and strategic meanings of policing. Our empirical evidence suggests that policing is not about disorderly places, nor about improving the quality of life, but about policing poor people in poor places. This strategy contradicts the policy rationale derived from Broken Windows theory, and deviates from the original emphasis on communities by focusing on people. Racially disparate policing reinforces perceptions by citizens in minority neighborhoods that they are under non-particularized suspicion and are therefore targeted for aggressive stop and frisk policing. Such broad targeting raises concerns about the legitimacy of law, threatens to weaken citizen participation in the co-production of*

* Jeffrey Fagan is a professor at the Mailman School of Public Health, Columbia University, and a visiting professor at Columbia Law School. Garth Davies is a doctoral candidate, School of Criminal Justice, Rutgers University. All opinions are those of the authors. Peter K. Manning provided helpful comments on this article. Brandon Garrett provided timely and thorough research assistance.

1. James Q. Wilson & George L. Kelling, *The Police and Neighborhood Safety: Broken Windows*, ATLANTIC MONTHLY, Mar. 1982, at 29-38 (using the analogy of a broken window to describe the relationship between disorder and crime).

2. *Id.*

3. Terry v. Ohio, 392 U.S. 1 (1968) (establishing *reasonable suspicion*, as opposed to the higher quantum of proof of *probable cause*, as the constitutional standard to govern stop and frisks).

security, and undercuts the broader social norms goals of contemporary policing.

When it comes to debating theories of crime and law, some people pretend that race does not matter at all, while others accord it undue, if not determinative, significance.[4] Unfortunately, recent events in policing seem to tip the balance of reality toward the latter view. There is now strong empirical evidence that individuals of color are more likely than white Americans to be stopped, questioned, searched, and arrested by police.[5] This occurs in part because of their race, in part because of heightened law enforcement intensity in minority communities, in part because of the temptation among law enforcement officers to simply "play the base rates" by stopping minority suspects because minorities commit

---

4. *See generally* RANDALL KENNEDY, RACE, CRIME, AND THE LAW (1997) (exploring the impact of race relations on criminal law and criminal justice); *see also* Kim Taylor-Thompson, *The Politics of Common Ground*, 111 HARV. L. REV. 1306 (1998) (emphasizing the role of race in criminal justice issues through a critical review of RACE, CRIME, AND THE LAW).

5. United States v. New Jersey, No. 99-5970 (MLC) (D. N.J. Dec. 30, 1999) (consent decree) (establishing the state of New Jersey's consent to comply with various procedures and policies to remedy racial profiling by the state police), http://www.usdoj.gov/crt/split/documents/jerseysa.htm; U.S. GEN. ACCOUNTING OFFICE, RACIAL PROFILING LIMITED DATA AVAILABLE ON MOTORIST STOPS, GAO-GGD-00-41, 7-13 (2000), *available at* http://www.gao.gov/AIndexFY00/title/tocR.htm; CIVIL RIGHTS BUREAU, OFFICE OF THE ATTORNEY GEN. OF THE STATE OF N.Y., THE NEW YORK CITY POLICE DEPARTMENT'S "STOP & FRISK" PRACTICES 89 (1999) [hereinafter OAG REPORT]; DAVID COLE, NO EQUAL JUSTICE: RACE AND CLASS IN THE AMERICAN CRIMINAL JUSTICE SYSTEM, 34-41 (1999) (describing the explicit use of race in criminal profiles by police departments in Maryland, Colorado, Louisiana, and New Jersey); Sean Hecker, *Race and Pretextual Traffic Stops: An Expanded Role for Civilian Review Boards*, 28 COLUM. HUM. RTS. L. REV. 551, 551 (1997); Kris Antonelli, *State Police Deny Searches are Race-Based; ACLU Again Challenges I-95 Stops*, BALT. SUN, Nov. 16, 1996, at 18B; David Kocieniewski & Robert Hanley, *Racial Profiling Was The Routine, New Jersey Finds*, N.Y. TIMES, Nov. 28, 2000, at A1; Barbara Whitaker, *San Diego Police Found to Stop Black and Latino Drivers Most*, N.Y. TIMES, Oct. 1, 2000, at A31; Jim Yardley, *Studies Find Race Disparities in Texas Traffic Stops*, N.Y. TIMES, Oct. 7, 2000, at A12. Similar patterns of stops, searches, and arrests of citizens have been observed in London. *See generally* DAVID SMITH ET AL., POLICE AND PEOPLE IN LONDON: VOLUME I: A SURVEY OF LONDONERS 89-119, tbl.IV.3 (1983) (showing racial disparity in police contacts with black citizens in London). The London survey was conducted in 1981-82, with a stratified random sample of 2420 Londoners ages fifteen and older. Minorities were over-sampled to ensure adequate representation in the study. Overall, 16% of Londoners were stopped in the twelve months preceding the survey. West Indians were slightly more likely to be stopped than whites (18% as compared with 14%), and Asians were least likely to be stopped (5%). The average number of stops was twice as high for West Indians (0.56) compared with whites (0.21) or Asians (0.8). The average number of arrests per person stopped was also far greater for West Indians (3.19) than for whites (1.46) or Asians (1.59). *Id.*

more crimes, and in part because of the tacit approval of these practices given by their superiors.[6]

Whether the legal system should consider race in its every day decision-making is a hotly contested and much-litigated issue.[7] Yet the modern practice of racial policing should surprise no one. Racial profiling is often defended as a useful means to detect criminal behavior.[8] The legal system has long used race as a signal of increased risk of criminality. Examples include: immigration exclusion and other discrimination against Chinese immigrants in the 19th century;[9] the racialization of the debate on the passage of the Harrison Narcotics Act;[10] the internment of the Japanese during World War II;[11] border interdictions to halt illegal immigration;[12]

---

6. *See generally* STATE POLICE REVIEW TEAM, OFFICE OF THE ATTORNEY GEN. OF THE STATE OF N.J., INTERIM REPORT OF THE STATE POLICE REVIEW TEAM REGARDING ALLEGATIONS OF RACIAL PROFILING (1999) (admitting that New Jersey State Police officers engaged in racial profiling, but also that profiling is part of the culture of the State Police), *available at* http://www.state.nj.us/lps/intm_419.pdf (Apr. 20, 1999); *see generally* Jeffrey Goldberg, *The Color of Suspicion*, N.Y. TIMES MAG., June 20, 1999, at 51 (examining various perspectives on racial profiling).

7. Brandon Garrett, *Standing while Black: Distinguishing* Lyons *in Racial Profiling Cases*, 100 COLUM. L. REV. 1815, 1816 n.5 (2000) (reviewing recent lawsuits and investigations of racial profiling). Consent decrees stemming from racial profiling have been signed in many cases. *E.g.*, United States v. New Jersey, No. 99-5970 (MLC) (D. N.J. Dec. 30, 1999) (consent decree entered); Memorandum of Agreement, Between the United States Department of Justice, Montgomery County, Maryland, the Montgomery County Department of Police, and the Fraternal Order of Police, Montgomery County Lodge 35, Inc., Jan. 14, 2000, http//www.usdoj.gov/crt/cor/Pubs/mcagrmt.htm; United States v. City of Pittsburgh, No. 97-0354 (W.D. Pa. Apr. 16, 1997) (consent decree entered); United States v. City of Steubenville, C2-97-966 (S.D. Ohio Sept. 3, 1997) (consent decree entered), http://usdoj.gov/cit/split/documents/steubensa.htm; United States v. City of Los Angeles, No. 00-11769 (C.D. Cal.) (consent decree entered). For reviews of consent decrees involving police departments generally, see Debra Livingston, *Police Reform and the Department of Justice: An Essay on Accountability*, 2 BUFF. CRIM. L. REV. 815 (1999); Myriam E. Gilles, *Reinventing Structural Reform Litigation: Deputizing Private Citizens in the Enforcement of Civil Right*, 100 COLUM. L. REV. 1384 (2000).

8. KENNEDY, *supra* note 4, at 145-46 (discussing race as a predictor of criminality). For a review of the historical uses of ethnic and racial exclusion in the United States based on attributions of greater danger to ethnic minorities, see generally SAMUEL WALKER ET AL., THE COLOR OF JUSTICE: RACE, ETHNICITY AND CRIME IN AMERICA (2d ed. 2000).

9. Yick Wo v. Hopkins, 118 U.S. 356 (1886) (inferring intentional discrimination against Chinese citizens from disparate enforcement of an ordinance banning laundries).

10. Harrison Narcotics Act, ch. 1, 38 Stat. 785 (1914); *see also* DAVID F. MUSTO, THE AMERICAN DISEASE 65 (1973) ("Cocaine raised the specter of the Wild Negro, opium the devious Chinese . . . .").

11. Korematsu v. United States, 323 U.S. 214 (1944) (finding forced internment troubling but ultimately upholding its constitutionality).

racial components of drug courier profiling;[13] and the so-called Carol Stuart stops in Boston.[14]

Generally, courts have refused to disallow the use of race as an indicia of criminality.[15] Most courts have accepted this practice, so long as (1) race alone is not the rationale for the interdiction, and (2) it is not done for purposes of racial harassment.[16] This practice has been reflected in case law as the sound exercise of "professional judgment" by police officers.[17]

---

12. United States v. Martinez-Fuerte, 428 U.S. 543, 556-57 (1976) (affirming the U.S. Border Patrol's right to conduct checkpoint stops of vehicles near the Mexican border with or without reasonable suspicion).

13. United States v. Harvey, 16 F.3d 109, 115 (6th Cir. 1994) (Keith, J., dissenting) ("African-Americans are more likely to be arrested because drug courier profiles reflect the erroneous assumption that one's race has a direct correlation to drug activity.").

14. MASS. ATTORNEY GEN.'S OFFICE, REPORT OF THE ATTORNEY GENERAL'S CIVIL RIGHTS DIVISION ON BOSTON POLICE DEPARTMENT PRACTICES (Dec. 18, 1990) (reporting results of an investigation into allegations that, in violation of constitutional mandates, the Boston Police Department "rounded up" African American men in the wake of the murder of Carol Stuart, a white woman).

Shortly before this article went to press, a sharply-divided United States Court of Appeals for the Second Circuit declined to reconsider its ruling upholding its dismissal of *Brown v. City of Oneonta*, 221 F.3d 329 (2000). The plaintiffs in *Brown* alleged that police unconstitutionally swept the 10,000-resident town and stopped and inspected the hands of black men after an elderly woman alleged she had been attacked in her home by a young black male who cut his hand during a struggle.

> The panel reaches a grave conclusion by holding that the police act constitutionally under the Fourteenth Amendment when, based on a witness's predominantly racial description, they stop every young African American male in town to determine whether he can exclude himself from a vague class of potential suspects that has been defined in overwhelmingly racial terms.

Brown v. City of Oneonta, — F.3d — (2d Cir. 2000), *available in* 2000 WL 1855047.

15. *See* Whren v. United States, 517 U.S. 806 (1996). In *Whren*, the U.S. Supreme Court ruled that as long as an officer observes a traffic violation, a traffic stop is constitutional, even if the officer has no intention to enforce the law the driver violated. Even if purely pretextual, a racially-motivated stop is constitutional under the Fourth Amendment if also motivated by a second, non-racial factor. The Court did state, however, that a stop motivated by race alone would violate Fourteenth Amendment protections. *Id.* at 813. COLE, *supra* note 5, at 39-40 (citing the extraordinarily high concentration of minority complainants in unsuccessful federal appellate cases involving pretextual traffic stops). *See also Harvey*, 16 F.3d at 115 (Keith, J., dissenting); KENNEDY, *supra* note 4, at 14 ("Racist perceptions of blacks have given energy to policies and practices (such as racial exclusion in housing, impoverished schooling, and stingy social welfare programs) that have facilitated the growth of egregious crime-spawning conditions that millions of Americans face in urban slums and rural backwaters across the nation.") (citation omitted).

16. *See Whren*, 517 U.S. at 813.

17. Although courts may be reluctant explicitly to identify and endorse the use of race as a proxy for criminal behavior, the factual underpinnings of many cases reveal tacit judicial approval of racial profiling. *E.g.*, Papachristou v. City of Jacksonville, 405

Contemporary criminal justice theory and practice accord with this view, but substitute sociological language for the more formal legal endorsement of race-based practices. In New York City, law enforcement strategies emphasize the aggressive patrol of areas containing manifestations of physical and social disorder. Thus, police aggressively enforce laws on public drinking and loitering. They also actively patrol neighborhoods with empty lots, abandoned cars, and dilapidated buildings. Collectively, these strategies are based on the "Broken Windows" theory, named after the influential essay on the contagious effects of unchecked signs of disorder.[18]

Beginning in 1994, officials altered the police strategies in New York City to address low-level disorder problems that might invite more serious crime problems.[19] These signs of disorder often are more prevalent in urban neighborhoods with elevated rates of pov-

---

U.S. 156 (1972) (reviewing the enforcement of a vague vagrancy ordinance against two black men accompanied by two white females); Florida v. J.L., 529 U.S. 266 (2000) (reviewing the adequacy of a stop and frisk based on an anonymous informant's description of a "young black male" wearing a plaid shirt and carrying a gun).

The "professional judgment" of Detective McFadden provided the basis for his stop and search of the defendant in *Terry v. Ohio*, 392 U.S. 1, 28 (1968). What has been lost in the *Terry* discourse in the ensuing years is the explicit racial component of the events. Terry was African American, McFadden was white. McFadden's "professional judgment" concerning Terry was based on the racial incongruity of Terry being observed outside a storefront in a commercial district far from the areas of Cleveland where most African Americans lived. Anthony C. Thompson, *Stopping the Usual Suspects: Race and the Fourth Amendment*, 74 N.Y.U. L. Rev. 956, 966 (1999). *But see Terry*, 392 U.S. at 5-7 (detailing the suspicious activity the *Terry* defendants engaged in after Detective McFadden, a thirty-nine year veteran of the police department, first observed them and felt "they didn't look right to [him] at the time").

In *Illinois v. Wardlow*, 528 U.S. 119, 124 (2000), the Court noted that although an individual's presence in a "high crime area" does not meet the standard for a particularized suspicion of criminal activity, a location's characteristics are relevant in determining whether an individual's behavior is sufficiently suspicious to warrant further investigation. Since "high crime areas" often are areas with concentrations of minority citizens, this logic places minority neighborhoods at risk for elevating the suspiciousness of its residents. *See e.g.*, Douglas S. Massey & Nancy A. Denton, American Apartheid: Segregation and the Making of the Underclass (1993).

18. Wilson & Kelling, *supra* note 1, at 31. *See generally* George L. Kelling & Catherine M. Coles, Fixing Broken Windows: Restoring Order and Reducing Crime in Our Communities (1996).

19. Bernard E. Harcourt, *Reflecting on the Subject: A Critique of the Social Influence Conception of Deterrence, the Broken Windows Theory, and Order-Maintenance Policing New York Style*, 97 Mich. L. Rev. 291, 292 (1998); Debra Livingston, *Police Discretion and the Quality of Life in Public Places: Courts, Communities, and the New Policing*, 97 Colum. L. Rev. 551, 556 n.14 (1997); Sarah E. Waldeck, *Cops, Community Policing, and the Social Norms Approach to Crime Control: Should One Make Us More Comfortable with the Others?*, 34 Ga. L. Rev. 1273, 1273 (2000).

erty and social fragmentation.[20] Accordingly, the implementation
of Broken Windows policies was disproportionately concentrated
in minority neighborhoods and conflated with poverty and other
signs of socio-economic disadvantage. Thus, what was constructed
as "order-maintenance policing" ("OMP") was widely perceived
among minority citizens as racial policing, or racial profiling.[21] The
fact that its principle tactic was an aggressive form of stop and frisk
policing involving intrusive *Terry* searches,[22] and that at least two
deaths of unarmed citizens of African descent were linked to
OMP,[23] further intensified perceptions of racial animus.[24]

---

20. WESLEY G. SKOGAN, DISORDER AND DECLINE: CRIME AND THE SPIRAL OF
DECAY IN AMERICAN NEIGHBORHOODS 59 (1990); Robert J. Sampson & Stephen W.
Raudenbush, *Systematic Social Observation of Public Spaces: A New Look at Disorder in Urban Neighborhoods*, 105 AM. J. SOCIOLOGY 603, 622-30 (1999); Stephen W.
Raudenbush & Robert J. Sampson, *Ecometrics: Toward a Science of Assessing Ecological Settings, with Application to the Systematic Social Observation of Neighborhoods*, 29 SOCIOLOGICAL METHODOLOGY 1 (1999).

21. OAG REPORT, *supra* note 5, at 74; David Kocieniewski, *Success of Elite Police
Unit Exacts a Toll on the Streets*, N.Y. TIMES, Feb. 15, 1999, at A1 (discussing reactions
of citizens to aggressive policing in New York City); Kit R. Roane, *Minority Private-
School Students Claim Police Harassment*, N.Y. TIMES, Mar. 26, 1999, at B5 (citing
complaints by minority students of indiscriminate and frequent police harassment).

22. There is an irony here about the use of such citizen detentions and searches as
a crime fighting tool. The *Terry* decision itself located the frisk less as an investigative
aid than as a protection for the patrolling officer: "The frisk . . . was essential to the
proper performance of the officer's investigatory duties, for without it the answer to
the police officer may be a bullet." Terry v. Ohio, 392 U.S. 1, 8 (1968) (citation omitted). That the stop and frisk engenders animosity was made explicit in the original
Terry decision. The Supreme Court in *Terry* noted that a frisk "is a serious intrusion
upon the sanctity of the person, which may inflict great indignity and arouse strong
resentment, and is not to be undertaken lightly." *Id.* at 17. The Court also noted that
Terry stops had the potential to inflict psychological harm: "Even a limited search . . .
constitutes a severe, though brief, intrusion upon cherished personal security, and it
must surely be an annoying, frightening, and perhaps humiliating experience." *Id.* at
24-25.

23. David Jackson, *Winning War on Crime Has a Price Giuliani Alienates Many in
New York City's Black and Hispanic Communities*, DENVER POST, Apr. 20, 2000, at
A23 (discussing the shootings by the New York City Police Department ("NYPD") of
Amadou Diallo and Patrick Dorismond); Symposium, *Is Our Drug Policy Effective?
Are There Alternatives?*, 28 FORDHAM URB. L.J. 3, 95 (2000) ("[A] team of under-
cover police approached a man [Patrick Dorismond] . . . even though they had no
reason to believe that he was involved in any criminal activity.").

24. Citizens who are stopped and frisked based on a profiling or racial policing
strategy understand that they have been singled out because of their race. These encounters have been termed "race-making situations." David R. James, *The Racial
Ghetto as a Race-Making Situation: The Effects of Residential Segregation on Racial
Inequalities and Racial Identity*, 19 LAW & SOC. INQUIRY 407, 420-29 (1994). The out-
rage of many minority citizens over the NYPD's policing of aggressive stop and frisks
reflects not only the emotional harm from being targeted because of one's race, but
also the fear that such situations can escalate into dangerously violent encounters. *See
generally* David A. Harris, *The Stories, the Statistics, and the Law: Why "Driving*

Moreover, by explicitly linking disorder to violence, OMP (as informed by Broken Windows theory) further focused police resources and efforts on the neighborhoods with the highest crime and violence rates.[25] That these were predominantly minority neighborhoods further reinforced the disproportionate exposure of New York City's minority citizens to policing. Thus, this construction of disorder broadened the concept to include places where violent and other serious crimes were most likely to occur. Those places tended to be ones with the highest concentrations of socially-disadvantaged minority populations.

In this paper, we assess empirical evidence designed to sort out these competing claims about the underlying theoretical basis for New York City's aggressive policing policy. We analyze patterns of stop and frisk activity to assess whether practice reflected the place-based strategies embodied in Broken Windows theory, or if instead, practice was focused on the social markers of race and disadvantage. We ask whether, after controlling for disorder, the city's stop and frisk policy is, in fact, a form of policing that disproportionately targets racial minorities. We begin by reviewing the history and evolution of these policies, showing the links between race, Broken Windows theory, and aggressive policing. In Part II, we review evidence of the racial skew in policing as reported in recent studies. In Part III, we offer the results of empirical tests of data conducted on trends and patterns of policing to resolve these competing claims about the motivating theories for the observed patterns. We find little evidence to support claims that policing targeted places and signs of physical disorder, and show instead that stops of citizens were more often concentrated in minority

---

While Black" Matters, 84 MINN. L. REV. 265, 273 (1999). The shared danger of profiling encounters reflects the concept of "linked fate" among residents of minority neighborhoods. "Linked fate" refers to the empathy that people have with family and friends. It can also exist among strangers. In the African American community, linked fate has its foundation in the fact that the life chances of African Americans historically have been shaped by race. MICHAEL C. DAWSON, BEHIND THE MULE: RACE AND CLASS IN AFRICAN-AMERICAN POLITICS 77 (1994). Linked fate suggests that when race over-determines an individual's life chances, it is much more efficient for that individual to use the relative and absolute status of the group as a proxy for individual utility. The long history of race-based constraints on life chances among blacks generates a certain efficiency in evaluating policies that affect minority individuals. *Id.*

25. OAG REPORT, *supra* note 5, at 53 (citing N.Y. CITY POLICE DEP'T, POLICE STRATEGY NO. 1: GETTING GUNS OFF THE STREETS OF NEW YORK (1994) (explicitly linking disorder to violence and rationalizing the concentration of order-maintenance policing ("OMP") strategies in the city's neighborhoods with the highest crime rates) [hereinafter POLICE STRATEGY NO.1].

neighborhoods characterized by poverty and social disadvantage. In Part IV, we conclude by returning to the theoretical arguments supporting current police policies. In this last section, we address claims about the positive link between aggressive policing and the prospects for creating social norms changes to restore social regulation of behavior. The counterfactual of crises in legitimacy provides the context for concluding remarks on race and policing in New York.

I. Disorder and Aggressive Policing in New York City

A. From Theory to Practice: Broken Windows and Order-Maintenance Policing

As stated, the policy of aggressive stop and frisk practices reflects theoretical and strategic innovations derived from what has become popularly known as Broken Windows theory.[26] The originators of the Broken Windows theory, James Q. Wilson and George L. Kelling, argued that police should address minor disorders to strengthen police-citizen interactions, and consequently, informal social control.[27] For Wilson and Kelling, signs of physical and social disorder invite criminal activity.[28] Disorder indicates to law-abiding citizens that their neighborhoods are dangerous places, leading to their withdrawal from informal social control and regulation.[29] The theory suggests that there is a tipping point at which disorder trumps order by defeating the willingness of citizens to interact with the police and with each other to co-produce security. Accordingly, disorder invites more disorder in a contagious process that progressively breaks down community standards and also sug-

---

26. Wilson & Kelling, *supra* note 1, at 31. For excellent reviews, see Livingston, *supra* note 19, at 578 (discussing the relationship between Broken Windows theory and current policing practices); Harcourt, *supra* note 19, at 301-08 (critiquing Broken Windows theory and empirical research claiming to support the link between disorder and crime); Tracey L. Meares & Dan M. Kahan, *Law and (Norms of) Order in the Inner City*, 32 Law & Soc'y Rev. 805 (1998) (discussing the link between social norms theory and law enforcement policies).

27. Wilson & Kelling, *supra* note 1, at 31; Livingston, *supra* note 19, at 576; Waldeck, *supra* note 19, at 1255.

28. Wilson & Kelling, *supra* note 1, at 32. They define "minor" disorder to include such problems and crimes as littering, loitering, public drinking, panhandling, teenage fighting on street corners, and prostitution. They also mention signs of physical disorder, including abandoned cars—with broken windows, naturally—and dilapidated buildings, also with broken windows.

29. *Id.* at 33 ("In response to fear, people avoid one another, weakening controls.").

gests to would-be criminals that crime will not be reported. Disorder ultimately invites criminal invasion.

Broken Windows theory comports well with social norms theories. In this framework, individuals form social norms through interactions with others in social spaces, creating norms of either legal or illegal behavior in their communities.[30] Wilson and Kelling argue that when police focus on repairing or removing these disorder problems, they combat crime by promoting the types of social interactions among law-abiding citizens that strengthen the dynamics of social regulation and produce security and social control.[31] To restate this in terms of Broken Windows theory, disorder conveys a social message that there is no effective social regulation of behavior in a neighborhood with such visible and prevalent signs of disorder.[32] In turn, disorder communicates the absence of restraints to others who may interpret this as either tolerance of, or an invitation to, criminal behavior. Thus, as both disorder and criminal behavior spread, they communicate a mutually reinforcing social norm regarding crime and social disorder, all the while communicating danger to those who would attempt to reinforce social norms that oppose crime and disorder.

Empirical support for Broken Windows and disorder theories of crime is reported by Wesley Skogan in an analysis of survey data collected in 1977 and 1983 in six cities.[33] Additional empirical support is reported by George L. Kelling and Catherine M. Coles.[34] Bernard Harcourt, however, reanalyzed Skogan's data and failed to replicate the results, citing numerous inconsistencies and errors in measurement.[35] Dan Kahan attributes New York City's crime decline in the 1990s to the adoption by its police department of a tactical strategy based on Broken Windows theory, although em-

---

30. Meares & Kahan, *supra* note 26, at 805. For an illustration based on ethnographic research, see ELIJAH ANDERSON, CODE OF THE STREET (1999).

31. Wilson & Kelling, *supra* note 1, at 35; ANDERSON, *supra* note 30, at 32; *see also* Harcourt, *supra* note 19, at 302-3. *See generally* Robert C. Ellickson, *Controlling Chronic Misconduct in City Spaces: Of Panhandlers, Skid Rows, and Public-Space Zoning,* 105 YALE L.J. 1165 (1996).

32. *See generally* Lawrence Lessig, *The Regulation of Social Meaning,* 62 U. CHI. L. REV. 943 (1995) (discussing the construction of social meaning); Ellickson, *supra* note 31.

33. SKOGAN, *supra* note 20. Surveys were conducted in Atlanta, Chicago, Houston, Newark, Philadelphia, and San Francisco. His basic model was a regression analysis predicting robbery rates from measures of social and physical disorder, controlling for characteristics of the cities derived from social disorganization theory: poverty, residential stability, and racial heterogeneity.

34. *See generally* KELLING & COLES, *supra* note 18.

35. Harcourt, *supra* note 19, at 312-39.

466   *FORDHAM URBAN LAW JOURNAL* [Vol. XXVIII

pirical and conceptual assessments of the crime decline contest that view.[36] Empirical work by Robert Sampson and Jacqueline Cohen provide indirect support for a Broken Windows model of policing by focusing on factors that influence perceptions of the tolerance of disorder, especially higher arrest ratios (relative to the crime rate).[37] Despite the implicit developmental and deontological underpinnings of Broken Windows theory (and corresponding social norms theories), none of the supportive studies included prospective tests of the effects of disorder on changes in crime rates in subsequent periods. In fact, all these studies rely on cross-sectional research that is unable to determine whether the observed relationships are temporally-ordered and therefore causally related, or if they are simply correlations whose causal order is unknown.[38]

The most comprehensive empirical test of the underlying premise of Broken Windows theory—that disorder gives rise to higher crime rates—was a study of disorder in Chicago neighborhoods by Robert Sampson and Stephen Raudenbush.[39] Rather than rely on either official records or self-reports, the researchers constructed highly reliable measures of social disorder from a randomized schedule of videotaping of locations. They combined these disorder measures with reports of social control mechanisms from a random sample of 3864 residents in 343 neighborhoods, and both self-reported and official records of crime. Sampson and Raudenbush re-

---

36. Dan M. Kahan, *Between Economics and Sociology: The New Path of Deterrence*, 95 Mich. L. Rev. 2477, 2488 n.63, n.65 (1997). Kahan states that the decline in crime must be attributable to the new policing strategy: order-maintenance policing. *Id.* *But see* Jeffrey Fagan et al., *Declining Homicide in New York City: A Tale of Two Trends*, 88 J. Crim. L. & Criminology 1277, 1285-86, 1289-91(1998) (claiming that changes in crime rates are actually predictable cyclical changes in violence rates, and that only gun crime rates have changed); Andrew Karmen, New York Murder Mystery 13-24 (2000) (discussing competing causal claims for the decline in New York City's homicide rate from 1991-98, but finding insufficient evidence to support any single explanation).

37. Robert J. Sampson & Jacqueline Cohen, *Deterrent Effects of the Police on Crime: A Replication and Theoretical Extension*, 22 Law & Soc. Rev. 163, 175-79 (1988) (reporting that more aggressive stop and frisk enforcement produces higher arrest ratios that, in turn, communicate a high punishment likelihood to would-be law violators).

38. For a general discussion of this type of validity threat in cross-sectional, non-experimental research designs, see generally Thomas D. Cook & Donald T. Campbell, Quasi-Experimentation Design and Analysis Issues For Field Settings (1979); Kenneth Rothman, Modern Epidemiology (1986); Leon Robertson, Injury Epidemiology (1992).

39. Sampson & Raudenbush, *supra* note 20 (reporting results of an observational survey of physical and social disorder in Chicago neighborhoods and its weak association with crime rates).

ported that social interactions and social controls among neighbors are more closely related to crime than is disorder, while these social processes—which they term "collective efficacy"—are unrelated to disorder. Similar to Harcourt's re-analysis of the Skogan data, Sampson and Raudenbush also discredit the relationship between crime and disorder.[40]

These empirical doubts about the efficacy of Broken Windows theory have not stopped its influence on American policing. The development of police strategies that operationalize Broken Windows theory proceeded apace in the past two decades.[41] It was widely translated into a police strategy known as "order-maintenance policing," or OMP.[42] At the same time, Broken Windows theory stimulated a body of academic writing on the subject of order maintenance.[43]

Under OMP, police aggressively enforce laws against social disorder with "zero tolerance" that requires arrest for any law infraction.[44] Widely viewed as an adaptation of an earlier movement

---

40. *Id.* at 603.

41. For example, Commissioner William Bratton had earlier implemented an OMP strategy while head of the New York City Transit Police, called the Clean Car Program ("CCP"). The strategy focused on ridding New York City's subway cars of graffiti. Maryalice Sloan-Hewitt & George L. Kelling, *Subway Graffiti in New York City: "Gettin' up" vs. "Meanin' it and Cleanin' it,"* in SITUATIONAL CRIME PREVENTION: SUCCESSFUL CASE STUDIES 242, 244-45 (Ronald V. Clarke, ed., 2d. ed. 1997).

42. Livingston, *supra* note 19, at 632.

43. *E.g.*, George L. Kelling, *Order Maintenance, the Quality of Urban Life, and Police: A Line of Argument,* in POLICE LEADERSHIP IN AMERICA 296 (William A. Geller ed., 1985); Carl B. Klockars, *Order Maintenance, the Quality of Urban Life, and Police: A Different Line of Argument,* in POLICE LEADERSHIP, *supra,* at 309; Carl B. Klockars, *Street Justice: Some Micro-Moral Reservations: Comment on Sykes,* 3 JUST. Q. 513 (1986); Gary W. Sykes, *Street Justice: A Moral Defense of Order Maintenance Policing,* 3 JUST. Q. 497 (1986) [hereinafter *Street Justice*]; Gary W. Sykes, *The Functional Nature of Police Reform: The "Myth" of Controlling the Police,* 2 JUST. Q. 51 (1985). *But see generally* Jack R. Greene & Ralph B. Taylor, *Community-Based Policing and Foot Patrol: Issues of Theory and Evaluation,* in COMMUNITY POLICING: RHETORIC OR REALITY, 195, 201-03 (Jack R. Greene & Stephen D. Mastrofski eds., 1988) [hereinafter COMMUNITY POLICING].

44. Definitions of the crimes that constitute disorder vary, but generally include: unlicensed peddling and vending, public drunkenness and open drinking, vandalism (including graffiti), public urination, loitering, littering, panhandling, prostitution, and menacing misbehavior. The latter often is symbolized by "squeegee" men who solicit money in return for unsolicited cleaning of motorists' windshields at stop lights. Cracking down on squeegee men represents the type of OMP enforcement that most closely expressed popular conceptions of the policy. KELLING & COLES, *supra* note 18, at 14-15; Livingston, *supra* note 19, at 553-54; Harcourt, *supra* note 19, at 297; Wilson & Kelling, *supra* note 1; WILLIAM BRATTON & PETER KNOBLER, TURNAROUND: HOW AMERICA'S TOP COP REVERSED THE CRIME EPIDEMIC 214 (1998) (discussing the NYPD's policy to rid the city of the squeegee people); William J. Brat-

toward "community policing,"[45] OMP advocates active engagement with and arrest of law violators. In more traditional community policing, police pursued ameliorative measures that also were consistent with Broken Windows theory, but avoided coercive encounters with citizens on the street.[46] These ameliorative measures were consistent with Broken Windows tenets that police should focus equally on protecting communities as well as protecting individuals.[47] Although community policing and OMP both derive from a social norms basis, the implementation of OMP in New York moved in a very different direction, exchanging amelioration of physical disorder for interdiction of social disorder.

Sarah Waldeck claims that this exchange resolved a conflict that arose in the occupational subculture of policing with the advent of community policing.[48] In addressing non-crime problems, police were reluctant to adhere to a new set of markers for performance and competence based on social interactions with law-abiding citizens.[49] By emphasizing the aggressive pursuit of social disorder, or disorderly persons, police returned to the more comfortable performance indicators of stops and arrests, while restoring to the workplace their traditional cultural dichotomy of "disorderly people and law abiders."[50] Thus, for example, while New York City police identified only seventy-five "squeegee" people,[51] the expanding definition of disorder meant that more and more people were disorderly and subject to aggressive police attention.

---

ton, *The New York City Police Department's Civil Enforcement of Quality-of-Life Crimes*, 3 J.L. & Pol'y 447, 447-48 (1995); N.Y. City Police Dep't, Police Strategy No. 5: Reclaiming the Public Spaces of New York 10-12 (1994) [hereinafter Police Strategy No. 5].

45. Livingston, *supra* note 19, at 562-91. While OMP emphasizes arrest, other forms of community policing eschew arrest in favor of building community contacts. *E.g.*, Wesley G. Skogan & Susan M. Hartnett, Community Policing, Chicago Style 8, 55-56 (1997).

46. These include, for example, cleaning up trash-strewn lots, painting over graffiti, and assisting housing inspectors to address code violations. *E.g.*, Livingston, *supra* note 19, at 584 (citation omitted); Herman Goldstein, Problem-Oriented Policing 134 (1990); George L. Kelling & Mark H. Moore, *From Political to Reform to Community: The Evolving Strategy of Police*, *in* Community Policing, *supra* note 43, at 3 (Jack R. Greene & Stephen D. Mastrofski eds., 1988); Stephen D. Mastrofski, *Community Policing as Reform: A Cautionary Tale*, *in* Community Policing, *supra* note 43, at 47, 67.

47. *See* Livingston, *supra* note 19, at 583 n.162.

48. Waldeck, *supra* note 19, at 1267-69.

49. *See id.* at 1267.

50. *Id.* at 1268, 1278.

51. Bratton & Knobler, *supra* note 44, at 214.

It is important to remember that Wilson and Kelling's original social science construction of Broken Windows theory had little to do with social disorder, especially with the aggressive interdiction of disorderly persons. Thus, as we shall see next, the evolution of OMP in New York resulted in a policy and style of policing that violated the subtle connection that Wilson and Kelling drew between crime and disorder, and that deviated in many important ways from its underlying social norms paradigm. As we show below, the exchange of physical disorder for social disorder signified nothing less than a theoretical paradigm shift from the original construction of Broken Windows theory to the more traditional and problematic policing of social disorganization.

B. Violence, Disorder, and Order-Maintenance Policing in New York City

Many observers have noted that OMP in New York City has eschewed (what is for police) the more esoteric dimensions of community policing targeted at physical disorder, for an aggressive policy of arrest and other traditional law enforcement tactics aimed squarely at social disorder. While remaining true to the origins of Broken Windows theory, there were strategic and tactical reasons to reconstruct the Broken Windows theory in this way.

Whereas community policing implies a partnership between police and community, the interpretation of community needs is one of the wild cards of the theory.[52] The partnership required that the parties respond both to a neighborhood's priorities regarding crime and to the more traditional police functions of detecting and deterring criminal behavior.[53] Community policing, then, often appeared to be a Solomonesque split between traditional police goals focusing on major crimes (e.g., murder and armed robbery) and the goals of community residents concerned with chronic low-level crimes and disorder problems.[54]

However, in shifting from community policing to OMP, police strategy in New York City redirected its strategic focus from remedying physical disorder to policing social disorder. The rationale for this shift from physical to social disorder was the theory that low-level crime—social disorder—nurtures and facilitates more serious crime.[55] George L. Kelling and Catherine M. Cole conceptu-

---

52. *See* Skogan & Hartnett, *supra* note 45, at 8.
53. BRATTON & KNOBLER, *supra* note 44, at 94-95.
54. *See generally* Goldstein, *supra* note 46.
55. Wilson & Kelling, *supra* note 1, at 34.

alized OMP as a cooperative variant on community policing: the enforcement of standards of conduct jointly defined by citizens and police.[56] Even so, this strategic shift did not necessarily imply a tactical change toward aggressive policing. Moreover, this tactical shift departed sharply from the Wilson and Kelling and the Kelling and Coles models of Broken Windows, as well as most contemporary models of community policing.[57] As conceptualized by Kelling and Coles, OMP involved the enforcement of these standards "through non-arrest approaches—education, persuasion, counseling, and ordering—so that arrest would only be resorted to when other approaches failed."[58]

The origins of the tactical shift are revealed in strategy documents issued by the New York City Police Department ("NYPD") in 1994.[59] According to the analysis by the Office of the Attorney General of the State of New York ("OAG Report"), these policies remain in effect today.[60] First, *Police Strategy No. 5, Reclaiming the Public Spaces of New York*,[61] articulates a reconstructed version of Broken Windows theory as the driving force in the development of policing policy. It states that the NYPD would apply its enforcement efforts to "reclaim the streets" by systematically and aggressively enforcing laws against low-level *social* disorder: graffiti, aggressive panhandling, fare beating, public drunkenness, unlicensed vending, public drinking, public urination, and other low-level misdemeanor offenses.[62]

Second, *Police Strategy No. 1, Getting Guns Off the Streets of New York*,[63] formalized the strategic focus on the eradication of gun violence through the tactical measure of intensifying efforts to seize illegal firearms. Homicide trends in New York City since 1985 provided strong empirical support for emphasizing gun violence in enforcement policy.[64] Nearly all the increases in homi-

---

56. KELLING & COLES, *supra* note 18, at 22-23.

57. *See* SKOGAN, *supra* note 20; Goldstein, *supra* note 46.

58. KELLING & COLES, *supra* note 18 at 23.

59. OAG REPORT, *supra* note 5.

60. *Id.* at 56-59.

61. POLICE STRATEGY NO. 5, *supra* note 44.

62. This aggressive approach to low-level disorder was "the linchpin of efforts now being undertaken by the New York City Police Department to reduce crime and fear in the city." *Id.*

63. POLICE STRATEGY NO. 1, *supra* note 25.

64. *See* ROBERT C. DAVIS & PEDRO MATEU-GELABERT, VERA INST. OF JUSTICE, RESPECTFUL AND EFFECTIVE POLICING: TWO EXAMPLES IN THE SOUTH BRONX 2, 3 fig.1a (1999) (charting "Homicides (Murder & Non-Negligent Manslaughter), 1978-1997") [hereinafter VERA REPORT].

cides, robberies, and assaults during this period were attributable to gun violence.[65] The political fallout of the homicide crisis lasted for several years more. The homicide crisis was a critical theme in the mayoral election campaign of 1993, and focused the attention of the incoming Giuliani administration's crime-control policy on gun violence.[66]

These two policies, articulated within a relatively brief period in the first few months of the new administration, explicitly cemented the marriage of OMP and "gun-oriented policing"[67] within policy. The logic of this approach was articulated in a series of documents and statements. "By working systematically and assertively to reduce the level of disorder in the city, the NYPD will act to undercut the ground on which more serious crimes seem possible and even permissible."[68] These tactical shifts were intended to raise the stakes for criminals who carried guns: "Stopping people on minor infractions also made it riskier for criminals to carry guns in public."[69] The policy assumed, quite explicitly, that would-be offenders would be deterred from carrying guns since they would be more likely to be stopped for minor crimes or infractions.

The net effect of this marriage was that Broken Windows theory was implemented out of context. Not only was Broken Windows theory recast from physical to social disorder, but community policing and disorder policing both were separated from the theory, reinvented, and implemented with very different tactics.[70]

First, the NYPD version of disorder policing rejected the emphasis on alternatives to arrest and prosecution—essential tenets of the original Broken Windows theory.[71] Although correcting disorder was the focus of policing, the tactic to achieve it was arrest, the most traditional of law enforcement tools. People who committed disorder offenses were questioned and checked for outstanding

---

65. Fagan et al., *supra* note 36, at 1289, 1298, 1304.

66. *See* ELI SILVERMAN, NYPD BATTLES CRIME: INNOVATIVE STRATEGIES IN POLICING 95 (1999); BRATTON & KNOBLER, *supra* note 44, at 219-20. *See generally* KARMEN, *supra* note 36.

67. Fagan et al., *supra* note 36, at 1322.

68. POLICE STRATEGY NO. 5, *supra* note 44.

69. VERA REPORT, *supra* note 64, at 1.

70. Waldeck, *supra* note 19, at 1274-75 n.89; *see also* Bratton, *supra* note 44, at 463-64. This version of community policing eschewed social work functions antithetical to the traditional definition of policing. These tactics robbed rank-and-file police of the activities—searches and arrests—that not only were the staple of police productivity, but also the stepladder to status on the force and advancement within the department. Among police administrators, the emerging paradigm of community policing took away their primary method of keeping order.

71. Waldeck, *supra* note 19, at 1274.

warrants. Those without identification were taken to a precinct, and many were held until fingerprint checks were completed.[72] In other words, disorder policing was used not to disrupt the developmental sequence of disorder and crime, but instead disorder offenses became opportunities to remove weapons and wanted criminals from the streets.

Second, community policing also was reinvented in this marriage. Community standards were no longer identified through structured and systematic interactions between police and community leaders. Instead, the NYPD turned to its sophisticated data-driven management accountability system—Compstat—to identify community needs. The result was that the locus of the standard-setting process shifted from police-community partnerships to precinct commanders.[73] Presumably, precinct commanders were still involved in their communities, developing plans and setting priorities for enforcement.[74] However, the precinct commanders, who continued to meet with community groups, were now accountable to the NYPD's operational hierarchy for both their successes and their failures to produce declining crime rates.[75] As a result, precinct commanders set the crime-fighting priorities for that precinct and developed overall plans of action, based on meeting NYPD priorities, rather than the standards set in cooperation with communities.[76]

## C.	Disorganization and Disorder: Competing Theories of Place and Crime

For decades before Broken Windows, criminological theories emphasized the notion of "place."[77] In the 1920s, Clifford Shaw

---

72. *Id.* at 1279. These tactics were developed and widely implemented in the transit police under Bratton's leadership in the early 1990s. BRATTON & KNOBLER, *supra* note 44, at 152.

73. BRATTON & KNOBLER, *supra* note 44, at 233.

74. *See id.*

75. *Id.*

76. OAG REPORT, *supra* note 5, at 54-56. According to the Report, accountability was implemented through Compstat meetings. Compstat ("comparison statistics") is a system of electronic computer mapping of weekly crime statistics within precincts and larger police commands. Monthly Compstat sessions focus on analysis of specific crime issues of any of the eight patrol boroughs. Each patrol bureau spans eight to ten precincts. Commanders are asked to explain, often on the spot and in front of an audience of the commissioner and other high ranking department personnel, changes in crime trends in their areas. *Id.*

77. "Place" in the criminological literature is an enduring concept that alternately refers to neighborhoods, larger sections of cities, or other aggregates of areas. *See generally* CLIFFORD R. SHAW & HENRY D. McKAY, JUVENILE DELINQUENCY AND

and Henry McKay showed that high rates of juvenile crime were persistent in specific neighborhoods over time, despite changes in the racial and ethnic composition of the persons who lived there. Shaw and McKay concluded that place, not the characteristics of the persons who live there, is implicated in crime. Factors such as poverty rates, a downward skewed age distribution, racial and ethnic heterogeneity, and population turnover (residential mobility) explain variations in crime rates across neighborhoods. Shaw and McKay defined the conditions that produced persistently elevated juvenile crime rates as social disorganization.[78]

Recent revisions to this theory emphasize the social organization—the actions of residents within neighborhoods to produce social control and realize their shared values—as protective against high crime rates. Robert Sampson, Stephen Raudenbush, and Felton Earls reported in a study of residents in 343 Chicago neighborhoods that social cohesion among neighbors is linked to lower levels of violence, net of poverty rates, demography, or other socioeconomic factors.[79] This dynamic conceptualization of neighborhood emphasizes social interactions among neighborhood residents, including:

> (1) the strength and interdependence of social networks; (2) the efficacy of collective supervision that residents exercise; (3) the personal responsibility they assume in addressing neighborhood problems; and (4) the level of resident participation in formal and informal organization such as churches, block clubs, and

URBAN AREAS: A STUDY OF RATES OF DELINQUENCY IN RELATION TO DIFFERENTIAL CHARACTERISTICS OF LOCAL COMMUNITIES IN AMERICAN CITIES (rev. ed. 1969) (presenting data on the stability of delinquency rates in Chicago neighborhoods across generations of residents of changing composition); ROBERT J. BURSIK JR. & HAROLD G. GRASMICK, NEIGHBORHOODS AND CRIME: THE DIMENSIONS OF EFFECTIVE COMMUNITY CONTROL (1993) (articulating a systemic theory of delinquency that includes elements of the physical attributes of neighborhoods, their social composition and demography, and the institutions that are influential for the people who live there); *Robert J. Sampson & Janet Lauritsen, Violent victimization and offending: Individual-, Situational-, and Community-Level Risk Factors, in* UNDERSTANDING AND PREVENTING VIOLENCE 1 (Albert J. Reiss Jr. & Jeffrey A. Roth, eds. 1994) (reviewing empirical studies that show a relationship between individuals and communities or neighborhoods and delinquency rates).

78. SHAW & MCKAY, *supra* note 77, at 383-87. Recent studies show that these factors are stable explanations over time of variations in crime and violence rates across cities and larger ecological aggregates. Kenneth Land et al., *Structural Covariates of Homicide Rates: Are There any Invariances Across Time and Space?*, 95 AM. J. SOC. 922 (1990).

79. Robert J. Sampson et al., *Neighborhoods and Violent Crime: A Multilevel Study of Collective Efficacy*, SCIENCE, Aug. 15, 1997, at 918 (examining neighborhoods in a way that ensured diversity by race, ethnicity, and class).

PTAs. The idea is that community-level social processes such as the level of supervision of teenage peer groups, the prevalence of friendship networks, and the level of residential participation in formal organizations, mediate the link often noted between individual-level factors, such as race and socioeconomic status, and crime.[80]

As Tracey Meares and others point out, the conditions that characterize poor, minority, inner-city communities generally conform to a place-based social organization model of crime. In urban areas, many poor people of color live in conditions of residential segregation, concentrated poverty, and unemployment that predict the breakdown of community social processes,[81] which in turn predict elevated crime rates.[82] For example, many poor African Americans live in the overwhelmingly poor communities marked by unemployment, family dislocation, and high residential turnover.[83] The challenges to social control in socially disorganized neighborhoods are greater for blacks and Hispanics than for whites.[84]

Social disorganization also predicts social and physical disorder. Both theoretically and empirically, disorder and disorganization are confounded. In the study of Chicago neighborhoods by Sampson and colleagues, they included in regression models measures traditionally associated with social disorganization theory to predict disorder in census tracts.[85] Neighborhood characteristics including concentrated disadvantage[86] and weak social ties (collective efficacy) were significant predictors of the rates of disorder. Disorder, however, did not predict rates of homicide, and only

---

80. Tracey Meares, *Place and Crime*, 73 Chi.-Kent L. Rev. 669, 673 (1998); *see also* Robert J. Sampson & William Julius Wilson, *Toward a Theory of Race, Crime, and Urban Inequality*, in Crime and Inequality 37, 45-48 (John Hagan & Ruth D. Peterson eds., 1995); Sampson et al., *supra* note 79.

81. Massey & Denton, *supra* note 17, at 130-31.

82. Sampson & Wilson, *supra* note 80; *see also* Robert J. Sampson, *Urban Black Violence: The Effect of Male Joblessness and Family Disruption*, 93 Am. J. Sociology 348 (1987) (discussing the effect of family disruption on crime independent of joblessness and welfare receipt).

83. Massey & Denton, *supra* note 17, at 166-67; William Julius Wilson, The Truly Disadvantaged: The Inner City, the Underclass, and Public Policy 20-62 (1987); James Short, Poverty, Ethnicity and Violent Crime (1997).

84. Meares, *supra* note 80, at 673-74; Sampson & Wilson, *supra* note 80, at 42 ("[R]acial differences in poverty and family disruption are so strong that the 'worst' urban contexts in which whites reside are considerably better than the average context of black communities."). *See generally* Sampson et al., *supra* note 79.

85. Sampson & Raudenbush, *supra* note 20, at 633-36, and tbl.6.

86. *Id.* This measure included tract-level rates of poverty and unemployment, single parent households, and receipt of public assistance. Racial concentration of blacks was a moderate contributor to the empirical derivation of this construct.

weakly predicted rates of robbery. After controlling for these neighborhood characteristics, the relationship between disorder and crime disappeared for four of their five empirical tests.[87]

Accordingly, social disorganization predicts crime and disorder, but disorder does not predict crime after controlling statistically for the effects of social disorganization. Sampson and colleagues conclude that: "Contrary to the Broken Windows theory . . . the relationship between public disorder and crime is spurious" for most crimes, and is weakly associated only with the crime of robbery.[88] Disorder is only a moderate predictor of robbery, and it co-varies with other neighborhood characteristics such as concentrated disadvantage. Disorder may have a cascading effect on antecedents of crime—encouraging business migration, for example—but it has very weak indirect effects on crime itself. Sampson and colleagues concluded that disorder takes a back seat to other factors, including structural disadvantage and social ties, in explaining crime rates. Controlling crime through disorder policing is, in their words, "simplistic and largely misplaced."[89] Disorder policing, or OMP, leaves the causes of crime untouched.

II. AGGRESSIVE POLICING: OMP, STREET STOPS, AND RACE

Under the tactical shift to order-maintenance policing in New York City, patrol was reinvented to include pro-active interdiction of persons suspected of violating both minor and serious crimes.[90] The importance of stop and frisk interventions to crime fighting was never formally acknowledged in official documents, but has been discussed in detail by the policy's architects and theorists. Kelling and Coles claim that for OMP to be successful, patrol officers should intervene in observed or suspected low-level disorder.[91]

Critics claim that OMP tactics increased the opportunity for pretextual stops leading to searches and arrests.[92] Stops for minor

---

87. *Id.* at 637.
88. *Id.* at 603, 636-37.
89. *Id.* at 638.
90. OAG REPORT, *supra* note 5, at 56-57.
91. KELLING & COLES, *supra* note 18, at 243-48; OAG REPORT, *supra* note 5, at 57; Waldeck, *supra* note 19, at 1282-83; *accord* James Q. Wilson, *Just Take Their Guns Away*, N.Y. TIMES MAG., Mar. 20, 1994, at 47 (stating that police should make street stop and frisks in order to find persons carrying illegal weapons, without stating a legal or practical rationale for these stops).
92. Waldeck, *supra* note 19, at 1282 ("Nor is there any doubt that the police use quality-of-life offenses as excuses to fish for drugs, guns, or evidence of a more serious crime.").

476   *FORDHAM URBAN LAW JOURNAL* [Vol. XXVIII

crimes or infractions were easier to justify under a lower constitutional standard (i.e., "reasonable suspicion") than stops for more
serious offenses. Accordingly, OMP stops provided opportunities
for police to check for warrants, and, again under reasonable suspicion standards, search suspects for contraband or weapons, and
make arrests. Many such offenses—such as public drinking or loitering—take place in public, making their observation easier and
an encounter with the putatively offending citizen more likely.

The result was a vast increase in misdemeanor arrests, but also a
sharp decline in their quality and sustainability in court. OMP has
been activated through vast increases in misdemeanor arrests of
adults, increasing from 129,404 in 1993 (the year prior to OMP implementation) to 181,736 in 1996, and 215,158 in 1998.[93] But the
evidentiary quality of arrests suffered as their number rose. As arrests increased under OMP, the rate at which prosecutors declined
to pursue these cases rose dramatically. In 1998, prosecutors dismissed 18,000 of the 345,000 misdemeanor and felony arrests, approximately twice the number dismissed in 1993.[94] Overall, more
than 140,000 cases completed in 1998 ended in dismissals, an increase of 60% compared with 1993.[95] Prosecutors say that refusals
to prosecute as well as the high dismissal rate can indicate a decline
in the quality of arrest.[96] Many of the declined cases, known as
"declined prosecutions" or "D.P.s" in the court, came from
predominantly minority neighborhoods, the focus of OMP efforts.[97] The punitive component of the D.P.s and dismissed arrests—being taken into custody, handcuffed, transported, booked,
often strip-searched, and jailed overnight—impregnates these
events with its own social meaning quite different from the origins
of Broken Windows theory.

---

93. DIV. OF CRIMINAL JUSTICE SERVS., STATE OF N.Y., CRIMINAL JUSTICE IN-
DICATORS: NEW YORK CITY, 1995-1999, *at* http://criminaljustice.state.ny.us/crimnet/
cjsa/areastat/areastat.htm (using search parameters: "Region: New York City," years
1995-1999) [hereinafter CJI: NEW YORK CITY].

94. Ford Fessenden & David Rohde, *Dismissed Before Reaching Court: Flawed
Arrests Rise in New York*, N.Y. TIMES, Aug. 23, 1999, at A1 (citing the sharp rise in
the number of arrests that prosecutors declined to prosecute in 1998). The number of
cases rejected by prosecutors rose by 41% in the Bronx and 23% in Manhattan, even
as the crime rate declined sharply in the same year. Approximately fifty persons each
day were arrested and booked, but then released—many spending a night in jail
before their cases were dismissed. *Id.*

95. *Id.*

96. *Id.*

97. *Id.*

Analyses of 1998 police stop and frisk reports—UF-250s— showed that OMP policing had drifted from street stops in quality of life crimes to widespread stops of citizens in search of guns.[98] Stop and frisk actions became the primary method for removing illegal handguns from the street. The OAG Report showed that from January 1998 through March 1999, weapons possession was suspected in more than one-third of documented stop and frisk encounters.[99]

The OAG Report also showed that the reconstructed OMP policy was implemented in a manner that was not race-neutral. The OAG Report showed that stops were disproportionately concentrated in the city's poorest neighborhoods, neighborhoods with high concentrations of racial minorities. Table 1 below shows the percentage of stops, according to the distribution of minority populations in the precincts. In precincts with the highest concentrations of minorities, stops of black and Hispanic suspects were highest (by percentage), as might be expected. However, in the thirteen precincts with the lowest minority populations,[100] stops of blacks and Hispanics were well above what their population percentage would predict. In those precincts, 30% of the persons "stopped" were black, more than ten times greater than their percentage of the overall population of those precincts.[101] Hispanics comprised 23.4% of the persons "stopped," more than three times their population share. Whites make up 80% of the population of those precincts, but only 41.5% of the persons "stopped." Even in precincts where neighborhoods had the lowest minority concentration, whites were stopped less. The pattern invokes an enduring empirical fact in criminological research: police officers are more likely to treat as suspicious persons who seem out of place from their surroundings.[102] To police officers, race serves as a marker of

---

98. OAG Report, *supra* note 5, at tbl.I.B.3.

99. *Id.* The Street Crime Unit was disproportionately responsible for the use of stop and frisk actions to search for guns. During the fifteen month study period in the OAG Report, the Street Crime Unit ("SCU") had a "particular emphasis on recovering illegal firearms." Its 435 officers (out of nearly 40,000 in the NYPD) effected more than 10% of all documented stop and frisk encounters citywide. *Id.* at 58-59.

100. *Id.* at tbl.I.A.2.

101. *Id.* The OAG Report established the population of each precinct, using census data for day and night populations. *Id.* at 96.

102. Jonathan Rubinstein, City Police 225 (1973); John van Maanen, *Working the Street: A Developmental View of Police Behavior, in* The Potential for Reform of Criminal Justice 83, 118 (Herbert Jacobs, ed. 1974).

where people "belong," and racial incongruity as a marker of suspicion.[103]

TABLE 1. DISTRIBUTION OF STOPS BY RACE OF SUSPECT AND RACIAL COMPOSITION OF PRECINCT (MANDATED REPORT STOPS ONLY)[104]

% Hispanic Population in Precinct	% Black Population in the Precinct		
	Over 40%	10% to 40%	Under 10%
Over 40%	57.0	38.0	17.1
	38.8	55.1	67.0
	3.3	4.9	10.1
	(4)	(11)	(3)
20% to 40%	74.6	31.6	29.5
	19.2	52.0	40.8
	2.9	12.7	22.3
	(2)	(6)	(6)
10% to 20%	84.8	56.9	22.9
	11.0	22.2	40.1
	2.9	18.2	26.3
	(8)	(9)	(5)
Less than 10%	91.6	74.7	30.0
	4.6	8.0	23.4
	2.0	15.4	41.5
	(6)	(2)	(13)
	Legend		% Black Suspects
			% Hispanic Suspects
			% White Suspects
			(Number of Precincts)

Racial incongruity is one of several patterns observed in the OAG Report that depict the racial component of OMP in New York. The ratio of 9.5 stops of black citizens for each arrest made was 20% higher than the 7.9 ratio for whites.[105] Such higher stop-arrest ratios suggest either that stops for blacks were pretextual and largely unfounded, or that police were less discriminating or skillful in assessing "suspicion" for minority citizens.

Stops, alone or in proportion to the population, tell only part of the story. The NYPD points out, for example, that the higher stop

---

103. Stephen Mastrofski et al., *Race and Every-Day Policing: A Research Perspective*, Presented at the 12th International Congress on Criminology, Seoul, Aug. 24-29, 1998. Anthony C. Thompson reminds us that racial incongruity was one of the markers that aroused the suspicion of Officer McFadden in the original *Terry* case. *See generally* Thompson, *supra* note 17, at 962-73 (discussing the racial dimensions of the original *Terry* case and the centrality of race to Fourth Amendment jurisprudence).

104. OAG REPORT, *supra* note 5, at tbl.I.A.2.

105. *Id.* at tbl.I.B.2.

rate for minorities reflects higher participation of blacks and Hispanics in crimes, especially in the city's highest crime neighborhoods. Using crime data on race- and crime-specific arrest rates within precincts, the OAG Report estimated the extent to which race- and crime-specific stops were predicted by crime, or whether actual stop rates exceeded the predicted stop rates. The results show that crime rates only partially explain stop rates overall, and fail to explain the rates at which minority citizens are "stopped" by the NYPD. After controlling for race- and crime-specific crime rates and the population composition of the precinct, the results showed that black and Hispanic citizens were significantly more likely to be stopped than were white citizens.[106] The overall differences between races were statistically significant, and were significant specifically for stops where the suspected crime was either violence or weapons possession.[107]

Table 2 illustrates the exponentiated coefficients—or comparative odds—from these models, showing the magnitude of the differences for each race- and crime-specific stop rate. This table only includes stops where reports were mandated by NYPD policy. The results are divided into three sections, according to the precinct's black population. This display illustrates the importance of concentration effects. Each coefficient shows the stop-rate adjusted for the crime rate, disaggregated by race of suspect and suspected crime. In other words, each table shows the rate at which blacks, Hispanics, and whites were "stopped" in proportion to the rate at which they were arrested for each crime type. Comparing the coefficient by race illustrates the magnitude of the differences between races.

---

106. *Id.* at tbl.I.C.1.
107. *Id.*

TABLE 2. LOG ODDS OF RACE- AND CRIME-SPECIFIC STOP RATES, CONTROLLING FOR 1997 RACE- AND CRIME-SPECIFIC ARREST RATES, BY BLACK POPULATION IN PRECINCT (MANDATED REPORT STOPS ONLY)[108]

Race of Suspect	Black Population in Precinct: Less Than 10% Suspected Crime			
	Violent	Weapon	Property	Drug
Black	0.37	2.17	0.26	0.10
Hispanic	0.32	1.87	0.39	0.11
White	0.11	0.97	0.33	0.10

Race of Suspect	Black Population in Precinct: From 10% to 40% Suspected Crime			
	Violent	Weapon	Property	Drug
Black	0.36	2.12	0.25	0.09
Hispanic	0.31	1.83	0.38	0.10
White	0.17	0.95	0.32	0.10

Race of Suspect	Black Population in Precinct: Greater Than 40% Suspected Crime			
	Violent	Weapon	Property	Drug
Black	0.30	1.76	0.21	0.08
Hispanic	0.26	1.52	0.31	0.09
White	0.14	0.79	0.27	0.08

For example, Table 2 shows that in precincts where the black population was less than 10%, blacks were 2.17 times more likely to be stopped for weapons offenses compared to the arrest rate for blacks for that crime. Whites were 0.97 times more likely to be stopped compared to the arrest rate for whites for that crime. Comparing the coefficients, blacks were more than twice as likely (2.17/0.97) to be stopped as whites for weapons offenses, relative to their race-specific arrest rates for that crime.

The comparisons throughout this table show the elevated rates at which blacks and Hispanics were stopped for suspected violence and weapons offenses as compared to stop rates for whites. In precincts with more than 40% black population, the black-white ratios were still more than twice as high for violent crimes (0.3/0.14) and nearly three times higher (1.76/0.79) for weapons offenses. The Hispanic-white ratios in these precincts were comparably disproportionate for stops for violent crimes (0.26/0.14) and for weapons offenses (1.52/0.79). The disparities were confined to these two crime types. The coefficients were either comparable or lower for

---

108. *See id.* at Appendix tbl.1.C.1.

whites where stops related to alleged drug or property crimes, regardless of precinct demography.

The higher-than-predicted stop rates of minorities suggest that the police had cast suspicion more often—than would be predicted by their crime participation—on the city's minority population.[109] Although race may not be determinative in the decision to stop a suspect, race certainly appeared to be a motivating factor in the patterns of stop and frisk interventions. The prominence of race in the decision to stop citizens may not rise to the threshold of racial profiling, but it does seem to create a racial classification of "suspicion."

To assess whether that suspicion met *Terry* standards of "reasonable suspicion," the OAG Report examined the stop rationales articulated by police officers on the UF-250 stop report form. The researchers examined the reasons that police officers provided for "stopping" civilians, and estimated the rate at which the reasons, as stated, met Fourth Amendment standards of "reasonable suspicion." The narrative rationales for "stops" came from a citywide sample of 10,000 coded and analyzed UF-250 forms from eight precincts plus a supplemental sample of cases across all precincts.[110] The narratives were coded into sixty-seven categories, and the OAG staff then determined whether the stated rationale in each category met *Terry* standards of "reasonable suspicion."[111] These codes were then collapsed into seven categories, or rationales, which were determined as either meeting or failing to meet *Terry* standards.[112]

Table 3, adopted from the OAG Report, shows that in nearly two-thirds of the stops, the articulated "reasonable suspicion" for the stop met *Terry* standards, and that racial disparities were small. However, stops of black suspects more often failed to meet *Terry*

---

109. *Id.* at 126-27.

110. *Id.* at 135-36. The researchers coded rationales for a citywide sample plus a supplemental sample of specifically chosen precincts. For the individual precinct sample, a purposive sample of eight precincts was selected—the 79th, 42nd, 30th, 43rd, 33rd, 107th, 72nd, and the 19th—based on variation in stop rates and population parameters. For each precinct, approximately half of the UF-250 forms were randomly sampled. In all, 4383 UF-250 forms were randomly sampled for the citywide analysis, including 3282 stops where reports were "mandated." *Id.* at 158-60.

111. *Id.* at 145, tbl.II.A.1.

112. *Id.* at 135-60, tbl.II.A.2. Categories where rationales were sufficient to meet *Terry* standards were: (1) crime observed, (2) suspect fit description, (3) weapon observed, (4) suspicious activity plus other criterion behavior. Categories where rationales failed to meet *Terry* standards included: (1) suspicious activity and (2) suspect in wrong place. *Id.* at tbl.II.A.2.

standards (15.4%) than did stops of whites (11.3%). In contrast, there were only minimal differences between stops involving Hispanic and whites suspects.

TABLE 3. ASSESSMENT OF *TERRY* RATIONALES FOR STOPS BY RACE OF SUSPECT, CITYWIDE SAMPLE (MANDATED REPORT STOPS ONLY)[113]

Assessment of Reasonable Suspicion Standard	Race of Person Stopped				
	Black	Hispanic	White	Other	Total
Facts, as stated, articulate reasonable suspicion	1,172 64.3%	690 65.4%	192 60.4%	60 69.8%	2,114 64.4%
Facts, as stated, do not articulate reasonable suspicion	281 15.4%	133 12.6%	36 11.3%	9 10.5%	459 14.0%
Insufficient information	370 20.3%	232 32.7%	90 28.3%	17 19.8%	709 21.6%
Total	1,823	1,055	318	86	3,282

The pattern of evidence in the OAG Report suggests that race evidently became a factor in "everyday policing" in New York City under OMP. Working within a legally permissible but lower standard of "reasonable" racial discrimination, where a second motivating factor (such as "reasonable suspicion") may be present, police over-stopped black and Hispanic citizens relative to their crime participation, well in excess of their white neighbors, and more often without constitutional justification. Black citizens in particular tend to generalize these experiences, with potentially toxic consequences for their perception of the legitimacy of the law.[114] Disproportionate stops of black citizens is an important "race-making" factor,[115] generalized through the sense of linked fate that many blacks share.[116] It conveys social stigma and under-

---

113. *See id.* at tbl.II.B.4.

114. Tracey Maclin, *Race and the Fourth Amendment*, 51 VAND. L. REV. 333, 386 (1998) ("Blacks correctly see pretextual traffic stops as another sign that police officers view blacks, particularly black males, as criminals who deserve singular scrutiny and treatment as second class citizens."). *See generally* David A. Harris, *"Driving While Black" and All Other Traffic Offenses: The Supreme Court and Pretextual Traffic Stops*, 87 J. CRIM. L. & CRIMINOLOGY 544, 571 (1997).

115. This term is borrowed from Professor David James, who has written of the ghetto as a "race-making situation." James, *supra* note 24, at 420-28.

116. DAWSON, *supra* note 24, at 77 (using the "linked fate" concept to explain the way that African Americans perceive what is in their individual self interest). Experiences such as "stop and frisk" encounters could easily undermine the social meaning of the OMP strategy. *Id.* at 80-84; *see also* JEFFREY FAGAN & TRACEY L. MEARES, PUNISHMENT, DETERRENCE AND SOCIAL CONTROL: THE PARADOX OF PUNISHMENT IN MINORITY COMMUNITIES (2000) (discussing how the perceived illegitimacy of the criminal justice system in the African American and Hispanic communities has kept

mines the perceived and attributed legitimacy of law and legal institutions necessary to promote compliance with the law. The harm to individuals stopped but not arrested cannot be discounted in a social framework where events and experiences are linked in this manner.[117]

III. RESOLVING COMPETING THEORETICAL CLAIMS ABOUT STOP AND FRISK ACTIVITY: EMPIRICAL RESULTS

Returning to OMP in New York City, then, we can ask whether the emphasis on disorder was, in fact, a strategy focused on policing poor people rather than disordered places. Of course, at the neighborhood level, race interacts with other neighborhood factors, ones that also correlate with social and physical disorder.[118] In the reconstructed Broken Windows theory that informed OMP in New York City, social disorder, or person-focused tactics, replaced physical disorder, or place-based tactics. Empirical evidence shows that the epidemiology of stop and frisk actions in turn was concentrated among minority persons in poor neighborhoods.[119] Accordingly, it appears that place was switched for race in the reality of OMP. Thus, what began as policing informed by a nuanced Broken Windows theory, in fact reflects criminological theories focused on social disorganization.

This raises two questions for understanding the racial patterns of policing. First, what are the net effects of race on patterns of policing after we control for disorder? If OMP was in fact targeted at disorder, race differences at the neighborhood level should disappear after we introduce measures of disorder. Unlike, for example, race-explicit drug-courier profiles, OMP should be racially and facially neutral once we control for the level of disorder in the neighborhood.

---

crime rates steady despite harsher sentencing), http://papers2.ssrn.com/paper. taf?abstract-id=223148.

117. William J. Stuntz, Terry's *Impossibility*, 72 ST. JOHN'S L. REV. 1213, 1218 (1998) (summarizing harms from encounters of innocent citizens with police, including violations of privacy, public shame at being singled out and treated like a criminal suspect, the emotional damage of discrimination, and the potential for police violence and physical injury).

118. Sampson & Raudenbush, *supra* note 20. *See generally* ROBERT J. BURSIK, JR. & HAROLD GRASMICK, NEIGHBORHOODS AND CRIME: THE DIMENSIONS OF EFFECTIVE COMMUNITY CONTROL (1993).

119. OAG REPORT, *supra* note 5, at 92-94 (citing New York City Police Commissioner Howard Safir's statement that minorities are more likely to be "stopped" because they live in high crime neighborhoods with an increased police presence).

Second, if disorder itself is predicted by neighborhood or ecological characteristics, factors that also are correlated with race, are these other factors significant predictors of stop and frisk patterns after we control for disorder? While some neighborhood characteristics are correlated with disorder, these factors also are part of competing theoretical explanations, explanations that are based on characteristics of persons, rather than places. Accordingly, we question whether OMP produces the dramatic racial disparities reported in the OAG Report because of the characteristics of people who live in the neighborhood, or whether these disparities reflect policing targeted in fact at disorder. Analytically, we can compare these two explanations to estimate the ecological locus of racial policing. The results of this competition follow, where we present findings of empirical tests designed to assess these competing claims about the theoretical meaning of OMP in New York City.

A. Social and Physical Disorder

Data on the social organization and physical characteristics of neighborhoods were obtained from the 1999 New York City Housing and Vacancy Survey ("HVS").[120] The HVS is sponsored by the New York City Department of Housing Preservation and Development ("HPD")[121] to comply with New York State and New York City's rent regulation laws. It is conducted every three years with respondents in a stratified random sample of New York City housing units. The sample is based on housing units recorded in the decennial census, and updated every three years as part of the enumeration process preceding the HVS. The HVS emulates the population dimensions of the decennial census and generates measures of household and person characteristics for the city.[122]

---

120. U.S. CENSUS BUREAU, DEP'T OF COMMERCE, 1999 NEW YORK CITY HOUSING AND VACANCY SURVEY (1999), *at* http://www.census.gov/hhes/www/nychvs.html [hereinafter NYC HOUSING SURVEY].

121. THE GREEN BOOK: OFFICIAL DIRECTORY OF THE CITY OF NEW YORK (2000) (providing names and contact information for HPD). The Department of Housing Preservation and Development is responsible for setting and administering housing policy in the city, including development of urban renewal programs, enforcement of civil codes for housing, management of city-owned properties, rehabilitation of abandoned buildings, and construction of low-income housing.

122. NYC HOUSING SURVEY, *supra* note 120, at Overview, http://www.census.gov/hhes/www/housing/nychvs/overview.html. Differences between the 1999 HVS and the 1990 census include interviewing procedures, staff experience and training, processing procedures, sample design, the sampling variability associated with the HVS and the sample data from the census, and the non-sampling errors associated with the HVS and the census.

The sample includes "vacant available for rent" units as well as occupied units. Both public and privately owned housing units, as well as in rem units,[123] are included. The public-use data set is made available by the U.S. Census Bureau, and includes weights to generate estimates of households and persons for the city. The response rate in the 1999 survey sample of 18,180 was 94%. Interviews were conducted between January and May, 1999 by "field representatives" hired by HPD.[124]

Measures of physical disorder and social structure were aggregated from individual-level responses in the HVS to sub-boroughs. The residential location of each respondent is coded to the borough (county) and the *community district* ("CD"), or sub-borough. CD's are administrative units of each borough; there are fifty-five in the city. Members of the councils of each CD meet periodically to assist city agencies in zoning and other regulatory planning functions. Sub-boroughs include one or two police precincts.

Measures of physical disorder in the sub-borough were computed from responses to items regarding the physical condition of the dwelling and the neighborhood. Respondents were asked to report whether there was damage or disrepair in the exterior walls and windows, stairwells and stairways, and floors. Respondents also were asked to report generally on the condition of other dwellings in their neighborhood: the presence of broken or boarded up windows, and whether the building was "deteriorated" or "dilapidated."[125] Responses were aggregated to the sub-borough level to measure the percentage of housing units with these characteristics.

To avoid redundancy among the disorder variables, a principle components factor analysis with varimax rotation[126] was completed to reduce the variables to a single dimension. The model yielded

---

123. In rem housing units are housing units that are acquired and owned by the City of New York following tax forfeitures or failure to pay other charges such as correcting violations of the housing codes. NYC HOUSING SURVEY, *supra* note 120, at H-2, Definitions of Rent Regulation Status, http://www.census.gov/hhes/www/housing/nychvs/defin99.html.

124. NYC HOUSING SURVEY, *supra* note 120, at Overview. Interviews were conducted to elicit information about the demographic characteristics of each household member, and the housing characteristics of the dwelling.

125. NYC HOUSING SURVEY, *supra* note 120, at Glossary, http://www.census.gov/hhes/www/housing/nychvs/gloss99.html. For vacant units, responses were recorded by the HPD field representatives.

126. "Varimax rotation" is a statistical procedure that permits the extraction of distinct factors or dimensions from a set of highly correlated variables, and assumes that the factors do not overlap statistically or conceptually. GERHARD ARMINGER ET AL., HANDBOOK OF STATISTICAL MODELING FOR THE SOCIAL AND BEHAVIORAL SCIENCES 205-6 (1995).

one factor explaining 85.9% of the variance. Factor coefficients ranged from 0.865 to 0.959, indicating uniform loading and high multicollinearity. Because of its conceptual clarity and importance to the construction of "physical disorder," we used the "broken windows" variable as the measure of disorder.[127]

Measures of social disorganization were computed using similar procedures. Both household and person characteristics were constructed by aggregating individual responses to sub-boroughs. Means and variances for the measures are shown in Appendix A, *infra.* A principle components factor analysis with varimax rotation was again completed and yielded three factors that explained 74.0% of the variance. The first factor describes neighborhoods characterized by concentrations of persons with low education, persons under- or unemployed, households receiving public assistance, households with Hispanic residents, and female-headed households. These neighborhoods also were characterized by low white population. The second factor describes neighborhoods with high racial fragmentation (racial heterogeneity)[128] and high concentrations of male population. These neighborhoods also were characterized by low black population. The third factor describes neighborhoods characterized by high concentrations of immigrants and residential mobility.[129]

These three factors reflect the classic dimensions of social disorganization.[130] The variables within factors were highly correlated, again permitting selection of specific variables to represent each factor. For conceptual clarity and theoretical specificity, we chose specific variables as measures of social disorganization: the percent of households with one or more persons receiving public assistance, racial fragmentation, and residential mobility.[131] Because of the importance of immigration to the social composition of New York City,[132] we included as a predictor the percentage of house-

---

127. Analyses available from authors.

128. *See* CHARLES LEWIS TAYLOR & MICHAEL C. HUDSON, WORLD HANDBOOK OF POLITICAL AND SOCIAL INDICATORS 216 (2d ed. 1972). Racial fragmentation is a measure of the racial heterogeneity within an area, and is computed as:
$$1 - ((P)^2)$$
Where P = proportion of each race within the spatial unit.

129. *Id.*

130. SHAW & MCKAY, *supra* note 77, at 183-89; SHORT, *supra* note 83, at 55; *see* Sampson & Lauritsen, *supra* note 77, at 1, 51-75; Meares, *supra* note 80, at 673.

131. SHAW & MCKAY, *supra* note 77, at 32, 37, 205.

132. I. M. Miyares & K. S. Gowen, Recreating Boundaries: The Geography of Latin American Immigrants to New York City, CLAG YEARBOOK 2431 (1998); *see* Arun Peter Lobo et al., *Immigration to the New York Metropolitan Region in the*

hold heads who were born outside the U.S. We also included two additional measures that are predictors of crime rates at the community level: the housing vacancy rate[133] and the percentage of housing units in the area that are public housing.[134]

Finally, we included a global measure of crime in the sub-borough: the count of 1997 arrests within each precinct, aggregated to the sub-borough. Arrest counts, published in the OAG Report,[135] were obtained by the OAG from the New York State Division of Criminal Justice Services. State crime counts include "finger-printable" crimes, or crimes that are punishable by jail or prison sentences.

B. Stops and Arrests

Counts and rates of stops and arrests within precincts were compiled from data published by the OAG.[136] In addition to stop counts, the ratio of stops to arrests was computed for each precinct and each type of crime. Cases involving stops that occurred from January 1998 - March 1999 were included. The data tables were compiled by the OAG from files created by the NYPD from UF-250 forms.[137] UF-250 forms are completed by officers following

---

1990's, in MIGRATION WORLD, Volume XXVII, No. 5. (1999); ARUN PETER LOBO ET AL., THE NEWEST NEW YORKERS 1990-1994: AN ANALYSIS OF IMMIGRATION TO NYC IN THE EARLY 1990s (1996); I. M. Miyares, *Little Odessa: Brighton Beach, Brooklyn: An Examination of the Former Soviet Refugee Economy in New York City*, 19 URB. GEOGRAPHY 518 (1998).

133. *See* Ralph B. Taylor, *The Impact of Crime on Communities*, 539 THE ANNALS OF THE AMER. ACAD. POL. & SOC. SCIENCE 28 (1995).

134. *E.g.*, TAMARA DUMANOVSKY ET AL., THE NEIGHBORHOOD CONTEXT OF CRIME IN NYC'S PUBLIC HOUSING PROJECTS (1999) (manuscript on file with author); TERENCE DUNWORTH & AARON SAIGER, NAT'L INST. OF JUSTICE, SUMMARY: DRUGS AND CRIME IN PUBLIC HOUSING: A THREE-CITY ANALYSIS, at viii (1994); Harold Holzman, *Criminological Research on Public Housing: Toward a Better Understanding of People, Places and Spaces*, 42 CRIME & DELINQUENCY 361 (1996).

135. OAG REPORT, *supra* note 5, at tbl.I.C.3; *see also id.* at 120 n. 25 (explaining that arrest counts for 1997 were used—instead of 1998 arrest data—to avoid autocorrelation between stops and arrests that both occurred in 1998). Arrest counts are preferable to crime complaint data, since many types of crime (such as drug crimes or minor property crimes) are not reported in citizen complaints to the police. *Id.* at 121. In addition, complaints often include crimes with no suspect information, while arrests include information on the demographic characteristics of the suspect. *See id.*

136. *Id.* at tbl.I.C.3. Race-specific rates for the total number of stops were computed from the percentages included in the table. The race-specific ratios of stops to arrests were computed from data in tbl.I.B.1 and I.B.2, and Appendix tbl.I.B.1 and I.B.2. tbl.I.B.2 also included data on weapons stops by race.

137. *Id.* at 88.

each stop event.[138] Both global stops and arrests were analyzed, as well as stops where the suspect was alleged to have a weapon. Weapons stops were analyzed separately because of the heavy emphasis on the control of gun violence in the formulation and implementation of NYPD policy.[139]

The analyses included only stops where a UF-250 form was mandated. NYPD policy mandates that officers complete a UF-250 under four specific circumstances: when (1) force is used in the course of the stop; (2) the suspect is frisked (i.e., pat down) and/or searched during the course of the stop;[140] (3) the suspect is arrested; or (4) the suspect refuses to identify him or herself.[141] Non-mandated reports also were submitted during this time, but compliance with reporting requirements when reports were not mandated was uneven, raising reliability problems in assessing the consistency of these reports across precincts.[142]

---

138. *Id.* at 63 (describing the UF-250 form and the NYPD policies regulating the filing of these reports). Although initially designed as a tool for investigation, completion of the UF-250 form has been required by the NYPD Patrol Guide since 1986. *Id.* at 65. In 1997, the police commissioner assigned a high priority to filing UF-250s. N.Y. City Police Dep't, Patrol Guide: Procedure No. 116-33 (effective Nov. 14, 1986) (detailing policy police officers, in certain circumstances, to document stop and frisk street encounters on the UF-250 form) [hereinafter Patrol Guide].

139. For a discussion of the policy, see Police Strategy No. 1, *supra* note 25, and OAG Report, *supra* note 5, at 53. The memo described the NYPD's plan to reduce gun violence by intensified efforts to find and seize illegal firearms. Guns and violent crime also were a primary focus of the NYPD's Street Crime Unit ("SCU"), an elite unit of plain-clothes officers tasked to "hot spots" of concentrated criminal activity. The SCU's "mission" is to "effect the arrests of violent street criminals, with a particular emphasis on recovering illegal firearms." OAG Report, *supra* note 5, at 53 n.32 (citing Police Commissioner Howard Safir, Statement Before the New York City Council Public Safety Committee (Apr. 19, 1999)) [hereinafter Safir Statement].

140. That is, searches inside his or her clothing.

141. Patrol Guide, *supra* note 138; OAG Report, *supra* note 5, at 63-64.

142. Analyses in the OAG Report show that whites were over-represented in cases involving non-mandated reports. OAG Report, *supra* note 5, at 95 n.9. Although whites comprised 12.9% of all cases and 10.4% of cases where reports were required, whites comprised 19.3% of cases where a form was not mandated. However, completion of non-mandated reports varied from precinct to precinct, when compared as a ratio to the number of stops with mandated reports. *See id.* at tbl.I.A.1. The OAG Report constructed two scenarios to explain the racial disparity in non-mandated reports. In one scenario, "the police completed non-mandated UF-250's for 'stops' of minorities and non-minorities at the same rate, but [found] that 'stops' of whites were less likely to rise to the more intrusive level of force, a frisk or an arrest." *Id.* at 95 n.9. In the second scenario, "the police were more likely to . . . complet[e] a UF-250 form . . . in a non-mandated situation when the person 'stopped' was white." *Id.* In either scenario, analyzing only mandated report cases—which by definition are more intrusive—would show greater racial disparity than would an analysis of all cases. *Id.*

C. Results

Two dimensions of police stops of citizens were computed to test the hypothesis that crime rates alone do not explain differences in stop rates by race or type of crime. First, comparisons of stop rates by race and type of crime are shown in Table 4.[143] Stop rates by race and type of crime are shown, and the overall race-specific crime rate is shown as a basis of comparison. We used the 1997 race-specific crime counts to compute a per capita stop rate over the fifteen month interval. The results show large disparities by race. Stop rates were nearly five times higher for blacks compared to non-Hispanic whites, and four times higher for Hispanics.[144] The citywide stop rate is heavily weighted by the concentration of stops among blacks and Hispanics. The disparities by race are consistent across crime types, and the heaviest disparities between stops of black and white citizens. For violence and weapons, stops of blacks occur at a rate ten times higher than the rate for whites, and more than twice as high as the rate for Hispanics. Disparities remain for other crime types, but are narrower. Comparisons of race-specific stop rates per 1000 population to arrest rates per 1000 population show that blacks and Hispanics were stopped at rates higher than their arrest rates.

---

143. *Id.* at 120 n.25 (describing types of crimes). Crimes were reported using four generic crime categories. *Violent crimes* included robbery, assault, homicide, kidnapping and sex crimes. *Weapons crimes* included arrests for both gun and other illegal weapons. *Property crimes* included larceny and burglary. *Drug crimes* included both possession and sale offenses. *Id.*

144. The OAG analysis constructed four categories of race from the eight recorded on the NYPD documentation in the UF-250 data: white, black, Hispanic white, Asian, American Indian, other, unknown. OAG REPORT, *supra* note 5. We use four: black, white, Hispanic, and other. The UF-250 form has no category for black Hispanics, so we were unable to determine whether officers classified black Hispanics as black or Hispanic, or whether officers were consistent in their classification decisions. *Id.* The NYPD classification is based on officers' observations, the Census Bureau classification is based on self-report. In constructing race-specific population rates from the HVS for the sub-boroughs, we classified both white and black Hispanics as black, consistent with classifications in the U.S. Census. The construction of the Hispanic classification from census data involves a two-stage process regarding both race and ethnicity. Once race is determined, a secondary question asks whether the individual identifies himself or herself as a person of "Hispanic origin."

TABLE 4. RACE-SPECIFIC AND CRIME-SPECIFIC STOP RATES PER 1,000 PERSONS, CRIME RATES PER 1,000 PERSONS, AND RACE-SPECIFIC POPULATION CITYWIDE[145]

Type of Crime	Stop Rate: Citywide	Stop Rate: Black	Stop Rate: Hispanic	Stop Rate: White	Stop Rate: Other
Violent	3.2	7.5	3.5	0.7	1.0
Property	2.0	3.1	2.6	1.1	0.9
Drug	1.4	2.7	1.8	0.6	0.3
Weapon	7.6	18.0	8.7	1.3	1.8
Quality of life offenses	1.3	1.8	1.5	0.1	0.5
All offenses	17.1	22.6	20.0	4.8	5.2
Total arrests	104,847	53,472	31,454	16,776	3,145
Arrest rate per 1,000 persons	14.1	29.0	15.1	6.0	4.4
1999 population	7,428,162	1,845,306	2,089,149	2,775,637	718,070

These differences are consistent with significant differences reported in the OAG Report.[146] Controlling for race- and crime-specific crime rates and population, that report showed that stop rates for blacks and Hispanics were significantly higher than the stop rates for whites.[147] These effects were most acute for stops for weapons and violent crimes.[148]

The second measure of police stop activity is the ratio of stops to arrests by race and type of crime. Once police officers decide to stop a citizen, the outcomes of those stops—including whether a frisk or search is conducted, and whether an arrest is made—should not differ by race. Presumably, the "reasonable suspicion" articulated in *Terry v. Ohio* and incorporated into both the formal training and professional judgment of police officers,[149] should lead to stops with race-neutral outcome probabilities. In other words, there is no rationale for police to exercise discretion differently by race that would lead to a higher rate of "false positives" for any racial group. Accordingly, stop rates should reflect a similar efficiency and strategic allocation of police efforts across races.

---

145. OAG REPORT, *supra* note 5, at tbl.I.A.1, tbl.I.A.5; DEP'T OF CITY PLANNING, CITY OF N.Y., 1990-99 POPULATION CHANGE ESTIMATES, *available at* http://www.ci.nyc.ny.us/html/dcp/pdf/9099pop.pdf.

146. OAG REPORT, *supra* note 5, at 94-95. Citywide, blacks constituted 50% of the total "stops" and 51% of the arrests for the covered period. Hispanics constituted 33% of all "stops" and 30% of all arrests. Whites constituted 13% of all "stops" and 16% of all arrests. However, this evidence of proportionality masks differences by neighborhood. *Id.* at 95 n.9, 123.

147. *Id.* at tbl.I.C.1 and I.C.2.

148. *Id.* at tbl.I.C.1 and I.C.2.

149. *See* Thompson, *supra* note 17, at 971.

Table 5 shows the ratio of stops to arrests by race of suspect and suspected charge. A higher rate indicates less efficiency in stops, or an excessive rate of stops needed to affect an arrest. A high stop rate may also indicate more indiscriminate stop practices, or simply broadened suspicion of individuals based on race alone.[150] Overall, the total stop-to-arrest ratio of blacks (7.3 stops per arrest) is 58.7% higher than the ratio for non-Hispanic whites (4.6); the ratio for Hispanics (6.4) is 39% higher than the rate for non-Hispanic whites. For weapons stops, the stop-to-arrest ratio for blacks is 18.7% higher than the ratio for whites, but the ratio for Hispanics is less than 23.0% higher.

TABLE 5. RACE- AND CRIME-SPECIFIC STOP-ARREST RATIOS CITYWIDE[151]

Type of Crime	Citywide	Black	Hispanic	White	Other
Weapon	16.5	16.5	17.1	13.9	17.3
All Stops	6.5	7.3	6.4	4.6	5.5

To test whether stops were proportionate to crime rates, and to assess factors that might explain stop rates higher than would be predicted by crime rates, multivariate analyses were completed incorporating three potential explanations: the crime rate within the sub-borough (or strategic theory), disorder (or place-based theory), or social disorganization (or person-based theory). Trends in both Tables 4 and 5 confirm the emphasis on weapons stops articulated in NYPD strategy memoranda. Accordingly, separate analyses were completed on the overall stop counts, and then on stops where weapons were the suspected charge or rationale for the stop.

Table 6 shows the bivariate correlations—the correlation between two variables—among these predictors and the outcome variables.[152] Correlations were statistically significant and in the predicted directions for stops overall and stops involving non-white

---

150. One could also argue that a higher stop rate for one group may indicate "under-stops" of other groups, or a reluctance to stop more often persons of one race or another. That is an unlikely explanation, however, since the OAG Report shows that the racial distribution of stops were consistent across precincts and stable over the fifteen months. *See* OAG REPORT, *supra* note 5, at 92-110. It is unlikely that the pattern of under-documentation or depressed stop rates for whites would remain so consistent across the NYPD's many precincts and neighborhoods.

151. OAG REPORT, *supra* note 5, at tbl.I.C.1.

152. For example, stop rates for whites were negatively correlated with vacancy rates, concentrations of public assistance recipients, and housing units with broken windows.

TABLE 6. CORRELATION MATRIX (PEARSON R, P)

	Total Arrests	% in Public Housing	Vacancy Rate	% Units with Broken Windows	% Receiving Public Assistance	Racial Fragmentation	Mobility	% Immigrants
ALL STOPS								
Stops - All	.707**	.474**	.397**	.461**	.573**	.082	-.039	.418**
Stops - Blacks	.582**	.361**	.477**	.423**	.474**	-.120	-.154	.259
Stops - Hispanics	.481**	.388**	.147	.337*	.502**	.236	.142	.418**
Stops - Whites	-.107	-.155	-.337*	-.344*	-.435**	.207	.025	-.033
Stops - Other	.098	.024	-.201	-.136	-.219	.371**	.009	-.126
WEAPONS								
Stops - All	.645**	.449**	.460**	.514**	.664**	-.017	-.124	.336*
Stops - Blacks	.509**	.321*	.462**	.425**	.495**	-.157	-.201	.169
Stops - Hispanics	.518**	.447**	.255	.429**	.641**	.185	.069	.451**
Stops - Whites	.052	-.094	-.244	-.204	-.230	.200	-.015	.015
Stops - Other	.223	-.008	-.110	-.065	-.076	.316*	.080	-.092

*   p < .05
** p < .01
*** p < .001

suspects. Stops involving whites either were not correlated with the disorder or disorganization variables, or were correlated negatively with disorganization variables.[153]

Results of multivariate tests of the relative contributions of crime, disorder, and disorganization to stop counts are shown in Table 7. A fixed effects Poisson regression analysis was used, with predictors from each of these three domains.[154] The model estimates the expected value of the number of events in relation to the causal factors and other explanatory variables of interest. The question in this analysis is whether the count of events (stops) in an area (sub-borough) is predicted by factors that might influence these events (arrest rates, social disorganization variables, and physical disorder variables). The baseline model tests the hypothesis that the race-specific stop count is proportional to the number of arrests in the area. The full model assesses whether factors beyond the arrest count predict the stop count in the area.

---

153. Overall, whites in New York City live in neighborhoods that are marked by the absence of social isolation or economic deprivation, as well as neighborhoods with lower crime rates. *See, e.g.*, JOHN MOLLENKOPF & MANUAL CASTELLS, DUAL CITY: RESTRUCTURING NEW YORK 29-31, 304-05 (1991). However, the correlation of stops of whites and crime rates in the neighborhood were not statistically significant. This may reflect the fact that whites often were stopped when they were observed in non-white neighborhoods, usually on suspicion of drugs. *Id.* This illustrates the "racial incongruity" source of disparity, where a stop is triggered by a racial "mismatch" of a person of one color moving through a neighborhood with population dominated by persons of another color. In the case of whites in non-white neighborhoods, it is often on suspicion of drug buying or possession. When black or Hispanic suspects are stopped in predominantly minority neighborhoods, it often is on suspicion of violence or weapons crimes. OAG REPORT, *supra* note 5, at 126-28, and tbl.I.C.1.

154. P. McCULLAGH & J. NELDER, GENERALIZED LINEAR MODELS 193-08 (1989); WILLIAM H. GREENE, ECONOMETRIC ANALYSIS (2d ed. 1993); PETER KENNEDY, A GUIDE TO ECONOMETRICS (3d ed. 1994). Poisson regression is an ideal method to analyze factors that predict counts of events, and determining the relationship of these counts to a set of explanatory or predictive variables. The loglinear Poisson model is the one utilized for these analyses. Standard errors are corrected for overdispersion.

TABLE 7. POISSON REGRESSION OF RACE-SPECIFIC STOPS FOR ALL STOPS AND WEAPONS STOPS ONLY [T, P(T)]

	All Stops				Weapons Stops			
	All Suspects	Black Suspects	Hispanic Suspects	White Suspects	All Suspects	Black Suspects	Hispanic Suspects	White Suspects
Intercept	12.71***	7.74***	3.47**	6.36***	8.86***	6.51***	2.18*	4.86***
1997 Arrests	4.61***	3.24**	3.16**	.81	4.20***	3.17**	3.79***	1.41
% in Public Housing	.30	.01	.28	.95	-.80	-.43	-.68	.16
Vacancy Rate	-1.21	.88	-3.73***	-.94	-.80	.80	-3.92***	-1.08
% Broken Windows	.90	-.71	2.09*	-.49	.45	-.83	2.20*	-.26
% Public Assistance	2.54*	1.55	3.50**	-2.09*	3.97***	2.24*	5.67***	-.79
Racial Fragmentation	1.72	-.11	2.92**	1.01	1.14	-.35	3.77***	1.12
Residential Mobility	-.61	-1.44	1.66	-.23	-1.38	-1.80	.96	-.61
% Immigrant	.05	-.56	1.26	.42	-.46	-.99	1.30	.31
-2 Log Likelihood	117.1	172.5	163.3	166.7	147.4	190.7	165.6	166.1
Model Chi-Square	16431.4	27870.4	12198.4	5281.7	12888.2	18624.2	4698.5	1542.9

*   p < .05
**   p < .01
***   p < .001

The results confirm the claim that the arrest rate predicts both total stops and weapons stops in the sub-boroughs. Arrests are a significant predictor of the total number of stops, the total number of weapons stops, and both total and weapons stops for black and Hispanic suspects. However, arrests fail to predict stops for whites. In part, this may reflect the low rate of stops of whites, or the heterogeneity of the locations of white stops. That is, stops of whites may include both "racial mismatch" stops of whites in non-white areas where crime rates may be elevated, but other types of stops occur as well, most in neighborhoods of varying crime rates. Some may simply be based on descriptions from complainants, and others based on the reasonable suspicion grounds articulated in *Terry*.

Crime rates *should* predict stop rates, and should take into account any differences by race in the likelihood that a citizen should be stopped relative to his or her propensity for crime commission. However, when factors other than crime rates affect stops, we attribute these additional factors to policy, or to other tacit assumptions about race, neighborhoods, and criminality. Table 7 shows that for stops overall, factors other than crime in the neighborhood predict the stop counts. For all suspects, after controlling for crime, stops within the sub-boroughs were predicted by their poverty rates. Accordingly, policing in the city's neighborhoods appears to reflect the economic status of people rather than the physical condition of its buildings.

When race-specific stop counts are considered, both disorder and disorganization variables predict stop counts for Hispanics, but not for blacks. The concentration of dwellings with broken windows, low vacancy rates, high concentration of persons in public housing, and racial heterogeneity all predict the stop count for Hispanics. The diversity of this pattern of predictors for Hispanics reflects the heterogeneity of residential patterns and socio-economic factors for Hispanics. For whites, stops are not predicted by crime, but instead are predicted by the absence of poverty. Again, this reflects the tendency for whites to live in areas that although not necessarily affluent, are less likely to be poor.

Finally, Table 7 shows a different picture for weapons stops. For weapons stops of all suspects generally and specifically of black suspects, poverty rates predicted stop counts, after controlling for crime. As above, policing weapons is concentrated in poor neighborhoods. Stop and frisk activity targeted at weapons seems focused on the economic status of people in neighborhoods, not the physical condition of their buildings. For stops of Hispanic suspects, weapons stops were predicted by both disorder and disorganization variables.

These patterns suggest that stop and frisk strategies have departed from their original Broken Windows underpinnings, and more closely resemble policing of poor people in poor places. How the policy in action evolved so far from its complex and nuanced theoretical origins is a potentially important tale. It is important to understand whether and how race became a marker of increased risk of criminality in this hothouse policy context, the ways in which race interacted with the social organization of policing to produce greater intensity of enforcement and over-enforcement against minority citizens, and the cultural and political dynamics that allow the conflation of race, poverty, and disorder in policing policy. These lessons await a different research paradigm, focused on the hot cognitions of police-citizen interactions, and the social contexts in which these events unfold.

IV. SOCIAL NORMS AND AGGRESSIVE POLICING

In New York, the application of Broken Windows theories through OMP strategies and stop and frisk tactics produced a style of racial policing with stigmatizing effects on minority communities. In fact, the implemented strategy departed sharply from the original design of Broken Windows theory, focusing more on the consequences of broken windows than their causes. The strategy as implemented was intensified surveillance and proactive engagement with citizens under a broad standard of "reasonable suspicion." The emphasis on persons rather than place, and the racial demography of places where OMP was most intense and active, suggest that the cues to which police responded were primarily tied to race as well as places that are defined by race. Not only is this a long way from Broken Windows theory, but it invites constitutional problems that can further distance police from minority citizens.[155] The drift from engagement with community in the co-production of security reflects two different dimensions of social norms, dimensions of both community and organization.

---

155. *See generally* OAG Report, *supra* note 5, at 15-44 (discussing Fourth and Fourteenth Amendment issues related to stop and frisk activity and racial profiling, respectively); Garrett, *supra* note 7, at 1829-34 (discussing equal protection issues in racial profiling cases).

A. Social Norms and Aggressive Policing Revisited

Although stop and frisk tactics likely contributed to the crime decline in New York, the precise contribution of these tactics is contested.[156] But there also is little doubt that there were social costs from the crackdown on crime that may compromise the original intent to redirect and rebuild social norms.[157] If the mechanism of decline is search, surveillance, and aggressive misdemeanor arrests, there is no causal path to declining crime that runs through order and social norms. As Harcourt observed, these efforts "have little to do with fixing broken windows and much more to do with arresting window breakers—or persons who look like they might break windows, or . . . strangers . . . or outsiders."[158]

The social norms approach underlying Broken Windows theory required that the cues of crime be removed and replaced with alternative cues that signaled order and social regulation. In the causal dynamic hypothesized by the theory, citizens engaged with police to enforce norms of orderliness, conveying a social meaning that influenced behavior of citizens in the orderly milieu.[159]

This construction of social control comports well with the dynamics of collective efficacy discussed by Sampson, Raudenbush, and Earls.[160] Citizen participation in the dynamics of informal social control, such as collective supervision of teenagers and citizen interventions in low-level crimes, are manifestations of the neigh-

---

156. Fagan et al., *supra* note 36, at 1322 (crediting the decline in gun violence in part to "gun-oriented policing" but acknowledging multiple causation by other social factors); Waldeck, *supra* note 19, at 1283-84 (citation omitted) (suggesting that the stop and frisk tactics produced a crackdown that deterred many from carrying weapons or drugs); Harcourt, *supra* note 19, at 339-40 (claiming that the huge increase in misdemeanor arrests under OMP produced a surveillance effect that depressed crime rates). *But see generally* KARMEN, *supra* note 36 (citing interactions among multiple causes for the crime decline that complicated attribution of effects to any single cause).

157. *See generally* Tom R. Tyler, *Public trust and confidence in legal authorities: What do people want from the law and legal institutions?*, in BEHAVIORAL SCIENCE AND THE LAW (forthcoming) (arguing that public views are primarily shaped by evaluating the fairness of police and court procedures). Neighborhood residents in high crime neighborhood often express satisfaction with the lowered crime rate, but greater distrust of police when aggressive stop, search, and arrest tactics are used. OAG REPORT, *supra* note 5, at 74-87.

158. Harcourt, *supra* note 19, at 342.

159. Kahan, *supra* note 36, at 2488; Meares & Kahan, *supra* note 26, at 823.

160. Sampson & Raudenbush, *supra* note 20, at 611-612 (discussing the link between disorder and "collective efficacy"); *see also* Robert J. Sampson et al., *supra* note 79, at 919-21 (showing evidence that crime rates fluctuate according to the neighborhood's collective efficacy, independent of poverty, racial composition, and other socio-demographic factors).

borhood's "collective efficacy" that reduces crime and disorder.[161] Collective behavior of this type may involve citizen-police interactions, but often these are citizen-initiated efforts, such as "phone trees" among residents to call police and report either physical or social disorder, citizen demands to enforce housing codes to rid neighborhoods of crack houses, advocacy in court proceedings for substantive punishment for chronic disorder offenders, and collective political activity on zoning and licensing.[162] However, neither collective efficacy nor social capital is likely to be increased by policing tactics that rely almost exclusively on stopping, searching, and arresting people. Wilson and Kelling, in the original *Broken Windows* essay, did not imagine a scenario where aggressive policing—in the absence of interaction with community groups or social agencies—would create enduring forms of social interaction by citizens to prevent and control crime.[163]

The incentives for people to engage with legal actors in social regulation and the co-production of security may lie in their evaluations of their treatment by the police. Fairness and crackdowns may be inconsistent, but at least citizens know they are tradeoffs. Recent work by Tom Tyler and colleagues in a survey of residents in three Oakland, California neighborhoods suggests that citizens' evaluations of legal actors are not linked to the outcomes of their court cases or interactions with police, or on the crime rate in their neighborhood.[164] They focus instead on the fairness of their treatment from those authorities.[165] Ronald Weitzer reaches the same conclusion in a survey of residents of three neighborhoods in Washington, D.C.[166] He reports contrasting evaluations of police services in two predominantly black neighborhoods. Proactive po-

---

161. Sampson & Raudenbush, *supra* note 20, at 612.

162. *Id.*

163. The original Broken Windows theory recognized that a disorder-focused policing strategy would "only be effective if applied in conjunction with a wide variety of other police tactics" and "pursued in partnership with . . . other social agencies." Waldeck, *supra* note 19, at 1270 (citation omitted). Waldeck shows that the social norms and tactics suggested by the original Broken Windows theory diverged sharply from the traditional social norms of policing as "crime-fighters" where the officer's "basic business" is arresting offenders. *Id.*; *see* George L. Kelling, *Toward New Images of Policing: Herman Goldstein's Problem-oriented Policing*, 17 LAW & SOC. INQUIRY 539, 540 (1992).

164. TYLER, *supra* note 157. Tyler also notes that some judgments are made on vicarious experiences of neighbors and friends, an illustration of the importance of linked fate. *Id.*

165. *Id.*

166. Ronald Weitzer, *Racialized Policing: Residents' Perceptions in Three Neighborhoods*, 34 LAW & SOC'Y REV. 129, 150-52 (2000).

licing of residents of a poor, high crime neighborhood elicited less favorable reactions to police than did the more reactive and respectful treatment of citizens in an "orderly" middle-class neighborhood.[167]

Such empirical findings suggest the viability and importance of an approach to social regulation based on procedural fairness. Procedural fairness—or better treatment—promotes greater trust and confidence in the law, and higher rates of compliance.[168]

These perceptions of law and legal actors have important implications about popular attributions of legitimacy to law. People who view the law as illegitimate are less likely to obey it, and people who view police officers and judges as lacking in legitimacy are less likely to follow their directives.[169] Although the law is based on the implicit or explicit threat of sanctioning for wrongdoing, the legal system depends heavily on voluntary compliance from most citizens to set and enforce norms, and to engage with the police in social control. Hence, lower levels of legitimacy make social regulation more costly and difficult, both materially and politically. The police depend heavily on the voluntary cooperation of citizens to fight crime. Citizens report crime and criminals, informally help to police their neighborhoods, and aid the courts as jurors and witnesses. Without these cooperative acts from the public, the police risk being seen as an intrusive force imposing order. And without these acts, the meaning of order becomes detached from its social basis and loses its moral weight to influence others in the community.

A social norms approach would invite policing of public order laws in the context of corresponding and contemporaneous extralegal social initiatives aimed at the same or parallel problems. These efforts reflect a more complex view of the interaction of crime and disorder, one that recognizes their spurious relationship to broader underlying social and physical conditions within neighborhoods. The legitimacy of the law benefits from the simultane-

---

167. *Id.* at 151. Weitzer's findings stand Broken Windows theory on its head by suggesting that the police may be reacting to the visible cues of crime and disorder, not just would-be criminals who might journey to a disorderly neighborhood to take advantage of crime opportunities. Weitzer's findings suggest that in neighborhoods with visible signs of disorder, police react with indiscriminate and widespread patterns of aggressive stops and interdiction of citizens.

168. Tom R. Tyler, Why People Obey the Law 172-73 (1990).

169. *Id.* at 172; Robert J. Sampson & Dawn Jeglum Bartusch, *Legal Cynicism and (Subcultural?) Tolerance of Deviance: The Neighborhood Context of Racial Differences*, 32 Law & Soc'y Rev. 777, 793-800 (1998); Tom R. Tyler et al., Social Justice in a Diverse Society 86 (1997).

ous and aligned actions of citizens and legal actors to promote social norms. While OMP approaches might promote a temporary reduction of crime through suppression, a legitimacy-focused approach promotes construction of social networks that integrate community-level social processes with the regulation of crime and disorder.

B. Organizational Norms

Explanations of the importance of race in police decision making—up and down the hierarchy within police organizations—focus on both the occupational culture and social norms of policing.[170] Although the empirical literature on police "subculture" offers inconsistent evidence of generalizable attitudes and beliefs, several studies show that the dynamics and structure of the police workplace may work to reinforce social (behavioral) norms, perceptions, and beliefs.[171] The separation of the policing and non-policing worlds is widely acknowledged, even in the era of reform and innovation.[172] The insularity of the police workplace leads to a closed system of ideas, a reluctance to question the statements or actions of fellow officers, and "matter of fact prejudices" that are reinforced through customs, rituals, and a shared language.[173] If the workplace is where citizens "acquire 'social capital' . . . and develop ties of empathy and solidarity with their fellow citizens,"[174] then the workplace may be the appropriate locus for efforts to change social norms supporting racial policing.

---

170. *See e.g.*, STATE POLICE REVIEW TEAM, *supra* note 6, at 33-34 (1999). *See generally* Jeffrey Goldberg, *supra* note 6; OAG REPORT, *supra* note 5, at Ch. III, Part III (discussing "Police Attitudes Toward Stop and Frisk"). "A recent survey of 650 Los Angeles Police Department officers found that 25% felt that racial bias (prejudice) on the part of officers toward minority citizens currently exists and contributes to a negative interaction between police and the community." REPORT OF THE INDEPENDENT COMMISSION ON THE LOS ANGELES POLICE DEPARTMENT 69 (1991). *But see* Steve Herbert, *Police Subculture Reconsidered*, 36 CRIMINOLOGY 343, 344 (1998) (claiming that norms within police departments are influenced by bureaucratic structures).

171. *See generally* BITTNER, *supra* note 102; ANTHONY V. BOUZA, THE POLICE MYSTIQUE: AN INSIDER'S LOOK AT COPS, CRIME AND THE CRIMINAL JUSTICE SYSTEM 6-7 (1990).

172. BITTNER, *supra* note 102, at 11; *see also* JEROME H. SKOLNICK & JAMES J. FYFE, ABOVE THE LAW: POLICE AND THE EXCESSIVE USE OF FORCE 242 (1993) (citation omitted).

173. POLICING: A VIEW FROM THE STREET 267-70 (Peter K. Manning & John Van Maanen, eds., 1978).

174. Cynthia L. Estlund, *Working Together: The Workplace, Civil Society, and the Law*, 89 GEORGETOWN L. REV. 1, 4 (2000) (describing the workplace as performing crucial functions of the civil society including fostering communication, connectedness, and empathy among diverse individuals).

The skewed version of Broken Windows theory implemented by the NYPD reinforced the crime-fighting image of policing rather than the alternative norms about alternative solutions to crime problems developed carefully in other community-policing models.[175] The "crime fighting" image included stereotypes of citizens and criminals, stereotypes pregnant with racial meaning.[176] After all, the emphasis on social manifestations of disorder, with its demographic and neighborhood correlates, confounded race and disorder, giving rise to broad suspicion of criminal activity and intensified enforcement in minority neighborhoods. Despite recognizing that some citizens were law-abiding and welcomed police presence, the broad reach of stop and frisk policing risked placing many law-abiders under suspicion.

Efforts to reform the police workplace to modify social norms that emphasize race as a risk factor for crime will require complicated and sustained efforts to "admi[t] the workplace into the realm of civil society . . . ."[177] Policing as a workplace is at once both regulated by the state but also subject to hierarchy, rules, coercion, formal sanctions, and restraint. Is social norms theory applicable to changing the everyday logic and rules of policing? The shift in police function to OMP did not significantly modify core police functions, and in turn it was unlikely to modify the occupational "frame of reference" about crime and race.[178] Accordingly, the older social norms that were reinforced by those police functions and rewards that remained intact. How then, to change those norms?[179]

Many efforts to curtail racial profiling have increasingly focused the role of statistics on police stops. Legislators in seven states have passed laws requiring police to keep statistics, and similar legislation is being considered in twenty-one additional states.[180] Rep-

---

175. Waldeck, *supra* note 19, at 1269-70.

176. Thompson, *supra* note 17 at 987-89 (discussing the processes of racial and other stereotyping that may unconsciously influence stop and arrest decision making).

177. Estlund, *supra* note 174, at 5.

178. POLICING: A VIEW FROM THE STREET, *supra* note 173, at 269.

179. Professor Waldeck suggests that changes in police functions, specifically a return to the original intent of community policing and its emphasis on alternatives, will promote changes in social norms based on a different functional definition of policing. Waldeck, *supra* note 19, at 1300-01. But we propose changes that do not necessarily involve substantive modifications in police functions that are disruptive of the structural relationships within police hierarchies and workplaces.

180. An Act Concerning Traffic Stops Statistics, 1999 Conn. Acts 99-198 (Reg. Sess.); An act concerning criminal procedure; relating to the collection of information on traffic stops, 1999 Kan. Sess. Laws 2683; N.C. GEN. STAT. § 114-10 (1999); 2000 Mo. Legis. Serv. 1053 (West); An Act Relating to Motor and Other Vehicles, 1999

resentative John Conyers, Jr. (D-MI) proposed similar legislation, the National Traffic Stops Statistics Study Act of 1998, which passed unanimously in the U.S. House of Representatives but was rejected in committee by the U.S. Senate.[181] One rationale for the emphasis on data collection is that statistics can lead to transparency in policing,[182] making decisions visible and publicly accountable. Statistics may enable police departments to evaluate their strategies, or assess whether there are disparity costs that come with successes of particular strategies. Data also make officers' actions transparent, making them more accountable for their decisions. As decisions and everyday actions become more democratic, social norms from community stakeholders will be infused into police norms.

But the dynamics of organizational change following the introduction of data raises several challenges. The organizational and democratic structures within which data are introduced, how data-driven facts are evaluated, and how their meaning is interpreted require experimentation to develop open forums for both internal organizational reflection and open policy debates.[183] How information is shared with community stakeholders, whether the agenda for analysis is shared with these groups, and how the findings of data analyses are translated into concrete measures for organizational change are part of a process of community participation that can "civilize" the police workplace through transparency, leading to democratic interactions focused on data-driven facts.[184] The ex-

---

R.I. Pub. Laws 7164; An Act Relating to reporting information on routine traffic enforcement, 1999 Wash. Legis. Serv. S.S.S.B. No. 6683 (SN); *see also* UNIV. OF MINN. LAW SCH., INSTITUTE OF RACE AND POVERTY'S RACIAL PROFILING DATA COLLECTION STATUS REPORT (indicating that bills have been introduced in Alabama, Arkansas, Florida, Iowa, Illinois, Indiana, Kansas, Kentucky, Maryland, Massachusetts, New Jersey, New York, Ohio, Oklahoma, Pennsylvania, Rhode Island, South Carolina, Tennessee, Utah, Wisconsin, and Virginia), http://www1.umn.edu/irp/ARB%20.html; Laura Gunderson, *Bill Aims to Track Racial Profiling*, PORTLAND OREGONIAN, Sept. 12, 2000 at B1 (describing proposed bill in Oregon, which following introduction, was hailed by state police and several major local police departments expressing interest in collecting data on stops).

181. *See* H.R. Rep. No. 105-435 (1998). The legislation passed unanimously in the House, but was voted down in the Senate Judiciary Committee due to opposition from police organizations. *E.g.*, Robert Cohen, *Racial profiling Allegations Spur Lawmakers to call for U.S. Study*, THE STAR-LEDGER, Apr. 14, 1999 at 7.

182. For illustrations of the uses of data to assess strategies, see Eric Luna, *Transparent Policing*, 85 IOWA L. REV. 1108, 1167-94 (2000).

183. Susan Sturm & Brandon Garrett. *Moving Beyond Racial Profiling in New Jersey*, PHILA. INQUIRER, Dec. 4, 2000, at A15.

184. Constructing these types of relationships is likely to be contested, even when consent decrees set forth a framework for data collection on stops and monitoring of

tent to which opportunities for community interaction with police are routinized and institutionalized can break down the insularity of police social norms at the top and bottom of its hierarchy.

statistical trends. National Public Radio ("NPR") reported that civil rights groups including the American Civil Liberties Union of Southern California, and plaintiffs in prior racial profiling litigation against the Los Angeles Police Department ("LAPD") have filed motions to be included as monitors in the consent decree involving the LAPD. *Morning Edition* (Nat'l Pub. Radio broadcast, Dec. 18, 2000) (discussing the LAPD consent decree described *supra* note 7), *audio clip of report available at* http://search.npr.org/cf/cmn/cmnps05fm.cfm?SegID=115661. In the wake of statements by President-elect Bush in the second presidential debate questioning the federal role in the reform of police departments, these groups are concerned that a court-appointed federal monitor will not effectively enforce the city's agreement. The NPR report quotes Mark Rosenbaum, legal director the Southern California ACLU, as stating that "[t]he decree fences out those individuals who have the greatest interest in the most conscientious enforcement . . . . " The NPR report quotes attorneys for the City of Los Angeles, who counter that "involving more people will lead to too much legal fighting and not improving policing. A federal judge will do the job on enforcing the court order, so no outside parties are needed." *Id.*

504 *FORDHAM URBAN LAW JOURNAL* [Vol. XXVIII

APPENDIX A. DESCRIPTIVE STATISTICS FOR NEIGHBORHOOD VARIABLES

Social Disorganization	Mean	Standard Deviation
% Non-Hispanic White	36.71	28.77
% Hispanic	27.34	20.50
% Black	26.77	27.00
Racial fragmentation	0.51	0.14
% Living in neighborhood < 6 months	25.57	9.32
% Living in residence < 4 years	39.81	4.60
% Immigrants	82.97	10.58
% Households with public assistance	18.88	13.81
% Not in labor force	40.76	8.19
% Worked less than 26 weeks past year	11.54	2.91
% Unemployed since 1997	38.22	8.65
% Education < less than HS graduate	27.69	12.72
Sex ratio: males: females	0.87	0.10
% Female headed households	21.71	10.97
% Population < 15 years old	22.42	6.63
Disorder		
% Dwellings with damaged exterior walls	3.24	17.71
% Dwellings with damaged exterior windows	2.80	19.11
% Dwelling with damaged stairways	5.69	23.17
% Dwellings with broken heat	13.58	34.26
% Dwellings with damaged floors	5.56	22.92
% Reporting any broken windows in neighborhood	8.89	28.46
% Reporting dilapidated buildings in neighborhood	7.78	26.79

[4]

INSIDE THE INTERROGATION ROOM*

RICHARD A. LEO**

I. INTRODUCTION

The "gap problem"—the gap between how law is written in the books and how it is actually practiced by legal actors in the social world—has been an ongoing concern to legal scholars at least since the advent of Legal Realism in the 1930s,[1] and has been the focus of countless empirical studies associated with the Law and Society Movement since the 1960s.[2] Nevertheless, the gap in our knowledge between legal ideals and empirical realities remains as wide as ever in the study of police interrogation. Recognizing the source of the gap problem in 1966, the *Miranda* Court wrote that "interrogation still takes place in privacy. Privacy results in secrecy and this in turn results in a gap in our knowledge as to what in fact goes on in the interrogation room."[3] Linking the gap problem to the secrecy of interrogation, the *Miranda* Court emphasized the absence of first-hand knowledge of actual police interrogation practices, issuing a clarion call for empirical research in this area.[4] Regrettably, this call has gone almost entirely unheeded in the three decades following the influential *Miranda* opinion. Although law libraries are overflowing with doctrinal analy-

---

* I thank the following individuals for offering helpful comments, criticisms, and suggestions on earlier versions of this paper: Mark Cooney, David T. Johnson, Richard Lempert, Gary Marx, Fred Pampel, Tom Scanlon, Lindsey Simon, Jerome Skolnick, Tom Tyler, Eric Wunsch, and Frank Zimring.

** Assistant Professor of Sociology and Adjoint Professor of Law, University of Colorado, Boulder. B.A., University of California, Berkeley, 1985; M.A., University of Chicago, 1989; J.D., University of California, Berkeley, 1994; Ph.D., University of California, Berkeley, 1994.

[1] AMERICAN LEGAL REALISM (William W. Fisher III et al. eds., 1993).

[2] LAW AND SOCIETY: READINGS ON THE SOCIAL STUDY OF LAW (Stewart Macaulay et al. eds., 3d ed. 1995). This edited volume excerpts numerous studies that illustrate the gap between how law is portrayed on the books and how it actually works in practice.

[3] Miranda v. Arizona, 384 U.S. 436, 448 (1966).

[4] *Id.* at 448-58.

ses of appellate court cases, there exist no contemporary descriptive or analytical studies of routine police interrogation practices in America. If, as William Hart has written, "no law-enforcement function has been more visited by controversy, confusion and court decisions than that of the interrogation of criminal suspects,"[5] then it is not only surprising but also disturbing to note just how little we know about everyday police interrogation practices in America.

To be sure, since 1966 there have been a few experimental studies of the social psychology of confessions,[6] several early evaluative studies of the judicial impact of the controversial *Miranda* decision on confession and conviction rates,[7] and a few socio-linguistic or "conversational" analyses of individual police interrogation transcripts.[8] But unlike their English counterparts,[9] American scholars have almost altogether ignored or avoided the empirical study of police interrogation practices and criminal confessions. In legal scholarship, there have been no *empirical* studies of police interrogation practices since the late 1960s.[10] Instead, law professors, lawyers, and law students have created a formidable law review literature that focuses almost entirely on the doctrinal and ethical aspects of interrogation and confession case law, rather than on the routine activities of legal actors and institutions.[11] Since traditional legal scholarship is based on an analysis of leading cases—which are unrepresentative of the larger universe of court cases and thus may depict atypical police practices as the norm—this literature is by itself both narrow and misleading. In short, we know scant more about actual police interrogation practices today than we did in 1966 when Justice Earl Warren lamented the gap

---

5 William Hart, *The Subtle Art of Persuasion,* POLICE MAG., Mar. 1981, at 7.

6 *See* LAWRENCE WRIGHTSMAN & SAUL KASSIN, CONFESSIONS IN THE COURTROOM (1993).

7 *See* OTIS STEPHENS, THE SUPREME COURT AND CONFESSIONS OF GUILT 165-200 (1973) (reviewing this literature).

8 *See* William Sanders, *Pumps and Pauses: Strategic Use of Conversational Structure in Interrogations in,* THE SOCIOLOGIST AS DETECTIVE: AN INTRODUCTION TO RESEARCH METHODS (William Sanders ed., 1976); D.R. Watson, *Some Features of the Elicitation of Confessions in Murder Interrogations, in* INTERACTION COMPETENCE (George Psathas ed., 1990); Maria T. Wowk, *Blame Allocation, Sex and Gender in a Murder Interrogation, in* WOMEN'S STUDIES INTERNATIONAL FORUM (1984).

9 In the last decade in England, there have been numerous empirical studies of police interrogation practices. For a review of this literature, see GISLI GUDJONSSON, THE PSYCHOLOGY OF INTERROGATIONS, CONFESSIONS AND TESTIMONY (1992).

10 However, one law professor has recently gathered data on police interrogation practices in Salt Lake City. *See* Paul Cassell & Brett Hayman, *Police Interrogation in the 1990s: An Empirical Study of the Effects of Miranda,* 43 UCLA L. REV. (forthcoming 1996) (manuscript on file with author).

11 The leading two contemporary scholars on police interrogation practices and criminal confessions in the legal literature are Yale Kamisar and Joseph Grano. *See* YALE KAMISAR, POLICE INTERROGATION AND CONFESSIONS (1980); JOSEPH GRANO, CONFESSIONS, TRUTH, AND THE LAW (1993).

problem in *Miranda v. Arizona.*

This Article, which is the first in a two-part series, will attempt to fill in some of the gaps in our knowledge of routine American police interrogation practices by describing and analyzing the characteristics, context, and outcome of interrogation and confession in ordinary criminal cases that are not likely to make the published record on appeal. The second Article will analyze the impact of the Court's ruling in *Miranda v. Arizona* on the behavior, attitudes, and culture of American police interrogators in the last thirty years.[12] Both articles are based on nine months (more than 500 hours) of fieldwork inside the Criminal Investigation Division (CID) of a major, urban police department I shall identify by the pseudonym "Laconia,"[13] where I contemporaneously observed 122 interrogations involving forty-five different detectives. In addition, I viewed thirty videotaped custodial interrogations performed by a police department I shall identify by the pseudonym "Southville"[14] and another thirty video taped interrogations performed by a police department I shall identify by the pseudonym "Northville."[15] For each interrogation, I recorded my observations qualitatively in the form of fieldnotes and quantitatively with a forty-seven question coding sheet. Thus, my field research represents a more general, multi-faceted and methodologically diverse study of the history and sociology of police interrogation in America.[16]

This Article takes the reader inside the interrogation room to understand the characteristics, context, and outcome of contemporary police interrogation practices in America. It is the only study to do so in more than twenty-five years, and the first ever to do so in any sustained, explicit, or comprehensive manner.[17] I hope to reorient

---

[12] Richard A. Leo, *The Impact of Miranda Revisited,* J. CRIM. L. & CRIMINOLOGY (forthcoming, Spring 1996).

[13] In 1990 Laconia had a population of 372,242—approximately 43% black, 28% white, 15% Hispanic, and 14% Asian/Pacific Islander. In 1992 there were 58,668 Part I offenses in Laconia (10,140 violent crimes and 48,546 property crimes), an official crime rate of 123 per 1,000 members of the population. *See* Richard A. Leo, Police Interrogation in America: A Study of Violence, Civility and Social Change 456 (1994) (unpublished Ph.D. dissertation, University of California (Berkeley)).

[14] In 1993 Southville had a population of 121,064. Fifty-one percent of Southville's residents were white, 24% Hispanic, 15% Asian, and 10% black. In 1993 there were 8,505 Part I offenses in Southville (1,298 violent crimes and 7,207 property crimes), and official crime rate of 70.3 per 1,000 members of the populaton. *See id.*

[15] By the end of 1993 Northville had a population of 116,148. Forty-six percent of Northville's residents were white, 21% Asian, 20% black, and 11% Hispanic. In 1993 there were 9,360 Part I crimes in Northville (1,613 violent crimes and 7,747 property crimes), an official crime rate of 80.78 per 1,000 members of the population. *See id.*

[16] *See id.*

[17] With the exception of my own empirically-grounded research on the history and

much of the research and discourse on police interrogation practices in legal scholarship from its near exclusive doctrinal (or "law-on-the-books") focus to a more empirically-grounded (or "law-in-action") perspective, which I believe is necessary to inform the legal, ethical, policy, and theoretical debates in the study of criminal procedure.

In Part II of this Article I discuss the potential sources of bias in my data and how I attempted to overcome them. In Part III, I quantitatively describe and analyze the patterns in police techniques, suspect behavior, and interrogation outcomes in all of the 182 cases I observed.[18] In Part IV, I analyze the effects of police interrogation practices, *Miranda* warnings, and incriminating statements on the subsequent stages of the criminal process, such as the adjudication of guilt, case disposition, and sentencing. Finally, in Part V of this Article I offer some concluding thoughts on the findings of this study.

II.   METHODOLOGICAL CAVEAT:
OBSERVER EFFECTS AND THE PROBLEM OF BIAS[19]

Participant observation may be the ideal method to get as close as possible to the phenomena the researcher intends to analyze and understand. This has been one of the underlying methodological assumptions in my empirical study of American police interrogation practices.[20] However, the problem of studying naturally occurring data confronts the participant observer. Consequently, the participant observer cannot control the parameters of his research nor the effects of his behavior on the research subjects.

It is a methodological truism that the field researcher inevitably influences the environment in which he participates during the very process of observation.[21] These so-called "observer effects" may "con-

---

sociology of American interrogation practices, see Richard A. Leo, *From Coercion to Deception: The Changing Nature of Police Interrogation in America, in* CRIME, LAW AND SOCIAL CHANGE (1992) [hereinafter *From Coercion to Deception*]; Richard A. Leo *Police Interrogation and Social Control, in* SOCIAL & LEGAL STUDIES (1994) [hereinafter *Social Control*], only two observational studies of police interrogation exist in the American literature. *See* Michael L. Wald et al., *Interrogations in New Haven: The Impact of Miranda,* 76 YALE L. J. 1519 (1967); and NEIL A. MILNER, THE COURT AND LOCAL LAW ENFORCEMENT: THE IMPACT OF MIRANDA (1971). Both studies rely on data that was collected more than 25 years ago, and neither one is an analysis of a major, urban police department.

[18] For a qualitative analysis of the patterns in police techniques, suspect behavior and interrogation outcomes I observed, see Leo, *supra* note 13, at 170-256; Leo, *Social Control, supra* note 17, at 99-113.

[19] For a full account of the methodological strategies, challenges, and limitations of my participant observation fieldwork, see Leo, *supra* note 13, at 451-95. *See also* Richard A. Leo, *Trial and Tribulations: Courts, Ethnography, and the Need for an Academic Researcher's Privilege,* AM. SOCIOLOGIST, Spring 1995, at 113-34.

[20] Leo, *supra* note 13.

[21] Melvin Pollner & Robert Emerson, *The Dynamics of Inclusion and Distance in Fieldwork*

taminate" the data that the participant observer seeks to collect. In the context of my research, my presence may have altered the behavior of the detectives during the custodial interrogations I observed. Indeed, whether the participant observer alters the behavior of law enforcement officers by his mere presence is a classic methodological problem that has bedeviled sociologists of policing since Westley's groundbreaking field research more than forty years ago.[22] It stands to reason that the presence of a third party influences police behavior, yet the precise outcome of this effect is often difficult, if not impossible, to accurately assess since participant observers usually lack any independent or hidden controls.

I do not believe that my presence in the interrogation room significantly altered the behavior of the detectives I observed. Although I will never know the true effect of my presence, I offer the following observations. First, I sometimes put my ear to the door and listened to those interrogations from which I was purposely excluded, and each time the *Miranda* warnings were given properly. Nor did I overhear any threats or promises. Conversely, I occasionally observed behavior inside the interrogation room—such as yelling, table pounding, or highly aggressive questioning—that straddled the margins of legality. After one such interrogation, one of the two interrogating detectives informed me that he could be fired if I reported his behavior to the Captain. As we will see in Part III of this Article, I viewed a few interrogations that were clearly "coercive" by the standards of contemporary appellate courts. In one of these interrogations, the primary detective ignored the suspect's repeated invocations of his *Miranda* rights to silence and counsel, though ultimately the detective failed to convince the suspect to talk. After the interrogation session, the detective asked me what I thought he could have done differently to elicit admissions. When I responded that it did not matter since any subsequent confession would have been suppressed by the court, the detective casually replied that neither one of us would have remembered the *Miranda* violations in court. That one of the detectives could so naturally assume that I would perjure myself to advance the cause of crime control is, I think, good evidence that my presence, at least in some instances, had little effect on the interrogation practices I was observing.[23]

Relations, in CONTEMPORARY FIELD RESEARCH (Robert Emerson ed., 1983).

[22] William A. Westley, *Violence and the Police*, 59 AM. J. Soc. 34 (1953).

[23] Other police field researchers have reported similar feelings of invisibility. For example, Richard Uviller writes: "For the most part, my presence was simply ignored while police activities were in progress." RICHARD UVILLER, TEMPERED ZEAL: A COLUMBIA LAW PROFESSOR'S YEAR ON THE STREETS WITH THE NEW YORK CITY POLICE xiii (1988). And David

Second, the more time I spent inside the CID, the more the detectives became accustomed to my presence. As I became part of the "furniture" inside the Laconia Police Department (LPD), the detectives frequently treated me as one of their own. They would, for example, describe their cases to me by penal code sections or their actions by police codes or jargon, apparently forgetting that I did not know what they meant. In addition, many of the detectives shared with me explicitly confidential information about their co-workers or superiors, information whose exposure could have damaged their reputations, if not their careers, within CID. At the same time, detectives told me of their own indiscretions and sometimes questionable behaviors, for which they could have been administratively sanctioned, and in some instances held civilly liable, had I publicly revealed their confidences. In a sense, then, I became the archetypical Simmelian observer to whom social secrets were entrusted.[24] Strangely and unexpectedly, I realized midway through my research that the police code of silence (perhaps more accurately described as a code of solidarity) applied to me as well.

Third, I interviewed prosecutors and public defenders who were knowledgeable of LPD custodial interrogation practices. They agreed with my general descriptions of police interrogation practices at LPD, confirming that the methods and techniques I observed were representative of what they knew of interrogation methods at LPD from their daily cases as well. Significantly, the public defenders—the most strident ideological critics of police in an adversarial system of criminal justice—generally spoke respectfully of custodial interrogation practices at LPD, agreeing that detectives rarely engage in any illegalities during custodial questioning. Nevertheless, despite these comments, and although I established high levels of trust with the LPD detectives and sometimes even felt literally invisible during the interrogations, inevitably my presence must have exerted some effect on their behavior.

That I tended to be (but was not always) excluded from the more serious cases raises the general methodological issue of bias, and more specifically the problem of the representativeness of my data within LPD and the generalizability of my findings beyond LPD. In field studies, the researcher can overcome these problems only in degrees. I was unable to select randomly those cases whose interrogations I observed for three reasons. First, I had no control over those interroga-

---

Simon writes: "I became a piece of furniture in the unit, a benign part of the detectives' daily scenery." DAVID SIMON, HOMICIDE: A YEAR ON THE KILLING STREETS 596 (1991).

[24] KURT WOLFF, THE SOCIOLOGY OF GEORG SIMMEL (1950).

tions from which some detectives chose to exclude me. Second, even in those cases in which I was allowed to attend the interrogation, the suspect had sometimes posted bail and left the jail prior to any custodial questioning. A class bias that is naturally present in the practice of interrogation at LPD was therefore inevitably present in my data. Third, occasionally circumstances conspired to provide me with a choice over which interrogations I would attend. Although sometimes hours would pass during which no interrogations would occur, at other times multiple interrogations would be occurring simultaneously. To correct for the inherent biases in my data, I always requested to sit in on the interrogation of the most serious cases available to me.[25] Nevertheless, the 122 interrogations I observed contemporaneously were still not entirely representative of the general category of interrogations occurring within LPD.

In addition, I attempted to correct for the bias against serious cases in the data I collected in my non-participant observations of sixty videotaped interrogations at the Southville and Northville Police Departments. I specifically requested videotapes of interrogations in the more serious felony crimes, especially homicide, rape, and assault, from these two departments. Observing the videotaped interrogations of two other police departments served as a check on any idiosyncratic interrogation practices at LPD.[26] Certainly the interrogation practices at LPD, which has been generally regarded as one of the most professional police departments in America during the last three decades, are not representative of the interrogation practices of all police departments in America. Nevertheless, observing the interrogation practices of two other police departments was one way I attempted to redress the intrinsic limitations of the case study method.

---

[25] I considered the seriousness of cases in the following order: 1) homicide, 2) sexual assault, 3) felony assault; 4) robbery, 5) property crimes.

[26] Although both the Southville and Northville Police Departments routinely videotape felony interrogations, neither department has a policy of storing their videotapes, and neither department permitted me to view videotaped interrogations in cases still pending. Therefore, neither department had many videotaped interrogations on hand from which I could choose to view cases. In Northville, I was provided with a master list of all the felony cases during the last several years in which interrogations had been videotaped. I was then permitted to meet with the evidence technician and retrieve as many tapes as we could locate. Unfortunately, most of the tapes had been destroyed once the case had been concluded. In Southville, the Captain of CID circulated a memo to the detectives, asking them to identify the homicide, sexual assault, and felony assault cases in which they had interrogated suspects. From this list, the Captain and I retrieved existing videotapes. While my fieldwork in Northville and Southville made up for some of the biases of my participant observations in Laconia, the method through which I obtained videotaped interrogations inevitably contained its own set of biases. Ultimately, I had little control over which videos both departments provided me.

III. The Context and Outcome of Police Interrogation: Exploring the Data

In all the interrogations I observed, both contemporaneously at LPD as well by videotape at the Southville and Northville Police Departments, I coded for a number of independent variables (e.g., class, race, gender, and social distance between the suspect and victim, strength of evidence against the suspect, and prior conviction record of the suspect) and a number of dependent variables (e.g., whether suspect waived/invoked *Miranda*, length of interrogation, outcome of interrogation, and ultimate case disposition). I now turn to a systematic analysis of these and other variables.

A brief statistical description of the demographic, legal, and case variables in my sample reveals the variation in my data and the typical characteristics of the suspect, victim, and interrogation procedures in the cases I observed. Slightly more than one-third (35%) of the interrogations were conducted in an interrogation room located inside the jail; the remaining (65%) were conducted in the interrogation rooms located inside the CID. In the large majority of interrogations (69%), one detective questioned the suspect; in the remaining interrogations (31%), two detectives conducted questioning. The primary detective was typically white (69%), though not infrequently African-American (19%) or Hispanic (12%); when present, the secondary detective was also white most of the time (65%) and African-American some of the time (19%). There was less variation in the gender of the detectives: virtually all (over 90% of the primary and 86% of the secondary detectives) were men. Most of the primary detectives had been police officers for between ten and twenty years (62%) and detectives for one to five years (61%); most secondary detectives had also been police officers for ten to twenty years (68%) but detectives for only zero to three years (54%).

The typical suspect in my sample was a young, lower or working class, African-American male. Although the age range spanned from the middle teens to the late sixties, approximately two-thirds (66%) of the suspects were less than thirty years old. More than 87% of the suspects were from the lower or working class; almost 12% were middle class; and only 1% were upper middle class.[27] Sixty-nine percent of the suspects were African-American, 14% were white, 13% were Hispanic, and the remaining 4% were either Asian or Native Ameri-

---

[27] I coded for the class status of the suspects in my sample by asking the primary detective to rate the suspect as either below middle class, middle class, or above middle class based on 1) the suspect's occupation and (2) the location of the victim's residence. The same procedure was followed to code for the class status of the victims in my sample.

can.[28] Thus, more than 85% of the suspects in my sample were minorities. As with the detectives who interrogated them, virtually all the suspects were male (more than 90%).

Unlike the suspects, the victims in my sample did not fit so clear a demographic profile, because many of the victims (more than 25%) were organizations. Excluding organizations, most of the victims came from the lower or working class (69%), a higher number of victims came from the middle class than did suspects (30%), but, as with suspects, only a negligible number were from the upper middle class (1%). Just as African-Americans comprised the largest racial group of suspects in my sample, so too were they more likely to be the victims of crime than any other racial group. Excluding organizations, a full 42% of the victims in my sample were African-American; 28% were white; 22% were Hispanic; and the remaining 8% were Asian. A far higher percentage of victims were likely to be female than were the suspects: excluding organizations, 39% of the victims were female while only 61% were male.

All the interrogations I observed were for felony offenses. A frequency distribution of these offenses, divided into five categories, is listed below in Table 1.[29]

Table 1

FREQUENCY DISTRIBUTION OF TYPE OF CRIME

Type of Crime	Freq.	Percent
Theft	9	4.95%
Burglary	21	11.54
Robbery	78	42.86
Assault	44	24.18
Homicide	22	12.09
Other	8	4.40
Total	182	100.00

[28] The non-minority (i.e., white) suspects in my sample were drawn disproportionately from the cases I observed at the Southville and Northville Police Departments. Although slightly more than two-thirds of the interrogations I observed occurred at the Laconia Police Department, only one-third (9/27) of the interrogations involving white suspects in my sample occurred at this department; 26% (7/27) occurred at the Southville Police Department; and 41% (11/27) occurred at the Northville Police Department.

[29] My division of criminal offenses into five primary categories parallels the categorization of offenses inside the Laconia CID Unit. The reader should note that allegations of rape or child molestation were classified as assaults. The few crimes in the "other" category were mostly drug offenses. Although these categories appear relatively straightforward, if multiple offenses were involved, the suspect was classified into the category representing the most serious offense. For example, if a suspect allegedly committed both a theft and a homicide, his crime was classified as a homicide.

While the type of crime I was likely to observe varied by department, 81% of the offenses were crimes against persons (e.g, robbery, assault, homicide), and the remaining 19% were crimes against property (e.g, burglary, theft).

Two potentially important case factors that may influence a suspect's treatment by legal authorities are the strength of the evidence and the suspect's prior criminal record. In 33% of the cases in my sample, the strength of the evidence against a suspect prior to an interrogation was weak (highly unlikely to lead to charging); in 32% of the cases the strength of the evidence was moderate (probably likely to lead to charging); and in 35% of the cases it was strong (highly likely to lead to charging). In 13% of the cases in my sample, the suspect did not have a prior criminal record; in 29% of the cases, the suspect had a misdemeanor record; and in 58% of the cases, the suspect had a felony record. Not surprisingly, almost 90% of the suspects interrogated were repeat players with prior criminal records. This variable distinguished the suspects from their victims. Almost 69% of the victims had no prior criminal record; approximately 15% had misdemeanor records; and approximately 16% had felony records.

The formal interrogation process must, of course, be preceded by the well-known *Miranda* warnings. Table 2 lists the frequency distribution for suspect's responses to *Miranda*.

Table 2
FREQUENCY DISTRIBUTION OF SUSPECT'S RESPONSE TO
MIRANDA WARNINGS

Suspect's Response To *Miranda* Warnings	Freq.	Percent
Waived	136	74.73%
Changed to Waive	1	0.55
Invoked	36	19.78
Changed to Invoke	2	1.10
Not Applicable	7	3.85
Total	182	100.00

In seven (almost 4%) of the cases I observed, the detective did not provide any *Miranda* warnings because the suspect technically was not "in custody" for the purpose of questioning.[30] Therefore, in these seven cases the detectives were not legally required to issue *Miranda*

---

[30] In other words, the suspect was neither under arrest nor was his freedom restrained "in any significant way" (in each case, the detective(s) informed the suspect that he did not have to answer their questions and that he was free to leave at any time).

warnings.[31] With the exception of these cases, the detective(s) read each of the fourfold *Miranda* warnings verbatim from a standard form prior to virtually every interrogation I observed.[32] A suspect might respond in one of four ways: waiving his rights, invoking them, or changing his initial response either to a waiver or an invocation. As Table 3 below indicates, 78% of my sample ultimately waived their *Miranda* rights, while 22% invoked one or more of their *Miranda* rights, thus indicating their refusal to cooperate with police questioning.

Table 3
FREQUENCY DISTRIBUTION OF SUSPECT'S ULTIMATE RESPONSE
TO *MIRANDA*

Whether Suspect Waived or Invoked	Freq.	Percent
Waived	137	78.29%
Invoked	38	21.71
Total	175	100.00

If a suspect chooses to waive his *Miranda* rights, the custodial interrogation formally begins. If a suspect chooses to invoke one or more of his *Miranda* rights, typically the detective terminates the interrogation and returns the suspect to jail (if he was under arrest). However, in seven (4%) of the cases I observed, the detectives questioned suspects even after receiving an invocation. In each of these cases, the detective(s) informed the suspect that any information the suspect provided to the detective could not and therefore would not be used against him in a court of law. The detective told the suspect that the sole purpose of questioning was to learn "what really happened." Of course, what the detectives knew and did not tell the suspect was that although the prosecution could not use such evidence as part of its case-in-chief, any information the suspect provided to the detective nevertheless could be used in a court of law to impeach the suspect's credibility, and indirectly incriminate the suspect if he chose to testify at trial.[33] In the remaining thirty-one cases in which the suspect invoked his *Miranda* rights at some point during questioning (82% of all

---

[31] *Miranda* warnings are legally required only "after a person has been taken into custody or otherwise deprived of his freedom of action in any significant way." Miranda v. Arizona, 384 U.S. 436, 444 (1966).

[32] In two of the burglary interrogations I observed, one investigator recited the *Miranda* warnings verbatim from memory. One robbery interrogator had the habit of reading the *Miranda* warnings from a standard form but crossing out (and thus not reading) the words "and will" in the second of the four warnings. *See* Leo, *supra* note 13, at 174-81.

[33] Harris v. New York, 401 U.S. 222 (1971).

cases in which a suspect invoked a *Miranda* right), the detective(s) promptly terminated the interrogation.

In any session in which the detective questioned a suspect beyond the *Miranda* warnings (whether or not a suspect invoked), I coded for twenty-five potential interrogation techniques.[34] Table 4 lists the frequency distribution for the total number of tactics employed by detectives during each interrogation. The number of tactics a detective employed per interrogation ranged from zero (e.g., the suspect spontaneously confessed or the detective did not genuinely try to elicit a confession) to fifteen. The cumulative percentage figure represents the percentage of interrogations in which detectives used at least that many interrogation tactics.

Table 4

FREQUENCY DISTRIBUTION OF TACTICS EMPLOYED PER INTERROGATION

Number of Interrogation Tactics Used by Detectives per Interrogation	Freq.	Percent	Cumulative Percentage
0	2	1.31%	—
1	8	5.23	99%
2	19	12.42	93
3	17	11.11	81
4	16	10.46	70
5	16	10.46	59
6	16	10.46	49
7	19	12.42	39
8	10	6.54	26
9	11	7.19	20
10	9	5.88	12
11	5	3.27	7
12	3	1.96	3
15	2	1.31	
Total	153	100.00	

The detectives employed a median of 5 and a mean of 5.62 tactics per interrogation. Clearly, however, the detectives used some interrogation tactics more frequently than others. Table 5 below lists each of the twenty-five tactics, and the frequency of their use during the interrogations I observed.

---

[34] I derived this list from the tactics (1) advocated in contemporary police interrogation training manuals; (2) taught in police interrogation training courses; and (3) used by police detectives in popular culture.

Table 5

TYPES OF INTERROGATION TACTICS AND THEIR FREQUENCY

Type of Interrogation Tactic	No. of Cases In Which Tactic Used	% of Cases In Which Tactic Used
TACTICS USED MOST OFTEN		
Appeal to the suspect's self-interest	134	88%
Confront suspect with existing evidence of guilt	130	85
TACTICS USED OFTEN		
Undermine suspect's confidence in denial of guilt	66	43
Identify contradictions in suspect's story	65	42
Any Behavioral Analysis Interview questions	61	40
Appeal to the importance of cooperation	56	37
Offer moral justifications/psychological excuses	52	34
Confront suspect with false evidence of guilt	46	30
Use praise or flattery	46	30
Appeal to detective's expertise/authority	45	29
Appeal to the suspect's conscience	35	23
Minimize the moral seriousness of the offense	33	22
TACTICS USED LEAST OFTEN		
Touch suspect in a friendly manner	17	11
Invoke metaphors of guilt	15	10
Minimize the facts/nature of the offense	9	6
Refer to physical symptoms of guilt	7	5
Exaggerate the facts/nature of the offense	6	4
Yell at suspect	5	3
Exaggerate the nature/purpose of questioning	3	2
Exaggerate the moral seriousness of the offense	3	2
Accuse suspect of other crimes	2	1
Attempt to confuse the suspect	1	1
Minimize the nature/purpose of questioning	1	1
Good cop/Bad cop routine	1	1
Touch suspect in an unfriendly manner	0	0

As Table 5 indicates, there is great variation in the distribution of the interrogation tactics I observed. A couple of the tactics were used in virtually all of the cases, several others were used in approximately one-third to one-half of the cases, a couple were used in approximately one-fifth of the cases, a few others were used only sparingly, and others virtually not at all. If a portrait of the typical interrogation emerges from the data, it involves a two-prong approach: the use of negative incentives (tactics that suggest the suspect should confess because of no other plausible course of action) and positive incentives (tactics that suggest the suspect will in some way feel better or benefit if he confesses). In my sample, detectives typically began the interrogation session by confronting the suspect with some form of evidence, whether true (85%) or false (30%), suggesting his guilt and then attempting to undermine the suspect's denial of involvement (43%), while identifying contradictions in the suspect's alibi or story (42%). But detectives relied on positive incentives as well, most often by appealing to the suspect's self-interest (88%), but also by frequently offering the suspect moral justifications or psychological excuses (34%), using praise or flattery (30%), minimizing the moral seriousness of the offense (22%), appealing to the importance of cooperation with legal authorities (37%) or appealing to the detective's expertise (29%), or appealing to the suspect's conscience (22%). In approximately 90% of the interrogations I observed, the detective confronted the suspect with evidence (whether true or false) of his guilt and then suggested that the suspect's self-interest would be advanced if he confessed.[35]

Of course, the interrogations in my sample also varied by length, ranging from literally seconds (when the suspect invoked before the detective even introduced himself) to four and one-half hours. Table 6 shows the frequency distribution of the length of the interrogations for those cases in which the detective chose to question a suspect (i.e., excluding the twenty-nine cases in my data in which the suspect invoked his *Miranda* rights, and the detective terminated all questioning). As Table 6 indicates, more than 70% of the interrogations in my sample lasted less than an hour, and only 8% lasted more than two hours.

Table 6
LENGTH OF INTERROGATION ONLY WHERE AN
INTERROGATION OCCURRED

Length of Interrogation	Freq.	Percent	Cum.
Less Than 30 Minutes	53	34.64%	34.64%
31-60 Minutes	56	36.60	71.24
1-2 Hours	32	20.92	92.16
More Than 2 Hours	12	7.84	100.00
Total	153	100.00	

[35] For a fuller description of contemporary American police interrogation techniques, see Leo, *Social Control, supra,* note 17, at 99-113.

The outcome of an interrogation is, of course, the most important aspect of questioning from the perspective of the police, and potentially the most important aspect of a case from the perspective of the suspect. In each interrogation, I coded for one of four possible outcomes: the suspect provided no information to the police that they considered incriminating (whether or not the suspect invoked); the suspect provided some information that police considered incriminating (whether or not intentionally) but did not directly admit to any of the elements of the crime;[36] the suspect admitted to some, but not all, of the elements of the crime; and the suspect provided a full confession to the detectives. Table 7 displays the frequency distribution for the outcome of the interrogations in my sample.

Table 7
OUTCOME OF INTERROGATIONS

Suspect's Response to Interrogation	Freq.	Percent
No Incriminating Statement	65	35.71%
Incriminating Statement	41	22.53
Partial Admission	32	17.58
Full Confession	44	24.18
Total	182	100.00

If an interrogation is successful when the suspect provides the detective(s) with at least some incriminating information, then almost two-thirds (64%) of the interrogations I observed produced a successful result. The rate of successful interrogations in this sample is notably higher than the success rate reported by Wald et al. (51%),[37] Younger (50%),[38] Neubauer (46%),[39] Seeburger and Wettick (38%)[40] or Leiken (32%),[41] but is slightly lower than the success rate reported by Witt[42] (67%).[43] If we exclude from my sample those cases ·in which

---

[36] Typically this consisted of implausible or contradictory denials that the detectives believed corroborated other evidence pointing to the suspect's guilt or that locked the suspect into a false alibi, and/or that could be used successfully to impeach a suspect's credibility, and thus incriminate him, in subsequent judicial proceedings.

[37] Wald et al., *supra* note 17, at 1566.

[38] Evelle Younger, *Results of a Survey Conducted in the District Attorney's Office of Los Angeles County Regarding the Effect of the Miranda Decision Upon the Prosecution of Felony Cases*, 5 AM. CRIM. L. Q. 32, 35 (1966).

[39] David W. Neubauer, *Confessions in Prairie City: Some Causes and Effects*, 65 J. CRIM. L. & CRIMINOLOGY 103, 104-06 (1974).

[40] Richard Seeburger & Stanton Wettick, *Miranda in Pittsburgh—A Statistical Study*, 29 U. PITT. L. REV. 1, 11 (1967).

[41] Lawrence S. Leiken, *Police Interrogation in Colorado: The Implementation of Miranda*, 47 DENV. L. J. 1, 13 (1970).

[42] James W. Witt, *Non-Coercive Interrogation and the Administration of Criminal Justice: The*

the police terminated questioning upon the invocation of a *Miranda* right (and thus the detective or detectives made no effort to incriminate the suspect), more than three-fourths (76%) of the interrogations I observed produced a successful result. To the extent that these studies are representative of general trends in American policing, detectives have become increasingly successful at eliciting incriminating information from criminal suspects.

Following a suspect's waiver of his *Miranda* rights, any information that he provides to a detective during custodial questioning— whether an incriminating denial, a partial admission, or a full confession—must be rendered "voluntarily" if it is to be used against that suspect in subsequent judicial proceedings.[44] In other words, the prosecutor will not be able to use any incriminating information police elicit from a custodial suspect if the interrogation methods they employed are deemed "coercive" by the courts. The issue of coercive questioning has been the fundamental concern of the appellate courts that have traditionally regulated police interrogation procedures in America.[45] Yet the meaning that courts have attributed to the concept of "coercion" has always been relative and historically contingent. How courts define the concept of "coercion" and where they draw the line between coercive and non-coercive interrogation tactics has varied dramatically in American history and continues to vary (from one jurisdiction to another as well as between courts within similar jurisdictions) in contemporary America.[46] For "coercion" in the context of interrogation is not an external thing one can indepen-

---

Impact of Miranda on Police Effectuality, 64 J. CRIM. L. & CRIMINOLOGY 320, 325 (1973).

[43] One must interpret these comparisons with some caution, for several of the researchers defined a successful interrogation differently or coded the outcomes of interrogations differently or relied on different methodologies when gathering their data. Witt uses a definition of success identical to my own (i.e., any interrogation yielding a confession, admission, or incriminating statement). *See* Witt, *supra* note 42, at 325. I computed the Wald et al. success rate by imposing on their data a definition of success identical to mine. *See* Wald et al., *supra* note 17, at 1566. Younger's definition of a successful interrogation—a confession, admission, or other (presumably incriminating) statement—appears similar to mine own. *See* Younger, *supra* note 38, at 35; *see also* Evelle J. Younger, *Interrogation of Criminal Defendants—Some Views on Miranda v. Arizona*, 35 FORDHAM L. REV. 255, 255-62 (1966). Neubauer's definition of a successful interrogation, which includes any confession, admission, or statement to police, appears more inclusive than mine because "statement to police" need not be incriminating. *See* Neubauer, *supra* note 39, at 104-106. By contrast, Seeburger & Wettick and Leiken employ a more exclusive definition of successful interrogations, which includes only confessions and admissions, not incriminating statements. *See* Seeburger & Wettick, *supra* note 40, at 10; Leiken, *supra* note 41, at 13. Despite the lack of identical definitions, however, these studies offer valuable data for rough comparisons of the efficacy of modern interrogation practices.

[44] Brown v. Mississippi, 297 U.S. 278 (1936).

[45] WAYNE LAFAVE & JEROLD ISRAEL, CRIMINAL PROCEDURE (2d ed. 1992).

[46] *See* Leo, *supra* note 13, at 12-66.

dently observe or something whose existence one can objectively verify, but rather a concept that courts attach to a variable and sometimes quite amorphous set of police behaviors.[47] In hard cases how courts draw the line between coercive and non-coercive interrogation methods depends on the judge's predisposition toward crime control or due process values and perhaps ultimately on the judge's philosophical conceptions of moral responsibility and the limits of human freedom.[48]

To operationalize the concept of "coercion," I attempted to capture those set of police behaviors and interrogation practices that contemporary appellate courts generally tend to label as "coercive." Thus, I coded any interrogation in my sample as "coercive" if at least one of the following ten conditions were present during the interrogation:

(1) The detective failed to read the *Miranda* warnings;

(2) The suspect was not permitted to invoke his *Miranda* rights;

(3) The detective touched the suspect in an unfriendly manner;

(4) The suspect was in obvious physical or psychological pain (whether or not related to the detective's actions);

(5) The detective threatened the suspect with physical or psychological harm;

(6) The detective promised the suspect leniency in exchange for an admission of guilt;

(7) The detective deprived the suspect of an essential necessity (such as water, food, or access to a bathroom);

(8) The detective's questioning manner was unrelenting, badgering or hostile;

(9) The interrogation lasted an unreasonable amount of time (more than six hours); or

(10) The suspect's will appeared to be overborne by some other factor or combination of factors.

Although some may disagree with where or how I chose to draw the line between coercive and non-coercive interrogations, I believe that I erred on the side of ruling as "coercive" questioning methods that many contemporary trial and appellate courts would otherwise deem to be non-coercive[49] and thus, my criteria for coercive tactics generally resolve any doubts in favor of the suspect, not the police. Nevertheless, in my sample of 182 custodial interrogations, police questioning methods in only four (or 2%) of the cases rose to the level of "coer-

---

47 *Id.*

48 *See* HERBERT PACKER, THE LIMITS OF THE CRIMINAL SANCTION (1968). To my knowledge, no one has empirically studied how judges reason, think about and distinguish "coercive" from "voluntary" confessions.

49 *See* YALE KAMISAR ET AL., MODERN CRIMINAL PROCEDURE: CASES, COMMENTS, QUESTIONS 452-61 (8th ed. 1994).

cion" according to these criteria.

Since four is too small a number to warrant any statistical analysis, I can only qualitatively describe the patterns, if any, I observed in these cases. All four cases involved the use of psychologically coercive methods; none involved the use of physically coercive methods. In one interrogation, detectives questioned a heroin addict who was quite obviously experiencing extremely painful withdrawal symptoms. While the detectives did nothing to contribute to the suspect's agony, they intentionally questioned him during the second day of his incarceration when they knew his withdrawal symptoms would be most acute. Although the police arrested the suspect on probable cause for felony gun possession, the detectives considered him a potential, not an actual, suspect in their robbery case. The detectives questioned him as if he were an informant, promising to release him just as soon as he provided them with information about a couple of robberies. Shortly thereafter, the police released the suspect from custody without charging him. In another case I coded as "coercive," two detectives employed the "good cop-bad cop" routine on a young gang member who witnessed a violent gang beating. As one detective kindly promised to release him from custody if he named the perpetrators of the assault, the other detective angrily threatened to provide the prosecutor with incriminating information that would send the suspect to prison. The suspect provided the detectives with the information they desired and was subsequently released without charge.

In another case, an alleged violent armed robbery by an individual with a long criminal record who had been recently released from prison, the detectives failed to acknowledge the suspect's repeated invocation of silence in response to the initial *Miranda* admonition. After repeatedly trying to talk the suspect out of waiving his *Miranda* rights, the detectives terminated their questioning after approximately five minutes. The suspect, against whom strong eyewitness evidence existed, was eventually charged by the prosecutor.[50] The last instance of a "coercive" interrogation in my sample involved a suspect who police arrested for selling drugs and offered an explicit promise of leniency if he became an informant and provided names of more highly placed drug dealers. The suspect refused to turn state's witness, and received a four year prison sentence instead.

Of course, four cases is too small a sample from which to draw any meaningful generalizations. If a common thread exists among these cases, however, it is that the detectives perceived that they had

---

[50] Due to a regretful error in note-taking, I was unable to track down the ultimate disposition of this case.

nothing to lose by exerting "coercive" means or intentionally eliciting an involuntary statement. For as all detectives know, witnesses do not enjoy the same constitutional protections as suspects, and the judicial suppression of a suspect's statement may not be very significant to the state's case when there exists other compelling physical evidence of a suspect's guilt. As in earlier studies,[51] the detectives did not, in this limited sample, appear to be any more likely to resort to coercive methods as a result of any personal or social characteristics of the suspect under questioning.

Police interrogation involves only one stage of the larger criminal process through which an individual may be convicted and ultimately incarcerated. The detective's primary goal during interrogation is to gather enough incriminating evidence to convince the prosecutor to file criminal charges against the suspect. Eventually, prosecutors charged 69% of the suspects in my sample and released the remaining 31%.[52] Of those individuals who were charged by prosecutors, 88.5% were convicted. Approximately 60% of the suspects in my entire sample were eventually convicted, though this figure includes only those cases whose dispositions were resolved (i.e., not pending trial or unknown) when I left the field altogether.[53] Eighty-five percent of those suspects received felonies while the remaining 15% received misdemeanors.

Whether or not a suspect was ultimately convicted of the offense for which he was under questioning, his case might be resolved by the criminal justice system in one of several ways: by dismissal; by a violation of parole or probation (in which the suspect is returned to prison for up to one year due to a prior conviction); by plea bargaining; or by trial. No charge or dismissal after charging occurred in approximately 38% of the cases in my sample; in approximately 10% of the cases the suspect violated his probation or parole from a prior conviction and was returned to prison; plea bargaining resolved approximately 43% of the cases; and in approximately 10% of the cases, the suspect's case was resolved by a trial.

---

51 *See* Wald et al., *supra* note 17.

52 I coded parole/probation violations as being charged, even though technically a suspect whose parole or probation is violated is not charged. Prosecutors may prefer to cite a parole/probation violation rather than charge a suspect for his current offense because the standard of proof for a violation is only "preponderance of evidence" (i.e., more likely than not) rather than "beyond a reasonable doubt," and thus violating a suspect's parole or probation typically results in the suspect's automatic re-incarceration for a previous conviction. Prosecutors "violated" the parole/probation of 18 (or approximately 10%) of the suspects in my sample.

53 Although I left the field in late September 1993 after nine months of fieldwork, I briefly returned to the Laconia, Southville, and Northville Police Departments in the spring of 1994 to collect information on outcomes for the outstanding cases in my sample.

The final stage of the criminal justice process for defendants is sentencing. In my sample, approximately 42% of the suspects were either not charged or not convicted and thus received no sentence. The other suspects in my sample received sentences ranging from probation to life imprisonment. Table 8 lists the length of sentence received by those suspects for whom dispositions were available at the time of this writing.[54] While there was considerable variation in the range of sentences in my sample, I have recoded them into four categories.

Table 8
LENGTH OF SENTENCE SUSPECT RECEIVED

Length of Suspect's Sentence	Freq.	Percent	Cum.
None	68	41.98%	41.98%
Low (Less Than One Year)	56	34.57	76.54
Medium (1-5 Years)	17	10.49	87.04
High (More than 5 Years)	21	12.96	100.00
Total	162	100.00	

IV. THE CONTEXT AND OUTCOME OF POLICE INTERROGATION: ANALYZING THE DATA

What explains how suspects respond to *Miranda* warnings? How do their responses vary by social, legal, and case factors? Are the differences statistically significant? How does a suspect's decision either to waive or invoke his *Miranda* rights affect the processing of his case, the likelihood of conviction, and the final case resolution? What explains how suspects respond to police questioning? Why do some suspects confess while others do not? Does the likelihood that a suspect will provide detectives with incriminating information vary by social, legal, and case factors? Are these differences statistically significant? Which interrogation tactics are likely to be most effective and ineffective in eliciting incriminating information from suspects? What explains the varying length of custodial interrogations and efforts detectives expend in trying to elicit incriminating information from criminal suspects? What effect does providing incriminating information to a detective have on the suspect's fate in the criminal justice system? These are among the questions that I will seek to answer in this section.

---

[54] *See supra* note 53.

A.   A SUSPECT'S RESPONSE TO *MIRANDA* AND ITS EFFECTS

Despite the passing of almost thirty years since their judicial creation, the *Miranda* warnings remain one of the most controversial issues in American criminal justice, even as *Miranda* has become settled
doctrine in the appellate courts, standard policy in police departments, and a household word in American popular culture.[55] The
conventional wisdom in legal and political scholarship is that virtually
all suspects waive their rights prior to interrogation and speak to the
police.[56] However, as we saw above, almost one-fourth of my sample
(22%) exercised their right to terminate police questioning, while
78% of the suspects chose to waive their *Miranda* rights. Nevertheless,
one might expect that certain individuals are more likely to waive
their rights than others. Indeed, the Warren Court in *Miranda* speculated that underprivileged suspects were less likely to comprehend or
exercise their constitutional rights to silence and counsel than their
more advantaged counterparts.[57] Though I tested for twelve social,
legal and case-specific variables, the only variable that exercised a statistically significant effect on the suspect's likelihood to waive or invoke his *Miranda* rights was whether a suspect had a prior criminal
record (p<.006). As Table 9 below indicates, while 89% of the suspects with a misdemeanor record and 92% of the suspects without any
record waived their *Miranda* rights, only 70% of the suspects with a
felony record waived their *Miranda* rights. Put another way, a suspect
with a felony record in my sample was almost four times as likely to
invoke his *Miranda* rights as a suspect with no prior record and almost
three times as likely to invoke as a suspect with a misdemeanor record.
This result confirms the findings of earlier studies,[58] as well as the
conventional wisdom among the detectives I studied, who complained
that ex-felons frequently refuse to talk to them as a matter of course.
The more experience a suspect has with the criminal justice system,
the more likely he is to take advantage of his *Miranda* rights to terminate questioning and seek counsel.

---

55 *See* FRED P. GRAHAM, THE SELF-INFLICTED WOUND (1970); LIVA BAKER, MIRANDA:
CRIME, LAW AND POLITICS (1983); Leo, *supra* note 12.

56 Leo, *supra* note 12.

57 Miranda v. Arizona, 384 U.S. 436, 471-73 (1966).

58 Wald et al., *supra* note 17, at 1562-77; Neubauer, *supra* note 39, at 106-07.

Table 9

SUSPECT'S RESPONSE TO *MIRANDA* BY PRIOR CRIMINAL RECORD

| Suspect's Prior Record | Whether Suspect Waived or Invoked | | |
	Waived	Invoked	Total
None	22	2	24
	91.67%	8.33%	100.00%
Misdemeanor	42	5	47
	89.36%	10.64%	100.00%
Felony	72	31	103
	69.90%	30.10%	100.00%
Total	136	38	174
	78.16%	21.84%	100.00%

Pearson chi2(2) = 10.1340 Pr = 0.006

At least as important as a suspect's response to the *Miranda* warnings is the effect that either a waiver or an invocation will exert on the processing of his case, the likelihood of conviction, and the final case resolution. While the police may consider a suspect's interrogation less likely to be successful if a suspect invokes his *Miranda* rights, this is neither necessarily nor obviously true. In my sample, the detectives acquired incriminating information against a suspect in six (approximately 16%) of the thirty-eight interrogations in which the suspect at some point invoked his *Miranda* rights.[59] Despite its potential effect on the outcome of an interrogation, a suspect's case was 4% less likely to be charged if he waived his *Miranda* rights than if he invoked his *Miranda* rights prior to or during interrogation (approximately 73% vs. 69%). While counterintuitive, this difference, as Table 10 below indicates, is not statistically significant and thus not significantly related to the prosecutor's decision to charge the suspect with a criminal offense.

---

[59] In my sample, detectives questioned seven suspects after they had invoked their *Miranda* rights and two suspects who subsequently invoked their *Miranda* rights. Of these nine cases, six suspects provided incriminating information to detectives.

Table 10

EFFECT OF SUSPECT'S RESPONSE TO *MIRANDA* ON PROSECUTOR'S
DECISION TO CHARGE CASE

Suspect's Response To *Miranda* Warnings	Whether Suspect was Charged by Prosecutor		
	Not charged	Charged	Total
Waived	42	95	137
	30.66%	69.34%	100.00%
Invoked	10	27	37
	27.03%	72.97%	100.00%
Total	52	122	174
	29.89%	70.11%	100.00%

Pearson chi2(1) = 0.1832 Pr = 0.669

While the suspects in my sample who waived their *Miranda* rights were only 4% less likely to be charged by the prosecution, they were approximately 10% more likely to be convicted of an offense than those who invoked their *Miranda* rights (63% vs 53%). This difference may seem large, but it is not statistically significant, as Table 11 below indicates.

Table 11

LIKELIHOOD OF CONVICTION BY RESPONSE TO *MIRANDA*

Suspect's Response To *Miranda* Warnings	Whether Suspect Was Convicted		
	Not Convicted	Convicted	Total
Waived	48	81	129
	37.21%	62.79%	100.00%
Invoked	15	17	32
	46.88%	53.13%	100.00%
Total	63	98	161
	39.13%	60.87%	100.00%

Pearson chi2(1) = 1.0057 Pr = 0.316

Although a suspect's response to *Miranda* is not significantly related to either the prosecutor's charging decision or the likelihood of conviction, it is significantly related to the process by which the suspect's case will be resolved (p<.024). As Table 12 below indicates, a suspect who waives *Miranda* is twice as likely to have his case resolved through plea bargaining, and this difference is highly significant (p<.009). And in my sample more than 98% of the plea bargains resulted in convictions. That a suspect's decision to waive his *Miranda* rights significantly increases the likelihood that his case will be resolved by plea bargaining confirms Neubauer's earlier finding,[60] and may be the most notable effect of a suspect's response to the pre-interrogation *Miranda* warnings. Presumably, the greater evidence accumulated against suspects who speak to their interrogators (and likely provide them with incriminating information) accounts for this statistically significant relationship. However, it is also possible that this relationship results from the selection bias created by *Miranda*; those suspects who waive their constitutional rights and allow police interrogation may be more cooperative individuals and thus more predisposed toward less adversarial means of case resolution such as plea bargaining, while those suspects who invoke their *Miranda* rights may be more inclined to press their claims aggressively through the court system.

Table 12

THE RELATIONSHIP BETWEEN *MIRANDA* AND PLEA BARGAINING

Suspect's Response To *Miranda* Warnings	Whether Suspect Case Was Resolved by Plea Bargaining		
	No	Yes	Total
Waived	69	65	134
	51.49%	48.51%	100.00%
Invoked	28	9	37
	75.68%	24.32%	100.00%
Total	97	74	171
	56.73%	43.27%	100.00%

Pearson chi2(1) = 6.9076   Pr = 0.009

The final stage of the criminal process in which a suspect's response to the *Miranda* waiver may exert an effect is sentencing. In particular, one might reasonably expect that suspects who waived their *Miranda* rights during interrogation would be likely to receive more severe sentences than those suspects who had invoked their rights. Although suspects who waive their *Miranda* warnings are more likely to receive punishment than their counterparts who invoke, the differences in the severity of punishment they receive are not statistically significant, as Table 13 indicates.

---

[60] Neubauer, *supra* note 39, at 109-10.

Table 13
RELATIONSHIP BETWEEN *MIRANDA* AND SENTENCE SEVERITY

Suspect's Response To *Miranda* Warnings	Severity of Suspect's Sentence				
	None	Low	Medium	High	Total
Waived	48	46	15	15	124
	38.71%	37.10%	12.10%	12.10%	100.00%
Invoked	15	9	2	6	32
	46.88%	28.13%	6.25%	18.75%	100.00%
Total	63	55	17	21	156
	40.38%	35.26%	10.90%	13.46%	100.00%

Pearson chi2(3) = 2.6350 Pr = 0.451

Even if we control for conviction (i.e. exclude from our analysis those suspects who were not convicted), the relationship between a suspect's response to the *Miranda* warnings and the severity of his sentence remains statistically insignificant ($p < .349$).

B. THE SUCCESS OF INTERROGATIONS

Why do some suspects confess while others manage to resist police pressures to incriminate themselves? What social and legal circumstances make the probability of a successful interrogation more or less likely?

Several earlier studies have attempted to answer these questions. Leiken found that younger suspects were much more likely to confess than older ones, and that suspects without a prior criminal record were slightly more likely to confess than suspects with a prior record.[61] The differences captured in his data, however, were not statistically significant at the .05 level.[62] Leiken also found that socially disadvantaged suspects (as measured by years of education) were no more likely to confess than more socially privileged suspects.[63] Neubauer found that suspects without criminal records were substantially more likely to confess than suspects with criminal records, and that suspects accused of property crimes were more likely to confess than suspects accused of crimes against persons.[64] But younger suspects were no more likely to confess than older ones nor were suspects from disadvantaged social groups any more likely to confess than suspects from privileged social groups.[65] Neubauer theorized that what really ex-

[61] Leiken, *supra* note 41, at 19-20.
[62] *Id.* at 19-21.
[63] *Id.* at 20.
[64] Neubauer, *supra* note 39, at 104.
[65] *Id.* at 105.

Police and Policing Law

plained the differential confession rate in his data was the evidence against a suspect prior to interrogation, which, he posited, was typically much higher in property crime cases than crimes against persons.[66] Like Leiken, however, Neubauer failed to provide tests of significance to support his assertions, and thus we do not know whether the strength of the associations in his data were arbitrary.

Employing more sophisticated methods, Wald et al. found that suspects without a prior record were significantly more likely to provide incriminating information during interrogation than suspects with prior criminal records, and that suspects were significantly more likely to provide incriminating information during interrogation the stronger the evidence against them prior to custodial questioning.[67] Additionally, in the more serious offenses suspects were significantly more likely to provide incriminating information during interrogation.[68] However, Wald et al. found no statistically significant relationship between either the suspects' race or age and their likelihood to confess.[69]

Unlike Wald et al., Leiken, and Neubauer, I examined the effects of a wide range of sociological and legal variables on the likelihood of successful interrogation outcomes. None of the sociological variables—the class, race, or gender of the suspects, victims, or officers—were significantly related to the likelihood of obtaining incriminating information from the suspect.[70] Neither were many of the legal and case specific variables.[71] Although my data confirm Neubauer's (unsubstantiated) assertion that the strength of the evidence against a suspect prior to interrogation is significantly higher in property crimes

---

[66] *Id.* at 106.

[67] Wald et al., *supra* note 17, at 1643-48.

[68] *Id.*

[69] *Id.* at 1644-46.

[70] Multivariate regression analyses confirmed the CHI2 finding that suspects' demographic data is not significantly related to successful interrogation outcomes.

[71] It is possible that unsuccessful or successful interrogation outcomes were accounted for by the suspect's innocence or guilt rather than by the length of interrogation or the number of tactics. Since I could not tell whether a suspect was innocent or guilty prior to his interrogation, this possibility cannot be altogether falsified. However, it seems highly unlikely for at least two reasons. First, many unsuccessful interrogations were the result of a suspect invoking his *Miranda* rights, and, as we have seen, suspects with prior felony records were four times more likely to invoke their *Miranda* rights than suspects without any prior criminal record, a finding that is statistically significant. It stands to reason that suspects with prior felony records, who were more likely to be guilty than suspects without a prior criminal record, thus accounted for a disproportionate number of the unsuccessful interrogation outcomes. Second, the strength of the evidence prior to the interrogation was the best indicator of the suspect's innocence or guilt prior to interrogation, and it was not significantly related to successful interrogation outcomes. When controlling for the strength of the evidence prior to the interrogation, however, the length of interrogation and number of tactics remain statistically significant at the .01 level.

than in crimes against persons (p<.028), they do not support his argument that there is a significant relationship between the type of crime and the likelihood of confession. Nor do my data confirm Leiken's assertion that younger suspects are much more likely to provide incriminating information during interrogation than older suspects. Nor do my data corroborate Wald et al.'s findings that the absence of a prior record, the strength of the evidence prior to questioning, and the seriousness of the offense exert a statistically significant effect on the likelihood that the suspect will provide incriminating information during interrogation.

The only variables in my sample that were significantly related to the likelihood of a successful interrogation were the number of tactics employed by detectives (p<.002), and the length of the interrogation (p<.000). That the number of tactics employed by detectives and the length of interrogation are significantly related to the likelihood of confession suggests that the effort and energy expended by detectives is one of the most important factors in explaining successful interrogation outcomes. The more interrogation tactics detectives use, the more likely they are to find something that works. The longer detectives interrogate, the more likely they are to wear the suspect down and elicit incriminating statements.

C. THE EFFECT OF INTERROGATION TACTICS

Although the earlier empirical studies mentioned above all analyzed the effect(s) of selected sociological and legal variables on the likelihood of confession, no study has ever examined (either qualitatively or quantitatively) the effect of interrogation tactics on the likelihood that suspects will provide incriminating information to detectives during interrogation. Yet according to the rhetoric of police interrogation training manuals and courses, as well as the conventional wisdom in police culture, the interrogation tactics that a detective uses should be the decisive influence in a suspect's decision to provide police with incriminating information.[72] The *Miranda* Court echoed a similar sentiment when it excoriated police interrogation training texts for compelling confessions through psychologically subtle and sophisticated questioning methods.[73] My statistical analysis in the previous section revealed that the number of interrogation tactics detectives employ during custodial questioning is significantly related to the likelihood of obtaining incriminating information from suspects (p<.002). Are certain interrogation methods and strategies

---

[72] *See* Leo, *supra* note 13, at 67-127.
[73] Miranda v. Arizona, 384 U.S. 436, 448-55 (1966).

also significantly likely to be effective at eliciting incriminating admissions from custodial suspects? And is the use of these and other interrogation tactics by detectives socially and/or legally patterned? In other words, under what circumstances or conditions do some interrogation tactics yield a statistically significant likelihood of eliciting incriminating information from a suspect?

As Table 14 indicates, when detectives employed certain interrogation tactics they were significantly likely to elicit incriminating information from suspects.[74] In particular, the tactic of identifying contradictions in the suspect's denial of involvement was successful at eliciting incriminating information in 91% of the interrogations in which it was used ($p<.000$); the tactic of offering the suspect a moral justification or psychological excuse for his behavior was successful in 90% of the interrogations ($p<.004$); the tactic of using praise or flattery was successful in 91% of the interrogations ($p<.005$); and the tactic of appealing to the suspect's conscience was successful in 97% of the interrogations in which it was used ($p<.001$). Although these four tactics were the only ones that exercised a statistically significant effect on successful interrogation outcomes in general, the tactic of appealing to the importance of cooperating with legal authorities ($p<.098$) and using Behavioral Analysis Interview questions[75] ($p<.090$) were also highly likely to be effective.

---

[74] Since 71 different detectives participated in the 182 interrogations in my sample, we can safely rule out the possibility that this table measures the techniques that only good interrogators use. Most of the interrogations in my sample did not involve the same officers. Moreover, as Table 5 indicates, several tactics were commonly used in a great many of the interrogations.

[75] The Behavioral Analysis Interview consists of a structured set of non-investigative hypothetical questions that are thought to evoke particular behavioral responses from which interrogators are taught to ascertain the truthfulness of suspects' responses and infer deception prior to commencing formal interrogation. *See* FRED E. INBAU ET AL., CRIMINAL INTERROGATION AND CONFESSIONS 63-68 (3d ed. 1986). Inbau et al. recommend approximately 15 questions to pose to the suspect, ranging from general questions, such as why does the suspect think someone would have committed the crime, to specific ones, such as would the suspect be willing to take a polygraph. Inbau et al. argue that guilty suspects react defensively and with discomfort to these questions; they equivocate, stall, and provide evasive or noncommittal answers. By contrast, innocent suspects are thought to produce cooperative, direct, and spontaneous responses to these questions. In their introductory and advanced training seminars, the Chicago-based firm of Reid & Associates advise interrogators to treat as guilty any suspect whose answers to four or more of the fifteen questions appear deceptive to the interrogator.

294 *RICHARD A. LEO* [Vol. 86

Table 14

THE EFFECT OF INDIVIDUAL INTERROGATION TACTICS

Interrogation Tactic	Success[76] Rate	CHI2[77]
MOST SUCCESSFUL INTERROGATION TACTICS		
Appeal to the suspect's conscience	97%	.001*
Identify contradictions in suspect's story	91	.000*
Use praise or flattery	91	.005*
Offer moral justifications/psychological excuses	90	.004*
LEAST SUCCESSFUL INTERROGATION TACTICS		
Touch suspect in a friendly manner	88%	.225
Invoke metaphors of guilt	87	.327
Any Behavioral Analysis Interview (BAI) questions	84	.090
Appeal to the importance of cooperation	84	.098
Appeal to detective's expertise/authority	84	.133
Confront suspect with false evidence of guilt	83	.241
Minimize the moral seriousness of the offense	81	.414
Undermine suspect's confidence in denial of guilt	80	.182
Confront suspect with existing evidence of guilt	78	.168
Appeal to the suspect's self-interest	77	.760

*p<.01

The effectiveness of specific interrogation tactics also varies by the social characteristics of the suspects under questioning as well as the legal characteristics of their cases. Table 15 displays the relationships between the techniques that are significantly likely to yield incriminating information by the social and legal variables in my data for which the number of observations available was large enough to warrant statistical analysis. These findings tell us not merely which police techniques are most likely to be successful, but also the tactics to which different suspects are most likely to be vulnerable. For example, younger suspects seemed far more vulnerable to appeals of conscience and justification, perhaps because they are more naive, inexperienced, or idealistic than older suspects, who, by contrast, seemed far more vulnerable to pragmatic appeals based on self-interest and the strength of evidence suggesting their guilt.

---

[76] As we saw in Table 7, detectives were successful at eliciting incriminating information in 64% of the cases in my sample. This figures rises to 76% if we exclude the cases in which suspects invoked one or more of their *Miranda* rights and questioning subsequently ceased. This figure, then, is the base rate of success against which the percentages in Table 14 should be compared.

[77] I excluded from my analysis any interrogation tactic that was not used in at least 15 (or approximately 10%) of the interrogations because otherwise the number was too small to permit adequate statistical analysis.

Interestingly, some interrogation techniques that were not generally significant become significantly likely to yield incriminating information under certain conditions. For example, suspects who are below middle class and suspects with prior felony records were significantly likely to be vulnerable to physical evidence ploys. Due to the lack of variation in many of the independent variables in my data, however, explicit comparisons in the efficacy of techniques and the vulnerability of suspects could not always be made. For example, we can see the specific tactics to which men, minorities, and below middle class suspects in my sample were most vulnerable, but I can provide no such data for their female, white, or middle class counterparts because so few of my subjects fell into these categories. Moreover, as we will see below, detectives were significantly likely to use more interrogation tactics against certain types of suspects and in certain types of cases, thus increasing the possible number of efficacious tactics in those cases and against those suspects. For example, detectives were significantly likely to use more interrogation tactics the more serious the crime (p<.042) as well as in those cases in which the strength of the evidence prior to the interrogation was not already high (p<.038).

Table 15
EFFECTIVENESS OF INTERROGATION TACTICS BY SOCIAL AND LEGAL
CHARACTERISTICS OF THE CASE

Variable/Successful Tactics	Success Rate	CHI2*
Younger Suspects (Less than 30 Years Old)		
Identify Contradictions	90%	.018
Use Praise or Flattery	93	.015
Offer Moral Rationalizations	97	.002
Appeal to Suspect's Conscience	100	.003
Older Suspects (Older than 30 years)		
BAI Questions	90	.024
Identify Contradictions	92	.004
Confronting Suspect with Existing Evidence	80	.004
Appeal to Suspect's Self-Interest	78	.048
Male Suspects		
Identify Contradictions	90	.001
Offer Suspect Moral Rationalizations	90	.008
Use Praise or Flattery	93	.004
Appeal to Suspect's Conscience	97	.001
Minority Suspects		
Identify Contradictions	93	.000
Offer Suspect Moral Rationalizations	93	.007
Use Praise or Flattery	91	.030
Appeal to Suspect's Conscience	100	.002
Appeal to Importance of Cooperation	88	.055

Suspects Below Middle Class		
Identify Contradictions	93%	.000
Confront Suspects with False Evidence	88	.050
Offer Suspect Moral Rationalizations	93	.001
Use Praise or Flattery	93	.004
Appeal to Suspect's Conscience	97	.002
Touch Suspect in a Friendly Manner	100	.028
Suspects With Prior Felony Records		
Use BAI Questions	94	.007
Identify Contradictions	95	.004
Confront Suspect with False Evidence	96	.027
Offer Suspect Moral Rationalizations	96	.013
Use Praise or Flattery	95	.033
Appeal to Suspect's Conscience	95	.030
Suspects Without Prior Felony Records		
Identify Contradictions	86	.031
Use Praise or Flattery	87	.044
Appeal to Suspect's Conscience	100	.009
Crimes Against Persons		
Identify Contradictions	90	.001
Offer Suspect Moral Rationalizations	90	.014
Use Praise or Flattery	91	.022
Appeal to Suspect's Conscience	97	.003
Appeal to Importance of Cooperation	86	.048
Crimes of Low or Medium Seriousness		
Identify Contradictions	97	.002
Offer Suspect Moral Rationalizations	93	.011
Appeal to Suspect's Conscience	100	.006
Crimes of High Seriousness		
Identify Contradictions	86	.054
Use Praise or Flattery	100	.016
Strength of Evidence is Low or Medium		
Prior to Interrogation		
Identify Contradictions	91	.001
Offer Suspect Moral Justifications	88	.036
Use Praise or Flattery	89	.031
Appeal to Suspect's Conscience	95	.013
Appeal to Importance of Cooperation	89	.008
Strength of Evidence is High		
Prior to Interrogation		
Offer Suspect Moral Rationalizations	95	.040
Appeal to Detective's Expertise	100	.042
Appeal to Suspect's Conscience	100	.033

*$p < .05$

D.   THE LENGTH AND EFFORT OF CUSTODIAL INTERROGATIONS

What factors determine the amount of time detectives put into interrogating suspects and attempting to elicit incriminating information from them? When are detectives more likely to interrogate suspects aggressively? How does the time and effort detectives expend during custodial questioning vary by the legal, case-specific, and sociological factors in my data? Which relationships are statistically significant?

My data revealed a statistically significant relationship between the amount of time detectives spend interrogating suspects and three other variables: the seriousness of the offense, the success of the interrogation, and the gender of the victim. The more serious the crime, the longer detectives spent attempting to elicit incriminating information from the suspect ($p<.002$). The high seriousness crimes were more than twice as likely to result in long interrogations (more than one hour) than low seriousness crimes (42% vs. 20%); conversely, a crime of low seriousness was approximately three times as likely to result in a short interrogation (less than thirty minutes) than a crime of high seriousness (53% vs. 18%). Not surprisingly, the length of the interrogation is also significantly related to its success ($p<.000$): successful interrogations were six times more likely to last more than one hour than unsuccessful ones (36% vs. 6%); conversely, unsuccessful interrogations were more than twice as likely to be under thirty minutes than successful ones (58% vs. 27%). Finally, the gender of the victim was also significantly related to the length of the interrogation in my sample ($p<.004$). If the gender of the victim was female, the interrogation was more than twice as likely to be long (46% vs. 21%). This finding is likely due to the interrogations of suspects accused of rape in my sample, interrogations which almost always lasted more than one hour and in which the victim was always female. However, this finding is difficult to assess because 89% of the suspects in my sample were men, thus rendering an extremely small comparison group.

Like the amount of time detectives spend interrogating suspects, the number of tactics detectives employ during custodial questioning was also significantly related to three independent variables: the seriousness of the offense, the race of the suspect, and the strength of evidence against a suspect. The more serious the offense, generally the more interrogation tactics detectives employ in their attempts to gather incriminating information from custodial suspects ($p<.042$). Interrogations for crimes of low seriousness were more than twice as likely to last under thirty minutes than either crimes of medium seriousness or high seriousness (53% vs. 26% vs. 23%). Not surprisingly, the number of interrogation tactics detectives employed during their interrogations of suspects accused of crimes against persons was significantly higher than for those accused of property crimes ($p<.008$). Detectives were also significantly likely to employ more tactics during their interrogation of minority suspects (p<.005). However, the small number of non-minority suspects makes this finding difficult to assess because 85% of the suspects in my sample were nonwhite, once again rendering an extremely small comparison group. Finally, the strength of the evidence against a suspect prior to questioning is significantly related to the number of tactics detectives are likely to employ during interrogation (p<.038). Generally, detectives tend to use fewer tactics when the evidence against a suspect is already strong and there appears to be little need to obtain more incriminating evidence. Detectives in my sample were more than twice as likely to use a high number of interrogation tactics when the evidence against the suspect prior to questioning was either weak or intermediate than when it was strong (47% vs. 22%).

E.   THE EFFECT OF CONFESSIONS ON CASE PROCESSING

What happens to suspects who incriminate themselves during interrogation? What effect does providing incriminating statements, admissions, and confessions in the interrogation room have on the likelihood that a suspect will subsequently be charged and convicted? The process through which a suspect's case is resolved? The severity of sentencing? Is it true, as critics have argued, that once a suspect confesses to police his case is largely over; in effect, the rest of the judicial process is mostly form rather than substance?[78]

This study suggests that confessions may well be the most damning and persuasive evidence of criminal guilt, a finding that confirms the beliefs of many detectives and prosecutors, as well as the outcome of mock jury experiments.[79] Incriminating statements provided to police during interrogation cast a long shadow over the defendant's fate within the criminal justice system. *Suspects who provide incriminating information to detectives are significantly more likely to be treated differently at every subsequent stage of the criminal process than those suspects who do not provide incriminating information during interrogation.* As Table 16 below indicates, suspects in my sample who incriminated themselves during interrogation were 20% more likely to be charged by prosecutors (p<.006);[80] 24% less likely to have their cases dismissed (p<.000); 25%

---

[78] *See* Charles Ogletree, *Are Confessions Really Good for the Soul?: A Proposal to Mirandize Miranda*, 100 HARV. L. REV. 1826 (1987); Arthur Sutherland, *Crime and Confession*, 79 HARV. L. REV. 21 (1965).

[79] *See* SIMON, *supra* note 23; Leo, *Social Control, supra* note 17, at 99; Gerald R. Miller & F. Joseph Boster, *Three Images of the Trial: Their Implications for Psychological Research, in* PSYCHOLOGY IN THE LEGAL PROCESS 19 (Bruce Dennis Sales ed., 1977).

[80] The statistically significant differences at this stage of the criminal process remained even when I recoded parole or probation violations as a decision by the prosecutor not to charge the suspect. Still, a suspect who provided police with incriminating information

Table 16

THE EFFECT OF PROVIDING INCRIMINATING STATEMENTS ON
CASE PROCESSING

Stage of Criminal Process	Percentages	CHI2
Whether Suspect Charged		.006*
Successful Interrogation	76%	
Unsuccessful Interrogation	56	
Whether Suspect's Case Was Dismissed		.001*
Successful Interrogation	29	
Unsuccessful Interrogation	53	
Whether Suspect's Case Resolved		.001*
By Plea Bargaining		
Successful Interrogation	52	
Unsuccessful Interrogation	27	
Whether Suspect Was Convicted		.001*
Successful Interrogation	69	
Unsuccessful Interrogation	43	
Severity of Sentence Received		.012*
NONE		
Successful Interrogation	33	
Unsuccessful Interrogation	57	
LOW SENTENCE (Less than One Year)		
Successful Interrogation	43	
Unsuccessful Interrogation	21	
MEDIUM SENTENCE (One to Five Years)		
Successful Interrogation	19	
Unsuccessful Interrogation	18	
LONG SENTENCE (More than Five Years)		
Successful Interrogation	13	
Unsuccessful Interrogation	13	

more likely to have their cases resolved by plea bargaining (p<.001); and 26% more likely to be found guilty and thus convicted (p<.001).[81] Suspects who incriminated themselves during interrogation were also significantly likely to receive more punishment following their conviction (p<.012). These findings confirm the view of many criminal justice professionals that what happens during police interrogation will be fateful for the subsequent processing of the suspect's case in the criminal justice system.[82]

---

during interrogation was 24% more likely than his tight-lipped counterpart to be charged by prosecutors (p<.002).

  [81] Moreover, if we examine only those cases in which the suspect spoke to detectives after the *Miranda* admonition (i.e., those cases in which an interrogation actually occurred), those suspects—whether or not they invoked their *Miranda* rights and whether or not they incriminated themselves—were 35% more likely to be eventually convicted (p<.000).

  [82] Multiple regression analyses that controlled for whether an interrogation was suc-

F.   SUMMARY

In sum, there are three sets of important findings. First, police use many of the standard interrogation tactics taught by training firms and advertised in training manuals; in my sample of cases the detectives employed an average of 5.62 tactics per interrogation. If a portrait of the typical interrogation emerges from the data, it involves a two-prong approach: the use of negative incentives (tactics that suggest the suspect should confess because no other course of action is plausible) and positive incentives (tactics that suggest the suspect will in some way feel better or benefit if he confesses). In approximately 90% of the interrogations I observed, the detectives confronted the suspect with some evidence (whether truthful or false) of his guilt and then suggested that the suspect's self-interest would be advanced if he confessed. Of the many interrogation tactics that detectives employed, only four were significantly likely to result in a successful interrogation: the appeal to the suspect's conscience (p<.001), identifying contradictions in the suspect's alibi (p<.000), the use of praise or flattery (p<.005), and offering moral justifications or psychological excuses to account for his behavior (p<.004).

The second important finding concerns the effects of *Miranda* on the criminal process. Almost one-fourth of the suspects in my sample chose to invoke their *Miranda* rights and thus either prevent or terminate police questioning. This is a far higher percentage than we might expect, since the conventional wisdom among police professionals and in the academic research literature is that virtually all suspects choose to waive their rights and speak to police.[83] Nevertheless, detectives successfully elicited incriminating information from suspects in 64% of the total number of cases in my sample, and in 76% of the cases in which any questioning occurred. The effects of *Miranda* on the subsequent processing of a suspect's case were limited, however. Suspects who waived their *Miranda* rights were 4% less likely to have their cases charged by prosecutors and 10% more likely to be convicted than suspects who invoked, but neither of these differences were statistically significant, nor was the relationship between a suspect's response to *Miranda* warnings and the severity of punishment statistically significant. The only statistically significant effect of *Miranda* in the criminal process was that suspects who waived their *Miranda* rights were twice as likely to have their case resolved by plea

---

cessful by the strength of the evidence prior to the interrogation confirmed the CHI2 findings in Table 16. In other words, as mentioned above, whether an interrogation is successful is significantly related at the .01 level to the likelihood that a suspect will be treated differently at every subsequent stage of the criminal process.

[83] Leo, *supra* note 12.

bargaining than suspects who invoked their *Miranda* rights (p<.009). And in my sample more than 98% of the plea bargains ultimately resulted in guilty verdicts.

The third, and perhaps most important, finding is that what happens inside an interrogation room exercises a statistically significant effect on the subsequent processing of a suspect's case at every stage in the criminal justice system. While a suspect's response to *Miranda* was not significantly likely to affect the subsequent processing of his case, a suspect's decision to provide detectives with incriminating information was fateful. Suspects who incriminated themselves during interrogation were significantly more likely to be charged by prosecutors (p<.006), significantly less likely to have their case dismissed (p<.000), significantly more likely to have their cases resolved by plea bargaining (p<.001), significantly more likely to be convicted (p<.001), and significantly more likely to receive more punishment than their counterparts who did not provide interrogators with any incriminating information (p<.012). These findings offer support for the widely held view among criminal justice officials that admissions and confessions are highly persuasive and damning evidence of guilt against a criminal suspect.[84]

V. CONCLUSION: CLOSING THE GAP

I began this Article by pointing to the familiar contrast between how law is written in the books and how it is actually practiced by legal actors in the social world, arguing that the gap in our knowledge between legal ideals and empirical realities remains as wide as ever in the study of American police interrogation. In this Article I have tried to fill in this gap—a gap that has widened considerably in the last two decades due to the complete absence of any empirical research on police interrogation practices—by providing quantitative data from the almost 200 interrogations I observed in nine months of participant observation fieldwork at three police departments. I have systematically described the patterns in police techniques, suspect behavior, and interrogation outcomes in all of the 182 cases I observed, and I have analyzed the effects of police interrogation practices, *Miranda* warnings, and incriminating statements on the subsequent stages of the criminal process in my entire sample. I have sought to bring the reader inside the interrogation room in order to understand the characteristics, context, and outcomes of interrogation and confession in ordinary criminal cases that are not likely to make the published record on appeal. Although this Article breaks

---

[84] Leo, *Social Control, supra* note 17, at 99.

new ground as the first empirical study of its type in more than two decades, our understanding of contemporary American police interrogation practices and outcomes remains highly incomplete. If we are to close the gap in our knowledge between the ideal and reality that the *Miranda* Court decried, we need more primary data and empirical studies of everyday police investigative practices, especially in other regions of the country.

This study offers a number of findings with important academic, legal, and policy implications. For example, the *Miranda* Court lamented the tactics advocated in police interrogation training manuals and texts for exploiting the weaknesses of criminal suspects and threatening to overbear their rational decision-making capacity.[85] Yet this study indicates that these techniques—undermining a suspect's confidence in his denial of guilt, offering moral justifications for his behavior, and confronting suspects with fabricated evidence of their guilt, to name but a few—appear to be exceedingly common in contemporary American police interrogations. In addition, this study suggests that detectives have become increasingly successful at eliciting incriminating information from custodial suspects in the last thirty years; that one in five custodial suspects invokes his or her constitutional right to avoid cooperating with custodial police questioning; that most of the suspects who invoke their *Miranda* rights to silence or counsel have prior criminal records; that very few everyday police interrogations are "coercive" by contemporary judicial standards; that the overwhelming majority of everyday police interrogations last less than one hour; and that suspects who provide incriminating information to detectives are significantly more likely to be treated differently at every subsequent stage of the criminal process (from charging to sentencing) than their counterparts who do not. These findings confirm the view of many criminal justice professionals that what happens inside the interrogation room exerts a fateful effect on the processing of a defendant's case at every subsequent stage in the criminal justice system.[86]

One might thus ask: what has been the effect of *Miranda?* It is to this question that I will turn in the second article of this two part series. In that article, I will examine the broader legal, social, and political context in which the empirical findings of this study must be interpreted. In particular, I will analyze the general impact of the *Miranda* warnings—which have remained an ongoing source of legal and political controversy since their judicial creation almost thirty years

---

[85] Leo, *supra* note 13, at 67-127.

[86] *See* Leo, *Social Control, supra* note 17, at 99; SIMON, *supra* note 23, at 193-207.

ago[87]—on the behavior, ideology, and culture of contemporary American police interrogators.

---

[87] *See supra* text at note 55.

[5]

SEARCH WARRANTS, MOTIONS TO SUPPRESS AND "LOST CASES:" THE EFFECTS OF THE EXCLUSIONARY RULE IN SEVEN JURISDICTIONS*

CRAIG D. UCHIDA** AND TIMOTHY S. BYNUM***

I. Introduction

Empirical studies that examine the effects of the exclusionary rule on search warrant cases are few and far between. Only a handful of researchers have studied the use of search warrants by law enforcement officers, and even fewer have looked systematically at the effects of the exclusionary sanction on their use.

Search warrants have become an important tool in law enforcement efforts to curtail illegal drug trafficking. During the late 1980s, a number of police agencies have increased their use of warrants. For example, Minneapolis narcotics detectives executed 123 warrants in 1987, 383 in 1988 and 425 in 1989. In San Diego, "crack abatement" detectives executed 143 warrants in 1989, compared to 67 in the previous year. In Denver, a "crack" task force of sixteen detectives executed 246 search warrants in 1988 and 350 in 1989.[1] However, little is known about the results of these warrants generally, in terms of arrests, prosecutions, motions to suppress, or "lost cases" due to the exclusionary sanction.

Questions about the effectiveness and necessity of the exclu-

* Prepared under Grant No. 85-IJ-CX-0015 from the National Institute of Justice (NIJ) to the Police Executive Research Forum (PERF). The opinions expressed herein are the authors' and not necessarily those of NIJ, Michigan State University, or PERF. The assistance of Dennis Rogan and Michael Wilson is gratefully acknowledged. We also thank three anonymous reviewers who helped to clarify issues, focus our thinking, and make this a better paper. Of course, any errors are ours, and ours alone.

** Ph.D., State University of New York at Albany, 1982; M.A., State University of New York at Albany, 1979; B.A., University of California at San Diego, 1976.

*** Professor, School of Criminal Justice, Michigan State University, East Lansing; Ph.D., Florida State University, 1977; M.S., Florida State University, 1974; A.B., Davidson College, 1970.

1 Private memoranda from the Minneapolis Police Department, San Diego Police Department, and Denver Police Department, on file at the offices of the *Journal of Criminal Law and Criminology*.

sionary rule continue to be raised outside scholarly circles and police agencies. Members of Congress continue to express interest in the rule—some wish to broaden its exceptions, while others try to maintain the status quo. Congressional interest is particularly evident in the "good faith exception,"[2] as both the House and Senate recently debated whether to expand the good faith notion to warrantless situations.[3] The United States Supreme Court continues to rule on fourth amendment cases as well.[4]

The use of search warrants and the exclusionary rule intersect when, during pretrial proceedings and courtroom arguments, motions to suppress evidence are raised to challenge both the methods and the results of searches conducted by police. Additionally, questions about a search's appropriateness are sometimes raised by defense counsel. At times, judges sustain these motions, but we do not know with precision how often and under what circumstances those rulings are made.

Given these compelling interests, the primary focus of this Article is to analyze systematically the effects of the exclusionary sanction on cases that emerge through search warrant applications. We examine the following research questions: Under what situations and circumstances are search warrants used? What are the outcomes? How often are motions to suppress physical evidence made by defendants? What is the success rate of the motions and what are the outcomes? To address these questions, we use data from 2,115 search warrant applications and interviews with 187 individuals from seven major criminal justice systems across the country. More specifically, to determine the effects of the exclusionary rule on search warrant-based cases, we examine and discuss the number of

---

[2] Debate over the definition and interpretation of the "good faith" exception has been as heated as debate over the exclusionary rule itself. For the most part, however, the good faith exception means that evidence obtained with a reasonable or good faith belief that the challenged search or seizure was consistent with the fourth amendment should not be excluded. For a more detailed discussion, see *infra* notes 40-41 and accompanying text.

[3] In October 1990, the House of Representatives approved a resolution that broadened the good faith exception to the exclusionary rule to cover warrantless searches as well as searches in which warrants are used. However, because a compromise could not be reached with the Senate, the exception was not included in the omnibus crime bill for fiscal year 1991. DRUG ENFORCEMENT REPORT, Oct. 30, 1990, at 1.

[4] Recent Supreme Court decisions on fourth amendment issues include United States v. Verdugo-Urquidez, 110 S. Ct. 1056 (1990) (fourth amendment not applicable to search by United States authorities in Mexico); Maryland v. Buie, 110 S. Ct. 1093 (1990) (fourth amendment permitted limited "protective sweep" in conjunction with in-home arrest); and Smith v. Ohio, 110 S. Ct. 1288 (1990) (warrantless search of suspect's bag not justified as search incident to lawful arrest).

arrestees, defendants, and "lost cases" as a result of successful motions to suppress evidence because of search and seizure problems.

II. LEGAL BACKGROUND

The fourth amendment guarantees the protection of individuals against unreasonable search and seizure.[5] These constitutional protections have traditionally been assured through the exercise of the exclusionary rule. Since the 1914 Supreme Court decision in *Weeks v. United States*,[6] evidence ruled to be seized in violation of the fourth amendment has been excluded from use in criminal prosecution in federal cases.

In 1949, the Supreme Court, in *Wolf v. Colorado*,[7] declared that the fourth amendment binds state and local law enforcement officers through the due process clause.[8] Despite the rationale of *Weeks*, however, the Court declined to extend the exclusionary rule to the states, thus leaving the states to fashion for themselves remedies for violations of the rule.[9] However, only twelve years later, in *Mapp v. Ohio*,[10] the Court overruled *Wolf* and extended the exclusionary rule to the states. In so ruling, the Court took into account: (1) the "imperative of judicial integrity;"[11] (2) a trend among states following *Wolf* to adopt the *Weeks* rule on the grounds that alternative remedies were inadequate;[12] (3) an assumption that states that admit illegally seized evidence encourage fourth amendment violations;[13] and (4) the absence of evidence, based on both the experience of the United States under *Weeks* and the states who voluntarily adopted *Weeks*, that the exclusionary rule impaired the effectiveness of law enforcement.[14]

---

[5] U.S. CONST. amend IV.

[6] 232 U.S. 383 (1914).

[7] 338 U.S. 25 (1949).

[8] *Id.* at 27-28.

[9] Several factors underlay the Court's decision in *Wolf*. First, the Court deferred to the principles of federalism. *Id.* at 28. Second, the Court believed that the rule excluded logically relevant evidence. *Id.* Third, 30 states had refused to extend *Weeks* to fourth amendment violations by state law enforcement officers, while only 17 had done so. *Id.* at 29. Finally, a number of alternative remedies to the rule were available in those states rejecting *Weeks*—remedies that, in the Court's view, were "equally effective" in discouraging fourth amendment violations "if consistently enforced." *Id.* at 31.

[10] 367 U.S. 643 (1961).

[11] *Id.* at 659 (quoting Elkins v. United States, 364 U.S. 206, 222 (1960)).

[12] The Court observed that "[w]hile in 1949, prior to the *Wolf* case, almost two-thirds of the states were opposed to the use of the exclusionary rule, now despite the *Wolf* case, more than half of those since passing upon it, by their own legislative or judicial decision, have wholly or partly adopted or adhered to the *Weeks* rule." 367 U.S. at 651.

[13] *Id.* at 656 (quoting *Elkins*, 364 U.S. at 217).

[14] *Id.* at 659-60.

Over the past thirty years, the appropriate application of the exclusionary rule and its rationale have been vigorously debated. Critics of the exclusionary rule maintain that its application has been too rigid and that substantial modifications are in order.[15] The critics believe that continuing court interpretations of the exclusionary rule have become increasingly complex and confusing. They further argue that the rule works to preserve the fourth amendment's guarantees only by imposing a high cost on society; specifically, by depriving the courts of reliable, and often direct evidence, a criminal is freed. Finally, they argue that there are few benefits to the rule: it assists those accused of crimes but does not deter police from unconstitutional conduct.

In contrast, proponents of the rule continue to argue that its preservation is essential to the protection of due process and individual rights.[16] Furthermore, they argue that evidence tends to show that exclusion does have a deterrent effect. Supporters point to the dramatic increase in the number of search warrants issued in the years after the *Mapp* decision as evidence of the tremendous impact that the Court's decision has had on police practices. Finally, they argue that police departments have increased the amount of training provided to their officers on how to comply with fourth amendment rulings.

Since the *Mapp* decision, the Supreme Court has continued to operationalize the exclusionary rule through a series of cases specifying the conditions and situations in which the rule does and does not apply. As Mertens and Wasserstrom point out, "exclusionary rule litigation provides the principal occasion for the articulation of fourth amendment standards. Without such litigation, it is unlikely that many of these fourth amendment issues would have been resolved."[17] The Court has carved out exceptions to the rule with regard to searches conducted incident to arrest,[18] in hot pursuit,[19] and

---

[15] *See, e.g.,* S. SCHLESINGER, EXCLUSIONARY INJUSTICE: THE PROBLEM OF ILLEGALLY OBTAINED EVIDENCE (1977); M. WILKEY, ENFORCING THE FOURTH AMENDMENT BY ALTERNATIVES TO THE EXCLUSIONARY RULE (1982); and Jensen & Hart, *The Good Faith Restatement of the Exclusionary Rule,* 73 J. CRIM. L. & CRIMINOLOGY 916 (1982).

[16] *See* Kamisar, *Does (Did) (Should) the Exclusionary Rule Rest on a "Principled Basis" Rather than an "Empirical Proposition"?,* 16 CREIGHTON L. REV. 565 (1983); LaFave, *The Fourth Amendment in an Imperfect World: On Drawing "Bright Lines" and "Good Faith",* 43 U. PITT. L. REV. 307 (1982); and Sachs, *The Exclusionary Rule: A Prosecutor's Defense,* 1 CRIM. JUST. ETHICS 28 (1982).

[17] Mertens & Wasserstrom, *The Good Faith Exception to the Exclusionary Rule: Deregulating the Police and Derailing the Law,* 70 GEO. L.J. 365, 402 (1981).

[18] *See, e.g.,* United States v. Robinson, 414 U.S. 218 (1973); Chimel v. California, 395 U.S. 752 (1969).

[19] Warden v. Hayden, 387 U.S. 294, 299 (1967).

seizure of items in plain view.[20] The Court has also refined the application of the exclusionary rule in grand jury and habeas corpus proceedings.[21] Additional decisions have further refined the search warrant procedure when informants are used.[22]

Since *Mapp*, the rationale for the rule has changed direction. In *Alderman v. United States*,[23] the Court, for the first time, suggested that the determination of whether to apply the exclusionary rule would turn on a balancing of the costs and benefits of exclusion. Justice White, writing for the majority, said:

> The deterrent values of preventing the incrimination of those whose rights the police have violated have been considered sufficient to justify the suppression of probative evidence even though the case against the defendant is weakened or destroyed. We adhere to that judgment. But we are not convinced that the additional benefits of extending the exclusionary rule to other defendants would justify further encroachment upon the public interest in prosecuting those accused of crime and having them acquitted or convicted on the basis of all the evidence which exposes the truth.[24]

The Court's decision in *United States v. Calandra*[25] further

---

[20] Ker v. California, 374 U.S. 23, 34 (1963).

[21] In United States v. Calandra, 414 U.S. 338, 349 (1974), the Court declared that the exclusionary rule did not apply to the presentation of illegally obtained evidence at grand jury proceedings. In Stone v. Powell, 428 U.S. 465, 494 (1977), the Court announced that state prisoners who had allegedly been convicted and imprisoned on illegally obtained evidence could no longer pursue their constitutional rights through the use of habeas corpus.

[22] In Illinois v. Gates, 462 U.S. 213, 230 (1983), the Court abandoned the "two-pronged" test of Aguilar v. Texas, 378 U.S. 108 (1964), and Spinelli v. United States, 393 U.S. 410 (1969). The "two-pronged" test required officers to establish either that their informant was credible (*i.e.*, generally trustworthy) or that the information was reliable (the "veracity" prong) *and* that the informer obtained the information in a reliable way ("the basis of knowledge" prong). In its place, the *Gates* Court adopted the "totality of the circumstances" standard to decide whether probable cause existed to issue a search warrant based on information provided by confidential or anonymous informants. Under the totality of circumstances approach,

> the task of the issuing magistrate is simply to make a practical, common-sense decision, whether given all the circumstances set forth in the affidavit before him, including the 'veracity' and 'basis of knowledge' of persons supplying hearsay information, there is a fair probability that contraband or evidence of a crime will be found in a particular place.

Gates, 462 U.S. at 238.

[23] 394 U.S. 165 (1969). The Court ruled that defendants whose fourth amendment rights were not violated lacked standing to move to suppress evidence obtained in violation of the fourth amendment rights of others. *Id.* at 171.

[24] *Id.* at 174-75.

[25] 414 U.S. 338 (1974). Both Canon, *Ideology and Reality in the Debate over the Exclusionary Rule: A Conservative Argument for its Retention*, 23 S. TEX. L.J. 559 (1982), and Nardulli, *The Societal Cost of the Exclusionary Rule: An Empirical Assessment*, 3 AM. B. FOUND. RES. J. 585 (1983), have commented that the Burger Court believed that the principal rationale for the rule was its value in deterring the police from the type of illegal behavior in

changed the basis for the exclusionary rule. In *Calandra*, the Court concluded that "the rule is a judicially created remedy designed to safeguard Fourth Amendment rights generally through its deterrent effect, rather than a personal constitutional right of the party aggrieved."[26] Thus, the Court articulated that the exclusionary rule was not a right conferred by the fourth amendment, but rather a remedy to effectuate fourth amendment rights. In addition, the *Calandra* Court all but abandoned the other bases for exclusion, emphasizing that the "rule's prime purpose is to deter future unlawful police conduct and thereby effectuate the guarantee of the Fourth Amendment against unreasonable searches and seizures."[27] The Court thus weighed the costs of exclusion in a particular context— the loss of highly probative evidence—against the likely benefits of exclusion—an increased deterrence of unlawful police behavior.

In subsequent cases, the Court has applied this cost-benefit/deterrence analysis to refuse to extend the scope of the exclusionary rule. In *United States v. Janis*,[28] the Court concluded that the rule's deterrent purpose would not be served by excluding evidence illegally seized by a state police officer from a federal civil tax proceeding. Similarly, in *Stone v. Powell*,[29] the Court held that where a state has provided a full and fair opportunity to litigate a fourth amendment claim, a state prisoner may not receive federal habeas corpus relief on the basis that illegally obtained evidence was introduced at his or her trial. In *Powell*, the Court further limited the "judicial integrity" justification for the exclusionary rule: "While courts, of course, must ever be concerned with preserving the integrity of the judicial process, this concern has limited force as a justification for the exclusion of highly probative evidence."[30] Finally, in

---

Calandra. Furthermore, Canon noted that "[b]y portraying the rule as a pragmatic social policy rather than a basic constitutional principle, its critics have shifted the scope of the debate from arguments about constitutional law and judicial integrity (where they lost) to arguments about the empirical data." Canon, this note, at 563. Potter Stewart has claimed that *Calandra* was "perhaps the most significant post-*Mapp* decision on the scope of the exclusionary rule." Stewart, *The Road to Mapp v. Ohio and Beyond: The Origins, Development and Future of the Exclusionary Rule in Search-and-Seizure Cases*, 83 COLUM. L. REV. 1365, 1390 (1983).

[26] 414 U.S. at 348. Commentators have pointed out that "the Court ruled that the accused has no personal constitutional right to have unlawfully-seized evidence excluded at trial. Therefore, because the Court commits no constitutional violation by admitting illegally seized evidence, judicial integrity comes into play only when the Court "encourages" constitutional violations." Mertens & Wasserstrom, *supra* note 17, at 386 n.100.

[27] 414 U.S. at 349-52.

[28] 428 U.S. 433 (1976).

[29] 428 U.S. 465 (1976).

[30] *Id.* at 485.

United States v. Havens,[31] the Court held that illegally obtained evidence could be used to impeach the testimony of the victim of the illegal search on the ground that the purpose of the exclusionary rule was adequately served by excluding the evidence from the case-in-chief.[32]

In *United States v. Leon,*[33] *Massachusetts v. Sheppard,*[34] and *Illinois v. Krull,*[35] the Supreme Court applied the good-faith exception to the exclusionary rule. In *Leon* and *Sheppard,* the Court permitted the admission of evidence secured through a search warrant even though the search warrant was faulty. The Court ruled that the officers who obtained the warrants had done so in "good faith," and thus the exclusionary rule should not apply.[36] Writing for the majority in *Leon,* Justice White first justified the Court's holding by concluding that the exclusionary rule was neither a "necessary corollary of the Fourth Amendment" nor "required by the conjunction of the Fourth and Fifth Amendments."[37] Justice White then weighed the costs and benefits of preventing the use of "inherently trustworthy tangible evidence." On the costs-side of the equation, the Court referred to the "substantial social costs of the exclusionary rule in terms of its interference with the criminal justice system's truth-finding function" and the result that "some guilty defendants may go free or receive reduced sentences."[38] On the benefits-side, the Court considered the deterrent effect of the exclusionary rule and found that it was "marginal or nonexistent in cases where evidence was obtained in objectively reasonable reliance on a subsequently invalidated search warrant . . . ."[39]

In *Illinois v. Krull,*[40] the Court ruled that the exclusionary rule did not apply to evidence seized during a warrantless search where the police conducted the search pursuant to, and with good faith reliance upon, a statute that authorized the warrantless administrative search, but which was later held unconstitutional. Justice Blackmun, writing for the majority, again used the cost-benefit rationale coupled with the deterrence argument as the basis for the decision. He wrote,

---

[31] 446 U.S. 620, 627 (1980).

[32] *Id.* at 627-28.

[33] 468 U.S. 897 (1984).

[34] 468 U.S. 981 (1984). *Sheppard* is the companion case of *Leon.*

[35] 480 U.S. 340 (1987).

[36] *Leon,* 468 U.S. at 905.

[37] *Id.* at 906.

[38] *Id.* at 907.

[39] *Id.* at 922.

[40] 480 U.S. 340 (1987).

Application of the exclusionary rule properly has been restricted to those situations in which its remedial purpose is effectively advanced. . . . The Court has examined whether the rule's deterrent effect will be achieved, and has weighed the likelihood of such deterrence against the costs of withholding reliable information from the truth-seeking process.[41]

By employing a cost-benefit approach, the Burger and Rehnquist Courts have not only changed the focus of their holdings on the exclusionary rule, but have also changed the focus of empirical research. The following sections take a closer look at the prior research in this area. We begin by focusing on studies that examine the impact of the exclusionary rule, and then discuss the research that analyzes the costs and benefits of the exclusionary sanction. Thereafter, we consider the importance of this Article within the context of search warrants and the exclusionary rule.

III. Prior Research

A. The Impact of the Exclusionary Rule

The focus of early research concerned the impact of the *Mapp* decision. Of specific interest in these studies was the implementation of search warrant procedures, the degree of compliance with the provisions of the *Mapp* decision, and the impact of the rule on case dispositions.

Columbia University Law School students provided the first empirical assessment of the effect of the exclusionary rule.[42] Specifically, they were interested in determining whether the *Mapp* decision altered police search and seizure practices. Using a before-after research design, the students examined the frequency of New York City misdemeanor narcotics offenses.

The authors expected to observe a change in the case disposition and frequency of arrest for narcotics in the post-*Mapp* period. Their data showed that the number of post-*Mapp* arrests declined by fifty percent for detectives in the Narcotics Bureau, but increased for arrests by uniformed officers and other detectives. The authors could not find a clear explanation for the differences within the police department. They could only speculate that the character of the Narcotics Bureau's duties differed from patrol or plainclothes officers.[43] Overall, although police practices did not change substantially as a result of *Mapp*, the authors suggested that the situation

---

[41] *Id.* at 347.

[42] Comment, *Effect of Mapp v. Ohio on Police Search and Seizure Practices in Narcotics Cases,* 4 Colum. J.L. Soc. Probs. 87 (1968).

[43] That is, the authors attributed the decrease in arrests to the specialized nature of

improved after *Mapp* because search and seizure practices were more strictly controlled.[44]

A broader effort to assess the deterrent effect of the exclusionary rule was conducted by Dallin Oaks,[45] who analyzed misdemeanor and felony arrests and convictions in Cincinnati, Chicago, and Washington, D.C. He determined that the exclusionary rule was applicable primarily in certain types of cases, particularly those involving narcotics, weapons, and gambling offenses. Oaks compiled arrest statistics from Cincinnati for the 1956-67 period and concluded that the imposition of the exclusionary rule in 1961 had virtually no effect on the propensity of the police to make arrests for narcotics and weapons offenses, though he conceded that the number of gambling arrests were affected. Oaks found differences between Chicago and Washington, D.C., in the proportion of cases where motions to suppress evidence due to search and seizure problems were brought (40% versus 16%, respectively); in the percent of motions granted (87% versus 20%); and in the percent of cases where a successful motion resulted in dismissal of the case (100% versus 50%). The primary reason for these differences was the more rigorous screening of cases in Washington, D.C. Oaks concluded that the filing of motions was not indicative of the actual impact of the exclusionary rule on case dispositions. He suggested, however, that these figures show that the rule had no deterrent effect on police practices; the data indicated that illegal search and seizures occurred quite frequently despite the rule.

Following in Oaks' footsteps, James E. Spiotto[46] studied motions to suppress to determine the impact of the exclusionary rule

---

the narcotics bureau, the "close-knit" character of the bureau, and the nature of the narcotics offenses themselves.

44 To assess the effect of *Mapp* on narcotics case dispositions, the authors examined court records for guilty pleas, dismissals, and motions to suppress evidence. In general, the authors found "the data indicate that defendants have fared better since *Mapp*." Comment, *supra* note 42, at 96. A sharp decrease occurred in guilty pleas, while increases occurred in successful motions to suppress and in "dismissals without explanation." These patterns led the authors to conclude that the changes since *Mapp* showed "the beneficial effects of greater respect for the civil liberties of criminal defendants . . . and represented a new obstacle to effective enforcement of narcotics laws." *Id.*

45 Oaks, *Studying the Exclusionary Rule in Search and Seizure*, 37 U. CHI. L. REV. 665 (1970).

46 Spiotto, *Search and Seizure: An Empirical Study of the Exclusionary Rule and Its Alternatives*, 2 J. LEGAL STUD. 243 (1973). Thomas Y. Davies, who critiqued Spiotto's work, noted that "in many respects James E. Spiotto's work was a continuation of that begun by Oaks." Critique, *On the Limitations of Empirical Evaluations of the Exclusionary Rule: A Critique of the Spiotto Research and United States v. Calandra*, 69 NW. U. L. REV. 740, 741 (1974). Davies pointed out that Spiotto used the Oaks data set from Chicago, that they worked together, and that both received grants from the Department of Justice.

on case processing over a twenty-year period. Using data from the Chicago courts, Spiotto argued that the best measurement of the impact of the exclusionary rule on police behavior was to observe the frequency of motions made before and after the introduction of the rule. If the rule had an apparent impact, he reasoned, then one would expect a decrease in the number of motions to suppress.[47] The results indicated a significant increase in motions to suppress for narcotics and weapons offenses, though gambling offenses experienced a substantial decline. A more important finding was that seventy-eight percent of the defendants who made a motion to suppress had a criminal record. Spiotto concluded that the rule had no deterrent effect on illegal search practices and that it exacted a high societal cost by freeing dangerous or guilty criminals.

Soon after Spiotto's work appeared, however, a critique written by Thomas Y. Davies warned that Spiotto's results should be viewed with caution for a variety of reasons.[48] First, the data were collected in a "haphazard fashion" and interpreted selectively.[49] Second, the research design contained a "critical" mistake regarding the date of the rule's introduction in Chicago: Illinois adopted the exclusionary rule in 1923, thirty-eight years prior to *Mapp*, not during the 1950-70 period that Spiotto claimed.[50] Third, Davies criticized the use of motions to suppress as valid indicators of illegal searches for the type of research question posed by Spiotto. Specifically, Davies argued that

> [m]otions to suppress cannot be used because they do not measure illegal searches prior to the introduction of the exclusionary rule. Although a form of the motion to suppress existed prior to the advent of the rule, the scope of cases where a motion to suppress could be raised increased dramatically following the introduction of the rule.[51]

Given his careful review of the data, Davies warned that "Spiotto's research . . . does not demonstrate the ineffectiveness of the exclu-

---

[47] In his analysis, Spiotto employed four different measures: (1) the number of defendants appearing in court; (2) the percentage of those defendants making motions; (3) percentage granted; and (4) the percentage of defendants with granted motions. Spiotto used data from 1950, 1969, and 1971 in Chicago, and focused on gambling, narcotics and weapons charges.

[48] Critique, *supra* note 46, at 762.

[49] Spiotto failed to control for population trends and increases in crime rates. During the twenty-year span of the study, the crime trends drastically increased, resulting in an increased number of motions to suppress.

[50] Clearly, this is an important error, for without data from the period prior to the implementation of the exclusionary rule, one cannot make inferences about its impact, particularly as Spiotto suggests.

[51] Critique, *supra* note 46, at 755.

sionary rule."[52]

In 1974, Bradley Canon reached different conclusions than Spiotto in his analysis of arrests, issued search warrants, changes in search and seizure policies, and successful motions to suppress evidence.[53] Canon found that changes in search and seizure practices could be attributed to *Mapp* and demonstrated that police compliance with search warrant procedures increased significantly between 1967 and 1973. He concluded that the exclusionary rule was more effective at the time of his study (1974) than it was shortly after the *Mapp* decision in 1961.

B. THE COST OF EXCLUSION

More recently, the focus of research on the exclusionary rule has shifted to its "cost" in terms of lost cases. Because the Supreme Court changed its exclusionary rule rationale in 1974,[54] researchers began to shift their emphasis to cost-benefit analyses and an examination of the deterrent effects of the rule. This change in emphasis is exemplified by research conducted by the General Accounting Office,[55] the National Institute of Justice,[56] Nardulli,[57] Davies,[58] and Orfield.[59]

The General Accounting Office study focused upon exclusion of cases in federal courts through declinations by United States Attorneys' Offices.[60] The GAO Report found that:

Of the 2,804 cases analyzed during the period July 1 through August

---

[52] *Id.* at 763.

[53] Canon, *Is the Exclusionary Rule in Failing Health? Some New Data and a Plea Against a Precipitous Conclusion*, 62 KY. L.J. 681 (1974). Canon collected crime data from 14 cities, sent questionnaires pertaining to search and seizure practices to police departments, prosecutors, and public defenders in over 130 cities, and interviewed police, prosecutors, and public defenders in 10 cities.

[54] *See supra* text accompanying notes 25 to 41.

[55] GENERAL ACCOUNTING OFFICE, REPORT OF THE COMPTROLLER GENERAL OF THE UNITED STATES, IMPACT OF THE EXCLUSIONARY RULE ON FEDERAL CRIMINAL PROSECUTIONS (1979) [hereinafter GAO REPORT].

[56] NATIONAL INSTITUTE OF JUSTICE, THE EFFECTS OF THE EXCLUSIONARY RULE: A STUDY IN CALIFORNIA (1982) [hereinafter NIJ REPORT].

[57] Nardulli, *supra* note 25.

[58] Davies, *A Hard Look at What We Know (and Still Need to Learn) About the "Costs" of the Exclusionary Rule: The NIJ Study and Other Studies of "Lost" Arrests*, 3 AM. B. FOUND. RES. J. 611 (1983).

[59] Orfield, *The Exclusionary Rule and Deterrence: An Empirical Study of Chicago Narcotics Officers*, 54 U. CHI. L. REV. 1016 (1987).

[60] GAO REPORT, *supra* note 55. The GAO received data from a national, stratified sample of 42 United States Attorney's Offices. Using the individual defendant as the sampling unit, cases were drawn from the period July 1 through August 31, 1978. In addition, questionnaires were sent to personnel in United States Attorneys Offices responsible for the cases to determine the role of the fourth amendment in decisions to

31, 1978, 16% of the defendants whose cases were accepted for prosecution filed some type of suppression motion, 11% cited the fourth amendment. However, only 0.4% of declined defendants' cases were declined due to fourth amendment search and seizure problems.[61]

In addition, the study found that successful motions were made in only 1.3% of prosecuted cases. Thus, the report concluded that the exclusionary rule had a minimal impact.

In contrast, three years later, an in-house research study conducted by the National Institute of Justice (NIJ) found that the rule had a major impact on the disposition of felony arrests.[62] A principal finding from this analysis indicated that 4.8% of all felony arrests rejected for prosecution were rejected because of search and seizure problems. In addition, 32.5% of all felony arrests for narcotics offenses were rejected for prosecution in one of the Los Angeles County District Attorney's Offices due to search problems, and 29% of similar cases were rejected in the other office studied. The NIJ Report also noted that about one-half of those defendants freed because of the exclusionary rule were subsequently arrested within two years of their release. The study concluded that the exclusionary rule is a major factor in the processing of felony cases and implied that it exacts a significant cost to the justice system in terms of lost arrests and cases.

Davies re-analyzed the NIJ data and reached different conclusions.[63] Davies severely criticized the NIJ study because it "suffers from inappropriate samples, from the omission of readily available

---

prosecute or not, the frequency of motions to suppress, and the impact of fourth amendment motions on criminal justice system resources and the disposition of defendants.

[61] *Id.* at 1.

[62] NIJ REPORT, *supra* note 56. In this analysis, the authors examined all California felony arrests that were rejected for prosecution for search and seizure problems between 1976 and 1979; all felony cases rejected in San Diego County in 1980; and a sample of cases rejected in two branches of the Los Angeles County District Attorney's Office. The authors also examined the prior and subsequent criminal activity of the defendants whose cases were excluded.

[63] Davies, *supra* note 58, at 611. Davies contested two major findings of the NIJ Report: (1) that 4.8% of arrests rejected by prosecutors were rejected because of illegal searches; and (2) that 30% of drug arrests were rejected by prosecutors because of illegal searches. In his re-analysis, Davies used a different baseline than the NIJ Report to determine the percentage of "lost arrests." The NIJ Report calculated that 4.8% of the declined cases (4,130 arrests rejected divided by 86,033 declined by prosecutors) were rejected because of the exclusionary rule. Davies found that only 0.8% (4,130 arrests rejected divided by 520,993 total arrests) of felony arrests were declined because of illegal search problems.

The NIJ Report estimated that 30% of drug arrests were rejected in California, based on data from two local prosecutor's offices in the Los Angeles area. Davies contends that the number of arrests (114 in one jurisdiction and 145 in another) was too small to represent a general estimate of the effects of the exclusionary rule in drug arrests. Davies used statewide data from the California Bureau of Criminal Statistics to

UCHIDA & BYNUM [Vol. 81

and highly pertinent data, and from a variety of analytical choices that produce a slanted interpretation of the data."[64] In his reanalysis, Davies found that prosecutors rejected only 0.8% of felony arrests because of illegal searches. Davies' reassessment also discovered that in felony drug arrests, the prosecutors rejected 2.4% of the arrests (not 30% as suggested by the NIJ study), the rejection rate for non-drug arrests was less than 0.3%, and the rate was even lower for violent crimes.[65] In addition, Davies found that by looking at the cumulative effect of the rule through all stages of the felony process in California, "only about 2.35% of felony arrests are lost because of illegal searches" and "[this estimate] is almost certainly somewhat inflated."[66] Finally, he concluded that available data showed that the cost of the exclusionary rule was marginal, especially in view of the ambiguous nature of the lost arrests.

Recent studies tend to agree with Davies' conclusions. Peter F. Nardulli's examination of the filing and outcomes of motions to suppress provided similar evidence that the rule exacted only marginal societal costs.[67] In his nine-county study of 7,500 felony court cases in Illinois, Michigan, and Pennsylvania, Nardulli analyzed the incidence of motions to suppress physical evidence, and for comparative purposes, motions to suppress confessions and identifications. The results showed that motions to suppress physical evidence were filed in less than 5% of all felony cases. Further, he noted that the success rate of such motions was quite marginal (only 0.69% of cases filed). Even when motions to suppress were successful, a number of defendants were still convicted without the excluded evidence. Nardulli concluded that the "cost" of the exclusionary rule was quite minimal in that less than 0.6% of all cases were lost due to the exclusion of evidence, and that most of these cases involved minor offenses and offenders.

Finally, one recent study concentrated solely on the deterrence rationale. Myron W. Orfield, Jr.,[68] interviewed narcotics detectives in Chicago and found that the exclusionary rule had "significant deterrent effects . . . [it] changed police, prosecutorial, and judicial procedures . . . it educated police officers in the requirements of the fourth amendment and punished them when they violated those

---

show that only 2.3% of drug arrests were rejected by prosecutors because of illegal searches over a five-year period.

[64] *Id.* at 619.

[65] *Id.* at 679-80.

[66] *Id.* at 655.

[67] Nardulli, *supra* note 25.

[68] Orfield, *supra* note 59.

requirements."[69]

These empirical studies have proven to be important in the on-going debate over the exclusionary rule. Both proponents and opponents of the rule, as well as members of the Supreme Court, have used these data in various ways.[70] Questions remain unanswered, however, particularly when we turn to the costs of exclusion using search warrants. In the next section, we briefly examine two prior studies of warrants that have a direct bearing on the current Article.

C. SEARCH WARRANT STUDIES

Richard Van Duizend and his colleagues at the National Center for State Courts[71] examined the search warrant process in seven cities across the country, and both dispelled and confirmed a number of myths associated with that process. For example, the researchers found that (1) search warrants were sought in relatively few cases; (2) warrants were diverse in their types of cases; (3) judge-shopping occurred by some law enforcement applicants; (4) warrant applications were rarely rejected by judges or magistrates; and (5) warrant applications were often based on unsworn hearsay from anonymous informants.

The study also attempted to determine whether issued warrants would be the subject of successful motions to suppress, and thus, constitute "lost" prosecutions. Examining 350 cases that resulted from issued warrants, the study reported that motions to suppress were filed in 40% of the cases, but only 5% (seventeen) of those motions were granted either fully or in part. Of particular importance was the finding that twelve of these seventeen cases still resulted in a conviction. The study concluded that search warrants

---

[69] *Id.* at 1017. Orfield based his study on one research question based on *Calandra* and three other court cases: Does the exclusionary rule deter unlawful police behavior? To answer this question, Orfield interviewed 26 Chicago narcotics officers in 1986 using a structured questionnaire. Questions were asked of officers regarding their views on training, experiences in court, their opinions of the exclusionary rule, and how it affects their work.

[70] For example, in United States v. Janis, after reviewing the various empirical studies of the rule's deterrent effects and criticisms of those studies, Justice Blackmun, writing for the Court, wrote: "The final conclusion is clear. No empirical researcher, proponent or opponent of the rule, has yet been able to establish with any assurance whether the rule has a deterrent effect." 428 U.S. 433, 450 n.22 (1976)

Additionally, Davies reported that the Solicitor General's Amicus Curiae Brief for the United States in Illinois v. Gates cited the GAO Report and the NIJ Report. Davies, *supra* note 58, at 615. Justice White, concurring in *Gates*, adopted the NIJ Report's findings. 462 U.S. at 257 n.13 (White, J., concurring).

[71] R. VAN DUIZEND, L. SUTTON & C. CARTER, THE SEARCH WARRANT PROCESS: PRECONCEPTIONS, PERCEPTIONS, AND PRACTICES (1986).

properly administered and supervised . . . can protect privacy and property rights without significantly interfering with the ability of police officers to conduct thorough and effective investigations of criminal activity. . . . Moreover, it was evident to us that the exclusionary rule, though seldom invoked, serves as an incentive for many police officers to follow the limits imposed by the Fourth Amendment as defined in their jurisdiction.[72]

The Van Duizend study raised important questions about the use of search warrants. Yet, it also issued methodological cautions that make general acceptance of the results somewhat problematic:

> The archival data were used principally to facilitate the exploration of significant patterns or the conspicuous absence of certain events (*e.g.*, successful suppression motions), and to be modestly demonstrative of overarching patterns. Owing to the fact that the cities used in this study are not necessarily representative of all cities and that the cases included in each city sample were not selected in strictly random fashion, statistical reliability of the archival data is not claimed.[73]

At six of seven sites, sixty-five to seventy-five search warrant applications were selected by the researchers on an *ad hoc* basis rather than through a systematic sampling procedure. This case selection bias leads to serious problems of interpretation. Another problem involves the unit of analysis. Because the primary concern was to examine search warrant applications, the researchers did not focus on individuals or their cases. For example, in the one intensively examined site, River City, 405 search warrant applications were examined, but a careful analysis of the persons involved in the cases was not conducted.

As the Van Duizend study neared completion, the United States Supreme Court released its decisions in *Leon* and *Sheppard*. The NIJ then commissioned the Police Executive Research Forum (PERF) to conduct an impact study.[74] In that project (conducted by the authors of this Article), the researchers used the same seven jurisdictions as the Van Duizend study and also conducted an intensive review of search warrant practices. The primary concern was the degree of change in such practices since the *Leon* decision.[75] Overall, the study found that the search warrant process did not change in the seven sites and across the country; that the number and con-

---

[72] *Id.* at 119.

[73] *Id.* at 10.

[74] *See* C. UCHIDA, T. BYNUM, D. ROGAN & D. MURASKY, THE EFFECTS OF UNITED STATES V. LEON ON POLICE SEARCH WARRANT POLICIES AND PRACTICES, FINAL REPORT (monograph prepared for Police Executive Research Forum 1986); *see also* Uchida, Bynum, Rogan & Murasky, *Acting in Good Faith: The Effects of United States v. Leon on Search Warrant Policies and Practices*, 30 ARIZ. L. REV. 467 (1988).

[75] We examined search warrant applications prior to and after *Leon*.

tent of warrants did not change from 1984 to 1985; and that the impact on judicial suppression of evidence was virtually non-existent. Because the focus of the study was the impact of the *Leon* ruling, the researchers did not carefully examine the cost of the exclusionary rule on search warrant activity. Like the Van Duizend *et al.* work before it, individual defendants and important research questions were all but ignored.

IV. RESEARCH DESIGN

Using the data from the *Leon* study, we now examine the following questions: Under what situations and circumstances are search warrants used? What are the outcomes? How often are motions to suppress physical evidence made by defendants? What is the success rate of the motions and what are the outcomes?

To answer these questions, we developed a research process that enabled us to focus on both the aggregate cost of the exclusionary rule and the rationale of the individual "lost" cases.

Unlike a number of previous empirical research efforts, we examined cases that resulted from search warrant applications. Our data included all search warrant applications for six months of 1984 and 1985 in seven sites (January through March of each year).

Second, most studies of the impact of the exclusionary rule only note whether a case was excluded and do not include any information regarding the seriousness of the violation itself. For example, we need to know why the exclusion occurred. A simple empirical tally of cases excluded tells us little of the police search process or the reasons behind a "lost case." Our purpose is to describe the "lost case" and to examine the rationale behind its exclusion.

Third, we distinguish this Article from Van Duizend *et al.* and our own previous work by focusing on individual cases and by avoiding case selection bias through the inclusion of all warrants in each of the seven sites for a six-month period.

A. THE SITES

We returned to the seven sites previously used in the Van Duizend *et al.* study in 1985. We agreed to allow the seven intensively studied sites anonymity.[76] They are referred to as Border City, For-

---

[76] While we recognize that the study is weakened somewhat by making these sites anonymous, the trade-off was not to conduct research in these settings at all. While members of four departments did not indicate a problem with disclosure, the others did, and we respect their decisions. We were given complete access to police and court

est City, Harbor City, Hill City, Mountain City, Plains City, and River City.

Border City, located in the western United States, is a large urban center with a diverse population. Forest City is characterized as a commercial center on the west coast, while Harbor City is a major eastern industrial city. Hill City is part of a large metropolitan area in the west. Mountain City, Plains City, and River City are the largest cities in their respective states, and serve as hubs of commercial activities.

Table 1 provides a comparison of the project sites regarding population and crime characteristics. In Table 1, we note the relative independence of city size, crime rate, and size of police force. Although Plains City, River City, and Border City all have similarly-sized police departments, they have widely different crime rates and populations. Interestingly, the smaller cities appear to have the higher rates of reported crime while the larger cities have among the lower rates of crime.

Table 1

CHARACTERISTICS OF PROJECT SITES

Site	Geographic Location	Population[1]	Index Crime Rate[2]	Number of Sworn Officers[3]
Border City	West	1,000,000	75	1500
Harbor City	Northeast	750,000	85	3000
River City	South	500,000	85	1500
Plains City	Midwest	500,000	105	1500
Forest City	Northwest	500,000	130	1000
Hill City	West	350,000	120	600
Mountain City	West	175,000	115	350

Source: FBI, CRIME IN THE UNITED STATES: 1985 (1986).

[1] 1985 estimate based on UCR.
[2] Rate is per 1,000 people.
[3] Numbers are based on 1985 estimate from UCR.

B. THE DATA

The data analyzed in this article were collected in 1985 and 1986. The principal data collection strategy consisted of an intense, in-depth study of search warrant activity in seven cities located throughout the country. In addition, interviews with key personnel throughout each criminal justice system were undertaken (N=187).

---

records and files, and personnel were willing to provide open interviews knowing that their statements would be held in confidence. As a result, we believe that the data we obtained are highly reliable and valid.

At each site, we reviewed all search warrant applications made during two three-month periods in 1984 and 1985. These applications were then tracked through the criminal justice system to their disposition, thus yielding a complete picture of warrant activity in these jurisdictions. A total of 2,115 warrant applications were examined, coded, keypunched, and analyzed. From these search warrants and the tracking of individual cases in each of the seven criminal justice systems, we were able to determine whether arrests occurred, cases were filed, motions were made, how courts ruled on motions, and the outcomes of the cases.

For this Article, we use two units of analysis—the primary warrant and the individual suspect. Primary search warrants are a subset of the total number of actual search warrant applications. Primary warrants were used because law enforcement officers, at times, wrote multiple warrants for the same case. On a number of occasions, officers were required to search more than one person, place, or vehicle. As a result, a number of search warrant applications were linked to the same case. When multiple warrants were related to one investigation, a "primary" warrant was selected to avoid overcounting and misrepresentation of warrant activity.[77]

To examine the effects of the exclusionary rule on individual cases, we used the individual suspect, arrestee, and defendant as our baseline. To determine how policies and practices regarding search warrants, motions to suppress, and lost cases were dealt with, we relied on information garnered through structured interviews with key personnel at each location. Police, prosecutors, defense attorneys, and judges were among those interviewed.

V. FINDINGS

A. SEARCH WARRANT ACTIVITY: A BRIEF OVERVIEW

Table 2 shows the warrant-based case flow or pipeline in each of the seven sites for the six month period of 1984 and 1985. As we discussed above, the unit of analysis is the "primary search war-

---

[77] Primary warrants were selected by the two Principal Investigators based on the warrant applications and affidavits. Where two or more warrant applications applied to the same individual, house, or vehicle, we examined both warrants or multiple warrants carefully, prior to coding information. All of the primary warrants were identical to the "secondary" or "tertiary warrants," except for the place to be searched. That is, the statements of probable cause, the type of informant, the officers writing the warrants, and the judges who signed the warrants were identical. This was a commonality among all sites. All warrants were coded and keypunched with the ability to determine during the data analysis how warrants might be linked to each other. This allowed us to validate the initial selection of primary warrants.

Table 2
PIPELINE OF SEARCH WARRANT ACTIVITY, SEVEN SITES
JANUARY TO MARCH, 1984 & 1985
(NUMBER OF WARRANTS & PERCENT OF PRIMARY WARRANTS)

	River	Mount	Plains	Border	Hill	Forest	Harbor	Totals
Total Warrants	234	85	300	310	254	208	724	2,115
Primary Warrants	191	70	264	265	233	182	543	1,748
Executed Warrants	141	68	253	234	198	176	511	1,511
	74%	97%	96%	88%	85%	97%	94%	86%
Warrants with at least 1 arrest	131	55	219	173	133	122	325	1,158
	69%	79%	83%	65%	57%	67%	60%	66%
Warrants with at least 1 case filed by D.A.	93	41	170	150	88	82	315	939
	49%	59%	64%	57%	38%	45%	58%	54%
Warrants with at least 1 motion to suppress	55	4	29	11	43	24	59	225
	29%	6%	11%	4%	18%	13%	11%	13%
Warrants with at least 1 successful motion to suppress	5	0	5	0	0	3	2	15
	3%	—	2%	—	—	2%	.4%	.9%

rant." Percentages within each of the columns are based on the number of primary warrants rather than the total number of warrants. For example, in River City, police officers wrote 234 total warrants, but conducted only 191 unique investigations (primary warrants), so these 191 primary warrants were used as the baseline.

Harbor City police officers wrote the highest number of warrant applications during this period, followed by officers in Border and Plains Cities. On average, 86% of all primary warrants were executed or served, ranging from a low of 74% in River City to a high of 97% in Mountain City. Similarly, warrant-based investigations led to an arrest almost two-thirds of the time, with Plains City officers (83%) making the most arrests. Offices of the district attorney filed cases in almost 54% of the warrants. The relatively low percentages of cases filed in Hill City (38%), Forest City (45%), and River City (49%) reflect the stringency of review and screening conducted in each of the offices of the district attorney.

Table 2 also shows the number and percentage of primary search warrants that were contested through motions to suppress. Overall, 225 primary warrants (13%) were contested by defendants. River City had the highest percentage of warrants challenged (29%), followed by Hill City (18%) and Forest City (13%). These motions were granted in 15 primary warrants (0.9%) and in only four of the seven sites (River City, Plains City, Forest City, and Harbor City).

Table 3 describes the overall situation further, by detailing individual-level information. Within the 1,748 primary warrants, police detained or arrested 2,276 total suspects. Of these, 1,672 were formally arrested by police and 1,355 (or 81%) became defendants (charged by the district attorney). Charging practices differed across sites. Harbor City, Mountain City, and Border City prosecutors accepted over 90% of the cases brought to their attention via arrest. Plains City, Forest City, Hill City, and River City district attorneys accepted fewer than 76% of the cases. Unfortunately, we do not know how many times prosecutors refused to file charges because there was a "bad" or faulty warrant, as opposed to other reasons for not prosecuting. Thus, we cannot assess the loss of arrestees where cases were never filed.

Table 3
PIPELINE OF SUSPECTS, ARRESTEES, AND DEFENDANTS
SEVEN SITES

	Total	River	Mount	Plains	Border	Hill	Forest	Harbor
# Suspects	2276	303	94	317	352	301	240	669
# Arrestees	1672	253	65	270	254	200	180	450
# Defendants	1355	155	63	204	234	128	132	439
Defendants as % of Arrestees	81.0	61.3	96.9	75.6	92.1	64.0	73.3	97.6
Defendants as % of Suspects	59.5	51.2	67.0	64.4	66.5	42.5	55.0	65.6

In terms of dispositions of search warrant-based cases, on average, 70% of the defendants were convicted of their crimes (Table 4). Mountain City and Forest City prosecutors convicted 82% and 81% of their defendants, respectively. Hill City and Harbor City had lower conviction rates (59% and 62%, respectively) and higher dismissal rates (29% and 24%) than the other cities. Acquittals by jury trial or bench trial averaged 3% across the sites, ranging from a low of 1% in Hill City to a high of 5% in River City.

In general, search warrant cases were subject to the exclusionary rule if the warrant did not meet the legal standard of probable cause. Supreme Court decisions in *Gates*,[78] *Leon*,[79] and *Sheppard*[80] provided the police with less rigid requirements to follow and more

---

[78] 462 U.S. 213 (1983).
[79] 468 U.S. 897 (1984).
[80] 468 U.S. 981 (1984).

Table 4
DISPOSITIONS OF DEFENDANTS
SEVEN SITES

	Total	River	Mount	Plains	Border	Hill	Forest	Harbor
# Defendants	1355	155	63	204	234	128	132	439
# Convicted[a]	839	113	45	127	155	57	80	262
	70%	75%	82%	75%	76%	59%	81%	62%
# Dismissed	238	25	8	32	28	28	17	100
	20%	17%	15%	19%	14%	29%	17%	24%
# Acquitted	38	8	2	6	5	1	2	14
	3%	5%	4%	4%	2%	1%	2%	3%
# Other[b]	78	3	0	5	16	10	0	44
	7%	2%	—	3%	8%	10%	—	10%
Missing cases	135	4	8	34	30	32	33	19

[a] includes those who pled guilty and those found guilty through trial
[b] includes defendants who were diverted for treatment or received a pre-trial "sentence" (e.g., probation before judgement in Harbor City)

incentives to seek more warrants. For example, in *Gates*, the Court established the "totality-of-circumstances" test, which directed the magistrate to "make a practical common-sense decision whether given all the circumstances set forth in the affidavit . . . [that] there is a fair probability that contraband or evidence of a crime will be found in a particular place."[81] Prior to *Gates*, police were required to describe both how the informant learned where the items were located and a basis for believing that the informant was credible or the information supplied was reliable.[82] Nonetheless, law enforcement officers are still required to provide the basis for using informants (*i.e.*, whether anonymous or confidential) within their warrants. In our interviews, police detectives and patrol officers indicated that they still followed the "two-pronged" test of *Aguilar-Spinelli* because it was well-defined and they were accustomed to writing warrants that laid out specific needs.

Leon and *Sheppard* theoretically provide police officers with added incentives to secure warrants. These incentives stem from the Court's ruling that evidence seized during a search conducted in objective, good-faith reliance on a warrant will be admitted at trial, even if the warrant is later found to be defective. Yet, even with the protection from subsequent motions to suppress, warrant activity did not increase; nor was *Leon* raised by prosecutors or judges when

---

81 *Gates*, 462 U.S. at 238.

82 *See supra* note 22 and accompanying text for a discussion of the *Aguilar-Spinelli* two-pronged test.

warrants were questioned post-*Leon*.[83]

To meet the probable cause standard in search warrants, law enforcement officers at each site recognized that they needed to follow certain procedural and substantive guidelines set by their respective state supreme courts as well as the United States Supreme Court. While these guidelines varied by site on specific dimensions, they were generalizable to a certain extent. For example, the warrant application usually consisted of two items: first, the formal search warrant, which had to be signed by a magistrate or judge and had to indicate the person, place, or vehicle to be searched and the types of items to be seized; and second, the affidavit, which provided more detailed support of the search warrant.

In preparing the affidavit, law enforcement officers provided information that established their credibility and veracity to the court. Officers included information about their background, the steps taken in the investigation, a description of the person or place to be searched and the items to be seized, and if necessary, information provided by informants.

Confidential informants were used over half of the time in Harbor, Hill and Border Cities, but less than a quarter of the time in Forest, Plains, and Mountain Cities. Table 5 shows the level of use

Table 5
USE OF CONFIDENTIAL INFORMANTS, SEVEN SITES
JANUARY TO MARCH, 1984 & 1985

	River	Mount	Plains	Border	Hill	Forest	Harbor
Primary Warrants	191	70	264	265	233	182	543
# Warrants with CI	90	12	67	141	140	42	326
Crime corroborated?	72	11	56	124	65	1	263
	80%	92%	84%	88%	46%	2%	81%
Site corroborated?	77	11	66	124	64	28	299
	86%	92%	99%	88%	46%	67%	92%
Material Seized	64	12	63	103	106	39	281
	71%	100%	94%	73%	76%	93%	86%
Arrest Made?	73	9	53	76	79	32	203
	81%	75%	79%	54%	56%	76%	62%
Case Filed?	56	9	37	69	49	19	198
	62%	75%	55%	49%	35%	45%	61%

of confidential informants (CIs) by site. Using the number of warrants with a CI as the unit of analysis, the data indicate that the quantity and quality of material within the affidavit varied by site and

---

[83] Uchida, Bynum, Rogan & Murasky, *supra* note 74, at 494.

by agency. In Forest City, police almost never corroborated information regarding the type of crime. Hill City officers did so less than 50% of the time, whereas, in the remaining five sites corroboration of the crime occurred in over 80% of the warrants using informants. The use of CIs, the levels of corroboration of the crime, and the location of the crime varied across the jurisdictions.

The outcomes of informant-based warrants also varied, but less dramatically than the corroboration of crime element. In Forest City, where crimes were least likely to be corroborated, an arrest took place in 93% of the warrants with CIs. At the same time, however, prosecutors were willing to file cases in only nineteen of thirty-two arrests (59%). In contrast, in Harbor City, officers made arrests in 203 of 326 warrants with CIs (62%) and prosecutors filed cases in 198 of the 203 arrests (98%).

In two jurisdictions, Border City and Mountain City, officers used standardized forms for their affidavits. In Border City, a district attorney developed five such forms, one each for homicide, narcotics, sex offenses, burglary, and auto theft. For the most part, these were "fill-in-the-blank" affidavits. Police simply filled in information about their background (*e.g.*, "I am a peace officer currently assigned to the —— division and have been so assigned for —— years"); the confidential informant (*e.g.*, "I have known the CI for about —"); the items to be seized; and the person or location to be searched.

In Mountain City, a detective developed a form that allowed officers not only to fill-in-the-blanks, but also provided a check-list for the evidence to be seized and the reliability of the confidential informant. Police in that jurisdiction explained that these standardized forms helped them to be more efficient and precise than is possible when writing new affidavits on each occasion. While some judges we interviewed expressed concern over the use of such forms because of problems in determining the truthfulness of the affidavits, others said that they were no different from the standardized language in affidavits generally. Furthermore, motions to suppress evidence based on a standardized form never appeared in any of the jurisdictions under scrutiny.

To ensure further that probable cause was established, in two sites, Plains and Border Cities, a member of the district attorney's staff reviewed and approved search warrant applications before they were submitted to a judge or magistrate. This arrangement was supported by formal agreements between the prosecutor's office and the police department, and by the twenty-four hour-a-day availability of a designated attorney. These full-time district attorney liaisons, whose offices were located within police headquarters, not only screened but also signed the warrant applications. Our interviews with police indicated that these district attorney liaisons provided assistance in determining probable cause and gave them confidence that evidence seized as a result of the warrant would not be suppressed at trial. In both sites, the police were enthusiastic about the support provided by the district attorney's offices.

In the other sites, a prosecutor was available to review a warrant application if desired by the officer. In Forest City, for example, the district attorney's office actively encouraged the police department to have its warrants reviewed by an assistant prosecutor. Moreover, if an assistant approved a warrant application, then it was the policy of the prosecutor's office to defend it in court from any challenges that may arise and to prosecute the case more vigorously. In contrast, in River City, we found that the police and prosecutor's office had very little contact regarding search warrants. In fact, police said that they seldom, if ever, asked the prosecutor's office for assistance.

In Mountain City, the police viewed district attorney input as "unnecessary." On occasion, however, an investigator would call the prosecutor's office for a cursory review. When they did call an attorney, detectives admitted to "attorney shopping;" that is, contacting a prosecutor whom they know would be less stringent in his or her review. In Hill City, where official departmental policy dictated that detectives call the district attorney's office for assistance and approval, detectives readily admitted that doing so "slowed the process" and did not follow that policy.

Once an internal and/or external review was completed, the officer usually presented a judge with the warrant and affidavit. The judge examined the documents and sometimes questioned the officer. Some police officers said that judges took, on average, about fifteen minutes to review the application. Others said that judges would spend five to thirty minutes reviewing a warrant, depending upon the length of the affidavit and also whether the judge knew the officer personally. Familiarity with the law enforcement officer sped up the process. According to officers in Harbor City, the credibility of the individual officer was of central importance to judicial review. They noted that it was imperative that the detective establish himself or herself as having credibility and reliability in court. Providing the judge with positive feedback about the execution of the warrant as well as being consistent and honest in situations not affiliated with warrant activity (*e.g.*, as a witness in a court case) established a "good" reputation with judges. In so doing, the police were confident that warrants would be approved.

In almost all of the applications, the judge, upon his or her determination of probable cause, signed the warrants. In only one instance did we find a rejected warrant application (out of 1,748 warrants). Rejected applications usually were either destroyed or revised by the police, and thus were not available for scrutiny. However, in Border City, where telephonic warrant applications are used, a transcript of one rejected warrant was on file.

Once the warrant was approved by a judge, the police had three to ten days to execute it. In most jurisdictions warrants were served within a day or two, but in Border City, detectives often waited the full length of time (ten days in this case) before serving the warrant. After executing the warrant, the officer had another ten days to file a "return" with the court. The return indicates whether the warrant was executed, the date and time of the execution, and an inventory of the items seized. In six of seven intensively studied jurisdictions, returns were filed regularly by the police. In River City, however, returns were often missing, resulting in problems for tracking cases.

Following the execution and filing of a search warrant, police often reported that arrests were usually made and criminal cases filed. According to our data, however, on average, only 54% of the primary warrants were actually filed for prosecution.

Once an individual was charged, the case fell within the guidelines of the criminal justice system. Arraignments, preliminary hearings, motion hearings, plea bargaining, trials (if necessary), and sentencing were conducted by the courts.

B.   MOTIONS TO SUPPRESS PHYSICAL EVIDENCE

At least one motion to suppress physical evidence was filed in 13% of all primary warrants.[84] River City defense attorneys filed motions in 29% of the primary warrants. Border City and Mountain City defendants were least likely to file motions, with Hill, Forest, Plains, and Harbor Cities falling within the ten and twenty percentiles (see to Table 2).

Motions to suppress physical evidence were raised as early as the preliminary hearing in most jurisdictions. These motions ranged from lengthy, detailed explanations to one-page "boiler plate" forms signed by a defense attorney. They also varied across and within jurisdictions. In River City, where defendants filed motions to suppress 57% of the time (Table 6), the motion itself was often only three paragraphs long, noting the name of the defendant,

---

[84] This figure is considerably lower than the 40% found by Van Duizend, *supra* note 71. This shows the selection bias within the Van Duizend study.

the grounds for the motion, and a request that an evidentiary hearing take place. At the evidentiary hearing, arguments would be raised by both the prosecution and defense counsel, and the judge would make a determination.

Table 6
DEFENDANTS AND MOTIONS TO SUPPRESS
SEVEN SITES

	Total	River	Mount	Plains	Border	Hill	Forest	Harbor
# Defendants	1355	155	63	204	234	128	132	439
# Defendants Who File MTS	317	88	7	35	14	57	37	79
% Defendants Who File MTS	23.4	56.8	11.1	17.2	6.0	44.5	28.0	18.0
# Defendants w/MTS Granted	27	12	0	7	0	0	6	2
% Granted (Defendants as base)	2.0	7.7	0	3.4	0	0	4.5	0.5
% Granted (Motions filed as base)	8.5	13.6	0	20.0	0	0	16.2	2.5

Mountain and Border Cities had the least amount of activity with regard to motions to suppress physical evidence. In Mountain City, defense attorneys claimed that trial court judges "always upheld searches regardless of what errors or lack of probable cause were found." As a result, members of the defense bar rarely made search and seizure an issue. The district attorney agreed with this attitude and further claimed that the judicial climate and legal community were "quite conservative." By this, he meant that both the prosecutors and defense attorneys were conservative in their political beliefs and presumed that search warrants were valid. In Mountain City, four warrants were challenged by seven defendants; two involved burglaries and two involved drugs. All seven defendants were denied their motions to suppress.

In Border City, the work of a district attorney liaison virtually assured that warrants would not be questioned regarding the probable cause standard. The district attorney liaison, permanently assigned to the police department, assisted the police by writing and processing warrants himself, thus reducing the likelihood of successful motions.[85] Defense attorneys were aware of this involve-

---

85 Officers would seek assistance from the district attorney liaison as an investigation unfolded. Once the need for a warrant was immediately apparent, the liaison and police officers would sit down together and write the warrant. The district attorney liaison

ment and were not likely to file motions to suppress (only 6% of the defendants file), which the judges, in turn, did not sustain.

Plains City, Forest City, and Hill City defense attorneys wrote lengthier, detailed briefs describing the reasons for the motions. At these sites, a number of motions cited a lack of probable cause in the warrant either because the police did not adequately corroborate the information provided by anonymous or confidential informants or because the "totality-of-circumstances" as articulated by the *Gates* decision was not met. A Hill City public defender related that he filed motions if he could "determine that the judge was misled or somehow deceived by the police officer in the written affidavit and/or if there was an inadequate description of the items to be seized."

In Hill City, the public defender's office was particularly active in filing motions to suppress physical evidence—defendants filed motions 45% of the time. However, judges did not grant the exclusion of the evidence in any of the cases. In Plains and Forest Cities, motions were successful on seven and six occasions, respectively.

To obtain an idea of the characteristics of the cases in which a motion to suppress evidence was made, the incidence of motions was examined by type of offense. Table 7 shows that motions were

Table 7
MOTIONS TO SUPPRESS BY TYPE OF OFFENSE
SEVEN SITES

	% of cases involving motions to suppress physical evidence						
Offense Type	River	Mount	Plains	Border	Hill	Forest	Harbor
Violent Crime	4.5	0	4.0	0.4	2.3	8.9	1.6
Property Crime	1.3	3.2	1.5	0.4	0	4.9	1.6
Drug Offense	31.6	3.2	7.4	1.3	32.0	13.0	9.8
Other	18.1	3.2	3.4	3.8	5.5	3.3	4.6
	N=155	N=63	N=204	N=234	N=128	N=132	N=439

filed most often in drug offenses[86] in six of the seven sites. The lone exception is Border City, where motions were more likely to be filed

---

would use a word processor with "boiler plate" language to assist in writing the warrant.

Plains City, which also had district attorney review, did not achieve similar results. However, in Plains City, the assistance of the district attorney liaison was less direct. Here, the police would seek advice after they had written the warrants themselves. The liaison would review the warrant for probable cause and then recommend changes or give approval through his or her signature.

[86] Drug offenses included both felonies and misdemeanors and involved possession and/or distribution of heroin, cocaine, marijuana, and other illicit drugs.

for "other" crimes.[87]

C. SUCCESSFUL MOTIONS AND CASE DISPOSITIONS

Motions to suppress were successful in only 0.9% of the primary warrants (15 of 1,748).[88] On an individual level, judges sustained motions for twenty-seven defendants, or 2% of all defendants. These figures varied across sites. In three locations, Mountain, Border, and Hill Cities, no motions were successful. River City had the most successes (twelve defendants), followed by Plains (seven), Forest (six) and Harbor Cities (two).

Table 8 provides a breakdown of the primary warrants, the defendant or co-defendant, the charges made by the prosecutor, and the dispositions of the defendants who were successful in suppressing evidence seized by police in four sites. As can be seen from the table, twenty-seven defendants were involved in the fifteen primary warrant cases.

In River City, twelve defendants successfully challenged the search warrants: five defendants were charged with obscenity;[89] five defendants were charged with possession of marijuana; and two were accused of fencing less than $25 worth of stolen property. The court dismissed eleven of the twelve cases as a result of the suppression of evidence. One individual was found guilty of possessing marijuana. His sentence included a fine of $500 and three years probation.

In Plains City, five defendants charged with cocaine possession in three separate cases (#134, #160, and #300) and two robbery defendants (cases #163 and #254) were successful in suppressing evidence. In case #134, involving three defendants, the defense counsel argued that the totality-of-circumstances test had not been fulfilled and that the information from a first-time confidential informant was not corroborated by police. The counsel also claimed that even under *Leon*, the good faith doctrine did not apply because of the reckless preparation of the warrant and the absence of a basis for an objective believe that probable cause existed. The judge agreed with the defendants and dismissed the case. In the two remaining cases of cocaine possession, the defendants successfully

---

87 "Other" crimes included firearms possession, gambling, pornography, petty larcenies, and the like.

88 In contrast, Van Duizend, *supra* note 71, found that motions to suppress were granted in 17 of 350 search warrant cases (5%).

89 In case #89, three defendants were charged with producing a pornographic movie, while in case #227, two defendants were accused of operating a movie house that showed a pornographic film.

Table 8
SUCCESSFUL MOTIONS TO SUPPRESS & THEIR OUTCOMES (BY SITE)

Primary Warrant #	Defendant	Charge	Disposition
River City			
89	#1	Obscenity	Dismissed
	#2	Obscenity	Dismissed
	#3	Obscenity	Dismissed
96	#1	Fencing	Dismissed
	#2	Fencing	Dismissed
149	#1	Marijuana	Dismissed
	#2	Marijuana	Dismissed
217	#1	Marijuana	Found guilty
	#2	Marijuana	Acquitted
	#3	Marijuana	Acquitted
227	#1	Obscenity	Dismissed
	#2	Obscenity	Dismissed
Plains City			
134	#1	Cocaine poss	Dismissed
	#2	Cocaine poss	Dismissed
	#3	Cocaine poss	Dismissed
160	#1	Cocaine poss	Dismissed
163	#1	Robbery	Pled Guilty
254	#1	Robbery	Pled Guilty
300	#1	Cocaine poss	Dismissed
Forest City			
34	#1	Marijuana	Dismissed
	#2	Marijuana	Dismissed
65	#1	Marijuana	Pending
	#2	Marijuana	Pending
80	#1	Marijuana	Dismissed
	#2	Marijuana	Dismissed
Harbor City			
45	#1	Marijuana	Dismissed
529	#1	Burglary	Pled Guilty

filed suppression motions based on a lack of corroboration of evidence provided by the confidential informant.

In the two warrants that were robbery-related (#163 and #254), even though the evidence seized was not allowed, because of lack of corroboration of the informants, eyewitness testimony and co-conspirator statements led the defendants to plead guilty.

In Forest City, the defendants who succeeded were all involved in marijuana "grow farms." Police had sought warrants for residences where defendants were allegedly growing marijuana in their basements. In cases resulting from primary warrants #34 and #65, judges ruled that the information obtained by police through confidential informants did not meet the *Aguilar-Spinelli* two-pronged test.[90] In case #80, the search warrant was not signed by a "neutral and detached magistrate" but by a judge pro tempore, who did not have the authority to issue a warrant. Four of the six defendants in these three distinct cases were released outright, while the other two (case #65) had their cases pending at the time of the data collection.

In Harbor City, two defendants succeeded in suppressing the evidence seized in two separate search warrant raids. A judge released one defendant (case #45, which involved a marijuana possession charge) after determining that the information from a CI was not sufficiently corroborated. The second defendant (case #529) pled guilty to a burglary charge despite having the evidence suppressed, for reasons not recorded by the court.

D. "LOST CASES"

Lost cases are those in which the court granted a motion to suppress and dismissed the case. Based on this definition, nineteen individual defendants were allowed "to go free" based on an exclusionary rule problem. This represents 1.4% of all defendants in our sample of search warrant-based cases (n=1,355). If we add the two acquittals from River City case #217, then the percentage increases to 1.5%.

Table 9 shows the numbers and percentages of lost cases by site. River City has the highest number of lost cases (eleven) and the leading percentage based on defendants (7.1%). Plains City has the highest percentage of successful defendants based on those who file a motion to suppress (20%).

In most of these "lost cases," the trial court judge determined that a police officer had not been able to properly establish probable cause. In one instance, the court ruled that a judge *pro tempore* was not a "neutral and detached magistrate" and thus did not have the authority to sign a warrant. Despite the ruling in *Leon*, which allowed for the good faith exception in search warrant situations, judges were willing to suppress the use of such evidence. "Technicalities," such as the lack of an inventory, or "return" sheet, were not part of the motions to suppress, nor were they incorporated into any decisions by judges.

---

90 In this jurisdiction, the state supreme court had not yet incorporated Illinois v. Gates, 462 U.S. 213 (1983). As a result, the *Aguilar-Spinelli* two-pronged test controlled probable cause determinations for search warrants.

Table 9
'LOST CASES'
SEVEN SITES

	River	Mount	Plains	Border	Hill	Forest	Harbor
Number of Lost Cases	11[a]	0	5	0	0	4	1
As % of defendants	7.1	0	2.5	0	0	3.3	0.2
As % of defendants who filed motions	12.5	0	20.0	0	0	10.8	1.3
As % of successful motions to suppress	91.7	0	71.4	0	0	66.7	50.0

[a] Includes 2 acquittals

VI. CONCLUSIONS

Our analysis has shown that motions to suppress were successful in only 0.9% of the primary warrants (15 of 1,748). Judges sustained motions for 2% of all defendants (27 of 1,355) in our warrant-based sample. Few cases were "lost" as a result of the exclusionary rule in seven jurisdictions when police used search warrants. Twenty-one of 1,355 defendants (1.5%) were "allowed to go free" as a result of a successful motion to suppress physical evidence. The most serious offenders who were released were those charged with possession of cocaine, a felony in Plains City. Others with successful motions were charged with obscenity (operating a pornographic movie house or producing a pornographic movie), fencing less than $25 worth of stolen property, and possessing less than an ounce of marijuana—clearly not major crimes.

Our results are consistent with the findings reported by Nardulli, Davies (in his re-analysis of the NIJ data), and the GAO Report. Nardulli indicated that motions were filed in about 5% of the 7,500 cases he studied, and were granted in 52 cases (or 0.7% of all cases). He also reported that convictions still occurred in some of these cases and that only 40 (of the 52) ended in nonconviction; accordingly, only 0.6% of all cases appeared to be "lost" because of the exclusionary rule. In addition, he reported that 80% of the lost cases involved non-serious crimes: 37% were drug related, 22% involved possession of a weapon, and 24% were for miscellaneous non-violent offenses. Similarly, the GAO Report found that 0.8% of arrests were lost because of illegal searches,[91] while Davies found a "cumulative loss" of 2.35% of arrests in his analysis of the NIJ Re-

---

[91] This figure is based on Davies' estimate of lost arrests. Davies, *supra* note 58, at 611.

port's California data. Our figure of 1.5% lost cases falls within the range of the Nardulli study (0.6%) and the Davies re-analysis (2.35%). Note, however, that our data reflect only search warrant based cases, not all cases filed within the jurisdictions.

We found other important results within the sites:

(1) In three of seven sites—Mountain, Hill, and Border Cities—defendants were not successful in their challenges to evidence seized by police as a result of search warrants.

(2) In Border City, the work of a district attorney liaison in writing search warrants with police officers reduced the chances that warrant-based evidence would be suppressed at trial.

(3) In Harbor City, we found that police were accomplished at writing warrant applications and conducted high quality investigations. As a result, only two motions were successful and only one case "lost" out of 439 search warrant applications during the six-month period of the study.

(4) Though Plains City officers worked with a district attorney liaison to meet the standards of the state courts, defendants had the highest percentage of successful motions to suppress (seven out of thirty-five, or 20%).

(5) River City's law enforcement and criminal justice communities were not aligned when it came to search warrants and the exclusionary rule. A poor and often antagonistic relationship existed between the police and the prosecutor. The police did not seek assistance in writing warrants. In our interviews, we found that police accused the district attorney's office of not prosecuting enough cases, while the district attorney accused the police of poor investigations. Defense attorneys filed a large number of motions to suppress (57% of defendants filed). Fourteen percent of those filing motions (or 8% of defendants) were successful in suppressing evidence. Of the twelve defendants who won, eleven were freed. At the same time, however, River City still maintained a high percentage of convictions (75% of defendants within our sample).

Given these findings, it is not surprising that we agree with the Van Duizend *et al.* conclusion that search warrants provide "clear and tangible records that facilitate *post hoc* evaluation of the original search."[92] We also agree with their finding that the "exclusionary rule, though seldom invoked, serves as an incentive for many police officers to follow the limits imposed by the Fourth Amendment as defined in their jurisdiction."[93] Our interviews indicated that police were willing to follow guidelines established by the Constitution, the district attorney's office, and the courts when writing search warrant applications. The willingness of officers in Border, Plains, and

---

[92] Van Duizend, *supra* note 71, at 106.
[93] *Id.* at 119.

Forest Cities to have warrants reviewed by prosecutors was a response, in part, to the exclusionary sanction. Police wanted to insure that warrants met the standards of probable cause and that evidence seized would not be later suppressed.

Our study also provides further evidence that the "cost" of the exclusionary rule in lost cases is slight when the police obtain a search warrant. While critics of the exclusionary rule argue that it imposes a high cost on society by depriving the courts of reliable evidence and allowing criminals freedom, we have found that, in fact, few criminals are freed, and when they are, their crimes are not serious. Thus, the cost to society is limited.

[6]

The Determinants of Deadly Force:
A Structural Analysis of Police Violence[1]

David Jacobs
Ohio State University

Robert M. O'Brien
University of Oregon

Political or threat explanations for the state's use of internal violence suggest that killings committed by the police should be greatest in stratified jurisdictions with more minorities. Additional political effects such as race of the city's mayor or reform political arrangements are examined. The level of interpersonal violence the police encounter and other problems in departmental environments should account for these killing rates as well. Tobit analyses of 170 cities show that racial inequality explains police killings. Interpersonal violence measured by the murder rate also accounts for this use of lethal force. Separate analyses of police killings of blacks show that cities with more blacks and a recent growth in the black population have higher police killing rates of blacks, but the presence of a black mayor reduces these killings. Such findings support latent and direct political explanations for the internal use of lethal force to preserve order.

What factors determine the amount of violence used by democratic states when they try to control their citizens? State coercion, particularly in the most developed societies, is rarely studied by sociologists, yet it may be a powerful explanation for social order. As Weber pointed out long ago, the

[1] We gratefully acknowledge financial support from the Harry Frank Guggenheim Foundation. We thank Pam Jackson and Gary LaFree for their comments on prior drafts and Stephen E. Haynes, Joe Stone, and James Ziliak for their advice. David Schlosberg and Scott Harris deserve our thanks for helping us collect the data. The data utilized in this research were made available in part by the Inter-University Consortium for Political and Social Research. The data from the Uniform Crime Reports, 1976–1986: Supplementary Homicide Reports were originally collected by the Federal Bureau of Investigation. Neither the consortium nor the collector bear any responsibility for the results or the interpretations presented here. Direct comments to David Jacobs, Department of Sociology, 300 Bricker Hall, 190 North Oval Mall, Ohio State University, Columbus, Ohio 43210-1358

American Journal of Sociology

crucial defining element of the state is its ability to call upon superior force in any dispute with internal or external rivals. Without this supremacy governments cease to exist. Even contemporary democratic states frequently command scarce resources from unwilling subjects with at least the threat of violence. Although modern democratic states avoid the military and employ domestic agencies like the police to control internal miscreants and dissidents, the primary activity that makes police organizations distinct is their use of force (Bittner 1990).

Perhaps what appears as a consensus within modern societies is deceiving because much of the domestic tranquillity we so frequently observe is based on accommodation rather than consent. Sociologists often respond by asserting that a society based on pure coercion would be inefficient. Goode (1972, p. 510) agrees, but answers that "sociologists have felt that force was a weak reed to lean on and no regime or society can rest on force alone. Indeed it cannot, but neither must it do so. None ever need try; rulers and conquerors . . . always command other resources." According to Goode, scholars who use the pure coercion argument to dispute the importance of force as a prerequisite for order have rejected an empty claim.

Although violence by social control agencies in advanced states is comparatively unusual, that does not make it ineffective. We may have been misled by the relative absence of conspicuous force in these societies. In any case, the discipline has neglected coercion and its chilling effects on nonconforming behavior, particularly in the most advanced industrial democracies. While we do not believe that coercion or its threat is the only important explanation for order, we suspect that further study of the conditions that lead to state violence will increase our understanding of how order is maintained in advanced societies.

Developments in historical political sociology have established the importance of political violence, but theoretical advances in the sociology of law and social control based on the work of Vold (1958), Dahrendorf (1959), Turk (1969), and Black (1976) furnish some of the more useful explanations for this outcome. Sociologists who stress coercive explanations for order often see the control agencies of the state as principally serving the interests of the privileged. According to this political threat view, a primary (but not the only) use of criminal law and law enforcement agencies is to maintain control over the "dangerous classes" who threaten public order.

Many Weberian and most neo-Marxist theorists who see coercion as a major way to preserve order think that differences in rewards are based on power (Lenski 1966; Collins 1975). According to this view, the privileged benefit greatly from existing arrangements while many citizens receive much less; inequality is an unstable condition that must be sustained by sanctions or their threat. If racial or economic disparities are at least partly sustained by coercion, enhanced state violence can be expected in areas where economic disparity and the menace of an underclass are greatest. We study such political explanations (and many others) for variation in the amount of internal state violence by looking at rates of lethal force within political subunits. This study assesses the determinants of the rate of killings committed by the police in 170 U.S. cities.

The conventional assumption is that police violence is a reaction to the violence the police encounter, so killings by police officers are a necessary response to the brutality they must control. A political approach suggests instead that police violence should be especially likely in areas where racial or economic divisions with political consequences are severe. If the privileged are threatened by the disorderly potential of a racial or economic underclass with little to lose and much to gain from redistributive violence, diminished efforts to control the police or demands that they be unfettered should be likely in racially or economically divided cities. Political explanations suggest that police killings will be most common in economically stratified cities with larger percentages of minorities because dominant groups have much to lose from threats to public order by a racial or economic underclass.

In this article we see if the police use of lethal force can be explained by political arrangements or by social divisions that are likely to have political consequences, but we also assess reactive accounts that stress interpersonal violence and other problems officers encounter in the urban environments they must police. Because race is such an important consideration in a study of police violence and because our initial results suggest that the determinants of police killings of blacks deserve separate study, we analyze the factors that explain these race-specific lethal force rates as well. Results from studies that assess many competing hypotheses are more accurate (Johnston 1984), so we use an inclusive strategy. This means the theoretical section that follows cannot focus on just a few explanations.

SOME TESTABLE HYPOTHESES

The Empirical Literature

Studies of the effects of racial and economic stratification on social control have examined the size of police departments. Some find minority threat to be the strongest explanation. Research by Liska, Lawrence, and Benson (1981) and Huff and Stahure (1980) on the per capita number of police, or Jackson's (1989) research on expenditures, shows that the percentage of blacks in a city is related to police strength. An analysis of metropolitan statistical areas (MSAs) found that, while percentage black mattered, eco-

American Journal of Sociology

nomic inequality was a stronger explanation for department size (Jacobs 1979). Also, inequality explains shifts in police strength over time (see Jacobs and Helms 1997). Disputes in this literature about the relative importance of inequality or minority presence have not been resolved.

The statistical studies of police killings are problematic. Kania and Mackey (1977) computed killings by the police in U.S. states. They ignore minorities and use welfare recipients to measure inequality, although the states with the greatest economic inequality had the smallest welfare roles (Dye 1969). Such problems make Kania and Mackey's rank order correlations too misleading to report. A reanalysis of the Kania and Mackey data (Jacobs and Britt 1979) using multiple regression finds that income inequality is the strongest explanation for police killings, but state-level data are not the ideal for this work, as they inappropriately combine many kinds of police departments that operate in disparate environments.

We use disaggregated city data (for a discussion of bias caused by aggregation, see Thiel [1971]), an imperfect unit of analysis that has advantages. This unit lets us treat police killings as an organizational outcome and analyze the environmental determinants of the lethal behavior of many individual departments.

Sherman and Langworthy (1979) and Liska and Yu (1992) appear to be the only multivariate city-level investigations. Both studies measured police killings by combining data from *Vital Statistics* with surveys of police departments, but the *Vital Statistics* estimates are about half as large as the estimates from either survey. The shared variance in the merged data that formed the dependent variables is extremely modest in both studies. In Sherman and Langworthy's study of 32 cities, the correlation between the estimates from their survey and the Vital Statistics estimates of police killings is .56; in Liska and Yu this correlation is .45. The problematic construction of both dependent variables plus the small number of cases and other difficulties make the inconsistent findings of these two investigations too questionable to report.

The problems identified in other studies suggest that an analysis of police killing rates in 170 cities based on a single comprehensive data source should yield more accurate results for the following reasons:

1. Information from disparate sources need not be combined to calculate the number of these lethal events.
2. Killings by the police need not be averaged across disparate departments that operate in extremely dissimilar environments because we analyze city rather than state data.
3. The large number of cases should produce superior statistical inferences and allow for the control of more explanations than those in the earlier research.

Deadly Force

4. Local conditions, made invisible by state-level data, can now be examined.

Finally, in contrast to past studies, we use an estimator designed to handle the censored dependent variables produced by using rates computed on these infrequent events.

Alternative Ways to Account for Police Killings

The theories we assess in this article fall into two broad categories: political explanations and reactive explanations. We begin by discussing *political threat explanations*. Killings by police officers may be especially likely where divisions based on racial or economic differences are greater because such divisions threaten dominant groups and undercut effective community controls over the police.

Second, reactive hypotheses that have nothing to do with social or political divisions may explain police violence. Reactive accounts suggest that the use of lethal force by the police should be most likely in areas where the police must control a violent population or where they must react to urban conditions that make their work difficult. We begin our theoretical discussion by talking about hypotheses that focus on social divisions that have political implications and hypotheses that are explicitly political. We finish by discussing some plausible reactive explanations for the use of lethal force by the police.

THREAT THEORIES

Race and Police Violence

The menace of a racial or economic underclass with an interest in redistributive violence may lead to violent law enforcement. Blalock (1967) argues that dominant populations will be threatened in areas with a larger racial underclass. Liska, Lawrence, and Sanchirico (1982) find that, with the crime rate held constant, fear of crime is associated with the percentage of African-Americans in cities. Departments should be more likely to use lethal force in cities with greater percentages of minorities because the threat posed by a large racial underclass may lead to harsh law enforcement measures. Threat theories also suggest that law enforcement should be more coercive in cities that have recently experienced growth in the percentage of black residents, because as the population of African-Americans increases, concerns about the prevalence of crime increase as well.

This and other versions of the threat hypothesis are plausible ways to

American Journal of Sociology

explain at least some killings committed by the police as long as a dis-
avowal is kept firmly in mind. It is *not* necessary to claim that privileged
groups make direct demands that the police use greater amounts of deadly
force. Without restraints, police violence is probable (Chevigny 1995). Officers are expected to preserve order rather than enforce the law (Bittner
1990), and violence is an efficient (but unfortunate) way to achieve this
end. Police behavior is not readily observed, yet extreme personal risks
are an inseparable part of this work. These personal risks give officers
reasons to use violence when it may not be warranted. Where the perceived threat of underclass violence is greater, all that is required for political explanations for police killings to hold is for the powerful to be less
willing to interfere with police methods. Hughes (1963) argues that a willingness to remain ignorant about the activities of the "dirty workers" is
a compelling explanation for much official brutality. Dominant groups in
cities with greater racial or economic disparities who are threatened by
these conditions *may* demand that the police be unfettered, but the political threat explanations tested in this article do not require such active
participation. Political divisions would still explain police killings if privileged groups only are less likely to interfere with police violence in cities
where they feel threatened by an underclass.[2]

The use of lethal force may be associated with political arrangements as
well. Wilson (1971) claims that cities with progressive "good government"
reforms have police departments that are comparatively insulated from
political restraints because reform administrative arrangements are less
responsive to majority pressure than more conventional political arrangements. This insulation may reduce community control over police violence, so cities with city manager or commission governments may have
higher police killing rates.[3]

We test a second explicitly political hypothesis by looking at the race
of the mayor. Police chiefs, who often originate and always enforce departmental policies that regulate officer proclivities to use force, serve at the

[2] Hence, external institutionalized controls on the police may be less effective in jurisdictions where privileged groups who could restrain the police use of deadly force
choose to remain ignorant about the methods these "dirty workers" use to maintain
order. Unfortunately, we cannot find systematic information about the presence of
external review boards.

[3] Chevigny (1995) and others claim that officers in Los Angeles were likely to use
violence because civil service policies made the removal of the chief extremely difficult. The public and their elected representatives in this exceptional city could not
control police violence because they could not remove the primary police administrator. Sampson and Cohen (1988) find that active police departments that make greater
numbers of arrests are likely to be found in cities with reform governments. It is
reasonable to believe that the more aggressive officers in these cities also may be more
likely to use lethal force.

Deadly Force

option of the mayor in almost all jurisdictions. If the mayor is black and probably dependent on minority votes, police administrators should have greater incentives to curb police violence. This condition should make them particularly likely to revise internal policies to achieve this goal. In our data, blacks are the victims of 53% of all killings by police, so the race of the mayor should matter.

Ethnographic and other work on the police shows that departmental regulations exercise strong controls on officer behavior (Rubenstein 1973; Fyfe 1982; Sherman 1983). It follows that police killings should be reduced in cities with a black mayor because the officer on the street should realize that violence against African-Americans will be more closely investigated and perhaps more severely sanctioned than it will be in cities with white mayors.

Inequality and Police Violence

Following Jacobs and Britt (1979), economic stratification should explain the amount of deadly force used by the police. The economic version of the political perspective on state violence holds that disparities in economic rewards produce a potentially unstable social order that must be maintained by force. Chambliss and Seidman (1980, p. 33) write that "the more economically stratified a society becomes, the more it becomes necessary for dominant groups to enforce through coercion the norms of conduct that guarantee their supremacy." Many neo-Marxists believe that, without the threat of coercion, unequal arrangements cannot be sustained.

Neo-Marxists do not have a monopoly on this view. Turk (1966, p. 349) observes that when there are greater differences in resources "normal legal procedures are likely to be unofficially abrogated in favor of summary and less costly procedures" because procedural law is expensive. For all of these reasons we expect that cities with greater economic differences between the affluent and the poor should have higher rates of killing by the police.

Theorists who stress coercion often see inequality as a potentially unstable condition that must be sustained by force or by its threat. Many of these theorists also hold that economic resources are a source of power. Because power is a relational asset that rests on differences in resources, inequality is unlikely to give the lower class or minorities greater control over the police for several reasons. First, because they have less power, people with the least resources should have a reduced ability to protect themselves from police violence in unequal areas. Second, if racial or economic inequality must be sustained by force, privileged groups in unequal cities will have less reason to interfere with police violence, and third, in unequal areas the privileged may indirectly encourage police killings

American Journal of Sociology

by demanding that restraints be removed so the police can maintain
order.

Yet hypotheses that focus only on economic inequality ignore the relative economic position of minorities. Such explanations assume that economic divisions between either poor whites or poor blacks and the affluent
have identical effects on social control agencies. We overcome this problem by looking at the effects of economic disparities between blacks and
whites. In cities where the ratio of black to white mean incomes most
favors whites, the relative number of police killings should be greater for
several reasons.

First, the greater the differences between black and white economic
resources, the more a relatively poor black underclass with less to lose
from redistributive violence should threaten privileged whites who, in this
situation, may be less willing to curb police violence. Second, both neo-
Marxists and sociologists who are not Marxists (e.g., Blalock 1967) view
power as at least partly based on differences in economic resources. Substantial differences in the economic resources of blacks and whites should
reduce the black population's political influence and thus their control
over police violence. Finally, racial inequality may lead threatened whites
to make direct demands that the police be unfettered to deal with the
threat posed by a potentially violent racial underclass.

Hence theorists who stress coercion often see inequality as a potentially
unstable condition that must be sustained by force or by its threat. Many
of these theorists also hold that economic resources are a source of power.
Because power is a relational asset that rests on differences in resources,
inequality is unlikely to give the lower class or minorities greater control
over the police for several reasons. First, because they have less power,
people with the least resources should have a reduced ability to protect
themselves from police violence in unequal areas. Second, if racial or economic inequality must be sustained by force, privileged groups in unequal
cities will have less reason to interfere with police violence, and third, in
unequal areas the privileged may indirectly encourage police killings
by demanding that restraints be removed so the police can maintain
order.

In his review of field studies that examined the use of lethal force, Sherman (1980b) concludes that about half of the people fired on by the police
did not have guns. The percentage shot while fleeing also was substantial.
He claims that these "executions without trial occur in response to crimes
against property without any defense justification" (p. 89). Sherman's conclusion that such deaths often result from overreaction leaves much variance for political (and other) hypotheses to explain after violence in departmental environments is held constant.

Deadly Force

REACTIVE HYPOTHESES

Civilian Violence and Violent Police Responses

Some police killings undoubtedly are a reaction to difficult conditions in departmental environments. If findings about social divisions or direct political hypotheses are to be credible, it is crucial to include extensive controls for these problematic urban conditions. For example, the police should be especially likely to use violent methods where they must deal with a violent population. This most fundamental reactive explanation suggests that police departments in cities with higher civilian murder rates should be more likely to use deadly force.

Family Strife and Police Violence

Sampson (1987) and others find that broken families lead to violent crime. We assess this effect in two ways. First, police killing rates may be greater in cities with larger percentages of female-headed families. Second, because much police work involves coping with violent domestic disputes and because these interventions often require force (Rubenstein 1973), police departments in cities with substantial divorce rates should be more likely to use lethal violence. For these reasons, we use both divorce rates and broken families to measure the intrafamily strife that may lead to more killings by police officers.

Population Density and Police Violence

Poverty or crowding, measured by dwelling units with more than a threshold number of people per room, may produce violent behavior that leads to violent responses by the police. Deadly force also may be likely in jurisdictions where departments have fewer officers relative to the population they must control. Finally, the police encounter heightened difficulties in larger cities in part because anonymity is enhanced. This relationship and the effectiveness of inexpensive informal controls in smaller cities suggests that greater amounts of deadly force can be expected in the most populous jurisdictions.

A SUMMARY OF THE HYPOTHESES

Political threat theories.—Police may use deadly force because they protect the interests of the privileged by keeping the redistributive violence of subordinate racial or economic groups in check. If the *economic* version is correct, the most economically unequal cities will

American Journal of Sociology

have the most police killings. If the *racial* version of this political
threat approach is correct, the following four relationships should hold.
(1) Police killing rates will be higher in cities with more blacks or
(2) in cities where growth in the percentage of black residents has been
pronounced. (3) We can expect a greater use of lethal force where there
are larger differences in the economic resources of blacks and whites.
(4) The police should not use lethal force as often in cities with a black
mayor.

   Reactive hypotheses.—The police may kill because they must protect
all groups from violence. If reactions to civilian violence explain police
violence, we can expect more police killings in the cities with the most
murders or in cities that are especially difficult to police for other reasons,
including family strife, poverty, and crowding. But, according to the reactive view, law-abiding citizens benefit from the public safety provided by
this seemingly necessary use of lethal violence.

METHODOLOGY

Research Design, Dependent Variable, and Estimation

Because the environmental approach has been so productive, most empirical studies of organizations stress environmental explanations. Sherman
(1986a) applies this logic to the police behavior when he says, "Theoretically the community level should be given the most attention. . . Rossi
[Berk, and Edison] (1974) found that in comparing city of employment and
officer's personal characteristics as explanations of the use of aggressive
detection tactics, 67 percent of the variance was uniquely attributable to
the city" (p. 94).

   Environmental factors ought to explain a police department's propensity to use lethal force as well, so we analyze the rate of police killings in
1980 in the 170 U.S. cities with a population greater than 100,000. The
data come from supplementary homicide reports that police departments
filed with the FBI. This information is likely to be accurate because such
homicides are difficult to conceal. The alternative information on police
killings relies on the erratic behavior of coroners and medical examiners
(Sherman and Langworthy 1979).

   Police killings are unusual events.[4] We therefore compute the total rate

---

[4] The mean number of *total* police killings across all 170 cities, 1980–86 is 9.68 compared to a mean of 1.99 for the *rates* per 100,000. The five cities with the highest
rates are Fort Lauderdale, 7.41; Dallas, 7.30; St. Louis, 7.17; Newark, 7.02; and New
Orleans, 6.83. It is interesting that Los Angeles ranked twentieth with a police killing
rate of 4.23, placing this city in the eighty-eighth percentile.

Deadly Force

of police killings per 100,000 residents in a city over seven years starting in 1980 and ending at 1986.[5] This aggregation is not novel (see Kania and Mackey 1977; Jacobs and Britt 1979; Liska and Yu 1992), but after computing these averages, 31 cities (18.3%) still had no police killings. Because ordinary least squares (OLS) gives inconsistent estimates when the dependent variable has many zero values, Tobit frequently is employed to deal with such censored dependent variables.

Tobit uses two formulas to predict values of the dependent variable—one for cases at the limit value (zero in this study) and another for cases above the limit (Roncek 1992, p. 503), so this procedure jointly calculates two effects. Tobit combines probit estimates of the probability that a case will have a nonlimit value for cases at the limit on the dependent variable with estimates of the effects of the explanatory variables on values of the dependent variable for cases with a nonlimit value on the dependent variable. We capitalize on the properties of this estimator because it is the most appropriate when the dependent variables are censored rates with large numbers of zeros (Roncek 1992; Greene 1993).[6]

We provide separate analyses of the rate of blacks killed by the police in the same period, but we must deal with an added methodological difficulty. Cities with a tiny black population can have extremely high rates of police killings of blacks. If a city has a small number of blacks, enormous rates can result from just one or two incidents over the entire seven-year period. To remove this distortion, we weight the Tobit equations explaining police killings of blacks by the number of blacks in a city. This procedure substantially reduces the effects of cities with few blacks and appropriately increases the influence of cities with a large number of black

---

[5] If we add three years and compute mean police killings from 1980 to 1989, the theoretical implications of the findings do not change, but we are dubious about such long lags. In any case, using these additional years to reduce the number of zeros in the dependent variable is ineffective. For example, 28 zeros remain in total police killing rates if police killings are averaged from 1980 to 1989 compared to 31 when the last year used is 1986. For these reasons, we handle zeros in the dependent variable by using Tobit. We do *not* average data for the regressors across multiple years because some theoretically important independent variables (e.g. Gini or the black/white income ratio) are available only for 1979. Averaging an independent variable over many years almost invariably increases that variable's explanatory power. Because multiple-year averages cannot be computed for every independent variable, they *must not* be used for any. We use city means for missing killings in 1982 for Houston and in 1984 and 1985 for Chicago, but these changes have infinitesimal effects on the results.

[6] For additional discussion and references to the many studies that have used Tobit, see Greene (1993) or any other standard econometrics text. For precedent in the use of this procedure by sociologists, see Walton and Ragin (1990), Roncek and Maier (1990), and Mosher and Hagan (1994). We use the Tobit routine in STATA ver. 5.0.

American Journal of Sociology

residents.[7] To correct skewed distributions, "1" is added to dependent variables and they are transformed into natural log form.

Measurement of Explanatory Variables

We measure minority presence with the percentage of blacks in a city (%BLACK). Squaring this variable weights the highest %BLACK values more heavily and puts greater emphasis on the largest black populations that should be most threatening (for precedent, see Jacobs and Helms [1996]). This transformation captures a crucial part of the threat hypotheses we are testing. We assess the effects of shifts in %BLACK with percentage change in %BLACK (indicated as %CHANGEB) as measured from 1970 to 1980. To correct for a modestly skewed distribution, this variable is in square root form.[8]

In supplemental (but unreported) analyses, we use the percentage of nonwhite population instead, but this measure gives almost identical results. If the separate combined percentage of white Hispanics and other racial minorities who are not black is added to equations that already contain the %BLACK variable, the nonwhite variable is insignificant. For these reasons, we measure minority effects with data on blacks.

We operationalize racial inequality with the ratio of black-to-white mean family incomes (ratios of medians give similar results) while aggregate inequality is measured with a Gini index calculated on household incomes as reported by the 1980 census. We include a dummy scored "1" for the presence of black mayors and a dummy for location in the South.[9] We measure poverty with the percentage of all families below the poverty line or with the percentage of impoverished black families. Following Sampson (1987), breakdowns in the family are assessed with the percentage of the population that is divorced or by the percentage of female-

---

[7] When we analyze police killings of blacks, we therefore follow econometric precedent and weight by the number of blacks to remove the effects of heteroscedasticity. Such weights appropriately reduce the effects of cities with few blacks and with extremely high police killing rates. Seventy cases, or 41.2% of the 170 cities, had no police killings of blacks, but weighting by the number of blacks substantially reduces the effects of these cases with zero values.

[8] Some variables are in square root or natural log form to correct for skewed distributions. These transformations reduce the effects of outliers and increase the likelihood of bivariate normality (Fox 1991).

[9] Dayton, Ohio, shifted from a black to a white mayor in the early 1980s during the years when yearly police killings were combined. If we alter the value of this case from "1" to "0" to reflect this shift, the results remain virtually identical. Unfortunately, we could not find data on the race of police chiefs or the racial makeup of departments in 1979 or 1980.

Deadly Force

headed black families. Crowding is measured with the natural log of the percentage of housing units with more than 1.01 residents per room.

We assess police strength with the number of police employees per 100,000 residents. We use total number of employees because departments substitute unsworn personnel for uniformed officers, but this choice does not matter. We measure violence in departmental environments with the murders per 100,000 residents.[10] Attempts to use violent crime rates or the robbery rates indicate that the murder rates are the best control. Murder rates (and the other explanatory variables in these 170 cities) are highly correlated from one year to the next, so we find that using either 1979 or 1980 rates furnishes almost identical results.

In the analyses of the police killings of blacks, we use the percentage of black families with a female head (because this variable has stronger effects than the black divorce rate), the black murder rate, which is computed by dividing the number of black offenders by the black population, and the percentage of black families who have incomes below the poverty line. Explanatory variables are measured in 1980.

Model Specification

One general specification of the Tobit model that predicts total police killings is

$$
\begin{aligned}
\text{POLKILL}_i = b_0 &+ b_1 \%\text{BLACK}_i^2 + b_2 \%\text{CHANGEB}_i \\
&+ b_3 \text{BLK/WHITEINC}_i + b_4 \text{MURDRT}_i \\
&+ b_5 \text{POP}_i + b_6 \text{DIVRC}_i \\
&+ b_7 \text{BLKMAYOR}_i + b_8 \text{SOUTH}_i \\
&+ b_9 \text{CITYGOV}_i + b_{10} \text{CROWDING}_i \\
&+ b_{11} \text{GINI, (or) } b_{11} \text{POV}_i + \text{RESIDUAL}_i,
\end{aligned}
\tag{1}
$$

where POLKILL is the natural log of the rate of police killings per 100,000 citizens plus one, %BLACK is the square of the percentage of blacks in the population, %CHANGEB is the square root of the percentage change in the percentage of blacks in the population, BLK/WHITEINC is black mean family income divided by white mean family income, MURDRT is the number of murders per 100,000 population, CITYGOV is a dummy scored "1" if a city has a city manager or a commission form of govern-

---

[10] Deaths caused by the police are removed from all independent variables that measure killings. Killings by police officers are eliminated from both the total murder rate and the black murder rate.

American Journal of Sociology

ment, POP is the natural log of population, DIVRC is the percentage of divorced persons in the population, BLKMAYOR is a dummy variable for a black mayor, SOUTH is a dummy for the South, CROWDING is the natural log of the percentage of housing units with more than 1.01 persons per room, GINI is the index of income inequality, and POV is the percentage of families with incomes below the poverty line.

Because they are too collinear to be used in the same equation, GINI and POV are given the same subscript and separated by *or*. In additional equations we enter the number of police employees per 100,000 population. Only the coefficients on the black/white income ratio, black mayors, and police employees per capita should be negative.

A general equation for the weighted (by the number of blacks) Tobit model predicting police killings of blacks is

$$
\begin{aligned}
\text{POLKILL}B_i = {} & b_0 + b_1 \%\text{BLACK}_i + b_2 \%\text{CHANGEB}_i \\
& + b_3 \text{BLK/WHITEINC}_i + b_4 \text{BLKMURDRT}_i \\
& + b_5 \text{POP}_i + b_6 \text{BLKFMLHD}_i \\
& + b_7 \text{BLKMAYOR}_i + b_8 \text{SOUTH}_i \\
& + b_9 \text{CITYGOV}_i + b_{10} \text{CROWDING}_i \\
& + b_{11} \text{GINI}_i \text{ (or) } b_{11} \text{POV}_i + \text{RESIDUAL}_{i,}
\end{aligned}
\tag{2}
$$

where POLKILLB is the natural log of the police killing rate of blacks per 100,000 blacks plus one, BLKMURDRT is the black murder rate, BLKFMLHD is the percentage of black families headed by a female, and the remaining variables are defined as above. Again we expect that only the black/white income ratio, black mayors, and police employees per capita should be inversely related to police killing rates of blacks.

ANALYSIS

Table 1 gives means and standard deviations for the variables. There is substantial variation in the dependent variable. Seven-year mean police killing rates across these 170 cities range between zero and 7.41 police killings per 100,000 residents.

Tobit Results

Total killings.—Table 2 presents the Tobit estimates of total police killing rates. Equation (1) in table 2 shows a restricted six-variable model. In equation (2) we add the black mayor measure and the dummy for location in the South. In equation (3) we add police employees per 100,000, reform

Deadly Force

TABLE 1

MEANS AND SDS OF VARIABLES

	Mean	SD
POLKILL, ...	.921	.602
BLK/WHITEINC, ...	.676	.134
%BLACK^2	631.460	940.786
%CHANGEB	10.422	4.456
DIVRC	10.035	2.457
MURDRT	14.524	11.029
Police employees per 100,000 population	259.347	96.746
POP	12.291	.752
GINI	.368	.036
BLKMAYOR	.065	.247
CITYGOV	.568	.497
CROWDING	1.431	.538
SOUTH	.361	.462
POV	11.066	4.788

NOTE.—Computed on 170 U.S cities with population over 100,000. Except for the income data used to compute inequality scores, explanatory variables are based on 1980 data.

political arrangements (CITYGOV), and the measure of income inequality (Gini). In equation (4) we drop police strength and add crowding. In equation (5) we substitute percent below the poverty line for Gini in an equation otherwise identical to equation (4).

These results show that murder rates, population, and divorce rates are consistent predictors of the use of lethal force by the police, but other environmental conditions that make police work more difficult do not matter.[11] Neither crowding, poverty, nor the relative size of departments explain this outcome. Some indicators of political divisions also do not predict these deaths. In contrast to Jacobs and Britt's (1979) results using state data, economic inequality is unrelated to police killings. Other racial and political variables that do not appear to influence the total rate of police killings include %BLACK, %CHANGEB, CITYGOV, and the presence of a black mayor.

Regardless of how the specifications are altered, the same four explana-

[11] Substituting the robbery rate or the violent crime rate in a specification otherwise the same as that used in eq. (4) of table 2 leads to identical theoretical implications, but the explanatory power is reduced. The robbery rates and the murder rates are too collinear to be used together, but forcing them into the same analysis does not alter the theoretical conclusions. The evidence strongly suggests that murder rates are the best indicator of the primary reactive explanation for police killing rates.

TABLE 2
TOBIT ANALYSES OF ALL KILLINGS BY POLICE OFFICERS

	(1)	(2)	(3)	(4)	(5)
Intercept	-1.9636*	-1.9887*	-2.2758	-2.3965	-2.5481**
	(-2.31)	(-2.27)	(-1.69)	(-1.76)	(-2.76)
%BLACK²	-.0568	-.0110	-.0187	.0021	-.0257
	(-.09)	(-.16)	(-.27)	(.03)	(-.35)
%CHANGEB	.0076	.0076	.0087	.0071	.0108
	(.74)	(.74)	(.82)	(.65)	(1.00)
BLK/WHITEINC	-1.4921***	-1.4692***	-1.4181**	-1.4001**	-1.5341***
	(-3.72)	(-3.33)	(-3.02)	(-2.77)	(-3.39)
MURDRT	.0262***	.0261***	.0252***	.0241***	.0210***
	(4.58)	(4.50)	(4.15)	(3.72)	(3.13)
POP	.2278***	.2291***	.2309***	.2411***	.2459***
	(3.65)	(3.63)	(3.56)	(3.72)	(3.81)
DIVRC	.0580***	.0573**	.0534**	.0529**	.0661**
	(3.16)	(3.01)	(2.63)	(2.52)	(2.89)
BLKMAYOR	...	.0292	.0232	.0147	.0221
		(.14)	(.11)	(.70)	(.11)
SOUTH	...	.0148	...	-.0060	-.0280
		(.14)		(-.06)	(-.27)
CITYGOV	...	...	.1373	.1141	.1329
			(1.46)	(1.22)	(1.40)
Police per 100,000 population	...	...	.0006	...	...
			(1.16)		
GINI	...	...	.1057	.3240	...
			(.96)	(.16)	
CROWDING	...	...	...	.0671	.0326
				(.74)	(.35)
POV	...	...	...	...	.0226
					(1.31)
Log likelihood	-138.55	-138.53	-137.05	-137.44	-136.59
χ²	95.89***	95.93***	98.89***	98.11***	99.81***

NOTE.—%CHANGEB is in square root form while %BLACK² has been divided by 10,000. Nos. in parentheses are t-values.
* $P \leq .05$; ** $P \leq .01$; *** $P \leq .001$.

Deadly Force

tory variables account for variation in police killings. The results suggest
that the police use of deadly force is greatest in the most populated cities
and in cities with the highest murder rates. Officers in communities with
larger divorce rates also are more likely to use lethal violence, but the
findings indicate that an important social division that is likely to have
political consequences explains this outcome as well. Police killings are
especially likely in cities where economic differences between blacks and
whites are most pronounced.

Because the racial inequality measure is theoretically important and
such a consistent predictor of the total rate of police killings and because
blacks are the victims of 53% of all of the police killings in our sample,
we next present separate analyses of the police use of lethal force against
African-Americans.

Police killings of African-Americans.—Table 3 shows the results of the
Tobit analyses of the use of lethal force against blacks. The explanatory
variables are similar to those in table 2, but we substitute the black murder
rate (BLKMURDRT) for the total murder rate and the black poverty rate
(BLKPOV) for the total poverty rate. Because the black divorce rate does
not explain police killings of blacks, we use the percentage of black families headed by a female instead. All models again are estimated with Tobit.
In these analyses, however, the equations are weighted by the number of
blacks in a city to correct the heteroscedasticity that results from a few
cases with extremely high black victimization rates that is largely an effect
of extremely small black populations in some cities.[12]

The specifications follow the pattern employed in table 2. Equation (1)
in table 3 presents another restricted model limited to six explanatory variables. In equation (2) we again add the presence of a black mayor and
the dummy for location in the South. In equation (3) we add police employees per 100,000, reform political arrangements, and the aggregate
measure of income inequality (Gini). In equation (4) we drop police
strength, and add crowding. In equation (5) we substitute the percentage
of black families below the poverty line for Gini in an equation otherwise
identical to equation (4).[13]

---

[12] Cities with the highest scores on police killings of blacks per 100,000 blacks are
Torrence, Calif., 228.65; Sunnyvale, Calif., 39.22; Amarillo, Texas, 22.48; Long Beach,
Calif., 21.18; Oklahoma City, 19.22; Arlington, Texas, 18.87; and Jacksonville, Fla.,
17.45. Both Torrence and Sunnyvale have fewer than 1,000 black residents and just
one (Sunnyvale) or two (Torrence) police killings between 1980 and 1986. This means
that a weighting scheme like the one we use that reduces the influence of these two
cases is appropriate. The mean *number* of police killings of blacks across these seven
years is 5.13. The mean *rate* of police killings of blacks is 5.94 per 100,000 blacks.

[13] The unweighted means and SDs for variables introduced in the analysis of police
killings of blacks are as follows: the mean of the natural log of police killing rates of

American Journal of Sociology

The explanatory variables that mattered when all police killings are analyzed continue to explain police killings of blacks despite the weighting and other changes. Blacks are more likely to be killed by the police in larger cities with higher black murder rates and more broken families, although the measure of broken families is different in these equations. Unreported findings show that the percentage of all female-headed families does not explain the total rate of police killings, but the results in table 3 show that the percentage of black families headed by a female is positively associated with police killings of blacks. The coefficients on these race-specific variables provide additional support for reactive explanations.

Some theoretically interesting contrasts are revealed by comparing the coefficients on the measures of political divisions and the coefficients on the direct measures of political effects in tables 2 and 3. The racial inequality variable is significant in both analyses, but the presence or absence of a black mayor does not influence total police killings. When the analysis is confined to the use of lethal force against blacks, however, we find that police killings are likely to be reduced when the most powerful political official in a city is an African-American. Finally, when we analyze all police killings, neither the percentage of blacks nor the percentage change in the percentage of the population that is black is significant. Yet when the police killing rates of blacks are at issue, both of these racial threat measures predict these deaths.

ALTERNATIVE TESTS

Because these findings provide insight about such an important outcome, we conducted sensitivity tests. The effects of additional explanatory variables were assessed in unreported equations. Residential segregation is not associated with either dependent variable. Unemployment rates, unemployment disaggregated by race, change in unemployment rates, either the rate or the number of police officers who were killed, and the presence of young males disaggregated by race have the same negligible effects on the total rates of police killings and police killings of blacks.[14] Using different combinations of the explanatory variables also does not alter the results. Finally, we could find no evidence for departures from linearity.

---

blacks plus one is 1.22 (SD 1.13); the mean of the black murder rate is 38.11 (SD 30.14); the mean of the percentage of female-headed black families is 27.49 (SD 7.05).

[14] Collinearity is not problematic in any of these analyses. *All* VIF scores are well below the threshold value of 10 that conservative statisticians advocate as an indicator of collinearity. This outcome and the stability of the results despite the many diverse specifications support a conclusion that this difficulty is not distorting our findings.

TABLE 3

WEIGHTED TOBIT ANALYSES OF POLICE KILLINGS OF BLACKS

	(1)	(2)	(3)	(4)	(5)
Intercept	-1.0300 (-1.50)	-2.0636* (-2.22)	-.8489 (-.60)	-1.4832 (-.98)	-1.9560 (-1.88)
%BLACK²	.1015** (2.93)	.1798*** (3.51)	.1752** (2.50)	.1855*** (3.27)	.1802*** (3.27)
%CHANGEB	.0680* (1.71)	.0707* (1.79)	.0791* (1.94)	.0680* (1.69)	.0695* (1.73)
BLK/WHITEINC	-1.6968*** (-3.54)	-1.5364** (-2.78)	-1.9731*** (-3.25)	-1.6803** (-2.62)	-1.5559** (-2.71)
BLKMURDR	.0160*** (5.79)	.0192*** (5.95)	.0202*** (6.23)	.0193*** (5.82)	.0194*** (5.75)
POP	.1219*** (3.20)	.1456*** (3.29)	.0988* (1.79)	.1495** (2.55)	.1416* (2.26)
BLKFMLHD	.0266* (2.20)	.0379** (2.90)	.0288* (2.00)	.0402** (2.71)	.0401** (2.51)
BLKMAYOR	...	-.3517* (-1.95)	-.4036* (-2.26)	-.3378* (-1.84)	-.3627* (-1.90)
SOUTH	...	.2003 (1.39)	...	.2121 (1.44)	.2167 (1.36)
CITYGOV	...	...	-.0193 (-.14)	-.0257 (-.19)	-.0322 (-.24)
Police per 100,000 population	...	...	.0003 (.45)	...	...
GINI	...	...	-.3579 (-.12)	-1.4271 (-.45)	...
CROWDING	...	...	...	.0078 (.05)	-.0029 (-.02)
BLKPOV	...	...	...	...	-.0036 (-.24)
Log likelihood	-158.93	-155.05	-155.88	-154.93	-155.00
χ²	60.63***	68.39***	66.74***	68.64***	68.49***

NOTE.—%CHANGEB is in square root form while %BLACK² has been divided by 10,000. Nos. in parentheses are t-values.
* $P \leq .05$; ** $P \leq .01$; *** $P \leq .001$.

American Journal of Sociology

To see if weighting leads to the contrasts between the unweighted findings reported in table 2 and the weighted findings reported in table 3,
we weighted the Tobit equations that predict total police killings by city
population. But when these weighted results are compared to the equivalent unweighted results in table 2, the same explanatory variables are significant.

We use principal components to combine Gini, the total (and, where
appropriate, the race-specific) poverty rates, and crowding to create a
comprehensive measure of the presence of an underclass, but these scales
have insignificant effects when their component variables are dropped
and the scales are added to the equations. When we reestimate the models
using White's (1980) correction for heteroscedasticity, the corrected t-val-
ues do not contradict the reported results.[15] The Tobit equations in the
tables also pass the link test (Pregibon 1980) for specification error.

In accord with the conventional wisdom, we find that measures of interpersonal violence in departmental environments and other problematic
urban conditions lead to more police killings, but racial threat effects and
one explicitly political indicator matter as well.

DISCUSSION

A Review of the Results

These findings are robust. When we substitute explanatory variables, the
results persist. The findings also hold when various sensitivity tests are
conducted. Plausible contrasts appear when different police killing rates
are analyzed. One explanation for these stable findings is the comparative
accuracy of supplemental homicide data on police killings. The number
of cities employed in this study probably contributes to the stability of
the findings as well and allows us to assess many competing explanations.
According to Johnston (1984), estimates based on comprehensive models
are less likely to be biased.[16]

---

[15] We analyze police killing rates rather than simple counts because the likelihood of
being killed by the police is theoretically more interesting. Analyses of the *number*
of police killings using negative binomial regression (an estimator similar to Poisson
regression but without such restrictive assumptions about the distribution of the dependent variable) nevertheless give results with the same theoretical implications as
those found using Tobit. Another check for distributional problems like heteroscedasticity involves transforming the dependent variables to ranks by rounding to the near-
est integer and then reestimating with ordinal probit. When this is done, the Tobit
findings reported in the tables persist.

[16] Johnston says, "It is more serious to omit relevant variables than to include irrelevant variables since in the former case the coefficients will be biased, the disturbance
variance overestimated, and conventional inference procedures rendered invalid,
while in the latter case the coefficients will be unbiased, the disturbance variance
properly estimated, and the inference procedures properly estimated. This constitutes

Deadly Force

The findings suggest that many of these lethal events stem from problematic urban conditions. The appropriate murder rates explain both total police killings and police killings of blacks. Population matters in all equations as well, so a conclusion that the police are more likely to use lethal force in the most populous cities seems warranted. This finding is plausible because anonymity and other conditions that increase the difficulties faced by the police are enhanced in larger cities.

Some of the remaining measures of problematic conditions in departmental environments do not influence the use of lethal force. Poverty rates, the number of police employees per 100,000, and crowding are unrelated to police killings. Higher divorce rates are associated with larger total police killing rates, however, and the presence of female-headed black families also predicts the police use of deadly force against blacks.

In contrast to Jacobs and Britt's (1979) state-level analysis, we find no evidence that aggregate inequality measured by the Gini index explains police killings. But studies that use cities often do not find that economic inequality predicts criminal justice outcomes. When the affluent suburbs and the central cities are combined by using data from MSAs, coefficients on economic inequality typically become stronger (Jacobs 1979). Limiting an analysis to cities excludes many prosperous residents who live in the suburbs, so community inequality probably is underestimated when researchers use city data. Yet it must be remembered that this is a post hoc explanation for a hypothesis that was ineffective.

The findings instead suggest that, at least during the 1980s, racial inequality (BLK/WHITEINC) is the kind of economic stratification that best explains the use of deadly force by the police. The results are consistent with a view that greater differences in the economic resources of blacks and whites reduce the black population's political influence and their ability to curb police violence. These findings also support a parallel hypothesis derived from threat theory that the willingness of dominant groups to interfere with harsh law enforcement methods is diminished in cities where differences in the economic resources of blacks and whites are most pronounced.

We also find that minority presence matters. While the percentage of blacks in the population is unrelated to total police killings, it has positive relationships with the use of deadly force against blacks. The latter result supports prior findings about the determinants of formal social control.

---

a fairly strong case for including rather than excluding relevant variables in equations. There is, however, a qualification. Adding extra variables, be they relevant or irrelevant, will lower the precision of estimation of the relevant coefficients" (1984, p. 262), so inclusive specifications typically provide more conservative significance tests.

American Journal of Sociology

According to these findings, cities with greater numbers of blacks tend to have stronger law enforcement agencies that operate in a more punitive fashion. The standard interpretation for such results hinges on threat effects. Following Blalock (1967), threat theorists argue that, where blacks are relatively numerous, white dominance is threatened, so whites use social control agencies to maintain their ascendant position. Our finding that change in the percentage of blacks in a city's population is positively associated with police killings of blacks after other factors are controlled provides additional support for this racial threat account.

Since they are often victims of crime, many blacks may support a stronger police force or other policies that offer the hope of reducing these risks. Studies of social control that find a positive relationship between the presence of blacks and police strength or arrest rates do not offer unequivocal support for the racial threat hypothesis because many African-Americans may see such measures as desirable. In contrast to the studies that analyzed these control outcomes, this study focuses on behavior that is far more likely to hurt blacks. A comparison of racial victimization rates shows that the rate of police killings of blacks per 100,000 blacks is much greater than the the the same rate for non-Hispanic whites (5.13 vs. .977). Because African-Americans have far less reason to condone the absence of restraints on police violence, an analysis of police killings offers a better test of racial threat theory than analyses of police strength or arrests.

Perhaps this disproportionate probability that blacks will be killed by the police is the main reason why the race of the mayor matters. While the relationships between the presence of reform political arrangements and police killings are negligible, our findings show that cities with a black mayor have fewer police killings of blacks. This finding is plausible because black mayors, who hire and fire police administrators, are likely to be dependent on black votes. Hence, black mayors have both the motive and the political resources to reduce police killings of blacks. These results suggest that social scientists should not overlook political factors when they analyze the determinants of police violence.

IMPLICATIONS AND CONCLUSIONS

The results reported above challenge views that focus only on economic inequality and ignore racial minorities. Arguments that economic gaps between either poor whites or poor blacks and the affluent have identical effects on repressive efforts to maintain order are not corroborated by findings that racial hypotheses explain police killings or by the weak associations between economic inequality and these lethal events, but they do show that racial inequality accounts for both the total rate of police kill-

Deadly Force

ings and the rate of blacks killed by the police. The persistence of all of these racial results after murder rates and other difficult urban conditions have been held constant, moreover, does not fit with the conventional wisdom that the use of deadly force by the police is only a reaction to the interpersonal violence they must control.

Macro studies such as this one can isolate general relationships, but aggregate data are unlikely to furnish information about the intervening links between structural explanations and political outcomes. The links between structural arrangements that give dominant races greater influence and outcomes that are consistent with their interests often must be inferred. In this case, we have suggested plausible mechanisms that explain how racial inequality and the other structural effects isolated in this study may lead to a greater use of deadly force.

We acknowledge, however, that ideological factors enumerated by Garland (1990) or by Savelsberg (1994) may complement our structural accounts. In racially stratified cities social distance and fear of an underclass may reduce an ability to see minorities and the poor as equally deserving of protection from executions without trial. Liska et al.'s (1982) finding that there is a positive association between minority presence and fear of crime that persists after the crime rates have been held constant fits with this view, but we have no evidence about beliefs.

This study nevertheless has important implications. Sociologists have not stressed coercion as an explanation for order in advanced societies. Perhaps the ubiquity of market exchanges has directed our attention away from force or its threat (Collins 1975). Because the violence used by contemporary control agencies is modest compared to times when rulers constructed states by forcefully subduing domestic rivals, students of advanced societies neglect these critical events (Tilly 1978).

Yet those who assume that state violence is unimportant forget that coercion, if used to regulate market exchanges, is the ultimate source of control in market economies. If most people realize that visible defiance of the state's coercive supremacy will be unprofitable, that does not mean that the threat of state violence no longer is an important explanation for social order. It suggests instead that we look closely at the political processes that determine how these critical resources are employed.

According to Weber, politics is the struggle for control over the coercive resources of the state. Since the police are to the state as the edge is to a knife (Bayley 1985), political explanations for police violence should be fruitful. Yet the political determinants of the behavior of social control agencies rarely are studied because social scientists often assume that state agencies charged with using domestic coercion serve universal interests. The results of this study and those found in other studies motivated by

American Journal of Sociology

a political approach to law enforcement challenge this view. By uncovering the racial and economic divisions that lead to harsh law enforcement methods, a relatively new research area that might be called the *political sociology of social control* has increased our knowledge about the coercive determinants of social order in modern societies.

This study extends this tradition by assessing the environmental determinants of police killings. A finding that the police use of lethal force varies with the degree of inequality between the races, the presence of blacks, and local political arrangements that increase black control over the behavior of law enforcement personnel supports political explanations for these violent events. Such results are consistent with claims that state violence is used in racially unequal jurisdictions to preserve the existing order. They also suggest that sociologists should not neglect the coercive foundations of domestic order particularly in advanced but racially divided societies like the United States.

REFERENCES

Bayley, David. 1985. *Patterns of Policing.* New Brunswick, N.J.: Rutgers University Press.
Bittner, Eon. 1990. "The Police on Skid Row." Pp. 30–62 in *Aspects Police Work,* edited by Eon Bittner. Boston: Northeastern University Press.
Black, Donald. 1976. *The Behavior of Law.* New York: Academic Press.
Blalock, Hubert. 1967. *Towards a Theory of Minority Group Relations.* New York: Capricorn Books.
Chambliss, William J., and R. Seidman. 1980. *Law, Order, and Power.* Reading, Mass.: Addison-Wesley.
Chevigny, Paul. 1995. *The Edge of the Knife.* New York: New Press.
Collins, Randall. 1975. *Conflict Sociology.* New York: Academic Press.
Dahrendorf, Ralf. 1959. *Class and Class Conflict in Industrial Societies.* Stanford, Calif.: Stanford University Press.
Dye, Thomas A. 1969. "Income Inequality and American State Politics." *American Political Science Review* 63:157–62.
Fox, John. 1991. *Regression Diagnostics.* Newbury Park, Calif.: Sage Publications.
Fyfe, James J. 1982. "Administrative Interventions on Police Shooting Discretion: An Empirical Examination." Pp. 258–81 in *Readings on Police Use of Deadly Force,* edited by James J. Fyfe. Washington, D.C.: Police Foundation.
Garland, David. 1990. *Punishment and Modern Society.* Chicago: University of Chicago Press.
Goode, William J. 1972. "The Place of Force in Modern Society." *American Sociological Review* 37:507–19.
Greene, William H. 1993. *Econometric Analysis.* New York: Macmillan.
Huff, C. Ronald, and John M. Stahure. 1980. "Police Employment and Suburban Crime." *Criminology* 17:461–70.
Hughes, Everett C. 1963. "Good People and Dirty Work." In *The Other Side,* edited by Howard Becker. New York: Free Press.
Jackson, Pamela I. 1989. *Minority Group Threat, Crime, and Policing.* New York: Praeger.

Deadly Force

Jacobs, David. 1979. "Inequality and Police Strength: Conflict Theory and Social Control in Metropolitan Areas." *American Sociological Review* 44:913–25.

Jacobs, David, and David W. Britt. 1979. "Inequality and the Police Use of Deadly Force." *Social Problems* 26:403–12.

Jacobs, David, and Ronald E. Helms. 1996. "Toward a Political Model of Incarceration: A Time-Series Examination of Multiple Explanations for Prison Admission Rates." *American Journal of Sociology* 102:323–57.

———. 1997. "Testing Coercive Explanations for Order: The Determinants of Law Enforcement Strength over Time." *Social Forces* 75:1361–92.

Johnston, J. 1984. *Econometric Methods.* New York: McGraw-Hill.

Kania, Richard, and Wade Mackey. 1977. "Police Violence as a Function of Community Characteristics." *Criminology* 15:27–48.

Lenski, Gerhard. 1966. *Power and Privilege.* New York: McGraw-Hill.

Liska, Allen E., J. J. Lawrence, and M. Benson. 1981. "Perspectives on the Legal Order." *American Journal of Sociology* 87:412–26.

Liska, Allen E., J. J. Lawrence, and A. Sanchirico. 1982. "Fear of Crime as a Social Fact." *Social Forces* 60:760–71.

Liska, Allen E., and Jiang Yu. 1992. "Specifying and Testing the Threat Hypothesis." Pp. 53–68 in *Social Threat and Social Control,* edited by Allen Liska. Albany: State University of New York Press.

Mosher, Clayton, and John Hagan. 1994. "Constituting Crime in Upper Canada: The Sentencing of Narcotics Offenders, circa 1908-1953." *Social Forces* 72:613–41.

Pregibon, D. 1980. "Goodness of Link Tests for Generalized Linear Models." *Applied Statistics* 20:15–24.

Roncek, Dennis W. 1992. "Learning More from Tobit Coefficients." *American Sociological Review* 57:503–7.

Roncek, Dennis W., and Pamula A. Maier. 1990. "Bars, Blocks, and Crimes Revisited: Linking the Theory of Routine Activities to the Empiricism of 'Hot Spots.'" *Criminology* 29:725–53.

Rossi, Peter H., Richard Berk, and B. K. Edison. 1974. *The Roots of Urban Discontent: Public Policy, Municipal Institutions, and the Ghetto.* New York: Wiley.

Rubinstein, Jonathan. 1973. *City Police.* New York: Farrar, Straus & Giroux.

Sampson, Robert J. 1987. "Urban Black Violence." *American Journal of Sociology* 93:348–82.

Sampson Robert J., and Jacqueline Cohen. 1988. "Deterrent Effects of the Police on Crime." *Law and Society Review* 22:163–89.

Savelsberg, Joachim J. 1994. "Knowledge, Domination, and Criminal Punishment." *American Journal of Sociology* 99:911–43.

Sherman, Lawrence W. 1980a. "Causes of Police Behavior." *Journal of Research in Crime and Delinquency* 17:69–100.

———. 1980b. "Execution without Trial: Police Homicide and the Constitution." *Vanderbilt Law Review* 33:71–100.

———. 1983. "Reducing Police Gun Use: Critical Events, Administrative Policy, and Organizational Change." Pp. 98–125 in *Control in the Police Organization,* edited by Maurice Punch. Cambridge, Mass.: MIT Press.

Sherman Lawrence W., and Robert H. Langworthy. 1979. "Measuring Homicide by Police Officers." *Journal of Criminal Law and Criminology* 70:546–60.

Theil, Henri. 1971. *Principles of Econometrics.* New York: Wiley.

Tilly, Charles. 1978. *From Mobilization to Revolution.* Reading, Mass.: Addison-Wesley.

Turk, Austen T. 1966. "Conflict and Criminality." *American Sociological Review* 31:338–52.

———. 1969. *Criminality and the Legal Order.* Chicago: Rand McNally.

American Journal of Sociology

Vold, George. 1958. *Theoretical Criminology.* New York: Oxford.

Walton, John, and Charles Ragin. 1990. "Global and National Sources of Political Protest: Third World Responses to Debt Crises." *American Sociological Review* 55: 876–90.

White, Halbert. 1980. "A Heteroscedasticity-Consistent Covariance Matrix and a Direct Test for Heteroscedasticity." *Econometrica* 48:817–38.

Wilson, James Q. 1971. *Varieties of Police Behavior.* New York: Atheneum.

Part III
Discretion in the Decision to Arrest

[7]

The Police and Nonenforcement of the Law—Part II

Wayne R. LaFave[*]

Introduction

The present article constitutes the second half of a two-part discussion[1] of the question: Should the police. under any circumstances, be entitled to exercise discretion as to when the criminal law is to be enforced, resulting in their sometimes neither arresting nor reporting an apparent criminal offender? In Part I the broader question of whether such invocation discretion has any place in the criminal administration process was discussed. Also considered there were the merits and evils of any such discretion at the police level, including an evaluation of the extent to which effective means for control of police discretion are provided by law.

Two conclusions reached therein were that instances of police nonenforcement are of extremely low visibility and that the means for challenge of specific instances of inaction are substantially limited. Thus, it should not be at all surprising that the law has seldom given recognition to either the existence or legitimacy of enforcement discretion in the hands of the police. The present article commences with an attempt to define the extent to which the law presently recognizes police discretion and provides norms for its exercise.

With this background, the balance of this article will be devoted to an analysis of police nonenforcement in current practice. Illustrative cases of nonenforcement, reflecting significant areas of police inaction discovered in extensive observation of many law enforcement agencies,[2] will be set forth. In discussing each of these prac-

[*] B.S., 1957, LL.B 1959, Univ. of Wisconsin; Knapp Fellow, Univ. of Wisconsin, 1959-60; Ass't Prof. of Law, Villanova Univ., 1960 61; Ass't Prof. of Law, Univ. of Illinois, 1961—. I am indebted to Mr. Hugh C. Morrison, a student at the Illinois College of Law, for research assistance in the preparation of this article.

[1] See 1962 Wis. L. Rev. 104.

[2] This article is a by-product of the author's participation in the analysis phase of the American Bar Foundation's Survey of the Administration of Criminal Justice in the United States. The ABF study, underwritten by a Ford Foundation grant, is concerned primarily with isolating and identifying the critical problems in current criminal justice administration. The complete study, to be published soon, is based upon detailed observation of the actual practices of police, prosecutors, courts and probation and parole agencies in selected areas of the United States. References herein to current enforcement practices are likewise based upon these observations.

tices, an attempt will be made to indicate specifically the kind of policy question involved.

However, as the criteria of decision are identified herein, the lack of any attempt by law enforcement agencies at rationalization of their noninvocation decisions must always be kept in mind. The listing of the various criteria may in itself give an impression that the current system is much more orderly than it is in fact. These criteria, then, are not necessarily criteria which have been expressly stated by the police and others as the actual bases for their decision making. Rather, they are set forth as being what appears to be the best explanation for why the criminal process is regularly not invoked in certain recurring situations. In this sense, the stated criteria come from the observers of the system, rather than directly from the actors in it.

I. POLICE DISCRETION AND THE LAW

A. Effect of Low Visibility

One principle consequence of the low visibility of pre-arrest decisions not to invoke the criminal process is the lack of any substantial guidance from the law on the legitimacy of such discretion. Law develops only from existing conflicts of such magnitude that individuals or groups are motivated to seek resolution of them from the legal process. Courts deal with cases or controversies, so judicial law-making can follow only from an individual dispute which is carried into the courts. Though some persons might be expected to call noninvocation into question—taxpayers, persons against whom the process *is* invoked, or others who feel they are adversely affected by the failure of enforcement—there are really few appellate level cases.[3] Low visibility in part accounts for this, as many of these possible litigants are not even aware of the noninvocation, while others who are aware feel they could not present sufficient proof in court.[4]

---

[3] The precise means of challenge in court were set forth in La Fave, *The Police and Nonenforcement of the Law: I* 1962 WIS. L. REV. 104.

Of the cases, most are cases of nonenforcement which all would agree occurred from corruption or clear neglect of duty, rather than an attempt to exercise discretion of the kind to be described herein. These opinions rarely speak to the problem of noninvocation in the absence of such circumstances.

[4] The problem of proof may be a considerable one. In People v. Winters, 171 Cal. App. 2d Supp. 876, 342 P.2d 538 (Super. Ct. 1959), a trial judge's dismissal of a case on grounds of discriminatory enforcement of gambling laws against Negroes was reversed on the basis that such intentional and purposeful discrimination had to be proved, judicial notice not being sufficient. In Bargain City U.S.A. v. Dilworth, 29 U.S.L. WEEK 2002 (Pa. C.P. June 10, 1960), prosecution under the Sunday blue laws was enjoined because of a deliberate policy of

Similarly, the legislature typically acts only in response to the known desires of a substantial or at least articulate segment of the community. Thus, legislative action presupposes a number of persons sufficiently interested in obtaining legislative declaration of a given principle that they will work together toward that end. Again, low visibility minimizes the chances of such interest groups developing. Groups objecting to invocation discretion have not taken form,[5] and while the police might be expected to work toward an express legislative grant of invocation discretion, they have been satisfied to continue with a system of uncertain authority but retained low visibility.

B. Legislation on Police Discretion

The above is not intended to suggest that the statute books of the several states are silent on the matter of police discretion. Exactly the contrary is true, and almost every state has passed some legislation relevant to this issue. However, a survey of these laws discloses a distinct lack of originality in the adoption of statutes concerning the powers and duties of the police agencies, suggesting the discretion question has not received careful legislative consideration. In addition, most of the applicable statutes have been on the books for a great many years, usually without benefit of any judicial interpretation as to whether they actually grant or deny police discretion. Thus, while a good case can be made for the proposition that the state legislatures have generally denied the police authority to not invoke the criminal process,[6] a review of all the applicable laws leaves the matter in some doubt.

The most convincing evidence that the police have been denied discretion comes from those statutes which set forth the duties of various police agencies. Some states impose a duty upon sheriffs[7]

---

selective enforcement, but the case is unusual in that the Police Commissioner had previously articulated a policy of enforcement directed only at large retail establishments because of limitations in resources.

It should be noted that limited visibility is not a characteristic exclusive to police decisions. In the most recent case of Oyler v. Boles, 82 Sup. Ct. 501 (1962), the Court observed that petitioners proof that 904 men with similar records had not been prosecuted under the recidivist statute (as petitioner had been) was insufficient, as "there is no indication that these records of previous convictions . . . were available to the prosecutors."

[5] Here again, groups might develop out of concern over corrupt law enforcement, which is another matter.

[6] See Goldstein, *Police Discretion Not to Invoke the Criminal Process: Low-Visibility Decisions in the Administration of Justice*, 69 YALE L.J. 543, 557 (1960).

[7] ARIZ. REV. STAT. ANN. § 11-441 (1956); ARK. STAT. ANN § 12-1110 (1947); CALIF. GOV'T CODE § 26601 (1943); IDAHO CODE § 31-2202 (1961); N.D. CODE § 11-15-03 (1960); UTAH CODE ANN. § 317-22-2 (1962); WASH. REV. CODE ANN. § 36.28.010 (1961).

or city police[8] to arrest "all" violators of the criminal law, while other states put such a duty in more limited terms, making the officers responsible to arrest "all felons"[9] or "all persons committing an offense in his presence."[10] A lesser number of statutes state the duty as being enforcement of "all" the criminal laws.[11] Seldom are the statutes setting forth police. duties phrased in permissive terms.[12]

It should also be mentioned that state statutes not infrequently impose a duty of full enforcement in some particular (and usually sensitive) area of the criminal law, such as gambling,[13] prostitution,[14] and narcotics[15] or liquor[16] violations. While these statutes do seem to demonstrate a special legislative desire for full enforcement in these areas, it of course does not necessarily follow that discretion *does* exist in the areas which have not been specifically enumerated in this manner. There is some evidence, however, that the police do conform to these particularized commands for

---

[8] COLO. REV. STAT. § 139-3-15 (1953); HAWAII REV. LAWS § 150-10(b) (1955); IOWA CODE ANN. § 748.4 (1950); NEB. REV. STAT. § 16-323 (1954); UTAH CODE ANN. § 10-6-66 (1962); WYO. STAT. § 7-155 (1957).

[9] MINN. STAT. ANN. § 387.03 (Supp. 1960); MO. REV. STAT. § 57.100 (1959); N.M. STAT. ANN. § 15-40-2 (1953).

[10] ILL. REV. STAT. tit. 38, § 655 (1961); IND. STAT. ANN. §§ 48-6107 (1950), 49-2802 (1951; NEB. REV. STAT. § 27-1706 (1956); OHIO REV. CODE ANN. § 2935.03 (1954).

[11] ALASKA COMP. LAWS ANN. § 40-12-8 (Supp. 1958); ARK. STAT. ANN. § 19-1705 (1947, Supp. 1961); COLO. REV. STAT. § 139-75-5 (1953); DEL. CODE ANN. tit., 11 § 8303 (1953); HAWAII REV. LAWS § 150-9 (1955); IDAHO CODE § 19-4804 (1948); KY. REV. STAT. ANN. § 70.570 (1960); MICH. STAT. ANN. § 5-1752 (1952); MO. ANN. STAT. § 85.060 (1952); OHIO REV. CODE ANN. § 737.11 (1954); VA. CODE § 15-557 (Supp. 1960); W. VA. CODE § 509 (1961).
Sometimes the statutes take different forms, such as requiring the police to "suppress and prevent all disturbances and disorder," MASS. ANN. LAWS ch. 41, § 98 (1961); or making it their duty "to report within 24 hours to the district attorney . . . every crime which shall come to his knowledge," LA. REV. STAT. § 15:575 (1950). The latter provision is an interesting one in that it suggests the police might properly refrain from arrest and instead refer the matter to the prosecutor for his invocation decision.

[12] The closest thing to express recognition of discretion in the police duty statutes is N.M. STAT. § 39-1-1 (1953), which makes it a police duty "to investigate all violations of the criminal laws . . . which are called to the attention of any such officer or of which he is aware, and it is also declared the duty of every such officer to diligently file a complaint or information, if the circumstances are such as to indicate to a reasonable prudent person that such action should be taken . . . ."
Statutes elsewhere are sometimes in permissive terms, such as those indicating the police "shall have power to arrest," KAN. GEN. STAT. §§ 13-623, 13-625 (1935); that the police "may arrest," S.D. CODE § 45.1133 (1939); or that the police are "empowered . . . to make arrests," PA. STAT. ANN. tit. 71, § 252 (1942).

[13] E.g., CALIF. PENAL CODE § 335 (1960); MISS. CODE ANN. § 2478 (1942).

[14] E.g., N.D. CODE § 44-04-06 (1960).

[15] E.g., ORE. REV. STAT. § 475.120 (1959).

[16] E.g., OKLA. STAT. ANN. tit. 37, § 88 (1953); R.I. GEN. LAWS § 3-12-1 (1956)

full enforcement while exercising considerable discretion in other enforcement areas.[17]

Over two-thirds of the states have passed general arrest statutes prescribing the circumstances under which all peace officers of the state can, without warrant, make an arrest. Of these, a great majority have phrased their arrest statutes in permissive terms, usually indicating that the police "may" arrest upon a given quantum of evidence.[18] By comparison, only a few states have declared that their police "shall" arrest upon a finding of such evidence.[19] Occasionally the courts have suggested that this permissive language must also be read as imposing a duty to arrest when the officer obtains the necessary evidence,[20] and other courts have made similar assertions with regard to common law arrest powers.[21]

With but few exceptions, the criminal statutes of the states make it an offense for an officer to refuse or neglect to make an arrest pursuant to a warrant directed to him.[22] This is entirely understandable, as once the decision to make an arrest has been reached in a given case by the responsible district attorney or magistrate, the police officer has only the ministerial duty of carrying out the

---

[17] Thus, while the police in Michigan exercise considerable discretion, the director of the Enforcement Division of the Michigan State Liquor Commission noted that local officers were resisting pressures for nonenforcement of the liquor laws because of the duty of full enforcement in the Liquor Control Act, MICH. STAT. ANN. § 18.971 (1957).

[18] ALA. CODE tit. 15, § 154 (1958); ALASKA COMP. LAWS ANN. § 66-5-30 (1958); ARIZ. REV. STAT. ANN. § 13-1403 (1956); ARK. STAT. ANN. § 19-1706 (1947); CALIF. PENAL CODE § 836 (1960); COLO. REV. STAT. § 39-2-20 (1960 Perm. Supp.); D.C. CODE § 4-141 (1961); FLA. STAT. ANN. § 530.15 (1960); HAWAII REV. LAWS § 255-5 (1955); IDAHO CODE § 19-603 (1961); ILL. REV. STAT. tit. 38, § 657 (1961); IND. STAT. § 9-1024 (1956); IOWA CODE ANN. § 755.4 (1950); LA. REV. STAT. § 15:60 (1950); MASS. ANN. LAWS ch. 276, § 28 (1956); MICH. STAT. ANN. § 28.874; MINN. STAT. ANN § 629.34 (1947); MISS. CODE ANN. § 2470 (1956); MONT. REV. CODES § 94-6003 (1947); NEV. REV. STAT. § 171.235 (1957); N.Y. CODE CRIM. PROC. § 177 (Supp. 1961); N.D. CODE § 29-06-15 (1960); OHIO REV. CODE ANN. § 2935.04 (1954); OKLA. STAT. ANN. tit. 22, § 196 (1937); ORE. REV. STAT. § 133.310 (1959); R.I. GEN. LAWS § 12-7-4 (1956); S.C. CODE § 17-253 (1952); S.D. CODE § 45,1133 (Supp. 1960); TENN. CODE ANN. § 40-803 (1955); TEX. CODE CRIM. PROC. art. 215 (1954); UTAH CODE ANN. § 77-13-3 (1953); VA. CODE § 52-20 (1958); W. VA. CODE § 489 (1961); WIS. STAT. ANN. § 954.03 (1961).

While the above statutes use the term "may," other statutes merely denote that "arrest is lawful whenever" certain evidence is available, DEL. CODE ANN. tit. 11, § 1906 (1953); N.H. REV. STAT. ANN. § 594.10 (1955).

[19] CONN. GEN. STAT. ANN. § 6-49 (1961); ME. REV. STAT. ch. 147, § 4 (1954); NEB. REV. STAT. § 29-401 (1956); N.C. GEN. STAT. § 15-41 (Supp. 1959); WYO. STAT. § 7-155 (1957). Of these, only the Connecticut and North Carolina statutes refer to other than persons "found" violating the law.

[20] Monson v. Boyd, 81 Idaho 575, 348 P.2d 93 (1959); Lees v. Colgan, 120 Cal. 262, 52 Pac. 502 (1898); Schultz v. United States Fid. & Gar. Co., 134 App. Div. 260, 118 N.Y.S. 977, aff'd. 201 N.Y. 230, 94 N.E. 601 (1909).

[21] E.g., Hoch v. State, 199 Wis. 63, 225 N.W. 191 (1929).

[22] E.g., N.M. STAT. § 40-31-9 (1953); N.D. CODE.§.12-17-02 (1960).

arrest directed on the face of the warrant.[23] Consequently, it may be of some significance that most of these states have not enacted a comparable statute imposing criminal sanctions for an officer failing to arrest without warrant when he was empowered to make such an arrest.[24] A few western states make it a crime if an officer "willfully refuses to . . . arrest any person charged with a criminal offense,"[25] but it is unclear whether the "charged" requirement means charged by the prosecutor, charged by the victim or other person actually desiring prosecution, or merely that the person be sufficiently guilty to allow a legal arrest without a warrant.[26] In a few other states it is an offense only if the officer should "neglect making an arrest for an offense . . . committed in his presence."[27] Similarly, only a few states expressly declare failure to make an arrest as grounds for removal.[28]

C. The Courts and Police Discretion

As a general proposition, it can be said that the courts have seldom recognized the existence of invocation discretion in the police. In part this is due to the fact that strong language denying the existence of such discretion has been employed in many opinions where it was apparent a clear abuse of authority was involved. For example, in one case of this kind the court stated emphatically:

> There is discretion to be exercised, but that discretion is reposed in [the legislature and city council]. They have left no room for the exercise of discretion on the part of officials charged especially with the duty of seeing that the laws are enforced.[29]

---

[23] Consequently it is generally agreed that the police officer can incur no liability if the warrant is fair on its face and he acts in accordance with it.

[24] Of course, it can hardly be contended that this conclusively establishes the existence of police discretion. It would be questionable policy, in an area such as this where the officer himself must weigh the evidence to determine if he can arrest, to leave the officer open to tort liability if. he erred in making an arrest and open to criminal liability if he erred in the other direction. Yet, criminal liability could be limited to those instances where the police officer failed to arrest knowing he could lawfully arrest. See statutes cited in note 25 *infra.*

[25] CALIF. PENAL CODE § 142 (1960); COLO. REV. STAT. § 40-7-34 (1953); IDAHO CODE § 18-701 (1947); NEV. REV. STAT. § 281.280 (1959).

[26] In the only case found in which an appellate court was interpreting this term in such a statute, it is observed that "it may be said that the words 'charged with criminal offense' limit the application of this statute to cases in which a formal charge has been made." Monson v. Boyd, 81 Idaho 575, 348 P.2d 93 (1959).

[27] D.C. CODE § 4-143 (1961); TEX. PENAL CODE art. 382 (1952).

[28] OKLA. STAT. ANN. tit. 11, § 577 (1959), removal for refusal "to make an arrest in the proper case"; W. VA. CODE § 509 (1961), for violation of the "duty to . . . arrest . . . any offender"; WYO. STAT. § 7-13 (1957), for failure to arrest for a violation in the officer's presence.

[29] State *ex rel.* Parker v. McKnaught, 152 Kan. 689, 107 P.2d 693 (1940).

Such language creates a sturdy barrier of stare decisis, tending to preclude recognition, in later cases, of circumstances where discretion might have been validly exercised.

Similarly, even within a single case a court may treat as identical the clearly improper failure to enforce the law and the lack of enforcement in other instances where some rational argument could be made in favor of noninvocation. A recent Wisconsin case provides an excellent example of this.[30] The court was reviewing the conviction of a sheriff for a number of alleged instances of misconduct in office. Along with counts of serious misconduct, such as allowing prostitution to continue in return for certain favors, was a charge that the sheriff failed to make an arrest in an assault case where the victim, the adult son of the offender, had indicated to the sheriff that he did not want to sign a complaint against his father. Noninvocation in such a case is certainly not unusual.[31] Yet the court held that such inaction justified conviction under the statute punishing a public official who "intentionally fails or refuses to perform a known, mandatory, nondiscretionary, ministerial duty of his office . . . ."[32]

Notwithstanding such approaches, some courts have nevertheless expressly recognized that some discretion, such as that involved in interpreting the legislative mandate,[33] must of necessity be exercised by the police.[34] However, this right has been carefully limited, and where the legislative mandate is clear and unambiguous, the police are not justified in concluding that the legislature does not contemplate enforcement as to conduct clearly within the scope of the statute.[35] But it has been suggested that such a presumption

---

[30] State v. Lombardi, 8 Wis. 2d 421, 99 N.W. 2d 829 (1959).

[31] See *infra* at 214.

[32] WIS. STAT. § 946.12(1) (1959).

[33] See La Fave, *supra* note 3, at 105.

[34] Thus, an officer has "the duty . . . of interpreting the statutes he is called upon to enforce. He must act according to his best lights. . . ." State *ex. rel.* Pacific American Fisheries v. Darwin, 81 Wash. 1, 13, 142 Pac. 441, 444 (1914). See also Jumonville v. Herbert, 170 So. 497 (La. App. 1936).

[35] Thus, a city ordinance providing that *no* person shall sell liquor without first obtaining a license may not be interpreted to exclude wholesale liquor dealers on the basis that it was the legislative intent that it apply only to saloon keepers. Such an ordinance imposes on the police ". . . an official duty . . . purely ministerial. No judicial discretion is anywhere involved." State *ex rel.* School Dist. of Omaha.v. Cummings, 17 Neb. 311, 313, 22 N.W. 545, 546 (1885). But see Rohrer v. Hasting Brewing Co., 83 Neb. 111, 119, 119 N.W. 27, 30 (1908), where the court, engaging in statutory interpretation under similar circumstances, relied on nonenforcement, stating:

"After a careful and deliberate consideration of all the legislative acts concerning said traffic and the conduct of the various officers whose duty it has been for the past 20 years to enforce those laws, we conclude that a corporation may be licensed to sell intoxicating liquors. . . ."

is justified if the legislation has remained unenforced for some substantial period of time.[36]

Nonenforcement as to certain clearly proscribed conduct because of limitations on enforcement resources might also be said to be a necessary discretionary power. Yet there has rarely been express recognition of this fact by the courts. An exception is the Michigan case of *Gowan v. Smith*,[37] where the court declared that the police commissioner

> is bound to use the discretion with which he is clothed. He is charged not alone with the execution of the liquor laws of the State within the city of Detroit, but he is likewise charged with the suppression of all crime and the conservation of the peace. To enable him to perform the duties imposed upon him by law, he is supplied with certain limited means. It is entirely obvious that he must exercise a sound discretion as to how those means shall be applied for the good of the community.[38]

Yet selective enforcement made necessary because of limited police resources has been found improper.[39]

If, as the *Gowan* case asserts, the police may exercise sound judgment as to how to apply their limited means, rather than expending their resources at random without striving for maximum effectiveness, the criteria to be used have not been clearly established by law. One court has suggested that it might be appropriate for the police to divert their resources away from those cases in which the possibilities of conviction seem slight.[40] Nonetheless,

---

See also People *ex rel.* Brown v. Kennedy, 102 Misc. 450, 169 N.Y.S. 1022 (Sup. Ct. 1918); Lay v. Common Council of Hoboken, 75 N.J.L. 315, 67 Atl. 1024 (1907).

[36] Thus, in refusing to mandamus the police, one court observed that "the ordinance [in question] seems, whether for adequate or inadequate reasons, to have been a dead letter for a number of years." Carmody v. City of Elmira, 160 Misc. 916, 290 N.Y.S. 1021, 1023 (Sup. Ct. 1936).

[37] 157 Mich. 443, 122 N.W. 286 (1909).

[38] *Id.* at 470, 122 N.W. at 297. While opinions expressly recognizing police discretion in this fashion are most unusual, it might be said that a number of courts have accomplished approximately the same result by denying to the relator the extraordinary writ requested on the grounds that such a remedy was not available to him. Compare State *ex rel.* Clark v. Police Bd. of Columbus, 10 Ohio Dec. Reprint 256 (C.P. 1888), where mandamus was granted to compel enforcement of blue laws, with State *ex rel.* Clark v. Murphy, 3 Ohio C.C.R. 332 (Cir. Ct. 1888), also arising in Columbus, where the court refused, on procedural grounds, to grant the writ to compel enforcement of the same laws.

[39] After the Philadelphia Police Commissioner, for lack of funds and personnel, adopted a policy of limited enforcement of the blue laws to large retail establishments, the Philadelphia Court of Common Pleas enjoined prosecution of a complaining defendant. Bargain City U.S.A. v. Dilworth, *supra* note 4.

[40] "If it be true that petit jurors will not convict in such cases, it might well be doubted whether it would be best to summarily arrest the parties. . . ." Graham v. Gaither, 140 Md. 330, 345, 117 Atl. 858, 863 (1922).

other courts have taken the position that the police have a duty to make arrests even in those cases where they are reasonably certain that the prosecutor or judge will dismiss.[41] It has similarly been held that the police are acting improperly if they divert their resources away from that enforcement which does not enjoy public support.[42]

Assuming that discretionary enforcement, for reason of limited resources or otherwise, is proper, the enforcement criteria must be consistent with constitutional guarantees. Thus the equal protection cases are relevant. The difficulty, however, is that the state cases on equal protection in law enforcement are far from consistent, making it unclear what invocation criteria actually violate the Constitution. Putting aside those cases holding that the equal protection clause has no application to discriminatory penal enforcement,[43] the only agreement is that it is merely purposeful and intentional discrimination which is prohibited.[44] It seems likely the requirement is only that criminal law administrators refrain from classifications impermissible to the legislature, such as race or religion, although some courts have stated other tests.[45] But, wherever the line is ultimately drawn, the equal protection cases do not answer the ultimate question of whether and when the police have discretion; they only identify certain enforcement criteria as unconstitutional.

In summation, then, the law on the subject of police discretion remains uncertain. The statutes of some states declare the police duty to be enforcement of all laws or arrest of all offenders, but almost all arrest laws are couched in permissive language. Except for failure to obey the command of a warrant, nonenforcement is seldom expressly proscribed by the criminal codes. Little recognition of police discretion is found in the case law, which for the

---

[41] Thus, "derelictions of other officials cannot excuse . . . failure to do what the law plainly required." State *ex rel.* Thompson v. Reichman, 8 Tenn: 653, 680, 188 S.W. 225, 232 (1916) (claimed courts would not convict); Goodell v. Woodbury, 71 N.H. 378, 52 Atl. 855 (1902) (suggested prosecutor would not charge).

[42] Clark v. Police Bd. of Columbus, *supra* note 38 (1888).

[43] See La Fave, *supra* note 3, at 135 n. 124.

[44] See Comment, 61 COLUM. L. REV. 1103, 1113 (1961).

[45] See La Fave, *supra* note 3, at 135 n. 128. The previously ambiguous Supreme Court position has been clarified by the most recent case of Oyler v. Boles, 82 Sup. Ct. 501 (1962). The Court there held that conscious exercise of some selectivity by state prosecuting authorities in application of a West Virginia recidivist statute was not, in itself, a violation of equal protection of the laws absent selection deliberately based upon unjustifiable standards such as race, religion, or other arbitrary classification.

most part only identifies some nonenforcement criteria of doubtful constitutionality.

II. Police Discretion in Practice: Noninvocation Because the Legislature May Not Desire Enforcement as to the Conduct in the Ordinary Case

As pointed out in Part I, it is necessary for the law enforcers to exercise discretion in interpreting the legislative mandate. In part, this involves the techniques of interpretation—the canons of construction and the like—usually thought of as necessary for an understanding of the actual meaning of words and phrases employed in legislation. But, the delimiting of enforcement by police and others in the criminal administration process, because it is thought there is not a real legislative desire for enforcement, goes beyond this. Thus, even if the language is without ambiguity, it may be thought that the conduct has been proscribed only as a cure for administrative enforcement problems, because of a desire to eliminate loopholes, or in order to reflect the ideals rather than immediate expectations of society. Yet another reason why the administrators of the criminal law may question whether the substantive law reflects the actual desires of the legislators is the fact that often the criminal proscriptions appear to be substantially outdated.

A. Ambiguity as to Whether Conduct Proscribed Because of Difficulties in Verbal Formulation

Illustration #1: A police officer received a complaint that an itinerant salesman was selling obscene magazines. The officer examined the material objected to, but was unable to determine whether such matter was covered by the rather ambiguous obscenity statute of the state. The officer refrained from making an arrest even though the salesman was about to leave the jurisdiction.

The objective of the law is guidance through the greatest possible clarity, certainty and reliability. In the criminal law, the principle of *nullem crimen sine lege* requires strict adherence to this objective. Thus, criminal statutes are strictly construed, impermissibly vague statutes are invalidated, and interpretation is limited to the ordinary meaning of the words rather than being aided by general purpose or "legislative intention."[46] Yet, even

---

[46] Indeed, there is rarely any evidence of legislative purpose available. Only the newer recodifications, which are few in number, typically contain supplemental legislative comments. *E.g.,* 5 Wis. Legis. Council, Judiciary Committee Report on the Criminal Code (1953); Proposed Illinois Revised Criminal Code of 1961 (Tentative final draft 1960).

in the criminal law, limitations on language make it impossible to achieve completely unambiguous definition even with the most careful legislative draftsmanship. This, together with the not too careful formulation of many criminal statutes, produces a significant element of uncertainty in the minds of those persons charged with the responsibility of enforcing the law.

Of central importance here is the question of how the ambiguity should be resolved at the arrest decision level. While a variety of positions might be taken, they would all seem to be somewhere between two extremes. On the one hand, it might be said that while the canon of strict construction and these other exacting interpretive devices are properly applied in court, they have no place at the arrest decision level. So viewed, the test for interpretation of ambiguous statutes, like that for proof of guilt, would be broader at the arrest point than at the conviction stage; the process in both respects being one of a series of more and more selective decisions. The rationale for such an attitude (aside from the obvious point that otherwise some of the guilty would escape punishment) is that if the exact boundaries of a particular statute are to be better defined, it is necessary for cases where doubt exists to reach a court of law.[47] The contrary view is that the criminal law is to be interpreted strictly not only by the courts, but by the police as well.[48] Implicit in this view is an attitude that the fair warning function of the law makes it improper for individuals who have engaged in conduct not clearly proscribed as criminal to be subjected to arrest, prosecution, and perhaps even conviction.[49]

Of course, an officer's choices are not always merely those of noninvocation by way of strict construction or invocation by employing a broader interpretation. Often it is possible for the officer, without arrest, to defer the interpretation question to another

---

[47] Not only will this allow judicial clarification, but, say the proponents of this view, "if a criminal law is . . . poorly defined . . . efforts by the police to achieve *full enforcement* should generate pressures for legislative action." Goldstein, *Police Discretion Not to Invoke the Criminal Process: Low-Visibility Decisions in the Administration of Justice,* 69 YALE L.J. 543, 586-87 (1960).

[48] Thus, Hall cautions the police that where the law is uncertain, "the law that must be enforced is the narrow, strict interpretation of the relevant statutes and decisions." Hall, *Police and Law in a Democratic Society,* 28 IND. L.J. 133, 171 (1953).

[49] "Erroneous conclusions of this kind may not reach the appellate court because the legal representation available to a defendant in many criminal cases is not likely to engage in careful law research, and thus may not call into issue prevailing assumptions as to the meaning of the substantive criminal law where that law is not clearly expressed." Remington & Rosenblum, *The Criminal Law and the Legislative Process,* 1960 U. ILL. L.F. 481, 488.

190   Wisconsin Law Review   [Vol. 1962

agency, such as the prosecutor's office, for a determination.[50] However, as in the above illustration, the need for immediate arrest does not always make this possible. In such a case the policeman is left with the question of whether an arrest should be made when it is not entirely clear that the conduct is within the legislative proscription.

The answer may well be that the police, for their own protection, are required to employ a very strict construction in doubtful cases. This is because some courts would hold that the officer, if brought to an accounting in a false arrest action, has been left no room for error. As was held in a recent Michigan case, "An officer of justice is bound to know the law, and if he makes an arrest which the facts on which he proceeds would not justify, if true, he is a wrongdoer."[51] The harshness of this rule is made clear in the Restatement concurrence that

> no protection is given to a peace officer who, however reasonably, acts under a mistake of law other than a mistake as to the validity of a statute or ordinance. Thus, an officer is not privileged to arrest another whom he reasonably suspects of having committed an act which the officer, through a mistake of law reasonable in one of his position, believes to be a common law felony. So too, a peace officer is not privileged to arrest another whom he reasonably suspects of having committed an act which the officer, through a mistaken construction of a statute, believes to have been a felony by such statute. And this is so although the reasonable character of the officer's mistake is proved by the fact that at the time of the arrest the statute is generally understood to make such an act a felony and is not judicially construed to the contrary until after the arrest is made.[52]

Thus, the law requires "certainty" in place of "reasonable cause" in the relationship between the suspected conduct and the substantive law.[53]

---

[50] Thus, officers in the Detroit censor bureau are not in the habit of making arrests without first obtaining a determination from the prosecutor that the objectionable material is covered by the obscenity statute. Similarly, complaints of questionable business practices are referred to the prosecutor's office in Detroit because of the difficult legal questions involved there. In Milwaukee it was also observed that those cases requiring careful statutory interpretation were regularly brought to the attention of the prosecutor before arrest—negligent homicide, obscene literature, embezzlement, violations of the blue sky laws, and other white collar crimes.

[51] Donovan v. Guy, 347 Mich. 457, 80 N.W.2d 190 (1956). Though this is the holding of the court, the facts of the case suggest that it is one in which the court could have said that there was not even "reasonable cause" for so believing.

[52] Restatement, Torts § 121, comment i (1934).

[53] "Reasonable cause" or "reasonable grounds to believe" is all that is usually required for felonies as to whether the conduct in fact occurred and whether the suspect was the actor.

It is difficult to describe the above requirement as a rule of conduct, as the criterion of whether an arrest should be made becomes
the outcome of the case following arrest. But, such a rule, to the
extent there is awareness of it by the police, certainly influences
their conduct, sometimes to the point that in cases of uncertainty
a more strict construction is employed by them than would be
utilized by the court at the adjudication level.[54] In view of such
consequences, it would seem that reconsideration of the sound-
ness of this doctrine is highly desirable.[55]

B. Conduct Possibly Proscribed as a Cure·
for Administrative Problems

Illustration #2: A police officer came upon a "bum," a man
wandering the streets clearly without any means of support.
Though such conduct is literally proscribed by the vagrancy
statute of the state, no arrest was made.

Because of uncertainties or restrictions in the law regarding the
extent to which pre-arraignment detention for purposes of investigation is proper, persons are sometimes detained by arrest (and
perhaps conviction) for an offense such as vagrancy or disorderly
conduct.[56] While sometimes such a charge is lodged even though
it appears clear that no conduct proscribed by these statutes has
taken place, on many other occasions the suspicious actions of the
suspect are sufficient in that they do fit within the literal legislative
proscription. That this could be so is apparent from the language
often used in these statutes, covering those "found loitering without visible means of support"[57] or persons "found in or loitering

---

[54] To the extent that observation of police practices reveals their usual attitude
in cases of ambiguity in the substantive law, it appears that the rules of strict
construction have become a principle governing the exercise of invocation discretion. It is unusual for either the prosecutor or court to find, as to a person
arrested, that the supposed conduct was not within the legislative proscription.
    However, sometimes cases are dismissed for policy reasons, but the reason given
is that the conduct did not violate the statute. Such concealment of the actual
reason is made necessary because the trial judge is not given the right to acquit
the guilty. State v. Evjue, 254 Wis. 581, 37 N.W.2d 50 (1949).
[55] While the police officer must make no mistakes in statutory interpretation,
his understanding of constitutional law need not be as great. The arrest is valid,
as to a statute later found to be unconstitutional, unless the statute is
clearly, on its face, unconstitutional. *E.g.,* Hill v. Taylor, 50 Mich. 549, 15 N.W.
899 (1883). This would appear to produce an anomalous situation in which, if
an officer arrests for conduct thought to be criminal, but the court declares the
statute unconstitutional, he is protected, while if the court should instead conclude that in order to find the statute constitutional it must construe it as not
covering this conduct, then the officer is liable.
[56] See Culombe v. Connecticut, 367 U.S. 568 (1961), for a most interesting fact
situation. See also note 59 *infra.*
[57] KAN. GEN. STAT. § 21-2409 (1949).

near any structure, vehicle or private grounds who is there without the consent of the owner and is unable to account for his presence."[58]

These very broad and rather ambiguous statutory provisions cover a wide range of conduct,[59] but because of the attitude that these statutes provide a necessary basis for the detention and investigation of suspicious characters no attempt is made at reform of these provisions.[60] The police reaction, however, is generally that these statutes were intended as and are in fact to be used as investigative devices. Consequently, a given individual who comes within these broad delineations will normally not be subjected to arrest absent other factors making it desirable to conduct an in-custody investigation of him.

C. *Conduct Possibly Proscribed in Order to Eliminate Loopholes*

Illustration #3: A police officer was led by a complainant to a private residence where the occupants could be observed through a large picture window playing poker for money. The officer refused to take any action against the card players, although the state statute expressly covered all forms of gambling.

Undoubtedly a narrower, more precise definition of certain criminal conduct has been resisted not because of any disagreement as to what conduct should be considered criminal, but rather be-

---

[58] WIS. STAT. § 947.02 (1959).

[59] This is not unusual. On these statutes elsewhere, and the problems which they create, see Foote, *Vagrancy-Type Law and Its Administration*, 104 U. PA. L. REV. 603 (1956); Perkins, *The Vagrancy Concept*, 9 HAST. L.J. 237 (1958); Sherry, *Vagrants, Rogues and Vagabonds—Old Concepts in Need of Revision*, 48 CALIF. L. REV. 557 (1960); Comment, 23 CALIF. L. REV. 506 (1935); Comment, 23 CALIF. L. REV. 616 (1935); Note, 59 YALE L.J. 1351 (1950).

[60] That recodification or other reconsideration of these provisions which does occur seems to reflect an awareness of these administrative problems, even if more clarity is achieved. In addition to the Wisconsin provision indicated above, another section was proposed at the time of the 1953 recodification to cover "a person who loiters on the streets, whose actions give rise to suspicion of wrongdoing and who is unable to give a satisfactory account of himself." 5 WIS. LEGIS. COUNCIL, JUDICIARY COMMITTEE REPORT ON CRIMINAL CODE 210 (1953). This proposal would seem to be an express recognition that the statute would be used to arrest and detain persons suspected of other criminal conduct.

When a proposed new California disorderly conduct statute was vetoed by the Governor because, in repealing the prior broad and ambiguous provisions, it "unfortunately removed from police control certain dangerous conduct, regulation of which is necessary in the public interest," the draftsman then added a section to the proposal in order to cover one "who loiters or wanders upon the streets or from place to place without apparent reason or business and who refuses to identify himself and to account for his presence when requested by any peace officer so to do." Sherry, *supra* note 59, at 569 n.67, 570-71.

cause of fears that any such restatement would create loopholes through which the guilty could regularly escape. In such a case, enforcement of the entire range of literally proscribed conduct would actually conflict with the true intention of the legislature.

The gambling laws serve as the best illustration of this. Frequently they are drawn in broad terms, covering all forms of gambling,[61] a sharp contrast to the American Bar Association sponsored Model Anti-Gambling Act optional provision, which exempts from prosecution gambling which is "incidental to a bona fide social relationship, is participated in by natural persons only, and in which no person is participating, directly or indirectly, in professional gambling."[62] However, the risks inherent in the latter formulation were well recognized by the draftsmen:

> The Commission has also had great difficulty with this problem of finding a formula which would exclude the social or casual gambler from prosecution and punishment, yet which would not result in opening a large breach in the statute for the benefit of professional gamblers and their patrons. The Commission recognizes that it is unrealistic to promulgate a law literally aimed at making a criminal offense of the friendly election bet, the private, social card game among friends, etc. Nevertheless, it is imperative to confront the professional gambler with a statutory facade that is wholly devoid of loopholes.
>
> It should be noted that the prosecuting attorneys who were asked for comment on prior drafts of the Model Act were also divided in their opinions as to the desirability of making an express exemption for the casual or social gambler. Many prosecutors were flatly opposed to any such exemption because it offered a loophole for the professional gambler.
>
> Many state laws at the present time penalize all forms of gambling without exceptions for the social gambler. It is doubtful whether the latter has been unduly harassed under such laws.[63]

The best summation of the observed practice is that it conforms to the ABA exempting provision, notwithstanding the broad coverage of the statutes in these states. Any difficulties in this area are apt to arise in terms of police definition of the boundary line between social gambling and professional gambling. Generally speaking, gambling occurring in private homes is exempted from enforcement,[64] but the police may be more particular when they learn

---

[61] Such broad coverage is the pattern in many states. 2 ABA COMM'N ON ORGANIZED CRIME, ORGANIZED CRIME AND LAW ENFORCEMENT 75 (1952).

[62] *Id.* at 74.

[63] *Id.* at 75.

[64] Some states have attempted by statute to exempt such gambling; *e.g.*, MONT. REV. CODE § 94-2403 (1947), excluding "all private homes."

professional games are being moved into private homes in order to avoid detection.[65] Gambling outside private homes is generally proceeded against, unless it is clear it is purely social in nature.[66] Professional gambling in so-called private clubs is a subject of strict enforcement and very active detection programs, though detection of such activity is obviously difficult. The police often find it difficult to decide whether minor gambling in such places as pool halls fits the "social gambling" test.[67]

> *Illustration #4:* A Negro approached a police officer and informed him that he had just been refused service in a nearby restaurant. The officer accompanied the complainant to the establishment, where the proprietor admitted that he had refused to serve the complainant. The officer then advised the proprietor of the state civil rights law, which makes it a misdemeanor to refuse public accommodations on the basis of race, creed or color. When the proprietor then agreed to serve

---

[65] One tactic observed when the police were called to such a gathering (often upon complaint of a noisy party) was for a number of the individuals in the group to be taken aside and asked to identify all other members of the group. This device, to some extent, allows the police to distinguish the mere gathering of a group of friends from the professional operations at which customers come and go at intervals and are not socially acquainted.

[66] Gambling tolerated in private homes may not be tolerated elsewhere, even though in private. Wichita detectives, in a hotel on another matter, overheard three men engaged in a crap game in a room, and arrested them although only ten cents was involved and the men said it was just a "friendly little game." Perhaps the fact that the conduct was not private enough, in that it could be overheard in the corridor, was a contributing factor.

[67] This gambling often is not professional in the sense that the proprietor receives any substantial income from the activity. He may receive no portion of the gambling money directly, but instead will receive a small sum from the players (not related to the amount bet or the amount won) for the use of the pool or card tables. Although the conduct may come to the attention of the police in the course of an inspection of such licensed premises, arrest is not likely as long as the social aspects outweigh the professional aspects. It is usually recognized that such activity is the equivalent of the at home social gambling engaged in by persons located at a higher level of the community class structure. The Michigan police on one occasion arrested eight persons engaged in minor gambling in a pool hall, but the prosecutor promptly refused a warrant on the basis that this type of activity was taking place in many homes in the area. It was intimated that the police intended to make no more such arrests in the future.
In one enforcement study it was noted that the kind of gambling against which the process was not invoked was that sanctified by the tradition of the people in the area. Esselstyn, Crime and Its Control in the Hinterland 201 (unpublished Ph.D. thesis, New York Univ. 1952). Elsewhere it has been observed that this tendency may go so far as to resut in nonenforcement against the numbers racket because this kind of gambling fits the prevailing pattern of behavior of the people involved. WHYTE, STREET CORNER SOCIETY 135 (2d ed. 1955). From the observations in the states studied, it did not appear that any such criterion was applied where there was a serious problem of professionalism: Thus, while playing the numbers is part of the usual behavior pattern of some minority groups in Detroit, there is vigorous enforcement against this conduct, just as there is against horse race books and other gambling operations of a clearly professional nature.

the Negro, the officer took no further action.

The police may not invoke the criminal process because they feel that the legislature did not intend for the conduct to be punished unless the violator was actually aware that it was proscribed by the criminal law. Except for some minor limitations,[68] the legislature may punish persons who have violated laws of which they are ignorant. Indeed, the doctrine of *ignorantia juris neminem excusat* makes this the intention of the legislature unless otherwise declared.[69] This doctrine can hardly be justified upon the fiction that everyone is presumed to know the law, but it has often been rationalized on the ground that effective administration of justice requires such a presumption.[70] Thus, it is not surprising that noninvocation sometimes results from an attitude that the doctrine was not excepted to by the legislature only because it would create an undesirable loophole.[71]

---

[68] Lambert v. California, 355 U.S. 225 (1957), held ignorance of the law should have been recognized as a defense in that case because the proscribed conduct was an omission—failure of a "convicted person" to register with the police in accordance with a Los Angeles ordinance.

[69] The legislature could do so:

"If the Legislature cannot, in good conscience, regard conduct whch it wishes to forbid as wrongful in itself, then it has always the option of declaring the conduct to be criminal only when the actor knows of its criminality or recklessly disregards the possibility that it is criminal. For knowing or reckless disregard of legal obligation affords an independent basis of blameworthiness justifying the actor's condemnation as a criminal, even when his conduct was not intrinsically antisocial. It is convenient to use the word "wilful" to describe this mode of culpability, although the term is by no means regularly so limited in conventional usage." Hart, *the Aims of the Criminal Law*, 23 Law & Contemp. Prob. 401, 418 (1958).

[70] Thus, Austin contended the doctrine was required because it was impossible to determine the relevant issue. "Whether the party was *really* ignorant of the law, and was *so* ignorant of its provisions, could scarcely be determined by any evidence accessible to others." As to showing the defendant was ignorant in not being aware, it would be "incumbent upon the tribunal to unravel his previous history, and to search his whole life for the elements of a just solution." 1 Austin, Lectures on Jurisprudence 498-99 (4th ed. 1879). "Without it justice could not be administered in our tribunals." 1 Bishop, Criminal Law § 294.1 (8th ed. 1892). For an excellent discussion of the doctrine and its rationale (including one by the author different than above) see Hall, General Principles of Criminal Law 376-414 (2d ed. 1960).

[71] Pound has criticized the "covering up" of cases where persons ignorant of the law are excused by conviction and pardon (as in the classic case of Rex v. Bailey Rus. & Ry. 1, 168 Eng. Rep. 651 (1800)) or by employing unwarranted presumptions and fictions. Pound, *Discretion, Dispensation and Mitigation: The Problem of the Individual Special Case*, 35 N.Y.U.L. Rev. 925, 936 (1960). Thus, he would allow exculpation for the express reason of lack of knowledge of the law, where appropriate, and perhaps he would approve of noninvocation on this score.

The Model Penal Code would recognize a limited defense here, allowing the defendant to show "by a preponderance of the evidence" that he held a "reasonable belief that [the] conduct does not legally constitute an offense" when "the statute or other enactment defining the offense is not known to the actor and has not been published or otherwise reasonably made available to him prior to the conduct alleged." Model Penal Code §§ 2.04(3), 2.04(4) (Tent. Draft No. 4, 1955).

But, when would the legislature perhaps not intend enforcement where the actor is unaware of the relevant substantive provision? Ignorance of the law, it is said, should hardly be excused as to acts "immoral regardless of the actor's ignorance of their being legally forbidden (e.g., the felonies and principle misdemeanors),"[72] as this is merely "a demand that every responsible member of the community understand and respect the community's moral values."[73] However, the theorists add that knowledge of the law ought be essential to culpability "where normal conscience (moral attitudes) and understanding cannot be relied upon to avoid the forbidden conduct."[74] To some, the latter group includes those offenses "merely *mala prohibita*,"[75] while others would attempt a more subtle distinction.[76]

Noninvocation by the police because of lack of knowledge on the part of the offender was not frequently observed, but it undoubtedly occurs from time to time. It can be expected to take place more often with enforcement agencies other than the regular police department, as "it is a frequent practice in the exercise of [business regulations] for field investigators to lay the foundation for future successful prosecution by establishing knowledge of regulations."[77] Yet, the police themselves sometimes have occasion to do likewise, particularly, as in the illustration, when the policy behind the statute suggests proceeding only against willful violators.

Beyond these two illustrations, broad legislative proscription in order to eliminate loopholes may well be the explanation for the breadth of other statutes, too. A statute may not be explicit as to the precise mental state involved for this very reason, but enforcement may be limited to those instances where there is an indication of unlawful intent.[78] The great mass of strict liability criminal

---

[72] HALL, *op. cit. supra* note 70, at 403.

[73] Hart, *supra* note 69, at 419.

[74] HALL, *op. cit. supra* note 70, at 404.

[75] Hart, *supra* note 69, at 419.

[76] HALL, *op. cit supra* note 70, at 402-08.

[77] *Id.* at 350. Empirical data to support this conclusion has been gathered for one jurisdiction. See Comment, 1956 WIS. L. REV. 625.

[78] See Remington & Rosenblum, *supra* note 49, at 490 n.26, for such objection by one law enforcement officer to the requiring of intent to commit a burglary in the Wisconsin burglarious tools statute.

In Michigan there is a statute prohibiting carrying a concealed weapon and another prohibiting carrying a concealed weapon with intent to use the same unlawfully. While the penalties are the same, the Detroit prosecutor's office will prosecute only for the latter. In addition to the hypothesis set forth in La Fave, *The Police and Nonenforcement of the Law: I,* 1962 WIS. L. REV. 104, 123 n.78, it appears this might be a case of enforcement narrower than a necessarily broad statute. While there was not complete police concurrence in the attitude of the prosecutor's office, it may well be that there was no real dis-

statutes are likewise probably explanable on this basis;[79] enforcement of these statutes usually being by a specialized agency rather than the police, actual enforcement levels were not observed.[80]

D. Conduct Possibly Proscribed Because of a Desire to Have the Substantive Law State the Ideals of the Community

Illustration #5: A local welfare director presented positive proof to the police that one of the local welfare recipients was engaging in an adulterous relationship. Notwithstanding a repetition of the complaint on another occasion, the police refrained from taking any action against the violator.

At one point in Part I, the question of what the criminal law actually is, both in terms of a command to the general public and a mandate to the law enforcers, was explored. An answer sometimes given is that, as to certain parts of the substantive criminal law, they are "state-declared ideals" rather than a declaration of immediate expectations to which conformance is to be required by the imposition of penal sanctions.[81] Thus, it is said that certain law-making is intended to educate, to guide the individual conscience, but is not intended to be used to coerce compliance.[82] The

---

agreement in the limitation of enforcement to unlawful intent cases, but only lack of agreement as to what cases sufficiently suggested unlawful intent to warrant prosecution.

[79] Attempts to justify strict liability statutes on this ground have been severely criticised in that "the convenience of investigators and prosecutors is not, in any event, the prime consideration in determining what conduct is criminal." Hart, *supra* note 69, at 423; HALL, *op. cit supra* note 70, at 342-51.

[80] However, a study made of the administration of the Wisconsin Food and Drug Act concluded:

"In actual effect then the principal functional significance of the liability without fault character of the food and drug sections is not to make possible wholesale convictions of inadvertent offenders untinted by subjective fault; it is rather to provide widened areas of administrative discretion within which the department of agriculture can administer and enforce the regulations with greater flexibility and effectiveness than would be possible if proof of subjective fault were necessary." Comment, 1956 WIS. L. REV. 625, 655.

[81] POUND, CRIMINAL JUSTICE IN AMERICA 67 (1930).

[82] "The Puritan conceived of laws simply as guides to the individual conscience. The individual will was not to be coerced. . . . But as all men's consciences were not enlightened, laws were proper to set men to thinking, to declare to them what their fellows thought on this point and that, and to afford guides to those whose consciences did not speak with assurance. . . . [M]any still think of law after the Puritan fashion." Pound, *The Limits of Effective Legal Action*, 3 A.B.A.J. 55 (1917).

Query whether legislation declaring it a crime to use artificial birth control devices, certainly an expression of the moral and religious views of a substantial segment of the community, known by the legislature to be completely unenforced but yet continued in effect notwithstanding numerous bills asking for repeal, is an illustration of just such a view of the law. See Poe v. Ullman, 367 U.S. 497, *rehearing denied,* 368 U.S. 869 (1961).

wisdom of using the criminal law for this purpose is frequently questioned, both on the ground that this educational objective cannot be realized and on the ground that it compounds the difficulties of law enforcement.[83] Yet it would be next to impossible to remove these provisions from the statute books. As Thurman Arnold has written:

> Most unenforced criminal laws survive in order to satisfy moral objections to established modes of conduct. They are unenforced because we want to continue our conduct, and unrepealed because we want to preserve our morals.[84]

The observation that these laws are not enforced is not a new one. It has been made repeatedly over the years,[85] though opinion differs as to whether the blame lies upon the legislators for making laws without regard to the practicalities of enforcement[86] or upon the nonenforcing administrators.[87]

---

[83] "However impressive the state-declared ideal may be to the contemplative observer, the spectacle of statutory precepts with penal sanctions, which are not and perhaps are not intended to be put in force in practice, casts doubt upon the whole penal code and educates in disrespect for law more than the high pronouncement can educate for virtue." POUND, *op. cit. supra* note 81, at 67.
See also Pound, *supra* note 82; Taft, *The Legislature and the Execution of the Laws*, 12 REP. PA. BAR ASS'N 239 (1906). Compare:
"Admitting that these moral qualities cannot be legislated into human beings by *fiat* of the State, does it necessarily follow that such legislation is futile and meddlesome? In other words, where legislation holds men to certain standards of conduct which have moral implications, must it be said that the purpose of such legislation is to instill into them the moral qualities on which such standards are based and that since moral qualities cannot be created by law, the legislation is therefore bad? . . . In other words, the aim of the law is not to accomplish the hopeless task of altering human character, but merely to insist on conformity of conduct to a standard deemed advisable for the protection of the other individuals who compose the community." Dickinson, *Legislation and the Effectiveness of Law*, 37 REP. PA. BAR ASS'N 337, 348-49 (1931).
[84] ARNOLD, THE SYMBOLS OF GOVERNMENT 160 (1935). See also, Cohen, *Positivism and the Limits of Idealism in the Law*, 27 COLUM. L. REV. 237, 246 (1927).
[85] See quote by the 17th century philosopher Spinoza in Cohen, *supra* note 84, at 247, for early recognition of this. See also, POUND, *op. cit. supra* note 81, at 67; ARNOLD, *op. cit. supra* note 84, at 160.
[86] "Successfully to understand the science of practical lawmaking requires close observation of the nature, customs and traditions of the people to be affected by the laws, the degree of efficiency of the persons to be charged with their execution, the method by which such executives are to be selected, the difficulties with which those violating the laws may be brought to justice, and many other circumstances . . . . The tendency of Legislatures in the enactment of such laws is to pass them and then rid themselves of the responsibilities for their enforcement by saying that the duty of enforcement rests on the executive and not on the legislative branch." Taft, *supra* note 83, at 244-45.
[87] "If we thus come to the conclusion that in the last analysis the effectiveness of law depends not so much on the nature of the subject-matter dealt with as on the particular forces of support or opposition which from time to time make for or against the enforcement of the law, it seems impossible

Much of the sexual misconduct between adults which is engaged in by consent and which is not abnormal or homosexual in nature is prohibited by statute. Yet, while again few of these violations come to the attention of the police, there is a very clear pattern of nonenforcement in this area. While some states prohibit single isolated acts of intercourse between nonmarried adults by fornication statutes,[88] this conduct is no more a matter of official concern there than in states without such a statute. Arrest for adultery is also very unusual, even where the police receive a complaint from an offended spouse[89] or other official agency.[90] Finally, even where the statutes do not require that cohabitation be open and notorious,[91] the police do not regularly invoke the process as to this conduct except in cases of substantially notorious cohabitation. As to all of these statutes, it might be said that they reflect the legislatively-expressed ideals of the community but yet are not to be used to force compliance by those who do not conform.

E. Conduct Possibly Presently Proscribed Only Because of Legislative Inaction

Illustration #6: A police officer came upon a merchant who was operating his business on Sunday. Such conduct was prohibited by a Sunday blue law, passed in 1860, covering all gainful employment. The officer knew that for years merchants had operated on Sunday. No action was taken.

It would be incorrect to assume that the sum total of all the existing criminal statutes of a given state reflects the current attitudes of the lawmakers there. Hundreds of laws are added to the statute books yearly, so that today's criminal law contains many

to say that legislation is futile merely for the reason that it deals with this or that subject-matter. . . .·What we need rather is to say that legislation is useless if no honest and sincere attempt is made to enforce it; but when that is the case the blame belongs to the administrative departments charged with enforcing the law, and not to the Legislature which enacted it." Dickinson, *supra* note 83, at 355.

[88] *E.g.*, Wis. Stat. § 944.15 (1959). Twenty-eight states consider single, isolated acts of sexual intercourse as no crime at all. Bensing, *A Comparative Study of American Sex Statutes*, 42 J. Crim. L., C. & P.S. 57, 69 (1951).

[89] For example; a policewoman in a Michigan county sheriff's department was heard to tell a telephone caller, "If you don't sign a delinquency complaint there's not much we can do for you." After the conversation was over the policewoman explained that the caller had found his wife and his sixteen year old daughter together with two young men in an automobile behind the tavern he owned, all engaged in sexual intercourse. She explained that the complainant had called once before and was told at that time that the only possible crime involved was contributing to the delinquency of a minor.

[90] See illustration· #5 in text.

[91] *E.g.*, Mich. Stat. Ann § 28.567. See· People v. Smith, 231 Mich. 221; 203 N.W. 869 (1925).

200   WISCONSIN LAW REVIEW   [Vol. 1962

provisions which found their way therein because of "the mood that dominated a tribunal or a legislature at strategic moments in the past, a flurry of public excitement on some single matter, [or] the imitative aspects of so much of our penal legislation."[92] Many of these statutes are forgotten in time, few are repealed, and over a period of years a great mass of legislation accumulates.

Legislative inaction on the problem of updating the criminal law is the rule country-wide. The legislators have instead devoted their time and energies to other activities more responsive to popular demand. Those few states which have accomplished recodification have done so only after very substantial periods of operation under admittedly obsolete statutes.[93] Even these states have not excised all the obsolete provisions, as a majority of the criminal proscriptions are usually found outside the criminal code itself.

A very substantial range of discretion is exercised by the police in not making arrests for conduct proscribed by statutes thought to be obsolete. Although no attempt has been made to categorize those provisions which the law enforcers treat as out of date, comparison of the observed practice with the entire range of legislative proscriptions leaves no doubt that this is so. In not invoking the process in these cases, the police are once again deciding as to what conduct the legislature does not desire enforcement in the ordinary case. Admittedly, this situation is different than noninvocation based upon actual interpretation of ambiguous language or noninvocation based upon conclusions that the statute was enacted for purposes other than full enforcement, both discussed earlier. Here police inaction is based upon the supposition that the statute involved would be repealed could the present legislature be sufficiently directed toward reconsideration of the provision. But, the present situation is analytically akin to the others in that, to the extent to which the police are correct in their beliefs, there is no

---

[92] Wechsler, *The Challenge of a Model Penal Code,* 65 HARV. L. REV. 1097, 1101 (1952).

[93] Thus the 1953 Wisconsin revision, which had among its objectives "simplifying the criminal law by removing obsolete material," was accomplished as to a body of laws which had not been thoroughly revised since their enactment in 1847. See 5 WIS. LEGIS. COUNCIL, JUDICIARY COMMITTEE REPORT ON THE CRIMINAL CODE i-ii (1953). Similarly, the 1961 Illinois revision was the first over-all revision of their Criminal Code since 1874, though the Judicial Council had reported the acute need for revision because of outdated laws to the governor and assembly in 1931, and though the state bar had presented drafts to the assembly in 1935, 1937, and 1939. PROPOSED ILLINOIS REVISED CRIMINAL CODE OF 1961, 3-4 (Tentative final draft 1960).

difference in policy judgment between the legislature and the police.[94]

Of course, these laws are still a part of the enforceable criminal law notwithstanding the circumstances of their continued existence. A legislative enactment cannot be rendered ineffective by nonuse or obsolescence, nor repealed by the failure of the administrators to enforce it.[95] This being so, there is no agreement on the propriety of police not arresting those violating statutes thought to be obsolete. Some think that only by such discretionary action, somewhere in the process, can we be freed from the ideas of past generations.[96] Implicit here is an attitude that the creation of sufficient incentive in the legislators to bring about repeal is not likely to be forthcoming. The following excerpt, though principally addressed to judicial nonenforcement, is a good statement of the directly contrary view.

> If the judiciary, influenced doubtless by the sincerest motives for the public welfare, did not tend to assume a quasi-legislative attitude in the interpretation and application of enactments of this character, the popular demand would necessitate the repeal of the laws in question . . . . Where the law, as declared, is judicially conformed to accord with the people's will, as conceived by the court, the generality of people remain in ignorance of their representatives' actual declarations. There is a necessary fiction in the administration of justice that all men know the law. The citizen who gains an actual knowledge of a law through its application to his own case and is dis-

---

[94] Furthermore, the level of nonenforcement of the obsolete law does not appear to change significantly depending upon the amount of enforcement resources provided, so this situation cannot be classified with those in the following section.

[95] District of Columbia v. John R. Thompson Co., 346 U.S. 100 (1953) (where it was no defense that the statute apparently had not been enforced for 78 years); Jayhawk Const. Co. v. City of Topeka, 176 Kan. 517, 271 P.2d 769 (1954); Board of County Road Comm'rs v. Michigan Pub. Serv. Comm'n, 349 Mich. 663, 85 N.W.2d 134 (1957); 1 SUTHERLAND, STATUTORY CONSTRUCTION § 2034 (3d ed. 1943).

> "On the Continent there was some speculation during the middle ages as to whether a law could become inoperative through long-continued desuetude. In England, however, the idea of prescription and the acquisition or loss of rights merely by the lapse of a particular length of time found little favour. . . . There was consequently no room for any theory that statutes might become obsolete. PLUCKNETT, A CONCISE HISTORY OF THE COMMON LAW 301 (2d ed. 1936).

A clear pattern of nonenforcement, however, may make it impossible for the statute's constitutionality to be challenged in court. Poe v. Ullman, *supra* note 82. Harlan, in dissent, said:

> "Indeed it appears that whereas appellants would surely have been entitled to review were this a new statute, . . . the State here is enabled to maintain at least some substantial measure of compliance with this statute and still obviate any review in this Court, by the device of purely discretionary prosecutorial inactivity." *Id.* at 537.

[96] POUND, *op. cit. supra* note 81, at 42.

satisfied therewith, may vote to compass its repeal. Knowledge in this regard is power. There is no more certain manner in which this knowledge can be disseminated than by the literal application and enforcement of all statutes by the courts.[97]

But, the one principal objection made to the latter view is that the harm from such enforcement program cannot be justified by the possible good in terms of an impetus toward law revision. Thus, even an opponent of police discretion has concluded that

> too many people have come to rely on the nonenforcement of too many "obsolete" laws to justify the embarrassment, discomfort, and misery which would follow implementation of *full enforcement* programs for every crime. *Full enforcement* is a program for the future. . . . when the states . . . enact new criminal codes clearing the books of obsolete offenses.[98]

Indeed, one court has expressed the position that for the law enforcers to proceed with enforcement, after a substantial period of nonenforcement of a statute as to which noncompliance has become a matter of custom, amounts to "a decision legislative in character" and therefore not correctly theirs to make.[99] The rationale of this position would seem to be that legislative acquiescence in the long continued practice of nonenforcement amounts to a legislative determination that enforcement is no longer desired, a policy the enforcement agencies would not be complying with by now proceeding against the conduct.[100]

---

[97] Mitchell, *Legislative and Judicial Desiderata*, 25 REP. N.Y.S.B.A. 289, 301 (1902). See also, Williams, *Turning a Blind Eye*, 1954 CRIM. L. REV. (Eng.) 271, 273; Goldstein, *supra* note 47, at 586-87; HAYEK, THE CONSTITUTION OF LIBERTY 155 (1960).

[98] Goldstein, *supra* note 47, at 588.

[99] In John R. Thompson Co. v. District of Columbia, 92 App. D.C. 34, 203 F.2d 579 (D.C. Cir. 1953), the court, although holding a criminal statute on refusal to serve a Negro unenforceable on other grounds, added:

"But we think it appropriate to comment, in this connection, that the enactments having lain unenforced for 78 years, in the face of a custom of race disassociation in the District, the decision of the municipal authorities to enforce them now, by the prosecution of the instant case, was, in effect, a decision legislative in character. That is to say, it was a determination that the enactments reflect a social policy which is now correct, although it was not correct—else the enactments would have been enforced—heretofore. Such a decision were better left, we think, to the Congress." *Id.* at 48, 203 F.2d at 592.

[100] If this position were accepted, it undoubtedly would have to be restricted to cases in which the inaction was based upon supposed obsolescence, and where lack of legislative complaint has the same basis. As the Supreme Court has observed, "We know that unquestioned powers are sometimes unexercised from lack of funds, motives of expediency, or the competition of more immediately important concerns." United States v. Morton Salt Co., 338 U.S. 632, 647-48 (1950).

III. Police Discretion in Practice: Noninvocation Because Limited Enforcement Resources Are Allocated to Other Conduct Thought More Deserving of Official Action

Once the police have determined what they perceive to be the conduct (of all that proscribed) as to which the legislature actually desires enforcement, further discretion is still exercised in carrying out the enforcement program. In the existing criminal justice system it can be no other way. As Thurman Arnold has said, denying discretion at this point ". . . is like directing a general to attack the enemy on all fronts at once."[101] The police and other enforcement agencies are given the general responsibility of maintaining law and order, are provided with a criminal law defining the various kinds of conduct against which they may properly proceed, and are then furnished with enforcement resources less than adequate to accomplish the entire task. Consequently, discretionary enforcement occurs in an attempt to realize the greatest results from these limited means. In this sense the budgetary appropriation is an establishment of policy (the general level of enforcement for which the public is willing to pay) and a delegation of power by the legislative to administrative branch.[102]

This selective enforcement program means that much of the criminal conduct coming to the attention of the police, by observation or even by complaint, cannot be subjected to official action. Often a warning is given; this is a form of action least demanding on the enforcement resources. Though the issuance of warnings generally takes place on a haphazard basis, it does appear sufficient as to certain trivial offenses, and consequently invocation is not thought necessary as to them. Even more serious offenses may not receive invocation when the police view the conduct as conforming to the norms of certain elements of the community thought not susceptible to change by more strict enforcement. Also, unless the offense is of a serious nature, the police do not consider it appropriate for consumption of their scarce resources when not even the victim is seriously interested in prosecution. Likewise, the victim, because of his own conduct, may not be thought worthy of receiving satisfaction by invocation of the criminal process. Factors such as

---

[101] Arnold, *op. cit. supra* note 84, at 153.

[102] See Wilson, Police Planning 20 (2d ed. 1957).

WISCONSIN LAW REVIEW   [Vol. 1962

these influence the police in their fashioning of enforcement priorities.[103]

Before proceeding to the particular criteria employed, one general observation can be made. Undoubtedly the arrest policies of the police affect greatly the rate of intake of the other agencies in the process—the prosecutor's office, the courts, the prisons and the correctional agencies. While the burden on these agencies is lessened by the various noninvocation decisions of the police, no affirmative evidence has been found indicating that the police follow a particular pattern of nonenforcement specifically to avoid a strain upon the resources of another agency. Rather, noninvocation is to conserve *police* enforcement resources, either those which would be used in the arrest-booking-detention process or those necessarily involved in later stages of the process.[104]

A. Triviality of Deviation Indicates Warning Will Suffice

Police manuals typically advise the officer that warning rather than arrest is appropriate where only minor violations are concerned.[105] In order to conserve resources for other, more serious conduct, warnings are frequently used where it is thought that the cost of invocation outweighs any benefits received thereby which could not be accomplished by this on-the-spot device.

Illustration #7: A police officer observed a motorist make an

---

[103] Of course, not all police attempts to allocate law enforcement resources can be said to involve arrest decisions. In a large part, priorities of enforcement are set by the manner in which a particular police agency is organized. The extent to which manpower is allocated to subagencies whose function is to discover particular kinds of crime may be particularly revealing.

[104] It should not be concluded, however, that the predictable action at these subsequent stages of the process has no bearing on police allocation of enforcement resources. It does in the sense that invocation is to be avoided where it is thought to be futile. If it is thought that charging or conviction is very unlikely, because of the attitudes of these later decision-makers, then perhaps no arrest will be made. Similarly, if the predictable punishment is thought to be inappropriate—either too strict or too lenient, invocation is less likely, unless the police have means of influencing the nature of the penalty. Also, if the conduct is such that it is thought the criminal process cannot provide the kind or amount of punishment, deterrence, or rehabilitation needed, the police may again devote their resources to other cases. Combinations of these factors will appear in the situations which follow.

[105] *E.g.,* Detroit and Milwaukee police are cautioned that "a polite warning" will suffice for "minor violations" and that arrests should not be made in such cases unless the violations are "willful or repeated." DETROIT, MICH., POLICE DEP'T, REVISED POLICE MANUAL, ch. 16, § 34 (1955); MILWAUKEE, WIS., POLICE DEP'T, RULES & REGULATIONS, Rule 30, § 31 (1950). Wichita police, in their "square deal code," are cautioned to "save unfortunate offenders from unnecessary humiliation, inconvenience and distress" and "never to arrest if a summons will suffice; never to summons if a warning would be better." WICHITA, KAN., POLICE DEP'T DUTY MANUAL i (undated).

illegal left turn. The officer stopped the driver, brought the violation to his attention, but did not make an arrest and did not write a ticket.

Use of the warning device for minor traffic offenses is a common occurrence. Indeed it is so well known that protests follow if an officer does invoke the process in such a case.[106] Even sharp critics of police nonenforcement acknowledge the necessity of employing such an alternative in these cases.[107] The great volume of these offenses does not allow otherwise.[108]

Officers engaged in traffic enforcement indicated it is entirely within the discretion of the individual patrolman whether to issue a warning rather than a regular citation in a particular case. Specific guidance as to what kinds of cases deserve warnings only is rarely given, except perhaps for an indication of toleration levels on speeding.[109] The result is that warnings are sometimes given for illegal turns, rolling stops, and the like, but the process is invoked against the identical conduct on other occasions, and it is not possible to determine any uniform enforcement pattern in this area. Invocation is the rule, however, if the violation created a condition in which a person was actually injured or was put in an unsafe situation.[110] Of course, when experience shows that a warning has not been effective against a particular violator, then actual invocation of the process against him can be expected.

Illustration #8: A police officer was called to a store where

---

[106] La Fave, *supra* note 78, at 129 n.98.

[107] *E.g.*, one writer, after asserting the police should enforce *all* the law, adds: "Nor is it really relevant to point out that the police in this country do already exercise some degree of discrimination in the enforcement of the law. Many traffic offenders, for example, receive a word of advice on the spot instead of a summons. That speaks merely for the good sense of the police, and for our good fortune in being served by sensible officers. The point is that these are exceptions to the general rule, and are made under strictly controlled conditions, for a particular purpose . . . ." Williams, *supra* note 97, at 272.
His justification for the exception seems questionable, as it is not readily apparent that there is any greater control over noninvocation here than in other areas.

[108] In one study it was concluded that in Berkeley, California, three million traffic violations were occurring daily, full enforcement of which would require 14,000 traffic officers. CALIF. STATE DEP'T OF EDUCATION, CALIF. PEACE OFFICERS TRAINING PUBLICATION NO. 71, POLICE SUPERVISORY CONTROL 26 (1957).

[109] *E.g.*, the radar unit in one Wisconsin community was instructed that, when operating in a 25 m.p.h. zone, speeds up to 32 m.p.h. were to be ignored, speeds from 32 to 38 m.p.h. were cases for warning cards, and speeds above 38 m.p.h. were to receive regular traffic citations.

[110] Observations accord with the statement of a sheriff in another state that "public safety is our rule" and that therefore a speeder on a lonely road would not be arrested but another driver at the same place and proceeding at the same speed would be if the traffic was heavy. Esselstyn, Crime and Its Control in the Hinterland 198 (unpublished Ph.D. thesis, New York Univ., 1952).

206   WISCONSIN LAW REVIEW   [Vol. 1962

a youth had been apprehended shoplifting some minor items. The officer administered a severe warning and then allowed the youth to go his way. No further action was contemplated, as the officer knew the youth had not been in trouble before.

That juvenile offenders receive special treatment is common knowledge. In particular, it is known that the juvenile is afforded different treatment later in the process—the juvenile court versus the criminal court—but it is not as frequently recognized that he may be specially treated at the outset so as to never enter the process at all. Rather, if the offense is not serious he may be given a warning and sent on his way. Warning without arrest frequently occurs in the smaller cities,[111] but in the larger metropolitan areas such as Detroit and Milwaukee the warning alternative is more apt to be selected after arrest except in the more minor cases.[112] Yet such dispositions by individual patrolmen are still numerous.[113]

The police deem it appropriate not to invoke as to petty juvenile

---

[111] Thus, the chief of police in a small Michigan city indicated that petty juvenile offenses are dealt with on an informal basis, and without the necessity of making an arrest. He further indicated that this method of settling these kinds of cases "behind the kitchen stove" is particularly suited to a small town, though it probably is not possible in a larger city.

[112] In a smaller town the officer may know on the spot whether the youth is a first offender or a habitual trouble-maker, or in any event may know he can easily locate the youth later if need be. But, arrest is likely in the larger city. The Detroit Police Manual instructs:

> "All violators under the age of twenty-one (21) years [who are guilty of purchasing, possessing, or transporting intoxicating beverages] shall be brought into the Precinct Station, and if it is determined that this is their first offense and there are no aggravated conditions involved, all such minors or juveniles may be released with a warning except juvenile girls [who will be transported home by the Women's Division]. . . .
>
> "The provisions of this procedure may be applied to other types of cases involving juveniles and minors found in disorderly parties or other difficulties where liquor violations are not involved." DETROIT, MICH., POLICE DEP'T, REVISED POLICE MANUAL, ch. 12, § 74 (1955).

The Milwaukee regulations put the invocation question in the hands of supervisory officers, suggesting arrest first is likely.

> "Whenever a juvenile case is brought before any commanding officer, and in his judgment the offense involved is of a minor nature and the case can consistently be kept out of the Juvenile Court, such commanding officer may release the offender with a reprimand." MILWAUKEE, WIS., POLICE DEP'T, RULES & REGULATIONS, Rule 32, § 9 (1950).

In Wichita, juvenile officers are told to "dispose of all juvenile offenders in the way that will be to the best interest of the offender and to society in general." WICHITA, KAN., POLICE DEP'T, DUTY MANUAL 61 (undated). Sometimes these juvenile officers do not enter the case until after arrest, but it is not uncommon for a patrolman in Wichita to radio for a juvenile officer and have him make the determination on the spot.

[113] See CARR, DELINQUENCY CONTROL 150 (1940), where it is said that in a city such as Detroit the police annually make from 10,000 to 14,000 non-official contacts in which a youngster may be reproved or admonished because of undesirable conduct. Of these, only one in three will be apprehended and placed in the detention home, and less than one in seven will be brought before juvenile court.

offenders for a number of reasons. It may be thought that resources can better be applied elsewhere because a severe warning is apt to accomplish just as much as a more involved process. Or, sometimes just the opposite occurs; no resources are expended because the police feel that the court will be too lenient, thereby accomplishing little.[114] Although the exact level of toleration of juvenile offenders cannot be stated with any great certainty, chances of invocation are great when force or violence has been used against an innocent victim outside the juvenile's social group. Nonviolent property crimes are considered less worthy of invocation unless the amount involved is great or the technique is professional in nature.[115] And of course the juvenile's past record is deemed to be very important; it is because of this factor that the invocation decision must sometimes wait until after arrest.[116]

Noninvocation to conserve resources because the triviality of the offense indicates the sufficiency of mere warning is of course not limited to the situations described above. It occurs as to other minor offenses as well. The policy factors usually involved are indicated by the above examples, however.

B. Conduct Not Thought to Deviate from the Standards of the Subgroup of the Community Involved

Illustration #9: A call came into the station of a precinct predominantly Negro in population that a stabbing had taken place. An officer reported to the address, an apartment, and

---

[114] Such opinions were not infrequently voiced by the police, and were particularly vehement when the police had expended a considerable amount of their resources. For example, one Detroit officer said, "We may go around here for months trying to figure out who in hell is committing a bunch of petty crimes. We finally may have apprehended the guy and brought him before a judge. But, since he is a juvenile, he probably gets off easy."

[115] Though the juvenile problem was not studied in great detail, the observations made seem entirely consistent with the conclusions reached in another study with such a focus. It was there noted that auto theft was considered serious by the police and that burglary and robbery generally resulted in invocation unless it was very minor and restitution was made. Sex relations between juveniles and without coercion do not often result in invocation unless abnormal in nature. Purse snatching is usually looked upon as a grave offense—an attack on the weaker sex—and restitution will rarely bar invocation. Shoplifting and other larceny is not generally considered worthy of invocation if the victim will accept restitution. The mode of commission of the offense may be significant. Carefully planned offenses professional in nature (such as burglary using burlary tools) are viewed as much more serious than offenses committed on impulse. Use of force is an important factor, as is the fact that the offense was committed at night. Goldman, The Differential Selection of Juvenile Offenders for Court Appearance 148-56 (unpublished Ph.D. thesis, Dep't of Sociology, Univ. of Chicago, 1950).

[116] While the taking of a juvenile offender to headquarters for a check on his record is an arrest, it may not be recorded as such if it is later decided that the youth will be released with a warning.

learned that a woman had seriously stabbed her husband with a pair of scissors. The parties were Negroes. The husband commented that there had been a little argument, and requested transportation to the hospital. The officer who served in the precinct for some time and was not unaccustomed to such a response when answering similar calls. Although the conduct constituted a felonious assault, no official action was taken.

Discrimination, or what might be called discrimination, may take many forms in law enforcement. One possibility, of course, is that members of minority groups may be arrested or perhaps carried even farther on in the process though they are guilty of no criminal conduct; this quite obviously is improper. A second possibility is unequal enforcement of the law with respect to minority groups in the sense that laws generally not enforced are enforced against minority groups. This, of course, is a serious matter, particularly since it is not likely that the arrested offenders will be able to prevent having the process invoked against them on this basis.[117] A third possibility, and the one under consideration here, is the failure to enforce certain laws only against members of certain minority groups.

This kind of unequal enforcement of the law against Negroes resulted in such offenses as bigamy and open and notorious cohabitation being overlooked by law enforcement officials,[118] and in arrests not being made for carrying knives or for robbery of other Negroes. However, this unequal enforcement is most strikingly illustrated by the repeated failure of the police to arrest Negroes guilty of felonious assault with knives or other such instruments upon their spouses or acquaintances unless the victim emphatically requests prosecution.

The typical officer, particularly if he has been assigned to a Negro area for any length of time, has become used to the double standard and applies it without quesction.[119] Whether settling dif-

---

[117] In People v. Winters, 171 Cal. App. 2d Supp. 876, 342 P.2d 538 (Super. Ct. 1959), the court reversed a Negro trial judge's dismissal of a case upon the basis of discriminatory enforcement of the gambling laws against Negroes, but without prejudice to the defendant's right to prove intentional or deliberate discriminatory enforcement, which would appear a formidable task.

[118] These offenses came to official attention principally when aid to dependent children was sought or when a domestic dispute was being dealt with.

[119] Certainly one exception was an officer who reflected that perhaps the department should begin signing complaints in these cases over the protest of the victim. This officer appeared principally concerned with cutting down the number of calls to the police. His thought that a change in policy would result in fewer victims calling the police is an interesting one. If this would be the result of this change in policy, it might be asked whether it is more desirable that Negro crime be more visible but judged by a lower standard, or less visible and thus often not judged at all.

ferences with a knife can properly be called the established standard of behavior for Negroes in these areas might be questioned, but this is certainly the conclusion the patrolman in the Negro area reaches after having responded to a great number of these incidents.[120] The police apparently feel that they are justified in refraining from taking a more active role in the case because they maintain that this is the method by which these people prefer to settle their differences. Added to this is the fact that in the usual case the victim of the felonious assault does not desire prosecution of the offender. Indeed, arrest of the offender often is not even desired; the police were called because the victim wanted free ambulance service to the hospital. Thus, while victim attitude is important elsewhere as well (as discussed in the immediately following section), only here does the victim regularly control the invocation process even in the more serious cases. Finally, with the Negro press sometimes accusing the police of discrimination solely because more Negro arrests are being made than white arrests,[121] these inter-Negro offenses where the victim does not desire prosecution appear to be the best instances in which not to make an arrest, thereby keeping down the Negro arrest statistics. The combination of these factors influences the police not to expend a substantial portion of their resources on inter-Negro crime.

Having said all this in explanation of the practice of not invoking the process against Negro offenders under the circumstances enumerated, it cannot be contended that this double standard of enforcement is justified. The basic question still remains: To what extent, if at all, is it appropriate to take into account the customs, practices and prevailing standard of conduct of an identifiable subcultural group in determining whether the process should

---

[120] Thus he does not come into contact with the law-abiding Negro, but only the law-breaking Negro.

[121] Frequent criticism of the Negro press was heard, not unlike that reported in another study which focused more directly on racial problems in law enforcement, KEPHART, RACIAL FACTORS AND URBAN LAW ENFORCEMENT (1957). There one Philadelphia policeman is quoted as saying:

"I don't know what the answer is. I think the Negro press plays up the wrong angle. Sometimes they hurt things instead of helping. It's got so now that some white cops hate to arrest a Negro. They know if there's any trouble the press will play it up to look bad for the cop." *Id.* at 66.

Similarly, a Negro patrolman, when asked if he was discouraged over the high Negro crime rate, replied:

"No, I don't get discouraged. It's just being handled all wrong. The cops, the magistrates, the judges—everybody's afraid to crack down, especially with the Negro Press yelling discrimination all the time." *Id.* at 119.

Kephart indicates that the police interviewed, of all ranks and both races, agreed on condemnation of local Negro newspapers. *Id.* at 147.

be invoked against a member of that group?[122] The nature of the problem is exposed very well by the comments of a Negro assistant prosecutor. Bringing up the difficulty of getting law enforcement officials, judges, juries, and the Negroes themselves to take Negro crimes of violence seriously, he said:

> Negroes have been struggling for many years to secure their civil and legal rights through such organizations as the NAACP, but there has been too little emphasis placed upon the Negro's duty to assume responsibility for acts of violence and not to expect differential treatment. But, it will take cooperation by the white people as well. There is too much of a tendency on the part of police officers, juries, and even judges to dismiss Negro crimes of violence with the saying, "It's only Negroes, and they've always been like that." Too many Negroes expect to escape lightly in crimes of this nature, and with some justification, as the whites in authority have actually condoned such offenses by taking them so lightly.

The dilemma he put is that the Negro continues to be judged by a different standard because he lives by a different standard, and he continues to live by a different standard because he is judged by a different standard.

C. Victim Does Not or Will Not Seriously Desire Prosecution

Another principal area in which the police believe it appropriate that enforcement resources not be expended in any substantial amount is that of the nonserious offense where the victim does not indicate a desire to expend his own time in the interest of successful prosecution. That police noninvocation should occur here in order to conserve resources is not surprising. The unwillingness of the victim may make conviction difficult or impossible. Also, with the victim not desiring prosecution, it is likely he contacted the authorities because of some other motive, as to which it is thought there is a lesser need for response by the criminal process. And, with many of these cases arising out of a private relationship, resolution of the difficulty without prosecution may appear to be a reasonable alternative.

1. Victim Interested Only in Restitution

---

[122] The criminal law has rarely considered cultural differences, although the problem has arisen when a given set of laws has been imposed upon territories with a population unlike that of the lawmakers. See Howard, *What Colour is the Reasonable Man"?*, 1961 Crim. L. Rev. (Eng.) 41; Marsack, *Provocation in Trials for Murder*, 1959 Crim. L. Rev. (Eng.) 697.

Illustration #10: A merchant called the police after having apprehended a shoplifter in his store. The officer asked the merchant whether he was willing to appear in court to testify, and the latter responded that he could not take time out from his work for this. The officer declined to arrest the shoplifter.

Illustration #11: A merchant turned over a "no account" check to the police, requesting apprehension of the writer. The merchant was asked whether he was willing to appear in court when the offender was prosecuted, and he responded that he only wanted to collect the amount of the check. The police refused to take any action.

The criminal process is usually not invoked as to minor offenses reported to the police, in which small amounts of property have been taken without force or violence, unless the victim sincerely indicates he desires prosecution and is willing to cooperate in the prosecution of the case. One kind of situation is that in which the police, after investigation of the offense, bring about the recovery of all or a substantial portion of the stolen property. In such a case it is most likely that the victim will express a desire that the matter be dropped, rather than take the time to appear in court, and the police usually do not invoke when such an attitude has been expressed. Cases of larceny and sometimes even burglary are concluded in this fashion.[123]

Probably the most significant category of conduct in which recovery of the property concludes the victim's interest in the case is shoplifting. To the extent that shoplifters are caught, they are usually apprehended in the act, meaning immediate recovery of the goods taken. Merchants generally indicate an unwillingness to prosecute at that point, asserting that they cannot afford the time away from the store to testify in court or the supposed loss of good will which would result.

The police may be equally hesitant to act when the victim has not yet recovered his property but appears to desire police assistance only for purposes of obtaining restitution. Thus, when a minor property crime is reported, the first inquiry concerns the willingness to prosecute. While this may occur in a great variety

---

[123] However, if in any of these cases the police have already expended considerable resources in investigating the offense, the police are less likely to defer to the victim's wishes. In fact, in such a case steps will probably be taken to commit the victim to participation in the prosecution.

of situations,[124] the most frequently recurring one is that of the report of a bad check by a merchant. For example, instructions for Detroit detectives handling bad check cases read, "Is the complainant willing to prosecute? (If the check is being reported merely as an aid to collection, the police department is not interested, and the check cannot be accepted as a complaint.)" Insuring that the complainant will prosecute is deemed most essential when some expense would be involved in preparing the case for prosecution.[125]

Sometimes bad check complainants are referred to the prosecutor's office. One reason for this is that going through the complaint-warrant process first tends to commit the complainant to carry out his promise to aid in prosecution of the offender. Secondly, to the extent that the criminal process is to be used *only* for restitution, not only do the police view this as an inappropriate object for the expenditure of their own resources (as opposed to those of the prosecutor's office), there is authority to the effect that an arrest to promote restitution is illegal.[126]

Thus, with the police viewing application of their resources to minor property crimes where the victim desires restitution as inappropriate, they can again devote more time to other offenses higher on the police priority list. Not only are they saved from the time which would have to be spent attempting to obtain a conviction in a case with a reluctant victim-witness, their policy

---

[124] Thus, when a woman called precinct headquarters and reported that in the course of paying for her meal in a restaurant she had been bilked out of some money, the lieutenant answering the call suggested she report to the station so that a complaint could be made out against the person who had cheated her. When the woman indicated she only wanted her money back, the lieutenant said, "Then, madam, you have the wrong department. Please call the lonely hearts club." He then hung up the phone.

[125] These instructions continue:

"It is well to caution the complainant that in the event that the check is drawn on an out-of-state bank account, unless the writer of the check admits that he has no account (or insufficient funds in that bank) it will be necessary for the county to bring in an officer from that bank to testify as to the status of the defendant's account (or lack of it). For that reason, the complainant may be required to post a cash bond guaranteeing prosecution in the case."

[126] Bergeron v. Peyton, 106 Wis. 377, 82 N.W. 291 (1900). There an officer took Bergeron to the bank where he had been overpaid on a check and when Bergeron refused to return the excess, the officer took him to the magistrate. Since the jury found the arrest was "for the sole purpose of compelling and inducing him to repay . . . the $43 thus overpaid," the court held the arrest illegal and the officer liable in damages, though the officer had taken the offender directly to the magistrate when he refused the opportunity to make restitution. But a Kansas case, apparently in answer to an assertion that an arrest had been made to influence payment of a debt, said that "if the arrest was lawful the motive for it was immaterial," but that the arrest must have been made "in good faith." Atchison, T. & S.F. Ry. v. Hinsdell, 76 Kans. 74, 90 Pac. 800 (1907).

of not aiding merchants seeking only restitution results in fewer complaints being made to the police.[127]

2. *Victim in Continuing Legitimate Relationship with Offender and Interested Primarily in Restitution or Vengeance*

> *Illustration #12:* An officer responded to a call only to learn that the complainant wanted his neighbor arrested for tearing down a part of his fence. The officer's investigation disclosed that this was merely the latest chapter in an ongoing neighborhood dispute between the complainant and offender. Although the property destruction was a criminal violation. the officer declined to take any official action.

A slightly different combination of factors may make for non-invocation when the criminal conduct occurs between two persons who are in a continuing legitimate relationship with each other— neighbors, landlord and tenant, parties to a contract, and the like. Generally, the feeling here is that, as long as the conduct is not serious, the dispute is principally private in nature, so that enforcement resources need not be diverted to it.

That the criminal process should not be invoked when the conduct involved only allows a possible civil action is clear. The police are warned against acting in such cases in the absence of a breach of the peace,[128] and do refuse assistance in these cases. However, invocation may also be denied where criminal conduct has taken place within this legitimate relationship and civil remedies are available to the injured party. The reason is essentially the same: not only does the presence of a civil remedy indicate invocation is unnecessary, it also suggests it would be unfair to allow the criminal process to be used to benefit one of these disputants. The fact the victim can bring an end to his difficulty by terminating the relationship is also often important. Thus a landlord was advised to evict his tenant when he wanted criminal action commenced against a member of the tenant's household who

---

[127] One inspector in the Detroit department read from some statistical sheets on his desk and then said, "There was an 11% drop in complaints, department-wide, from 1955 to 1956. This was due to greater selectivity in taking a case from a merchant who would indicate from the outset that he would be unwilling to prosecute on an NSF check."

[128] Detroit police are told:

> "Members of the Department shall render no assistance whatever in civil cases, or advise parties involved, except to prevent a breach of the peace or to quell a disturbance actually commenced." Detroit, Mich., Police Dep't, Revised Police Manual, ch. 10, § 25 (1955).

Similarly, in Wichita the police are instructed:

> "Officers shall not render assistance in civil cases, except to prevent an immediate breach of the peace or to quell a disturbance actually commenced." Wichita, Kan., Police Dep't, Duty Manual 11 (undated).

caused malicious damage to the premises,[129] and an employer was told he could handle the situation when a burglary was found to be an "inside job" perpetrated by an employee.

Here again, when such an offense is reported to the police, the initial inquiry is apt to concern the victim's desire for prosecution. However, the police may here discourage the complainant even if he expressly asserts he desires and will cooperate in the prosecution of the offender. For one thing, they feel that the victim is often motivated by spite, and that prosecution would only strain a necessary continuing relationship (such as that of neighbors). Also, the continuing relationship makes it more likely that the parties involved will subsequently reach an amicable solution, at which point the victim would no longer desire prosecution.

3. Victim a Member of Offender's Family

Illustration #13: A call was received at precinct reporting a disturbance of the peace. The officer responding to the call found that the disturbance was due to a family squabble. Although the husband was still slapping his wife when the officer appeared on the scene, the officer did not make an arrest, but merely restored order and then went on his way.

The police are sometimes advised to avoid arrest in domestic disputes where possible. For example, the Detroit Police Manual provides:

> When a police officer is called to a disturbance in a private home having family difficulties, he should recognize the sanctity of the home and endeavor diplomatically to quell the disturbance and create peace without making an arrest.
>
> In any case where an officer suspects that a disturbance may result in the injury of any person, it is advisable for the officer to take the person causing such disturbance into custody, at least temporarily, even though it may be against the wishes of the family involved.[130]

This is the policy generally followed elsewhere as well. Officers called to a household where an assault and battery or similar

---

[129] The Michigan state policeman responding to the call learned the landlord's primary interest was having his door replaced. The trooper advised,

"That won't do very much good. He probably is smart enough to know that there is not much that can be done unless you swear out a complaint form. And then if you do that there is no telling what will happen after that. If the man does go to jail for 30 days, you still haven't got your door repaired, and in a sense you are still paying for it because you are supporting him while he is in jail. It may be that you will have to handle this case civilly. Frankly, I think the best thing for you to do would be to order these people to move and get rid of the problem that way."

[130] DETROIT, MICH. POLICE DEP'T. REVISED POLICE MANUAL, ch. 16 · 5· 22 (1955).

offense has taken place or is occurring usually attempt to restore order, using whatever means other than arrest are possible to prevent a recurrence. The police dislike becoming involved in these family disputes,[131] and calls for service may be refused when it does not appear that arrest is essential to maintaining order. This is particularly true during periods of heavy demands upon police services.

In these intrafamily disturbances involving criminal conduct not of a serious nature—minor assaults and the like, direct invocation by the police is unlikely in the absence of an expressed desire by the offended spouse for prosecution.[132] Even if the victim-spouse asserts a desire to prosecute, the officers may still refrain from arresting if it appears likely the victim will later change his or her mind. Because the police believe it is futile to expend resources on cases where the victim will later refuse to cooperate in prosecution, steps are sometimes taken to commit the victim presently indicating a desire for prosecution.[133]

D. Victim's Own Conduct Disentitles Him to Prosecution

Illustration #14: A man entered a precinct station and complained that he had just been cheated out of $20. Asked to explain, he said that he had given the money to a prostitute who had agreed to meet him at a certain time and place, but that she had failed to appear. The police, although familiar with this kind of practice, subjected the complainant to some ridicule, suggested he had learned his lesson, and sent him on his way.

---

[131] Confirming the observations from these three states is the statement of a police official quoted in another study: "You know, if there is one thing these men hate more than anything else it is to go out on a call for a family quarrel. You ought to see their faces when they hear the call come over the radio." Westley, The Police: A Sociological Study of Law, Custom and Morality 115 (unpublished Ph.D. thesis, Dep't of Sociology, Univ. of Chicago, 1951).

[132] Undoubtedly the law could be drafted so as to require such demand by the spouse here, just as with adultery or intra-family thefts. See MODEL PENAL CODE §§ 206.13(4), 207.1, comment 10 (Tent. Draft No. 4, 1955).

[133] Thus in Wichita, if the officer doubts such a presently manifested desire, the victim-spouse may be taken to the station immediately to sign a complaint before arrest, or the victim might be arrested in an attempt to insure appearance in court the following day. In Milwaukee the victim's true desires are determined by the police officer giving the spouse a referral memorandum which may be used to obtain a warrant, but the clerk of municipal court (who issues warrants in both ordinance and statute violation cases) will issue warrants for common drunk or assault upon complaint of a spouse only after a three-day "cooling-off" period. In Detroit the police go to lengths to discourage prosecution, but they may refer the spouse to the misdemeanor complaint bureau, which does undertake to mediate more serious family disputes. The full burden is on the victim to do so, however, and no arrest is made where mediation is the goal.

In allocating scarce enforcement resources to conduct most deserving of official action, the police place situations where the offense was brought about in part by the conduct of the victim low on their priority list. If the victim has knowingly and voluntarily placed himself in such a position that commission of the offense against him is possible, the process may not be invoked against the offender for this reason. We are not here concerned with the multitude of offenses which involve what might be termed a willing victim—prostitution, gambling, sale of narcotics and illegal liquor, and the like—but rather with those cases in which the victim actually complains about the offense committed after having placed himself in such a position as to make its commission possible. Such is the case, for example, where a prostitute is mistreated as a direct result of her illegal activity, or in a fight where both parties are at fault. But the most frequently observed occurrence is the man who has been tricked out of funds given to a prostitute or pimp. In this kind of case, the most frequent police reaction is that found in the illustration above. If some official action is taken it rarely goes beyond detaining of the prostitute long enough to obtain return of the money.[134]

IV. POLICE DISCRETION IN PRACTICE: NONINVOCATION BECAUSE THERE ARE REASONS FOR NOT INVOKING THE PROCESS EVEN WITH SUFFICIENT RESOURCES

Assuming it is possible to determine the scope of the proscriptions intended by the legislature, and further assuming that sufficient enforcement resources are available to allow invocation against all conduct proscribed, there would undoubtedly still be a substantial range of discretion exercised whereby the process often would not be invoked. We have just noted in the previous section various reasons why some criminal conduct is placed low on the enforcement priority scale. Given adequate resources, the

---

[134] The officers who do this but refuse to invoke the full process probably do so because of past knowledge that such a case cannot be successfully prosecuted. It is likely that the prosecutor will not approve prosecution where the complainant does not have "clean hands," and the judges are not prone to convict in these kinds of cases. For example, in one case the judge asked the complainant to explain what had happened. The complainant stated that this man took $15 from him after saying that he could obtain some girls for them. The judge asked if this was on promise that he would lead them to some girls. The complainant answered in the affirmative and indicated that the individual disappeared with the money. The judge asked once again, "And you gave him the money?" The complainant answered, "Yes." The judge said, "And you did this on Hastings Street?" Again the complainant nodded in the affirmative. The judge then said, "Case dismissed."

reasons there presented as to why invocation is less appropriate or effective as to this conduct would still influence some noninvocation, though clearly the tolerance level would be lower. In addition, other reasons totally unrelated to problems of resource allocation—such as the impossibility of legal rules which take account of the particular circumstances of the individual case—also account for noninvocation.

A. Subjecting this Conduct to the Criminal Process Would be Inappropriate or Ineffective

Illustration #15: A police patrol came upon a number of skid row bums in an intoxicated condition. The officers knew them all, having found them all in a similar state on numerous other occasions. Although all of them were violating the statutes on public drunkeness and habitual drunkeness, no arrests were made. Another intoxicated derelict was found passed out on the sidewalk, and he was arrested for his own safety, but was immediately released the following morning.

Even with sufficient resources available, the prior observations suggest the police would in some situations view invocation as a futile and frustrating act, accomplishing little or nothing. This is because the circumstances may indicate that the available and predictable punishment or treatment is not likely to be effective or appropriate. More specifically, the following police attitudes have already been noted: (1) that invocation is futile because subsequent agencies in the process will be too lenient; (2) that invocation is futile because there does not exist within the present system any effective means of dealing with the conduct; or (3) that invocation would allow the criminal process to be inappropriately used for private ends.

As observed earlier, communication between the police and subsequent agencies in the process is very weak.[135] A particular officer's knowledge of how the prosecutor or judge will react to a given case is based only on hearsay or his own limited observations. But, whether accurate or not, the police officer often has a prognostication as to what the action of these agencies will be. If his prediction is one of what he views to be leniency so extreme as to be ineffective, he may forego invocation even if sufficient resources are available.

Even if the subsequent agencies are willing to use the best al-

---

[135] See La Fave, *The Police and Nonenforcement of the Law: I,* 1962 WIS. L. REV. 104, 122.

ternatives available for purposes of punishment, deterrence, or treatment, the police may still doubt whether invocation would be effective. Thus, habitual drunkards often are not arrested for the simple reason that means within the criminal process to treat the alcoholic successfully are usually lacking.[130] Even the drunk who is "down and out" and arrested for his own safety often is sent through the "golden rule" process, resulting in his release the following morning.[137]

Finally, police nonenforcement even with sufficient resources can be expected because of the previously noted attitude that, notwithstanding the fact a crime has been committed, some uses of the criminal process would still be considered inappropriate. Most obvious here is the frequently repeated police assertion that the criminal process should not aid a person who only desires restitution.

B. Noninvocation Would Prevent Loss of Public Respect and Support

Illustration #16: A police officer came upon open gambling in a local tavern. The community is known as a "wide-open town," and much of the revenue in the city comes from operation of gambling and entertainment houses. A considerable majority of the community appears to favor the continuance of such conditions. No arrest was made.

The effect upon law enforcement of public attitudes concerning what laws should and should not be enforced has long been recog-

---

[130] However, as to some other forms of conduct which the criminal process is often said to be incapable of effectively handling, drug addiction (See JOINT COMM. OF ABA & AMA ON NARCOTIC DRUGS, DRUG ADDICTION: CRIME OR DISEASE? (1961) and many citations therein.) or homosexuality (See Comment, 70 YALE L.J. 623 (1961), and numerous citations therein), it is unusual to find acknowledgement of this at the police level.

[137] In Detroit, those intoxicated persons who are arrested but are not to be subjected to prosecution are termed "golden rule drunks." A substantial number of intoxicated persons arrested are so treated, as the following statistics demonstrate:.

Year:	1951	1952	1953	1954	1955	1956
Golden rule:	9,303	8,064	8,592	7,249	6,626	5,865
Drunks prosecuted:	8,443	7,840	10,181	10,124	10,513	8,665

DETROIT, MICH., POLICE DEP'T, 91st STATISTICAL ANNUAL REPORT, Table III-B (1956).

Drunks are sent through the "golden rule" process because it is thought nothing is to be gained from prosecution or conviction. If a drunk is prosecuted, it probably is because: (a) he is a habitual; (b) he is "down and out" in the sense that he needs medical treatment, etc.; (c) he was belligerent; or (d) he requested incarceration (not uncommon in the winter months).

In Massachusetts, it is provided by law that the judge shall determine where an arrested drunk should be released without prosecution. MASS. ANN. LAWS, ch. 272 §§ 44-46 (1956).

nized as an important problem.[138] While it is indeed important, it tends to have less of an effect in day-to-day law enforcement because of nonenforcement decisions of the kind which have been discussed up to this point. When the police fail to invoke where there is doubt as to the actual legislative desire for enforcement and where it is thought enforcement resources are needed more elsewhere, much of the law enforcement program which the public would most likely find objectionable—social gambling, minor traffic violations, and the like—has been eliminated.[139] This is not to say, however, that public pressures do not actually affect current law enforcement. Variations in local attitudes clearly bring about differences in local enforcement levels. While most of these pressures might be thought to converge upon the prosecutor, an elected official, at least one authority has asserted that it is the individual policeman "who usually determines how far popular attitudes shall control."[140]

Law enforcement agencies in this country are often structured so as to be subject to popular control. Popular election of the sheriff is the general rule, and has been in this country since early times because of the unpopularity of the colonial governors.[141] The selection of an appointed police administrator, such as the local chief, is apt to involve careful consideration of how responsive the various candidates would likely be to local opinion.[142] Possible candidates for the job may be limited to local residents, just as membership in the department usually is, in order to insure a department more responsive to local wishes.[143] Also of utmost importance is the fact that our whole scheme of police organization is largely based upon the concept of local autonomy and control. Decentralization and fragmentation "are the most striking char-

---

[138] See, *e.g.*, Smith, Police Systems in the United States 5-7, 18-19, 285-86, 366-67 (1940); Arnold, The Symbols of Government, ch. 7 (1935).

[139] Indeed, these factors may be traced back to public opinion, as legislative desires and budget appropriations are likewise responsive to it.

[140] Smith, *op. cit. supra* note 138, at 19-20.

[141] *Id.* at 84-85. Thus one study concludes: "In summary it would appear that as chief conservator of the peace of this county the social function of the sheriff is not to enforce the law but to keep that kind and degree of peace which the people want kept." Esselstyn, *op. cit. supra* note 110, at 239.

[142] Thus, open recruitment of a new chief of police is usually opposed. "More than any other position in the municipality, it seems as if the citizen wants to feel assured that the police chief understands the community and its feelings." Sherwood, *Roles of City Manager and Police*, Public Management 110 (May 1959).

[143] See Smith, *op. cit. supra* note 138, at 162, 246. He notes that if public opinion *is* to be interpreted by the police administrator to determine the extent and direction of popular control, then a local resident can probably do this better. But, he adds, popular control is not always the most vital issue.

acteristics of American police patterns, since no other part of the world has carried local autonomy in police management to such extreme lengths."[144]

Therefore, an appropriate question which can be asked is whether the structure of the police organization should be such as to maximize or minimize the necessity of the police reacting to community pressures. Necessary reliance upon public support may have some benefits: it may insure "reasonable" law enforcement and may provide protection from "unfair" enforcement methods.[145] Yet is is obviously inconsistent with full enforcement of legislative proscriptions. One might take the position that this is also desirable; that the police *should* proceed to enforce the law in accordance with the desires of the local population. As such, the criminal law would have to be viewed not as a mandate for uniform enforcement throughout the state, but rather a restriction upon what conduct the localities could impose serious sanctions. That complete state-wide uniformity is not contemplated in the present system seems apparent: local government can, within limits, pass ordinances which impose minor sanctions on conduct not prohibited by the criminal law; local government can likewise pass ordinances as to conduct prohibited by the criminal law, thereby providing an alternative basis of action with a lesser penalty involved; and local government has been given the purse strings on the local police department, by which it can make anything near full enforcement of all the state laws impossible. However, it is one thing to admit that these devices have been given to the local legislative body—city council, county board, and the like; it is another to assert that police administrators should directly attempt to ascertain the desires of the local citizenry and fashion their enforcement program accordingly. Not only may the extreme lack of uniformity throughout the state which could result have adverse affects, there are obviously numerous other problems involved in such an attempt.[146] But it is no answer to assert that law

---

[144] *Id.* at 342.

[145] Not all would agree that popular control brings about police fairness. Some are of the view that the general public does not care how the police treat persons as long as they restrict their activities to those the public thinks are criminals. See Westley, *op. cit. supra* note 131, at 118.

[146] For one thing, how are the desires of the majority of the local populace determined? May not enforcement really reflect the desires of a vocal and influential minority? Cannot more pressure usually be mobilized against enforcement of a particular kind than for enforcement? For example, in a Kansas city, after the police received complaints that a number of youths were causing minor property damage and disturbing the peace because of their drag-racing and similar activities in a particular neighborhood, arrests were made of some of the

enforcement should proceed without any regard to public opinion. Not only is this more than can be expected of the official who continues in his job only with public approval, but public cooperation is an essential ingredient of law enforcement. "In a democratic society, the corollary is the dependence of professional police upon the public with regard to detection, evidence, financial support, and in last analysis, the police job itself."[147]

Public pressures upon the police for nonenforcement where there would otherwise be enforcement are explainable for a number of reasons. These reasons in turn explain why the pressures can be expected to be greatest as to certain offenses. For one thing, the average citizen does not really appreciate the need for enforcement in some areas. Thus, where the traffic laws and other safety regulations are violated, "there is serious menace to the general security in ways which the ordinary citizen, under the ordinary circumstances of his experience, does not perceive readily, and is not likely to appreciate until a gross instance or a wholesale disaster shocks the conscience of the community into a spasm of activity."[148] Secondly, restrictions of these types apply to the day-to-day conduct of most citizens, "the old easy division of the community into lawbreakers and law observers has thus been destroyed," and enforcement thereby may "prove irritating to the sensibilities of people who believe that they have a right to be let alone."[149] Finally, public knowledge of less than full enforcement in some areas makes for great resistance to invocation by the individual offender. Thus the area of traffic enforcement is made most dif-

offenders. Because of this action, however, the police received severe criticism from the parents of those arrested and also from the local newspapers. Because of this criticism the police stopped making arrests of the hot-rodders.

[147] Hall, *Police and Law in a Democratic Society*, 28 IND. L.J. 135, 143 (1953). Thus, one leading police official flatly asserts, "The police cannot progress ahead of public sentiment." Wilson, POLICE PLANNING 48 (2d ed. 1957).

This dilemma can be reduced down to the need of the individual officer to have the approval of the people on his beat. As Whyte concluded in his study of an Italian slum he called Cornerville:

"There are prevalent in society two general conceptions of the duties of the police officer. Middle-class people feel that he should enforce the law without fear or favor. Cornerville people and many of the officers themselves believe that the policeman should have the confidence of the people in his area so that he can settle many difficulties in a personal manner without making arrests. These two conceptions are in a large measure contradictory. The policeman who takes a strictly legalistic view of his duties cuts himself off from the personal relations necessary to enable him to serve as mediator of disputes in his area. The policeman who develops close ties with local people is unable to act against them with the vigor prescribed by the law." WHYTE, STREET CORNER SOCIETY 136 (2d ed. 1955).

[148] POUND, CRIMINAL JUSTICE IN AMERICA 19 (1930).

[149] SMITH, *op. cit. supra* note 138, at 10, 18.

ficult because it is generally recognized that the police engage in the practice of warning offending drivers,[150] while public pressures diminish in other areas where the police have successfully convinced the general public that they have no discretionary power.[151]

C. Noninvocation Would Allow the System to Receive an Affirmative Benefit Outweighing the Risk from Inaction

Illustration #17: In a routine frisk of a group of persons found under suspicious circumstances, a small quantity of narcotics was found on one of them. The officers recognized this man as one who from time to time informed the police on narcotics peddlers. No arrest was made.

The problem involved here is not entirely unlike the one just discussed above. Some tempering of law enforcement to suit public opinion might be rationalized on the basis that public cooperation is a necessary ingredient of effective enforcement in other, more important areas. Likewise, noninvocation may occur with respect to particular individuals who are thought to be in a position to aid in the detection, arrest and conviction of other offenders. This

---

[150] In Wichita the point has been reached where the police often avoid arresting for traffic offenses because of the loss of respect engendered by such action. Assigning men to traffic work has become a personnel problem because the officers are subjected to considerable abuse and vituperation by the citizenry. When a traffic offender is written up, the officer has to really "sell" the ticket, sometimes talking to the offender for up to fifteen minutes. In Milwaukee traffic violators sometimes complain to police supervisors that the process was invoked against them instead of a mere warning given. Another study has also concluded that "for the policeman the traffic violator represents an unpleasant experience." Westley, *op. cit. supra* note 131, at 109.

[151] For example, the director of the Enforcement Division of the Michigan State Liquor Commission noted that not infrequently local groups have attempted to exert pressure upon local law enforcement officers because of their strict enforcement of the Liquor Control Act. He indicated that these local officials have been able to successfully overcome this pressure by emphasizing the fact that they have no discretion in this area. To bolster their position, they are able to assert that they are themselves subject to arrest and prosecution in the event they do not proceed against a known violation of this act. This is so because one section of the act makes it a misdemeanor for "sheriffs . . . and their deputies . . ., village marshals, constables, officers or. members of the village or city police, and members of the department of state police" to "neglect or refuse to perform the duties imposed" by the act. Mich. Stat. Ann. § 18.971 (1957). Though no officer has ever been proceeded against under this statute, the Director was certain it had been effective in terms of enabling local police to repel pressure for less than full enforcement.

Presumably an officer in Michigan could base his enforcement against any kind of conduct upon another statute which declares it to be a misdemeanor for an officer to neglect to perform a duty enjoined upon him by law. Mich. Stat. Ann. § 28.746. This statute probably would not be as helpful, as (a) it does not itself declare full enforcement to be the officer's duty; and (b) assuming it does require full enforcement, knowledge that the law is not fully enforced as to all conduct would make it apparent the statute is not the effective sanction the officer asserts it to be.

preferred treatment may occur at a number of different decision points in the process. Persons who have provided information for the police may receive a lighter sentence or may be placed on probation; the giving of testimony in court may result from a grant of immunity by the prosecutor[152] or a more informal agreement not to prosecute. The concern here, however, is with the decision not to arrest persons thought to be furnishing some law enforcement agency with information helpful in enforcing the law against others.

Substantial use is made of informants.[153] They are most often used in narcotics enforcement, but are also used to a lesser degree with respect to liquor, gambling, vice, and similar offenses. Informants not only provide the police with information obtained from persons with whom they associate, but are also utilized in setting up purchases of illegal goods, in eliciting information from suspects, some of whom are in custody, and in actually making purchases of narcotics and the like. Officers engaged in enforcement in the areas mentioned strongly support the use of informants. Particularly with respect to narcotics enforcement, the police take the position that effective enforcement requires the continued use of these informers. Great care is taken to protect the identity of informants, so that usually only one detective is aware of a particular person's contributions as an informant.[154]

Police informants assist in enforcement in return for some kind of compensation. While some informers are paid money for their assistance,[155] a good number of them, especially in the narcotics area, are rewarded for past, present, or future information by being granted immunity from arrest notwithstanding the fact they have engaged in criminal conduct. Thus, the standard practice is that a *user* of narcotics is considered immune from arrest, though it is known he is using or presently possesses narcotics, if this person is on a continuing basis supplying the officers responsible for nar-

---

[152] See 2 ABA COMM'N ON ORGANIZED CRIME, ORGANIZED CRIME AND LAW ENFORCEMENT 157-86 (1953). The concern with proper controls over any such arrangement whereby one person is not proceeded against because he aids in enforcement against others is reflected therein; the model act set forth there provides for control over the prosecutor, with alternative provisions requiring either prior approval of the Attorney General or a court finding that immunity would not be "clearly contrary to the public interest."

[153] In accord with the observed practice are those reported in DEUTSCH, THE TROUBLE WITH COPS 98 (2d ed. 1955); Kooken, *Ethics in Police Service*, 38 J. CRIM L. & C. 172, 174-75 (1947).

[154] Police are cautioned not to "burn" an informant by disclosing his identity. See KENNEY, A GUIDE FOR POLICE PLANNING: NARCOTICS OPERATIONS 10-11 (1954).

[155] Most departments appeared to have a substantial amount of money available for this purpose.

cotics enforcement with information directed toward the apprehension of sellers of narcotics. Other kinds of conduct may also be tolerated by the police where engaged in by persons providing information: a numbers writer may not be arrested because he furnishes information on blind pigs, crap games, and prostitutes; even the fixing of traffic tickets may be prompted by the fact the offender has been a good source of information.

The exact extent of arrest immunity which all informants enjoy—that is, what kind of offenses they can commit and with what frequency and still be immune from apprehension—is difficult to assess. It undoubtedly varies somewhat, depending upon the precise value of the informant. As a general rule, however, it would seem that immunity would hardly be granted for offenses just as serious or more serious than those for which information is given (but there might be a difference of opinion on the relative seriousness of some different kinds of conduct), as then little if anything would be accomplished. Thus informants used to apprehend narcotics sellers are themselves expected to refrain from selling. It also appears that informants are expected to confine their criminal activities to those kinds of offenses which do not involve committing a crime against an unwilling victim who would report the same to the department and expect action upon it. Thus, one does not find burglars or similar such offenders being granted immunity, rather it is prostitutes, numbers writers, and the like who are allowed to carry on their activities because they supply information.[156]

The granting of arrest immunity to informants in exchange for information is, for the most part, a decision made by the individual officer involved. Most of these decisions are made within a narcotics or vice bureau of a police department, and there is little indication that the policy is given detailed consideration by anyone higher than the head of such bureau. There is no consultation outside the police department.[157]

---

[156] Admittedly, the latter types are more likely to become informants in the first instance. However, it was noted that when they overstepped the boundary, so that the police received a specific complaint as to their activity, then the immunity was apt to end. Thus, one Detroit addict who was well known to detectives because he had worked for them as an informant was immediately arrested when he was reported for shoplifting, and the detectives indicated that they were not interested in any "deals" regardless of how much new information he promised.

[157] Consultation outside the police agency is unlikely, even when it is a matter of releasing a person already held. It has been said that such an informer program, when established by the police, "constitutes a usurpation of legislative function," but that such a program could properly be initiated by prosecutor or court.

Any policy of granting immunity from arrest to persons supplying the police with ,information presents problems of a serious nature to the police and to the criminal justice system as a whole. The problems relate not only to the questionable propriety of such a policy, but also to the problems of implementing it, assuming the policy is a wise one.

In the first place, any such arrest immunity program is difficult to carry out, as each police officer can hardly be expected to know each and every person that is considered valuable enough to some part of the department to warrant not invoking the process against him. Officers assigned to a particular unit may not be aware of those individuals serving·other units, as considerable care is taken in concealing the identity of police informers. The problem is complicated by the fact that it is also deemed desirable to grant immunity to persons serving other law enforcement agencies. One result is that persons who have been granted immunity are sometimes arrested because the officer is unaware of their informer status.[158] More serious, however, is the fact that this general confusion over who is and who is not an informant results in persons who in fact are not informants being granted immunity by unsuspecting officers. It is not uncommon for the police, upon questioning individuals on the street, to be told "I'm working for the Bureau," or "I'm working for Sergeant Smith's crew."[159] The only way in which the patrolmen can be sure that these persons are in fact informants is by checking with the agency for which they claim to be working. It does not appear that such a check is usually made when the person has not already been arrested, but it is made as to persons already in custody who then allege they are supposed to be immune.

Not only is coordination between units of a department difficult, it is also questionable whether particular informant programs reflect the attitude of all parts of a given department. To the ex-

---

Goldstein, *Police Discretion Not to Invoke the Criminal Process: Low-Visibility Decisions in the Administration of Justice,* 69 YALE L.J. 543, 568-69 (1960).

[158] Thus a federal informant was arrested by Detroit officers on the basis of information provided by a Detroit informant. After consultation with the federal narcotics agents the case was not prosecuted.

[159] For example, after Detroit officers stopped a vehicle in order to question the occupants, each of the individuals was searched separately. The driver of the car informed the officers that he was working for the narcotics bureau and was trying to get a buy off the other fellow in the car. The other fellow, who was seated in the car, was questioned separately and informed the officers that he, too, was an informant—but for the federal agency, and that he was associating with this fellow in hopes that he would obtain some information relating to the sale of narcotics.

226 WISCONSIN LAW REVIEW [Vol. 1962

tent that immunity of certain persons makes one unit's job easier, it may complicate the enforcement job of another unit. Toleration of one class of offenders in order to obtain information about another class of offenders is not condoned by an entire department, as a rule, but rather depends upon the bias of a particular unit, depending upon the job that unit has to perform.[160] The result is that in some sections of a department the complaint may be heard that too strict enforcement has dried up many good sources of information, while other members of the force feel the information received did not justify immunity.[161]

Finally, even if the program could be carried out without difficulty, and even if there were more uniformity within a department as to the value of a given type of trading of information for arrest immunity, the question remains as to whether the practice can be justified. While the narcotics informant program, for example, makes narcotics enforcement easier, little attempt has been made to determine whether the program actually contributes significantly to deterring the narcotics traffic. It is not clear that the policy has been reviewed with a view to deciding whether the benefits derived from the program sufficiently offset the fact that the opportunity to rehabilitate many narcotics users is forfeited.[162] While the present program may be the most desirable alternative, it does not appear to exist as a result of any detailed, well-consid-

---

[160] Another study reports that for this reason detectives and officers granting immunity to informants try to conceal this tactic from others in the department. Westley, *op. cit. supra* note 131, at 69, 73.

[161] A supervisory officer of the Detroit homicide bureau objected, "All sources of information are dried up. In the past one used to be able to stop pimps, whores, on the street and get something from them. Now they won't talk at all. We, as detectives, are not concerned with that aspect of police work. We feel it is much more important to catch murderers and stick-up men even if it means allowing a pimp or whore to operate another week or so before they get caught."

In response to this attitude, a high official in the department indicated that in his view the opportunity to have a source of information available did not justify leaving these undesirable characters on the streets. Rather, he thought these persons should have no immunity, and that the detectives should "have to get out and work instead of waiting for the telephone to ring."

[162] Not only is there deprivation of the opportunity to rehabilitate the person in terms of his addiction, but the police are also taking a calculated risk that the addict will not indulge in more serious kinds of criminality while he remains free. For example, one addict who was still free because of his being a source of information was apprehended for shoplifting; but he and others could resort to yet more serious conduct in order to obtain money needed to satisfy their addiction. If the informant program is desirable, this may suggest that furnishing informants with narcotics might be preferable to allowing the addict to remain free without access to the quantity of drugs he needs to satisfy his craving.

ered policy-making.[163]

D. Invocation Would Cause Harm to the Offender or Victim Outweighing the Risk from Inaction

Illustration #18: A woman returned home from work in a disheveled condition and told her husband that she had been kidnapped and raped. The husband called the police, and they began an investigation. Upon questioning the woman the following day, some discrepancies in her story developed, and she finally admitted that she and a man had engaged in lovemaking by mutual consent, and that she had concocted the story in order to explain her absence to her husband. Since proceeding against the woman for a false felony report would have endangered her marriage, the police decided to take no action.

Of concern here are those situations in which the police do not invoke the criminal process because they believe the cost to the suspect or others which would result from invocation outweighs the risk which would be created by not subjecting the offender to the criminal process. The risk created would typically relate to the likelihood of repeated criminal conduct by the suspect if he is not subjected to the process, but may also include such things as the risk that the system will suffer a loss of respect as a result.[164] The cost may be the predictable sanction imposed by the court, or it may be the particular hardship which would be imposed on the suspect by arrest because of the circumstances of the particular case. The arrest of a vagrant on suspicion of theft is obviously a different case from the arrest of a local banker on the same charge. The cost may also relate to the hardship to others, such as the victim or the family of the suspect or victim.

One kind of cost-risk balancing resulting in noninvocation may arise out of a disagreement between the police and the judges or legislature on what the given penalty should be for certain criminal violations. If the predictable punishment is viewed as excessive, the police may choose not to arrest rather than subject the offender to it. Disagreement between the police and legislature occurs when the *necessary* punishment is believed to be inappropriate to the

---

[163] For one view on the questions of whether the program fulfills the retributive, restraining, and reformative functions of the state narcotics laws, and whether it implements the deterrent function of criminal law administration, see Goldstein, *supra* note 157, at 569-72.

[164] Thus, arrest, charging, conviction and punishment may be deemed necessary notwithstanding the fact there does not appear to be any risk of further violation by the offender. See Mead, *The Psychology of Punitive Justice*, 23 AM. J. SOCIOLOGY 577 (1918).

conduct involved. Thus, the elimination of discretion at the judicial level may result in discretion being assumed at an earlier and less visible point in the process. For example, Wisconsin law requires that the license of a juvenile driver be suspended or revoked for any moving violation;[105] the result is that traffic officers are apt to merely warn the youth unless the violation is really serious.[106] Disagreement between police and judge occurs when the judge does have the power to impose a more lenient penalty, but it is thought he will not do so. The police not infrequently spare traffic violators and minor juvenile offenders from arrest on this score,[107] and this may occur as to other offenses as well.

But, as the illustration indicates, perhaps of even more interest is the case of noninvocation because of the circumstances of the individual case. The need for such individualized treatment is well recognized at the sentencing stage, where discretion is provided to allow imposition of a sentence based upon the individual circumstances involved.[108] While there is agreement that "the power of adjusting the operation of legal precepts to the exigencies of special circumstances is unavoidable if there is to be a complete system of justice according to law,"[109] undoubtedly not all would agree that noninvocation on this basis is justified.[110] The case for noninvocation at the arrest level to save persons from excessive harm is stated thusly by Justice Breitel:

> Discretion too must play its role very early—at the inception of a criminal matter. Criminal proceedings, by their very nature, are summary and often effected in immediate pursuit of the wrong and the wrongdoer. Mere arrest may destroy reputation, or cause the loss of a job, or visit grave injury upon a family. Hailing the arrestee promptly before a magistrate, though serving due process, may be no boon indeed, to the innocent or technical violator.[171]

[105] Wis. Stat. § 48.36 (1959).

[106] Similarly, at the 1956 Wisconsin Traffic Court Conference in Madison, one county judge suggested that high minimum sentences for traffic offenses cause what he termed "court on the highway," with traffic officers often deciding not to invoke the full process for this reason.

[107] It is interesting to note that noninvocation because it is thought the penalty will be too light also occurs in these areas. This suggests that in these areas there is considerable variation in penalties applied by different judges, and also considerable difference of opinion by police as to what punishment is appropriate.

[108] There is not agreement upon what the limits upon individualizing should be, however. See Hall, General Principles of Criminal Law 56 (2d ed. 1960).

[109] Pound, *Discretion, Dispensation and Mitigation: The Problem of the Individual Special Case*, 35 N.Y.U.L. Rev. 925, 936-37 (1960).

[170] E.g., Hall contends only "mitigation" is proper when these special circumstances are shown. Hall, *op. cit. supra* note 168, at 55.

[171] Breitel, *Controls in Criminal Law Enforcement*, 27 U. Chi. L. Rev. 427, 431 (1960).

While noninvocation sometimes occurs because the unique circumstances of the individual case indicate excessive harm would follow, it does not appear to occur with any regularity at the arrest decision level for the simple reason that these relevant circumstances are usually not known at this time. Yet, as the illustration demonstrates, sometimes the case develops in such a way that these circumstances are known early. This case also clearly shows that the mere fact of arrest, even though it had later been determined that the woman would not be prosecuted, would have undoubtedly been sufficient to bring about the harm which the police intended to prevent.

V. Police Discretion in Practice: Arrest Because of the Circumstances of the Particular Case, Though the Process Would Not Otherwise Ordinarily be Invoked

The preceding discussion has centered upon those instances in which the police exercise discretion resulting in a decision not to invoke the criminal process. These cases of noninvocation present serious questions concerning the validity of current nonenforcement practices. But, even if discretion may be legitimately exercised, clearly sound criteria are needed whereby some offenders are proceeded against and some are not. Particularly in view of the equal protection guarantee, it is not enough that some justification be shown for not proceeding against certain kinds of conduct in the ordinary case. Careful scrutiny is also needed of those situations where, because of some circumstance of the individual case, the process is invoked notwithstanding the fact that ordinarily the police do not proceed against the conduct involved. It is these kinds of cases which are considered herein.

A. Arrest to Avoid a Strain Upon Available Resources

Illustration #19: The police received a call of a disturbance at a particular address and reported to the scene. It proved to be the usual family squabble, involving a minor assault on a spouse. Although the usual procedure was to merely restore order and then leave, the officers recalled they had received repeated calls to this particular address in the past, so an arrest of the offender was made.

It was noted earlier that arrests may not be made with respect to certain types of frequently recurring conduct of a less serious nature because invoking the process against this conduct would present too great a strain upon the resources of one or more agencies in the criminal justice system. Involved here is the converse of that situation, the arrest of persons not ordinarily arrested because it is felt that such action is necessary in order to minimize the necessity of responding to future calls for police action concerning this kind of conduct or concerning the particular offender.

As the illustration suggests, such action is most noticeable in the area of enforcement concerning domestic disturbances, which is usually not a subject of invocation. However, if the police have had to respond to the same address on a number of prior occasions, an arrest will be made. Thus, as to this same kind of frequently recurring conduct, there may be a police response to the strain upon their resources by selecting out for enforcement those individuals who from past experience, appear to be most responsible for this diversion of police resources in that they have been the subject of repeated calls for police service. These individuals may be selected out for arrest in hopes that such a tactic will result in no further police calls from that particular residence.[172]

If it is felt within a particular department that an inordinate amount of their resources is being expended in dealing with certain conduct, there may be a general reversal of this policy of nonenforcement. Thus in one community the chief of police directed that an arrest was to be made in all cases where a policeman was called to a domestic dispute, his hope being that this would put an end to calls for police service in most of these cases. The chief's action here reflects dissatisfaction with the necessity of diverting the resources of law enforcement from functions that only the criminal law can handle to problems such as the arbitration of marital disputes, which are more in the nature of social services. Yet the solution, at least in terms of short-run results, seems to be one of responding to these disputes in such a way that they

---

[172] Actually, whether arrest in these cases will be resorted to depends in part on whether there are any alternative means available for solving the problem. Because in Detroit there is an alternative, the use of the misdemeanor complaint bureau, it appears that arrest in an attempt to foreclose further requests for police service at a particular household is not as frequent a practice as noted elsewhere. Rather, in such a case the patrolman will refer the matter to the bureau.

This bureau is staffed by detectives who have considerable competence in handling family disputes because of their specialization in this kind of problem. At an informal hearing at which the husband and wife appear, the detectives may attempt to resolve the problem or may decide to refer the case to some social agency, to some other agency within the criminal justice system, or may suggest that the parties consult an attorney. In this way, the necessity for any further police services is minimized. But in any event, the wife is made aware of the fact that this bureau is the appropriate agency to handle such problems, so that in the future she will contact this bureau rather than call the precinct for police service.

are in every case treated as purely criminal matters, resulting always in arrest. Whether this is outweighed by the possibility that the police in the long run would no longer be called upon to perform this function of arbitration, thereby accomplishing the desired result of lessening the strain upon law enforcement resources, is unclear.[173] It also might be asked whether it is important that some other agency fill the gap resulting from police abdication of this function. [174]

B. Arrest to Maintain Respect for the Police

Illustration #20: A police patrol car clocked a driver at 39 m.p.h. in a 30 m.p.h. zone. They pulled the car over and indicated prior to leaving the squad car that they would only issue a warning. When the deputies approached, the driver said in a sarcastic tone, "What in hell have I done now?" Because of the driver's belligerent attitude a speeding ticket was issued.

The maintenance of respect is sometimes viewed as an important objective of police action.[175] As already noted, an arrest may not be made where it is thought that invocation would result in the loss of public respect and support. Similarly, an arrest may be made of a person who ordinarily would not be arrested because such action is deemed necessary to the maintenance of respect for the police or the law enforcement system as a whole. A "spite arrest," the taking of a person into custody merely because he has incurred the disfavor of a particular officer, certainly is subject to criticism. However, it is not so clear that it is improper to make an arrest of a person guilty of criminal conduct not usually proceeded against, where failure to do so would result in the loss of respect for the police by persons observing this instance of inaction. Nor is it clear that it is improper to arrest a person, assuming sufficient probability of guilt, because he has not extended to the police a reasonable amount of courtesy and cooperation, though in the absence of such lack of respect no arrest would have been

---

[173] For a report of a drop in intrafamily assaults in Oakland, Calif., after a similar policy change from nonenforcement to enforcement, including the necessary query of whether the drop really represents a decrease in *actual* or *reported* assaults, see Goldstein, *supra* note 158, at 577-80.

[174] For a discussion of other similar problems emminating from law enforcement agencies performing functions in the nature of social services, see Allen, *The Borderland of the Criminal Law: Problems of "Socializing" Criminal Justice,* 32 Social Serv. Rev. 107 (1958).

[175] "The decision upon the part of the individual policeman as to what kind of action to take in a specific situation involves the interrelation of three variables: the enforcement of the law, the maintenance of respect for the police, and the apprehension of the felon." Westley, *op. cit. supra* note 131, at 197.

made. This occurs most frequently as to drunks, traffic violators,[176] and juvenile offenders,[177] but the attitude of the offender is an important factor in the determination of whether an arrest will be made in all minor offenses.[178]

C. Arrest to Maintain Public Image of Full Enforcement

Illustration #21: The police were aware of the operation of a private card game in which there was no house card. Since this operation therefore qualified as mere social gambling, no action was taken against the offenders. However, the operators of the game made no attempt at all to conceal the operation, and it was soon apparent to the general public that the police must be aware of it. Upon learning these added facts, the police arrested the gamblers.

The concern here is with a criterion akin to the one which has just been discussed. They are distinguishable, however, in that the previous section was concerned with the need to maintain respect for the police, while here the concern is with the need to maintain respect for the law itself. Admittedly, the similarity of the two criteria will often result in similar application.

The maintenance of a public image of full enforcement, that is, maintenance of respect for the law itself, requires that the law sometimes be enforced against conduct not ordinarily proceeded against because the particular circumstances indicate that knowledge of the police inaction will become known to the general public. The extremes to which such an attitude may be carried has been aptly described by Thurman Arnold in the following terms:

> It is important to keep in mind that we are concerned with Law Enforcement as a sort of creed, and not with the enforcement of any particular rule. When, by imperceptible graduations, emphasis is changed from the purpose or merits of a rule itself to the notion that the very prestige of government depends on enforcements as a kind of ceremonial, to be ob-

---

[176] Another study likewise noted that traffic violators who talked back or claimed to know more about the law than the officer were arrested. *Id.* at 153.

[177] Another study concludes: "Almost all police officials agree that defiance on the part of a boy will lead to juvenile court quicker than anything else. Such damage to the dignity of the police will lead to court referral even in minor cases." Goldman, The Differential Selection of Juvenile Offenders for Court Appearance 145 (unpublished Ph.D. thesis, Dep't of Sociology, Univ. of Chicago, 1950).

[178] The observed practice would appear to conform to Westley's conclusion: "The emphasis placed on the maintenance of respect for the police makes the attitude of the offender a major factor in the policeman's decision as to whether he will act against him except in the case of crimes on the felony level. Thus there is a tendency to let the respectful offender off easily, but to give the works to the disrespectful offender." Westley, *op. cit. supra* note 131, at 297.

served even toward obnoxious legislation—when the enforcement becomes directed, not to preserve public safety or convenience, but to justify a moral attitude toward law regardless of public convenience—then the common-sense idea with which we started has become the mystical ideal called Law Enforcement.[179]

Obviously such a strict attitude of full enforcement is not presently being taken. The point to be made here, however, is that a move toward fuller enforcement is sometimes made necessary in particular instances where the nonenforcement policy would otherwise become visible to a substantial segment of the public.

Under such circumstances, enforcement appears to follow so that the people will know that the law is being enforced, irrespective of whether the public actually desires enforcement in this area.[180] However, it is possible for the police to maintain a reasonably good image of full enforcement in the public eye while at the same time following a policy of nonenforcement in many areas, as many instances of failure to invoke the process are not visible in the way that continued open gambling is. Enforcement in some areas must sometimes be set at a higher level than would otherwise be considered proper because public attention has been directed toward certain criminal conduct.[181]

The police desire to maintain this public image is certainly understandable, and cannot be labelled as deception. Even if all were to agree that less than full enforcement was proper as to particular kinds of conduct, it does not necessarily follow that public knowledge of this fact would make the task of law enforcement any easier. Widespread recognition of the exercise of discretion by the police not to enforce might actually make impartiality more difficult. As was noted earlier, public pressures on the police for nonenforcement in individual cases becomes greatest when the conduct involved is generally recognized as being of a type which does not receive full enforcement. And, *thinking in broader terms, there*

---

[179] Arnold, *op. cit. supra* note 138, at 152. His chapter 7 explores this matter in more detail, and is an excellent statement.

[180] Because in some cases observed the most vocal groups in the community and the greatest concentration of pressure appeared to be for nonenforcement, it seems that it is more evident than usual that the real purpose for the enforcement was to promote this image of full enforcement.

[181] "Elsewhere, a twelve year old boy was arrested for taking liberties with a six year old girl. Examination showed that he had not raped or otherwise physically harmed the child. Although the boy came from a good home and the police authorities thought that the act was one of curiosity rather than evil intent, the boy was committed to the juvenile court. Such action was deemed necessary because of the disturbed state of the public resulting from the newspaper accounts of a brutal sex killing in a nearby community." Goldman, *op. cit. supra* note 177, at 144.

may well be something to the assertion that "the worst evil of disregard for some laws is that it destroys respect for all law."[182]

D. Arrest Because of Opportunity to Punish Offender the System Desires to Punish

Illustration #22: The police learned of a minor property theft, but the victim was not interested in prosecution, so in accord with the usual policy no arrest was planned. But, it was then learned that the offender was known to the police as a "bad actor," and that the police had been unsuccessful in obtaining his conviction for other, more serious offenses. Because of this an arrest was made.

The point to be made here is a simple one, but yet needs to be made in order to explain some instances in which arrests are made though the conduct, by application of the criteria already stated, is not the kind of conduct against which the process is ordinarily invoked. If there is a particular individual who is thought to be responsible for one or more offenses which are of public concern, but for one reason or another it is not possible for this individual to be dealt with by the system for these offenses, then the process may be invoked against him for engaging in certain conduct which ordinarily would not result in arrest. As such, the large body of usually unenforced criminal laws becomes "an arsenal of weapons with which to incarcerate certain dangerous individuals who are bothering society."[183] Thurman Arnold has observed:

> [S]o far as the effect of the number of criminal laws on policemen or the prosecutor is concerned, they are more apt to be a help than a hindrance. Such persons are trying to apprehend individuals who at the time happen to be considered dangerous to society, and the wider the selection of laws which they have, the more chance there is of conviction.[184]

The great disparity between the law in the books and the law usually enforced, insofar as it aids in the apprehension and punishment of criminals that cannot otherwise be dealt with, might be

---

[182] ARNOLD, *op. cit. supra* note 138, at 151, quoting a statement made by Pres. Hoover in connection with the report of the Wickersham Commission.
"For the police to ignore breaches of a particular law, for whatever reason, is to offer a license to sections of the community to violate those laws at will. Further, it is to demand that the rest of the community ignore the breaches also. . . . If public servants such as the police are to choose which laws to enforce and which to ignore, then naturally the public will make such a choice too." Williams, *Turning a Blind Eye,* 1954 CRIM. L. REV. (Eng.) 271.
[183] ARNOLD, *op. cit. supra* note 138, at 153.
[184] *Id.* at 160.

said to be beneficial. This, however, does not alone justify the existence of such a system. It may confer too much discretion upon the police. "A discretion to withhold a punishment may result in just as much arbitrary power as discretion to use extra-legal punishment," one writer has noted.[185] And, such a system always makes it possible for these laws to be applied on unfair bases, such as race.[186] Yet it is equally unclear that the possibility that law enforcement officers may take the "arsenal of weapons" approach to the criminal law itself warrants repeal of many of the substantive provisions. While exclusion from a criminal code of some conduct is sometimes explained on this basis,[187] it is not entirely clear that all of the statutes used as an arsenal against criminals could be removed without serious consequences.[188]

E. Arrest to Aid in Investigation of Another Offense or Offender

Illustration #23: Narcotics officers were following a person suspected of carrying narcotics. The officers lacked grounds to arrest, however. Observing the suspect commit a minor traffic violation (one which ordinarily would result in a mere warning), the officers placed the suspect under arrest and searched the car for narcotics.

Illustration #24: Officers noted a man with a jacket on his arm get out of an out-of-state car in the pawn shop district. The suspect, when questioned, indicated he had no employment but had come to the city to find same. He could provide no identification, but explained this by saying his wallet had recently been stolen. He was somewhat evasive in answering other questions, so the police arrested him for vagrancy.

Illustration #25: Officers had reasonable grounds to believe that a particular suspect was responsible for a recent homicide. However, desiring an opportunity to conduct a further in-custody investigation, the suspect was arrested on a vagrancy charge and then convicted. The murder investigation was continued while the suspect served out his vagrancy sentence.

---

[185] Hargrove, *Police Discretion*, 25 Sol. 337 (1958).

[186] See People v. Winters, 171 Cal. App. 2d Supp. 876, 342 P.2d 538 (Super. Ct. 1959).

[187] The Model Penal Code, in omitting some sex offenses, presents the argument that they are used for purpose of discriminatory enforcement. See Model Penal Code § 204-10 (Tent. Draft No. 4, 1955).

[188] For example, we have already noted above that the laws on bad checks and theft, usually not invoked in certain circumstances, are so used. And, all recall the use of the income tax laws to deal with known gangsters. For a more detailed discussion of this problem, see Remington & Rosenblum, *The Criminal Law and the Legislative Process*, 1960 U. Ill. L.F. 481, 493-94 (1960):

An arrest may be made for conduct not ordinarily subjected to the process because such arrest facilitates the investigation of another offense, one which is subjected to the process. As the illustrations indicate, the investigation of the other offense may be aided because (1) it is now possible to search the suspect incident to the arrest; (2) it is now possible to legally take the person into custody; or (3) it is now possible to detain the suspect longer than otherwise possible.

Arrest for conduct not normally proceeded against in order to aid investigation in either of these three ways might be subject to severe crictism. As to the arrest for offense *A* in order to conduct a search relating to offense *B*, the courts admittedly have usually upheld such searches. But, more and more courts are now requiring that the search be shown to relate either to a seeking of evidence on offense *A* or to protection of the arresting officer.[189] Thus arrest of a driver for failing to come to a complete stop does not warrant search of the trunk of the car. Perhaps even more important, however, is that there is some evidence that courts may now invalidate any search in this kind of case merely because the motive behind the arrest was the seeking of evidence on another offense.[190]

As to arrest for offense *A* because the person is suspected of offense *B* but cannot be arrested for offense *B* because of lack of evidence, this question has seldom reached the appellate courts. An exception is a California case in which the testimony of the arresting officers frankly revealed that the vagrant would *not* have been arrested *except* for the desire to investigate. Said the court:

> Whether this is an entirely commendable attitude toward the appellant's class of misdemeanants we need not stop to consider; but we think the admitted fact that the appellant would not have been arrested if he had confined himself to vagrancy did not render his arrest for that offense illegal.[191]

In sharp contrast is the following attitude of an English court:

> It seems to me to be an abuse of the process of the criminal

---

[189] See Note, 1959 Wis. L. Rev. 347. It is observed therein that few courts have analyzed these kinds of cases carefully, most being satisfied to merely declare that a search incident to an arrest is valid. Since that note was written some states have switched to the stricter approach, *e.g.*, People v. Mayo, 19 Ill. 2d 136, 166 N.E.2d 440 (1960); People v. Watkins, 19 Ill. 2d 11, 166 N.E.2d 433 (1960); People v. Gonzales, 356 Mich. 247, 97 N.W.2d 16 (1959).

[190] *E.g.*, Gilbert v. United States, 291 F.2d 586 (9th Cir. 1961), *appeal pending;* Taglavore v. United States, 291 F.2d 262 (9th Cir. 1961).

[191] People v. Craig, 152 Cal. 42, 47, 91 Pac. 997, 1000 (1907).

law to use the purely formal charge of a trifling offense upon which there is no real intention to proceed, as a cover for putting the person charged under arrest, and obtaining from that person incriminating statements, not in relation to the charge laid. . .but in relation to a more serious and altogether different offense.[192]

In support of the practice of making an otherwise legal arrest where another offense is suspected, it might be said that some sections of the criminal code were adopted by the legislature for exactly such a purpose. Indeed, sometimes evidence of this can be obtained.[193] While the commentators are not in agreement on the legitimacy of such a purpose,[194] probably the most valid criticism made is that questioning the appropriateness of adopting substantive provisions to solve procedural problems. Says one writer on the subject:

> If it is necessary to . . . legalize arrest for mere suspicion, then the grave policy and constitutional problems posed by such suggestions should be faced. If present restrictions on the laws of attempts or arrest place too onerous a burden upon the police because of the nature of modern crime, then such propositions should be discussed and resolved on their merits as, for example, the proposals in the Uniform Arrest Act.[195]

The arrest and conviction (or arrest and obtaining of a continuance) on a minor charge in order to provide ample time for an in-custody investigation of another offense poses substantially the same kind of problem. In a recent Supreme Court case a suspect was arrested for questioning concerning a double murder-

---

[192] Rex v. Dick [1947] 2 D. L. R. 213, 225 (Ont. Ct. App.), quoted in Culombe v. Connecticut, 367 U.S. 568, 632 n.95 (1961).

[193] "The underlying purpose [of the vagrancy laws] is to relieve the police of the necessity of proving that criminals have committed or are planning to commit specific crimes." N.Y. LAW REVISION COMM'N REPORT 591 (1935).

[194] Compare: "Arrest of a person who is not known to have committed a crime simply to discover whether he might possibly have done so someplace . . . is clearly unjustifiable," Comment, 23 CALIF. L. REV. 506 (1935), with:
"If a crime is specified for which the officer has power to arrest on reasonable suspicion, the mere fact that the person arrested is subsequently charged with a different crime does not make the arrest wrongful, for *non constat* that the officer did not reasonably believe that the stated crime had been committed when he made the arrest. . . . So it seems that an otherwise valid arrest on a minor charge is not rendered illegal by the fact that the real or principal motive of the police is to prevent the suspect's escaping from justice on some major charge which they are preparing against him. . . . This means that there is no legal objection to the practice of making a 'holding charge,' provided of course that the holding charge is a genuine one and that it operates to justify the detention." Williams, *Requisites of a Valid Arrest*, 1954 CRIM L. REV. (Eng.) 6, 17.

[195] Foote, *Vagrancy-Type Law and Its Administration*, 104 U. PA. L. REV. 603, 649 (1956).

robbery which took place without witnesses. The arrest occurred Saturday night, on Monday morning the suspect was booked for a breach of the peace, and on Tuesday morning he was taken into police court on this charge. At the suggestion of the investigating officer, the prosecutor moved for a continuance, which was granted without the defendant having an opportunity to contest the motion or participate in the proceedings in any way. Said the Court of this procedure:

> Instead of bringing him before a magistrate with reasonable promptness, as Connecticut law requires, to be duly presented for the grave crimes of which he was in fact suspected (and for which he had been arrested under the felony-arrest statute), he was taken before the New Britain Police Court on the palpable ruse of a breach-of-the-peace charge concocted to give the police time to pursue their investigation. This device is admitted. . . . [I]t kept Culombe in police hands without any of the protections that a proper magistrate's hearing would have assured him. Certainly, had he been brought before it charged with murder instead of an insignificant misdemeanor no court would have failed to warn Culombe of his rights and arrange for appointment of counsel.[196]

This reasoning is interesting, as it would seem to apply even though the charge on which the suspect is actually taken into Court is fully substantiated, and even though the person's detention is brought about by actual conviction. The court seems to be of the view that whatever other legal reasons might exist for detention, if it is used for investigative purposes it must include the protections ordinarily available to one arrested and detained for the offense being investigated.

CONCLUSION

The realities of current criminal justice administration make it imperative that the police exercise discretion in performing the law enforcement task; and, as the above discussion of current practice makes apparent, a broad range of discretion in fact has been assumed by the police.

That the present system does and must include discretionary power raises questions of a most serious nature. As Herbert Wechsler has written:

> There are, of course, important differences between the law in action and the law in books in this as in other fields. The

---

[196] Culombe v. Connecticut, 367 U.S. 568, 631 (1961).

soundest paper system would be totally impoverished by an inadequate administration, and sensible administration may get good results despite glaring defects in law. Abusive definitions of the scope of criminality may have their teeth drawn by the agencies of prosecution in refusing to proceed. . . . [But there is] no assurance that the possible correctives will be used in situations where upon the merits they ought' to be or that their application will be principled and free from favor or abuse. A society that holds, as we do, to belief in law cannot regard with unconcern the fact that prosecuting agencies can exercise so large an influence on dispositions that involve the penal sanction, without reference to any norms but those that they may create for themselves. Whatever one would hold as to the need for discretion of this order in a proper system or the wisdom of attempting regulation of its exercise, it is quite clear that its existence cannot be accepted as a substitute for a sufficient law. Indeed, one of the major consequences of the state of penal law today is that administration has so largely come to dominate the field without effective guidance from the law. This is to say that to a large extent we have, in this important sense, abandoned law—and this within an area where our fundamental teaching calls most strongly for its vigorous supremacy.[197]

The need for discretionary enforcement, even at the police level, does not mean that law *must* be abandoned. Rather, there is as great a need for legal principles and legal controls governing non-enforcement as there is for such standards and sanctions in the area of affirmative criminal law enforcement. Whether offenders are subjected to the criminal process by means which are fundamentally unfair, or whether offenders are excluded from the process by resort to unsound criteria, the consequences to a democratic society are equally serious.

The first step is to elevate police discretion from the *sub rosa* position it now occupies; the role of the police as decision-makers must be expressly recognized. Then, as has been found possible with respect to other administrative agencies, the areas in which discretion properly may be exercised must be delimited, principles to govern its exercise must be established, and effective means of control must be discovered. Only then can it be said with certainty that police nonenforcement does not contravene some of our most cherished democratic values.

---

[197] Wechsler, *The Challenge of a Model Penal Code*, 65 HARV. L. REV. 1097, 1101-02 (1952).

[8]

Revisiting the Decision to Arrest:
Comparing Beat and Community Officers

Kenneth J. Novak
James Frank
Brad W. Smith
Robin Shepard Engel

During the past 30 years, an expanding body of literature has evolved that examines the correlates of officers' decisions to arrest. This study extends this line of inquiry by investigating the influence of situational- and community-level variables on the arrest decisions of officers in an agency that has implemented community policing. Using data collected through systematic social observations of the police, the authors examine the direct effects of officers' assignment on the decision to arrest. In addition, the authors explore whether conventional arrest predictors vary between community and beat officers and, if so, the extent and nature of the variance. The findings generally suggest that there is no significant direct influence of assignment on arrest decisions. However, substantive differences in the decision-making process are revealed among predictors of arrest across assignments.

Since the American Bar Foundation sponsored a series of studies spanning the criminal justice system in the 1950s, academics and criminal justice practitioners have generally recognized that criminal justice officials exercise a considerable amount of discretion in the activities they perform, the manner in which they interact with citizens, and the processes by which they invoke and uphold the law (Bernard & Engel, 2001; Remmington, 1990; Walker, 1992). This "discovery" of discretion was particularly important in

KENNETH J. NOVAK: Department of Sociology/Criminal Justice & Criminology, University of Missouri–Kansas City. **JAMES FRANK**: Division of Criminal Justice, University of Cincinnati. **BRAD W. SMITH**: Department of Criminal Justice, Wayne State University. **ROBIN SHEPARD ENGEL**: Department of Sociology, Pennsylvania State University.

This work was supported by the National Institute of Justice Grant Number 96-IJ-CX-0075. Points of view are those of the authors and do not necessarily represent the view of the U.S. Department of Justice or the National Institute of Justice. A previous version of this article was presented at the annual meetings of the American Society of Criminology, Washington D.C., November 1998. We wish to thank John D. Wooldredge and Francis T. Cullen for their comments and suggestions. Please submit all correspondence to Kenneth J. Novak, 5100 Rockhill Rd., 208 Haag Hall, Kansas City, MO 64110; phone: 816-235-1599; e-mail: novakk@umkc.edu.

the field of policing, where it is generally acknowledged that the lowest level workers within police departments' organizational hierarchies have the greatest amounts of discretion over critical decisions. Evidence concerning the existence of discretion was initially demonstrated by the relatively infrequent use of arrest powers during encounters with citizens. For example, Reiss (1971) reported that officers only rarely made arrests of citizens, even when there were legal grounds to do so. Operating as street-level bureaucrats (Lipsky, 1980; Prottas, 1978), patrol officers are the gatekeepers of the criminal justice system. That is, the quantity of law (Black, 1980) that citizens receive is decided nearly exclusively by patrol officers at the street level.

Officers' frequent use of discretion, coupled with the importance of their decisions to invoke the criminal justice system, have led police researchers to examine extensively the use of arrest by officers. During the past 40 years, a large body of research has developed that contributes significantly to the understanding of police officers' decisions to invoke the criminal justice system (see Brooks, 1997; Riksheim & Chermak, 1993; and Sherman, 1980, for extensive literature reviews of police behavior). Nevertheless, recent changes in policing strategies and philosophies have challenged our understanding of and ability to predict officers' decision making. Departments across the country have adopted changes in their missions, strategies, and tactics during a time generally recognized as the community era in policing (Kelling & Moore, 1988). Indeed, administrators have hailed community-oriented policing as the preferred policing strategy (Rosenbaum & Lurigio, 1994) and subsequently report widespread implementation of this new model of policing. Despite this assertion, exactly how community policing has affected the day-to-day activities of police officers and whether it affects the way officers and citizens interact remains largely unknown.

Furthermore, officers' decision making in the era of community policing is particularly important for the police policy maker. Liability attached to police officers' behavior is enormous, and the potential liability involving improper police activities is estimated to be more than $780 billion (Kappeler, 1993). Community policing is designed to increase the level of discretion of the line officer, increase the frequency of officer-citizen encounters, decrease officer accountability, and thus increase organizational exposure to civil liability (Worrall & Marenin, 1998). Police policy makers should understand police officer behavior to ensure officers are not systematically engaging in unfair, immoral, or illegal types of behavior. Understanding officer-citizen interactions can assist administrators in monitoring and reducing organizational liability.

Various police behaviors have been empirically studied (e.g., traffic stops, use of force, gaining citizen compliance), which provides useful information to guide the present inquiry. This study, however, focuses specifically on decisions by police officers to take suspects into custody via arrest, thus depriving them (at least temporarily) of their freedom. Examining individual arrest decision making is not particularly innovative, as prior researchers have extensively addressed this issue. With the exception of research conducted by Mastrofski, Worden, and Snipes (1995), prior research has been unable to examine empirically possible changes in arrest practices during the community policing era.

This study attempts to fill this void by examining the influences of police arrest practices in the Cincinnati Police Division (CPD), a large, urban department that has implemented community policing. Using contemporary data collected through systematic social observations of police officers, situational- and community-level correlates of officer arrest decisions are examined. If community policing indeed affects the way police officers and citizens interact at the street level, it is reasonable to believe these changes will manifest themselves when comparing the correlates of arrest between officers actively engaging in community policing to those engaging in more traditional reactive/beat styles of policing. The context of this research differs from prior research in that we compare officers with different ascribed roles within the police organization rather than comparing officers with different attitudes toward community policing. We speculate that these roles manifest themselves in officers' decision making and affect how officers interact with citizens. Differences in police-citizen interactions, we believe, will lead to direct differences in officers' decisions to formally invoke the criminal justice system through the use of arrest.

COMMUNITY POLICING AND
THE DECISION TO ARREST

Regardless of how community policing is implemented, administrators have made several broad and sweeping generalizations regarding its anticipated effect. One claim is that community policing will lead to crime prevention and a reduction in overall crime. Another claim is that it builds more confidence and trust between citizens and the police. Still another claim is that it potentially affects the way in which police exercise discretion and social control, including the use of arrest. If community policing does not in reality achieve these outcomes, one might legitimately question whether it should be continued as the preferred method of service delivery. In other words, without realizing these outcomes, community policing is merely symbolic and represents more "rhetoric than reality" (Bayley, 1988).

Discussing its central philosophical themes, Cordner (1995) remarked that under community policing, the general goals of policing broaden to include more non–law enforcement tasks. It also encourages differential enforcement contingent on community values and norms. This differential policing will primarily affect the manner in which officers address minor offenses, local ordinances, and disorders. The types of interactions and encounters in which officers and citizens engage would also most likely change. Furthermore, police should use community residents to set priorities and reinforce neighborhood values. As such, it is plausible to infer that there will be an increase in the quantity and quality of police-citizen interactions and thus a change in the relationship between the police and the public (Eck & Rosenbaum, 1994; Goldstein, 1987; Skolnick & Bayley, 1987). What remains largely unknown, however, is how community policing is translated into practice, how it has affected policing at the street level, whether it has changed the way police officers and members of the public interact, and whether arrest decisions by community policing and beat officers are premised on the same factors.

Can researchers and administrators expect the arrest practices of officers to change under the implementation of community policing? Admittedly, this is a difficult question. One possible assertion is that the decision to arrest will not differ between officers practicing traditional policing and those practicing community policing. This may be due to the fact that community policing does not change the basic nature of policing, and officers' discretion is constrained by the nature of crime, the law, and occupational socialization. In contrast, a number of theoretical assertions have been offered that suggest community policing may influence arrest decisions. For example, assignment as a community policing officer might encourage underenforcement of the law in an effort to build community partnerships that might be compromised by more aggressive policing tactics (Bayley, 1988). Alternatively, officers practicing community policing may make more arrests for relatively minor infractions (Bratton & Knobler, 1998; Wilson & Kelling, 1982). Central to the discussion of these hypotheses is how community policing is defined and implemented within departments.

Mastrofski and his colleagues (1995) have suggested that community policing may be generally defined and implemented as three different models: broken windows, community-building, and problem-oriented policing. They described the broken windows model as stressing aggressive enforcement of minor crimes and disorders and suggested that this approach "might increase the total number of arrests" but also might "decrease the probability of arrest in some situations because officers are to intervene at lower thresholds of disorder and to use intrusions short of arrest" (p. 540; also see Crank, 1994). In contrast, they described the community-building model as focusing on crime prevention, victim assistance, and the building of rapport with citizens, while it "deemphasizes law enforcement activities" (Mastrofski et al., 1995, p. 540). Last, they described the problem-oriented policing model as using a number of tactics to address the underlying causes of problems. Accordingly, advocates of this model "urge police to invoke the criminal sanction more sparingly and to give greater play to other methods" (Mastrofski et al., 1995, p. 541). Collectively, these hypotheses suggest that police departments implementing aggressive order maintenance models of community policing should expect increases in the use of arrest, whereas those departments implementing community-building and/or problem-solving models should expect decreases in the use of arrest.

Although none of these assertions have been thoroughly subjected to empirical scrutiny, there exists some evidence that suggests community policing policies do influence officers' arrest decisions. Mastrofski and colleagues (1995) examined the arrest decisions of officers who reported both favorable and unfavorable attitudes toward community policing within a department that had implemented the community building model of community policing (Richmond, Virginia, police department). They found that officers with more favorable attitudes toward community policing were "more selective in making arrests" compared to those officers with less favorable attitudes. Moreover, they reported that arrest decisions for officers with less favorable views toward community policing were more strongly influenced by legal characteristics compared to those with positive views. Neither group, however, was strongly influenced by extralegal factors. They concluded that "in a time of community policing, officers who support it do manifest some arrest decision patterns distinguishable from those of colleagues who adhere to a more traditional view of law enforcement" (p. 539). These researchers, however, were unable to thoroughly describe the arrest patterns for officers with positive views of community policing, commenting, "community-oriented officers 'march to the beat of a different drummer' . . . but our model gives a poor account of that 'beat'" (p. 556). Their results indicate that although we know much about officers' decision making prior to the implementation of community policing initiatives, factors influencing officers' discretion in the era of community policing are open for debate.

CORRELATES OF ARREST IN THE
COMMUNITY POLICING ERA

A great deal of prior research has examined the factors that influence officers' decision making, particularly officers' decisions to arrest. Directly related to the present inquiry is the influence of organizational assignments (as community or beat officers) on officer behavior. We expect that organizational assignment as community policing officers will result in behavioral differences when compared to beat officers. Indeed, recent research examining the time officers spent conducting community policing activities, problem-solving activities, and encounters with citizens suggested that officers with community policing assignments spent "less 'face time' with the public and more time 'behind the scenes'" (Parks, Mastrofski, DeJong, & Gray, 1999, p. 514) when compared to 911 responders. We further expect that differences in assignments will influence officers' decisions to arrest directly and indirectly through other correlates of police behavior, including legal factors, situational factors, and community context.

Situational Factors

Reviews of police research generally suggest that legal variables (e.g., seriousness of the offense, amount of evidence, the presence of a weapon, etc.) have a relatively strong and consistent influence over officer decision making vis-à-vis suspects (Black, 1971; Black & Reiss, 1970; Smith, 1984; Smith & Klein, 1983; Smith & Visher, 1981; Smith, Visher, & Davidson, 1984; Sykes, Fox, & Clark, 1985; Worden, 1989). One might speculate that legal variables will have a significant influence over officers' behavior regardless of community policing. Ultimately, community policing officers are still police officers who have been socialized within the same organization, with similar constraints, expectations, rewards, and so forth as their counterparts. Thus, legal factors may have equal influence regardless of assignment. Mastrofski et al. (1995), however, found that offense seriousness was not significantly related to arrest decisions for officers with positive attitudes toward community policing. They argued that the behavior of officers who embrace community policing may be influenced by information beyond legal factors.

The research available on the influence of other situational variables (i.e., characteristics of the suspect, characteristics of the victim, characteristics of the situation) over police behavior has been somewhat mixed. Particularly controversial is the potential effect that suspects' characteristics have over police behavior. Whereas some researchers have reported that citizens encountered by police who were racial minorities (Lundman, 1979, 1998; Smith et al., 1984; Smith & Klein, 1984; Smith & Visher, 1981), male (Visher, 1983; Worden & Shepard, 1996), juvenile (Black, 1976; Mastrofski et al., 1995), disrespectful (Engel, Sobol, & Worden, 2000; Lundman, 1994, 1996a, 1996b, 1998; Worden & Shepard, 1996), and intoxicated (Engel et al., 2000; Mastrofski et al., 1995) were significantly more likely to be arrested, other research suggests that these extralegal factors do not have a strong influence over officers' behaviors (Klinger, 1994, 1996a, 1996b).

One of the concerns surrounding the implementation of community policing is the influence that suspects' characteristics might have over officers' behavior as discretion is increased through innovative strategies and organizational changes associated with community policing. As Bayley (1988) warned, "community policing may weaken the rule of law in the sense of equal protection and evenhanded enforcement" (p. 231). As a result, one might speculate that suspects' characteristics would have a stronger influence over officers' behavior in the community policing era. Alternatively, because of their closer and consultive relationship with citizens, community officers may look beyond certain discriminatory factors. These factors may matter less in predicting encounter outcomes for community officers due to higher levels of tolerance toward unconventional citizens or those citizens generally considered by police to be less respectable (e.g., juveniles, minorities, lower income and homeless persons, mentally disordered persons, etc.). In addition, due to the relationship community officers enjoy with citizens, they may be more predisposed to follow citizens' requests and preferences, which have been shown in past research to influence officers' behavior (Mastrofski, Snipes, Parks, & Maxwell, 2000; Smith & Klein, 1983, 1984; Smith & Visher, 1981; Worden, 1989; Worden & Pollitz, 1984).

In addition, other characteristics of the social setting may influence arrest. Community officers may be more successful in negotiating what Sykes and Brent (1980) described as definitional or imperative regulation. If citizens comply with officers' requests, the escalation of control often stops. If citizens are noncompliant, however, the encounter intensifies and officers often rely on coercive control of the citizen through legal sanction, arrest, or use of force. Community policing officers may be more likely to secure compliance from citizens for a number of reasons. First, the "police and the public are encouraged to become closely acquainted so that they will be mutually accountable" (Mastrofski, Snipes, & Supina, 1996, p. 270); therefore, community police officers should have more nonthreatening interactions with citizens. Second, community officers are assigned to communities over a long period of time to build rapport, which might translate into a lesser need for the use of coercive techniques. Beat officers, although assigned to the same district for a long period of time, are not necessarily assigned to the same community on a daily basis because their beat assignment may vary. Thus, community officers, by virtue of their assignment, are provided a greater opportunity to get to know community residents on a more intimate level, and this should in turn allow for the officer to me more successful in gaining complaisance during encounters with the public. In short, citizens may grant compliance to community officers, whereas beat officers may not be able to attain this imperative regulation. The only evidence addressing this hypothesis reported that officers' attitudes toward community- oriented policing did not have a significant effect on the likelihood of citizen compliance (McCluskey, Mastrofski, & Parks, 1999). However, this research measured officers' attitudes but not their assignment as community policing or traditional beat officers.

Community Context

Variations in the neighborhood context of police-citizen encounters may also influence police officer behavior. There are at least two rationales for examining the effects of neighborhood-level characteristics on officer behavior. First, there is a hypothesized relationship between levels of neighborhood informal social control and the exercise of formal social control by police officers. Essentially, in communities where there is less informal social control, there is a greater need for formal social control, such as official police intervention (Bursik, 1986; Schuerman & Kobrin, 1986). Second, citizen expectations of police officer priorities have been found to differ based on racial and economic characteristics of communities (Alpert & Dunham, 1988; Alpert, Dunham, & Piquero, 1997; Skogan & Hartnett, 1997). As such, communities differ in what they desire police officers to do and the priorities police officers should promote. In short, neighborhood disorganization may have a significant and positive influence on the arrest practices of traditional officers but may not manifest itself for community policing officers.

Community context may influence officers' behavior in one of two different ways. On one hand, police-citizen encounters occurring in neighborhoods characterized by high levels of disorganization (i.e., high residential mobility, single-parent households, poverty, racial heterogeneity, and renter-occupied households) may involve a greater use of legal dispositions because local informal social control mechanisms may be weak. On the other hand, police-citizen interactions in disorganized communities may elicit a less vigorous response from officers. Klinger (1997) hypothesized that within police districts with higher rates of crime, a low level of deviance or less serious crimes may be met by informal police responses. In other words, crimes occurring in high-crime-rate or disorganized areas would evoke a more lenient response. In communities where there are high levels of crime, officers may be less likely to initiate an arrest for relatively minor crime because the action may not have violated a threshold for conduct in that community. Thus, officers would be less likely to arrest a citizen in this community and more likely to issue a warning, command the citizen to cease the behavior, or use some other type of order-maintenance technique. He suggested that district-level work norms influence how officers would respond to deviance with alternatives beyond arrest.

Extant research on the relationships between structural characteristics and arrest is inconsistent. For instance, racial conflict theory stated that racial minorities are seen as threats to the majority as well as local agents of formal social control (Black, 1976; Brandl, Chamlin, & Frank, 1995; Turk, 1969). Citizens encountered by police in communities with high economic distress have been found more likely to receive coercive dispositions (Smith, 1984; Smith et al., 1984; Smith & Klein, 1984). Finally, single family households represent decreased levels of guardianship and observation of persons in the community, particularly juveniles. This factor has been found to be related to increased crime rates, lower levels of informal social control, and greater opportunity for offending and victimization.

Although the above review suggests that community characteristics influence the behavior of officers engaging in traditional, incident-driven policing, it is unknown if community context influences the behavior of officers practicing community policing. Because community policing implies that officers will become closer to citizens and will better understand community norms, community factors that have in the past influenced arrest dispositions may not have the same effect in encounters involving community officers.

Limits of Existing Research

Although prior research on officer behavior has contributed significantly to our understanding of police-citizen encounters, several limitations exist. First, many of the conclusions that have been drawn and the conventional wisdom that has been established regarding the correlates of police behavior are based on data collected before the shift to community-oriented policing. As Fyfe (1996) acknowledged regarding the generalization of findings from studies conducted in the late 1970s through the mid-1980s, "all that has happened to policing since collection of the data that now form the conventional wisdom makes it unwise to generalize from them to either 1985 or the present" (p. 339). Indeed, contemporary empirical research supports contentions that officers who believe in the underlying concepts of community policing use different decision-making structures than their counterparts when deciding whether to arrest citizens (Mastrofski et al., 1995); therefore, correlates that previously were found to predict behavior may differ between officers practicing community-oriented policing and officers performing more traditional reactive policing.

Second, because community-oriented policing suggests that a closer relationship exists between the police and citizens, police may be interacting with their constituents on a more intimate level than before. This, coupled with the long-term orientation of patrols in neighborhoods, may minimize the importance of citizen characteristics in arrest decisions and encounters more generally because community officers are likely to have more information about the citizens they encounter and may be less likely to rely on ascribed traits. Alternatively, as some critics of community policing have speculated, this intimate connection with the community might serve to enhance officers' decision making based on suspects' characteristics. The current research available has not adequately tested these hypotheses.

Third, prior operationalizations of neighborhood may have been imperfect (Klinger, 1997). Research stated that the neighborhood should serve a locally relevant function and that the members should share common interests and beliefs (Duffee, 1990; Flynn, 1998; Hillery, 1955). Extant research has operationalized neighborhood as larger, arbitrary, macrogeographic units, such as police beats, census block groups, or enumeration districts (see Smith, 1986). The use of neighborhoods, which exert their own political influence on local government, may yield differing results when examining the influence of community-level variables on police officer behavior.

Finally, the findings reported from the only empirical study available that has addressed some of these issues during the community policing era—Mastrofski et al. (1995)—are somewhat limited. This research did not examine the differing influences of community factors on officers' behavior. For reasons articulated above, we believe this to be an important omission.

Furthermore, the research conducted by Mastrofski and his colleagues (1995) explored variations in arrest practices between officers who expressed favorable or unfavorable attitudes toward community policing. Prior to this research, however, police research has been unable to establish a strong relationship between police officer attitudes and behavior (Meyers, Heeren, & Hingston, 1989; Smith & Klein, 1983; Snipes & Mastrofski, 1990; Stith, 1990; Worden, 1989). Indeed, the influence between officers' attitudes and behavior has been continually questioned. Therefore, one might expect that organizational assignments as community policing officers (although certainly correlated with officers' attitudes toward community policing) might be a stronger measure of officers' behavior.

These limitations are addressed in the present inquiry. Using contemporary data collected from a department actively engaged in community policing, this article examines the correlates of arrest, including situational and community characteristics. The logistical regression analyses examine the factors related to the arrest decision between officers assigned as community police officers and those engaged in traditional beat style of policing.

METHOD

Research Site

Data for this study were collected from systematic observations of officers from the CPD. The CPD is the largest police agency within Hamilton County, Ohio, with 996 sworn officers. It is a full-service police department serving a city of approximately 364,000 citizens, including an African American population of 37.9%. In 1991, the department began implementing community policing on a limited scale and was expanded to every community in the city by 1994 (for more information, see Frank, Brandl, & Watkins, 1997).

All officers who participated in this study were assigned to the Patrol Bureau at the time of observation. The first type of officers observed was beat officers. These officers typically performed all duties associated with traditional line-level police officers, particularly responding to calls for service. The second type of officers observed was community-oriented policing (COP) officers. These officers were assigned to a specific community (or in some cases, several communities) and were expected to perform community policing functions, including becoming acquainted with citizens in their assigned neighborhood, identifying neighborhood problems, forging partnerships with citizens to develop solutions to neighborhood problems, networking with local service agencies to assist in problem solving, representing the division at community meetings, preparing and sharing crime statistics with citizens, conducting security surveys, and developing initiatives to improve opportunities for youth, along with some of the general duties common to all officers in the Patrol Bureau. To facilitate the performance of these duties, community officers did not rotate shifts or neighborhoods and were largely freed from responding to calls for service.[1] Administrators described community policing in Cincinnati as focusing on community building; however, in practice, community policing could be more accurately described as a hybrid between community building and problem solving. Incidentally, these two ingredients (community building and problem solving) are the same two factors identified by the Community Policing Consortium (1994) required to institute community policing. Officers were largely left to their own devices regarding the delivery of services and the modification of tactics according to community conditions and the demands of residents.

Data

Data used in this study came from two different sources: social observations of police officers and the U.S. Census. Between April 1997 and April 1998, trained observers conducted observations during 442 shifts with CPD officers. The division's organizational arrangement could be considered as specialist in nature in that officers were assigned as either community policing officers or beat officers in each neighborhood in the city. Observations were conducted with both COP and beat officers.

Because extant literature suggests that officers' routines and behavior may vary by neighborhood characteristics, we sought to observe COP and beat officers in similar environmental contexts to make direct comparisons. COP officers and beat officers worked in the same beats and neighborhoods, so both COP officers and their complementary beat officer were observed. COP and beat officers observed in this study had similar demographic characteristics, including gender (COP: 80% male; beat: 83% male), race (COP: 52% White; beat: 65% White), and length of service (COP: $\bar{x} = 7.65$; beat: $\bar{x} = 6.42$). Cincinnati contains 52 designated neighborhoods that are well defined both politically and geographically.[2] A random sample of 32 COP officers was selected for inclusion in the study. Because COP officers work either first shift (7:00 a.m. to 3:00 p.m.) or second shift (3:00 p.m. to 11:00 p.m.), observations of beat officers were also constrained to these time periods. Trained researchers accompanied COP officers during 206 shifts and beat officers during 236 shifts, observing 1,103 and 1,568 police-citizen encounters, respectively.[3]

To identify structural differences in communities, block group–level data were collected from the 1990 census. Community boundaries were obtained from the CPD, whose officers realigned assignments, beats, and districts to conform to the neighborhood parameters designated by the city planning commission. Maps obtained from the police division were compared with block group census maps to determine block groups that corresponded with neighborhoods in Cincinnati. These group data were aggregated to the neighborhood level.

The unit of analysis for this study was the interaction between the police and a member of the public. Certainly, not all interactions between the police and the public end in arrest, and in fact, not all encounters could be reasonably expected to end in arrest. This sample consists of encounters where probable cause to believe the citizen committed a criminal offense was present during the encounter.[4] Of the 1,103 interactions between COP officers and citizens, there were 104 interactions where probable cause was present. Of the 1,568 interactions between beat officers and citizens, there were 230 involving probable cause.

Variables

Table 1 presents the descriptive statistics for the variables used in this analysis.[5] The dichotomous dependent variable indicates whether the officer arrested any citizen involved in the encounter. The officer's assignment is measured as a dichotomous variable, where 0 = community policing officer and 1 = beat officer. Situational-level correlates include two legal variables, offense seriousness and evidence critera. Offense seriousness is measured on a 2-point scale, in which 0 = minor offenses or misdemeanors and 1 = serious offenses or felonies.[6] The evidence variable is measured as an additive scale ranging from 0 to 4 based on the amount of evidence present at the encounter. Four different types of evidence are included: (a) whether the officer observed the citizen engage in an illegal act or viewed circumstantial evidence of an illegal act, (b) whether the officer observed physical evidence that implicated the citizen to an offense, (c) whether the officer heard claims from others that implicated the citizen in an offense, and (d) whether the officer heard the citizen confess to the offense.[7]

Citizens' demographic characteristics are measured as dichotomous variables, including gender (0 = male, 1 = female), race (0 = White, 1 = non-White), and age (0 = nonjuvenile, 1 = juvenile). Demeanor is also measured as a dichotomous variable, whereby 0 = deferential or civil and 1 = moderately or highly disrespectful.[8] Interaction-phase crime (Klinger, 1994) is measured as whether the citizen engaged in criminal activity during the encounter, such as assaulting another citizen, assaulting the officer, fleeing from the officer, or resisting arrest (0 = no interaction-phase crime, 1 = interaction-phase crime). In addition, whether the officer exercised order maintenance techniques during the encounter (0 = no order maintenance techniques used, 1 = officer attempted order maintenance)[9] as well as whether the citizen complied with these directives (0 = citizen complied with directives, 1 = citizen did not comply with directives) are also included in the analysis. The rationale is if the officer attempted to direct the citizen to do some act, the officer

TABLE 1: Description and Frequency of Variables

		Frequency	
		Beat	Community-Oriented Policing
	Values	Beat Officers (1)	Policing Officers (0)
Dependent variable			
Arrest	0 = No	150 (65.2)	77 (74.0)
	1 = Yes	80 (34.8)	27 (26.0)
Situational level			
Offense	0 = Minor offense/misdemeanor	208 (90.4)	96 (92.3)
seriousness	1 = Serious offense/felony	22 (9.6)	8 (7.7)
Evidence	0 = No evidence observed	20 (8.7)	4 (3.8)
	1 = One evidence criterion	62 (27.0)	45 (43.3)
	2 = Two evidence criteria	67 (29.1)	30 (28.8)
	3 = Three evidence criteria	56 (24.3)	20 (19.2)
	4 = Four evidence criteria	25 (10.9)	5 (4.8)
Citizen gender	0 = Male	157 (68.3)	85 (81.7)
	1 = Female	73 (31.7)	19 (18.3)
Citizen race	0 = White	81 (35.2)	40 (38.5)
	1 = Non-White	149 (64.8)	64 (61.5)
Citizen age	0 = Age 18 and older	191 (83.0)	63 (60.6)
(Juvenile)	1 = Preschool to age 17	39 (17.0)	41 (39.4)
Citizen	0 = Deferential	182 (79.1)	84 (80.8)
demeanor	1 = Not deferential	48 (20.9)	20 (19.2)
Interaction-	0 = No crime	210 (91.3)	91 (87.5)
phase crime	1 = Nonviolent crime	20 (8.7)	13 (12.5)
Citizen	0 = No	191 (83.0)	92 (88.5)
intoxication	1 = Yes	39 (17.0)	12 (11.5)
Preference	0 = No	200 (87.0)	95 (91.3)
for arrest	1 = Yes	30 (13.0)	9 (8.7)
Order	0 = No order maintenance	130 (56.5)	39 (37.5)
maintenance	1 = Order maintenance	100 (43.5)	65 (62.5)
Noncompliance	0 = Citizen complied	193 (83.9)	96 (92.3)
	1 = Citizen did not comply	37 (16.1)	8 (7.7)
Community level			
Residential	Percentage	$\bar{x}$ = .52,	$\bar{x}$ = .51,
Mobility		SD = .08	SD = .08
Community	Factor	$\bar{x}$ = .72,	$\bar{x}$ = 1.44,
Factor		SD = .74	SD = .59
n		230	104

was giving the citizen an opportunity to avoid arrest. Furthermore, if the citizen acquiesced with these commands, there was a diminished necessity for arrest. Successful attainment of imperative regulation should decrease the likelihood of arrest. Variables also indicated whether citizens displayed any visible signs of intoxication (0 = not intoxicated, 1 = intoxicated) and whether a victim/witness preferred arrest (0 = no preference, 1 = preference for arrest).

Community-level correlates are also described in Table 1. Data were collected on residential stability, economic distress, racial composition, proportion of single family households, proportion of renter-occupied households, and the poverty level of communities.[10] To avoid problems associated with multicollinearity, these community-level variables were factor analyzed. One of these variables, the percentage of the population living in the community for less than 5 years (i.e., residential mobility), did not load onto the main factor and therefore is analyzed as a separate variable. The remaining variables were combined into one factor score. Principal components factor analysis indicated that these variables tap the same dimension, with the eigenvalue equal to 3.014. The remaining factors all had eigenvalues of less than 0.668. The total item intercorrelation suggests there is internal consistency with these four items and that they tap the same underlying construct (Cronbach's standardized alpha = 0.864). The items addressing community disorganization loaded on the factor between 0.787 and 0.948.

Analyses

In the analyses that follow, a series of logistical regression models are estimated that include situational- and community-level variables. Due to the multilevel nature of the data, hierarchical linear models (HLM) were initially estimated.[11] After estimating an unconditional HLM model in which no predictors were included, we were able to estimate the conditional models, which included only unmanipulated situational-level predictors. However, upon examination of the chi-square statistic for the y intercept, we observed a nonsignificant value (direct-effects model: $x^2 = 1.76491, p > .05$; beat officer model: $x^2 = 0.12452, p > .05$; COP officer model: $x^2 = 0.555, p > .05$). This indicates that after accounting for the variation explained by the situational variables, there is no significant amount of variation in the outcome variable left to be explained by the aggregate predictors. Stated differently, conducting a HLM analysis while including both levels of data would not significantly contribute to the prediction in arrest decision making, and therefore, multilevel modeling was not necessary.[12]

Using logistical regression, a direct-effects model was first estimated for the correlates to examine the direct effects of assignment on decisions to arrest. Thereafter, conditional-effects models are estimated for encounters involving beat and COP officers separately to examine the interaction effect of assignment on the different correlates of arrest. Finally, comparisons of the coefficients for COP and beat officers were made using an equation derived by Clogg, Petkova, and Haritou (1995) to test for significant differences in the correlates of behavior between officers.[13] The log odds of the coefficients are also presented. This value, *Exp(b)*, indicates the odds of experiencing a change in *y* (arrest) for every unit change in *x* (independent variable). These statistics reveal whether the individual correlate exerts a different substantive influence on officers' arrest decisions.

RESULTS

Table 2 presents the direct effects logistical regression analysis for situational- and community-level correlates. Of particular importance is the insignificant relationship between officer assignment and decisions to arrest. Several situational-level variables, however, are significant predictors of decisions to arrest. Evidence is positively related to arrest ($b = .472, p < .05$), whereas male citizens ($b = -1.340, p < .01$) and juveniles ($b = 1.300, p < .01$) are significantly more likely to be arrested than females or adults. In addition, citizens who display signs of intoxication are significantly more likely to be arrested ($b = 2.195, p < .01$) as are citizens who display a hostile demeanor ($b = .846, p < .05$) and citizens who are noncompliant with requests made by officers ($b = 2.204, p < .01$). During encounters where officers do not attempt order maintenance techniques, citizens are significantly more likely to be arrested than citizens confronted during other encounters ($b = -1.577, p < .01$). Finally, officers are more likely to arrest citizens during encounters where a victim or witness specifically requests such action ($b = 2.885, p < .01$). Although several situational-level correlates are related to decision making in the direct-effects model, arrest decisions do not vary significantly due to the community-level characteristics.

To examine the interaction effects of assignment on arrest decisions, separate models were estimated for COP and beat officers. These subsequent analyses allow for a comparison of independent variables on decisions to arrest across organizational assignment. The estimates for the conditional effects models are displayed in Table 3.

In the model for encounters between beat officers and citizens, males are significantly more likely to be arrested than are females ($b = -1.231, p < .01$). Intoxicated citizens encountered by beat officers are also more likely to be arrested than are their counterparts ($b = 2.933, p < .01$) as well as citizens who

TABLE 2:   Direct Effects of the Logistical Regression Analysis for Correlates of
           Arrest ($N = 329$)

	b	SE
Constant	−5.531**	1.348
Officer assignment	−.015	.404
Offense seriousness	.949	.559
Evidence	.472**	.167
Citizen gender	−1.340**	.427
Citizen race	.822*	.430
Citizen age	1.300**	.408
Citizen intoxication	2.195**	.548
Demeanor	.846*	.431
Citizen noncompliance	2.204**	.479
Interaction-phase crime	2.249**	.548
Victim preference	2.884**	.522
Order maintenance	−1.577**	.399
Residential mobility	2.516	2.129
Community factor	−.038	.293
Model χ^2	172.990**	
Pseudo R^2	.374	

*$p < .05.$ **$p < .01.$

display a hostile demeanor ($b = 1.108$, $p < .05$). Beat officers who do not attempt order maintenance techniques during encounters are more likely to ultimately arrest the citizen involved in the encounter ($b = -2.157$, $p < .01$); likewise, citizens who, when given a directive, remain noncompliant ($b = 2.608$, $p < .01$) are significantly more likely to be arrested.

Table 3 also displays the estimates for COP officers. Unlike the model estimated for beat officers, few of the situational-level correlates are significant predictors of arrest. Only four predictor variables are significant, one of which was not significant in the beat officer model. Specifically, COP officers are more likely to take juveniles into custody ($b = 1.683$, $p < .05$). Similar to beat officers, when citizens comply with order maintenance requests the encounter is less likely to end in arrest ($b = 2.223$, $p < .05$). During encounters where a victim or witness requests arrest, COP officers are much more likely than not to follow through with the request ($b = 4.191$, $p < .01$) as well as make an arrest when there is a crime committed in the presence of the officer ($b = 2.805$, $p < .05$). The final column in Table 3 provides a comparison of coefficients between the multiplicative models for beat and COP officers. Although the models estimated for beat officers appear to be very different

TABLE 3: Conditional Effects of the Logistical Regression Analysis for Correlates of Arrest

	Beat Officers			Community-Oriented Policing Officers			
	b	SE	Exp(b)	b	SE	Exp(b)	t
Constant	−6.221**	1.65		−4.869	3.193		
Offense seriousness	1.136	.678	3.113	1.203	1.307	3.330	−.045
Evidence	.380*	.190	1.466	.767	.413	2.153	−.842
Citizen gender	−1.231*	.564	.292	−2.373	1.268	.093	.823
Citizen race	1.123*	.564	3.075	.313	.875	1.367	.778
Citizen age	1.103*	.535	3.014	1.683*	.833	5.381	−.586
Citizen intoxication	2.932**	.623	18.770	.079	1.085	1.082	2.280*
Demeanor	1.108*	.547	3.029	.377	.833	1.458	.734
Noncompliance	2.608**	.597	13.577	2.223*	1.131	9.237	.301
Interaction-phase crime	2.072**	.762	7.944	2.805**	1.074	16.530	−.556
Victim preference	3.034**	.639	20.780	4.191**	1.377	66.111	−.762
Order maintenance	−2.157**	.539	.116	−.763	.761	.466	−1.495
Residential mobility	4.248	2.620	9.967	−3.006	5.257	.049	1.235
Community factor	−.327	.361	.363	.791	.635	.213	−1.530
Model χ^2	135.084**			49.711**			
Pseudo R^2	.546			.461			
n	226			103			

*$p < .05$. **$p < .01$.

from the models estimated for COP officers, only one factor exerts a significantly different affect on decision making. Specifically, citizens who displayed visible signs of intoxication are significantly more likely to be
arrested by beat officers but not COP officers ($t = 2.280$, $p < .05$).

Table 3 also presents the log-odds coefficient change for each situational
independent variable across officer assignment, Exp(b). Although few of the
comparisons of coefficients reveal significant differences, some substantive
effects are displayed. Specifically, citizen intoxication increases the likelihood of arrest by a factor of 18.8 for beat officer encounters but only by a factor of 1.1 for COP officers. Hostile citizens are 3.0 times more likely to be
arrested by beat officers but only 1.5 times more likely to be arrested by COP
officers. Finally, during encounters where victims or witnesses request an
arrest, beat officers are 20.8 times more likely to make an arrest. However,
there is a 66.1 factor increase in arrest during encounters with COP officers.

DISCUSSION

Similarities Between Officers

This study examines situational- and community-level factors that influence the decision-making processes of police officers during encounters with citizens. The findings suggest that assignment as a community policing officer has no direct effect on officers' decisions to arrest. This conflicts with hypotheses that community policing officers would be less likely to make arrests and more likely to use nonlegal remedies during encounters (Bayley, 1988; Cordner, 1995). The analyses indicate that in Cincinnati, beat officers and community policing officers perform at parity when exercising this type of coercive control over citizens.

The data also show that when citizens fail to comply with officer directives, they are more likely to be arrested, regardless of officer assignment. If citizens did not comply with these orders, officers invoked coercive regulation by making an arrest. Regardless of assignment, when a victim or citizen present at the scene requested arrest of a suspect, officers were more likely to follow this request. However, it is interesting to note the difference in log-odds between officers. When victims or witnesses communicate a preference for arrest during encounters with beat officers, the officers are 10 times more likely to arrest the citizen. The influence was much greater for COP officers, in which they were 66.1 times more likely to arrest the citizen. It appears that COP officers are much more likely to comply with the requests of victims and witnesses than their counterparts, perhaps indicating that these officers are more conscious of the preferences of members of the public.

Several conclusions can be drawn from the analyses of aggregate-level predictors. Community-level crime rates do not significantly affect arrest decision making in any of the models. Neither beat officers nor COP officers are more likely to make arrests in communities with greater residential mobility. Citizens encountered in communities with greater values on the community factor are neither more nor less likely to be arrested by both beat and COP officers.

Differences Between Officers

Factors that influenced the decision to arrest appear to differ between COP and beat officers. Several of the predictors are only statistically significant for beat officer encounters. Specifically, strength of evidence, gender, race, intoxication, demeanor, interaction-phase crime, and whether the officer attempted order maintenance are all significantly related to arrest. In contrast, citizen age and interaction-phase crime are only related to COP officer decisions to arrest. The data also revealed that beat officers are significantly more likely to arrest citizens when they do not first attempt to exercise order maintenance during the encounter. If citizens complied with these orders, officers were not compelled to actuate an arrest. It should be noted that only one of these differences—the influence of intoxication—is statistically significant. However, there are clearly substantive differences between officers' assignments in the degree of influence these correlates exert on arrest decisions.

These findings both confirm and call into question results reported in the extant literature. They support prior research that has reported levels of evidence to be positively related to arrest. As the number of evidence criteria increased, beat officers were more likely to make an arrest. This was not the case for COP officers, although the influence of evidence did not differ significantly between organizational assignments. Thus, the data revealed the more important legal variable to be the amount of evidence that alleged the citizen had committed an offense versus the severity of the offense itself. The findings also provide mixed conclusions regarding the influence of citizens' demographic characteristics. The multiplicative analyses revealed beat officers are more likely to arrest male citizens than female citizens. In contrast, COP officers are more likely to arrest juveniles than are beat officers. Therefore, it appears that COP officers are not more likely to play a role of mentor or agent of diversion than are their counterparts, as Bazemore and Senjo (1997) have suggested. This may indicate COP officers are more likely to take a "get tough" approach on juvenile crime, rather than diversion from the criminal justice system. It is plausible that COP officers, because of their different role in the community, may be placing juvenile crime and hooliganism as a priority for enforcement. These data were collected as part of a larger study. Results from a survey of Cincinnati citizens (not reported here) indicated residents may feel juvenile crime is a problem in their community. Specifically, when citizens were asked, "How big of a problem is kids hanging out on the street bothering people?" more than 47.3% indicated this was a "big problem" or "somewhat of a problem." Thus, the COP officer may be viewed as acting more in accordance with citizens' priorities than are beat officers (Frank, Novak, & Smith, in press).

Intoxicated citizens encountered by beat officers are significantly more likely to be arrested, whereas this relationship is not observed for COP officers. Intoxicated citizens are 18.8 times more likely to be arrested during encounters with beat officers, but only 1.1 times more likely to be arrested by COP officers. Furthermore, citizen intoxication exerted a significantly different influence on the decision to arrest based on officer assignment.

In addition, the influence of citizens' demeanor is particularly noteworthy. Similar to the conclusions of most prior research, beat officers are significantly more likely to arrest hostile citizens. At the same time, hostility did not significantly influence the decision making of COP officers. When confronting a hostile citizen, beat officers are 3.0 times more likely to actuate an arrest, whereas COP officers are only 1.5 times more likely to arrest. Combined, these analyses imply that COP officers may be more tolerant of both intoxicated and hostile citizen behavior and may not simply arrest citizens who flunk the attitude test (Brown, 1981). This may be due to community officers' desires to refrain from arresting citizens in an effort to strengthen police-citizen relationships. In any case, the findings suggest that beat officers and COP officers interact with inebriated and disrespectful citizens differently.

CONCLUSIONS AND POLICY IMPLICATIONS

These results present several implications. First, policy makers may use these results to understand more fully the behavior in an organization that engages in community policing by creating a separate unit or split shift within the department. Community policing officers arrested citizens at a slightly lower rate as their counterparts (26% vs. 34.8%) and engaged less frequently in encounters in which arrest was a possible disposition. Specifically, beat officers engaged in encounters that could end in arrest once every 1.05 shifts, whereas COP officers engaged in similar encounters once every 2 shifts. Although the opportunity to make an arrest may be a product of their position within the organization, explaining their reduced proclivity to exercise arrest powers is somewhat more difficult. Because COP officers volunteered for the position, differences in the arrest rate may be due to cognitive differences within the officer. It is equally plausible that variation may be explained by additional training and practice in community policing. Furthermore, multivariate analyses show that COP officers use slightly different decision-making processes than their counterparts do. Although officer assignment does not have a direct influence on arrest decision making, it appears that there is some different decision-making processes being employed by COP and beat officers. This is congruent with the hypothesized impact of community policing on the decision to arrest, and our results confirm the conclusion that perhaps some officers use different decision-making criteria during these encounters. Officers actively engaging in community policing may be interacting with citizens in a subtly different fashion and using different dimensions of the encounter as critical decision criteria.

Second, liability associated with organizational change is more complex in the community policing era. One of the chief concerns related to community policing is that officers will be freer to apply the law in a discriminatory fashion. As Bayley (1988) cautioned, such increased discretion inherent to community policing may manifest in a weakening of the equal protection of law or evenhanded enforcement. This unequal protection could lead to civil liability filings through Title 42 of the United States Code, Section 1983 (Hughes, 2000; Worrall & Marenin, 1998).[14] Our results do not confirm these fears, because beat officers are more likely to use indicators such as minority status, gender, intoxication, and hostile demeanor when making their decision to arrest. COP officers are less likely to use discriminatory factors (such as race or gender) and signs of nonconformity (including intoxication and hostile demeanor) when making their decisions to arrest, indicating the increased discretion inherent to community policing may be exercised in an evenhanded fashion. Furthermore, COP officers are more likely to act on the preferences of the victim or a witness, indicating they are more responsive to the community that they serve. These results are surely comforting to proponents of community policing.

Third, the role of community in community-oriented policing remains uncertain. Using traditional measures of social organization, these structural correlates had no explanatory power when considering arrest decisions. It appears that using traditional measures of structural variation as a vehicle for differentiating communities has little use. Perhaps other measures of community variation or community needs such as described by Skogan and Hartnett (1997) should be developed to examine if officers do differentiate individual decisions to arrest based on neighborhood context. Factors noted by Klinger (1997), such as work group norms or district-level culture, may need to be controlled to uncover variations in arrest decisions during police-citizen interactions.

Fourth, the relationship between order maintenance, citizen compliance, and arrest decisions for beat officers is worthy of further exploration. Decisions made by both beat officers and citizens early in an encounter influence whether the encounter ends in arrests. During these encounters, there are two opportunities to avoid official state intervention. If beat officers choose to exercise order maintenance, then arrest is often avoided. Likewise, if citizens recognize these directives as an opportunity to bypass arrest, citizens are given an out, and the result is a corresponding decreased likelihood of arrest. Empirical research has begun to explore the relationship between officer directives and citizen acquiescence (McCluskey et al., 1999). Using this information, policy makers may train officers in skills to limit using arrest and official sanctioning of citizens while achieving the larger goal of social harmony. Reducing the exercise of formal application of the law is in line with the tenets of community-oriented policing.

If community policing is the paradigm of the future, understanding and predicting the decision to take a citizen into custody becomes a paramount concern. Over the past 30 years, researchers and practitioners have more fully begun to understand the complex decision making of American police. Just as observers of the police began to understand discretion of officers as street-level bureaucrats, community policing promises to suddenly make these tasks more challenging. Given divergences of our results from prior research, perhaps the most significant conclusion we can make is that we still have a lot to learn. The impact of community policing on decision-making processes is quite complex and may vary by police department. Certainly, further exploration into these (and other) matters are warranted before researchers and policy makers can truly claim to understand community policing at the street level. Whether complexity in individual arrest decision making is a virtue or a vice remains unanswered, but certainly, future research will attempt to filter these muddy waters.

NOTES

1. Community-oriented policing (COP) officers obtained their assignment through an intradivision bid and review process. After officers applied for the position of COP officer, community policing sergeants, other division supervisors, and members of the community where the officer would be assigned interviewed them. This group selects an officer for the assignment, and then officers are provided an additional 40 hours of academy training geared toward community policing and problem solving (all officers in the Cincinnati Police Department received 8 hours of community policing and problem-solving training through in-service training).

2. At this point, it is important to discuss more fully communities in Cincinnati. Cincinnati residents, when asked where they live, are most likely to identify themselves as residents of a particular neighborhood; in other words, they cognitively identify themselves with a specific neighborhood. Communities in Cincinnati are recognized by the city as separate political entities, whereas each community has one council that exerts political and fiscal influence on the city government. The history of these communities dates back to the early 1900s, when these communities were separate villages or cities not yet incorporated by the city (Thomas, 1986). These communities have particular relevance for community policing and the current examination due to the fact that the Cincinnati Police Department assigned community-oriented policing officers to particular communities to work collectively with the community councils to identify problems and form solutions. As such, these communities do not merely represent macrogeographic units, such as police beats, census block groups, or enumeration districts, as prior operationalizations of community have suggested.

3. None of the police-citizen encounters observed included both a community-oriented policing and a beat officer at the same time. Additional officers at the encounter and time of day offered no explanatory value in predicting arrest decision making and therefore are not included in the multivariate analyses.

4. Whereas other research limited their sample to all encounters between the police and suspects, we felt there were many encounters where the citizen was defined as a suspect in a crime yet no probable cause existed that would lead to an arrest. Probable cause is required by statute to actuate an arrest, and if no probable cause existed during an encounter, it is reasonable to infer that arrest was not a viable option for the officer, and therefore, an analysis that included such events would be meaningless. Including citizens in the sample where no probable cause was present effectively eliminates the ability of the officer to make an arrest. Although a probable cause is a lucid concept that is open to debate whether it exists (such as in court), researchers were trained in techniques on how to determine whether officers had the legal right to actuate an arrest, and when researchers were unsure, they asked the officers probing questions regarding their legal right to make an arrest. Of the 289 encounters between the police and suspects where no probable cause was identified, none of the citizens were arrested.

5. In addition to situational- and community-level correlates of behavior, prior research has also explored the influence of individual officer characteristics and organizational characteristics as explanatory variables. Individual-level variables were not included for several reasons. There is less theoretical reason to believe the influence of characteristics, such as officers' race, gender, or length of service, should differ between community-oriented policing and beat officers. Indeed, individual-level correlates offer little additional explanatory power to the present analysis. In separate analyses using these correlates, the individual-level correlates offered little significant or consistent predictive power (Novak, 1999, pp. 208-210). In the interest of parsimony, only situational- and community-level exogenous variables are used.

6. Although Klinger (1994) has criticized previous research for using dichotomous measures for crime seriousness, we use this measure for two reasons. First, because our sample excludes encounters where probable cause for arrest is not established, the "no crime" category of a scaled variable is automatically excluded. Second, other research has shown that "the 'crude indicators' used in previous studies capture a substantial proportion of the variation in seriousness" (Worden & Shepard, 1996, p. 100). Therefore, we believe this dichotomous measure adequately captures the seriousness of pre-intervention-phase crime.

7. In encounters where the citizen was arrested, observers coded the presence of evidence prior to the arrest. This operationalization of evidence assumes all evidence criteria are given equal explanatory value, or in other words, it measures the quantity rather than the quality of evidence. Unfortunately, the existing data did not allow for further analysis of evidence quality. This variable is similar to the evidence strength correlate used by Mastrofski, Worden, and Snipes (1995, pp. 547-549); however, our variable equally weighs all evidence criteria. Furthermore and similar to Mastrofski et al., a score of 0 does not mean there was no evidence indicating the citizen committed a crime; it simply means none of these evidence criteria were observed during the encounter. In their sample of suspects, 40.1% of the encounters had no evidence.

8. The measurement of demeanor has recently provided a source of controversy. Several other operationalizations of the variable have been used in extant research examining the influence of demeanor. Lundman (1994) argued, "There is no basis for arguing that one representation is superior to another" (p. 637), and in the current data, different measurements of the same construct revealed high levels of intercorrelation. In most of the recent research, demeanor has been operationalized as a dichotomous variable, representing either disrespect or politeness (Worden & Shepard, 1996), because the differences in citizen demeanor is a matter "of kind rather than degree, for the measurement of which an ordinal scale is inappropriate" (Worden, Shepard, & Mastrofski, 1996, p. 330). In other words, ordinal scales may fail to capture the threshold of antagonism that would most likely affect an officer's behavior.

9. Order maintenance is distinguished as whether the officer suggested, requested, negotiated, commanded, or threatened citizens to take some action. These requests are often intended

to return a situation to a state of normality. Although normality can be reached through the application of arrest, order maintenance is a tactic available to officers to achieve this end short of taking a person into custody. Therefore, order maintenance was operationalized as whether an officer requested a citizen to (a) leave another person alone, (b) cease disorderly behavior, (c) cease illegal behavior, or (d) control another person or problem maker. These particular requests were specifically designed to return an encounter to a state of homeostasis. Variables such as demeanor, order maintenance, and compliance were included only if they were observed before arrest.

10. Whereas Klinger (1997) indicated aggregate-level crime rates would influence the vigor of officers' responses, we included a series of structural characteristics in lieu of crime rates. When crime rates were included in the models, harmful levels of collinearity were detected. Communities with high levels of disorganization also had correspondingly high levels of Part I and Part II crimes, therefore making our structural characteristics proxies for aggregate-level crime rates.

11. For a more detailed description of hierarchical linear models building, see Bryk and Raudenbush (1992). Given the data, it normally would be necessary to estimate a hierarchical linear model for several reasons. Heteroskedasticity often exists among the aggregate-level variables. This is particularly true for aggregate-level correlates measured as proportions, because the denominator in the proportion drives the magnitude of the overall estimate. In other words, communities with greater numbers of observed encounters will include larger denominators in the proportions. Summary statistics calculated with smaller numbers are less stable. A consequence of this is an inflated standard error for the aggregate predictors, thus making it more difficult to reject the null hypotheses (Hanushek & Jackson, 1977). In addition, including individual- and aggregate-level variables in a pooled model results in biased statistical tests. The sample size of the community-level variables is artificially inflated to the sample size of the individual-level variables, making it easier to reject the null hypothesis.

12. We also estimated two-stage, weighted least squares models that included both situational- and aggregate-level predictors to address similar issues related to multilevel analyses. These models also indicate that community-level predictors provide no significant contribution to explaining variation in officers' decisions to arrest. Also, it could be suggested that officer assignment is actually another level of analysis. However, most officers encountered less than three arrest-eligible citizens, and thus, multilevel analyses would likely provide unstable estimates.

13. The equation $z = \frac{b1 - b2}{seb1 + seb2}$ is most appropriate and will be used due to sample size, as described in Brame, Paternoster, Mazerolle, and Piquero (1998).

14. Under Title 42 U.S.C., Section 1983, citizens can seek relief from officials who violate their constitutional rights under the guise of their governmental positions. Section 1983 outlines a procedure that individuals can follow to seekm compensation for violations of their constitutional rights. There are two essential components of Section 1983, namely, (a) the defendant must be acting under the color of law, and (b) there must be a violation of a constitutional or federally protected right. Because community policing increases the ability of the line officer to make decisions while loosening oversight by supervisors, officers are in effect implementing organizational policy in which the officer, supervisor, department, and municipality may be held liable.

REFERENCES

Alpert, G. P., & Dunham, R. G.. (1988). *Policing multi-ethnic neighborhoods: The Miami study and findings for law enforcement in the United States.* Westport, CT: Greenwood.

Alpert, G. P., Dunham, R. G., & Piquero, A. (1997). On the study of neighborhood and the police. In G. P. Alpert & A. Piquero (Eds.), *Community policing: Contemporary readings* (pp. 309-326). Prospect Heights, IL: Waveland.

Bayley, D. H. (1988). Community policing: A report from the devil's advocate. In J. R. Greene & S. D. Mastrofski (Eds.), *Community policing: Rhetoric or reality* (pp. 225-238) New York: Praeger.

Bazemore, G., & Senjo, S. (1997). Police encounters with juveniles revisited: An exploratory study of themes and styles in community policing. *Policing: An International Journal of Police Strategy and Management, 20,* 60-82.

Bernard, T. J., & Engel, R. S. (2001). Conceptualizing criminal justice theory. *Justice Quarterly, 18,* 1-30.

Black, D. (1971). The social organization of arrest. *Stanford Law Review, 23,* 1087-1111.

Black, D. (1976). *The behavior of law.* New York: Academic Press.

Black, D. (1980). *The manners and customs of the police.* San Diego, CA: Academic Press.

Black, D., & Reiss, A. J. (1970). Police control of juveniles. *American Sociological Review, 35,* 63-77.

Brame, R., Paternoster R., Mazerolle, P., & Piquero, A. (1998). Testing for the equality of maximum-likelihood regression coefficients between two independent equations. *Journal of Quantitative Criminology, 14,* 245-261.

Brandl, S. G., Chamlin, M. B., & Frank, J. (1995). Aggregation bias and the capacity for formal crime control: The determinants of total and disaggregated police force size in Milwaukee, 1934-1987. *Justice Quarterly, 12,* 543-562.

Bratton, W. J., & Knobler, P. (1998). *Turnaround: How America's top cop reversed the crime epidemic.* New York: Random House.

Brooks, L. W. (1997). Police discretionary behavior. In R. G. Dunham & G. P. Alpert (Eds.), *Critical issues in policing* (pp. 149-166). Prospect Heights, IL: Waveland.

Brown, M. (1981). *Working the street: Police discretion and the dilemmas of reform.* New York: Russell Sage.

Bryk, A. S., & Raudenbush, S. W. (1992). *Hierarchical linear models: Applications and data analysis methods.* Newbury Park, CA: Sage.

Bursik, R. J. (1986). Ecological stability and the dynamics of delinquency. In A. J. Reiss, Jr., & M. Tonry (Eds.), *Communities and crime* (pp. 35-66). Chicago: University of Chicago Press.

Buzawa, E. S., & Austin. T. (1993). Determining police response to domestic violence victims. *American Behavioral Scientist, 36,* 610-623.

Clogg, C. C., Petkova, E., & Haritou, A. (1995). Statistical methods for comparing regression coefficients between models. *American Journal of Sociology, 100,* 1261-1293.

Cordner, G. W. (1995). Community policing: Elements and effects. *Police Forum, 5,* 1-8.

Duffee, D. (1990). *Explaining criminal justice.* Prospect Heights, IL: Waveland.

Eck, J. E., & Rosenbaum, D. P. (1994). The new police order: Effectiveness, equity and efficiency in community policing. In D. P. Rosenbaum (Ed.), *The challenge of community policing: Testing the promises* (pp. 3-26). Thousand Oaks, CA: Sage.

Engel, R. S., Sobol J. J., & Worden. R. E. (2000). Further exploration of the demeanor hypothesis: The interaction effects of suspects' characteristics and demeanor on police behavior. *Justice Quarterly*, *17*, 235-258.

Flynn, D. W. (1998). *Defining the "community" in community policing*. Washington, DC: Police Executive Research Forum.

Frank, J., Brandl, S., & Watkins, R. C. (1997). The content of community policing: A comparison of the daily activities of community and "beat" officers. *Policing: An International Journal of Police Strategies and Management*, *20*, 716-728.

Frank, J., K. J. Novak, & B. Smith. (in press). *Street-level policing in Cincinnati: The content of community and traditional policing and the perceptions of policing audiences*. Washington. DC: National Institute of Justice.

Fyfe, J. J. (1996). Methodology, substance and demeanor in police observational research: A response to Lundman and others. *Journal of Research in Crime and Delinquency*, *33*. 337-348.

Goldstein, J. (1960). Police discretion not to invoke the criminal process: Low visibility decisions in the administration of justice. *Yale Law Journal*, *69*. 543-594.

Goldstein, H. (1987). Toward community-oriented policing: Potential, basic requirements and threshold questions. *Crime & Delinquency*, *33*. 6-30.

Hanushek, E. A., & Jackson, J. E. (1977). *Statistical methods for social scientists*. New York: Academic Press.

Hillery, G. A. (1955). Definitions of community: Areas of agreement. *Rural Sociology*, *20*, 111-123.

Hughes. T. A. (2000). *Community policing and federal civil liability under 42 USC 1983*. Unpublished doctoral dissertation, University of Cincinnati.

Kappeler, V. E. (1993). *Critical issues in police civil liability*. Prospect Heights, IL: Waveland.

Kelling, G. L., & Moore, M. H. (1988). The evolving strategy of policing. In *Perspectives on policing*. Washington, DC: National Institute of Justice.

Klinger, D. A. (1994). Demeanor or crime? Why "hostile" citizens are more likely to be arrested. *Criminology*, *32*, 475-493.

Klinger, D. A. (1996a). Bringing crime back in: Toward a better understanding of police arrest decisions. *Journal of Research in Crime and Delinquency*, *33*, 333-336.

Klinger. D. A. (1996b). More on demeanor and arrest in Dade County. *Criminology*, *34*, 61-82.

Klinger, D. A. (1997). Negotiating order in patrol work: An ecological theory of police response to deviance. *Criminology*, *35*, 277-306.

Lipsky, M. (1980). *Street-level bureaucracy: Dilemmas of the individual in public services*. New York: Russell Sage.

Lundman, R. J. (1979). Organizational norms and police discretion: An observational study of police work with traffic law violators. *Criminology*, *17*, 159-171.

Lundman, R. L. (1994). Demeanor or crime? The midwest city police-citizen encounters study. *Criminology*, *32*, 631-656.

Lundman, R. J. (1996a). Demeanor or crime? The Midwest city police-citizen encounters study. *Criminology*, *32*, 631-656.

Lundman, R. J. (1996b). Extralegal variables and arrest. *Journal of Research in Crime and Delinquency*, *33*, 349-353.

Lundman, R. J. (1998). City police and drunk driving: Baseline data. *Justice Quarterly*, *15*, 527-546.

McCluskey, J. D., Mastrofski, S. D., & Parks, R. B. (1999). To acquiesce or rebel: Predicting citizen compliance with police requests. *Police Quarterly*, *2*, 389-416.

Mastrofski, S. D. (1992). What does community policing mean for daily police work? *National Institute of Justice Journal No. 225.* Washington, DC: National Institute of Justice.

Mastrofski, S. D., Snipes, J. B., Parks, R. B., & Maxwell, C. D. (2000). The helping hand of the law: Police control of citizens on request. *Criminology, 38,* 307-342.

Mastrofski, S. D., Snipes, J. B., & Supina, A. E. (1996). Compliance on demand: The public's response to specific police requests. *Journal of Research in Crime and Delinquency, 33,* 269-305.

Mastrofski, S. D., Worden, R. E., & Snipes, J. B. (1995). Law enforcement in a time of community policing. *Criminology, 33,* 539-563.

Meyers, A. R., Heeren, T., & Hingson, R. (1989). Discretionary leniency in police enforcement of laws against drinking and driving: Two examples from the state of Maine, USA. *Journal of Criminal Justice, 17,* 179-186.

Novak, K. J. (1999). *Assessing police-citizen encounters: Do community and beat officers differ?* Unpublished doctoral dissertation, University of Cincinnati.

Parks, R. B., Mastrofski, S. D., DeJong, C., & Gray, M. K. (1999). How officers spend their time with the community. *Justice Quarterly, 16,* 483-518.

Prottas, J. M. (1978). The power of the street-level bureaucrat in public service bureaucracies. *Urban Quarterly Affairs, 13,* 285-312.

Reiss, A. J. (1971). *The police and the public.* New Haven, CT: Yale University.

Remmington, F. J. (1990). Development of criminal justice as an academic field. *Journal of Criminal Justice Education, 1,* 9-20.

Riksheim, E. C., & Chermak, S. M. (1993). Causes of police behavior revisited. *Journal of Criminal Justice, 21,* 353-382.

Rosenbaum, D. P., & Lurigio, A. J. (1994). An inside look at community policing reform: Definitions, organizational change, and evaluation findings. *Crime & Delinquency, 40,* 299-314.

Schuerman, L., & Kobrin, S. (1986). Communities and careers in crime. In A. J. Reiss, Jr., & M. Tonry (Eds.), *Crime and justice: A review of research: Vol. 8: Communities and crime* (pp. 67-100). Chicago: University of Chicago Press.

Shaw, C. R., & McKay, H. D. (1942). *Juvenile delinquency and urban areas.* Chicago: University of Chicago Press.

Sherman, L. W. (1980). Causes of police behavior: The current state of quantitative research. *Journal of Research in Crime and Delinquency, 17,* 69-100.

Skogan, W. G., & Hartnett, S. M. (1997). *Community policing, Chicago style.* New York: Oxford University Press.

Skolnick, J. H., & Bayley, D. H. (1987). Theme and variation in community policing. In M. Tonry & N. Morris (Eds.), *Crime and justice* (pp. 1-37). Chicago: University of Chicago Press.

Smith, D. A. (1984). The organizational context of legal control. *Criminology, 22,* 19-38.

Smith, D. A. (1984). Police control of interpersonal disputes. *Social Problems, 31,* 468-481.

Smith, D. A. (1986). The neighborhood context of police behavior. In A. J. Reiss, Jr., & M. Tonry (Eds.), *Crime and Justice: A review of research: Vol. 8: Communities and crime.* Chicago: University of Chicago Press.

Smith, D. A., & Klein, J. R. (1983). Police agency characteristics and arrest decisions. In G. P. Whitaker & C. D. Phillips (Eds.), *Evaluating performance of criminal justice agencies* (pp. 63-97). Beverly Hills, CA: Sage.

Smith, D. A., & Visher, C. A. (1981). Street level justice: Situational determinants of police arrest decisions. *Social Problems, 29,* 167-177.

Smith, D. A., Visher, C. A., & Davidson, L. A. (1984). Equity and discretionary justice: The influence of race on police arrest decisions. *Journal of Criminal Law and Criminology, 75,* 234-249.

Snipes, J. B., & Mastrofski, S. D. (1990). An empirical test of Muir's typology of police officers. *American Journal of Criminal Justice, 14*, 268-296.

Stith, S. M. (1990). Police response to domestic violence: The influence of individual and familial factors. *Violence and Victims, 5*, 37-49.

Sykes, R. E., & Brent, E. E. (1980). The regulation of interaction by police: A systems view of taking charge. *Criminology, 18*, 182-197.

Sykes, R. E., Fox, J. C., & Clark, J. P. (1985). A socio-legal theory of police discretion. In A. S. Blumberg & E. Niederhoffer (Eds.), *The ambivalent force: Perspective on the police* (3rd ed., pp. 171-183). Fort Worth, TX: Harcourt Brace College.

Thomas, J. C. (1986). *Between citizen and city: Neighborhood organizations and urban politics in Cincinnati.* Lawrence: University Press of Kansas.

Turk, A. (1969). *Criminality and legal order.* Chicago: Rand McNally.

Visher, C. A. (1983). Gender, police arrest decisions and notions of chivalry. *Criminology, 21*, 5-28.

Walker, S. (1992). Origins of the contemporary criminal justice paradigm: The American Bar Foundation survey, 1953-1969. *Justice Quarterly, 9*, 47-76.

Wilson, J. Q., & Kelling, G. L. (1982). Broken windows: The police and neighborhood safety. *Atlantic Monthly*, pp. 29-38.

Worden, R. E. (1989). Situational and attitudinal explanations of police behavior: A theoretical reappraisal and empirical assessment. *Law and Society Review, 23*, 667-711.

Worden, R. E., & Pollitz, A. A. (1984). Police arrests in domestic disturbances: A further look. *Law and Society Review, 18*, 105-119.

Worden, R. E., & Shepard, R. L. (1996). Demeanor, crime and police behavior: A reexamination of police services study data. *Criminology, 34*, 83-105.

Worden, R. E., Shepard, R. L., & Mastrofski, S. D. (1996). On the meaning and measurement of suspects' demeanor toward the police: A comment on "demeanor and arrest." *Journal of Research in Crime and Delinquency, 33*, 324-332.

Worrall, J. L., & Marenin, O. (1998). Emerging liability issues in the implementation and adoption of community oriented policing. *Policing: An International Journal of Police Strategies and Management, 21*, 121-136.

[9]

THE HELPING HAND OF THE LAW: POLICE CONTROL OF CITIZENS ON REQUEST*

STEPHEN D. MASTROFSKI
George Mason University

JEFFREY B. SNIPES
Stanford University

ROGER B. PARKS
Indiana University

CHRISTOPHER D. MAXWELL
Michigan State University

This study examines how patrol officers respond to citizens' requests that officers control another citizen—by advising or persuading them, warning or threatening them, making them leave someone alone or leave the scene, or arresting them. Data are drawn from field observations conducted in Indianapolis, Indiana, in 1996 and St. Petersburg, Florida, in 1997. Officers granted the request for the most restrictive form of control requested by the citizen in 70% of the 396 observed cases. Several factors were modeled to determine their influence on officers' decisions to grant or deny the most restrictive request. These factors include legal considerations, need, factors that attenuate the impact of law or need, the social relationship between the requester and target of control, and personal characteristics of the officer. Multivariate analysis shows that the most influential factors were legal considerations. When citizens requested an arrest, the likelihood that the police would be responsive dropped considerably. However, as the evidence of a legal violation against the targeted citizen increased, so did the odds of an arrest. Officers were less likely to grant the requests of citizens having a close relationship with the person targeted for control, disrespectful of the police, or intoxicated or mentally ill. The race, wealth, and organization affiliation of citizen adversaries had little impact on the police decision. Male officers, officers with fewer years

* This research is based on data from the Project on Policing Neighborhoods, directed by Stephen D. Mastrofski, Roger B. Parks, Albert J. Reiss, Jr., and Robert E. Worden. The project was supported by Grant 95-IJ-CX-0071 by the National Institute of Justice, Office of Justice Programs, U.S. Department of Justice. Points of view in this document are those of the authors and do not necessarily represent the official position or policies of the U.S. Department of Justice. The authors appreciate the comments of the editor and the anonymous reviewers of earlier drafts of the article.

of police experience, and officers with a stronger proclivity to commu-
nity policing, had significantly greater odds of giving citizens what they
requested. The implications of the findings for research and policy are
discussed.

Most research on police behavior examines what officers do *to* people,
not what they do *for* them. In a society that prizes individual liberty, most
studies of police focus on what they do to restrict that liberty: stop, investigate, search, arrest, and otherwise coerce people. This interest derives
from two concerns about the exercise of police power: whether a constable
overstepped his or her authority to intrude, and whether this intrusion
produced felicitous results, such as a diminution of offensive behavior or
an increase in public contentment. Such inquiries consider the classic tension in a democracy between balancing the rights of an individual's liberty
with society's need for peace, order, and lawfulness.

What such inquiries ignore is another tension, one emanating from the
conflict between private parties. Often, police are summoned by one
party to assist in some claim or grievance against another, the utmost concern of the complainant being how to secure personal relief or benefit, not
the commonweal. The Anglo-American criminal law originated as a
mechanism for personal relief by which individuals might mobilize law
enforcement officials, such as the sheriff (usually for a fee), to secure persons and evidence associated with wrongdoing against the aggrieved party.
This practice persisted well into nineteenth century America (Lane,
1992:6). More recently, the criminal law changed to stress society's primacy as the offended party, with victim complainants relegated to the supporting role of providing evidence of the suspect's guilt and the extent of
harm caused, but this does not alter the fact that police are usually mobilized because individuals seek personal benefit (Reiss, 1971a:173). Securing that benefit often comes at some cost to another's liberty. From the
complainant's perspective, when the police protect them, the service they
receive is unambiguous. If we frame our understanding of the problem as
one of what police do *for* the supplicant rather than merely what they do
to the target of the supplicant's request, we explicitly acknowledge that
police are in the business of authoritatively allocating value to individuals.
That is, they are engaged in an inherently political enterprise. This
approach helps us see more clearly who benefits by the mobilization of
one of the state's most powerful agents.

Consider the following vignettes, drawn from field research over the
past 20 years.

- A security guard asks police to arrest a juvenile caught shoplifting in a
  department store. The guard has a videotape of the theft.

POLICE CONTROL OF CITIZENS 309

- Police respond to a woman's call to arrest her estranged husband, who has broken into her residence. The police arrive to find the man on the porch, his hand bleeding badly. He reports that his wife stabbed him. The police handcuff the man and take him inside to talk to his wife. She says that her husband came to kidnap their infant daughter. The husband's story is that he came to get the baby because she is always on crack cocaine and neglects the child. When he picked up the baby, she grabbed the infant and threw her against the wall. The officers see the child, who appears to have suffered severe brain damage. Hearing this from her husband, the woman screams in anger and demands that the police arrest him.

- A man complains that his neighbor's dog was coming into his yard and trashing it. He asks police to warn the neighbor that he will get a citation if he does not keep his dog in his own yard.

- A woman asks the officer to run her neighbors out of the area because they are from another planet. They make her pets behave "funny," and they "mess" with her television reception.

- A mother has found a sexually suggestive note from a boy at school in her adolescent daughter's book bag. The mother asks the police to counsel the daughter about the risks of engaging in sex.

- A home owner asks the police to run a group of teenagers off of his street corner because they are dealing drugs and making the corner unpleasant.

- A woman asks police to make her husband get out of their car so that she can drive it to work. They are having an argument, and he refuses to relinquish the car. She says that he does not work and that she has to get to work to support their five children.

- A customer in a corner grocery store wants the police to make the store owner refund him 25 cents because the pinball machine he was playing malfunctioned. The store owner refuses to provide the refund because he merely rents the space to the owner of the machine. He told the customer to contact the owner of the machine for the refund. The customer has raised a ruckus and refuses to leave until he receives his quarter. Now, the store owner wants the police to evict the customer.

These vignettes illustrate the diverse circumstances confronting police when asked to control someone else. Situations vary in the seriousness, the factual ambiguity about who did what, and the moral ambiguity concerning the right thing to do. Although they raise many issues about what *should* be done, our interest here is only to account for whose requests are fulfilled and whose are not. That is, who wins, who loses, and why? To what extent are police choices governed by the law? By the requester's need? By the participants' demeanor? By their personal characteristics? By the officer's own predisposition? Answers to these questions will lead us to a better understanding of this underexplored aspect of police discretion and will add to our knowledge of the behavior of law.

We first explore the nature of these requests. Next, we consider what prior research suggests about the decision to grant or deny these requests. Then, we present evidence from a systematic observation of patrol officers recently conducted in two cities engaged in implementing community policing in the 1990s.

REQUESTS TO CONTROL OTHERS

Much public policing involves citizens engaging the police to take care of things that seem awry. Such requests alert the police to many situations that would otherwise escape their attention, and by voicing those requests, citizens indicate that someone wants the police to do something. This action infuses American policing with a strong popular character, for it is the principal means by which the typical patrol officer gains entrée to the private affairs of the public (Black, 1980; Reiss, 1971a). Sometimes, summoners have not formed a clear view of what they want the police to do, from either a lack of detailed knowledge of the circumstances (such as when a neighbor reports something next door that sounds like domestic violence) or ignorance of the police authority and capacity to act. Sometimes requesters defer to the police to determine what, if anything, should be done. What the citizen wants of police may be articulated at the outset, or it may emerge through the course of conversation, an exchange of information, and the clarification of facts, rights, and responsibilities by both parties. This process can be exhortatory or negotiated, and sometimes the citizen may never articulate a specific request.

We are concerned with those occasions when the citizen makes clear a specific request for a police action intended to control another citizen. Such occasions afford us the opportunity to see whether the state's agent fulfills a request that requires infringement on the freedom of another. Fulfilling those requests imposes two kinds of costs: the expenditure of public resources required to fulfill the request and the degree of imposition on the targeted citizen. The state's financial cost of restricting citizens' freedoms is generally related to the degree of restriction imposed.

POLICE CONTROL OF CITIZENS 311

Both costs may enter into an officer's choice of response, reflecting concern for what the law permits and requires, for what satisfies justice, for efficient use of the officer's time, and for the kind of work the officer prefers to do.

The forms of control that citizens requisition may vary in the degree to which they restrict the freedom of the targeted party. Figure 1 depicts several points along an ordinal scale of the restrictiveness of the request. When police merely offer advice or attempt to persuade a citizen, their effort is an expression of their preference that, on the surface at least, leaves the targeted citizen with the choice of what to do. The mother who asked the officer to counsel her daughter on the risks of teen sex was asking for this kind of control. Because it is an officer of the law offering counsel, a more authoritative and perhaps even unspoken coercive element exists, but it is less so than when the officer makes such a demand or request accompanied with an explicit threat or warning. The man who wanted his neighbor's dog chained asked the police to make clear the legal consequences of a failure to do so. Citizens desiring an even greater level of control may ask that police make someone leave the scene, such as the homeowner who asked the officer to banish the drug-dealing teenagers from the street corner. One of the most restrictive demands a citizen can make of the police is to arrest another, such as the security guard requested for the shoplifter. Taking someone into custody is a severe deprivation of freedom and the preliminary step in mobilizing the criminal process that may provide even greater loss of freedom and property. Thus, the degree of requested control defines the degree of intrusion the requester desires of police and serves as the frame of reference regarding the quantity of law that the requester wishes to mobilize against the target (Black, 1976). The availability of this range in police authority is known to most citizens seeking to calibrate the amount of law mobilized on their behalf.

Figure 1. Requests for Control of Other Citizens: A Scale

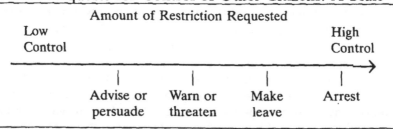

	Amount of Restriction Requested	
Low Control		High Control
Advise or persuade	Warn or threaten	Make leave	Arrest

To place our research question in a larger framework of dispute settlement, we note that the situations concerning us are those in which

            MASTROFSKI ET AL.

the requesters seek a specific, partisan response from police; they seek an advocate (pleading the requester's case), an ally (perhaps risking injury), or a surrogate (relieving the requester of all responsibility and risk) (Black, 1993:ch. 6). From the citizen's perspective, granting the request is nearly always a partisan act. The police officer, however, may decide the case by employing any of a wide range of criteria. The officer may act out a partisan role, or the officer may fulfill a nonpartisan, "settlement" role (Black, 1993:121). Whereas a partisan response may be justified on a wide range of grounds, including familiarity with the parties and biases about their characteristics, the settlement role requires an *a priori* neutrality and a decision on the merits of the case according to standards enjoying some degree of legitimacy in the larger society. The more visible the officer's actions are to outsiders—especially to the police department hierarchy, the courts, and other government agencies—the greater the pressure on the officer to present his or her actions as nonpartisan, framed in the role of peacemaker, mediator, arbitrator, or judge. High-visibility police responses, such as making an arrest, thus increase the likelihood that officers will respond according to criteria, such as the law, that can support the appearance of nonpartisanship.

ACCOUNTING FOR THE POLICE RESPONSE TO CITIZENS' REQUESTS TO CONTROL OTHERS

We group the influences on the police response into five categories, each representing a type of system or source for structuring police discretion. We discuss the implications of each category in terms articulated by Donald Black, who has presented a comprehensive theoretical framework for explaining the behavior of law. Black (1976) defines the behavior of law as governmental social control. Law may vary in quantity (more versus less control) and quality (e.g., penal, compensatory, therapeutic, and conciliatory). We are concerned with measuring the responsiveness of police in terms of their willingness to grant requests to control others, ranging from little or no explicit penal imposition (advising or persuading) to a highly penal one (making an arrest) (Black, 1980:138).

Black's "purely sociological" strategy for predicting behavior is to locate all relevant aspects of social life in different dimensions of social space. Vertical space differentiates people according to their wealth. Horizontal space distinguishes people according to social morphology: the distribution of labor, how they participate in social life (e.g., neighboring behavior), and the degree of intimacy that exists between them. Symbolic space is the cultural dimension of life, measured by how much of a given culture a person has or how conventional one's culture is. Corporate space is defined by the power or potential for collective action (e.g., belonging to

POLICE CONTROL OF CITIZENS 313

an organization). Normative space is a broad category defined by various ways of exerting social control (e.g., law, psychotherapy, bureaucracy, etiquette, ethics), all of which define or react to deviant behavior. Each type of social control is more or less powerful, depending on the setting (i.e., varying with the unit of social organization, time, and place). People's exposure to different forms of social control varies, so that at any given time, someone is more or less influenced by it and defined as more or less deviant. Black develops a large number of propositions about the impact of these social dimensions on the behavior of law. We will consider some of these propositions as they pertain to the categories that we have identified for predicting police responsiveness to citizens' requests to control others.

LEGAL STANDARDS

The law and various aspects of the legal system set forth technical standards and expectations that stipulate or guide the officer's actions in a number of domains. It represents an official normative source for defining what is deviant; it is, by definition, legitimate. Whatever the limits of the law in governing the police, it remains the most powerful symbol for controlling them in contemporary America, or at least justifying their behavior *ex post facto* (Black, 1980:180). Many legal standards issue from statutes and jurisprudence, the kinds of rules and precedents in which law schools immerse their students. The law is nearly mute about most of the points on the scale. Indeed, the criminal law devotes virtually all of its attention to arrest, offering scarcely more than a whisper on banishment (except for protection from abuse orders), and nothing about threats, warnings, advice, and persuasion. As a general principle, the law requires that officers gather and weigh the evidence that might justify restricting a citizen's freedom, greater restrictions requiring higher evidentiary standards. Consequently, the very nature of the restriction requested frames the legal standard for fulfillment. Higher standards imply more rejected requests, assuming that citizens are more inclined to seek justice that incorporates a broader set of norms than embodied in the law (Black, 1980:ch. 6). The state exercises greater selectivity, not only to protect citizens' rights in a democracy, but also to husband its limited resources to restrict liberty. The law protects citizens, and it protects the state.

Some prior research on police arrest behavior suggests that the strength of evidence against the targeted citizen is a powerful predictor of arrest (Black, 1980:103; Mastrofski et al., 1995), but complainants can also influence the officer's choice (Black, 1980; Smith, 1986). Their expressed preference for an arrest signals the presence of a willing witness and increases the likelihood of arrest, and in many circumstances in which control of another is requested, the officer observes evidence of the *requester's*

314   MASTROFSKI ET AL.

wrongdoing as well. This action may reduce the credibility of the complainant's claims, forcing the officer to consider a more complex situation, such as whether the complaint is motivated by the desire for revenge or whether the target acted in self-defense.

NEED

American policing has entered a time when reformers have shifted the meaning of the term professionalism from being a "snappy bureaucrat" (Bittner, 1970:53) to being a well-trained decision maker, acting like a clinician serving clients based on their informed judgment of what they "need" (Mastrofski, 1998:174). Officers may thus supplement or supplant legal requirements with their reading of the need for intervention (Reiss, 1971a:181). For example, officers may decide to make an arrest in a domestic dispute for which little or no evidence exists, because they fear that if they do not arrest, someone will get seriously hurt later. As we construe it, need is not necessarily defined officially, but it too constitutes a justification for action that officers may muster to defend their choices. The definition of "need" is usually left to the officer's discretion, although these individual choices occur in larger cultural and normative contexts. For example, the need to control others may be defined by the requester's vulnerability and the degree of threat presented by the target. What defines vulnerability and threat can vary with the society. Similarly, the seriousness of the harm to the requester may be placed in social space by the interaction of different normative systems of social control—the law and local custom, for example. American policing is continually awash in waves of reform, many of which may not yet be articulated in law or bureaucratic rules, but which nonetheless vie for normative supremacy in society and in the police department. The movements to protect women and children from abuse by others in the household exert normative pressures that attempt to shape the occupation's definition of "need" for protection.

SITUATIONAL ATTENUATORS OF LAW AND NEED

Officers acting on either legal or need criteria are generally considered to be acting in accordance with the expectations of the highest established standards of the occupation. However, no matter how compelling the case for either the law or need, citizens can behave in ways that attenuate the potency of these influences. Targeted citizens with a weak legal case against them or appearing not to be a threat may nonetheless neutralize the relevance of this information by acting disrespectfully to the police (Brown, 1981). A citizen's failure to defer to police authority is well established as a predictor of police sanctioning behavior (Worden et al., 1996), which may be extended to the other party in a dispute, the complainants, who by their demeanor influence the officer's receptivity to the request. Arguably, those complainants appearing mentally ill or intoxicated are also discredited as worthy supplicants (Teplin, 1986). In Black's terms, all of these situational attenuators locate the citizen in normative social space. Considerable consensus exists among police that situational attenuators should "trump" legal and need considerations (Brown, 1981; Rubinstein, 1973; Van Maanen, 1974), although such justifications lack the front-stage stature that law or professional ideals provide.

REQUESTER-TARGET SOCIAL RELATIONSHIPS

Black's theory of the behavior of law places importance on how parties to a dispute relate to each other in social space (1976). Those individuals in higher social strata, as distinguished, for example, by wealth, are hypothesized to fare better before legal decision makers than those in lower social strata. Those individuals at the cultural center (e.g., in a hegemonic racial group) should receive more favorable law than those further from the center. And the more organization behind citizens, the greater their prospects to have their way. Representatives of business and government organizations are thus predicted to receive more responsive policing than their customers and clients. Finally, the more intimate the relationship between disputing parties, the more reluctant are legal actors to intrude. Black emphasizes that the social characteristics of adversaries in a dispute are only interpretable when compared with each other (1989:9). One must know, for example, the social status of the requester relative to that of the target when attempting to predict the police response. The pairing most likely to receive a positive police response is high-status requester and low-status target. The least likely pairing is a low-status requester and a high-status target. Those individuals in the middle are like-status pairings, with the higher status pairing having a greater probability of a positive response. In this case, disputes among higher status individuals are presumably accorded greater merit than disputes between lower status individuals. These social relationships have no standing in the law, but they are presumed to reflect powerful behavioral tendencies in legal actors that originate from broader influences that stratify and culturally segment society.

OFFICER PREDISPOSITIONS

A great deal of social science presumes that the characteristics of legal decision makers matter, independent of whatever the case at hand may present. Black's conceptual approach to characterizing legal official "third parties" to a dispute is to locate them in social space, just as he does the disputants (1993:122–123). For example, officers are expected to be predisposed to act on cultural expectations related to gender: greater aggression and overt coercion for male instead of female officers (Martin and Jurik, 1996; Worden, 1993:209). African-American officers are expected to be more responsive to requests from African Americans than white officers. Some reformers expect a college education to promote more tolerant, service-oriented policing (Worden, 1990:566ff), but we begin with the assumption that higher education serves to differentiate people culturally. Officers with a college education are more culturally distant from citizens without a college education and are therefore less inclined to a supportive response. Officers assigned to specialist positions with the explicit responsibility of "customer service" are placed by their departments in a normative space that should predispose them more favorably to citizens' requests. Officers who have received more indoctrination in such a customer-service approach have been more strongly socialized to be responsive than those with less indoctrination. Community policing is the current reform movement that attempts to define the officers' work role in such customer-service terms (Sparrow et al., 1990:145). Officers who have been indoctrinated in and embrace community policing values should therefore be more inclined to render such assistance than those with less indoctrination and commitment. On the other hand, the cumulative influence of an informal normative system, the occupational subculture, may isolate and alienate officers from the public, deflating their "service ideals" about being responsive to citizens' requests (Van Maanen, 1974). More years of experience means increased exposure to subcultural values, diminishing the officer's willingness to take actions that require more "work" (Mastrofski et al., 1994).

Of course, many of the characteristics discussed above have been presented in a different conceptual framework—one that is psychological rather than sociological (Black, 1976:8). Some researchers argue that officers develop personal predispositions that may be independent of their location in social space. These predispositions operate through decision frames and algorithms (Stalans and Finn, 1995) shaped by officers' upbringing and work experiences (Broderick, 1987; Brown, 1981; Muir, 1977; White, 1972; Worden, 1995). Regardless of the conceptual framework in which officer characteristics are placed—sociological or psychological—research has shown their influence on police behavior to be weak or nonexistent. Most of the research attempting to establish the effects of individual officer characteristics has focused on gender, race, education, length of service, and attitudes about police work and the public. With few exceptions, individual characteristics have not proven to be strong or consistent predictors of officer behavior, especially when situational factors are taken into account (Riksheim and Chermak, 1993; but cf. Mastrofski et al., 1994, 1995). One might argue that this result reflects the overwhelming impact of the police occupational subculture, which impels officers to a high degree of conformity, regardless of their individual variation. However, research on individual officer effects is plagued with suboptimal measures of the characteristics that are relevant to the police behavior in question and design limitations (inadequate sample size, inability to control for other influences).

RESEARCH SITES

This study is about individual officer behavior, but we need to frame it in the larger context of the communities and organizations from which our data are drawn. Indianapolis, Indiana, and St. Petersburg, Florida, served as the sites for data collection for the Project on Policing Neighborhoods (POPN), conducted in 1996 and 1997, respectively. These sites were selected because both were implementing community policing, both were diverse in the race and wealth of their residents, and both were receptive to hosting a large research project.

Table 1 shows some of the features of each community and police department. The chiefs of both departments had secured their jobs largely on their reputations for promoting community policing, and both chiefs listed improving community relations as their top priority. Both departments had stressed the need to decentralize service delivery decisions to the district level, and both departments attempted to achieve long-term stability in officers' beat assignments to facilitate closer police-community working relations.

St. Petersburg developed an international reputation as a leader in the implementation of community policing, especially emphasizing "problem solving" and geographic deployment of officers and supervisors as its central features. Indianapolis's chief stressed a more diffuse approach to community policing, one that exhorted officers to engage in higher levels of "traditional" law enforcement activity (making suspect stops, arrests, and seizures of drugs and guns) to improve quality of life in the neighborhoods, as well as using alternatives, such as code enforcement to shut down problem properties. Both departments appointed a subset of patrol officers to serve as community policing specialists, relieved of the responsibility to respond to routine calls for service to engage in the department's priorities for community policing. In Indianapolis, about 5% of the patrol force received this assignment, in St. Petersburg, about 22%. Indianapolis

Table 1. Characteristics of Indianapolis and St. Petersburg

Characteristic	Indianapolis	St. Petersburg
Population of service area (1995 estimated)	377,723	240,318
% of population that is minority (1990)	39	24
% of population that is unemployed (1990)	8	5
% of population that is 50% below poverty level (1990)	9	6
% of families with children that are headed by a female (1990)	17	10
UCR Index crime rate/1,000 residents (1996)	100	99
UCR Index crime rate/officer (1996)	37	47
Form of city government (1996/1997)	Strong mayor	Strong mayor
Number of full-time sworn officers (1996)	1,013	505
Number of full-time sworn officers in patrol (1996/1997)	492	283
% of patrol officers who are minority (1996/1997)	21	22
% of patrol officers who are female (1996/1997)	17	13
% of patrol officers with 4-year college degrees (1996/1997)	36	26
Number of training hours required for recruit officers (1993)	1,392	1,280
Year community policing implementation initiated	1992	1990
Number of community policing specialists (1996/1997)	24	63
Number of patrol districts/beats (1996/1997)	4/50	3/48

specialists operated together in teams with other specialists. St. Petersburg's community policing officers worked in teams with other generalist patrol officers assigned to the same territory.

The top leaders of both departments, but especially St. Petersburg's, stressed the importance of "empowering" patrol officers to exercise initiative in deciding which problems in their assigned beats should receive priority and gave greater leeway to individual community policing officers in choosing how to do it. Leaders of both departments said that community policing was a philosophy that should guide the practices of all officers, not just the specialists. Aside from reformulating department mission statements, the details of general patrol officers' performance expectations under the community policing philosophy were communicated through basic training in the principles of community policing, revised performance evaluation criteria (St. Petersburg only), and repeated exhortation from top management to work with the community.

Racial issues have particular relevance at these sites because a large proportion of the police interactions observed involved one or more minority citizens, nearly all of whom were African American. The police of both cities were closely scrutinized by groups interested in their treatment of minorities. Minority spokespersons in both cities received considerable publicity for their claims that members of their race were not receiving equal treatment from the police. About a year before our study, Indianapolis police dealt with a relatively small civil disturbance in which the treatment of minorities was an issue. Several months before our field research began there, St. Petersburg made the national news when an officer shot and killed a black motorist. A civil disturbance ensued that resulted in several properties being burned, rocks and bottles thrown, and the department mobilized for riot duty. Less than a year later, St. Petersburg's mayor appointed the city's first African-American chief.

Both departments made community policing an important element in their efforts to improve relations with minority group citizens. Although dealing with allegations of police abuse and incivility toward minority suspects was an issue in both communities, both departments were also pressured by minority group leaders to increase the quality and quantity of protection against drugs, violence, and quality-of-life offenses in predominantly minority areas. Leaders in both communities spoke of their desire that their officers be responsive to victims' needs and enhance the quality of life in neighborhoods, especially those most socially and economically distressed.

The leadership in both departments in this study aspired to similar objectives through the vehicle of "community policing," a reform intended to temper the legalistic, bureaucratic pressures that had shaped both agencies over many years. The current direction of leadership resonated with Wilson's (1968) characterization of the "service-style" department: a commitment to improving relations with the community, establishing stronger "partnerships" with community organizations, and increasing the level of officer productivity in ways that would be measurable and visible. The departments differed somewhat in their programs and structures, but for the purposes of this study, no *a priori* reasons exist to expect different patterns in police responsiveness to citizens' requests to control other citizens.

Recapping the paper's core proposition, we suggest that whether the police grant a citizen's request to control another depends on a range of predictors that can be classified into five categories: legal standards, need, behaviors and conditions of the parties that attenuate the law and need, the social relationship between the disputants, and the officer's predisposition. Drawing on Black's theory of law, we have characterized specific concepts within each category as kinds of "social space" and have set forth propositions about the direction of the relationship between indicators and the police response. The professional history, combined with the current community policing orientation of both departments, leads us to expect that legal considerations and need would be relatively important predictors of police behavior. Whether they overshadow the effects of factors associated with the police subculture (legal and need attenuators) and the class and race-based tensions in these communities will be an issue of particular concern.

DATA

To capture a range in socioeconomic conditions, 12 beats in each city were selected for systematic observation. Sampled beats were matched as closely as possible across the two sites according to degree of socioeconomic distress. Socioeconomic distress was measured as the sum of the percentages of families with children headed by a single female, the adult population that is unemployed, and the population below 50% of the poverty level. This index is similar to the one used by Sampson et al. (1997). The sample excluded those beats with the lowest socioeconomic distress so that observations would concentrate in those areas where police-citizen interactions were most frequent. Field observers were graduate students and honors undergraduates with a semester's training in systematic observation of the police plus on-site orientation rides.

Systematic observations were conducted in summer months according to procedures originally set forth by Reiss (1971b) and detailed elsewhere (Mastrofski et al., 1998). Field researchers accompanied patrol officers throughout a matched sample of work shifts in each of the selected beats of a city. They took brief field notes and then spent the next day at the research office, transcribing notes into detailed accounts and coding them according to a protocol. Observation sessions oversampled the busier days and times of the week. Both general patrol officers and community policing officers were observed in rough proportion to their representation in the personnel allocation to the study beats. Approximately 240 hours of observation were conducted for officers assigned to each of the selected beats.

Observers noted all officers' encounters with members of the public. An encounter was a face-to-face communication between officers and citizens that was more than a passing greeting. Observers recorded police contact with approximately 6,500 citizens in Indianapolis and 5,500 citizens in St. Petersburg. Those events ranged from less than a minute to several hours. Researchers guaranteed that officers' identity would be protected. In only about one-half of 1% of the officers' encounters with the public did observers detect evidence suggesting that officers had changed their behavior because of the researcher's presence. In fact, field observers noted many instances of police behavior that could have been cause for disciplinary action, a phenomenon noted in previous field studies of patrol officers (Reiss, 1968). Observers characteristically reported cordial relations with officers during ridealongs. They reported that only 12% of their observation sessions began with the officer displaying a negative attitude about the observer's presence, and this dropped to only 2% by the end of the observation session.

Data are also drawn from in-person interviews of patrol officers conducted in a private room by researchers who did not conduct field observations. These surveys took approximately 25 minutes, covering the officers' views and experiences on the beats they served, the work of police, the department, and community policing. Interview data were merged with observation data for this analysis with few cases lost because of officers who refused or were otherwise unavailable for interview.

The focus for this article is on police-citizen interactions during which the citizen asked officers to control another citizen. Excluded are those encounters with more than one officer present in which the officer selected for observation did not take or share the decision-making lead, usually because the observed officer served as a back-up to another officer already present. We wanted to observe what officers did when the citizen targeted for control was present at the scene of the encounter, so we excluded encounters in which the targeted citizen was not present. At these sites, 396 citizens asked 172 officers to control another citizen present during the encounter. The requester-officer dyad serves as the unit of analysis.

VARIABLES

CITIZEN REQUEST AND POLICE RESPONSE

Observers distinguished four kinds of requests to control another citizen. They reflect the scale points shown in Figure 1. Table 2 shows the frequency that each type of request was voiced and the percentage of those requests that police fulfilled. The police response was initially grouped into three categories: (1) ignoring the request or explicitly refusing to comply, (2) partial fulfillment (taking observable steps to fulfill the request, but not completing it in the citizen's presence) or promising to fulfill the request at some future time, and (3) complete fulfillment of the citizen's request. Seventy-four percent of the cases in category (2) were partial fulfillment.

322   MASTROFSKI ET AL.

Table 2.   Citizens' Requests to Control Others and the
           Police Response

Type of Request	# Requests	% Not Fulfilled	% Partially Fulfilled/Promised	% Completely Fulfilled
Advise/persuade	249	27	26	48
Warn/threaten	81	30	37	33
Make leave/ leave alone	174	27	14	59
Arrest	101	49	16	36
Most restrictive request	396	30	22	48

The most frequently voiced requests—for advice or persuasion of the
targeted party—required the least restriction by the responding officers.
Making someone leave or not bother them was the second most popular
request. The third most frequent request was for an arrest, although it was
much less frequent than the previous two requests. Slightly less popular
than arrests were requests to warn or threaten the targeted citizen. Thus,
citizens usually asked for a form of control less restrictive than arrest; yet,
arrest requests still accounted for one-fourth of all those observed. The
police were very likely to make some *positive gesture* (fulfill, partially fulfill or promise to fulfill) for any request except an arrest.

Some citizens made more than one request—37% in Indianapolis and
41% in St. Petersburg. Multiple requests require a more complicated
measure of the police response, because the police could fulfill all, some,
or none of the requests. Of those multiple-request cases, police were
strongly inclined to fulfill either all or none; 92% were handled this way in
each city. We desire a parsimonious way of measuring police assistance
across single- and multiple-request cases. For each requester, we selected
the request that required the most control, because that establishes the
outer boundary of the citizen's expressed preferences. We want to know
the police response to the citizen's most demanding desire.

The rate of full police compliance with the most restrictive request in
our data is similar to the compliance rate reported by Black (1980:160) in
field observations from the 1960s (48% and 52%, respectively). However,
the partial/promised compliance rate in our data is considerably higher
(22% versus 2%), making the likelihood of a positive response significantly higher in these data than those reported by Black, who concluded
that in disputes, complainants "generally do not receive what they want
from police" (1980:188).

POLICE CONTROL OF CITIZENS 323

PREDICTOR VARIABLES

Table 3 defines the variables used to predict the police response to the citizen's request. The second column shows the expected direction of effects. Table 4 provides descriptive statistics for all variables.

Table 3. Description of Predictor Variables

Variable	Direction of Expected Effect	Definition
Legal Considerations		
Evidence of target's violation	+	Strength of evidence of target's legal violation
Evidence of requester's legal violation	–	Strength of evidence of requester's legal violation
Arrest requested	–	Citizen requested target's arrest
Need		
Young or elderly requester	+	Requester is < = 12 or > = 60 years old
Female requester	+	Requester is female
Male target	+	Target is male
Intoxicated target	+	Target shows behavioral effects of drug/alcohol intoxication
Serious problem	+	Problem at hand is serious (danger to life or health, major property loss, or carrying significant criminal penalties)
Situational Attenuators		
Target disrespectful of police	+	Target shows disrespect to police
Requester disrespectful of police	–	Requester shows disrespect to police
Requester intoxicated/ mentally ill	–	Requester shows behavioral effects of drug/alcohol intoxication or mental illness
Requester-Target Social Relationship		

324   MASTROFSKI ET AL.

Status pairing by race (pro-responsiveness)	+	1 = requester minority/target white; 2 = requester minority/target minority; 3 = requester white/target white; 4 = requester white/target minority
Status pairing by wealth (pro-responsiveness)	+	1 = requester low/target high; 2 = requester low/target low; 3 = requester high/target high; 4 = requester high/target low
Status pairing by organization affiliation (pro-responsiveness)	+	1 = requester not org./target org.; 2 = requester not org./target not org.; 3 = requester org./target org.; 4 = requester org./target not org.
Close relationship	–	Requester and target are intimates, family, friends, neighbors, or coworkers
Officer's predisposition		
Male officer	+	Officer is male
College degree	–	Officer has bachelor's degree or higher
Years of police experience	–	Years of experience in any police department
Proclivity to community policing	+	Amount of community policing training × officer's willingness to handle disputes, nuisances, and minor disorders
Community policing job assignment	+	Officer is freed from responsibility for answering routine calls for service to engage in community policing

LEGAL CONSIDERATIONS

The criminal law as a normative system requires officers to act on evidence of wrongdoing, not hunches or biases; stronger evidence constitutes a stronger justification for restrictive action. Evidence strength is calculated as a summative index of the evidence of the target's or requester's violation of the law. The following points were assigned for each factor present and then summed: officer observed citizen perform an illegal act (3), citizen gave officer a full confession (2), citizen gave officer a partial

Table 4. Descriptive Statistics

Variable	Range	Mean	S.D.
Dependent Variables			
Officer fulfilled most restrictive request	0–1	.70	.46
Officer response to most restrictive request	0–2	1.18	.86
Legal Considerations			
Evidence of target's legal violation	0–7	.94	1.26
Evidence of requester's legal violation	0–6	.32	.87
Arrest requested	0–1	.26	.44
Need			
Young or elderly requester	0–1	.08	.26
Female requester	0–1	.56	.50
Male target	0–1	.63	.48
Intoxicated target	0–1	.20	.40
Serious problem	0–1	.33	.47
Situational Attenuators			
Target disrespectful of police	0–1	.14	.34
Requester disrespectful of police	0–1	.10	.30
Requester intoxicated/mentally ill	0–1	.11	.32
Requester-Target Social Relationship			
Status pairing by race (hi = pro-responsive)	1–4	2.52	.78
Status pairing by wealth (hi = pro-responsive)	1–4	2.62	.82
Status pairing by organization (hi = pro-responsive)	1–4	2.30	.74
Close relationship	0–1	.70	.46
Officer's Predisposition			
Male officer	0–1	.80	.40
College degree	0–1	.34	.47
Years of police experience	0–31	8.43	6.70
Proclivity to community policing	2–90	33.01	17.43
Community policing job assignment	0–1	.07	.26

confession (1), officer observed physical evidence implicating citizen (1), officer heard testimony from other citizens implicating the citizen (1). Requesting an arrest also has legal implications. Presumably, it fortifies the prospective prosecution of the target because it signifies a willing witness (Mastrofski et al., 1995:541), but taken in the context of the other lesser degrees of control, such a request is more closely scrutinized. Because the criminal law is based on the principle of proportionality, a citizen seeking an arrest sets a much higher legal standard for the requested intervention than lower levels of control. Setting higher standards requires more police selectivity, thus reducing the chances of a positive response. Whether the citizen requested an arrest is entered as a dummy variable.

326   MASTROFSKI ET AL.

NEED

The cultural norms of contemporary American society play a powerful
role in defining need. Police officers draw on these norms but must nearly
always rely on limited information to make judgments about need, using
readily observable characteristics to classify people (Bittner, 1970).
Regardless of the objective risks, society perceives the very young and the
elderly as more vulnerable than all others. Female requesters are perceived as more vulnerable than males, whereas male targets are perceived
as more threatening than female targets (Katz, 1988; Tedeschi and Felson,
1994:255). Intoxicated targets are construed as more threatening, because
they are less controllable (Muir, 1977:127; Tedeschi and Felson,
1994:197–201). Serious problems increase the stakes in the situation by
the severity of harm that is threatened (Mastrofski et al., 1996:287).

SITUATIONAL ATTENUATORS

These variables locate citizens in normative social space, ones that have
consistently shown a strong likelihood to increase the probability that
police will punish offenders (Riksheim and Chermak, 1993; Worden et al.,
1996). Citizens were considered disrespectful to police if they called the
officer names, made derogatory or belittling statements, issued slurs,
spoke in a loud voice, or ignored police commands or queries. Being argu-
mentative was not considered disrespectful unless it included one of the
above.

REQUESTER-TARGET SOCIAL RELATIONSHIP

These variables reflect the relationship of the requester to the target in
several dimensions of social space. Race pairings are ordered to reflect
Black's hypotheses about the law acting to benefit those in the hegemonic
culture over those at the cultural periphery. Nearly all minority citizens
were African Americans. Pairings by wealth are ordered to reflect Black's
notion that the law operates to benefit those individuals of higher wealth
when in conflict with those of lower wealth. Nearly all "high" wealth citizens appeared to be middle income; low wealth citizens were considered
to be at a subsistence level or lower. Pairings by organization affiliation
reflect Black's notion that citizens from organizations get more favorable
law over those without organization affiliation. The final variable in this
group reflects the degree of intimacy or the closeness of the relationship
between the requester and target—in Black's terms, a measure of the horizontal social distance between them.

POLICE CONTROL OF CITIZENS 327

Four characteristics are used as proxies to measure officers' predispositions: the officer's sex, education, years of experience, and job assignment. The proclivity to community policing is the interaction of two terms: the amount of training on community policing principles the officer had received in the previous three years multiplied by the officer's acceptance of minor disputes and quality-of-life problems as a part of their work. The training scale was ordinal: (1) none, (2) less than a day, (3) 1–2 days, (4) 3–5 days, and (5) more than 5 days. The measure of officer's attitude about minor disputes and quality-of-life problems was an additive scale comprising officers' views about how often they should be expected to do something about public nuisances, neighbor disputes, family disputes, litter and trash, parents who do not control their kids, and nuisance businesses that cause lots of problems for neighbors: (0) never, (1) sometimes, (2) much of the time, and (3) always. The reliability coefficient for this measure was .72 for all Indianapolis patrol officers interviewed and .82 for all St. Petersburg officers interviewed.

In terms of Black's framework, gender and college education place officers in specific cultural spaces (1980:174). Females are expected to be less coercive and, therefore, less inclined to fulfill requests to restrict the target. College-educated officers are expected to be more culturally distant from most center-city citizens they encounter and, therefore, on average less inclined to fulfill their requests. Officers having received specialist community policing job assignments and more community policing training are in normative spaces that dictate or encourage responsiveness to citizens' requests, but officers with more years of experience are expected to reflect the declining influence of the idealism that active intervention constitutes service delivery, thus diminishing the likelihood of a positive response.

ANALYSIS OF POLICE RESPONSE TO CITIZENS' REQUESTS

Table 5 provides a summary of the nature of the situations confronting officers in our sample. The largest portion (42%) were disputes in which no violence or threat of violence exists; nearly two-thirds of these were domestic. The second largest category was assaults (26%), nearly half of which were domestic. Public disorders and assistance comprised the next two largest categories (11 and 10%, respectively). Serious thefts, minor violations, and other serious offenses constituted the remainder, each comprising 5% or less of the sample. This diverse sample, like patrol work, generally, is dominated by minor disorders, squabbles, and concerns, a significant proportion of which are domestic in nature. Relatively few of the

Table 5.   Positive Police Response by Type of Problem

	Problem Not Serious			Problem Serious			
		Public	Minor		Serious		
	Assistance	Disorder	Disputes	Violations	Assaults	Theft	Other	Total
(*N*)	(39)	(44)	(165)	(18)	(103)	(14)	(7)	(396)
% of Sample	9.8	11.1	41.7	4.5	26.0	5.1	1.8	100.0
% Positive Response	66.7	84.1	66.1	100.0	66.0	70.0	85.7	70.2

Assistance: Missing persons, medical, mentally disordered, disabled, return missing/stolen property, damaged property, traffic accident, protection/escort, exchange information, miscellaneous assistance.
Public disorder: Drunk, disorderly, loitering, begging, noise, prostitution, obscene activity, littering, miscellaneous minor disorders.
Disputes: Disputes not involving violence or threat of violence.
Minor Violations: Shoplifting, bad check, refuse to pay, trespassing, traffic/parking offense.
Assaults: Using violence against a person, kidnaping, child abuse, threats to injure, injured persons.
Serious Theft: Motor vehicle theft, theft from motor vehicle, burglary, purse snatching.
Other: Illicit drugs, fleeing police, leaving the scene of an accident.

cases, even those classified as "serious," would appear on the nightly news in these cities. The police are thus thrust into a lot of conflict where the stakes appear to be low and undramatic. The likelihood of a positive police response does not appear to be strongly related to problem seriousness. Officers responded positively in all of the minor violations but only 66% of the assaults and 70% of the serious thefts.

Two kinds of multivariate analysis were performed, each based on a different set of assumptions about the metric of the dependent variable. First, the dependent variable was treated as an ordinal variable: (0) request not fulfilled, (1) request promised or partially fulfilled, and (2) request completely fulfilled. This dependent variable was regressed on predictor variables using an ordered probit. The ordered probit, which imposes more stringent metric requirements, produced a model with predicted maximum probability outcomes that placed all cases into either the 0 or 2 categories. Further analysis revealed that cases with observed outcomes in category 1 (partially fulfilled or promised) were appropriately grouped with category 2. The patterning of officers' responses was similar for both categories 1 and 2. We next defined the dependent variable as a dichotomous variable, receiving a value of 1 when police responded positively to the citizen's most restrictive request (fulfilled completely, partially, or promised), and otherwise receiving a value of 0. The results of the two regressions were similar, with only a few differences in levels of statistical significance. We report the results of both the logistic regression and ordered probit, but we concentrate our discussion on the former, which makes less demanding assumptions about the metric of the dependent variable, noting any substantive differences from the ordered probit.[1] Effects were estimated using a single model that includes both sites.[2] Table 6 portrays the effects of each variable by the regression coefficient, standard error, odds ratio, and the standardized regression coefficient (logistic regression only) (Menard, 1995). Analysis of tolerances reveals no serious multicollinearity problems. Because all of the variables have a specific expected direction of effect, we use a one-tailed test for statistical significance.

Legal considerations were the most powerful predictors of the police response, all variables showing relationships in the hypothesized direction. The evidence against the target was a relatively powerful predictor, more than doubling the odds that police would respond positively for each unit increase in the five-point evidence strength scale. Evidence of the requester's wrongdoing was a significant, but less powerful predictor. Asking for an arrest greatly reduced the odds that officers would grant the request for control. If an arrest request frames the issue more clearly in legal terms, we would expect that evidence strength against the target

---

1. The independent variables in our model were collected at two levels of measurement. Data on the police officer's predispositions were collected at the officer level, whereas all other data were collected at the encounter level. Some officers encountered more than one citizen, and therefore, their data on predispositions were duplicated each time they appeared in an encounter. As a result, the usual multivariate regression methods may be inappropriate for modeling these duplicated data, because these regression techniques may understate the size of the standard error for each police officer measure (Bryk and Raudenbush, 1992). However, in both departments, relatively few officers encountered more than two citizens. Only 18 of the 172 officers were observed with five or more citizens. Three-fourths of the officers encountered two or fewer citizens. The potential for underestimating standard errors using nonhierarchical logistical regression is thus greatly reduced. Nevertheless, we went forward with a hierarchical linear model (HLM). Given the small number of encounters per officer and the skewed distribution of several independent variables, we had to reduce drastically the number of independent measures in our HLM and increase three-fold the number of interactions before the model would converge. We found that in our most complete converged model only 1 out of the 171 police officers had a sufficient number of encounters to generate regression coefficients for the encounter-level measures. Because of this small number of level-two units, not one of the encounter-level coefficients had a reliability estimate above .05. The converged model produced no substantive findings different from those that we found using the single-level logistic regression we report in Table 5. For the sake of parsimony, we have limited our paper to a single-level analysis.

2. No *a priori* reasons exist to expect strong differences in the pattern of effects between sites. Including a site as a dummy variable in the model did not significantly increase the model's explanatory power. Estimating effects separately for each site produced some differences in patterns of effect, but only 2 of the 20 coefficients showed statistically significant differences between the two cities, a result with a probability only slightly greater than chance at the conventional $p < .05$ level.

Table 6. Coefficients Representing Effects of Independent Variables on Police Fulfillment of the Citizen's Request to Control Another

Variable (Range)	Logistic Regression				Ordered Probit		
	B	S.E.	Odds Ratio	Std. Coeff.	B	S.E.	Odds Ratio
Legal Considerations							
Evidence of target's legal violation (0–7)	.87*	.18	2.40	.36	.36*	.07	1.40
Evidence of requester's legal violation (0–6)	-.30*	.16	.74	-.08	-.10	.08	.90
Arrest requested (0,1)	-2.16*	.37	.12	-.31	-.94*	.18	.16
Need							
Young or elderly requester (0,1)	-.54	.51	.58	-.05	-.27	.24	.76
Female requester (0,1)	.21	.29	1.23	.03	.01	.14	1.01
Male target (0,1)	-.20	.30	.82	-.03	.11	.14	1.11
Intoxicated target (0,1)	.30	.38	1.35	.04	.33*	.19	1.39
Serious problem (0,1)	-.06	.33	.94	-.01	-.09	.15	.91
Situational Attenuators							
Target disrespectful of police (0,1)	-.03	.46	.97	-.00	.32	.21	1.38
Requester disrespectful of police (0,1)	-.78*	.44	.46	-.08	-.53*	.24	.59
Requester intoxicated/mentally ill (0,1)	-1.34*	.43	.26	-.14	-.53*	.21	.59
Requester-Target Social Relationship							
Status pairing by race (1–4)	.14	.19	1.15	.04	.04	.09	1.04
Status pairing by wealth (1–4)	.12	.19	1.13	.03	.07	.09	1.07
Status pairing by organization (1–4)	.06	.26	1.07	.02	.13	.11	1.14
Close relationship (0,1)	-.66*	.35	.52	-.10	-.04	.17	.66
Officer Predispositions							
Male officer (0,1)	.75*	.35	2.11	.10	.30*	.18	1.35
College degree (0,1)	-.42	.31	.66	-.07	-.18	.15	.84
Years of police experience (0–31)	-.07*	.02	.94	-.15	-.03*	.01	.97
Proclivity to community policing (2–90)	.02*	.01	1.02	.09	.01*	.00	1.01
Community policing job assignment (0,1)	-.67	.50	.51	-.06	-.16	.24	.85
$N = 396$			$R^2_L = .26$				$R^2_L = .30$

*$p < .05$, one-tailed.

would have a stronger effect in those cases than in instances when lower levels of control were sought (the effect revealed in Table 7). This result is also the case when the interaction effects for arrest request and evidence strength are tested in the multivariate model ($p < .05$). Taken together, the three legal variables uniquely accounted for half of the explained variance in the dependent variable; all other variables accounted for about 35% of the explained variance, and both legal and all other variables shared the remainder of the explained variance.

Table 7. Percent of Citizens Whose Requests Were Granted by Evidence Score and Type of Request

	Low Evidence		High Evidence	
	%	*(N)*	%	*(N)*
Arrest not requested	73	(237)	93	(58)
Arrest requested	30	(64)	89	(37)

Note: Low evidence scores were 0 or 1; high evidence scores were 2–7. Percentage differences between all column cells are significant at $p < .05$. The difference between row percentages is significant for low evidence, but not for high evidence.

Need, as we measured it, did not appear to figure largely in the officers' decision to grant the citizen's requests. No indicators of need showed a significant effect in the logistic regression and only one did in the ordered probit (intoxicated target, in the predicted direction). In St. Petersburg, when the target was male, the police were substantially less likely to grant a request to control him, and this effect was significantly different from that shown in Indianapolis.

Two measures of the attenuation of the effects of law and need showed a significant effect. Requesters with a condition suggesting that their requests are less credible or worthy (those intoxicated or evidencing mental illness) were much less likely to have their requests fulfilled. Also, as predicted, disrespectful requesters were less likely to have their wishes granted.[3] Contrary to what research on the sanctioning of suspects shows, a disrespectful target did not significantly affect the odds of granting another citizen's request to control that target.

Only one of the requester-target relationship variables evidenced significant effects, a close relationship between the requester and target (only in the logistic regression). The largest difference across sites was the race pairing. In St. Petersburg, the racial pairing of requester and target

---

3. The effects of this variable differed significantly at the two sites. Disrespectful requesters in Indianapolis, but not St. Petersburg, had a greatly reduced chance of having their requests fulfilled.

had a statistically significant effect in the hypothesized direction, but it was distinguishable from the Indianapolis coefficient only at $p < .10$. The possibility that the nature of the racial pairing of citizens interacts with the race of the officer was also considered, but the interaction term was not significant in either city when it replaced the main-effects racial-pairing term in the model. Other models were estimated testing only for main effects of citizen and officer race, producing no significant effects.

Three indicators of officer predisposition showed significant effects. Male officers had twice the odds of female officers in fulfilling the request to control another. The greater inclination of males to grant the request holds across low and high evidence levels and whether an arrest or some other form of control was requested, indicating that males are more likely to intervene on the requester's behalf regardless of the legal implications of the situation. As officers' years of police experience increased, their responsiveness to the controlling request declined. Officers with a stronger proclivity for community policing were more responsive to requests. Neither a community policing specialist job assignment nor a college degree showed a significant impact.

DISCUSSION

Unlike most prior research on police, we have defined officers' discretion not by how much control they exert, but rather, whether they will grant one citizen's request to control another. Who gets what they asked for? Citizens with the evidence on their side, asking for less than the full measure of the criminal sanction (arrest), credible or "worthy" (not intoxicated, mentally ill, or disrespectful), not targeting someone with whom they had a close relationship, and getting an officer with certain characteristics (male, few years of experience, and predisposed to favor community policing). Citizens exhibiting need or social status according to wealth, race, or organization affiliation appeared to enjoy no strong advantage in getting what they requested, although race did show a significant effect in St. Petersburg. We discuss these findings below.

Our analysis shows that police are generally responsive to requests to control others, and that the requesters most likely to receive a positive response are those seeking less than the maximum police control (arrest). This situation casts a somewhat different light on the now well-established relationship between the presence of a citizen asking for another's arrest and the likelihood that the police will make that arrest (Riksheim and Chermak, 1993:366; Mastrofski et al., 1995). Police may be more likely to arrest when a complainant requests it, but our analysis clearly shows that requests for this form of control are the least successful. Such requests are more susceptible to the influence of evidentiary strength than requests for the mobilization of less control. As predicted, requests for more law place police more squarely into the nonpartisan role. Police, even those in organizations that pursue community policing, may be influenced by citizens' desires to impose the most extreme restriction on their adversary's freedom, but officers act more to screen out such requests than to accommodate them. Their role is thus more accurately portrayed as legal gatekeeper than responsive public servant. It puts the "radically democratic character" of the police response to complainants' preferences for arrest (Black, 1980:102) in a broader framework. Officers serve more to modulate than amplify the public's will, at least when enacting the most extreme form of control we have considered. In keeping the peace, they soften the blows that might otherwise fall between disputants, reducing vigilantism and the prospects for a Hobbesian struggle of all against all (Black, 1980:198).

By concentrating almost exclusively on arrest as the principal form of police control, researchers have ignored the more frequent occasions when citizens seek to mobilize *some* law on their behalf. Our study shows that it is easier to mobilize the police to intrude on others when citizens ask them to use "less law" in Black's terms. This pattern has been noted in systematic observation of the police conducted in the 1960s (Black, 1980:161). One interpretation is that citizens make many requests, especially for arrest, that are legally unsupported. Another is that officers decline to arrest, even when such action is legally warranted. Reformers concerned about the police response to domestic violence have expended considerable effort to increase the pressure on police to arrest by lobbying for new laws and pushing for stricter enforcement (Sherman, 1992). This campaign may have encouraged the public to solicit an arrest response more often than before, perhaps disproportionately to what the law will support. Legal reforms may stimulate popular expectations that far exceed the willingness and capacity of legal institutions to respond.

Here, we have examined a broader range of citizen conflict situations than domestic disputes. We have not attempted to make judgments about whether the observed circumstances crossed a specific legal threshold to justify the requested police intrusion, but we have merely noted the relatively strong effects of legal variables on the officer's response. The much weaker effects of other situational factors, such as need, citizen demeanor, and disputants' personal characteristics, indicate that factors we associate with legal decision making dominated the officers' response. In terms of Black's theory of law, legalistic norms about the distribution of social control in the observed cases dominated the selection of the police response, outweighing by far the weaker effects of other normative systems associated with the police subculture (e.g., punishing disrespectful individuals).

Further, indicators of the citizens' social status (race, wealth, and organization affiliation) showed no appreciable or, in the case of race, consistent effect. Why racial pairings should show the hypothesized effect in St. Petersburg but not Indianapolis is a matter about which we can only speculate. Racial tensions were evidenced in both cities, but the distance in social space between minorities and whites may have been greater in St. Petersburg. Given that the difference in race effects between the two cities did not achieve the standard level of significance, we view this finding with caution and regard it as suggestive only. In general, then, our results reinforce the findings of most prior quantitative studies based on systematic observation that citizens' social status is a weak and inconsistent predictor of police behavior (Riksheim and Chermak, 1993).

Our results provide a somewhat different picture than presented in Black's analysis of the police response to disputes. Distinguishing complaints according to the severity of the offense and grounds for arrest, Black found no relationship between the legal status of the complaint and the likelihood of arrest. He concluded, "[T]he written law seems to have limited value as a predictor of what the police will do from one case to the next" (1980:186). The difference in our conclusions and his are not surprising, given the trend of the past two decades to promote the use of law and public agents enacting it to resolve disputes, even some that seem minor. Reforms, such as those that expanded the domain of the criminal law in domestic abuse cases, have also created tremendous pressure on the police to treat these disputes as criminal. That officers attend to legal concerns more than any others seems a natural outgrowth of that pressure. Regardless of recent community policing efforts to debureaucratize and mitigate legalistic tendencies of American police (Mastrofski, 1998), the twentieth century trend has been one in which the police "have adapted the practice of policing to the legalistic demands of the formal legal system" (Reiss, 1992:83). The law may not govern police, but our evidence reinforces the view that it is a powerful influence on their behavior (Herbert, 1998; Klinger, 1996; Reiss and Bordua, 1967:32–40).

With the exception of the closeness of the relationship between the disputants and a race effect in St. Petersburg, the results do not support the proposition that the social relationships among disputants strongly influence the behavior of law (Black, 1976). Otherwise, pairings by race, wealth, and organizational representation evidenced neither strong nor significant effects, and the closeness of the relationship, though significant, was relatively weak, which is contrary to Black's (1980) conclusions from systematic observation of the police handling of disputes and to some claims of unequal protection and unequal enforcement according to citizens' race (Kennedy, 1997). Several reasons may account for this difference. First, the police Black studied in the 1960s may have used different decision algorithms than those we studied in the 1990s. As suggested above, police of the 1990s may be more legalistic and thereby less prone to influence by citizens' personal characteristics, a finding that two of us noted in an earlier analysis of police arrest practices (Mastrofski et al., 1995). Unfortunately, despite its groundbreaking theoretical contribution, Black's analysis makes it difficult to assess this claim. He serially tested bivariate relationships between citizens' social characteristics and police behavior. The effects of independent variables were not simultaneously controlled, which is likely to overstate the effects that are uniquely attributable to any single variable. Specifically, his analysis did not simultaneously control for the effects of legal variables. Including these variables might have illuminated spurious relationships between social characteristics and police behavior.

Unlike most previous studies, our results suggest that some decision-maker characteristics do pattern police choices about who gets what. The two indicators that reflect the organization's efforts to move officers into the community policing normative space both showed the predicted effects, albeit only the individual's proclivity to community policing was significant. That male officers are more likely than female officers to fulfill these requests raises intriguing questions for future inquiry. Does this characteristic reflect a greater reticence among women officers to fulfill citizens' requests—structured perhaps by a different sense of justice than embraced by male officers (Gilligan, 1982)? Or does it issue from a tendency to be less controlling in general than males, regardless of whether someone solicits it? More police experience makes officers less inclined to responsiveness to the citizen's request, which could be the result of increasing cynicism—or wisdom, depending on one's perspective—accruing over the years about the futility of intervention, and it may also reflect a diminution in the officer's willingness to do time-consuming work. The proclivity to engage in community policing makes officers more susceptible to citizens' entreaties to provide a controlling intervention. This result is consistent with the expectations of many contemporary reformers, but from these data, we cannot know the extent to which these departments' community policing programs caused or strengthened these views or to what extent officers came to hold them independent of management efforts to transform them.

Few systematic studies of police discretion explore in depth the complainant's behavior, beyond preference for an arrest; they concentrate instead on the suspect or target of the complainant's request (Riksheim and Chermak, 1993). Our analysis indicates that some police decision making in these cases does turn on the target to whom the requester directs police attention. Evidence of the target's wrongdoing was a relatively strong predictor of the police response. However, a display of disrespect by the target did not appear to figure powerfully in the officers' choice when the strength of evidence was taken into account.[4] On the other hand, the evidence against the requester, the requester's credibility or worthiness, and the requester's display of disrespect were more powerful and significant. In adversarial situations, how *requesters* present themselves to police thus appears to matter, independent of the evidence about the grievance.

The generalizability of these findings is limited. Black (1995:834) argues that the direction of the effects of social space predictors is constant across different societies, but we have reason to expect that the relative *strength* of influence will vary according to community environment, organizational policies, and structures (Reiss and Bordua, 1967). For example, Wilson (1968:157–171) found that police agencies that had been remodeled according to "good government" standards were less inclined to make arrests for certain disorders according to the suspect's race than those departments that remained unreformed. Reformed departments were more responsive to legal norms of equal treatment, regardless of social standing. The only subsequent effort to test various implications of Wilson's organizational effects thesis found mixed results, some situational influences being uniform across all types of police departments and others varying significantly with the type of department (Smith, 1984).

Given that both departments in our sample conformed to Wilson's service style, we cannot test his thesis, but this organizational characterization points to hypotheses about what we might expect in markedly different types of agencies. Service-style agencies are those that have undergone legalistic reforms, but whose leaders seek to smooth the impersonal edge of bureaucracy with more responsiveness to citizens. They take law enforcement as seriously as do purely legalistic agencies, but they resort more often to informal resolutions, customized to the needs of their clients (Wilson, 1968:200ff). This action would account for the relatively strong influence of legal factors in our sample and the tendency to deny more requests for arrest than requests for less formal means of control. We expect that "watchman"-style departments, those that remain unmoved by legalistic reform pressures, would show markedly weaker effects from legal factors, while showing much stronger effects among those promoted by the police subculture (situational attenuators) and social status of the

---

4. We cannot distinguish the separate effects of disrespect and evidence strength in the cases in which they overlap (Worden et al., 1996:327). If one selects a somewhat arbitrary dichotomization of evidence scores into those with a score below 2 (no or weak evidence) and those with a score of 2 or higher, only 6% of all 396 cases had both high evidence scores and were disrespectful.

participants. We would have expected need considerations to show stronger effects in service-style departments than they did in our sample, because such departments promote a professionalism that responds to citizen needs. However, the absence in both departments of policies identifying need criteria and when and how to employ alternatives to arrest may account for the lack of effects in our sample. Finally, these departments' efforts to "empower" rank-and-file officers to use their judgment in handling citizens' problems may account for the strength of some officer predisposition variables. Given a greater sense of freedom, officers might have been more inclined to act on their personal preferences. The community policing values actively promoted in both departments do show significant effects in the direction desired by management. We speculate that legalistic agencies that do not promote the empowerment of their rank and file will show weaker effects of individual officers' personal predispositions.

In addition to testing this model in a variety of departments, future research could also compare effects across different neighborhood ecologies. Klinger (1997) argues that levels and standards of social deviance vary across police districts within a city, and that these affect officers' views of their work: for example, what constitutes "normal" deviance, the deservedness of victims, and what constitutes a worthwhile police response. These views are the building blocks of informal rules of police behavior, "negotiated" within distinct work groups that vary according to district. This model is said to account for why police are more lenient in high- instead of low-crime areas. We conjecture that a number of standards derived from our model of police responsiveness to citizens may vary ecologically within a large city. Thresholds and attenuators of need (especially what constitutes disrespect) seem likely to vary by area, producing different results accordingly. For example, in areas where officers are accustomed to frequent incivility from habitués, they may be less inclined to overlook a given instance of disrespect than in areas where such behavior is rare—sensitizing them rather than acclimatizing them to these affronts.

SOME POLICY IMPLICATIONS

Our observations were made in departments that, like many others in the United States, were implementing community policing, the dominant American police reform movement at the turn of the century. Community policing places a high value on citizens as "coproducers" of public order and safety. Under community policing, citizens are encouraged to call on the police to act against other citizens threatening that order and safety. To the extent that police departments respond favorably to such requests, it amplifies the citizen's part in mobilizing law. We found that officers with a proclivity for community policing were more inclined to be responsive to citizens' requests, but the scope of these effects was greatly overshadowed by those of legal considerations. In these two agencies, the anticipated tendency of community policing to amplify the democratic character of the mobilization of police assistance seems bounded by legal constraints. Would this limitation be so in departments in which the organization sought a closer balance between commitment-to-community policing and legal constraints? One might find such agencies among Wilson's (1968) watchman-style departments and those service-style agencies that are able to secure a much stronger rank-and-file commitment to the police-community partnership practices advocated by community policing reformers.

Public officials and policy analysts might be prompted to take some encouragement from our results and conclude that things are as they should be: More than anything else, police are influenced more by legal concerns than citizens' personal characteristics. But being influenced by the law is not the same as following its specific standards. We did not establish whether probable cause existed for an arrest, whether a sufficient evidentiary basis existed to justify banishing the target, and so on. Applying such thresholds and, indeed, establishing whether they can even be applied reliably, is an entirely different enterprise. In a broader context, readers are cautioned not to assume that police officers who are more responsive to citizens' requests to control others are necessarily "better" than those less responsive. Citizens may ask for many things that are trivial, unwarranted, illegal, or unjust. The police, after all, are here to act for us when the better angels of our nature are not.

Determining precisely which requests are worthy requires value choices that, in turn, must be legitimated and then articulated in ways that officers can apply. But police work operates in a *moral* realm that is only loosely bound by laws, department rules, and professional standards (Muir, 1977:ch. 11), and often those legitimate sources intended to guide discretion are fraught with ambiguity and conflict. Many police husband their coercive authority (for reasons admirable and otherwise), often using less than the law allows or even requires—when it provides any guidance at all (Brown, 1981; Reiss, 1971a:135). Whether officers act in accordance with whatever consensus society has mustered is a question worthy of future pursuit. Legal criteria are but one standard and perhaps not the most compelling in many cases. Doing what is legally required may fall far short of what the highest professional standards prescribe (Bittner, 1983; Klockars, 1994). Our crude measures of need that justify a positive response may not have captured the sorts of factors that are most compelling to a professional approach. Also, most of the control police exert on

POLICE CONTROL OF CITIZENS 339

some citizens on behalf of other citizens occurs under circumstances for which neither the law nor professional standards are now clearly articulated (Bayley and Bittner, 1984). Further, professional standards may well be at odds with certain popular expectations about what the police should do. Thus, the first step in making judgments about the *merit* of the police response to these requests will be to establish principles by which police performance can be judged. That will be an important step toward performance evaluation in commonplace situations that comprise so much of police work and remain virtually unexamined and unevaluated.

REFERENCES

Bayley, David and Egon Bittner
 1984 Learning the skills of policing. Law and Contemporary Problems 47:35–59.

Bittner, Egon
 1970 The Functions of Police in Modern Society. Bethesda, Md.: U.S. National Institute of Mental Health.
 1983 Legality and Workmanship. In Maurice Punch (ed.), Control in the Police Organization. Cambridge, Mass.: MIT Press.

Black, Donald
 1976 The Behavior of Law. New York: Academic Press.
 1980 The Manners and Customs of the Police. New York: Academic Press.
 1989 Sociological Justice. New York: Oxford University Press.
 1993 The Social Structure of Right and Wrong. San Diego, Calif.: Academic Press.
 1995 The epistemology of pure sociology. Law and Social Inquiry 20:829–870.

Broderick, John
 1987 Police in a Time of Change. 2d ed. Prospect Heights, Ill.: Waveland Press.

Brown, Michael K.
 1981 Working the Streets. New York: Russell Sage Foundation.

Bryk, Anthony S. and S. W. Raudenbush
 1992 Hierarchical Linear Models: Applications and Data Analysis Methods. Newbury Park, Calif.: Sage.

Gilligan, Carol
 1982 In a Different Voice: Psychological Theory and Women's Development. Cambridge, Mass.: Harvard University Press.

Herbert, Steve
 1998 Police subculture reconsidered. Criminology 36:343–369.

Katz, Jack
 1988 Seductions of Crime: Moral and Sensual Attractions of Doing Evil. New York: Basic Books.

Kennedy, Randall
 1997 Race, Crime, and the Law. New York: Vintage.

340   MASTROFSKI ET AL.

Klinger, David A.
  1996   Bringing crime back in: Toward a better understanding of police arrest
            decisions. Journal of Research in Crime and Delinquency 33:333–336.
  1997   Negotiating order in patrol work: An ecological theory of police response
            to deviance. Criminology 35:277–306.

Klockars, Carl B.
  1994   A theory of excessive force and its control. In William A. Geller and
            Hans Toch (eds.), And Justice for All. Washington, D.C.: Police
            Executive Research Forum.

Lane, Roger
  1992   Urban police and crime in nineteenth century America. In Michael Tonry
            and Norval Morris (eds.), Modern Policing. Chicago, Ill.: University of
            Chicago Press.

Martin, Susan E. and Nancy C. Jurik
  1996   Doing Justice, Doing Gender: Women in Law and Criminal Justice
            Occupations. Thousand Oaks, Calif.: Sage.

Mastrofski, Stephen D.
  1998   Community policing and police organization structure. In Jean-Paul
            Brodeur (ed.), Community Policing and the Evaluation of Police Service
            Delivery. Thousand Oaks, Calif.: Sage.

Mastrofski, Stephen D., R. Richard Ritti, and Jeffrey B. Snipes
  1994   Expectancy theory and police productivity in DUI enforcement. Law and
            Society Review 28:113–148.

Mastrofski, Stephen D., Jeffrey B. Snipes, and Anne E. Supina
  1996   Compliance on demand: The public's response to specific police requests.
            Journal of Research in Crime and Delinquency 33:269–305.

Mastrofski, Stephen D., Robert E. Worden, and Jeffrey B. Snipes
  1995   Law enforcement in a time of community policing. Criminology
            33:539–563.

Mastrofski, Stephen D., Roger B. Parks, Albert J. Reiss, Jr., Robert E. Worden,
Christina DeJong, Jeffrey B. Snipes, and William Terrill
  1998   Systematic Social Observation of Public Police: Applying Field Research
            Methods to Policy Issues. Washington, D.C.: National Institute of Justice.

Menard, Scott
  1995   Applied Logistic Regression Analysis. Thousand Oaks, Calif.: Sage
            Publications.

Muir, William K., Jr.
  1977   Police: Streetcorner Politicians. Chicago, Ill.: Chicago University Press.

Reiss, Albert J., Jr.
  1968   Police Brutality: Answers to Key Questions. New Brunswick, N.J.:
            Transaction.
  1971a   The Police and the Public. New Haven, Conn.: Yale University Press.
  1971b   Systematic observation of natural social phenomena. In Hebert L.
            Costner (ed.), Sociological Methodology 1971. San Francisco, Calif.:
            Jossey-Bass.

POLICE CONTROL OF CITIZENS   341

1992   Police organization in the twentieth century. In Michael Tonry and
        Norval Morris (eds.), Modern Policing. Chicago, Ill.: University of
        Chicago Press.

Reiss, Albert J., Jr. and David J. Bordua
1967   Environment and organization: A perspective on police. In David J.
        Bordua (ed.), The Police: Six Sociological Essays. New York: Wiley.

Riksheim, Eric and Steven Chermak
1993   Causes of police behavior revisited. Journal of Criminal Justice
        21:353–382.

Rubinstein, Jonathan
1973   City Police. New York: Farrar, Straus, and Giroux.

Sampson, Robert J., Stephen W. Raudenbush, and Felton Earls
1997   Neighborhoods and violent crime: A multilevel study of collective
        efficacy. Science 277:918–924.

Sherman, Lawrence W.
1992   Policing Domestic Violence: Experiments and Dilemmas. New York: Free
        Press.

Smith, Douglas A.
1984   The organizational context of legal control. Criminology 22:19–38.
1986   The neighborhood context of police behavior. In Albert J. Reiss, Jr. and
        Michael Tonry (eds.), Communities and Crime. Chicago, Ill.: University
        of Chicago Press.

Sparrow, Malcolm K., Mark H. Moore, and David B. Kennedy
1990   Beyond 911: A New Era for Policing. New York: Basic Books.

Stalans, Loretta J. and Mary A. Finn
1995   How novice and experienced officers interpret wife assaults: Normative
        and efficiency frames. Law and Society Review 29:287–321.

Tedeschi, James T. and Richard B. Felson
1994   Violence, Aggression, & Coercive Actions. Washington, D.C.: American
        Psychological Association.

Teplin, Linda
1986   Keeping the Peace. Washington, D.C.: U.S. Government Printing Office.

Van Maanen, John
1974   Working the street: A developmental view of police behavior. In Herbert
        Jacob (ed.), The Potential for Reform in Criminal Justice. Beverly Hills,
        Calif.: Sage.

White, Susan
1972   A perspective on police professionalism. Law and Society Review
        7:61–85.

Wilson, James Q.
1968   Varieties of Police Behavior. Cambridge, Mass.: Harvard University
        Press.

Worden, Alissa
1993   The attitudes of women and men in policing: Testing conventional and
        contemporary wisdom. Criminology 31:203–241.

342   MASTROFSKI ET AL.

Worden, Robert E.
   1990   A badge and a baccalaureate: Policies, hypotheses, and further evidence. Justice Quarterly 7:565–592.
   1995   Police officers' belief systems: A framework for analysis. American Journal of Police 14:49–81.
Worden, Robert E., Robin L. Shepard, and Stephen D. Mastrofski
   1996   On the meaning and measurement of suspects' demeanor toward the police: A comment on "Demeanor and Arrest." Journal of Research in Crime and Delinquency 33:324–332.

Stephen D. Mastrofski is Professor of Public and International Affairs and Director of the Administration of Justice Program at George Mason University. His research interests include testing theories of police behavior, applying organization theory to criminal justice reform, measuring the performance of police organizations, and field research methods on crime and justice topics.

Jeffrey B. Snipes is a law student at Stanford University and a candidate for the doctoral degree in the School of Criminal Justice at the University at Albany.

Roger B. Parks is Professor in the School of Public and Environmental Affairs at Indiana University-Bloomington.

Christopher D. Maxwell is Assistant Professor in the School of Criminal Justice at Michigan State University. His research interests include the social control and criminal justice response to violence between intimates, the efficacy of aggression and delinquency prevention programs, and the impact of social and ecological contexts on patterns of delinquency, crime, and criminal justice decision making.

[10]

Policing Identities: Cop Decision Making and the Constitution of Citizens

Trish Oberweis and Michael Musheno

We examine police decision making by focusing on police stories and drawing together contemporary thought about identities and police subculture. Our inquiry suggests that police decision making is both improvisational and patterned. Cops are moral agents who tag people with identities as they project identities of their own. They do engage in raw forms of division or stereotyping, marking some as others to be feared and themselves as protectors of society, while exercising their coercive powers to punish "the bad." Due, in part, to the many ways that they identify themselves, cops also connect with people as unique individuals, including individuals whose categorical identities (e.g., drug dealers) put them at the margins of society. Rather than using their coercive powers to repress these individuals, cops infuse them with certain virtues (e.g., good family men) while cutting them breaks. As they complicate representations of themselves, cops also project complex notions of law and legality. Moral discourse seems to infuse their judgments, while they invoke law strategically as a tool to enforce their moral judgments.

The marginalistic integration of individuals in the state's utility is not obtained in the modern state by the form of the ethical community which was characteristic of the Greek city. It is obtained in this new

Trish Oberweis is the project manager at the American Justice Institute, San Francisco. **Michael Musheno** is professor of justice studies and public affairs and director of the Center for Urban Inquiry at Arizona State University. The authors are grateful to M. A. Bortner, Steve Herbert, Nancy Jurik, Suzanne Leland, Steven Maynard-Moody, Peter Manning, and the anonymous reviewers for comments on earlier drafts of this manuscript. The research related to this article was supported by a National Science Foundation Grant, Law and Social Sciences Program, Grant number SBR-9511169.

political rationality by a certain specific technique called then, and at
this moment, the police.

—Foucault, The Political Technology of Individuals

Police decision making is about policing identities; it is about the constitution of citizens or subjects who are wedded to the administrative apparatus of the state. Examining stories told to us by police officers, we find
that police decision making is richly normative and contingent rather than
narrowly rule driven and fixed. When police come into contact with citizens, they render moral judgments and concoct actions as they tag people
with identities and project identities of their own.

Our identity framework embraces a sociology of culture that treats culture as particular, fractured, and contingent (see Garfinkel 1967; Swidler
1968; Sewell 1992; or Gamson 1992).[1] It builds on the works specific to
police culture that depict cop decision making as "both guided and improvisational" (Shearing and Ericson 1991, 500; also Manning 1989; Van
Maanen 1978) and which recognize that "while coherence is at times obvious in the police world . . . conflict is also always present" (Herbert 1997,
146). It draws on police stories as a valuable source for gaining access to the
"practical reasoning" of cops engaged in their trade.[2]

Police engage in raw forms of division, marking some as others to be
feared (e.g., urban youth gang members), and "put themselves forward as the
protectors of 'what is in us more than ourselves,' that is, that which makes
us part of the nation" (Salecl 1994, 205). But, police identity is not monolithic, as cops have more than just professional identities. Due, in part, to
the many ways they identify themselves, cops connect with people as
unique individuals and sometimes defy the simple coercive politics of stereotyping whole groups as "bad." Here, they bond with people whose categorical identities (e.g., illegal aliens, drug dealers) put them at the margins of

---

1. While others have invoked the importance of "social" identities to understand policing (e.g., Crank 1997, 5), only a few have taken up identities (see, for example, the classic
study "The Asshole" by Van Maanan 1978) that are particularly reflective of current thinking
about the meaning of identity and how identities are acted out in the everyday.

2. We are guided by Shearing and Ericson, who regard police stories as revealing of cops'
practical reasoning or their improvising norms and action (1991, 482). They critique the
scholarship on police decision making that presumes action follows rules, even those scholars
who have posited the importance of local rules devised at the organizational level and modified by what is often referenced as the "police subculture" (see Manning 1977). Even when
scholars have observed the centrality of police stories to the "craft" of policing, they are reluctant to view this form of communication as constitutive of the practical reasoning of cops, in
part because police scholars themselves embrace the importance of rule-driven decision making to liberal democracy (see Bayley and Bittner 1984). The significance of stories to understanding normativity and action is well recognized today in sociolegal studies (e.g., Ewick and
Silbey 1998; Conley and O'Barr 1998), and in policy inquiry (e.g., Schram and Neisser 1977).
We embrace these writings as well as the early groundbreaking work of Shearing and Ericson
that is specific to policing, and suggest that police stories reveal the importance of identity
and identification to their practical reasoning.

society. Woven into these improvisations of policing is the recognition of particular individuals as having certain virtues (e.g., good family men), and for them, police act by cutting breaks or by going out of their way to find services.

Classifying some whose categorical identities put them at the margins as worthy individuals needing services or deserving breaks preserves the ranks of society while creating the illusion that individual virtue coupled with timely state action enable movement from the margin to the center of society. We argue that while appearing to be the warm, friendly face of policing, these communicative processes and the exceptionalism they produce are better understood as crucial to the making of state-centered subjects, including citizens who are simultaneously cops.

Before turning to our empirical observations, we lay out our conceptualizations of identity and police. We do this because our perspectives are distinct from mainstream liberal understandings of these topics. As we show below, our perspective is grounded instead in literatures that oppose liberal conceptions of the self and the state.

CONCEPTUALIZING IDENTITY

Identity is how we come to recognize ourselves and each other. It is the composite of all the multiple and intersecting subject positions that one actor occupies, either by chance or by choice. All of us belong to certain groups; this is to say that we all occupy particular subject positions. The authors are white, well-educated, middle-class heterosexuals. One of us is female and the other is male. Each of these group memberships (middle-class, white, heterosexual, male/female) represents what we are calling a "subject position." These subject positions are constituted through an ever-changing process of social meaning making; they often define our expectations as well as what others will expect of us. They provide a way of organizing the social world, of endowing both ourselves and other social actors with more particularized meaning.

Each subject position tells us, to some degree, who we are in relation to others, how to behave, and how to expect others to behave. Thus, subject positions come with expectations that are largely socially agreed upon. They are brought to life through personalized meaning as individuals struggle to take up their positions in ways that both fit with all the other subject positions defining that actor and also which adequately portray any particular subject position, allowing other actors to recognize that position and to act accordingly. For example, the occupational subject position "professor" could be taken up in any number of ways, but to be successful, the performance must be recognized as "professorial."

We draw a distinction between the term "subject position" and the term "role," which rests on a very different notion of the subject. Subject positions are often categories that might elsewhere be called roles: each term refers to a similar list of words (e.g., professor, woman, etc.). However, in choosing the term "subject position," we are making a different assumption about human actors than we feel the term "role" permits. "Roles" can be chosen and played, exchanged one for another at any time. This implies some human agent, separable from the roles, who is able to put on first one role and then perhaps another. We wish to distance ourselves from this notion of the autonomous self or liberal subject.[3] Instead, our assumptions are that the actor is always and only the interactive total of her/his subject positions and that there is no self beyond the intertwined subjectivities themselves, no rational actor hiding behind the scenes. The distinction between identities and roles, then, rests on differing assumptions about human subjectivity.

Returning to our example, any particular professor must "be" a professor in ways that are congruent with the other subject positions that that professor holds (e.g., female, heterosexual). Simultaneously, that actor must act in a manner sufficiently congruent with cultural expectations of professors to be recognized as such (e.g., stands in the front of the classroom, gives and grades assignments, and more subtly, is kempt and attentive, carries books or paper or chalk). Thus, the identity process works in both directions, both as a means for actors to know how to act and also as a means to recognize the acts of others. In this way, identity provides a profoundly definitional but largely uncognized framework. From this perspective, then, identity—the total mixture of subject positions and their domains of social connotations—is the flexible bedrock of social order, giving shape and continuity to social relationships, including the relationship to one's self.

Chantal Mouffe offers a more philosophical explanation:

> The social agent is constituted by an ensemble of "subject positions" that can never be totally fixed in a closed system of differences. . . . The "identity" of such a multiple and contradictory subject is therefore always contingent and precarious, temporarily fixed at the intersection of those subject positions and dependent on specific forms of identification. (Mouffe 1995, 33)

Thus, we are never only women or men, only a member of a race or nation or profession. These identifications intersect,[4] mutually defining the way

---

3. For a discussion, see Lovibond (1993, 390) or Pauline Marie Rosenau (1992, specifically chap. 3, "Subverting the Subject").

4. Again, we are using the term *identification* to refer to at least two directions of identity making: we identify ourselves and act accordingly, and we are also identified by others according to how we act/appear. The act of identification in either direction can be more or less

each subject position becomes part of a nonfixed whole. The ways in which a woman, for example, takes up her femaleness depends on her racial, national, and/or professional positionings, and vice versa. The multiple subject positions that combine to create an identity thus do not coexist, but interexist. They are not separate entities, but rather determine each other in a constant process of formation and transformation, with each new act or performance by the actor. Identity is thus unstable and always momentary, depending on context for clarity.

Our conception of identity insists on this basic dynamism: Identities are interactive. Within the same individual, one particular subject position, in our case "police officer," might be taken up one way by one officer and differently by another officer, depending on what other subject positions (such as race, age, rank, sex, etc.) are interacting with the occupational subject position. It may even be—and often is—taken up differently by the same officer at different times. Across individuals, we see the importance of context. The combination of localized social relations, events, and territory make some particular identities more directly germane and others relevant only indirectly at any particular moment.

Contemporary feminist, queer, and antiracist theory focuses on the ways that identity excludes (see Halley 1993; Hall 1996; or Butler 1990). Descending from a Derridean logic of différance, these theorists tend to focus largely on who might be excluded from an invocation of a "we," identified as some identity group. As people sharing a given subject position define themselves as a "we," they do so only by simultaneously defining an excluded "they." It is a politics of exclusion based on otherness. In other words, identity tends to be seen as something that divides people across (perhaps arbitrary) attributes. Judith Butler, speaking about the subject of feminism, describes the problem: "The minute that the category of women gets invoked as *describing* the constituency for which feminism speaks, an internal debate invariably begins over what the descriptive content of that term will be. . . . Identity categories are never merely descriptive, but always normative, and as such, exclusionary" (Butler 1992, 15–16). Thus, the terrain of identity is itself not neutral but political. Lines are drawn between "us" and "them," and sides must be taken (indeed, are often experienced as already having been taken). In this sense, identity divides people from each other by its inherent inclusions and exclusions.

However, identity is not only about division. Cornel West suggests that "in talking about identity, we have to begin to look at the various ways in which human beings have constructed their desire for recognition, associ-

---

rigid. (This is particularly clear in the example of defining "homosexuality" [see Halley 1993]). Subjects can identify themselves and others more or less according to stereotyped images that flatten identities and make rigid what is permeable. In this sense, rigid identifiers are not unlike stereotypes.

ation and protection over time and in space, always in circumstances not of their own choosing." For West, identity facilitates social coherence. "Identity is about binding," he argues, "and it means, on the one hand, that you can be bound. . . . But it also means that you can be held together" (1995, 16). Thus, identity is a means of connection, too. We pay attention to the ebb and flow of both identity division *and* connection in the context of the everyday life of policing. Focusing on police officers, we are able to explore the connotations of binding and dividing as microprocesses at work in the construction of state subjects or citizens. We offer identity-driven insight into the informalities of the formal practice of law enforcement, a practice of (re)constituting social order through the "policing" of identity. Our focus includes both citizens and agents as political subjects and conceives of each such that "state agent" and "citizen" are not always mutually exclusive labels. Particularly, police officers are simultaneously state actors and state subjects, or citizens.

ABOUT POLICE AND POLICING

Louis Althusser has suggested that one primary activity of the state is the reproduction of the relations of production. The police play a crucial role in such reproduction. The state's reiteration of itself requires "a reproduction of its submission to the rules of the established order" (Althusser 1991, 127). He argues that this process of reproducing social order "is secured by the exercise of State power in the State Apparatuses, on the one hand the (Repressive) State Apparatus, on the other the Ideological State Apparatus" (1991, 141). The police play a unique role in this process, as they are both agents of the state as well as state subjects, ideologically constituted in and through the same apparatuses as other subjects. Unlike other subjects, however, police are granted the authority to repressively and violently constitute other subjects within the state's order. Althusser explains that although "the (Repressive) State Apparatus functions massively and predominantly *by repression* (including physical repression) . . . the police also function by ideology both to ensure their own cohesion and reproduction, and in the 'values' they propound externally" (1991, 138).

Similarly, Foucault suggests that "the aim of this new art of governing . . . is to reinforce the state itself" (1988, 150). He defines the police as governors,[5] explaining that the "police govern not by the law but by a spe-

---

5. In tracing the genealogy of police and policing in France and Germany, Foucault shows that from the sixteenth century onward the term *police* referred to the entire state administrative apparatus and *policing* to the full range of state administrative activities (1988, 154–55). While the naming of agencies of the state has become more specified and the numbers of state agencies have proliferated from the eighteenth century onward in the West, we take the position that policing remains the task of all state agencies, or in Foucault's words, what the "police are concerned with is men's coexistence in a territory, their relationships to

cific, a permanent, and a positive intervention in the behavior of individuals" (1988, 159). This is how it comes to pass that for Foucault, "the problem of a permanent intervention of the state in social processes, even without the form of the law, is . . . characteristic of our modern politics and of political problematics" (1988, 159). The police must enforce not only law, *but also order*. The order police enforce is the state's order.

Rather than protectors of freedom or doers of justice, Foucault's police are protectors and perpetuators of the state. They are among the state's administrators. For him, the population of citizens is "nothing more than what the state takes care of for its own sake" (1988, 160). Thus, police as agents of the state are part of the process of creating subjects who, in turn, legitimate the state administrative apparatus and its authority (see also Crank 1994). It is this perspective, a critical perspective of policing, that we embrace. This process of creating subjects includes moments in which the police make connections with citizens and withhold their coercive powers, in effect potentially strengthening the rules through exceptionalism. Through stories about their work, the officers in this study provided illustrations of such moments.

EXAMINING POLICE DECISION MAKING

To inquire about citizen making, we follow the suggestions of Shearing and Ericson by "examining police stories as stories . . . that is, as figurative forms with their own logic" that reveal their "practical reasoning" (Shearing and Ericson 1991, 489). In viewing police stories from the perspective of identity, we suggest that what police think ought to be done and what they do in particular situations depends, in part, on who is involved.[6] This officer's story illustrates the point.

> I got a call for a criminal damage report. Well, it was a dispute between two neighbors. . . . So when I got there, I noticed that the front door had

---

property, what they produce, what is exchanged in the market, and so on" (1988, 155). We focus on the activities of officers in a contemporary police agency while anticipating that they, like their counterparts in other state agencies (e.g., welfare offices), are attendant to the full range of tasks outlined by Foucault in his essay on "The Political Technology of Individuals" (1988). Currently, in collaboration with others, we are conducting parallel research in other state agencies, including a public school and two agencies that deal with vocational rehabilitation.

6. The work of Shearing and Ericson (1991) has been important in challenging the prevailing views that police decision making is structured by an externalized body of rules, and/or that some fixed "police culture" produces "informal" rules that the police then follow. Rather, they see the police as "active participants in the construction of action" and view police culture as "gambits and strategies" rather than some organic whole. Building on Shearing and Ericson, we think that the multiplicity and fluidity of identities provide insight into how police construct action and constitute cultures of policing. We elaborate on this view and relate it to the police literature in the conclusion below.

> *lipstick written on it and in real big letters it said, "I know you have my coat*
> *and my stereo. You better give it back." It was the size of the whole front*
> *door in real dark red lipstick.* So I contacted the girl that lived there. She was
> a white female student whose parents were from the area. She was in her
> early 20s, nice looking girl, you know, typical college. "Yeah, my neighbor
> . . . she had her stereo stolen and she had her jacket stolen and now she
> thinks we did it. . . . *We know she's the one who wrote the lipstick because*
> *she's left messages on our machine saying, 'I know you have my coat and my*
> *stereo. . . . You better give it back.'"*
>
> So, basically I had a criminal damage and I could've easily arrested, but
> . . . she agreed and the victim agreed that once they leave that evening, she
> would clean the door and all that, and then she agreed to give the victim $30
> right there while I was there. . . . I don't think on another day I would have
> arrested in this scenario, but in a lot of criminal damage cases like that, the
> normal routine would be just to arrest the person. . . . I'd have to put a little
> more thought into the decision had the suspect been male, because physically
> he'd be more capable of hurting someone there. But, as long as, you know,
> he didn't seem insane, it didn't seem like there was no threat of violence. I
> guess I probably would put more thought into the fact that he's male.[7]

And so we insist: identity matters, in a definitional way. In this case,
cultural representations about women and femininity are conjoined with
the action the officer (and, by extension, the state) took in defining the
situation, its characters, and action plot. The officer's common sense about
what course of action he should take was closely related to matters of identity. Police, by virtue of their profession, find themselves in a relatively
unique, although certainly not unified position, compared to other American citizens. As agents of the state with coercive powers, police are authoritative directors and choreographers who mark and divide citizens. But these
officers are also state subjects, themselves marked and divided by others.
Officers, too, are located in other subject positions that may bind them to
and divide them from other officers and citizens in an infinite array of inter-
connections. We suggest that this contradictory location of being both
agent and subject of the state shapes how individual officers enforce *order* as
well as law. Below, we examine these thick processes of identity bonds and
divisions as they emerge from the stories the officers tell about their work.

We spent six months in the field with the officers of two squads of a
police department in a metropolis of the western United States, riding in
patrol cars, attending briefings, interviewing. and generally hanging out.[8]

---

7. Italics indicate passages that were replicated verbatim from the transformed stories
told to us by officers. Indented passages that are not italicized are excerpted from the more
traditional interviews. See our appendix for a description of the process the stories underwent.

8. We found evidence that police officers may be well disciplined by social scientists.
The law enforcement agency we concentrated on, like many others, has given considerable
access to researchers. Nearly all the officers in the two squads had the view that ride-alongs
and interviews must be the key to advancing our knowledge about their work. They expected

After getting to know them and letting them get to know us, we selected a subset of 10 officers from the squads not only for their willingness to talk to us and for their verbal animation, but also partially with the goal of diversifying storytellers across several identity categories, such as race, sex, rank, age, and sexual preference. Still, the majority were predictably white, male, street-level officers whom we presumed to be heterosexual.[9] (See table 1 for breakdowns according to these factors.) As we talked with the officers, other social categories began to emerge as important sources of identity: religion, marital status, parenthood, and even (usually the lack of) membership in the department's special assignment teams.

Characteristics of Police Officers/Storytellers

Race	
Hispanic	1
African American	1
White	7
Other	1
Sex	
Female	3
Male	7
Rank	
Officer	7
Sergeant	2
Lieutenant	1
Age	Mid-20s to early 50s
Sexual preference	
Presumed to be heterosexual	7
Presumed to be homosexual or bisexual	2
Not sure	1

We asked these officers to tell us work-related stories about their interactions with people on the street and in the hallways of their department.[10] Transcripts of these storytelling sessions, worked into written

---

us to do a lot of riding, and we did. But we told them that our central interest was in stories, particularly the stories they tell one another. We are quite confident that they did eventually tell us such stories, in part, because we came to hear the same plots repeated and, in some cases, the same events retold by a number of officers. But, all along, the officers thought that the stories had to be secondary to the data we collected through observation and interviews. For a discussion of the historical tendency of researchers to treat stories as insignificant and the implications of this, see Shearing and Ericson 1991, 487–91.

9. Those who mentioned having opposite-sex spouses or children and one man who talked about gays in the department using us-them terminology were presumed to be heterosexual. Those categorized as homo- or bisexual were explicit about such self-identification. One woman's actions and affiliations at the department suggest that she may be a lesbian, but she never told us so, and so her identity remains ambiguous on this dimension.

10. *Narratives* or *stories*, used interchangeably here, are part of people's routine communications (see White 1987). Moreover, they both constitute and carry information about culture, as known by the storyteller. Ewick and Silbey write, "stories people tell about

narratives, were returned to officers, who added or subtracted information as they wished. Identities of characters were probed where necessary. (See appendix for a more complete description of the research process.) The result was 20 stories about work matters within the department, on the street, and at the intersections between the street and the politics of the department. The remainder of the paper looks at these stories through the framework of identity.[11] Does identity appear as a salient dimension in the stories and, if so, how does the performance of identities bind people together and how does it divide? How does identity operate in the daily work of police officers? How do they negotiate their own and others' identities in the stories they have chosen to tell? What are the implications of these processes for making citizens? To address these questions, we examined stories first for descriptions of police enacting their occupational identities in various ways, binding them to the community of police officers and other uniformed state agents. Similarly, we examine affirmations of other identities that mediate occupational identification as moments of division between officers. Some stories included descriptions of events or themes that reflected a simultaneous binding and dividing of officers.

COP IDENTITY

Certainly, our stories reflected a great deal of solidarity among officers, and officers made decisions to protect that unity.

> It looked like a plain suicide, which is really all that it was. Tragic suicide, but really nothing more complicated than that. They had to go through his property and other things, his dresser and things of that effect to look for any suicide notes or anything that may have foretold what was to happen. As he was doing this, in a pair of the fireman's socks, he found a small vial of cocaine and instead of turning it over to the wife or letting the family know about it or anything to that effect, he just got a hold of the prosecutor and they decided just to get rid of it and be done with it and throw it away, which is exactly what happened. And here was a case where you really could have turned that thing into a big mess.

---

themselves and their lives both constitute and interpret those lives; the stories describe the world as it is lived and understood by the storyteller" (Ewick and Silbey 1995, 198). It is in this sense that we use the term story. The assumption that we make is that stories contain elements of Ewick and Silbey' s "hegemonic tales," that they represent particular information about doing culture. In this sense, then, "the work is itself already a copy" (Machery, cited in Young 1985). A story, then, is a particularized representation of both the social and the particular.

    11. Our intention is not to be reductionist. While our focus is on describing how identity shapes action, certainly we recognize that the actions in the stories are not purely identity driven. For example, Steve Herbert (1998; 1997) shows how territory and space define the action norms that police invoke when working the streets. Situational factors of all kinds have a hand in the outcomes.

The family was never informed of the drug find, and because of the "fraternity" of uniformed emergency workers, the deceased fireman's identity as one of the "good guys" was never challenged. The story of the fireman's suicide and the vial of cocaine marks the territory of police exceptionalism in which officers withhold their coercive powers to serve their invocations of the cause of "justice." In this instance, the officer demonstrates police compassion by referencing concern for "wife" and "family" coping with "tragic" suicide. In making an exception, the officer mutes the routine of police intrusiveness into the lives of friends and lovers of criminal suspects, thus softening the state's coercive capacities, while reinforcing dominant notions of family and constructions of tragedies.

Police routinely engage in this process of identifying who deserves a softening of the state's coercive powers, dividing some from others. Several "suspicious behaviors" were listed as criteria for making these routine distinctions between kinds of people. Language was revealed more than once, with one officer specifically saying that particular phrases, such as "Wut up?" and others that might stereotypically be associated with *the* voice of African Americans, were criteria of suspiciousness to him. Another officer we'll call Craig talked about objects, particularly cars:

> Craig said that everyone is prejudiced, especially police officers. They are not necessarily prejudiced on the basis of skin color or religion, etc., but they are prejudiced against the 'criminal element.' At the time he was telling me this, an older car—maybe an '88 Pontiac Grand Am— drove past. It lacked hub caps and had some parts of a different color, indicating a visit to the junk yard to repair damage. 'There's a criminal's car,' Craig said. Picking out criminals is like a prejudice, he told me, but it's not exactly that. Criminals are not likely to drive around in a Lexus. If they are, those are the hard ones to catch. (Field notes following the ride-along)

Thus, internal to the stories and conversations, the condition of one's car or a simple turn of phrase (assuming language is what the invocation of those phrases was actually about) is enmeshed with the evaluations of people and the actions taken by police. Through this power of determination, police create a gulf between themselves and other citizens.

Despite the potential for isolation from the rest of (the nonpolicing) society, some officers were extremely committed to their professional identities, acting in ways that clearly elevated police status over other identifications. In one story, an officer had to break a love bond in order to preserve his identity as an officer. The officer and dog were the canine unit on call for the department when an armed individual took refuge in a stranger's home, resulting in a volatile situation with potential hostages.

> *Lt. Grangier asked our team leader, Gould, what he wanted to do next, and he said that he wanted to send our canine in to check the door entry to see if the suspect was still alive. . . . At that point I had a real kind of sick feeling in my stomach because I knew if the suspect was alive that he was going to kill my dog. I thought about it, and my first thought was I'm not going to send him into a situation like this. . . . I decided to go ahead and send him in because this was a crisis situation. You could be fired at the scene if you refuse a direct order according to the general orders of operations that were written at that time. So, I sent my canine in, and it was kind of a strange one because I had already done over 300 searches with him, building searches with him, and every time I sent him in, I followed right in after him. . . . The dog went in about 30 seconds; then I heard a gunshot and a yelp, and I recalled the dog two or three times, and he came back to me. . . . The dog died about a half hour or so later at the vet's. The bullet just bounced around and hit a lot of the main organs and there was nothing they could do. . . . I don't know. Sometimes I wonder about the decision and if it was the right one or not. . . . I did not know how much of an impact it would have until it was my dog, how important this dog was to me, how close we really were, how much of a friendship I had with the dog.*

The performance of his police identity bound this officer to his fellow officers in such a way that his allegiance to them was maintained throughout the crisis, despite the huge cost. The story illustrates the salience of occupational identity and the partial coercion involved in evoking that salience. At the same time, however, the story reveals that this coercion is internalized as normal. Indeed, the officer acknowledges his own agency in the events and takes responsibility for the decision to send in his dog. Thus, the state is not made to appear as a seamless web of domination, but rather as a legitimate authority to be voluntarily obliged.[12]

Another officer committed herself even more deeply to her identity as a police officer when she shot and killed an assailant. The words she recalls telling herself at the time are revealing about how her actions connect to her identity.

> *I'm being honest with you here. I was thinking, "Hey, shit. Frankly, I don't want to be here," and for a fleeting moment I just wanted to get the hell out of there. I remember thinking, "There's something wrong with this guy. I want to get the hell out of here." He's coming at us with this weird sort of gait and these black eyes, and there's something wrong with him. He's not listening to us. Let's get the hell out of here, but I knew I couldn't. So, for a fleeting moment we kind of retreat. I realized that, you know, you can't really run away. This is your job. You're going to have to handle it, but I would rather not have been there. Unfortunately that is my job, and I remember having to tell myself, "Susan, this is your job. You have to handle this."*

---

12. Theoretical support comes from Althusser 1991.

Thus, despite whatever other identities might have been salient, she defined the situation in terms of her police identity and eventually invoked the ultimate power of the state, killing the assailant and clearly committing herself to her police identity: her job, her duty, her performance of self.

Officers are bound together through their identification as officers, as is evident from the examples above. However, the police identity is far from homogenous, as other identifications combine with occupational identity, dividing officers from each other and binding them to other social affiliations. Even the way that different people took up the identity of "officer" reveals the simultaneity of binding and division. Although the following two officers react differently, both officers must explicitly manage the social isolation and coercive powers that accompany one's identification with policing. One officer told us this during a ride-along:

> When I'm off duty at home, . . . when we go out to restaurants, I never sit where they put the menu. I always have to sit in certain spots. I have to have a good view of the door, the front door. My back has to be to a corner. It's just a type of . . . it's a lifestyle. And that's what I am is a police officer, and I see people off duty that I've arrested before. A lot of times they don't recognize me without my uniform, but I carry a gun everywhere I go.

He seems unable to abandon, even temporarily, his occupational identity. Another officer, however, handles her police identity differently. In field notes after a ride-along with her, one of us wrote this:

> She indicated that while going to the university, she found herself deceiving fellow students about her being a police officer. And, even now, while pursuing a master's, she conceals her identity as a cop. She said that being a cop "tags your identity" in the minds of others. People either really like that you are a cop and want to talk about it, or they instantly distance themselves.

Both officers addressed the issue of how they handled themselves while off duty, but each took a different approach, one being consumed by his police identity and the other explicitly and intentionally putting it aside when she leaves work.

We locate "officer" as one among many mutually defining subject positions occupied by an "individual." Thus, to take on police identity or be associated with it is not the same as identifying only as a cop and only with other cops. To bind together is not to homogenize, and to "identify as" is not to become "identical to." Instead, we found differences among officers as they are associated with other identity categories and/or affirm them.

THE CITIZEN IN THE COP

Like other studies (i.e., Reuss-Ianni 1983), we found some division between street-level officers and the command staff. The timing of our fieldwork was such that we watched the creation of an association of officers that linked itself to other police and fire fighters' unions in the metropolitan area. A very involved officer told us about the union in one of his stories.

> *I guess it started somewhere around '94–'95. A gentleman was hired to do a reclassification study on the police department. . . . Well, as a result of this study, commanders got a raise, lieutenants got a raise, and sergeants got a raise. The officers were not given a raise. . . . That, in addition to other problems we were having, caused the officers to say, "Let's get to together and discuss what's going on." This time the atmosphere was a lot different. A lot of the officers didn't feel intimidated. There were a lot more things to discuss, and so we held a meeting and about 60 officers showed up . . . .*
>
> *The general feeling was that we needed to start a union. We talked to a lot of officers and we could see that the support was there. We had another meeting, and we decided that yes, we are going to form an association, and we started collecting names of officers who were interested in joining. We collected over 100 names. Pretty close to 130.*

Thus, officers divided across rank lines, in the sense that officers were forming a union that excluded, and perhaps would even be somewhat antagonistic to, command staff.

Other identifications divided officers from each other and bound some to identities that were not occupational. One female officer, for example, told us a story about gender and work.

> *This is definitely an organization where you can pursue opportunities that are available to you, but . . . when I pursued those opportunities, they haven't always been accepted with open arms. And sometimes it would seem that that's because I'm a woman. There's been openings that I haven't applied for, but that I know other female officers have applied for—for example within the narcotics division—that they simply won't allow a woman into. Actually, I think a woman could do a fine job as a decoy in a lot of those cases. There's been one person who is a peer of mine and our careers have pretty much paralleled. We did go for a couple of the same opportunities whereas maybe he was chosen and I wasn't. I'm not meaning to sound bitter, but after three or four of those kinds of incidents, you've got to kind of wonder what's going on.*

Thus, for her, femaleness divided her from other officers, making her a particular kind of officer. This particular officer indicated a very high identification with women outside the department, as well. She told us in her initial interview, "I tend to be more, gravitate more towards women. I personally like upwardly mobile women. The climbers, the shakers, the movers."

Moreover, this officer told one of us a story fragment while on a ride-along about how being a female gave her an advantage in some circumstances, helped her identify with and bind herself to the citizens of her community as a woman as much as or more than as an officer. She explained what happened at a domestic violence scene, in which the female victim was extremely upset but apparently not seriously physically injured. The goal was to get the victim into inpatient psychiatric treatment.

> *It's just kind of a matter of who you latch onto first at the scene. And John latched onto the victim . . . and I ended up with somebody else. So I never saw the victim. Well, John came out of the room and said she's not going to go to Mercyville voluntarily, you know, so now we have to try to get an emergency medical admission and what have you and I said to him, "Well, John, do you mind if I go in and talk to her?" I didn't want to step on his toes or anything like that. And I think it was simply because I was a woman. I stepped in there and she instantly related to me and within two minutes I said to her, "Do you want to go to Mercyville?" and she agreed.*

Here, the process of identification binds and divides in complex and fluid ways. The officer was bound to other officers as she arrived at the scene, demonstrated by her knowledge and willingness to address the situation in police style (i.e., each officer "latched onto" somebody at the scene and worked team style to gather information). As she decided that her identity as a woman might be more effective in connecting with the victim, she was divided from the other officers, and simultaneously was bound to another (white) woman.[13]

Race, too, was important to the fabric of identity that divided some officers from others, both on the street and in-house. The matter of race inside the department was addressed very explicitly by one African American officer. He told us a story that began with his career, 16 years ago. It is the story of getting the organization actively involved in antiracism. He began by recounting a racist incident between himself and another officer.

> *We went to a baseball game, our squad did. . . . And that same officer that I felt had been prejudiced was there . . . . So at the baseball game, it was very apparent he had been drinking a lot. He was becoming very belligerent and loud. After the game, we were walking down the walkway to the parking lot and he was behind me, and there was another officer from my squad walking side by side with me with his wife. Well, the officer walking behind*

---

13. This is not to suggest that being a cop can be completely separated from being female, or vice versa, merely that various qualities of membership are highlighted in varying intensities.

> *me, he all of the sudden puts his arm on my right shoulder and he says to me, "How much money do you have, nigger?" I was shocked, and I turned around to see who it was, and it was this other officer. I pulled my shoulder away from him, and I just kept walking to my car.*

He recognized his division from the rest of the department. *I was one of two black officers working in the Glenville Police Department.*[14] The rest of the story was a description of how this officer has tried, without much success, to lead his department to hiring a more diverse group of officers.

> *I continue to ask, "Why has it taken so long to hire minorities?" So, I'll give you an example. After I was hired, 10 years later, a third black officer was hired. In those 10 years, I continued to ask, "What is the problem? Why can't you find minorities?" The answer was, "We can't find any qualified." I myself was asked to be a recruiter. So I went to a recruitment class the department held and was told that they would send me to college fraternities and various African American associations as a recruiter for the police department. Well, I waited and waited, and pretty close to a year went by and there was nothing.*

Again from this story the theme emerges that identity divides some people from others. For this officer, racial affiliation separated him from some fellow officers, but bound him to other minority officers, even if they were not African American in particular. Interestingly, there seemed to be an antagonism rather than a connection between the minority officers, female and male, and a growing population of white lesbian officers, a point we take up below.

A mainstream view among officers seems to be that recruitment into the ranks is highly selective and determined entirely on the basis of merit. The relatively small number of African American and Hispanic police officers in the ranks is believed to be due to a process that judges all applicants blindly and objectively. Officers believe that minorities who apply tend to be less qualified than the pool of Anglo applicants. Some of these officers hold the view that the department fails to recruit qualified minorities, while others take the position that the ratio of minorities to the citizenry is roughly equivalent, indicating a difference in perspective as to whether the department should make more of an effort to find qualified minorities.

Some white male and female officers who hold the view that the process of selecting officers is based on individual merit take a different stance with regard to the way people receive special assignments (e.g., narcotics). Specifically, they believe that special assignments are distributed *subjectively*, despite similar testing and oral board procedures. According to a

---

14. Glenville is the fictitious name we've chosen for this police department.

number of them, special assignment is controlled by a "good old boy" net-work of senior, white males with rank that enables a select number of of-ficers, mostly white males who hang out with the seniors or come from the ranks of the senior officers, to circulate across assignments. One female of-ficer told us this, in a story about sexist promotional habits:

> *It does seem that as a woman I have to work a little bit harder to prove myself as far as moving up the ladder around here. . . . Again, in another incident, this person was recently promoted. What happened was that there were opportunities, and a letter of interest was put out, and if anybody wanted to apply for the position, they could do so. Several people did. But this particular officer, I feel, was kind of hand chosen before that process even got done.*

In another instance, Officer Bolt, who is young, white, and male, reveals that he, too, felt victimized by a good old boys' network. He told us during an interview that a lot of the competition for promotion is determined by the good old boys. He went to great extremes, even spending a good deal of his off-duty time making himself the most qualified candidate for a promo-tion, but the job was given to someone Officer Bolt believed to be less deserving.

> *He didn't want it as much as me and that was obvious because of the prepa-ration that he did and that he didn't do. I had a real problem with that, and that gave me a real bad outlook on the department. You know, it's not what you know; it's who you know. It goes beyond the testing policy.*

According to newer-to-the-ranks white males and white female officers hired in the past decade, then, the hiring process that includes them and excludes most minorities is fair, or based on objective standards, while the processes for determining special assignments is unfair, based on the subjec-tive judgments of an identity group marked by whiteness, generational dif-ference, and strong occupational bonds.

Male minority officers see the preferences within special assignments as reflective of a larger system of racial discrimination that includes the recruitment of citizens into the ranks. They do not affiliate with white les-bian officers because of their judgments about recruitment. Some minority officers define the situation in terms of competition, and believe special efforts have been made to recruit lesbians into the department at the ex-pense of minorities. These officers point to the relatively large investment the department makes at gay pride events, by donating time and setting up a recruitment booth that actually generates good contacts, and they compare that investment to the recruitment efforts with regard to minority officers. Several officers made the comment that despite a dire need for Spanish-speaking, bicultural officers and the very low number of black officers, "alternative" recruitment efforts were directed more toward homosexuals than toward people of color. An African American officer became active in the recruiting process hoping to rectify the problem:

> As far as the recruitment at the university career day, I felt that was a waste because they have our booth next to top law enforcement agencies, like FBI or Big City Police Department and then you have other companies not in law enforcement nearby, like the big engineering companies. And the whole time I was there maybe five minorities stopped by, just to pick up a brochure to look at. I never once got to address the African American groups and fraternities on campus. . . . I think I did it about three times, and each time I did it, I came away with the feeling that this is a waste. The recruitment is not being done right.

PARTICULARIZED INCLUSIONS AND EXCLUSIONS ON THE STREETS AND IN THE HALLWAY

Race divided officers not just within the ranks. Stories also demonstrated that race matters on the street. But the following stories also reveal the particularized classifications embedded in police decision making and how these means of identification affirm the citizenship of some while excluding others from membership. For example, in a case involving a working-class Hispanic man who confessed to being a marijuana dealer, officers disagreed on how to proceed. Two of the man's marijuana affiliates came to his house to rob and kill him. Due to a great size advantage, Francisco was able to grab his assailants' gun and fire shots at them. The Hispanic officer[15] who told us the story felt that *Francisco had been through enough. Francisco had been traumatized, upset, fearful for his life, and he was just defending himself. Period. He had every right to shoot.* He wanted no charges to be brought against Francisco, either regarding his drug violations or for his unsafe firing of a gun.

The marijuana business is dismissed as a class problem, although perhaps the male requirement to provide for one's family may have played into the connection as well.

---

15. The Hispanic officer defined himself as "working class" in conversations with us and in interview sessions with him. In fact, several officers in the two squads asserted a working-class identity, to our surprise. They chose the territory of their squads in part because it is inhabited by other "working joes." They referenced other space as alien to their self-identity—affluent neighborhoods full of professionals, doctors, lawyers and scientists—and viewed many calls from such areas as "petty."

> *He had a wife and a baby and wasn't able to make ends meet. So he started dealing small amounts of marijuana. . . . Francisco was just doing the best he could. These were terrible burdens he had on his back, for a 28-year-old guy. He also had his little sister living with him. She was still in high school. I'm not sure where the parents were, but he was raising his little sister. . . . He had a little brother living with him and his brother was in high school. . . . He had a little family situation set up there and he was trying to make ends meet. I've seen people that have worked hard during their lifetimes, like Francisco had.*

The supervisors did not share the officer's view that Francisco should go free. The officer himself points to the intersection of race, ethnicity, and class in narrating the discrepancy of opinion. *The supervisors were adamant that Francisco be arrested. I didn't care for that idea. I think [that] to them, Francisco was seen as a semi-literate Hispanic. These were white supervisors making the decision.* The connection between the officer and Francisco in this story demonstrates the division among officers across other identity dimensions and the alternative connections that the officer might make as daily decisions are being made and citizens are being identified as criminal or not criminal.

The story of Francisco is, in part, about police exceptionalism—that is, coercive powers are withheld to the benefit of a citizen occupying marginal cultural space. The officer bonded sufficiently with Francisco that he risks severe consequences for negating charges that superiors expected him to file, and he therefore, is acting contrary to his self-interest. At the same time, it is a story about the construction of a political subject who receives his just deserts because he exhibits a work ethic and family commitment that enfolds him—along with the officer as subject—into the mainstream fabric of sociocultural (hard-working immigrant) and normative orderings (just deserts). The benevolence of the police is foregrounded by the officer as agent, and yet, his identification of those who tried to rob and kill Francisco excludes other individuals and marks them as particularly requiring coercive police action. The officer describes one of the "bad guys" this way:

> *Steve . . . deserves trouble. He had been involved in other shootings. Steve had told another homicide detective before that he was untouchable because his family was judicial. [In a different incident,] he pulled up to a stop sign and ran it and saw some people from another car with a gun. They started shooting at him with high-capacity 9mms. Steve seemed to have nine lives. One went across him and hit his girlfriend in the face and eventually she wound up with paralysis and nerve damage. His brother was hit twice in the back of the head in the back seat. . . . You'd think that he'd go to the hospital. Not Steve. Steve drives down the street, parks the vehicle, and goes to a safe place and starts changing tires. He's got two bleeding people in his car and he's changing tires.*

The following excerpts from one lieutenant's story highlight the importance of identity in defining an individual as criminal or not.

> We have an officer who had a domestic violence situation. I don't want to go into what it was about, but they were having domestic problems. He and his wife were not getting along well. They were in the process of getting a divorce, and things were not going well. There was a very young child involved in it. He [the officer] was just losing it. He made a series of phone calls. Not a good idea, granted. She, of course, filed a police report in Jefferson City. He winds up being charged [and convicted] with making harassing phone calls. Well, she gets linked up with, of all people, an ex-convict, which is not like his [the officer's] thing to decide, but that's who's raising his son now. And his son is still involved, and they're still trying to write the visitation issues. And he starts yelling at her . . . and the next thing you know they're in a big argument in which our officer is probably the aggressor. There's no physical contact or anything. It's just loud. So, they wanted to file a complaint. Now he's convicted again. What do we do with this guy? Two convictions now. Two convictions on a police officer. Is this about his ability to be a police officer, or is this about his broken heart? Wait a minute, let's just put this in the proper perspective. I'm saying this is not a professional issue. It's a personal issue. How is he a police officer when he's convicted of these things? When he comes here, he's a police officer. Well, if we can say about a month after this thing is dealt with that he winds up at a call where he saves somebody's life, then we save face, too. Interesting, eh?

What is compelling about this story is that two men, both convicted of lawbreaking, are identified quite differently by this lieutenant. One is an "ex-convict" whose identity is an added source of frustration, in part, because his status as a convict throws into question his ability to raise a child. At the same time, however, the *officer's* convictions are the result of a "broken heart," a "personal" rather than "professional" problem. His indignation at having an "ex-convict" raise his son is legitimated by the lieutenant's telling of the story. In this way, the officer's identity as a cop protected him from the social stigma that accompanies being identified by the police as a criminal. He remains an agent of the state while his subject position is constituted as a troubled worker in *need* of help. The state administrative apparatus, as manifested in the story by the lieutenant, is presented as caring for one of its workers while, at the same time, the territory of coercive engagement is marked in the referencing of another individual as an ex-con.

As a last example of the simultaneous processes of binding and dividing, we turn to the group of lesbians who work in the Glenville Police Department. Because her partner required surgery and after care, a lesbian officer approached her lieutenant, who is also homosexual, and requested a family emergency leave day, which is a paid day reserved for "family" emergencies. In the following excerpt, the lieutenant reports what the officer, who we'll call Joan, said:

> *"I think the right thing for us to do is that I should be afforded the same opportunities toward emergency leave for a family situation as others in this agency are allowed to do." [Joan] reminded me by way of example. A sergeant [Al] had just recently married, maybe four or five years ago. She said, "Here we have a sergeant who's been married four or five years, and he recently took family emergency leave for something. Who knows what it is. Well, I'm here to tell you that me and my partner have been together for over nine years, so I have been involved in a domestic relationship for longer than even [Al], and he gets the paid benefits. Why shouldn't I?" I said, "You're right. You're absolutely right."*

The officer got the paid day. She defined her family situation as similar to the situation of a heterosexual officer and his family. The lieutenant accepted this definition. Thus, like the male officer in the department, she was entitled to the benefit. At its core, the officer's argument uses the logic that she, as an officer, should be entitled to the same city benefits that other officers—and one in particular—received, binding her to other officers as a whole and one male officer specifically, for the political end of getting benefits. At the same time, however, making explicit that she is homosexual simultaneously divides her from the exemplified officer, as well as other officers, producing a binary between heterosexual and homosexual officers.

CONCLUSION

Our analysis suggests that cops' identities as cops are strong, even as officers find different ways to manage their occupational identities. Several of the narratives suggest that occupational identity defines, indeed trumps, other reactions. For example, one of the officers told a story about his inability to abandon, even temporarily, his occupational identity. Even when off duty and at a restaurant with his spouse, he would always sit so as to have a good view of the front door. A female officer's story of killing an assailant is deeply interwoven with her realization about the salience of her cop identity. Other stories reveal the strength of the bonds among officers, including a strong tendency of cops to withhold their coercive powers when dealing with citizen-cops, as was revealed in the story about the police officer who was "the aggressor" in a series of family violence events.

At the same time, our analysis suggests that different cops act out their occupational identities in different ways. For example, contrast the way of the cop who always positions himself to see the front door in a restaurant with that of the cop who conceals her identity as a police officer while attending a university. Police are part of an organizational culture, but "different individuals . . . possess different amounts and types of cultural resources" (Herbert 1998, 346).

In addition to drawing on their occupational identities differently, cops are not uniform in the norms and primary values they use to render judgments about citizens and fellow officers. Steve Herbert finds that police officers employ a web of "normative orders," each representing "a set of rules and practices centered on a primary value" (1998, 4). He uncovers six normative orderings at work—law, bureaucratic control, adventure/machismo, safety, competence, and morality—and argues that conflicts arise among officers over which set of rules and practices should be used in what street contexts (Herbert 1998, 361–64). Herbert's framework, grounded in the study of space and territoriality, is illuminating, but it gives limited insight into *how* cops manage their conflicts over norms and the contexts that seem to invite police officers to use one normative order over another. Herbert writes, "Just which order, or combination of orders, will capture a particular officer's allegiance at any given time eludes prediction" (1998, 171).

Our work suggests that the invocation of norms is strongly bundled with processes of identification. How cops identify with one another and the people they encounter on the streets is wrapped up or ontologically interwoven with the action norms they invoke. At times, cops use crude notions of "badness" in combination with broad categorizations, denying the uniqueness of individuals, and enfolding them into social categories already marked for exclusion and the invocation of coercion (e.g., homeless vs. homeowner; illegal alien vs. citizen). Indeed, some report that police have become more skilled in constructing these categories through the invocation of a discourse of war, and use paramilitary strategies to enforce the boundaries they themselves have been active agents in constructing (see Fishman 1978; Ericson 1991; Welch, Fenwick, and Roberts 1998; or Zatz 1987).

At the same time, we draw attention to a more subtle process of identification at work in modern policing that enables management of conflicts. Police engage in an ongoing negotiation of their own subject positions as they interact with fellow officers in the hallways of their department and engage people in the streets. Through the dynamics of binding with the particularities of individuals, cops sometimes withhold their coercive powers, creating moments when they define themselves in relation to civilians with complex identities. Yet, at the same time, these actions divide further, revealing police as highly adept at classification and its attendant political rationality. For example, in the story of Francisco, his violent acts are exempted while he is affirmed as a worthy citizen, due, in part, to his work ethic and family orientation. At the same time, the violence of Francisco's assailants is condemned, and they are vilified as unworthy subjects with particularized attributes and pursued with the full force of police coercive capacities.

Even as they are particularistic, the classifications that arise from these subtle processes of binding and dividing reinforce rather than fracture dominating identity tropes (e.g., white middle-class lesbianism) and norms (e.g., justice of deserts). Officers reposition themselves, often moment to moment, in relation to the administrative apparatus they occupy and reveal a range of identities that counter categorical thinking about who cops are. Privileging the particulars of some citizens while at the same time revealing the particularities of their own identities may enable police to generate necessary support from the diversity of working- and middle-class communities occupying contemporary urban space.

As they complicate representations of themselves, cops also project complex notions about law and legality. We are struck by the significance of moral discourse, particularly in contrast to legal discourse, in how cops frame their justifications for action. Cops appear to make judgments about the relativity of people—their similarity or incomprehensibility—more than they tend to evaluate people's actions in relationship to legal codes and rights. Law is often invoked in the stories strategically—that is, as a tool to be used to punish the unworthy or as a hurdle to get around so that the worthy can be helped rather than punished.

Our observation that morality is more significant than law in the practical reasoning of cops could be interpreted as a reflection wholly consistent with contemporary sociolegal thought about "legality." Patricia Ewick and Susan Silbey reference *legality* as "the meanings, sources of authority, and cultural practices that are commonly recognized as legal, regardless of who employs them or for what ends" (1998, 22). Cops are a critical source of legal authority, and their action norms, even when expressed in moral terms, are commonly recognized as legal expressions that carry significant weight. Moreover, some contemporary sociolegal scholars hold that law has no normative center and, instead, is contradictory in what it projects as guiding principles. But we think it is important to pay attention to the salience of normative orderings and agree with Steve Herbert that it is possible to distinguish one from another in tracking the expressive judgments of state agents and citizens alike. Failing to do so is to privilege a normative ordering as having no discernable contours and, ultimately, to risk rendering law meaningless as an intellectual construct.[16]

16. For a different view, see Sarat 1990.

920   LAW AND SOCIAL INQUIRY

REFERENCES

Althusser, Louis. 1991. Ideology and Ideological State Apparatuses (Notes Toward an Investigation)" In *Lenin and Philosophy, and Other Essays*, trans. Ben Brewster, 121–73. London: New Left Books.

Bayley, David, and Egon Bittner. 1984. Learning the Skills of Policing. *Law and Contemporary Problems* 47:35–59.

Butler, Judith. 1990. *Gender Trouble: Feminism and the Subversion of Identity*. New York: Routledge.

———. 1992. Contingent Foundations: Feminism and the Question of Postmodernism. In *Feminists Theorize the Political*, ed. Judith Butler and Joan W. Scott, 3–21. New York: Routledge.

Conley, John, and William O'Barr. 1998. *Just Words: Law, Language, and Power*. Chicago: University of Chicago Press.

Crank, John P. 1994. Watchman and Community: Myth and Institutionalization in Policing. *Law and Society Review* 28: 325–52.

———. 1997. *Understanding Police Culture*. Cincinnati, Ohio: Anderson Publishing.

Ericson, Richard. 1991. *Representing Order: Crime, Law, and Justice in the News Media*. Toronto, Ont.: Toronto University Press.

Ewick, Patricia, and Susan Silbey. 1995. Subversive Stories and Hegemonic Tales: Toward a Sociology of Narrative. *Law and Society Review*, 29:197–227.

———. 1998. *The Common Place of Law*. Chicago: University of Chicago Press.

Fishman, Mark. 1978. Crime Waves as Ideology. *Social Problems* 25:531–43.

Foucault, Michel. 1988. The Political Technology of Individuals. In *Technologies of the Self*, ed. Luther H. Martin, Huck Gutman, and Patrick H. Hutton, 145–62. Amherst: University of Massachusetts Press.

Gamson, William. 1992. *Talking Politics*. New York: Cambridge University Press.

Garfinkel, Harold. 1967. *Studies in Ethnomethodology*. Englewood Cliffs, N.J.: Prentice Hall.

Hall, Stuart. 1996. Introduction: Who Needs Identity? In *Questions of Cultural Identity*, ed. Stuart Hall and Paul du Gay, 1–17. London: Sage Press.

Halley, Janet M. 1993. The Construction of Heterosexuality. In *Fear of a Queer Planet*, ed. Michael Warner, 82–104. Minneapolis: University of Minnesota Press.

Herbert, Steve. 1997. *Policing Space: Territoriality and the Los Angeles Police Department*. Minneapolis: University of Minnesota Press.

———. 1998. Police Subculture Reconsidered. *Criminology* 36:343–69.

Lovibond, Sabrina. 1993. Feminism and Postmodernism. In *Postmodernism: A Reader*, ed. Thomas Docherty, 390–414. New York: Columbia University Press.

Manning, Peter. 1977. *Police Work*. Cambridge, Mass.: MIT Press.

———. 1989. Occupational Culture. In *Encyclopedia of Police Science*, ed. William Bailey. New York: Garland.

Meyer, John C. 1995. Tell Me a Story: Eliciting Organizational Values from Narratives. *Communication Quarterly* 43:210–24.

Mouffe, Chantal. 1995. Democratic Politics and the Question of Identity. In *The Identity in Question*, ed. John Rajchman, 33–46. New York: Routledge.

Reuss-Ianni, Elizabeth. 1983. *Two Cultures of Policing: Street Cops and Management Cops*. New Brunswick, N.J.: Transaction Books.

Riessman, Catherine Kohler. 1993. *Narrative Analysis*. Newbury Park, N.J.: Sage Publications.

Rosenau, Pauline Marie. 1992. *Post-Modernism and the Social Sciences: Insights, Inroads, and Intrusions*. Princeton, N.J.: Princeton University Press.

Salecl, Renata. 1994. The Crisis of Identity and the Struggle for New Hegemony in the Former Yugoslavia. In *The Making of Political Identity*, ed. Ernesto Laclau, 205–32. London: Verso.

Sarat, Austin. 1990. 'The Law is All Over:' Power, Resistence, and the Legal Consciousness of the Welfare Poor. *Yale Journal of Law and Humanities* 2:343–79.

Schram, Sanford, and Phillip Neisser. 1977. Introduction to Tales of the State. In *Tales of the State: Narrative in Contemporary U.S. Politics and Public Policy*, ed. Sanford Schram and Phillip Neisser. Oxford, England: Rowman and Littlefield.

Sewell, William. 1992. A Theory of Structure: Duality, Agency and Transformation. *American Journal of Sociology* 98:1–23.

Shearing, Clifford, and Richard Ericson. 1991. Culture as Figurative Action. *British Journal of Sociology* 42:482–506.

Swidler, Ann. 1968. Culture in Action: Symbols and Strategies. *American Sociological Review* 51:273–86.

Van Maanen, John. 1978. The Asshole. In *Policing: A View from the Streets*, ed. John Van Maanen and Peter Manning. Santa Monica, Calif.: Goodyear Publishing.

Welch, Michael, Melissa Fenwick, and Meredith Roberts. 1998. State Managers, Intellectuals, and the Media: A Context Analysis of Ideology in Experts' Quotes in Feature Newspaper Articles on Crime. *Justice Quarterly* 15: 219–42.

West, Cornel. 1995. A Matter of Life and Death. In *The Identity in Question*, ed. John Rajchman, 33–46. New York: Routledge.

White, Hayden. 1987. *The Content of the Form*. Baltimore, Md.: Johns Hopkins University Press.

Young, Robert, ed. 1985. *Untying the Text: A Post-Structuralist Reader*. Boston: Routledge and Kegan Paul.

Zatz, Marjorie. 1987. Chicano Youth Gangs and Crime: The Creation of a Moral Panic. *Contemporary Crises* 2:129–58.

APPENDIX: A WORD ON NARRATIVE METHOD

Officers from three squads were asked by their superiors to participate in the project. Participating officers took one or both of us on at least one ride-along and were interviewed at that time about their histories and work as police officers as well as about how they define themselves. From these interviews as well as our field notes and experiences, 11 storytellers were chosen. One of these retired, but the remaining 10 agreed to participate. They were asked to tell us stories about fairness and unfairness and how they used their discretion. Stories could pertain to events occurring either inside the department or on the street.

Narrative methods take everyday experience as data. Storytelling is an almost reflexive means to relate personal experiences. Catherine Kohler Riessman explains: "A teller in a conversation takes a listener into a past time or 'world' and recapitulates what happened." (1993, 2), giving subjective order to events and experiences. Authorship of the experiences to be included or excluded in a story belongs to the storyteller. Through stories, participants can relate their everyday, subjective experiences. Riessman goes on to suggest that because the "approach gives prominence to human agency and imagination, it is well suited to studies of subjectivity and agency" (1993, 5). Moreover, "narratives bridge the gap between daily social interaction and large-scale social structures" (Ewick and Silbey 1995, 198). They navigate between the particular, routine lives of the characters in the story and the broader, sociohistorical context that infuses the specifics of a story with social meaning. Specific everyday events are thus situated into the broader social background from which they emerge.

Officers themselves decided which of their many work stories to share with us and how such stories should be relayed, deliberately highlighting the events and characters in particular ways. Thus, when officers shared their stories—from the first telling—they constructed them in meaningful ways, laden with the narrator's assumptions about and viewpoints on the events. For example, one officer whose agenda involved getting the department to hire more minorities took advantage of finding a place to speak. He told stories about what he defined as unfair hiring procedures and expressed a gratitude that someone was willing to listen. He used his stories to construct one aspect of the department in order to make his perspective heard. Another officer recognized the political implications of her story when she expressed her concern that a story might paint the department as sexist, which she said she did not want to do, despite her story's explicitly sexist plot.

Finally, a fairly common concern from our storytellers was that their stories would be boring. Several officers (and especially two young white male officers) were very concerned that their stories would not be exciting enough to compare with the image of policing. One rescheduled with Trish at least three times, telling her that he wanted to go back through his computer notes to find sufficiently exciting stories. Even as Trish rode along with this officer, he expressed a concern that the ride-along would be too boring. He said that ordinarily, he would be doing some routine visits to local apartment complexes, making a pitch for the managers to cooperate with the police in a community policing project designed to reduce crime. Thus, the stories, even as they were being recorded for the first time, were careful constructions by officers, with the intention of creating some particular picture (i.e., of racist hiring practices, sexist promotions in an otherwise unsexist organization, or the exciting work of police officers).

Officers told us these stories in tape-recorded sessions, most of which took place in interview rooms at the station or substations. However, one officer held nearly every session in his squad car. Transcripts were created and manipulated from their original (largely one-sided) dialogue into a straight narrative. Basically, this consisted of eliminating some of the repetition that is part of oral communication but that does not read well as written narrative. The other main manipulation was to integrate responses to probes asked at the end of the session at some logical point in the narrative. Such manipulations by the research team do change the story. Simply moving from an oral to a written tradition changes the story. We do not believe that the researchers should have full authorial license to manipulate the stories, yet it seemed imperative to bring the data into a grammatical form that could then be shared on paper. What the officers first constructed as an oral representation, the researchers reconstructed as a written text and then, later, represented through the analytical framework of a binding and dividing identity politics.

Our reconstruction was subject to the storyteller's final approval. Once the story was coherent as a narrative, we returned it to the storyteller for corrections and clarifications. All changes from this session were applied to the story, and the result of this process is what we counted as story data.

Transformations to the story were carefully considered.[17] Particularly because of the way the stories were solicited, with officers having several days to plan out and even write down a story to tell us (among other reasons), we view the stories as constructed representations. We took the verbiage of the transcript and transformed it into (our version of) a written story. This allowed the additional information gained during follow

---

17. By contrast, see John C. Meyer's article, "Tell Me a Story" (1995), in which he analyzed interviews. One drawback to using the interviews and determining which pieces within them are to be called stories is that the power to determine lies with the researcher. The two-step process—transforming the interviews into stories and then asking participants to review them—serves as a check on the researchers' creation of data. Although initially it seems counterintuitive, we believe that transforming the stories into a written tradition and giving greater control over what counts as a story to the participants gives them more control over the data than the seemingly less obtrusive method of analyzing interviews for the story fragments that the researchers identify.

up probes to be inserted at its logical point in the story. It also allowed officers to be comfortable as they read their own texts, making changes here and there. Thus, officers retained control over their texts. After the interview transcripts were made into narratives, officers reviewed them with the understanding that they were to change anything that was inaccurate or inappropriate. Any changes they made were incorporated into their texts.

Aside from the stories, much of our analysis relied on field notes from the time we spent interacting with officers and their daily routines. These field notes served as backdrops to our understandings and interpretations of the stories. Without the extended period of observation and repeated review of the field notes, we would lack a nuanced understanding of the events of the stories. The most obvious example of the interwoven analysis of the stories and the notes would be that had we not done the observations, we might very well have articulated a professional identity centered on the daily excitement of police work. Instead, we found that daily work time is spent filling out paperwork, waiting for something to happen, or assisting with car breakdowns and other "unexciting" but certainly important aspects of police work. Thus, to thicken our readings of the officer's stories, we drew heavily on each other's field notes, which captured important insights into the kinds of constructions we perceived police to be advocating.

[11]

Morality in Law Enforcement: Chasing "Bad Guys" with the Los Angeles Police Department

Steve Herbert

Police officers regularly construct their work in terms of a morality that is so pronounced that it must arise from unique aspects of their role in society. I draw on fieldwork conducted in a patrol division of the Los Angeles Police Department to develop an explanation for the prevalence of police morality. Three components of the police function create potent dilemmas that their morality helps ameliorate: the contradiction between the police's ostensible aim to prevent crime and their inability to do so; the imperative that they run roughshod over the ambiguity inherent in most situations they handle; and the fact that they invariably act against at least one citizen's interest, often with recourse to a coercive force that can maim or kill. Reliance on moralistic understandings for the police's mission provides a salve for these difficulties; however, it can also work to harm police-community relations. Paradoxically, the police's reliance on morality can encourage or condone overly aggressive actions that are, in fact, contradictory to the virtuous self-definition officers often construct.

Legality and morality are intimately connected. Most legal rules contain implicit or explicit normative messages; they point to proper behavior that ostensibly best serves social needs. It is not surprising, therefore, that the enforcement of law is often understood by police officers as a moral as well as a legalistic enterprise. As Silver (1967) pointed out, the growth of modern policing developed in tandem with a more pervasive sense of moral order created and protected by the state. Or, as Corrigan and Sayer (1985:4) have argued more generally: "Moral regulation is coextensive with state formation, and state forms are always animated and legitimated by a particular moral ethos."

The role of the state in creating a moral order, in part through creating a legal order, is a long-standing focus of major social theoretic work, including that of Durkheim (1986), Weber (1954), and Foucault (1990; see also Donzelot 1979; Polsky 1991). These works share an interest in the ways in which power

My thanks to Katherine Beckett and two anonymous reviewers for helpful comments on earlier versions of this essay. Address correspondence to Steve Herbert, Department of Criminal Justice, Indiana University, Sycamore Hall 302, Bloomington, IN 47405-2601; e-mail Herbert@indiana.edu.

marries with morality to imprint itself indelibly on the citizenry. The state's legal order is understood as part of an attempt to create a more peaceable populace that abides by a presumably morally justified set of rules and regulations. Without this sense of moral justification, state power would seem nakedly coercive and thus illegitimate; public assent would wither.

One of the moralistic ways that nation-states acquire public loyalty is through the construction of enemies. In the process of defining inferior others, nation-states simultaneously construct themselves as unique repositories of virtue, and thus compel compliance to their morally laudable aims (see Campbell 1992; Dalby 1990). Boundaries are constructed between pure and polluted (Douglas 1966, 1973), between good and evil, and the favored nation shines in the comparison. Internally, the state's moral aims work toward the construction of the model, normal citizen, who is well schooled, well behaved, and willing to sacrifice for the nation's welfare. This normality is, again, constructed in tandem with a contrasting pathology (Durkheim 1938), and those perceived as incorrigible are sanctioned and/or banished.

State rule thus requires and daily enacts morality, often through the construction and enforcement of its legal structure. It trains attention on those both within and without the state's boundaries, regularly trumpeting virtue by denigrating evil. This is certainly true of police officers, who serve as the state's principal internal cartographers in marking the boundaries between normal and pathological. Officers are preeminently focused on those who violate moral-cum-legal codes, and define their actions as part of an attempt to protect the good through expunging the evil.

A sense of moral fervor clearly attends much police behavior (Reiss & Bordua 1967; Skolnick & Fyfe 1993; Van Maanen 1978; Westley 1970); officers regularly draw on an abiding reservoir of virtue to sustain and justify their actions as part of a vital mission (Reiner 1992). Indeed, this sense of morality seems unusually pronounced in police subculture. This raises two provocative questions: What accounts for the regular and emphatic invocation of moralistic dictums to guide and justify police actions? And what influence does their morality have on police officers' practices?

Previous work on the police, as mentioned, has drawn attention to the extent of police moralism, particularly to the extent that it contributes to the development of an "us versus them" mentality (Niederhoffer 1967; Skolnick 1966; Westley 1970); only police officers, from this perspective, understand their particular mission, and hence they are isolated from the rest of the misguided populace. Van Maanen (1978) also points to one of the key advantages for the police of drawing sharp moral characterizations—it provides ample justification for whatever actions they choose to take, a point I develop further later in this article. However, none of the works that discuss police morality fully develop an explanation for its pronounced presence in officers' daily lives or fully discuss its implications for daily practice.

I draw below on field observations of officers in the Los Angeles Police Department (LAPD) to illustrate the centrality of morality to everyday understandings and justifications of police actions.[1] I follow with a three-pronged explanation of the prevalence of this fervent morality. More specifically, I focus on (1) the contradiction between stated police aims and the near impossibility of achieving those aims; (2) the inherent ambiguity in many situations that officers encounter, which must be ignored if the officers wish to effect speedy resolution; and (3) the inescapable demand that officers act against at least one person's interest in most situations, often with recourse to coercive and, ultimately, lethal force. All these fundamental constituents of the police's daily practice produce tensions, frustrations, and dilemmas that an overarching, trans-situational morality helps to ameliorate.

The final sections of the article consider the consequences of the prevalence of police morality, especially in terms of tensions between officers and minority communities, and also review the paradoxes that are central to that morality. Central here is the fundamental importance of coercive force to the police's function in society (Bittner 1970). On the one hand, the moral code regularly invoked by officers tends to sanitize or divert attention away from the tools of force they often wield. On the other hand, coercive force in a society that values peace is always difficult to justify unambiguously, and thus makes the police's omnipresent moralism ever uneasy.

I. Morality in Policing

> *It is early in the morning, and the attending officers seem a bit listless as the sergeant begins roll-call training. His topic for the day is traffic stops of passenger vans. He reminds the officers that traffic stops should never be considered routine in Los Ange-*

---

[1] The fieldwork, in a single patrol division from August 1993 to March 1994, consisted primarily of 35 ride-alongs of an average length of six hours with sergeants, who served as supervisors of patrol officers in the field, and 20 ride-alongs of a average length of four hours with Senior Lead Officers, who are responsible for police-community relations and for monitoring locations of ongoing criminal activity. The ride-alongs stretched across different shifts, although they were primarily concentrated in the evening hours. In addition, I spent four evenings observing dispatch operations in the Communications Division, did single ride-alongs with specialized units focused on narcotics, vice, and street gangs, and rode in Air Support helicopters twice. I carried a small notebook while on the ride-alongs, which I used to jot down brief notations of events and conversations. These were later developed into fieldnotes which served as the data base for the analysis, and the sources of the vignettes described here (Herbert 1996). The vignettes are set off in italic type.

*les, because one could quite likely "have something more" than
just a moving violation. He places great emphasis on how to
approach a van safely, given its large number of doors and windows. Any of these portals, he cautions, could be conduits for an
attack. Thus, officers should approach cautiously and vigi-
lantly. Throughout his monologue, he makes repeated references
to the "evil" that stalks the streets of Los Angeles, to the various
people "who do not have a life" and therefore might just attack a
police officer wantonly. In fact, some people might be heartless
enough to indoctrinate young children into attacking the police;
presumably this means that officers should not relax even if a
van is full of kids.*

The sergeant's goal is to underline tactics to ensure officer
safety, but he punctuates his remarks with repeated moralistic in-
vectives against those the officers encounter daily on the streets.
The sergeant simultaneously seeks to caution the officers and
also to explain just why they need to be careful: there is evil out
there, ready to overpower the unsuspecting. Indeed, evil can
come disguised as a seemingly wholesome family enjoying a drive
in their passenger van.

The discourse of evil is remarkably common in police discourse. The term "bad guy" is ubiquitous in police parlance, occasionally supplemented by such terms as "punk," "idiot,"
"knucklehead," or "terrorist." Another term commonly used,
"predator," is quite evocative in displaying a sense of evil devour-
ing good; like carnivores attacking prey, these dastardly fiends
probe for vulnerable spots among the populace and attack for no
logical reason. Observations of police in "Union City" provided
Van Maanen (1978) insight into the ubiquitous usage of a similar
term, "asshole," a category police reserved for any who refused to
accede to officer prescriptions. This category, he argues, not only
helps to justify a variety of police actions but also to increase an
internal sense of police validity.

Recourse to "evil" as an explanation for the seeming chaos
that Los Angeles officers encounter on the streets is long-standing. Note the following comments, one from William Parker,
chief from 1949 to 1966, the other from one of his successors,
Daryl Gates, who served from 1979 to 1992:

> There are wicked men with evil hearts who sustain themselves
> by preying upon society. There are men who lack control over
> their strong passions, and thus we have vicious assaults, many
> times amounting to the destruction of the life of a fellow man.
>
>   To control and repress these evil forces, police forces have
> existed, in some form or another, throughout recorded history.
> (Wilson 1957:5)

> Society flinches from the truth; we do our very best to find psy-
> chological and sociological reasons to excuse behavior that our

minds won't accept for what it is. You walk into court and you have all these attorneys explaining away all of the things that you can sum up in one simple word: Evil. (Gates 1992:165)[2]

As Douglas (1966) suggests, the construction of morality often rests on such stark distinctions between pure and impure. In this case, the distinction is between good and evil, between those who share a concern for their fellow citizens and those who are fundamentally, irrationally, and irrevocably opposed to common standards of behavior and decency. And it is the police's unique and valorous duty to intercede between these two groups, to protect the one by detecting and banishing the other. It is perhaps easier, from this perspective, to understand officers' regular complaints about a lax judicial system that, in their view, enables evil to seep quickly back out of jail and to repollute otherwise peaceable neighborhoods. The power to banish some to jail allows officers to draw a boundary between pure and polluted and to nourish their morality with a sense of a clear victory over evil. If, however, suspects reappear quickly back onto the streets, the boundary erodes and with it the officers' sense of virtue.

Officers are particularly concerned about those they consider most vulnerable to "predators"—children and the elderly. An officer explains his concern about dice games in a fast-food outlet's parking lot; he wouldn't, he says, want his children to see that. Another officer makes the same complaint about alleged drug sales occurring across the street from an elementary school, and indicates that she will exert pressure on the dealers to convince them to relocate. A third officer keeps a similarly watchful eye on a group of young men who regularly gather in front of the home of an elderly woman. The woman has called the patrol station and complained that she is so afraid of the group that she will not leave her house. Enraged and protective, the officer informs the young men that unless they gather elsewhere, "Somehow, some way, you are going to jail."

Officers, in other words, act not just to enforce legal codes but to buttress wider notions of moral correctness (Banton 1964; Bittner 1967). Thus, the legal action of, say, arresting a spousal abuser is justified not just as a legal proscription but as a morally laudable act.

The sergeant is one of three officers who arrive simultaneously at a call about an alleged domestic incident. Their knock on the door is answered by the man of the house, who invites them into the living room. There they discover his wife with a fresh bruise above her eye. They also notice that the phone has been pulled from the wall. Their initial questions elicit little re-

---

[2] The extent of this moralizing from the leadership suggests that perhaps the LAPD is unique in the extent to which it constructs the world in stark terms. However, as mentioned, police morality has been noted by numerous researchers as a pronounced aspect of the social world of a variety of police departments.

sponse, so they take the woman into a back bedroom, where she admits that she called the police and that her husband is the author of her injury. The officers inform her that California law requires that her husband be arrested. The woman protests. The sergeant explains that the law provides them no leeway. Further, he says that what her husband has done "simply isn't right" and that his time in jail will enable her "to sleep in peace."

In this situation, the officers define their legally required act in larger moralistic terms and justify their actions as a prophylactic against unwanted violence that allows a woman to get some restful sleep. The police's sense of moral virtue in protecting good from harm rests most fundamentally in their acceptance of the unfortunate necessity that they may have to pay the "ultimate sacrifice" in enacting their responsibilities.

A sergeant is responsible for overseeing a "scenario" at a training event. In the scenario, a pair of officers is called to a home. When they arrive, they find a pair of officers, a man and a woman, play-acting a domestic dispute. The dispute quickly escalates when the man pulls a gun and points it at the woman. The officers are thus confronted with an important and sudden decision: whether to shoot the man. The decision is not simple, because the officers may fear the outcome should they not fire accurately. They could inadvertently wound the woman, or if they miss altogether, they could compel the man to shoot them instead. After witnessing several teams handle this scenario, the sergeant discusses the patterns he observed. Most striking to him was the generational difference between older officers, who usually chose to shoot, and younger ones, who typically demurred. He credits the fallout from the Rodney King beating as the key factor; younger officers, he reasons, are socialized into a different ethic that intensifies concern about inappropriate uses of force. For his part, the officer says simply, "I'm the police." It is his final comment.

The sergeant condenses a powerful sentiment in three simple words. He states, quite flatly, that it is his solemn duty not to fear potential damage to his personal safety or career advancement when a need for potentially lethal force is evident. For him, it is part of his sworn mandate to so endanger himself if the welfare of a tormented citizen is at stake. It is a central component of his virtue as a police officer that he will sustain such risks to protect good from evil.

But note that police morality is not monolithic. It is not necessarily embraced avidly by all officers, and may also be differentially employed across the varied populations of the city. Police officers do characterize various communities and social classes, and their moral characteristics, in markedly different terms (Alpert & Dunham 1988; Banton 1964; Bayley & Mendelsohn 1968; Bittner 1967; Brooks 1989; Manning 1993; Sacks 1972; Werthman & Piliavin 1967). Also, the high-minded moralism of an overtly self-sacrificing officer runs counter to another motivation commonly found in police organizations—the desire to lie low and avoid trouble. The "CYA [Cover Your Ass] syndrome" afflicts officers who live primarily in fear of administrative censure and thus avoid all situations that involve risks that might later be second guessed (Brown 1981; Kappeler, Sluder, & Alpert 1994; Reuss-Ianni 1983). This syndrome is also regularly displayed around the LAPD, as in other police organizations. If not monolithic, however, police morality is still robust in both its construction and consequences, and thus merits closer attention.

II. Explaining Police Morality

Police officers, then, regularly nest discussions and justifications of their actions within a discourse of morality that portrays them as proud and noble warriors protecting the peace from the chaotic and turbulent anarchy of evil. Why, however, is such an ardent moralism so prominent in police subculture? The answer, in short, is that the stated aims of police departments are generally unattainable and that police work is inescapably ambiguous and ultimately coercive. These factors lead to tensions and dilemmas that officers can minimize through recourse to an overarching morality that provides a secure and even glorious rationale for their ever disputable and ultimately ineffective actions. Morality, in other words, works as a functional adaptation to the inevitable uncertainties and failures that police officers daily must face.

A. The Problematic Rationale for Modern Policing

Advocates of modern, professionalized policing pitched their enterprise as one focused on crime prevention. The tools of this technologically sophisticated force—the radios, the patrol cars, the helicopters, the well-equipped crime labs—would combine to enable officers to easily capture and convict offenders. Such demonstrated success would convince would-be criminals to desist lest they ensure their own imprisonment (Walker 1977).

The effectiveness of modern police forces was clearly overdrawn; little evidence exists to substantiate its crime-fighting claims (Bayley 1994; Kelling 1983; Manning 1977).[3] Put simply, variations in policing have little impact on crime rates. Departments advertising themselves as primarily focused on reducing

---

[3] Sherman (1992) has attempted to make the case that police intervention can work to reduce crime. However, he is hard put to find examples of clear police successes or to find examples of strategies that would work in numerous locations.

806   **Morality in Law Enforcement**

levels of criminal activity thus place themselves in a tenuous political position, because they cannot ultimately deliver the goods (Manning 1977).

The irony is not lost on some police officers, who from their daily practice become aware that their crime-fighting efforts are mostly ineffectual. Many wish to place regular surveillance on "problem areas" to "put the heat" on those who are engaged in, say, open drug sales. But such strict surveillance cannot be maintained forever, and thus the sales are difficult to snuff out fully. Further, many recognize that success in one area may only mean that the perpetrators will move to another area and become the problem of some other officer. And police officers can, of course, do little to address problems of poverty, poor education, and community disenfranchisement.

Police officers are thus put in a difficult position: They are given a task they cannot accomplish. Widely publicized as engaged in an important effort to rid society of the plague of crime and equipped handsomely to succeed in that mission, they are ultimately ineffectual, due to factors completely beyond their control. This startling contradiction between public image and actual practice can, however, be skirted with regular recourse to the discourse of an ardent morality. When "victories" do occur, when "predators" are in fact captured, officers perhaps overstate their significance with well-worn moralistic messages to help stave off a sense of incompetence that would accompany any more rational evaluation of their overall effectiveness. Caught between their image as crime fighters and the structural impediments to success, officers attempt to resurrect the nobility of their efforts by exaggerating the significance of their occasional triumphs. Their moralistic proclamations of good trumping evil provide a comforting refuge from the overall impotence of their crime-reduction capacities and allow them to ignore the vast chasm that divides their oft-stated goals and their actual success. Of course, the inability of the police to reduce crime rates to any significant extent does not necessarily lead to the construction of sharply defined categories of good and evil. However, understanding policing as ultimately concerned with the preservation of such grand values as liberty and peace through engaging the "enemy" who would destroy those values does have the effect of minimizing any sense of impotence that might result from a more sober assessment of the police's crime-fighting work.

B. Running Roughshod over Ambiguity

Police officers are regularly asked to resolve social situations that are chaotic and confused. They find themselves in the middle of disputes between spouses and partners, landlords and tenants, proprietors and customers, and countless others, and are subjected to loud and complicated claims and counterclaims. Faced with such situations, officers must not only attempt to untangle the web the disputants discursively create, but also must act quickly, decisively, and, it is hoped, fairly. In most cases, officers have other calls pending and cannot afford to burrow deep to the wellsprings of the dispute, even if they were inclined or skilled enough to do so. If complainants' stories differ, as they often do, then officers must make instant decisions about whose character is more worthy of respect, and thus which version to treat most seriously. As Bittner (1990:11) succinctly puts it: "The mission of the police is limited to imposing provisional solutions to uncontexted emergencies."

> *The sergeant accepts a call that is billed as a domestic dispute. Normally, he would not take such a call because he rides alone; domestic disputes are understood by officers to be often volatile and thus more than a single officer can handle. However, his reading of the information given him by the dispatcher is that this is actually a landlord-tenant dispute. This turns out to be not exactly accurate, although the key issue is indeed real estate.*
>
> *When he arrives, one woman emerges from the house in question and another from a car parked across the street. An elderly man remains seated in the parked car. A shouted exchange erupts between the women, during which they promise to alter each other's physical appearance. The sergeants impels the second woman to return to her car while he gets one side of the story.*
>
> *The current dispute began when a friend of the man seated in the car attempted to enter the guest quarters behind the house in question, apparently to retrieve some of the man's belongings. It turns out that the elderly man used to own the house but deeded it over to the woman who now resides there; she, in fact, is his niece. The niece claims that her uncle had remarried a few years ago and deeded the house to her so that his new wife would not simply divorce him and take over the house. The divorce did ultimately occur, and the woman seated in the car is a new romantic interest.*
>
> *The niece presents paperwork that appears to prove her rightful ownership of the property. The sergeant briefly inspects the documents and finds them legitimate, although he notes the presence of some white-out on one line. Still, he basically upholds the niece's position.*
>
> *The couple in the car have emerged by this point, and the man is muttering constantly if incomprehensibly, betraying a seeming senility. The sergeant encourages him to spend some time to retrieve his property from the premises and counsels him to challenge the niece in a more formal legal process if he feels his claim is warranted. The sergeant remains at the house during the 15 minutes the man uses to retrieve some clothing to ensure that*

808   **Morality in Law Enforcement**

the dispute does not become inflamed, but leaves when the man completes the retrieval.

In a remarkably short time, the sergeant must attempt to calm the situation, gain an understanding of its significant dynamics, and make a decision. This dispute is entangled in a confusing family history made more complicated by the questionable documents and the elderly man's incoherence. And the stakes—ownership of a valuable piece of property—are quite high.

But the sergeant must act, and does so to the best of his ability. The niece appears to have the more legitimate stake, but the sergeant is doubtful enough to counsel the old man strongly to take the case to a higher authority. He then grants the man the right to accomplish his short-term goal of retrieving his goods, and ensures that this can occur peaceably.

> _The sergeant is called to the parking lot of a mini-mall by a patrol officer team. They are handling a complaint by a woman who maintains she was harassed on the basis of sexual orientation. Another patron in the mall was angered when he thought she cut him off in the tight maneuvering for parking spaces. In his tirade against her that followed, he referred to her as a "fat dyke bitch." The woman now is displaying a pamphlet from a local gay and lesbian resource center that discusses legal proscriptions against such harassment, and insisting that the officers arrest the man. They are reluctant to do so, and seek the sergeant's imprimatur for their decision._
>
> _The sergeant agrees with the officers, and explains to the woman that the man did not know her and thus did not know anything definitive about her sexual orientation. Further, he notes that the dispute was really about a parking space, not sexual orientation. This contrasts, he maintains, to the sort of acts the law was intended to address: groups willfully and consciously seeking homosexuals for overt harassment._
>
> _However, the officers do address her feelings by summoning the man from inside the mall, explaining the situation to him, and persuading him to apologize. After he does so, the officers leave the scene._

In the span of only 10 minutes, the officers define the situation, establish a course of action, and attempt to justify that action to the people involved. This process involves quickly deciding for themselves the most important issues at stake, the best interpretation of those issues in terms of the law, and the best means to bring some resolution. This is obviously a situation open to varying interpretations, and their chosen course of action may betray an absence of sympathy for victims of harassment based on sexual orientation. Either way, however, the process is a decidedly speedy one in which a delicate situation is resolved hastily and with minimal attention to the entire range of issues at stake.

Regardless of the logic employed by the officers here, both situations illustrate the type of inchoate and complex situations they regularly face. Disputes are rarely simple, and evolve from a host of circumstances that officers cannot fully decode. Further, these disputes can be inflamed by such larger dynamics as homophobia, racism, or long-standing familial tensions. The situations officers face, in short, are inherently and irrevocably ambiguous.

But officers must ignore much of this ambiguity if they are to be effective in restoring order and if they are to keep up with their call load. Effectiveness often rests on decisiveness, so officers cannot hem and haw their way to a half-hearted decision. And their increasing queue of yet-unanswered calls places urgency on handling the dispute in the most parsimonious way possible.

The ambiguity inherent in the vast majority of police calls contrasts sharply with the clear-cut boundaries of good and evil that officers regularly construct in their moralistic discourse. Indeed, the contrast is probably not accidental. The overarching, trans-situational morality that officers construct seems a perfect antidote to any qualms that might arise from them running roughshod over the ambiguity in the disputes or other calls officers handle. Cast in terms of the broad and potent categories of good and evil, officers' actions take on a markedly less ambiguous character and provide a powerful justification for acts that may ultimately be open to question.

C. The Inevitable Harms of Policing

Regardless of the aims of police actions, many resolutions that officers accomplish come at the expense of one of the parties involved. Of course, many cases the police handle, particularly the more mundane order-maintenance tasks that occupy much of their attention, do not have a clear opposition of interests and/or a high level of tension. However, officers regularly encounter situations that are confused and highly charged. This is most likely when those involved tell diametrically opposed versions of events and desired outcomes. In some cases, officers do attempt to reach a resolution that can receive some minimal degree of communal consent, but time pressures often dictate a more brusque response. In many cases, of course, there is a clear victim and perpetrator, so swift restraint of the latter is not fundamentally in question; the harm caused by jailing is not something that would trouble officers. But given the ambiguity discussed above, actions that clearly favor one party over another are not always easy to justify.

The potential unease that might accompany acting against one party's interest is compounded for officers by the coercive means to which they often resort to eventuate their desired outcome. Resistance to police commands is inevitable, and officers possess a wide array of tactics and tools to ensure their ultimate authority. It is this coercive authority that distinguishes the police from other social agencies (Bittner 1970) and explains their importance in upholding the state's legal and moral rule. But coercive force is obviously harmful to the individual involved, and its use makes clear the extent to which the police can deleteriously affect members of the citizenry.

It is therefore not surprising that officers spend much time discussing whether and how to use force. During the fieldwork, I observed a number of roll-call discussions that focused on recent shootings within the department. Lieutenants and sergeants reviewed each situation, explaining how the officers acted and how those actions were or were not justified. This training is motivated both to ensure that officers prevail in any confrontations with armed and dangerous suspects and to prevent any unnecessary use of force. Supervisors would continually remind officers that in any postincident investigation, "every shot must be accounted for." In other words, officers would be expected to justify each shot they fired as a responsible and reasonable use of force that did not unnecessarily endanger the wrong people.

In many cases, however, the use of force is not seen in such wary terms but is a badge of distinction that officers wear proudly. Officers are referred to as "ghetto gunfighters" who have fallen victim to the "John Wayne Syndrome." For these hard-charging officers, occasional uses of force are necessary to fight evil and earn internal distinction. The majority of officers, however, do not fall into this category; indeed, many officers try to avoid working with their more aggressive counterparts because they fear the potential damage to their career that an out-of-control partner might cause.

Still, the enforcement of police authority often involves making some persons suffer by denying them pursuit of their preferred path of action and/or physically restraining them. This compounds the unease stemming from the ambiguity inherent in most situations officers encounter; not only must officers act decisively in confused situations, but they must also often act against one party's interest, sometimes with recourse to coercive and ultimately lethal force. Further, because police officers serve as a key mechanism of the state's coercive apparatus, they attract potentially lethal attention themselves from those who resist police authority. Officers are never unaware of the potential danger they face at a moment's notice. Given this unavoidable mandate—to ensure order via coercive force in often-inchoate settings at the risk of their own lives—it is perhaps understandable why officers take refuge in a moralistic discursive universe that avoids the irresolvable questions of whether this or that use of force is justified, and instead posit a more simplistic good/evil frame by which actions can be interpreted. This moralistic universe also defines a life lost in the line of duty as not a mere death but as a sacrifice for a large and worthy cause. An ardent morality provides officers a cushioned escape from the conundrums their social role foists on them, a retreat where they can wash away the difficult particularities of actual situations and thus helps them adapt to the reality of the potentially lethal risks they daily assume.

III. The Implications and Paradoxes of Police Morality

Given the facts that police officers must quickly and coercively create order in ambiguous situations and that they are presumed to prevent crime when they cannot actually do so, it is easier to understand why simplistic moral frames might work to reduce their level of tension, why such moral frames might serve as an adaptive response to the inescapable and interminable anxieties of daily police practice. The difficult and easily questioned decisions they must constantly make are rendered less troublesome if they are nested in a broader and simpler discourse that bluntly describes behavior as either good or evil. The societal role of the police to create order coercively perhaps explains why their morality should be so singularly pronounced; the burden of their unique responsibility is alleviated by continually reinforcing the overall worth of their mission.

Police morality often yields laudable efforts. One can easily sympathize with an old woman who fears leaving her home and thus can endorse strong efforts on an officer's part to reduce her anxiety. In many cases, officers identify those who are most vulnerable—typically the elderly and children—and operate primarily to ensure their welfare. Given a strong desire to do good, many officers involve themselves deeply in their communities or work long hours. Indeed, many LAPD officers understood the recent inability of the officers' union to gain wide support for a "sickout" as a function of the inextinguishable desire of officers to serve; they simply could not condone leaving the citizenry unprotected. Similarly, officers worked many extra hours after the Northridge earthquake with little complaint.

But the dangers of excessive moralizing are equally clear. It is understandable why officers might regularly vilify those they define as their opponents. If the "bad guys" are defined as essentially evil, then officers' responses are more easily justified. Even if, say, the use of force was bit excessive, it was the perpetrator who initiated the encounter and who sought to harm the community. And whatever the officer did, he/she was ultimately mo-

812   **Morality in Law Enforcement**

tivated by the praiseworthy virtue of protecting the good from
the depredations of evil. As Van Maanen (1978:234) put it, "In

Police officers are perhaps unique in the extent to which they must regularly wrestle with the ambiguous nature of human reality. To the degree, however, that they use a structured morality to avoid the difficult task of discriminatingly interpreting social action, they are unable to police with the measured and delicate hand of a true professional. Officers pass the murkiness of the social world through the prism of their morality to reduce phenomena to a narrower spectrum of black-white/good-evil images. This is a comforting exercise but an ultimately troublesome one.

This discussion reveals the central paradox at the heart of police morality. In using their morality to render the social world in more sharply categorical terms, officers are led to enact or condone practices that are inconsistent with their virtuous self-definition. Their muscular morality enables them to justify various actions that are perpetually questionable and that almost unavoidably harm at least one citizen. They can therefore easily transform condemnable actions into condonable ones by excusing police excesses as first and foremost acts to uphold the good. It was Rodney King, after all, who terrorized a suburban Los Angeles community with his reckless driving, and it was those officers' duty to restrain him in whatever way they could. By couching their actions as tactics in the monumental battle to stave off evil, officers can lose the capacity to read nuance in the social landscape or even to cast a critical eye on their own behavior. Police actions that are, in fact, inconsistent with the moral cast that molds their self-interpretation can be reinterpreted as excusable given the larger fight for virtue that defines their mission.

An integral part of the tension within police morality is the seeming incompatibility of coercive force, which can maim and kill, and the pursuit of peace, order, and the good. The difficulty of balancing the harm of lethal force against the larger social aims for which it is ostensibly employed is perhaps the most basic dilemma facing police officers (Muir 1977). On the one hand, officers wish to portray themselves as saviors for the troubled and the vulnerable, the "thin blue line" that protects the orderly from the chaotic. On the other hand, the police exist primarily as a repository of legitimate coercive force, which they stand ready to employ on extremely short notice. The tension between these two is usefully illustrated in the following incident.

> *A group of officers have followed a trail of clues from a shooting at a hamburger stand to a young woman's apartment. She is the girlfriend of the registered owner of a truck seen speeding from the scene. Because it is a fresh pursuit, the officers do not need a search warrant to enter the woman's house. She, however, is reluctant to open the door. The officers are polite and explain why they are there. They also attempt to compel her cooperation by discussing the general comfort the police bring her in times of*

trouble. "We are the police," one officer reminds her, "the people you call when you need help and protection."

When this effort to create trust does not work, the officers inform her that the manager of the apartment building is on his way, and he will grant them legal access to her apartment. This is enough to convince her to open the door. Once inside, the officers search the apartment with aggressive thoroughness, overturning furniture and tossing items from closets. Two officers take the young woman into a back room where they press her for information about the suspect's whereabouts. One officer is overheard telling the woman that unless she tells them what they want to know, "We will thump you so hard it will hurt to sit down." The woman seems genuinely unable to provide them with any information, but she and the other three people in the apartment are taken to the station for further questioning.

The officers' early invocation of the cherished protective role of police in society was obviously motivated by a desire to talk their way into the woman's apartment. Still, the contrast between their advertised ability to comfort and the actual threat they pose to the woman's property and physical well-being is stark. Regardless of how much they may try to convince the woman to see the police as the ultimate source of community protection, the officers quickly reveal the coercive heart of their occupation by trashing the apartment and threatening physical harm. The facade of benevolence crumbles in the earthquake of strong-armed policing.

On the other hand, as I have suggested, the benevolent aspects of policing are often genuine, real, and commendable. To the extent, however, that officers' good/evil categories are inflexible, they undercut the very morality they attempt to claim for themselves. The pervasiveness of police morality is undoubtedly related to the coercive tasks society relegates to them, enabling officers to assuage their sense of responsibility or guilt when they must harm another. But the soil of the police's moral high ground is ever unstable, precisely because of their coercive function. The fact that the police can cause harm to others gives rise to the comforting refuge of their morality, but their capacity to maim and kill also threatens to undercut that morality. An uneasy tension is thus built into the core of the police's moral vision, as they try to obscure what they cannot escape. Whether police officers can be successfully trained to adopt the more nuanced and mature perspective that Muir sometimes observed is an open question. The track record of contemporary policing, especially in Los Angeles, suggests that it is a challenge worth addressing.

IV. Conclusion

The importance of morality for justifying and promoting state rule is obvious and is the focus of much scholarly attention. The legal order, for example, is not just a dry-as-dust set of stodgy regulations but an attempt to structure virtue into the populace. The precise mechanisms through which this morality is inculcated into the citizenry are certainly worthy of our attention, because to study them is to reveal the actual work that states must accomplish to sustain themselves. One can thus avoid reifying the state as some sort of coherent, transcendent unity, and instead focus on the actual practices by which state rule is created and maintained (Abrams 1988).

It is therefore important to investigate how the state, through its legal order, aims its focus on its subject population and attempts to mold a model citizenry through its various proscriptions, how it seeks to make a moral order more pervasive and binding. But it is useful not only to focus on the state's external relations but also to investigate the *internal* processes through which state legal actors justify their actions, often with recourse to moralistic dictums. Police officers, for example, drink regularly from the fount of morality and replenish their internal esprit de corps by invoking a larger virtue that their actions serve. Given its prevalence and seeming power, this morality deserves explanation.

My suggestion is that this morality flows from three fundamental constituents of modern policing: the gap between the stated goals of the police and their inability to achieve them; the inherent ambiguity in most police-citizen encounters that officers must ignore to affect order quickly; and the inevitable harm that police actions, coercive or otherwise, cause some citizens. Police officers are thus placed in a difficult position. They are asked to arrest crime when they cannot, they are required to enforce order when denied the time and tools to unearth the full range of disordering influences, and they are compelled to use coercive force in quickly developing and uncertain circumstances. The combination of these factors can create potent dilemmas, whose intricacies can be simplified and disquiet can be eased through an equally potent morality. Cast in terms not of ambiguity and contradiction but rather in the rigid categories of good and evil, police actions are more easily justified, even if they overstretch certain bounds. Thus, a use of force that perhaps was not fully necessary given a complete understanding of the event in question is more easily condoned if understood as ultimately motivated by a desire to expunge evil from otherwise peaceable streets. Individual excesses are the price one pays in the ongoing effort to clean the city of the polluting stains of the irrational and chaotic.

On the one hand, police morality can be both understood and, at times, applauded; officers who work long hours and are genuinely motivated to improve people's quality of life deserve our fullest appreciation. And their willingness to insert themselves in dangerous situations where our fundamental physical well-being is at stake is extremely laudable. On the other hand, police morality, to the extent that it too crudely categorizes individuals and their actions, threatens to condone needlessly aggressive or insensitive treatment of some members of the citizenry. It undoubtedly has contributed to the sort of police-minority tensions that rage in Los Angeles and other cities. The drive to reduce ambiguity is perhaps necessary given the dilemmas officers face, but in erasing gray areas from their world-views, officers are led to enforce order in ways that are, paradoxically, inimicable to their moral definition of themselves. Thus, the morality of officers is born from unique aspects of the police's role in society but also can exacerbate the intensity of the moral dilemmas they regularly confront.

Any efforts to reform the police must be attentive to their morally created world-view and to the ways it shapes their everyday practice. The challenge is to ratify the officers' understandable need to imbue their work with a sense of overarching purpose while encouraging an openness to ambiguity that would discourage too-simplistic categorizations of people and events. In a sense, officers need to be encouraged not to allow their fervent morality to contribute to actions that are inconsistent with that morality. Police morality needs to be saved from itself in order to actually allow the work it ostensibly encourages.

References

Abrams, Philip (1988) "Notes on the Difficulty of Studying the State," 1 *J. of Historical Sociology* 58.

Alpert, Geoffrey, & Roger Dunham (1988) *Policing Multi-ethnic Neighborhoods.* New York: Greenwood Press.

Banton, Michael (1964) *The Policeman in the Community.* London: Tavistock.

Bayley, David (1994) *Police for the Future.* New York: Oxford Univ. Press.

Bayley, David, & Harold Mendelsohn (1968) *Minorities and the Police: Confrontation in America.* New York: Free Press.

Bittner, Egon (1967) "The Police in Skid-Row: A Study of Peacekeeping," 32 *American Sociological Rev.* 699.

———— (1970) *The Functions of Police in Modern Society: A Review of Background Factors, Current Practices and Possible Role Models.* Chevy Chase, MD: Center for Studies of Crime & Delinquency, National Institute of Mental Health.

———— (1990) *Aspects of Police Work.* Boston: Northeastern Univ. Press.

Bordua, David Joseph, ed. (1967) *The Police: Six Sociological Essays.* New York: John Wiley & Sons.

Brooks, Laurie (1989) "Police Discretionary Behavior: A Study of Style," in R. Dunham & G. Alpert, eds., *Critical Issues in Policing: Contemporary Readings.* Prospect Heights, IL: Waveland Press.

Brown, Michael (1981) *Working the Street: Police Discretion and the Dilemmas of Reform.* New York: Russell Sage Foundation.

Campbell, David (1992) *Writing Security: United States Foreign Policy and the Policies of Identity.* Minneapolis: Univ. of Minnesota Press.

Corrigan, Philip, & Derek Sayer (1985) *The Great Arch: English State Formation as Cultural Revolution.* Oxford: Basil Blackwell.

Cray, Ed (1972) *The Enemy in the Streets: Police Malpractice in America.* Garden City, NY: Anchor Books.

Dalby, Simon (1990) *Creating the Second Cold War: The Discourse of Politics.* London: Pinter.

Donzelot, Jacques (1979) *The Policing of Families.* New York: Pantheon.

Douglas, Mary (1966) *Purity and Danger: Analyses of Concepts of Pollution and Taboo.* London: Routledge & Kegan Paul.

—— (1973) *Natural Symbols: Explorations in Cosmology.* London: Barrie & Jenkins.

Durkheim, Emile (1938) *The Rules of Sociological Method.* Chicago: Univ. of Chicago Press.

—— (1986) *Durkheim on Politics and the State.* Stanford, CA: Stanford Univ. Press.

Foucault, Michel (1990) *The History of Sexuality,* vol. 1. New York: Vintage Books.

Gates, Daryl (1992) *Chief: My Life in the LAPD.* New York: Bantam Books.

Herbert, Steve (1995) "The Trials of Laurence Powell: Law, Space and a 'Big Time Use of Force,'" 13 *Environment & Planning D: Society & Space* 185.

—— (1996) *Policing Space: Territoriality and the Los Angeles Police Department.* Minneapolis: Univ. of Minnesota Press.

Kappeler, Victor E., Richard D. Sluder, & Geoffrey P. Alpert (1994) *Forces of Deviance: Understanding the Dark Side of Policing.* Prospect Heights, IL: Waveland Press.

Kelling, George (1983) "On the Accomplishments of the Police," in M. Punch, ed., *Control in the Police Organization.* Cambridge, MA: MIT Press.

Manning, Peter (1977) *Police Work: The Social Organization of Policing.* Cambridge, MA: MIT Press.

—— (1993) "Violence and Symbolic Violence," 3 *Police Forum* 1.

Muir, William (1977) *Police: Streetcorner Politicians.* Chicago: Univ. of Chicago Press.

Niederhoffer, Arthur (1967) *Behind the Shield: The Police in Urban Society.* Garden City, NY: Doubleday & Co.

Polsky, Andrew J. (1991) *The Rise of the Therapeutic State.* Princeton, NJ: Princeton Univ. Press.

Raine, Walter (1967) *The Perception of Police Brutality in South Central Los Angeles.* Los Angeles: Institute of Government and Public Affairs, Univ. of California.

Reiner, Robert (1992) *The Politics of the Police.* Toronto: Univ. of Toronto Press.

Reiss, Albert, & David Bordua (1967) "Environment and Organization: A Perspective on the Police," in Bordua 1967.

Reuss-Ianni, Elizabeth (1983) *Two Cultures of Policing: Street Cops and Management Officers.* New Brunswick, NJ: Transaction Books.

Sacks, Harvey (1972) "Notes on Police Assessment of Moral Character," in D. Sudnow, ed., *Studies in Social Interaction.* New York: Free Press.

Sherman, Lawrence (1992) "Attacking Crime: Police and Crime Control," in M. Tonry & N. Morris, eds., *Modern Policing.* Chicago: Univ. of Chicago Press.

Silver, Allan (1967) "The Demand for Order in Civil Society," in Bordua 1967.

Skolnick, Jerome (1966) *Justice without Trial.* New York: John Wiley & Sons.

Skolnick, Jerome, & James Fyfe (1993) *Above the Law: Police and the Excessive Use of Force.* New York: Free Press.

818   **Morality in Law Enforcement**

U.S. Commission on Civil Rights, California Advisory Committee (1963) *Police-Minority Relations in Los Angeles and the San Francisco Bay Area.* Washington: U.S. Commission on Civil Rights.

Van Maanen, John (1978) "The Asshole," in J. Van Maanen & P. Manning, eds., *Policing: A View from the Street.* Santa Monica, CA: Goodyear Publishing.

Walker, Samuel (1977) *A Critical History of Police Reform: The Emergence of Professionalism.* Lexington, MA: Lexington Books.

Weber, Max (1954) *Max Weber on Law in Economy and Society.* New York: Simon & Schuster.

Werthman, Carl, & Irving Piliavin (1967) "Gang Members and the Police," in Bordua 1967.

Westley, William (1970) *Violence and the Police: A Sociological Study of Law, Custom, and Morality.* Cambridge, MA: MIT Press.

Wilson, O. W. (1957) *Parker on Police.* Springfield, IL: Charles C. Thomas.

[12]

DEMEANOR OR CRIME? THE MIDWEST CITY POLICE-CITIZEN ENCOUNTERS STUDY*

RICHARD J. LUNDMAN
The Ohio State University

There is agreement in the literature on policing that demeanor and other extralegal variables help determine police decisions. A recent challenge to that agreement has been issued, however. Klinger (1994) has asserted that nearly all previous quantitative analyses of the effects of demeanor and other extralegal variables are fatally flawed because they failed to limit demeanor to spoken words and failed to control for crime. He concluded that all previous research is suspect until additional analyses of the data sets used in previous research and new observational research are presented. This research starts the first of these tasks by reporting additional analyses of data from three previously published papers based on the Midwest City Police-Citizen Encounters Study. With demeanor limited to spoken words and crime partially controlled, the reanalyzed data suggest that the effects of demeanor depend on how demeanor is represented and, to a lesser extent, model specification. Consequently, caution with respect to existing reports of the effects of demeanor and other extralegal variables remains necessary. In addition, carefully controlling for crime and limiting demeanor to spoken words may not be the only problems surrounding efforts to assess the effects of demeanor. This research suggests that multiple representations of demeanor and more fully specified models may be important as well.

There is agreement in the literature on policing that demeanor and other extralegal variables help determine police decisions. Much of that agreement stems from a collection of quantitative studies consistently linking extralegal variables, such as demeanor, with arrest and other formal police actions (Black, 1971, 1980; Black and Reiss, 1970; Pastor, 1978; Piliavin and Briar, 1964; Smith, 1984, 1986, 1987; Smith and Klein, 1983, 1984, 1986, 1987; Smith and Visher, 1981; Smith, et al., 1984; Sykes, et al., 1976; Visher, 1983; Worden, 1989; Worden and Politz, 1984). Qualitative researchers also have long reported that extralegal factors, including demeanor, help explain police actions (Bayley, 1991:39; Goldman, 1963; Rubinstein, 1973:155; Skolnick and Bayley, 1986:168; Skolnick and Fyfe,

---

* The anonymous reviewers provided extraordinarily helpful comments on earlier versions of this paper. I am responsible for the mistakes that remain.

1993:90; Stark, 1972:61; Van Maanen, 1978; Westley, 1970; Wilson, 1968:36–37). Muir (1977:160), for example, observed: "Ever since God investigated Adam, police . . . have performed 'attitude tests' because they have always had to make judgments." And police say that attitude matters (Baker, 1985:209–243; Bouza, 1990:78; Fletcher, 1990:17; Holdaway, 1983:27; Rothmiller, 1992:36–38). The words of a Chicago police officer are especially instructive: "People write their own tickets. They really do. Your conduct to me will predict how I'll act to you. The ultimate outcome of that traffic stop is always in your hands. Your attitude writes your ticket" (Fletcher, 1991:249).

A recent challenge to this agreement has been issued, however. Klinger (1994) has asserted that nearly all previous quantitative analyses of the effects of demeanor share two fatal flaws. First, "measures of . . . [demeanor] . . . often include criminal conduct." Second, "criminal conduct is not controlled adequately when the effects of demeanor on arrest are estimated" (p. 477). He backs his assertions with supportive findings. Using data collected during observation of Metro-Dade County (Florida) police in the mid–1980s, Klinger demonstrated that "demeanor . . . does not exert an independent effect on arrest, once crime has explained as much as it can" (p. 489). He concluded that all previous reports of the independent effects of demeanor and other extralegal variables are suspect until two types of additional research are presented. The first is "additional analyses of the data sets . . . used in previous research . . . to learn whether the reported findings hold when only legal displays of hostility are counted as demeanor and when crime is controlled comprehensively." The second is "additional projects . . . in which observers carefully measure . . . demeanor . . . and . . . crime" (p. 490).

THE CURRENT RESEARCH

This research starts the first of the tasks suggested by Klinger by reporting additional analyses of one of the data sets used in previous research—the Midwest City Police-Citizen Encounters Study.

MIDWEST CITY POLICE-CITIZEN ENCOUNTERS STUDY

During a 15-month period beginning in June 1970, a group of seven observers under the direction of Richard E. Sykes and John P. Clark accompanied police patrol officers in a large midwestern city (Sykes and Brent, 1983; Sykes and Clark, 1975). In 1970 "Midwest City" had a population of over 500,000 and was located in a metropolitan area of over 2 million people. The observers trained for three months prior to the start of the project and then observed a stratified random sample of police officers in patrol cars. With prior permission but without prior notice as to specific precinct and cruiser, observers rode in randomly selected patrol cars for full-eight-hour shifts. A total of 365 eight-hour shifts were observed.

A wide variety of data were encoded by the observers, either as a police-citizen encounter took place or immediately after. Situational factors immediately encoded included the nature of the offense or problem that initially brought police and citizens together (e.g., a citizen-initiated public drunkenness encounter or a police-initiated traffic law violation encounter). Interaction was described using codes representing deferent, polite, and impolite statements and entered as the interaction took place. Other actions also were immediately encoded, including criminal acts occurring once an encounter had begun. Outcome was encoded at the conclusion of each encounter, ranging from release to arrest for criminal encounters and from verbal warning to ticket for traffic law violation encounters. Data describing the sex, race, age, and social class of the alleged violator were collected by the observers using visual and audial information and recorded following each encounter. Interobserver reliability for the many factors encoded was regularly assessed and the coefficients for the data reported averaged about .70 (Sykes and Brent, 1983:273–277).

Publication using the data assembled during the Midwest City Police-Citizen Encounters Study has been relatively frequent (Sykes and Brent, 1983; Sykes and Clark, 1975; Sykes et al., 1976). Along with the early research of others (e.g., Black, 1980; Reiss, 1971), the Sykes and Clark Midwest City data have been an important source of information about the work and, especially, the factors shaping the decisions of urban police patrol officers in the very early 1970s (see Sherman, 1980).

DATA

I reanalyze data from three previously published papers based on the Midwest City Police-Citizen Encounters Study. The first examined police exercise of arrest discretion during encounters with public drunkenness offenders (Lundman, 1974). The second replicated earlier research by Black and Reiss (1970) and examined police exercise of arrest discretion with juvenile offenders (Lundman et al., 1978). The third detailed police exercise of discretion in encounters with traffic law violators (Lundman, 1979).

The previously published studies display the characteristics Klinger correctly argues flaw previous research. They did not clearly control for the seriousness of the initial offense, and they did not control for additional crimes taking place during an encounter. Consequently, they did not disentangle legally permissible hostile demeanor from initial and additional

634 LUNDMAN

criminal deeds. In addition, they placed exclusive faith in simple percentages, an approach that appears hopelessly naive when viewed from the perspective of contemporary multivariate modeling techniques. Thus, they did not firmly establish the independent effects of demeanor and other extralegal variables, net of crime.

LOGIC OF THE REANALYSIS

My reanalysis attempts to fix some of these problems. When variation in initial crime exists, I try to control for it by distinguishing between the felony and nonfelony offenses that first brought police and citizens together. If an additional crime took place once an encounter began, I represent it. I limit my measures of demeanor to spoken words. The representations of initial crime, encounter crime, and demeanor are complemented by a standard set of demographic variables—the sex, race, age, and social class of the alleged offender. I replace the simple percentages with multivariate logistic regression.

The reanalysis does not fix all of the problems, however. Because the studies to be reexamined were limited to particular types of encounters, there is little variation in initial crime. Only 7 of the public drunkenness encounters ($N = 195$) and 18 of the juvenile encounters ($N = 200$) involved felonies. All of the rest were nonfelony and other minor offenses. None of the traffic law violation encounters ($N = 290$) involved felony offenses.

In addition, I have no clear way of distinguishing the seriousness of the initial offense that gave rise to the encounter, other than the crude distinction between felony and nonfelony. For the misdemeanor public drunkenness encounters, for example, I am unable to represent degree of offender intoxication. In traffic law violation encounters involving speeding, I do not know how many miles per hour (mph) over the speed limit the offender was driving.

Encounter crime was a very rare event, and when it occurred, it was very minor. Only 11 of the public drunkenness encounters involved additional crimes, and all of them were very simple attempted assaults that police quickly foiled. Only one of the juvenile encounters involved an additional crime, and it too was an attempted simple assault that failed. None of the traffic law violation encounters involved additional crimes. While these encounter crimes are separately represented and therefore not a direct part of the measures of demeanor, they were infrequent, minor, and mostly unsuccessful.

I am unable to determine whether hostile demeanor came before or after arrest or a traffic ticket. This was also a problem with other early research (e.g., Black, 1980; Black and Reiss, 1970; Pastor, 1978). Klinger (1994) noted, however, that demeanor tends to be a "stable commodity," which suggests that impolite words come before arrest (also see Sykes and Clark, 1975). That is my observational experience as well. Most offenders are deflated by the decision to arrest or ticket. Few suddenly become bolder. Still, causal order must be inferred and that is a problem.

Finally, it cannot be assumed that all of the alleged offenders involved in the encounters to be examined were actually seen by Midwest City police as suspects. If they were, it cannot be assumed that all were guilty, even if they were arrested. Street cops are curious creatures (Skolnick, 1966:42–70), and most like to talk (Muir, 1977:227–235). At least some traffic law violation encounters are seen by police as an opportunity to satisfy their curiosity and, assuming nothing out of the ordinary is found, talk. Equally important, when street cops do make an arrest, prosecutors reject many for lack of sufficient evidence (Boland et al., 1992).

It is important to note, however, that while the problems Klinger identified are not solved here, they are addressed. The indicators of demeanor are limited to spoken words. The effects of demeanor and other extralegal variables are examined with some elements of initial and additional crime partially controlled. Multivariate modeling replaces simple percentages, and the models include important demographic variables that previous research has shown sometimes shape police exercise of discretion (Black, 1971; Pastor, 1978; Worden, 1989).

VARIABLES AND CODING

The dependent variable is the dispositional decision made by the police officer(s) handling the encounter. For the public drunkenness and juvenile encounters, Arrest (yes = 1, no = 0) is the dichotomous dependent variable. For the traffic law violation encounters, Ticket (yes = 1, no = 0) is the dichotomous dependent variable. (See the appendix for the frequency distributions of the dichotomous and categorical variables and for the zero-order effects of the independent variables.)

The first two independent variables attempt to control for initial and additional crime. To represent the rare felony offenses, Felony is a dummy coded variable (yes = 1, no = 0). Encounter Crime also is dummy coded (yes = 1, no = 0) and represents the handful of encounters with minor additional crimes.

The standard demographic variables direct attention to the characteristics of the alleged offender. Sex is a dummy coded variable (male = 1, female = 0). Race-ethnicity involves three categories (African-American, Native American, and white) and is represented using two dummy variables and white as the omitted reference category (African-American, where yes = 1, else = 0; Native American, where yes = 1, else = 0). Age is coded to approximate an ordinal variable (senior = 5, adult = 4, young adult = 3, adolescent = 2, child = 1), as is Class (declassified = 3, blue collar = 2, white collar = 1).

For the traffic law violation encounters, there were no felony offenses, no additional crimes, and no method of determining the seriousness of the traffic law violation (e.g., mph over the speed limit). There were, however, important differences in the circumstances surrounding the start of some of the encounters and the differences are represented. A monthly quota system shaped the writing of traffic tickets by Midwest City police (also see Petersen, 1971). Traffic tickets were counted for each officer and posted by name in precinct roll call rooms each month. Patrol officers in Midwest City resisted quota demands during the first half of each month by making fewer traffic stops and writing fewer tickets. They also acted apart from organizational norms and did not target African-American, poor, or impolite drivers. During the last half of each month, Midwest City police paid for their earlier autonomy by making more stops and writing more tickets. They also followed organizational norms and wrote more tickets for African-American, poor, and impolite drivers. Quota is therefore a dichotomous variable (month days 16–end = 1, month days 1–15 = 0). Three interaction terms represent the effects identified in the simple percentage data originally reported —Quota by African-American, Quota by Class, and Quota by the indicators of demeanor described next.

The independent variable of primary interest is demeanor. Each uninterrupted statement directed by an alleged violator to an officer was immediately content analyzed by an observer and placed into one of three mutually exclusive interactional categories. The polite interactional category included "civil interaction conducted in normal tone of voice with normal emotional load . . . [including] . . . questions, statements of facts, excuses, and explanations, as long as stated in civil, non-hostile, non-highly emotional tone." "Somewhat deferent" involved "more than usual cooperation," and "very deferent" included "elevation or recognition of the face of the other by acting very subservient." "Somewhat impolite" involved "non-aggressive, non-compliance . . . disagreement with high emotional load," and "very impolite" included "calling names, ridiculing the other, personal vituperation . . . [and] . . . humbling the other."

The statements advanced by offenders to police during encounters are initially represented using three dummy variables and entirely polite encounters as the omitted reference category (Impolite, where one or more impolite statements and no deferent statements = 1, else = 0; Deferent, where one or more deferent statements and no impolite statements = 1, else = 0; Mixed, where one or more impolite and one or more deferent statements = 1, else = 0). The reference category therefore consists of encounters in which violators made only polite statements. "Impolite" captures encounters with at least one impolite statement, no deferent statements, and a variable number of polite statements. "Deferent" includes only encounters with at least one deferent statement, no impolite statements, and a variable number of polite statements. "Mixed" includes encounters in which violators shifted interactional gears during the course of an encounter by being impolite at one point, deferent at another, and typically, polite at still another. One advantage of this representation is that mixed interaction encounters are clearly distinguished rather than being placed into either the impolite or deferent category.

Demeanor, however, has been represented in a variety of ways in previous research, and there is no basis for arguing that one representation is superior to another. Black and Reiss (1970:74–75), for example, represented encounters on the basis of the "suspect's degree of deference toward the police . . . civil . . . neither strikingly respectful nor disrespectful . . . very deferential . . . [and] . . . antagonistic." Pastor (1978:377) classified encounters using four categories—"friendly-cooperative . . . neutral-resigned . . . hostile-abusive . . . and violent." Klinger (1994:484) represented demeanor during encounters using three categories—civil, moderately hostile, and highly hostile.

I therefore include four additional representations of demeanor. It is possible to represent hostile demeanor as a continuous variable composed of the number of impolite statements. Number Impolite is that continuous variable. Dummy Impolite is a dichotomous variable (one or more impolite statements during an encounter = 1, no impolite statements = 0). The variable GT Av. Impolite also is dichotomous (greater than average impolite encounters = 1, average or below = 0). Hostile Demeanor replicates Klinger's (1994) representation (entirely polite, including deferent, encounters = 1, encounters with at least one somewhat impolite statement = 2, encounters with at least one very impolite statement = 3).

DATA ANALYSIS

Because the dependent variables are dichotomous and the independent variables categorical or continuous, I analyzed the data using logistic regression, which is intended for use with a dichotomous dependent variable (Aldrich and Nelson, 1984). In logistic regression, parameters are estimated using a maximum likelihood procedure, which provides a number of desirable properties, including an asymptotic distribution and efficiency (Feinberg, 1980). Further, the logistic coefficient divided by its standard error follows a standard t distribution. Thus, the statistical significance as well as the direction of each independent variable can be assessed.

To facilitate understanding of the effects of demeanor and other extralegal variables, I estimate the parameters of several different models by manipulating entry of the independent variables. Entered first are the indicators of demeanor to establish baseline effects and to replicate the zero-order data originally reported. Entered next are the incomplete indicators of initial and additional crime to assess the effects of demeanor with crime partially controlled. If previous research has indeed been fatally flawed by the failure to control for crime, the initial effects of demeanor should at least be reduced once the partial controls for crime have been introduced. The initial models are then respecified by deleting the crime indicators and adding the standard demographic variables. This provides an opportunity to determine whether the failure to control effectively for important demographic variables also flaws previous research. Finally, full models consisting of the indicators of demeanor, initial and additional crime, and the demographic variables are examined. In these full models the independent effects of demeanor are assessed, net of the partial controls for crime and the more complete controls for the demographic variables.

FINDINGS

PUBLIC DRUNKENNESS ENCOUNTERS

For the public drunkenness encounters, all of the indicators of demeanor are in the expected positive direction and nearly all are statistically significant (model 1, sections A–E of Table 1). Only the continuous Number Impolite indicator of demeanor is not significant. Partially controlling for initial and additional crime (model 2, sections A–E of Table 1) does not alter the direction of the demeanor indicators, but it does alter the statistical significance of two representations. Thus, the Impolite and Hostile Demeanor representations are not statistically significant with crime partially controlled. Removing the crime indicators and adding the demographic variables (model 3, sections A–E of Table 1) also does not change the direction of the indicators of demeanor. But adding the demographic variables surfaces the Deferent indicator of demeanor (section A of Table 1) and strips the Hostile Demeanor and GT Av. Impolite indicators of significance. In the full model (model 4, sections A–E of Table 1), only the Deferent, Mixed, and GT Av. Impolite indicators of demeanor are significant. The Native American and Class variables are statistically significant in all of the full models as well.

Based upon reanalysis of the public drunkenness encounters, the issue with respect to demeanor does not exclusively seem to be the failure to control for crime, although controlling for crime is clearly important. Instead, two additional issues may be just as important. Representation of demeanor appears to be one. Model specification seems to be a second.

DEMEANOR OR CRIME? 639

Table 1. Public Drunkenness Encounters: Multivariate Logistic Regression Models of Arrest on Explanatory Variables (N = 195)

Explanatory Variable	Models			
	1	2	3	4
A				
Demeanor				
Deferent	.66	.77	1.02*	1.30*
	(.47)	(.48)	(.51)	(.53)
Impolite	.79*	.47	.61	.18
	(.45)	(.51)	(.48)	(.55)
Mixed	.98*	1.02*	1.05*	1.10*
	(.39)	(.41)	(.41)	(.44)
Offense				
Felony		8.19		9.10
		(13.76)		(13.24)
Encounter Crime		.27		.44
		(.69)		(.76)
Demographic				
Sex			.26	.46
			(.58)	(.65)
African-American			.17	-.36
			(.60)	(.73)
Native American			1.14*	1.34*
			(.41)	(.44)
Age			-.08	.07
			(.26)	(.35)
Class			.58*	.75*
			(.33)	(.35)
B				
Demeanor				
Number Impolite	.01	.01	.00	.00
	(.01)	(.01)	(.01)	(.01)
Offense				
Felony		8.08		8.72
		(13.82)		(13.30)
Encounter Crime		.49		.66
		(.67)		(.70)
Demographic				
Sex			.31	.48
			(.57)	(.62)
African-American			.11	-.48
			(.57)	(.70)
Native American			.99*	1.03*
			(.39)	(.40)
Age			-.05	.03
			(.25)	(.27)
Class			.54*	.71*
			(.32)	(.34)
C				
Demeanor				
Dummy Impolite	.71*	.60*	.62*	.43
	(.31)	(.33)	(.33)	(.35)
Offense				
Felony		7.94		8.55

640   **LUNDMAN**

Table 1 (continued)

Explanatory Variable	Models			
	1	2	3	4
Encounter Crime		(13.79) .30 (.68)		(13.39) .52 (.71)
Demographic				
Sex			.24 (.57)	.42 (.63)
African-American			.06 (.58)	−.48 (.70)
Native American			.93* (.39)	.98* (.40)
Age			−.11 (.25)	.00 (.27)
Class			.55* (.33)	.70* (.35)

D

	1	2	3	4
Demeanor				
GT Av. Impolite	.70* (.36)	.77* (.38)	.64 (.38)	.67* (.40)
Offense				
Felony		8.18 (13.76)		8.80 (13.28)
Encounter Crime		.22 (.69)		.41 (.74)
Demographic				
Sex			.25 (.57)	.42 (.63)
African-American			.11 (.58)	−.49 (.71)
Native American			1.01* (.39)	1.03* (.40)
Age			−.07 (.25)	.02 (.27)
Class			.51 (.33)	.67* (.35)

E

	1	2	3	4
Demeanor				
Hostile Demeanor	.37* (.21)	.34 (.22)	.31 (.22)	.25 (.23)
Offense				
Felony		8.05 (13.84)		8.66 (13.36)
Encounter Crime		.31 (.69)		.52 (.72)
Demographic				
Sex			.25 (.57)	.42 (.63)
African-American			.06 (.58)	−.50 (.71)
Native American			.96* (.39)	1.00* (.40)
Age			−.08 (.25)	.02 (.27)

DEMEANOR OR CRIME? 641

Table 1 (continued)

	Models			
Explanatory Variable	1	2	3	4
Class			.53* (.33)	.70* (.34)

NOTE: All models estimated with constant (not shown). Standard errors in parentheses.
* $p < .05$ (one tailed).

JUVENILE ENCOUNTERS

A minority of the juvenile offenders were in contact with Midwest City police because of alleged felonies ($N = 18$). Unlike the public drunkenness encounters, however, initial crime is significantly and consistently linked with arrest (see the Felony logit coefficients, Table 2). Encounter Crime was a very rare event ($N = 1$) and its logit coefficient is therefore not significant. None of the demographic variables is consistently and significantly linked with arrest.

Table 2. Juvenile Encounters: Multivariate Logistic Regression Models of Arrest on Explanatory Variables ($N = 200$)

	Models			
Explanatory Variable	1	2	3	4
		A		
Demeanor				
Deferent	.13 (.50)	.38 (.71)	−.05 (.53)	.13 (.75)
Impolite	−5.19 (16.40)	−5.18 (27.03)	−5.62 (16.10)	−5.49 (26.62)
Mixed	1.36* (.47)	1.79* (.65)	1.18* (.51)	1.44* (.68)
Offense				
Felony		5.40* (1.10)		5.44* (1.12)
Encounter Crime		5.83 (60.44)		6.19 (60.44)
Demographic				
Sex			−.41 (.64)	−.92 (.75)
African-American			1.26* (.55)	1.20* (.73)
Native American			2.24* (.99)	1.65 (1.33)
Age			.46 (.57)	−.26 (.65)
Class			.03 (.49)	−.45 (.62)

642   **LUNDMAN**

Table 2 (continued)

		Mo	dels	
Explanatory Variable	1	2	3	4
		B		
Demeanor				
Number Impolite	.06	.09	.04	.06
	(.04)	(.06)	(.04)	(.07)
Offense				
Felony		5.26*		5.42*
		(1.07)		(1.11)
Encounter Crime		3.55		3.99
		(22.26)		(22.26)
Demographic				
Sex			−.55	−1.08
			(.61)	(.72)
African-American			1.11*	1.25*
			(.55)	(.71)
Native American			2.28*	1.74
			(.98)	(1.46)
Age			.36	−.31
			(.55)	(.64)
Class			−.10	−.54
			(.46)	(.60)
		C		
Demeanor				
Dummy Impolite	1.11*	1.44*	.95*	1.19*
	(.43)	(.57)	(.46)	(.60)
Offense				
Felony		5.39*		5.49*
		(1.09)		(1.12)
Encounter Crime		3.69		4.15
		(22.26)		(22.26)
Demographic				
Sex			−.38	−.92
			(.63)	(.74)
African-American			1.13*	1.10
			(.54)	(.72)
Native American			2.32*	1.83
			(.97)	(1.32)
Age			.44	−.32
			(.56)	(.64)
Class			−.12	−.63
			(.46)	(.59)
		D		
Demeanor				
GT Av. Impolite	1.17*	1.50*	.95*	1.19*
	(.46)	(.60)	(.49)	(.64)
Offense				
Felony		5.38*		5.43*
		(1.08)		(1.11)
Encounter Crime		3.64		4.13
		(22.26)		(22.26)
Demographic				
Sex			−.37	−.84
			(.63)	(.74)
African-American			1.15*	1.15
			(.53)	(.71)

DEMEANOR OR CRIME? 643

Table 2 (continued)

Explanatory Variable	Models			
	1	2	3	4
Native American			2.26*	1.72
			(.97)	(1.34)
Age			.33	−.43
			(.56)	(.64)
Class			−.10	−.55
			(.46)	(.59)
		E		
Demeanor				
Hostile Demeanor	.78*	.85*	.65*	.74
	(.33)	(.44)	(.35)	(.48)
Offense				
Felony		5.28*		5.44*
		(1.08)		(1.11)
Encounter Crime		3.65		4.13
		(22.26)		(22.26)
Demographic				
Sex			−.47	−1.03
			(.62)	(.73)
African-American			1.10*	1.10
			(.54)	(.72)
Native American			2.41*	2.08
			(.96)	(1.29)
Age			.40	−.35
			(.56)	(.64)
Class			−.12	−.68
			(.46)	(.59)

NOTE: All models estimated with constant (not shown). Standard errors in parentheses.
* $p < .05$ (one tailed).

The indicators of demeanor again suggest that how this variable is represented is important. With Entirely Polite as the reference category, only Mixed encounters were significantly more likely to end in arrest in all of the models. Among the alternative representations, the Dummy Impolite and the GT Av. Impolite operationalizations also are significant in all of the models but Number Impolite is not.

Model specification also is important in the juvenile encounters as illustrated by the effects of Hostile Demeanor. It is significant with crime partially controlled or with the important demographic variables more fully controlled. Hostile Demeanor is not significant in the full model with the offense and demographic variables entered.

As was the case with the public drunkenness encounters, the juvenile encounters suggest that in addition to controlling for crime, issues of representation and, to a lesser extent, model specification are important when assessing the effects of demeanor.

644 LUNDMAN

TRAFFIC LAW VIOLATION ENCOUNTERS

The simple percentage data originally reported indicated that interaction effects were important but direct effects were not (also see appendix). Such is the case for most of the multivariate data in Table 3. None of the independent variables has consistent and statistically significant direct effects. But the interaction of Quota and Class is significant in all of the models, and the interaction of Quota and African-American is not significant in any of the models.

Table 3. Traffic Law Violation Encounters: Multivariate Logistic Regression Models of Arrest on Explanatory Variables ($N = 290$)

Explanatory Variable	Models				
	1	2	3	4	5
			A		
Demeanor					
Deferent	−.16	−.16	−.16	−.15	−.26
	(.25)	(.25)	(.26)	(.26)	(.40)
Impolite	−1.34*	−1.37*	−1.41*	−1.40*	−5.92
	(.81)	(.81)	(.82)	(.82)	(11.12)
Mixed	.57	.57	.54	.54	.32
	(.43)	(.43)	(.44)	(.45)	(.74)
Offense					
Quota		.37		.38	−2.02*
		(.24)		(.25)	(.90)
Demographic					
Sex			.31	.29	.36
			(.36)	(.36)	(.37)
African-American			.20	.21	.12
			(.41)	(.41)	(.68)
Native American			−1.76	−1.79	−2.11*
			(1.10)	(1.11)	(1.13)
Age			.06	.02	.09
			(.18)	(.18)	(.19)
Class			.09	.05	−.61
			(.25)	(.25)	(.39)
Quota by					
Deferent					.10
					(.53)
Impolite					5.08
					(11.15)
Mixed					1.92*
					(1.02)
African-American					.33
					(.88)
Class					1.35*
					(.52)
.					
			B		
Demeanor					
Number Impolite	−.00	−.00	−.01	−.01	−.31
	(.09)	(.09)	(.09)	(.09)	(.36)
Offense					

DEMEANOR OR CRIME? 645

Table 3 (continued)

Explanatory Variable	Models				
	1	2	3	4	5
Quota		.37		.38	−1.68*
		(.24)		(.24)	(.82)
Demographic					
Sex			.25	.24	.29
			(.35)	(.35)	(.36)
African-American			.27	.28	.09
			(.40)	(.40)	(.66)
Native American			−1.78	−1.80	−2.04*
			(1.10)	(1.10)	(1.12)
Age			.02	−.01	.01
			(.17)	(.18)	(.18)
Class			.06	.02	−.60
			(.25)	(.25)	(.38)
Quota by					
Number Impolite					.58
					(.40)
African-American					.40
					(.85)
Class					1.19*
					(.50)
			C		
Demeanor[a]					
Dummy Impolite	.17	.16	.13	.13	−.62
	(.35)	(.35)	(.36)	(.36)	(.67)
Offense					
Quota		.36		.38	−1.77*
		(.24)		(.24)	(.83)
Demographic					
Sex			.27	.26	.31
			(.36)	(.36)	(.36)
African-American			.26	.27	.13
			(.40)	(.40)	(.67)
Native American			−1.75	−1.77	−2.05*
			(1.10)	(1.11)	(1.12)
Age			.01	−.02	.04
			(.18)	(.18)	(.18)
Class			.04	.00	−.62
			(.25)	(.25)	(.38)
Quota by					
Dummy Impolite					1.49*
					(.83)
African-American					.38
					(.86)
Class					1.23*
					(.51)
			D		
Demeanor[a]					
GT Av. Impolite	.17	.16	.13	.13	−.62
	(.35)	(.35)	(.36)	(.36)	(.67)
Offense					
Quota		.36		.38	−1.77*
		(.24)		(.24)	(.83)
Demographic					
Sex			.27	.26	.31
			(.36)	(.36)	(.36)

646   LUNDMAN

Table 3 (continued)

	Models				
Explanatory Variable	1	2	3	4	5
African-American			.26	.27	.13
			(.40)	(.40)	(.67)
Native American			-1.75	-1.77	-2.05*
			(1.10)	(1.11)	(1.12)
Age			.01	-.02	.04
			(.18)	(.18)	(.18)
Class			.04	.00	-.62
			(.25)	(.25)	(.38)
Quota by					
GT Av. Impolite					1.49*
					(.83)
African-American					.38
					(.86)
Class					1.23*
					(.51)
		E			
Demeanor					
Hostile Demeanor	.15	.15	.12	.12	-.65
	(.33)	(.33)	(.33)	(.34)	(.63)
Offense					
Quota		.37		.38	-1.79*
		(.24)		(.24)	(.83)
Demographic					
Sex			.27	.26	.33
			(.36)	(.36)	(.37)
African-American			.26	.27	.13
			(.40)	(.40)	(.67)
Native American			-1.75	-1.78	-2.05*
			(1.10)	(1.11)	(1.12)
Age			.02	-.02	.04
			(.18)	(.18)	(.18)
Class			.04	.00	-.61
			(.25)	(.25)	(.38)
Quota by					
Hostile Demeanor					1.54*
					(.79)
African-American					.39
					(.86)
Class					1.23*
					(.51)

NOTE: All models estimated with constant (not shown). Standard errors in parentheses.
* Dummy Impolite and GT Av. Impolite have the same values for the traffic law violation encounters. That is why the logit coefficients are exactly the same.
* $p < .05$ (one tailed).

The patterns traced by the various representations of demeanor (in interaction with Quota) are now familiar. Whether demeanor matters is a function of how demeanor is represented. The Mixed and GT Av. Impolite representations are significant, as they were in the public drunkenness and juvenile encounters. The Hostile Demeanor representation also is significant, which has not previously been the case. Only the continuous Number Impolite representation is not significant, which has previously been the case as well.

DEMEANOR OR CRIME?   647

DISCUSSION

The reanalyzed data yield two initial observations. First, extralegal factors, including demeanor, may shape police exercise of discretion with initial and additional crime partially controlled and important demographic variables more fully controlled. In all three of the reanalyses, some representations of demeanor and some extralegal variables were significantly linked with formal police action. Second, the effects of demeanor depend on model specification and, especially, representation. While demeanor was consistently linked with arrest, statistical significance was clearly a function of representation.

This second observation warrants brief illustration. Consider again the data in the tables. If only the Number Impolite representation of demeanor had been presented, the conclusion would have been that demeanor does not matter. If only the GT Av. Impolite representation had been presented, the conclusion would have been that demeanor does matter. What the data suggest is that the effects of demeanor depend on how it is represented.

These initial observations raise two additional issues. The first is making sense of the various representations of demeanor. The second is why the Midwest City data provide some limited support for demeanor and other extralegal variables and the Metro–Dade data do not.

DEMEANOR AND REPRESENTATION

Making sense of varying representations of demeanor requires an understanding of why police officers may attend to demeanor in the first place. The existing answer is that when offenders are impolite, police get angry and then they get even (see Stark, 1972:59–60; Wilson, 1968:36–37). From this perspective, the manifest purpose of an arrest or a ticket is to punish an impolite offender for being in "contempt of cop" (Rothmiller, 1992:36–38).

Police attention to attitude, however, may serve a latent purpose as well (Merton, 1967:114–138). Unintended and unrecognized by police, getting angry and then getting even may function to identify the handful of offenders who require formal police action. The next four paragraphs in this section stitch together some of the essential elements of this expanded image of the importance of demeanor; the fifth paragraph returns to the issue of demeanor and representation.

A starting point is a clear understanding of the nature of police patrol work. Most of the problems police deal with involve minor violations of criminal or traffic laws (see Cumming et al., 1965; Hernandez, 1989:64; Sherman, 1992). There are few organizational (Rubinstein, 1973:153–154) or peer (Mastrofski and Parks, 1990) rewards for undertaking formal actions in these situations; justice does not require formal action (Bayley, 1991:98–115); and most of these minor problems are self-correcting in the wake of police words and deeds that routinely fall far short of formal action (Muir, 1977:77–81).

Although most of these problems are self-correcting, a minority are not. Some recur, others grow worse, and the police sometimes get called back. For the public drunkenness encounters examined, for example, most of those who were publicly drunk knew or quickly learned the situational rules of the police game and disappeared when told to do so (also see Skolnick and Bayley, 1986:40–43). A minority did not. Some public drunkenness offenders remained visible, others caused still more problems, and the police got called back. Similarly, most traffic law violators caught speeding appeared to listen to police words of warning and, even without a ticket, signaled repentance by listening carefully and driving away slowly (also see Bayley, 1991:39–40). A minority seemed oblivious to police words and sped away as soon as the police officer had clearly finished.

A highly useful skill for police is to find the few among the many who require formal action. That is, the few public drunks among the many for whom arrest is the only sure way of reducing visibility. The few juvenile offenders for whom arrest is the only certain method of keeping a problem from recurring. The few speeders for whom a ticket is the only possible way of securing even a modest reduction in average driving speed.

Finding the few is not easy because there are no formal guidelines. In this circumstance, attending to attitude may serve the latent function of helping police find the handful who require intervention. A public drunk who has a "bad attitude" is perhaps more likely to stay visible once a police officer has left. Juveniles in need of "attitude adjustment" may well be more likely to persist in their troublesome ways once police are gone. A driver who "flunks the attitude test" is possibly a driver for whom simple words of warning are nothing more than simple inconvenience. After all, if someone is "crazy-brave" (Muir, 1977:145) enough to be impolite to the police, there is good reason to worry about what else they might be capable of doing once the police are gone and only mere mortals remain.

When viewed from this perspective, the various representations of demeanor appear to tell a consistent tale. Two of the representations are always significant—Mixed and GT Av. Impolite—and both are difficult types of citizen interaction for police. Mixed encounters are interactional roller coasters for police as alleged offenders move between deferent, polite, and impolite statements. By operational definition, GT Av. Impolite encounters are difficult because they involve more than the average number of impolite statements. It was my experience that these types of encounters made Midwest City police angry, and the data show that they got even by undertaking formal actions significantly more often. It is also possible that Midwest City police found the few among the many, although their screening actions were neither intended nor recognized.

WHY THE MIDWEST CITY DATA AND NOT THE METRO-DADE DATA?

One obvious issue that remains is why the Midwest City data yield some limited support for existing arguments about the importance of extralegal variables and the Metro-Dade data do not. The possibilities are several. Three seem especially important and of the three, one can almost certainly be assessed.

There are important differences in place and time. The Midwest City data were collected in a relatively large city with a small minority population, in the very early 1970s, and thus at a time when all of the police patrol officers were male and only one was African-American. The Metro-Dade data were collected in a major metropolitan area with a large minority population, in the mid-1980s, and thus at a time when more of the police were female, African-American, and Hispanic (Bureau of the Census, 1987:29; Federal Bureau of Investigation, 1986:313; Flanagan and McGarrell 1986:58). These important differences in place and time could help explain the differences in findings. Midwest City's homogenous police department was a highly cohesive group (Skolnick, 1966:52–53), and there was strong agreement among the officers that attitude was important. Metro-Dade's demographically diverse police department was less visibly cohesive and conceivably less likely to evidence consensus on a variety of factors (Walker 1992:334–335), including demeanor.

The types of encounters examined also are clearly different. The Metro-Dade data were limited to disputes between citizens. The reanalyzed Midwest City data involved public drunkenness, juvenile, and traffic law violation encounters. The clear differences in types of encounters may well explain the differences in findings. Disputes, for example, may present fewer opportunities for formal police action than traffic law violation encounters wherein a ticket is without exception a possible outcome.

Different multivariate models were specified to assess the effects of demeanor. The models generated using the Midwest City data included partial controls for initial and additional crime, standard demographic variables, and multiple representations of demeanor. The models generated using the Metro-Dade data included initial and additional crime, whether an officer had received special training, and a single representation of demeanor. Hence, variations in model specification may explain the observed differences in findings, and it is possible to do more than simply speculate whether this might be the case. The Metro-Dade data permit at least a dummy impolite alternative representation of demeanor

650 LUNDMAN

and they may permit others. Equally important, because the Metro-Dade data were collected using conventional observational techniques, standard demographic information was probably obtained. It would be useful to reexamine the Metro-Dade data using models that include alternative representations of demeanor and standard demographic variables.

SUMMARY AND CONCLUSIONS

This paper examined whether demeanor and other extralegal variables exert effects on police exercise of discretion. The indicators of demeanor were limited to spoken words and initial and additional crime were partially controlled. The results suggest that the effects of demeanor depend on how demeanor is represented and, to a lesser extent, the specification of models. Some demographic factors also appear to be important when crime is partially controlled, but none of them consistently showed a significant effect.

Consequently, caution with respect to existing reports of the effects of demeanor remains necessary. This research involved weak controls for crime and an inferred linkage between offender attitude and police decisions. It also suggests that other problems may plague previous research on the effects of demeanor. They include how demeanor is represented and how models estimating demeanor are specified.

Some of the elements of an agenda for future research on the effects of demeanor and other extralegal variables are therefore clear. As Klinger (1994) correctly argued, comprehensively controlling for crime and limiting demeanor to legally permissible spoken words are essential. This research suggests that multiple representations of demeanor and more fully specified models may be important as well.

REFERENCES

Aldrich, John H. and Forrest D. Nelson
  1984   Linear Probability, Logit, and Probit Models. Beverly Hills, Calif.: Sage.

Baker, Mark
  1985   Cops. New York: Simon & Schuster.

Bayley, David
  1991   Forces of Order: Policing Modern Japan. Berkeley: University of
          California Press.

Black, Donald
  1971   The social organization of arrest. Stanford Law Review 23:1087–1111.
  1980   The Manners and Customs of the Police. New York: Academic Press.

Black, Donald and Albert J. Reiss, Jr.
  1970   Police control of juveniles. American Sociological Review 35:63–77.

DEMEANOR OR CRIME? 651

Boland, Barbara, Paul Mahanna, and Ronald Sones
  1992   The Prosecution of Felony Arrests, 1988. Washington, D.C.: U.S.
          Department of Justice.

Bouza, Anthony V.
  1990   The Police Mystique. New York: Plenum.

Bureau of the Census
  1986   Statistical Abstract of the United States, 1985. Washington, D.C.: U.S.
          Government Printing Office.

Cumming, Elaine, Ian Cumming, and Laura Edell
  1963   The policeman as philosopher, guide, and friend. Social Problems
          12:276–286.

Federal Bureau of Investigation
  1986   Crime in the United States, 1985: Uniform Crime Reports. Washington,
          D.C.: U.S. Government Printing Office.

Feinberg, Stephen E.
  1980   The Analysis of Cross-Classified Categorical Data. Cambridge, Mass.:
          MIT Press.

Flanagan, Timothy J. and Edmund F. McGarrell
  1986   Sourcebook of Criminal Justice Statistics—1985. Washington, D.C.: U.S.
          Government Printing Office.

Fletcher, Connie
  1990   What Cops Know. New York: Villard Books.
  1991   Pure Cop. New York: Villard Books.

Holdaway, Simon
  1983   Inside the British Police: A Force at Work. Oxford: Basil Blackwell.

Klinger, David A.
  1994   Demeanor or crime? An inquiry into why "hostile" citizens are more
          likely to be arrested. Criminology 32:475–493.

Goldman, Nathan
  1963   The Differential Selection of Juvenile Offenders for Court Appearance.
          New York: National Council on Crime and Delinquency.

Hernandez, James, Jr.
  1989   The Custer Syndrome: The American Public vs. The Police. Salem,
          Wisc.: Sheffield Publishing.

Lundman, Richard J.
  1974   Routine police arrest practices: A commonweal perspective. Social
          Problems 22:127–141.
  1979   Organizational norms and police discretion: An observational study of
          police work with traffic law violators. Criminology 17:159–171.

Lundman, Richard J., Richard E. Sykes, and John P. Clark
  1978   Police control of juveniles: A replication. Journal of Research in Crime
          and Delinquency 15:74–91.

Mastrofski, Stephen and Roger B. Parks
  1990   Improving observational studies of police. Criminology 28:475–496.

Merton, Robert K.
  1967   On Theoretical Sociology. New York: Free Press.

652   LUNDMAN

Muir, William K.
  1977   Police: Streetcorner Politicians. Chicago: University of Chicago Press.

Pastor, Paul
  1978   Mobilization in public drunkenness control: A comparison of legal and
            medical approaches. Social Problems 25:373–384.

Petersen, David
  1971   Informal norms and police practices: The traffic quota system. Sociology
            and Social Research 55:354–362.

Piliavin, Irving and Scott Briar
  1964   Police encounters with juveniles. American Journal of Sociology
            70:206–214.

Reiss, Albert J., Jr.
  1971   The Police and the Public. New Haven: Yale University Press.

Rothmiller, Mike, with Ivan G. Goldman
  1992   L.A. Secret Police: Inside the LAPD Elite Spy Network. New York:
            Pocket Books.

Rubinstein, Jonathan
  1973   City Police. New York: Farrar, Strauss & Giroux.

Sherman, Lawrence W.
  1980   Causes of police behavior: The current state of quantitative research.
            Journal of Research in Crime and Delinquency 17:69–100.
  1992   Attacking crime: Policing and crime control. In Michael Tonry and
            Norval Morris (eds.), Modern Policing. Chicago: University of Chicago
            Press.

Skolnick, Jerome H.
  1966   Justice Without Trial. New York: John Wiley & Sons.

Skolnick, Jerome H. and David Bayley
  1986   The New Blue Line: Police Innovation in Six American Cities. New
            York: Free Press.

Skolnick, Jerome H. and James Fyfe
  1993   Above the Law: Police and the Use of Excessive Force. New York: Free
            Press.

Smith, Douglas A.
  1984   The organizational context of legal control. Criminology 22:19–38.

Smith, Douglas A. and Jody R. Klein
  1983   Police agency characteristics and arrest decisions. In Gordon P. Whitaker
            and Charles D. Phillips (eds.), Evaluating Performance in Criminal Justice
            Agencies. Beverly Hills, Calif.: Sage.
  1984   Police control of interpersonal disputes. Social Problems 31:468–481.
  1986   The neighborhood context of police behavior. In Albert J. Reiss, Jr. and
            Michael Tonry (eds.), Communities and Crime. Chicago: University of
            Chicago Press.
  1987   Police response to interpersonal violence: Defining the parameters of
            legal control. Social Forces 65:767–782.

Smith, Douglas A. and Christy A. Visher
  1981   Street-level justice: Situational determinants of police arrest decisions.
            Social Problems 29:167–177.

DEMEANOR OR CRIME? 653

Smith, Douglas A., Christy A. Visher, and Laura Davidson
    1984   Equity and discretionary justice: The influence of race on police arrest decisions. The Journal of Criminal Law and Criminology 75:234–249.

Stark, Rodney E.
    1972   Police Riots. Belmont, Calif.: Wadsworth.

Sykes, Richard E. and Edward E. Brent
    1983   Policing: A Social Behaviorist Perspective. New Brunswick, N.J.: Rutgers University Press.

Sykes, Richard E. and John P. Clark
    1975   A theory of deference exchange in police-citizen encounters. American Journal of Sociology 81:584–600.

Sykes, Richard E., James C. Fox, and John P. Clark
    1976   A socio-legal theory of police discretion. In Arthur Niederhoffer and Abraham S. Blumberg (eds.), The Ambivalent Force: Perspectives on the Police. 2d ed. Hinsdale, Ill.: Dryden Press.

Van Maanen, John
    1978   The asshole. In Peter K. Manning and John Van Maanen (eds.), Policing: A View from the Street. Santa Monica, Calif.: Goodyear.

Visher, Christy A.
    1983   Sex, police arrest decisions, and notions of chivalry. Criminology 21:5–28.

Walker, Samuel
    1992   The Police in America: An Introduction. 2d ed. New York: McGraw-Hill.

Westley, William A.
    1970   Violence and the Police. Cambridge, Mass.: MIT Press.

Wilson, James Q.
    1968   Varieties of Police Behavior. Cambridge, Mass.: Harvard University Press.

Worden, Robert E.
    1989   Situational and attitudinal explanations of police behavior: A theoretical reappraisal and empirical assessment. Law & Society Review 23:667–711.

Worden, Robert E. and Alissa A. Politz
    1984   Police arrests in domestic disturbances: A further look. Law & Society Review 18:105–119.

Richard J. Lundman is Professor in the Department of Sociology at The Ohio State University. His current research focuses on the effects of work group demographics on police productivity and newspaper coverage of homicide.

654   LUNDMAN

Appendix.   Variables, Coding, Frequencies, and Percentage
            Ending in Formal Police Action (Arrest or
            Ticket), by Data Set (and Quota for Traffic
            Law Violation Encounters)

Variable	Coding	Frequency	Percent Ending in Formal Action
Public Drunkenness Encounters (*N* = 195)			
Dependent			
Arrest			
Yes	1		31.3
No	0		68.7
Demeanor			
Deferent	1	29	34.5
Impolite	1	32	37.5
Mixed	1	50	42.0
Polite (Ref. Category)		84	21.4
Dummy Impolite			
≥ 1	1	82	40.2
None	0	113	24.8
GT Av. Impolite			
Yes	1	41	43.9
No	0	154	27.9
Hostile Demeanor			
Very Impolite	3	28	35.7
Somewhat Impolite	2	54	42.6
Entirely Polite	1	113	24.8
Offense			
Felony			
Yes	1	7	100.0
No	0	188	28.7
Encounter Crime			
Yes	1	11	45.5
No	0	184	30.4
Demographic			
Sex			
Male	1	176	31.8
Female	0	19	26.3
Race-Ethnicity			
African-American	1	17	29.4
Native American	1	39	51.3
White (Ref. Category)		139	25.9
Age			
Senior	5	10	20.0
Adult	4	117	35.0
Young Adult	3	53	26.4
Adolescent	2	15	26.7
Child	1	0	
Class			
Declassified	3	45	48.9
Blue Collar	2	133	25.6
White Collar	1	17	29.4
Juvenile Encounters (*N* = 200)			
Dependent			
Arrest			
Yes	1		15.5
No	0		84.5
Demeanor			
Deferent	1	53	13.2
Impolite	1	5	0.0

DEMEANOR OR CRIME? 655

Appendix (continued)

Variable	Coding	Frequency	Percent Ending in Formal Action
Mixed	1	32	34.4
Polite (Ref. Category)		110	11.8
Dummy Impolite			
≥ 1	1	37	29.7
None	0	163	12.3
GT Av. Impolite			
Yes	1	28	32.1
No	0	172	12.8
Hostile Demeanor			
Very Impolite	3	7	28.6
Somewhat Impolite	2	30	30.0
Entirely Polite	1	163	12.3
Offense			
Felony			
Yes	1	18	94.4
No	0	182	7.7
Encounter Crime			
Yes	1	1	(1)
No	0	199	15.1
Demographic			
Sex			
Male	1	179	15.1
Female	0	21	19.0
Race-Ethnicity			
African-American	1	23	30.4
Native American	1	5	60.0
White (Ref. Category)		172	12.2
Age			
Senior	5	0	
Adult	4	0	
Young Adult	3	0	
Adolescent	2	162	16.0
Child	1	38	13.2
Class			
Declassified	3	3	(1)
Blue Collar	2	151	15.2
White Collar	1	46	15.2

		Quota = 0 (N = 125)		Quota = 1 (N = 165)	
		NC	%	NC	%
Traffic Law Violation Encounters					
Dependent					
Ticket					
Yes	1		42.4		51.5
No	0				
Demeanor					
Deferent	1	51	43.1	65	46.2
Impolite	1	4	(0)	6	33.3
Mixed	1	11	36.4	16	81.3
Polite (Ref. Category)		59	45.8	78	51.3
Dummy Impolite					
≥ 1	1	15	26.7	22	68.2
None	0	110	44.5	143	49.0
GT Av. Impolite					
Yes	1	15	26.7	22	68.2
No	0	110	44.5	143	49.0

656 LUNDMAN

Appendix (continued)

		Quota = 0 (N = 125)		Quota = 1 (N = 165)	
		NC	%	NC	%
Hostile Demeanor					
Very Impolite	3	1	(0)	1	(1)
Somewhat Impolite	2	14	28.6	21	66.7
Entirely Polite	1	110	44.5	143	49.0
Offense					
Quota					
Days 16-end	1			165	51.5
Days 1-15	0	125	42.4		
Demographic					
Sex					
Male	1	106	42.5	144	52.8
Female	0	19	42.1	21	42.9
Race-Ethnicity					
African-American	1	12	41.7	17	64.7
Native American	1	2	(0)	5	20.0
White (Ref. Category)		111	43.2	143	51.0
Age					
Senior	5	2	(1)	3	(1)
Adult	4	37	43.2	68	48.5
Young Adult	3	67	41.8	75	56.0
Adolescent	2	19	42.1	19	47.4
Child	1	0		0	
Class					
Declassified	3	0		1	(0)
Blue Collar	2	66	34.8	103	57.3
White Collar	1	59	50.8	61	42.6

[13]

The Effect of Different Police Enforcement Policies on the Control of Prostitution

E. NICK LARSEN*
Department of Sociology
University of Lethbridge

Cet article présente une analyse comparative du contrôle de la prostitution dans quatre villes canadiennes en utilisant le contrôle policier comme variable indépendante. Plusieurs études canadiennes récentes sur la prostitution ont évalué le bien-fondé de la loi actuelle, et la majorité des analystes ont conclut qu'il faut décriminaliser la prostitution. Cependant, notre analyse fait l'hypothèse qu'il est peu probable que la loi soit bientôt changée, et montre que la police canadienne possède déjà la discrétion légale voulue pour décider quand et où la loi doit être mise en application. Notre article présente une analyse qualitative des modes de contrôle policiers dans quatre villes (Vancouver, Edmonton, Winnipeg et Toronto) allant d'un contrôle très strict des prostituées et des consommateurs à une tolérance sélective et à la négotiation entre les différents groupes affectés. À partir de cette analyse, l'auteur conclut que la façon la plus appropriée de réduire les problèmes et les conflits politiques associés à la prostitution implique une tolérance sélective, combinée à une négociation entre les prostituées et les divers groupes touchés. L'article conclut par une discussion, basée sur une orientation féministe, des raisons expliquant pourquoi les tentatives de supprimer la prostitution ne fonctionneront pas et pourquoi les prostituées doivent être partie prenante de toute discussion concernant le contrôle de la prostitution.

This article conducts a comparative analysis of prostitution control in four Canadian cities using police enforcement policies as the independent variable. Most recent Canadian prostitution research has centred on assessing the adequacy of the existing law, and the majority of analysts have concluded that most prostitution offences ought to be decriminalized. However, the analysis in this article assumes that the law is unlikely to be changed in the near future, and instead argues that Canadian police already possess sufficient legal discretion to decide when and where they will enforce the law. The article conducts a qualitative analysis of police enforcement policies (in Vancouver, Edmonton, Winnipeg and Toronto) ranging from strict enforcement of the law against prostitutes, customers and both prostitutes and customers through to various forms of selective toleration and negotiation among the various affected groups. Based on this analysis, the writer concludes that the most effective way of reducing both the nuisance and the political conflict associated with prostitution involves selective toleration, combined with negotiation between prostitutes and other affected groups. The article concludes with a feminist oriented discussion of the reasons why attempts to suppress prostitution will not work and why the prostitutes themselves must be part of any discussions regarding the control of prostitution.

Introduction

The area of police decision making represents an increasingly important aspect of public policy formulation which is frequently ignored by Canadian policy researchers. This neglect is unfortunate since there is significant evidence to suggest that

the police possess significant legal autonomy over the implementation of criminal
laws. This autonomy is particularly important with respect to controversial but relatively minor offences such as prostitution.
In many respects, the contradiction between prostitution's relatively minor legal
status and the fact that street prostitution
is a significant problem in many large
Canadian cities creates a frustrating
dilemma for Canadian police forces. On one
hand, prostitution's minor legal status
limits both the priority which the police can
assign to prostitution control and their ability to deal effectively with it.[1] On the other
hand, street prostitution is usually concentrated in business and residential areas
near city centres, and this creates conflict
with the people who live and work in these
areas. This conflict forces police to choose
between expending large amounts of resources on what is legally a minor offence,
or being accused of failing to protect the
public and maintain order. In this respect,
police are often caught between liberal and
civil rights groups, who oppose increased
police enforcement, and residents and business owners who want the problem solved.
In recent years, feminist groups have in-
jected another dimension into an already
complex issue. This has further increased
the political factors with which Canadian
police must contend, and makes it imperative that they develop rational comprehensive policies to control street prostitution.

The intent of this article is to conduct a
comparative analysis of the manner in
which police in Vancouver, Edmonton,
Winnipeg and Toronto implemented recent
changes to Canada's prostitution laws.
Popularly referred to as Bill C-49, these
changes effectively criminalized all public
communication for the purposes of prostitution.[2] The impetus for this legislation can
be traced to the public clamour which arose
after the 1978 *Hutt* decision weakened the
previous anti-soliciting provisions contained in section 195.1 of the *Criminal
Code*.[3] Although there is considerable disagreement regarding the degree to which

the *Hutt* decision was responsible for the resulting prostitution problem,[4] there is little
doubt that it appeared to correlate with an
increase in the levels of street prostitution.
Canadian police forces almost universally
condemned the decision and blamed it for
the sudden increase in street prostitution
in many large cities. This instigated a political process which ultimately led to an in-
depth investigation of the entire prostitution issue by a non-parliamentary Special
Committee (hereafter referred to as the
Fraser Committee) (Larsen, 1995). Although the Fraser Committee concluded
that the best way to control prostitution
was to decriminalize most prostitution activities,[5] the federal government instead
enacted Bill C-49. This law clearly represents one of the toughest approaches to
prostitution control in western societies,
and it's proclamation on December 28, 1985
engendered bitter controversy.[6] Although
most Canadian police forces and many residents and business groups welcomed the
new law, many other groups argued that
the law was neither necessary nor likely to
solve the problems associated with street
prostitution.

As a result of the above controversy, the
Federal Department of Justice announced
that an evaluation of the law would be commenced within three years of its proclamation. This evaluation was duly completed
during 1987 and 1988 and the final report
was published in 1989 (Fleischman, 1989).
In general, the official evaluation concluded that Bill C-49 was almost completely ineffective in reducing the numbers of
prostitutes working in Vancouver and
Toronto. It also concluded that 'land use
conflicts' between street prostitutes and
residents and business people remained
high (Fleischman, 1989:76). Although it is
more difficult to draw conclusions about
Winnipeg since it was not a major evaluation site, the Winnipeg study did suggest
that the law's effect on levels of prostitution
had been temporary at best (Brannigan,
Knafla and Levy, 1989:212). Edmonton was
not included in the evaluation at all, and

thus there is no previously published evaluation of Bill C-49 in Edmonton. In addition to the official evaluation, several academics have also conducted independent evaluations and/or published articles dealing with various aspects of the law's implementation.[7] The academic articles have generally focused on more narrow issues. For example, Lowman (1991:322–24) argues that Vancouver police exhibited a greater gender bias against female customers than occurred in either Toronto or Montreal. He further notes that there was a class bias with respect to the male customers charged, and that lower class men were the most likely to be charged. O'Connell (1988) makes the same general point and argues that the new law has increased the levels of violence against prostitutes. While a detailed review of the literature is beyond the scope of this discussion, there is near unanimous agreement about the general ineffectiveness of the law.

Interestingly enough, despite the voluminous amount of research published to date, there has been little attempt to focus on police enforcement strategies as an independent variable. Inasmuch as the police were a major force behind the enactment of Bill C-49, there are several important questions which must be answered regarding the influence of *specific* police enforcement strategies on the effectiveness of the law. Inasmuch as Bill C-49 appeared to give police exactly what they had demanded in the post-*Hutt* debate (Larsen, 1992a), its implementation provides an ideal opportunity to address these questions. Accordingly, this discussion will outline the approaches taken by the different police forces and attempt to assess their relative effectiveness at reducing the numbers of visible prostitutes and the degree of conflict over prostitution. An attempt will also be made to assess the degree to which police forces developed comprehensive policies regarding the implementation of the law and the extent to which the police adopted political positions independent of their political masters. Finally, this article will conclude with several recommendations for future prostitution control policies.

Methodology for the Present Study

This article is based primarily on a qualitative research study carried out in the cities of Vancouver, Edmonton, Winnipeg and Toronto during 1989. The following methodological steps were used to conduct the research for this article.

1. An in-depth media search was conducted in all four cities to provide detailed information on the topic area. This search used the *Canadian News Index* to provide an exhaustive listing of all prostitution-related media articles between 1986 and 1989. While the main data-gathering technique was to review the contents of the articles themselves, the overall tone and media stance was also analysed. This step has been repeated in all cities every year until 1995.

2. A series of in-depth unstructured interviews was conducted with selected individuals identified as playing significant roles with respect to the issue. The aim of this step was to obtain information on the implementation of Bill C-49 from the perspective of the different interest groups which were involved. This survey included police officials, officials in the Federal Ministry of Justice and the appropriate provincial Ministries of the Attorney General, municipal politicians and local interest groups. An attempt was made to maximize the representativeness of the sample by employing a modified quota sample which included informants from all categories of groups in proportion to their numbers and perceived importance. However, because of the small sample size and the tendency of potential informants to 'self select' out of the interviews, it was not always possible to maintain the quotas to the end.[8] The interviews were unstructured and the questions were largely open-ended during the initial part of each interview. However, towards the

end of each interview, an attempt was made to structure the overall content, using a prepared questionnaire as a guide. In addition, the following steps were included as part of this survey:

a) The prepared questionnaire was mailed to those potential informants who had expressed a willingness to participate in this study but who were unavailable for personal interviews.

b) Follow-up questions were directed at certain individuals who had been identified as particularly reliable and/or helpful sources. These follow-up questions generally involved issues which had come to light as the research progressed, and thus had been omitted from the initial interviews. In certain instances, selected individuals were treated as 'key informants' and used to verify and/or cross-check information obtained from other sources. This step was repeated on a smaller scale in 1992–93 in all cities except Edmonton.

3. Regular walking patrols were conducted through the prostitution strolls in all cities. An attempt was made to systematically 'sample' all strolls at a variety of different times (i.e. afternoon, early evening, late night and early morning). The methodological technique involved a type of participant observation in which the walking pace, the distance from working prostitutes, and the amount of eye contact with prostitutes were all varied. The goal was to ascertain the degree of harassment to ordinary passers-by in the prostitution areas.[9] The patrols were carried out for 7 to 10 day periods in all cities in 1989. They were repeated in Vancouver in 1992 and have been periodically carried out in Toronto and Winnipeg from 1989 to 1995. They have not been repeated in Edmonton.

4. Existing documents were analysed to provide detailed information on the implementation of Bill C-49 as well as additional insights into the positions of various groups and organizations. This information was used to cross-check and verify the information obtained from the interviews. As well, the results obtained from each type of document were compared to those obtained from other types wherever possible. The following types of documents were included in this step:
– the minutes of municipal council meetings
– position papers published by community groups
– research reports
– committee reports

The Communicating Law in Vancouver

The Vancouver police implemented Bill C-49 by conducting several major sweeps against female prostitutes during January, 1986. Although both the number of arrests and the number of visible prostitutes were initially very low, it appears that prostitutes had intentionally stayed off the streets until they had a sense of how police would enforce the new law.[10] The number of arrests quickly increased once they returned to the streets, and the police charged over 90 prostitutes during January, 1986 (Lowman, 1989:A525). Although the number of arrests declined in subsequent months, largely as a result of several Provincial Court decisions invalidating parts of the law, the numbers of visible prostitutes continued to increase (Lowman, 1989:A527).[11] Although the court challenges were quickly over-ruled by the BC Supreme Court, and the police adopted even tougher measures against prostitutes, the conflict over street prostitution continued to escalate. Prosecutors began routinely asking that area restrictions be made part of probation orders for convicted prostitutes, even though this tactic simply pushed most prostitutes to the edge of the restricted area (*Vancouver Sun* (*VS*), May 9, 1986, p.A3).[12] The fact that the area restrictions did not apply to customers ensured that there was a steady supply of customers, and prostitutes quickly developed new strategies to avoid arrest.[13] This gender bias was reinforced by the fact that Vancouver police laid far fewer charges against customers (Lowman, 1989:A525), and many commentators argued that prostitutes would remain on the street as long as there was business.[14]

The conflict continued to escalate during 1987 and many community groups were arguing that Bill C-49 was clearly a sham. This was particularly true of the Mount Pleasant area, a working class neighbourhood near the city centre. The Vancouver Police had stopped responding to prostitution-related calls from Mount Pleasant, and many residents became convinced that the Vancouver police were using the area as a 'dumping ground' for street prostitution because of its lower social economic status.[15] In response to these criticisms, the police established the Mount Pleasant Task Force to co-ordinate enforcement efforts during the summer months of 1986 to 1988. The Task Force experimented with several 'harassment' tactics and organized periodic 'blitzs' against prospective customers.[16] In addition, they stepped up the frequency of visible uniformed patrols near where prostitutes were working to discourage customers from cruising the area.[17] Although the Task Force was reasonably effective, it is important to note that these tactics were not dependent on Bill C-49, and could have been used before it was implemented. Further, the activities of the Task Force displaced large numbers of prostitutes into the 'Downtown Eastside' area, including the respectable working class area known as Strathcona.[18]

The scenario which developed in Strathcona differed significantly from other areas, largely because both the residents and the police adopted radically different attitudes towards the problem. Instead of adopting confrontational tactics, residents and prostitutes negotiated compromise agreements outlining where the prostitutes could work. This approach was reinforced when police became involved and suggested that patrol personnel would tolerate some

prostitution if the prostitutes stayed away from schools and residential areas (*VS*, Apr. 20 1988, p.B5).[19] These tactics have been continued by the uniformed patrol team responsible for the area, and recent research indicates that the police have extended their liaison work with prostitutes to include regular consultations with the affected groups.[20] Thus, although there continue to be significant amounts of prostitution activity in the Strathcona area, there is remarkably little conflict.[21]

In summarizing this discussion of Bill C-49 in Vancouver, it is clear that the new law was not effective in reducing the numbers of street prostitutes in Vancouver.[22] Although it did give the police somewhat greater ability to control the areas in which prostitutes worked, and thus helped to quiet public controversy, harassment tactics using traffic codes and other non-criminal laws were far more effective. The most effective solution, however, involved the negotiation and other 'social work' tactics practised by the police and residents in Strathcona. While these tactics did not appear to reduce the numbers of prostitutes, they did minimize conflict. Unfortunately, this tactic has been limited to the Strathcona area, as residents and patrol teams in other areas have been unwilling to adopt it. As a result, conflict continues in the Mount Pleasant area, and there is an ongoing media debate regarding the best approach to the problem.[23]

The Communicating Law in Toronto

The initial implementation of Bill C-49 in Toronto appeared to involve much more planning and co-ordination than had been evident in Vancouver. After consultation with the prosecutor's office and other groups, the Toronto police announced that they intended to concentrate on customers, and that they would co-operate with social service programs designed to help prostitutes change their lifestyles (*Toronto Star* (*TS*) Jan. 26, 1986, p.A6). The police quickly adopted a pattern of arresting more customers than was occurring in Vancouver and this tactic succeeded in deterring many customers from cruising the strolls. Although the numbers of prostitutes working the streets also dropped drastically,[24] this success was short-lived. Many of the prostitutes who temporarily vacated the streets moved into escort agencies and massage parlours, a move which increased the number of pimps and their ability to dominate the prostitution trade.[25] The police subsequently placed greater emphasis on escort agencies, which forced prostitutes back on the street, where they adopted new tactics to cope with police surveillance. A Provincial court decision overturning Bill C-49 further increased the number of prostitutes and customers returning to the streets. At this point, the police changed their tactics and began concentrating on female prostitutes, but the evidence suggests that their efforts simply displaced many prostitutes to other areas. By August of 1986, street prostitution had again become a major problem and the police conducted a prolonged series of sweeps, in which female prostitutes were the major targets. Although Toronto police adopted many of the tactics being used in Vancouver,[26] the increased police activity failed to significantly affect the prostitution trade (*TS*, Aug. 22, 1986, p.A1).

The controversy and conflict regarding street prostitution intensified in 1987 despite much more aggressive enforcement of Bill C-49. The Toronto police formed the Police-Community Prostitution Committee to facilitate co-operation and information sharing with residents and business owners, the Crown Attorney's office and local politicians. The one group which was not included were the prostitutes themselves and this may explain why this Committee was less successful than the one in the Strathcona area of Vancouver. Further, although this Committee likely represented a genuine effort to deal effectively with citizens' concerns, it also was clearly an attempt to appease some of the most

vocal groups and to subvert local political activity to serve the interests of the police. In this respect, it was relatively successful at minimizing public criticism of the police, and directing public lobbying efforts against politicians.[27]

Although the police were able to minimize public conflict, they were not able to reduce the number of prostitutes. Despite their aggressive enforcement of Bill C-49, the number of prostitutes on the streets doubled between January and October of 1987 (*Globe & Mail (G & M)*, Oct.15, 1987, p.A3). The fact that most of this increase occurred after the police shifted their emphasis from customers to prostitutes underscored the futility of tougher laws against prostitution. Although the police ultimately returned to their previous concentration on customers, there is little evidence to suggest that this was effective. Although conviction rates remained high, the number of visible prostitutes also remained high.[28] Further, public dissatisfaction began to grow and the Police-Community Liaison Committee was no longer able to contain it. In order to appear more effective, Toronto police instituted a practice of moving prostitutes from area to area, never allowing them to stay in one area for lengthy periods of time.[29] These practices have been continued to the present time, and although some prostitution activity has even been displaced into Toronto's outer suburbs, this has simply spread the nuisance problem over a larger area. The Toronto media continue to debate the prostitution issue and there are constant reports of conflict between residents and prostitutes. In this respect, it is instructive that local politicians have started calling for legalized 'zones of tolerance' and bawdy houses (*G & M*, Oct. 26, 1991, p.A10).

The Communicating Law in Winnipeg

The implementation of Bill C-49 in Winnipeg tended to follow the patterns evident in Vancouver and Toronto. Although the Winnipeg Police were somewhat unique in that they explicitly instituted a short 'period of grace' following the proclamation of the law, their subsequent enforcement of the law against prostitutes and customers quickly drove most prostitutes off the streets (*Winnipeg Free Press* (*WFP*), Jan 14, 1986, p.3).[30] However, although the prostitution issue remained quiet in the main female stroll,[31] controversy quickly arose in two other prostitution areas. The first instance involved complaints from residents of the Hill area about prostitution-related activities in the lanes and parking lots surrounding the Legislative Buildings.[32] The police responded by setting up road blocks and conducting traffic checks and other harassment activities. Although this temporarily alleviated the problem, it reappeared again in early fall when residents renewed their complaints. This precipitated several public meetings involving residents, the police and the gay community. Numerous possible solutions were discussed, and ultimately the City of Winnipeg installed permanent traffic barriers to prevent motorists from cruising through the area. Although this tactic simply displaced the prostitutes and their customers into a more heavily populated part of the area, changes in attitudes by prostitutes, combined with stepped up police patrols, apparently solved the problem. There has been no further public controversy, and some observers credit the involvement of the gay community for the success of the negotiations (*WFP*, Sept. 26, 1986, p.3).[33]

The success of the police action in the Hill area stands in stark contrast to the situation which arose in the 'lo-track' area during this time period.[34] In this case, a police attempt to clean up the Main Street strip displaced many prostitutes into the adjacent residential area. This led to conflict with residents, who complained that the police were ignoring the problem because of their poor economic status (*WFP*, Oct 17, 1986, p.3). The police responded

with a series of sweeps against female prostitutes, and although this crackdown was largely ineffective, it destroyed their previously good relationship with the prostitute community. POWER quickly condemned the police for ignoring male customers and also accused them of ignoring assaults against prostitutes.[35] Although the police denied both accusations, their relationship with the prostitutes deteriorated sharply after this point. The situation was exacerbated by the attitudes of residents and business owners in the area, many of whom exhibited very inflexible attitudes towards the prostitutes.[36] Thus, the problem has not been resolved and conflict over prostitution continues in the area to the present time.

In summarizing the discussion of Bill C-49 in Winnipeg, it is clear that the law was not effective in reducing the amount of street prostitution. Although there is little firm evidence regarding levels of street prostitution before and after the law, most observers agree that there has been no long-term reduction in the numbers of visible prostitutes (*WFP*, Nov. 23, 1988, p.1).[37] Further, despite aggressive enforcement of the law in Winnipeg, it actually appeared less effective than the more tolerant approach taken by the police in Calgary.[38] In terms of reducing political conflict, a clear class bias emerged in which the police were much more responsive to public concerns from the middle class Hill area than they were to those emanating from the 'lo-track' area. The police continue to argue that they are unable to control prostitution because of the overly lenient attitudes of the courts and call for even tougher laws to deal with the issue. There is an ongoing media debate regarding street prostitution and recent polls have indicated that a majority of the public are in favour of legalized red light areas (*WFP*, March 10, 1994, pp.D8–D9). However, the Winnipeg police have indicated that they have no intention of tolerating prostitution in any area of the city (*WFP*, April 25, 1994, p.C10).

The Communicating Law in Edmonton

The implementation of Bill C-49 in Edmonton parallelled the situation which occurred in the other cities. The Edmonton Police initially eschewed the major sweeps which were taking place in Vancouver and Toronto, and adopted a 'routine enforcement' approach which concentrated on female prostitutes. Although the numbers of prostitutes on the streets declined drastically immediately following the implementation of the law,[39] they quickly increased again once prostitutes became accustomed to police activity. Although the Edmonton Police subsequently stepped up their enforcement activities, and experimented with a variety of harassment tactics, there is little evidence that these tactics exerted any long-term effect.[40] Indeed, police activities simply displaced the prostitutes into other areas (*Edmonton Journal (EJ)*, Sept. 6, 1987, p.A1) and the familiar class bias developed insofar as the police appeared to place a greater emphasis on middle class areas than they did on lower and working class areas.[41] However, once the working class residents organized into lobby groups, the police adopted a stated policy of using traffic checks and other harassment tactics to routinely displace the prostitutes from one area to another.[42] These harassment tactics were supplemented by periodic sweeps against both prostitutes and customers. Although this response initially appeared to satisfy both the working class residents and the Jasper Avenue business owners,[43] the problem was never permanently solved and street prostitution periodically re-surfaces as a political issue in Edmonton.[44]

In concluding this discussion of Bill C-49 in Edmonton, several important issues need to be emphasized. First, despite public and political pressure, the Edmonton Police did not take a particularly hard line in enforcing the law.[45] Indeed, Edmonton Police publicly stated that prostitution could only be repressed by using huge amounts of police resources which would detract from more important police operations (*EJ*, Sept. 9, 1988, p.A1). Further, the Edmonton Police intentionally maintained a good relationship with the street prostitutes.[46] Although this policy was partially motivated by the increasingly critical reaction of the media to police crackdowns on prostitution,[47] it clearly assisted the police when they decided to negotiate with prostitutes in an attempt to minimize the nuisance associated with street prostitution. Although this practice never reached the level of the Strathcona area of Vancouver, it nevertheless appeared relatively successfully in defusing some of the tensions.[48] Thus, although the overall scope of the negotiation was quite limited, it represents the one tactic which appeared to minimize conflict over the issue.

Summary and Conclusions

The analysis in this article has focused on the degree to which different police enforcement strategies reduced prostitution and/or the amount of conflict over the issue. Inasmuch as these two criteria were also the stated goals enshrined in Bill C-49, it is considered important to first summarize the degree to which the enforcement of Bill C-49 helped achieve these goals before discussing broader issues relating to the control of prostitution.[49] In this respect, although there were many specific differences in the way Bill C-49 was implemented in the four cities, the same general pattern emerged in which levels of street prostitution initially plummeted but quickly rebounded to previous (or even higher) levels. Further, although Toronto's emphasis on customers was initially more effective than Vancouver's focus on female prostitutes, neither approach was successful over the long term. Similarly, there was no significant difference in effectiveness noted between routine enforcement and major sweeps. In all cities, prostitutes quickly adapted to routine enforcement activities and the long-term effect of major sweeps was extremely limited. Thus, the evidence collected in this study appears to indicate that the enforcement of Bill C-49 was almost completely ineffective at reducing either the levels of street prostitution or the conflict associated with it. This finding generally supports the official evaluation conducted by the Department of Justice and other published studies.

The almost complete failure of one of the toughest prostitution laws in western societies can be explained with reference to selected aspects of feminist theory. However, before these issues can be discussed, it is important to examine two enforcement tactics which were relatively effective. Once it became clear that Bill C-49 was not having the desired effect, all police departments in this study adopted harassment tactics to deter both prostitutes and their customers. These tactics, which included traffic stops and the aggressive deployment of uniformed patrols near where prostitutes were working, displaced prostitutes to different areas. This reduced public pressure on the police, and all police departments gradually adopted the practice of routinely displacing prostitution from one area to another so that the nuisance associated with street prostitution would not be imposed on any one area for a prolonged period of time. Although this tactic did not reduce the overall number of prostitutes, it was somewhat effective at reducing the conflict associated with prostitution. However, it is important to note that these harassment tactics were not dependent on Bill C-49 and could have been used before the law was implemented. Although some police officials have argued that these tactics require the enforcement threat of Bill C-49 to make them work successfully, most prostitutes argue that it is a fact that business plummets under harassment conditions which forces them move to another area.[50]

Although the harassment tactics reduced the conflict associated with street prostitution, they did not significantly reduce the overall nuisance effect of street prostitution. All they really accomplished was to keep the nuisance effect moving from area to area so that public complaints and political activity were minimized. Moreover, this reduction in public pressure was accomplished at the expense of large amounts of police resources which diverted attention away from other more serious offences. Although the Edmonton police were the only force to publicly complain about the amount of attention that they were forced to give to prostitution control, officers in other forces also made the same point in private interviews.[51] In addition, the harassment tactics created unnecessary problems for prostitutes, and led to civil rights abuses in extreme cases. Various informants attested to witnessing verbal abuse directed against prostitutes and potential customers, and in some cases illegal searches. The inappropriateness of utilizing such tactics to suppress a summary offence such as prostitution is accentuated by the fact that they were marginally effective in any case.

Another approach which was somewhat more effective involved negotiation between prostitutes and various other interest groups. This strategy was most successful in the Strathcona area of Vancouver, where the patrol units have taken a very proactive approach to working with both prostitutes and residents. As a result, conflict over street prostitution has been largely eliminated despite the fact that the actual levels of street prostitution remain high. Negotiation was also used on a smaller scale in Edmonton and Winnipeg, where it helped defuse some of the tension on a short-term basis. However, because the practice was discontinued after a short period of time, conflict in these cities has periodically reappeared. Finally, although the Toronto police adopted the most ambitious approach to negotiating with residents and business groups, their attempts were less successful than in the other cities, largely because they failed to include prostitutes in the negotiation process.

This latter point appears to be the key

48 E. Nick Larsen

variable in terms of effectively controlling the nuisance associated with street prostitution. It is also crucial to achieving 'successful' prostitution control as defined in much broader terms than those currently under discussion in this article. While a detailed discussion of feminist theory is clearly beyond the scope of this analysis, it is considered crucial to situate the remainder of this discussion within one major precept of feminist analysis as it relates to prostitution. In this respect, most feminists would argue that prostitutes are generally oppressed women who become involved in prostitution because they have no other economic options (Cooper, 1989; Freeman, 1989; Shaver, 1988).[52] This is the major reason why most of the tactics discussed in this article were largely ineffective in reducing either the numbers of prostitutes or the conflict associated with street prostitution. Simply stated, any attempt to control prostitution without taking into account the interests of prostitutes is doomed to failure because 'leaving the business' is simply not a viable option for most prostitutes. This explains why the negotiations in Vancouver, Edmonton and Winnipeg, which included prostitutes, were more successful than those in Toronto, which excluded them. Most prostitutes' spokespersons interviewed in this study have continually reiterated that they simply want a location where they can conduct business without undue police interference, and that they are willing to co-operate with other affected groups in order to achieve this.[53]

The above discussion leads to the conclusion that prostitution itself cannot be eliminated through legal prohibitions, and thus police efforts should be aimed at managing it to achieve a compromise between the rights and interests of all affected groups.[54] This will only be accomplished if the rights of prostitutes are considered as equally important as the rights of residents and business owners. Since prostitution itself is perfectly legal in Canada, it is logical that prostitutes should be permitted to operate as long as they meet certain condi-

tions designed to protect the rights and interests of other groups.[55] This concept is not in itself particularly radical, as many other writers have suggested that some form of zoning is the best approach to controlling the nuisance of street prostitution. Indeed, the Fraser Committee discussed earlier recommended that most prostitution activities be decriminalized and that prostitutes be allowed to work legally in fixed off-street locations. Unfortunately, actual legal zoning is not possible unless prostitution itself is decriminalized[56] and this is unlikely to happen in the near future. This conclusion would appear to lead the discussion into a stalemate; however, the police have sufficient legal discretion to decide the conditions under which they are going to enforce Bill C-49. Thus, the obvious solution to the dilemma is for the police to establish public guidelines stipulating where and under what conditions Bill C-49 will be stringently enforced, and under what conditions prostitution will be tolerated. The public proclamation of such guidelines will permit prostitutes (and their customers) to modify their behaviour to meet the guidelines.[57]

There are several additional recommendations which are necessary to ensure the success of the approach articulated above. First, based on the evidence discussed in this article, it is considered mandatory that this policy be developed in consultation with all of the affected groups, including prostitutes. It is also important that these groups be encouraged to open a dialogue with each other as well as with the police.[58] Second, the guidelines must be imposed on all components of the police, as previous negotiations were sometimes undermined by a lack of co-ordination and co-operation between Vice Squads and patrol units in some cities. Finally, inasmuch as street prostitution is more dangerous for prostitutes and also more likely to cause conflict with other groups, every attempt should be made to encourage off-street prostitution in the form of escort agencies and/or bawdy houses.[59] In order to prevent pimps and organized crime from controlling off-street prostitution, it is recommended that police forces develop strategies to effectively monitor escort agencies and bawdy houses without forcing prostitutes out on the street. In this respect, the periodic crackdowns against bawdy houses and escort agencies in Vancouver and Toronto clearly worked against the primary goal of reducing street prostitution, as well as indicated that the police in these cities had failed to develop a coherent strategy for dealing with the issue.

In closing this discussion, the writer is well aware that the above suggestions will undoubtedly provoke a negative reaction from the police on the grounds that they cannot legally agree not to enforce a specific law. Although this is their standard argument regarding the issue of tolerance, it must be pointed out that the police routinely establish policies which stipulate that certain offences will not be enforced in certain circumstances. Further, it can be argued that the implementation of the approach articulated in this article would offer several practical advantages for the police aside from greater effectiveness in the management of prostitution. In this respect, there is increasing evidence that Canadian public opinion favours some form of quasi-legal toleration as long as it effectively controls the nuisance associated with street prostitution. Moreover, the media debate discussed in the preceding pages suggests that municipal politicians are also willing to accept some form of 'formalized' toleration. Thus, even if the strategy did not work, the police would be able to argue that they had simply been attempting to implement the expressed wishes of the public and their political masters, and could 'legitimately' demand an even tougher approach to the problem. In either case, i.e. either the strategy works or it does not, the public proclamation of an intent to tolerate prostitution under certain circumstances might finally force the federal government to clarify prostitution's legal status. Aside from the other issues discussed in this ar-

ticle, this would constitute a desirable end in itself.

Notes

* The empirical research conducted in this study was partially funded by research grants from the Criminology Research Centre at the University of Manitoba and a SSHRC grant administered by Brock University. The author would like to thank Professor John Lowman of the School of Criminology at Simon Fraser University for sharing previously published research on the topic. In addition, the suggestions of the anonymous reviewers were particularly helpful in re-focusing the analysis in parts of this article.

1 The most commonly charged prostitution-related activity is 'communicating for the purposes of prostitution' as outlined in S. 212.1 of the *Criminal Code*. This is a 'summary' offence which precludes arrest on 'reasonable' grounds and does not permit offenders to be fingerprinted. Thus, the police must resort to time-consuming entrapment tactics and are unable to properly identify prostitutes because many of them use several aliases.

2 Bill C-49 Provisions:
(1) Every person who in a public place or in any place open to public view:
a) stops or attempts to stop any motor vehicle, impedes the free flow of pedestrian or vehicular traffic or ingress to or egress from premises adjacent to that place, or
b) Stops or attempts to stop any person or in any manner communicates or attempts to communicate with any person
for the purpose of engaging in prostitution or of obtaining the sexual services of a prostitute is guilty of an offence punishable on summary conviction.
(2) In this section, 'public place' includes any place to which the public have access as of right or by invitation, express or implied,and any motor vehicle located in a public place or in any place open to public view.

3 *Hutt v. The Queen* (1978), 32 C.C.C. (2d) 418. This decision by the Supreme Court of Canada ruled that 'soliciting for the purposes of prostitution' was only an offence if it was 'pressing and persistent'.

4 See for example: Lowman (1986). Lowman argues that the Vancouver problems were more closely related to the closure of two nightclubs which catered to prostitutes and their customers. This action drove large numbers of prostitutes onto the street, where they migrated to business and residential areas. See also Larsen (1992a). Larsen links the problem to patterns of gentrification occurring in major cities. This process, which peaked

during the late 1970s and early 1980s, saw previously run-down houses in prostitution areas bought and renovated by middle-class professionals, who then lobbied for the removal of the prostitutes.

5   In particular, the Fraser Committee recommended that prostitutes be allowed to work legally in fixed indoor locations and that prostitution generally should be controlled by using the same laws which were used to regulate business generally (Larsen, 1995).

6   It should be noted that Bill C-49 legally became S. 195.1 of the *Canadian Criminal Code* once it was proclaimed. However, the numbering of the section changed during the time period covered by this article and the term Bill C-49 will be used throughout to avoid ambiguity or confusion.

7   It should be noted that the evaluation was mandated by the legislation itself. The evaluation was supervised by the Department of Justice but was carried out by independent contractors. The major sites were Vancouver, Calgary (which also included brief assessments of Regina and Winnipeg), Toronto (including several smaller centres in Ontario), Montreal (including Quebec City and several smaller centres) and Halifax. It should be noted that many of the contractors were university academics, who have since updated their original work and published academic articles. Thus the academic literature is generally not independent of the official evaluation.

8   In general, politicians were the most likely to decline to participate while the local interest groups were the least likely to opt out.

9   Given that the strolls were in residential and business areas in all four cities, this was seen as crucial to determining the level of nuisance associated with street prostitution.

10 This information is derived from a private interview with Marie Arrington, President of the Vancouver chapter of Prostitutes and Other Women for Equal Rights (POWER). All informants will be identified in detail in a footnote the first time they are cited and thereafter by their name alone.

11 The situation was exacerbated when Mayor Mike Harcourt directed the Vancouver Police to move against several bawdy houses and forced even more prostitutes out on the street (*Vancouver Sun*, Mar. 27, 1986, p.A3). Considering that the major goal was to keep prostitutes off the street, this action suggests that the Vancouver Police and City Council had failed to develop a coherent strategy for dealing with prostitution.

12 In fact, the area restrictions may have exacerbated the problem by expanding the red light area. Referred to by some as the 'creeping red light district' phenomenon, it spread the problem of street prostitution over a larger area and actually increased the amount of public outcry.

13 Marie Arrington and S/Sgt. Thompson (Team 6 – Vancouver Police) both argued that prostitutes were able to develop coping strategies to minimize the possibility of arrest.

14 The practice was also criticized by prostitutes' spokespersons and some defence lawyers because it contravened the principle of equal enforcement (Marie Arrington, President of POWER; Tony Serka and Bridget Eider, Defence Attorneys).

15 This information was provided by Tim Agg and Phylis Alfeld, leaders of two community organizations which were created by residents to attempt to do something about the prostitution problem in Mount Pleasant. Although these organizations were in fact dominated by professionals moving into the area, there was significant participation from the original working class residents. In any case, the perception that the area was working class still remained in the minds of police and politicians. (Libby Davies, Vancouver Alderperson)

16 In some instances, these tactics extended to questionable and even illegal behaviour on the part of the police. For example, the video 'Anywhere But Here' interviewed informants who witnessed police officers searching prostitutes' purses and scattering the contents on the ground. Such activities are clearly illegal, and all the more extreme considering that the women had simply been standing quietly on street corners.

17 S/Sgt Thompson, Prostitution Liaison Officer for Team 6.

18 This area was located along the Vancouver Harbour and near Chinatown. It encompassed skid row, a large area of public housing, some established working class residential districts and the trendy restaurant and shopping area known as 'Gastown'. Although the area had always contained significant amounts of prostitution, the transient nature of the population, combined with a preponderance of seedy bars and other transient oriented businesses, minimized conflict.

19 It should be noted that although the majority of the evidence supports the scenario outlined above, there was some disagreement about the effectiveness of the initial police response to the Strathcona situation. A group of Strathcona residents who were unhappy with the levels of street prostitution in the area organized the Strathcona Prostitution Action Committee (SPAC) in May of 1988. The group organized a short lobbying campaign aimed at Vancouver Police and City Hall. This quickly resulted in the formation of a Special Police Liaison Committee for Strathcona which met with the dissatisfied residents and drew up a plan of increased uniformed patrols. Three area prostitutes also attended the meeting and participated in the discussion and negotiations over the problem (Vancouver City Manager's Report to Council, August 26, 1988). This appeared to re-

solve the issue, as there was no further indication of trouble in the area.

20 Cst. Griff Simons, Team 3, Vancouver Police. In a 1992 interview, Constable Simons stated that he and his partner made a point of developing rapport with prostitutes in their area so as to facilitate their co-operation. They also attended monthly liaison meetings with prostitutes, residents and business owners. This approach is apparently working well, and several informants from various organization in the area expressed satisfaction with the police activity. Further, one community leader informed this writer that they were very satisfied with the willingness of prostitutes to co-operate. (Muggs Sigurdson, Strathcona Resident, Interview conducted in February, 1992.)

21 This assertion is based on a series of interviews conducted in 1992. It is also noteworthy that there has been little mention of the Strathcona area in the media since 1988.

22 In addition to the qualitative information gathered for this study, the official evaluation conducted by the Department of Justice came to similar conclusions. For example, although the average number of visible prostitutes did decline in 1986, it rebounded to even higher levels in 1987. (The figures were 1985–44.0, 1986–23.6, 1987–54.2.) (Lowman, 1989:95).

23 An additional aspect of police enforcement patterns detracted from any attempt to mediate a solution in Mount Pleasant. The Vice squad was much more active in Mount Pleasant than it was in Strathcona. The Vice Squad consistently refused to become involved in any negotiations over prostitution and this scuttled an attempt to establish an informal 'red light district' in Mount Pleasant prior to the implementation of the law (Larsen, 1992a). Although the Vice Squad operated in Strathcona, it had less effect there. (S/Sgt Jim Maitland, Vancouver Police Vice Squad – Interview in February, 1992.)

24 In April, the police announced that the numbers of prostitutes had dropped to approximately one third of their pre-Bill C-49 levels (200–300 vs. 600–700) (*Toronto Strar (TS)* Apr. 27, 1986, p.A8). The police claimed that their strategy of going after the customers was effective because middle class customers (often with families) were much more easily deterred than prostitutes, most of whom already had long criminal records.

25 This was because pimps now found it easier to control their girls than when they were on the streets. While a prostitute working the streets could 'turn tricks' without giving her pimp his share, this would be more difficult in an agency where the pimp could monitor all calls without leaving the office. The police were virtually powerless to intervene since it was all underground, and they lacked an effective way of monitoring the activi-

ties of the pimps (*TS*, Apr. 27, 1986, p.A8).

26 For example, they instituted the practice of detaining arrested prostitutes overnight, despite the fact that persons charged with summary offences are normally released on appearance notices. They also asked the courts to impose a 9:00 pm curfew, combined with area restrictions, as conditions of bail (*Globe & Mail*, Aug. 23, 1986, p.A6).

27 A senior Toronto police Superintendent informed this writer that he regularly used the committee to 'make noise' when he wanted something from City Hall.

28 This assertion is also supported by the evaluation conducted by the Department of Justice, which found that the numbers of prostitutes and their working hours had not been significantly reduced by the law (Moyer and Carrington, 1989).

29 S/Insp Jim Clark, OIC – Toronto Police Morality Division, Interview in June 1989; S/Supt John Getty, Chair – Police-Community Liaison Committee, Interviews in June 1989 & June 1992.

30 The Winnipeg Police announced that they could find no evidence that prostitutes were moving into hotels and escort agencies or that pimps were taking over the prostitution scene in Winnipeg (*WFP*, Jan 14, 1986, p.3).

31 Referred to as the 'hi-track,' this stroll was centred on Albert Street, an area of restaurants and boutiques near the downtown and adjacent to City Hall and Chinatown. Many of the area merchants welcomed the prostitutes because they attracted street traffic which was good for business.

32 The Hill area located near the legislature in downtown Winnipeg is the centre of the male prostitution in Winnipeg. The males were frequently drunk (as opposed to being on drugs) and were very noisy. They also made a practice of turning tricks in full view of apartment windows and passing traffic.

33 It is worth emphasizing that the Hill area is noted for a high percentage of gay residents, and that their willingness to negotiate with the prostitutes facilitated a resolution to the issue. It is also significant that the gay community has played a significant role in counselling male prostitutes and that this has helped gain their co-operation.

34 The 'lo-track' area is a lower/working class residential area near skid row. It is used primarily by younger, less expensive female prostitutes and male transvestites.

35 *WFP*, Oct. 19, 1986, p.3. Debbie Reynolds, President of POWER, also repeated these accusations in a 1989 interview.

36 In a 1989 interview, Inspector Ray Johns, current OIC of the Vice Division suggested that the attitudes of residents and business owners was at least partially responsible for the controversy.

37 This conclusion was also supported by statements

from the Winnipeg Police and representatives of POWER.

38 This conclusion is based on the research conducted for the Minister of Justice evaluation. This evaluation compared the effect of Bill C-49 in Winnipeg, where the police had devoted considerable efforts to enforcing it, to Calgary, where the police had given it a much lower priority. Changes in the numbers of street prostitutes were about the same in both cities, thus convincing the researchers that the law had not exerted a major impact on street prostitution in the Prairie Region (Brannigan, Knafla and Levy, 1989).

39 For example, on February 7, 1986, the police estimated that the numbers of prostitutes working Edmonton's streets on an average night had been reduced from 40–50 to six or seven (*Edmonton Journal (EJ)*, Feb. 7, 1986, p.B7). Since it appeared that the street prostitutes were not being displaced into escort agencies or bars, the Edmonton Police were generally happy with the law during the first few weeks of its operation.

40 S/Sgt Whitton, Edmonton Police Morality Squad – Interview conducted in August, 1989.

41 For example, the police quickly responded to complaints from the middle-class residents in Riverdale and business owners along Jasper Avenue, but appeared more inclined to tolerate prostitution in the working class Boyle-McCaully area (*EJ*, Sept. 5, 1987, p.B1; *EJ*, Sept 8, 1987, p.A1).

42 The City also installed traffic barriers in the prostitution areas but these proved almost completely ineffective (Rick Milligan – Edmonton City Engineer, Interview conducted in August, 1989).

43 Karen Dandemueller and Ruth Gelderman (Residents' Groups Spokespersons) and Claude Buzon (Jasper Avenue Restaurant Owner) – Interviews conducted in August, 1989.

44 One of the more recent instances of political conflict occurred in early 1993, when residents and business owners in the Queen Mary and Central McDougal areas lobbied the police to get rid of the prostitutes and drug dealers infesting their neighbourhood. Although the police crackdown remedied the situation somewhat, the police themselves described it as a never-ending problem that could never be cured completely (*Alberta Report*, June 21, 1993, p.14).

45 For example, they often gave out appearance notices to prostitutes charged twice in the same night (*EJ*, Sept. 11, 1987, p.B1). In addition, the practice of seeking area restrictions as probation and/or bail conditions was never adopted in Edmonton (Mike Allen, Senior Crown Attorney – Interview conducted in August, 1995).

46 For example, Anne Dolina, spokesperson for the Alliance for the Safety of Prostitutes (ASP), publicly commended the Edmonton Police for their enlightened approach and obvious desire to main-

tain a good working relationship with prostitutes (*EJ*, May 24, 1988, p.A1). This policy was also confirmed by S/Sgt. Whitton and Insp. Noel Day of the Edmonton Police Morality Squad.

47 John Geiger, Columnist for the *Edmonton Journal* – Interview conducted in August, 1995. Interestingly, Geiger maintained that the police actually caused most of the prostitution problem when they drove prostitutes out of a run-down area near the main police station. He argued that this area was a perfect spot for prostitution since it contained mostly parking lots and seedy businesses, whose owners were unconcerned about the prostitutes. Unfortunately, the police action displaced the prostitutes into other areas, where they were unwelcome.

48 Ruth Gelderman – Telephone Interview conducted in August, 1989. Gelderman spoke highly of the work carried out by Community Service Officers, who acted as a liaison between the police and the public on a wide range of issues. However, she also suggested that they were sometimes undermined by the Morality Squad, who sometimes conducted sweeps while the CSOs were trying to negotiate with the prostitutes.

49 The adoption of these two criteria is not intended to denigrate the importance of other possible goals. For example, prostitutes' spokespersons and many feminist writers have argued that the reduction of violence against prostitutes should be a primary goal. Although the present writer completely supports this argument, there is currently a lack of accurate data to assess this issue. See Larsen (1995) for a more detailed discussion of violence, and the current problems which exist in assessing whether violence has increased since Bill C-49 was implemented.

50 In fact, these tactics were used by police prior to Bill C-49 but were initially abandoned in favour of strict enforcement when the law was proclaimed. The success of these tactics was similar in both cases, a factor which further weakens police contentions that Bill C-49 was needed to make them work. (See Larsen, 1992a, for a discussion of the pre-Bill C-49 situation.)

51 Police officials in Vancouver and Winnipeg suggested to this writer that many of the 'problems' associated with street prostitution were caused by the intolerance of residents. Indeed, routine walking patrols conducted as part of this study did not encounter or witness significant amounts of noise or disruption attributable to street prostitution activities.

52 It must be noted that Shaver takes a slightly different approach to the question of feminism and prostitution. She criticizes many of the feminist assumptions about the degrading and exploitive nature of prostitution and argues that some prostitutes do enter it as a matter of choice. She

also strongly suggests that Canadian feminists need to defend the existence of prostitution, and is in favour of maintaining it as an occupation for women who wish to enter it voluntarily.

53 This point was made by Marie Arrington, President of POWER, Vancouver, Debbie Reynolds, President of POWER, Winnipeg, and Valerie Scott, President of the Canadian Organization for the Rights of Prostitutes (CORP) in Toronto. Although Ann Dolina, President of the Alliance for the Safety of Prostitutes (ASP) in Edmonton was unavailable for a private interview, she made a similar statement to the *Edmonton Journal* (*EJ*, May 24, 1988, p.A1).

54 Although this writer has argued elsewhere that most prostitution-related activities should be decriminalized (Larsen, 1992b;1995), the focus here is on police enforcement policies. Thus, the current law is accepted as a 'given' which is largely outside the control of the police. However, as noted in the introduction, the police have significant autonomy to control the implementation of Bill C-49 and the following recommendations are considered within the legal discretion of the police to administer justice.

55 See *Anywhere But Here* (video of the B.C. Learning Resources Institute, Vancouver, 1992) for a more detailed discussion of the anomalies created by prostitution's uncertain legal status. See also Shaver (1994). Shaver argues that prostitution per se is not necessarily different from other occupations, but that its current legal status makes it unnecessarily problematic.

56 In *R. vs Westendorp*, the Supreme Court of Canada ruled that municipal governments cannot use bylaws to control prostitution because some aspects of the trade are covered by the *Criminal Code*.

57 This recommendation parallels the discussion by Lowman (1992a;1992b) and Matthews (1992; 1993). While Lowman and Matthews were debating the creation of red light districts through zoning laws, their discussion also applies to police decision-making. Although Matthews (1992:20) argues that the police should limit themselves to identifying where prostitution is not permitted (which he refers to as 'negative zoning'), Lowman (1992a:14) favours specifying the conditions under which it is legally permitted.

58 Indeed, the success of the Strathcona experiment can be partially attributed to the fact that negotiation was started by residents and prostitutes prior to police involvement.

59 This recommendation is not intended to suggest that the police should attempt to completely eliminate street prostitution. Rather, the goal should be to minimize the amount of street prostitution and utilize negotiation to minimize conflict over the remaining street prostitution. For a variety of reasons, some prostitutes will be unable or unwilling to operate in off-street locations (Lowman, 1992a:14–15).

References

Brannigan, A., L. Knafla and C. Levy (1989) *Street Prostitution: Assessing the Impact of the Law* (Ottawa: Minister of Supply and Services Canada).

Cooper, B. (1989) 'Prostitution: A Feminist Analysis,' *Women's Rights Law Reporter*, VII:99–119.

Fleischman, J. (1989) *Street Prostitution: Assessing the Impact of the Law: Synthesis Report* (Ottawa: Department of Justice Canada).

Freeman, J. (1989) 'The Feminist Debate over Prostitution Reform: Prostitutes Rights Groups, Radical Feminists and the |Im|possibility of Consent,' *Berkeley Women's Law Journal*, V:75.

Larsen, E.N. (1992a) 'The Politics of Prostitution Control: Interest Group Politics in Four Canadian Cities,' *International Journal of Urban and Regional Research*, XVI:169.

—— (1992b) 'Its Time to Legalize Prostitution,' *Policy Options*, Sept. 1992, p.21.

—— (1995) 'The Limits of the Law: A Critical Analysis of Prostitution Control in Three Canadian Cities.' Forthcoming, *Hybrid: The University of Pennsylvania Journal of Law and Social Change*.

Lowman, J. (1986) 'Street Prostitution in Vancouver: Notes on the Genesis of a Social Problem,' *Canadian Journal of Criminology*, XXVIII:1:1–16.

—— (1989) *Street Prostitution: Assessing the Impact of the Law – Vancouver* (Ottawa: Department of Justice)

—— (1991) 'Punishing Prostitutes and their Customers: The Legacy of the Badgley Committee, the Fraser Committee and Bill C-49.' Pp.299–328 in L. Samuelson and B. Schissel (eds.), *Criminal Justice Sentencing and Reform* (Toronto: Garamond Press).

—— (1992a) 'Street Prostitution Control: Some Canadian Reflections on the Finsbury Park Experience,' *The British Journal of Criminology*, XXXII:1:1–17.

—— (1992b) 'Against Street Prostitution,' *British Journal of Criminology*, XXXII: 3:400.

Matthews, R. (1992) 'Regulating Street Prostitution and Kerb-Crawling: A Reply to John

Lowman,' *British Journal of Sociology*, XXXII:1:18–22.

—— (1993) 'Against Street Prostitution,' *British Journal of Criminology*, XXXIII: 4:601.

Moyer, S. and P. Carrington (1989) *Street Prostitution: Assessing the Impact of the Law – Toronto* (Ottawa: Supply and Services, Canada)

O'Connell, S. (1988) 'The Impact of Bill C-49 on Street Prostitution: "What's Law Got to Do With It?,"' *Journal of Law and Public Policy*, IV:109–45.

Shaver, F. (1988) 'A Critique of the Feminist Charges Against Prostitution,' *Atlantis*, XIV:2:82–89.

—— (1994) 'The Regulation of Prostitution: Avoiding the Morality Traps,' *Canadian Journal of Law and Society*, IX:1:123–45.

Part IV
Discretion, Race and Gender

[14]

How Novice and Experienced Officers Interpret Wife Assaults: Normative and Efficiency Frames

Loretta J. Stalans   Mary A. Finn

Prior research has speculated about, but has not provided systematic empirical data on, how officers use their prior knowledge to interpret wife assault situations and how these interpretations shape their responses. Our findings challenge claims that officers' reluctance to pursue formal arrest stems primarily from their proclivity to blame victims. By manipulating whether or not a wife exhibited abnormal behavior, we show that experienced officers do not focus on whether wives can control their "provoking" actions and are to blame; instead they consider the relative credibility and dangerousness of the husband. Prior experience with handling wife assault situations thus shifts the focus of decisionmaking from normative considerations such as blameworthiness to efficiency considerations such as substantiating claims for successful prosecution. However, both novice and experienced officers base their arrest decisions on prior beliefs about whether wives provoke their husbands when wives have alcohol problems. Our findings indicate that future research can profitably examine how prior knowledge shapes interpretations to gain a better understanding of police decisionmaking.

Police calls about violence in domestic situations generally have been handled through informal mediation and separation of disputants (e.g., Berk & Loseke 1981; Dobash & Dobash 1979; Muir 1977; Worden 1989) and overwhelmingly involve men who have physically attacked women (Bell & Bell 1991). Academic researchers (e.g., Sherman & Berk 1984), feminist groups, and civil liability suits filed for failure to provide equal protection in the 1980s challenged the informal handling of wife assaults.[1] (See

A college and university research grant from Georgia State University supported this research. We gratefully acknowledge and thank the participating officers, and the Clayton County, Fulton County, and North Central Public Safety Training Centers for their support and cooperation. The order of authorship indicates level of contribution: The first author proposed the conceptual framework, analyzed the data, and wrote the paper. The second author refined and clarified aspects of the analysis and writing. Both authors contributed equally to the development of materials and measures and to the data collection and coding. We thank four anonymous reviewers and Mark Dantzer for constructive comments that clarified our exposition and thinking. Address correspondence and requests to Loretta Stalans, Loyola University, Dept. of Criminal Justice, 820 N. Michigan, Chicago, IL 60611.

[1] We use the more specific term "wife assault" to highlight the criminal and gender-based nature of the offense. Wife assault also limits the issue to married females; many

Hanmer, Radford, & Stanko 1989a for a history of the movement
to bring policy reforms to the handling of wife assaults.) These
sources catalyzed changes in state laws to allow and encourage
police officers to use arrest when probable cause existed without
obtaining the victim's consent or preference (Hirschel & Hutchinson 1991; Law Enforcement News 1987).

Officers, however, still have much choice about when evidence meets the standard of probable cause (Baumgartner 1992;
Ferraro 1993). Also, some states have enacted primary aggressor
provisions to handle situations where disputants provide conflicting stories. These provisions further increase the complexity and
discretionary nature of officers' decisionmaking. Georgia's statute, for example (Family Violence Act of Georgia 1991), instructs
officers to determine who is the primary aggressor based on normative considerations such as blameworthiness (i.e., whether injuries were inflicted in self-defense), dangerousness considerations such as the likelihood of future violence, and evidentiary
considerations such as the visibility and severity of injuries.[2]
These statutes, however, provide little guidance on the relative
importance of normative, dangerousness, and evidentiary considerations.

How do officers interpret potential wife assault situations
when husbands and wives provide conflicting testimony and both
claim self-defense? Some observational field research suggests
that officers make decisions based on beliefs about gender roles,
battered women, social class, and the sanctity of the family (Black
1980; Ferraro 1989a, 1989b; Martin 1976), and on role orientations, which are formed from general attitudes about people and
from departmental training and experience (e.g., Muir 1977;
White 1972). Research that systematically measures officers' role
orientations and attitudes, however, indicates that situational features predict officers' decisions much better than do officers' attitudes (for a review and empirical support see Riksheim &
Chermak 1993; Worden 1989). A more complete understanding
of police decisionmaking requires empirical data on how officers
use their prior knowledge and the disputants' actions to interpret the conflicting testimony, and how these interpretations de-

---

laws cover only domestic violence for married couples and fail to recognize the rights of
cohabiting couples.

　　[2] Georgia's primary aggressor statute states:

　　Where complaints of family violence are received from two or more opposing
parties, the officer shall evaluate each complaint separately to attempt to determine who was the primary aggressor. If the officer determines that one of the
parties was the primary physical aggressor, the officer shall not be required to
arrest any other person believed to have committed an act of family violence
during the incident. In determining whether a person is a primary physical
aggressor, an officer shall consider: (1) prior family violence involving either
party; (2) the relative severity of the injuries inflicted on each person; (3) the
potential for future injury; and (4) whether one of the parties acted in self-
defense.

termine their decisions (Mastrofski & Parks 1990 and Worden 1989 make similar arguments for police decisionmaking in general).

We demonstrate how novice and experienced officers' prior knowledge and the appropriateness of wives' actions interact to shape interpretations and responses to wife assaults. Much prior research finds that officers consider the victims' actions and characteristics and are less likely to take formal action when wives' actions deviate from what they consider to be appropriate behavior (e.g., Black 1980; Ferraro 1989a, 1989b; Muir 1977; Waaland & Keely 1985). We use signs of mental illness to operationalize instances when wives' actions deviate from social norms, because this operationalization allows us to show how stereotyped images of mentally ill persons affect decisions and to test competing claims about how officers make decisions. Some scholars claim that officers blame women because they believe women can control their provoking actions or can leave the situation (e.g., Ferraro 1989b; Hilton 1993a; Jaffe et al. 1993), whereas other scholars claim that officers make decisions based more on efficiency concerns such as credibility and dangerousness (e.g., Berk & Loseke 1981; Black 1980; Smith 1987). The atypical situation of a hallucinating wife provides a situation in which normative and efficiency considerations conflict. Officers perceive hallucinating wives as unable to understand that violence is wrong and as unable to control their actions, which are two normative considerations suggesting that men unjustifiably inflicted physical injuries on women even if the women provoked them. On the other hand, officers also perceive hallucinating wives as untruthful and dangerous, which results in a low probability of husbands being successfully prosecuted. This atypical situation thus allows a more controlled test of the relative importance novice and experienced officers generally place on normative and efficiency concerns across situations. Moreover, we show that both novice and experienced officers in situations involving alcohol abuse use beliefs about women's proclivity to provoke men because they see this situation as representing the typical wife assault.

We first outline a conceptual framework and its associated hypotheses that explains how officers interpret wife assault situations. We then provide a description of the sample, hypothetical scripts, and measures of officers' responses and inferences. Finally, we present the results and reflect on their implications.

I. Conceptual Framework

Schema theory describes how people form knowledge systems and how the context determines which knowledge structures are used to interpret a situation. Schema theory has received much empirical support in laboratory studies in psychology (for reviews see Black, Galambos, & Read 1984; Fiske & Neuberg 1990; Fiske & Taylor 1991; Rumlehart 1984) and has been used to examine how laypersons and legal officials make decisions (e.g., Carroll et al. 1982; Lurigio & Carroll 1985; Chi, Glaser, & Farr 1988; Stalans & Lurigio 1990). We provide a brief discussion of its assumptions and demonstrate the connection between schema theory and ideas in sociolegal research about how officers make decisions.

Schema theory delineates two types of knowledge that people have in memory. One is "content knowledge"—knowledge about categories or groups of people and events (Rumlehart 1984; Fiske & Taylor 1991). Many studies on how officials make decisions suggest that they use prior knowledge about the different categories of people and events (Black 1980; Emerson 1969, 1983; Drass & Spencer 1987; Ferraro 1989a; Gilboy 1991; Hawkins 1992a; Lurigio & Carroll 1985; Muir 1977; Smith 1987; Stalans & Lurigio 1990: Sudnow 1965). The other knowledge system—"procedural knowledge" or "frames"—holds rules about the relevant information and inferences needed to arrive at a decision (Hawkins 1992a; Lurigio & Stalans 1990; Manning & Hawkins 1990). Frames are connected to individuals' worldviews, values, and concerns that help define the meaning of different situations, and are content-free knowledge structures that contain rules about what questions are relevant to ask and what criteria are relevant to consider in making a decision.

A. Officers' Knowledge about Categories

When officers can categorize a specific wife assault situation as an example of a category, they use their prior knowledge about the category to interpret the conflicting stories and assign less relevance to the presented physical evidence (e.g., Fiske & Neuberg 1990; Stalans & Lurigio 1990; Sudnow 1965). Both novice and experienced officers acquire beliefs about mentally ill persons, social classes, race, and battered wives from earlier socialization and media stories. Drawing on schema theory and prior research, we can make several predictions about how knowledge about mentally ill persons, typical wife assaults, and social class differences shape interpretations of conflicting stories. Table 1 provides a summary of these hypotheses. Hypotheses 1–4 describe the expected effects of this categorical knowledge on officers' interpretations and responses to specific wife assault situations. For example, officers may conclude from their stereotyped images of mentally ill persons that a wife who is hallucinating usually is violent, unpredictable, and untruthful even though she has bruises and lacerations to the face and neck (Desforges et al. 1993; Scheff 1984). Schema theory suggests that

officers will use beliefs about whether wives typically provoke
their husbands into violence when characteristics of a specific situation indicate that the situation is representative of the typical
battered wife (Black 1980; Drass & Spencer 1987; Ferraro 1989a;
Stalans 1988). Often these beliefs are centered on normative
concerns about how people should behave. For example, Ferraro
and Pope (1993:105) concluded: "Police stereotypes of battered
women are related to their assumptions of 'rational' human action and deserving victims."

Table 1. Hypotheses about the Relationship among Experience, Prior
Knowledge, and Interpretations of Specific Situations

Hypothesis 1:	Both novice and experienced officers will perceive wives who have hal-lucinations or alcoholism as less truthful and more dangerous than wives who do not. Officers will perceive wives having hallucinations as less in control of their actions. Officers will perceive wives with unusual startled responses compared with normal wives as more credible, less dangerous, and more in control of their actions.
Hypothesis 2:	Officers' inferences about credibility and dangerousness will shape their decisions to recommend mental health treatment and to recom-mend shelters. Experienced officers share common knowledge about when these recommendations should be made; hence, experienced officers' decisions should be more predictable than novice officers' decisions.
Hypothesis 3:	Both novice and experienced officers will use their prior knowledge about whether women in typical wife assault situations provoke men's violence toward them when situational features allow officers to catego-rize the situation as "typical." We explore whether a wife's alcoholism, unusual startled responses, or no deviant behavior serve as cues that allow officers to classify the situation as typical.
Hypothesis 4:	Officers hold beliefs that couples in poverty are more mutually habitu-ally violent than are middle-class couples. Based on this belief, officers will be less likely to use wives' actions to predict the dangerousness of a poverty-stricken husband than the dangerousness of a middle-class hus-band.
Hypothesis 5:	Experienced officers will place more importance on whether claims can be substantiated and successfully prosecuted and less importance on blameworthiness in selecting responses to handle wife assaults than will novice officers. These different frames also will define effectiveness of arrest. Novice officers will perceive arrest to be more effective when the husband understands violence is wrong, whereas experienced officers will perceive the opposite.
Hypothesis 6:	Experienced officers will be less likely to arrest when the wife is halluci-nating than will novice officers. This difference occurs because exper-ienced officers conclude that the wife is relatively less credible and more dangerous than the husband whereas novice officers are more likely to conclude the husband acted unjustifiably when he injured his wife, who could not control her provoking behavior.

Some categories such as social class, gender, and race are
chronically accessible and may automatically inform inferences
(Fiske & Taylor 1991). Prior research (Black 1980; Ferraro
1989a, 1989b; Smith 1987) suggests that officers believe couples
in poverty are more habitually violent than are middle-income
couples. This knowledge leads them to arrest poverty-stricken

husbands less often than middle-income husbands. Social and economic characteristics also allow officers to classify cases as normal or deviant (Black 1980; Ferraro 1989a, 1989b; Manning 1977; Muir 1977). Ferraro (1989a:67) concludes: "Deviants serve as the 'other' for police officers; they are publicly intoxicated or high, homeless, involved in crime, live in run-down houses, have atypical family structures, and/or speak foreign languages."

B. Two Frames: Normative and Efficiency

Officers sometimes are faced with situations that cannot be easily categorized or typified into their specific knowledge about wife assault cases. In these situations, they rely more on their frames to organize and interpret testimonial and physical evidence. Drawing on prior research on officers' decisionmaking, we describe two ideal frames that officers may bring to wife assault situations. Individual officers may give different weight to these two frames. In describing these frames, we cite research that has speculated about what inferences officers make but has not provided direct empirical support for these speculations.

Normative Frame

Some research claims that officers often blame women for the violence (e.g., Ferraro & Pope 1993; Hatty 1989; Jaffe et al. 1993; Saunders & Size 1986; Stith 1990; for a review see Hilton 1993a). Ferraro (1993:169) highlights the central issue officers with a normative frame focus on: "When officers arrive at a 'family fight,' they decide who is most to blame for the problem. If they view each partner as equally liable, both parties will be arrested." Officers employing a normative frame attend more to the appropriateness of each disputant's actions based on societal norms (e.g., Ferraro 1989a; Smith 1987; Hawkins 1992a). Officers assess the moral character of the disputants (Hawkins 1992a), whether the husband or wife *should* have acted differently. They base their decision on a moral or normative basis more than on a practical basis of whether either disputant *could* have acted differently. They will arrest a husband when he should have acted otherwise and a wife acted justifiably, and will not arrest a husband when a wife committed a more unjustified action that was within her control. Officers may see inflicted injuries as deserved when husbands acted in self-defense or were provoked into anger by wives who committed unjustifiable actions such as adultery (e.g., Saunders & Size 1986). Officers may see inflicted injuries as undeserved when husbands inflict injuries on wives who have mental illnesses that make them unable to control their actions or are physically ill (e.g., Dobash & Dobash 1979).

Officers may claim that they usually either try to mete out justice or usually try to provide help. Prior research, for example, has identified two types of officers—tough cops and problem solvers—who use normative framing but claim to strive toward meting out justice or providing help, respectively (White 1972; Worden & Pollitz 1984). Whereas previous research has assumed that officers respond consistently across situations to achieve their stated objective (Black 1980; Smith 1987; Worden & Pollitz 1984), we argue that objectives serve to rationalize, not guide, decisions (see also Hawkins 1992a). Muir (1977:88–91) provides an example of how a problem solver uses a normative frame and can become a "tough cop" in certain situations:

> Officer Frank Carpasso . . . "was out there to help people." . . . In a situation where information was so elusive, helter-skelter, and subjective, asking "Who's to blame for hurting the kids?" centered the matter. . . . Carpasso tended to approach situations, looking for favorites to pamper. If the boy played his cards right, he could get Carpasso to . . . go to bat with the Youth Authority to divert him from jail. . . . But if there were favorites, there were also heels, against whom Carpasso carried out his moral mandate to be forceful.

Both tough cops and problem solvers base decisions on an assessment of blameworthiness from the presented evidence and their prior beliefs about categories of people and events. An important feature of our research, which distinguishes it from much previous research on police decisionmaking, is that we examine consistency in the ways officers ask questions, interpret information, and form responses.[3]

Efficiency Frame

Whereas officers with a normative frame unravel the past to determine whether the person primarily responsible for the occurrence of the injuries should be blamed, officers with an efficiency frame consider the immediate present and near future situation. (For a detailed discussion of the conceptual difference between responsibility and blame, see Shaver 1985.) Officers with an efficiency frame are pragmatic thinkers who are concerned with job security and material rewards and recognition the limited resources in the criminal justice system (Berk & Loseke 1981) and in the community (Bittner 1990; Teplin 1984b; Teplin & Pruett 1992). To minimize the likelihood of glaring errors and bad media publicity, officers assess the likeli-

---

[3] Drawing on schema theory and naturalistic research (e.g., Manning & Hawkins 1990; Hawkins 1992a), we adopt an approach where a frame can lead to quite divergent responses depending on the situation. Some prior research (Black 1980; Smith 1987; Worden & Pollitz 1984), which has used the terms "role orientations" and "styles of control," connects how officers interpret situations to one and only one outcome (e.g., Black's penal style is manifested by arrest and focuses on blameworthiness). Officers, however, can arrive at the same response by interpreting situations variously.

hood that the husband or wife will inflict severe harm in the near future (e.g., Berk & Loseke 1981; Bittner 1967; Teplin 1984b) and determine whether claims can be substantiated and successfully prosecuted in court (e.g., Ferraro & Pope 1993; Worden 1989).

C. How Professional Socialization Changes Framing

From earlier socialization, both novice and experienced officers have acquired both normative framing and certain aspects of efficiency framing such as concern about dangerousness. However, from their socialization into the profession, experienced officers also have acquired other aspects of efficiency framing such as the need to use arrests sparingly and to substantiate claims. For example, novice officers quickly learn from conversations with experienced officers that "gung-ho" attitudes make them the object of fellow officers' jokes because their eagerness violates the informal norm to "lay low and avoid trouble" (Van Maanen 1974). Rookie officers learn through direct and vicarious experiences that they must use arrest sparingly and as last resorts (Berk & Loseke 1981; Bittner 1967, 1990; Muir 1977; Teplin 1984b), because an arrest takes much time to process and takes them away from backing up fellow officers, from handling their share of calls, from helping other citizens, and from being available for "big pinches" (Van Maanen 1974). Novice officers also learn what it takes to establish probable cause and "how to . . . avoid unnecessary or fruitless effort, and write reports that will reduce the risks of a negative response from the police hierarchy" (Mastrofski, Ritti, & Snipes 1994:126–27).

Schema theory proposes that the priority placed on each of these frames will depend on the frequency of use in the officers' daily and professional lives, on the salience of characteristics associated with future dangerousness (e.g., a weapon), on the officers' attitudes toward their job, and on the salience of normative and instrumental framing in recent high-profile wife assault cases (e.g., Stalans & Lurigio 1990). Most police departments base raises and promotions on efficiency concerns and place more emphasis both in informal and formal training on efficiency concerns such as substantiating claims and protecting society than on normative concerns about the wrongfulness of an action. Experienced officers, then, receive much exposure to efficiency framing. Through the salience of efficiency framing, experienced officers consider the broader administrative and professional context in making decisions about how to handle specific wife assaults (e.g., Gilboy 1991; Simon 1976; Worden 1989).

Given this organizational context, it is understandable that the shift toward holding attitudes that place more importance on

self-interested and efficiency concerns than on a pursuit of justice is relatively swift, occurring within one year of job experience
(Fielding 1986, 1988). Compared with novice officers, those with
one or more years of experience more often take no action and
see their inaction as deriving from a more realistic view of the
criminal justice system and their perception of police work as a
job with instrumental benefits (Van Maanen 1975; Fielding &
Fielding 1991). Novice police officers, perhaps because of their
normative concerns, are more likely to arrest suspects including
special groups such as fellow officers and elderly individuals than
are officers with at least one year of experience (Tuohy et al.
1993).

This previous research provides only indirect support for how
professionalization changes the way officers interpret and handle
specific cases. From this research and schema theory, we propose
hypotheses 5 and 6 (see Table 1). Compared with novice officers,
experienced officers will place more emphasis on efficiency because of its connection to instrumental benefit and widespread
use in organizational matters, whereas novice officers, underex-
posed to organizational concerns, frame decisions based on earlier socialization. Contrary to prior feminist research (e.g., Hanmer et al. 1989a), hypothesis 6 suggests that experienced officers
do not distinguish between wives who can and cannot control
their provoking behavior.

II. Data Collection

A. Respondents' Training and Experience

Officers ($N = 128$) serving the North Georgia area received
credit toward their mandatory in-service or mandated training
hours for participating in this study. Most officers were male
(82.8%) and Caucasian (57.3%). The age of officers ranged from
19 to 55 ($M = 36.14$; SD = 19.87). Officers were classified into one
of three groups based on their answers to questions about experience and training: untrained novice officers ($N = 34$), trained
novice officers ($N = 45$), and trained experienced officers ($N = 49$). Novice officers are those with less than a year of actual policing experience and who have handled fewer than 10 domestic
violence calls. Experienced officers usually had handled more
than 100 domestic violence calls and had between 1 and 33 years
of experience; over half had 9 or more years; we defined "experienced" as at least 1 year of experience because prior research
suggested that officers' shift toward placing more importance on
efficiency framing occurs within a year (Fielding & Fielding
1991). The untrained officers had not received any formal training on domestic violence from the police academy. The trained
officers had received formal training on domestic violence. Most

experienced officers had acquired their formal academy training in domestic violence an average of 8 months prior to the data collection. Conversely, trained novice officers had received their formal academy training in domestic violence an average of 2 weeks prior to data collection.

Formal training at the police academy consisted of a four-hour lecture course on the Family Violence Act of Georgia. The lectures covered both general substantive matters and specific concerns. On general matters, officers learned about the content of the law, including the primary aggressor clause; they were told that the primary goals are to establish order and protect the life, liberty, and property of others; and they were reminded of the need to establish the facts in a situation. They were also told about various categories of disputants, including information about the battered wife syndrome. On the specific side, they received step-by-step instructions on how to complete necessary reports and how to protect their own safety by, for example, checking the dwelling for other occupants and keeping disputants in view. They were also warned of the increased danger in domestic violence situations involving a disputant with alcoholism.

B. Research Design and Scripts

Respondents were each randomly assigned to read one of the eight scripts. Respondents were told that the study was examining how officers made decisions about domestic violence situations. Officers were assured that there were no right or wrong answers and that their responses would be confidential and anonymous. Each one then read the assigned script and wrote down their thoughts as they came to mind. They then answered open-ended questions about how they would handle the situation and closed-ended questions assessing the mediating inferences to their decisions.

We attempted to simulate as much as possible the actual interview process that police officers use to investigate a domestic violence call. We believe our simulation allowed officers to project themselves into the script and to respond to it as if they were handling a real call.[4] Two features of the script varied across subjects. Subjects either received a script describing a lower-income couple or a middle-income couple, which was conveyed through language and employment (see appendix). There were also four

---

[4] The generalizability of our results is an empirical issue; supporting the possible robustness of our findings is the fact that they buttress claims and extend themes in observational field research. To prepare our instrument, we interviewed experienced officers ($N = 80$) about the typical questions and procedures in domestic disputes. From the coding of the officers' responses to open-ended questions, we then incorporated the questions and procedures that were used by many officers or are part of the standard police report form. This procedure ensures that the questions officers usually ask have been covered in the scripts.

versions of the wife's actions that were indicative of her mental state; these versions will be described later. This 2×4 between-subjects design thus resulted in eight scripts varying by the couple's social class and the wife's mental state.

The scripts shared several features, which are set out in Table 2. We focused exclusively on situations where wives displayed moderately severe injuries because most police calls involve injured wives, not injured husbands (Bell & Bell 1991). The values of the other features were chosen to create an ambiguous situation where neither arrest nor an informal method is an obvious response. For example, we examined situations where a weapon is not present because the presence of a weapon is less frequent and often leads to arrest (e.g., Worden 1989). The blameworthiness of each disputant also is not clear because the two disputants give conflicting stories about how the argument and violence occurred. Because these two versions of the stories are central to officers' inferences about credibility and blame, we provide in the appendix a detailed description using the script of the low-income couple.

Table 2. Common Features in the Hypothetical Scripts

	Operationalization	Situational Category
1.	Wife has bruises to face and neck	Injury
2.	No weapon is present or used	Weapon
3.	Disputants neither request an arrest nor request no intervention	Citizens' request
4.	Both disputants are present	Suspect present
5.	Both display respectful attitudes toward officers	Attitude toward police
6.	There is no property damage	Property damage
7.	Neighbor phones the police	Complainant
8.	Disputants are antagonistic toward each other	Antagonism between disputants
9.	Conflicting stories about how the injuries occurred	Whether disputants agree about how injuries occurred

The manipulations of the wife's actions that are associated with a mental disorder were inserted throughout the script.[5] The

---

[5] To provide construct validity to our manipulations of mental state, two advanced clinical psychology students assisted in the development of the manipulations. Five other advanced clinical psychology students, who were unaware of the study, independently rated the husband and wife on the presence and type of mental illness after being instructed on the definition of mental illness. Using Teplin's (1984b) criteria for the presence of mental illness, we defined mental illness as having one symptom of a severe mental disorder when this symptom cannot be attributed to the current social context. Teplin (1984b) found that there was 93.4% agreement on the presence of severe mental illness between this definition and the NIMH Diagnostic Interview Schedule. All five raters agreed on the presence/absence of signs of mental illness and the type of mental illness signs for each of our manipulations. Officers rated the wife as more mentally ill when she had hallucinations (M = 6.53) or unusual startled responses (M = 3.02) or alcoholism (M = 2.56) than when she was normal (M=1.90; ts (122) = 12.55, 3.02, 1.65, ps < .01, .05, respectively. Most officers spontaneously wrote that a wife was mentally ill when she was hallucinating (78.8%) but not when she had unusual startled responses (6.3%) or alcoholism (0%). Officers' experience and the couple's social class did not affect officers' perceptions of mental illness.

script described in the appendix is labeled the normal condition because the wife shows no signs of severe thought or perceptual disturbances, delusions, alcoholism, or extreme inappropriate expressions of emotions. Many domestic violence situations, however, involve wives who act inconsistently with societal norms for appropriate behavior and thoughts. Because a domestic violence victim may be perceived differently when her behavior violates societal norms for appropriate behavior, we focused on three kinds of mental disorders.

One of the most frequent occurrences in wife assault is the intoxication of the wife and/or the husband (Barnett & Fagan 1993; Roy 1988). We manipulated whether the wife showed signs of alcohol dependence such as impaired functioning, denial of problem, and use of alcohol on a daily basis. The husband described the wife's drinking problem: "She was already drinking heavily when I got home. Her drinking is really getting out of control again. It used to just be weekends, but now it seems she drinks all the time." The wife responded with slightly slurred speech, and beer cans were visible. When asked how often she drinks, the wife replied, "Only a little every day."

Are officers able to recognize signs of repeat abuse? The battered spouse syndrome is a mental disorder that develops after one or more traumatic stressful events (American Psychiatric Association 1987; Walker 1984). One central feature of battered spouse syndrome is an overreaction to nonthreatening stimuli; this reaction is called "unusual startled response." We manipulated whether the wife displayed unusual startled responses. The wife was described as displaying jerking motions and appearing startled in response to nonthreatening stimuli. For example, Officer Johnson drops a piece of paper on the floor and Mrs. Jones jumps and curls her feet under her on the couch.

Sometimes women who are victims of domestic violence have perceptual and thought disorders. Research on police handling of mentally ill persons has usually focused on the handling of suspects rather than the handling of victims (e.g., Bittner 1967, 1990; Teplin 1984a, 1984b; Teplin & Pruett 1992). Samples of psychiatric patients, however, reveal that a substantial percentage of these patients have been victims of wife assault (Carlile 1991; Yellowlees & Kaushik 1992). We chose an obvious sign of severe perceptual disorder: "hearing voice." In the perceptual disorder condition, the wife turned from others and engaged in conversation with a person who is not present (a dead mother). For example, "She suddenly stops pacing and turns away from Officer Kelly and whispers, 'I know. I know. I know. Please be quiet.' "

III. Data Analysis Strategy

We employed measures from both open-ended and closed-ended questions to assess the relevant inferences associated with the two frames. We first describe how we coded the thought protocols and then briefly describe the measures associated with each frame and those that assessed officers' content knowledge.

A. Coding of Thought Protocols

As they were reading the script, respondents wrote down their thoughts, opinions, and decisions as they came to mind. After reading the script, respondents answered three other open-ended questions which provided additional measures of spontaneous thoughts.[6] To code the thought protocols, we developed a coding scheme containing 14 concepts such as the blameworthiness of each disputant, pattern of physical abuse in the home, and future dangerousness.[7] The coding scheme was both reliable[8] and exhaustive (99% of the statements could be coded into at least one category).

---

[6] Because the officers' open-ended responses as they were reading the script probably captured only the most central thoughts, we used three open-ended questions to probe for additional information about how they made their decisions. These questions were:

  a) How would you handle this domestic violence call?

  b) Did you consider any alternative response(s)? What were these responses and why did you decide not to use them?

  c) Did you need either additional information or questions asked? If yes, what additional information did you need or what additional questions did you want the police officers to ask?

Open-ended questions do not impose concepts on respondents, whereas closed-ended questions (e.g., ratings of the husband's truthfulness) impose concepts that respondents may have not considered before we posed the question.

[7] The conceptual categories are: (1) helping couple to find way to resolve their problems; (2) mentioned one or more causes of the couple's problem; (3) blameworthiness of husband or wife; (4) mentioned alcohol or drug problems; (5) mental illness; (6) injured party's actions are typical of battered spouse; (7) pattern of physical abuse in settling disagreements; (8) credibility of disputants; (9) likelihood of future violence; (10) disputant's capability of handling disputes; (11) seriousness of injury; (12) cited family violence act as a reason for arrest; (13) conditional dispositions; and (14) demographic, physical, and social characteristics. Each category captured both the absence or presence of a concept (e.g., credibility) and the valuative and descriptive nature of the inferences (e.g., husband is lying). Under some categories, e.g., causes of the couple's problems, coders could check more than one options; the options included financial difficulties, alcohol problem of wife or couple, poor communication, use of drugs, mental illness of wife, stressful environment, husband's attitude toward wife, and wife's attitude toward husband.

[8] Two coders separately read and coded 70 of the thought protocols. Coders used the context surrounding a phrase to interpret its meaning. The kappa coefficients ranged from .72 to 1.00 and measured the amount of agreement between the two coders. Kappas can range from 0 to 1.00, and coefficients above .70 indicate adequate reliability.

B. Measurement of Inferences and Prior Knowledge

Normative Frame

The normative frame proposes that officers judge whether each disputant's actions were justifiable or unjustifiable, which is the essence of placing blame. From the open-ended responses, we coded whether the officer indicated the husband acted unjustifiably in resorting to violence and should have taken a different course.[9] To assess blameworthiness, officers may assess how much the husband and the wife understand that violence is wrong, which was measured with a closed-ended question. To be considered blameworthy, individuals must be able to understand the wrongfulness of their actions from a moral and legal perspective. In the legal system, for example, juveniles who do not understand the consequences of their actions are less blameworthy than adults who do. Officers may determine blameworthiness in part by inferring whether the wife has hit the husband in the past (measured here with a closed-ended question) and whether the husband has repeatedly abused the wife (assessed here from open-ended responses).

Efficiency Frame

To determine blameworthiness and to determine whether the disputants can handle the wife assault themselves, officers must assess whether each disputant has the ability to control his/her own actions; we measured these inferences with closed-ended questions. Because officers employing an efficiency frame are pragmatic thinkers, they use arrest sparingly when it can be effective at reducing the likelihood of further violence (measured using the difference between two closed-ended questions).[10] Officers also must judge the "dangerousness" of the wife

---

9 Statements that the husband *should have* or *ought to have* done something differently or foreseen the consequences were coded as blaming the husband. Examples of statements placing blame on the husband are:

> As for Mr. Jones' contention that she attacked him first, there are no marks on Mr. Jones to support this. And even if she had attacked first, the extent of her injuries well exceeds any force he may have used in self-defense.

> No matter how mad you get it does not justify you to beat someone as bad as it seemed from the looks of her.

> He knows his wife is having a hard time with her mother's death so he should be very patient with her. He had no right to hit her.

> No one deserves to be beaten in an argument, especially your spouse.

A dichotomous measure represented inferences about husband's blameworthiness: 0 = did not mention (82.0%); 1 = blamed husband (18.0%).

10 Officers were asked to assess the likelihood of future violence without intervention and with arrest ("If the husband [is arrested; remains in the home], how likely is it that he will in the future inflict severe harm on his wife?"). Respondents provided their answers using 1–7 Likert scales where 1 is "not at all likely" and 7 is "extremely likely." To create a measure of perceived effectiveness of arrest, we subtracted the likelihood without

and the husband, and were asked to rate the husband and the wife separately on aggressiveness and dangerousness to family and other people.[11] To obtain a successful prosecution, officers also must infer who is telling the truth and whether enough hard evidence exists to support probable cause. In the closed-ended questions, respondents rated the husband and wife separately on their responsibility for the violence, their truthfulness, and their believability; we created a scale of the wife's credibility relative to the husband's credibility.[12] From the open-ended measures, we created a dichotomous measure of whether the respondent mentioned credibility or visible injuries to substantiate claims with mentioning coded as 1 (44.5%) and not mentioning coded as 0 (54.7%). This open-ended measure is related to inferences about credibility and the wife's dangerousness. Wives who are perceived as dangerous are seen as creating the violence and as having less credibility to substantiate claims.[13]

Content Knowledge about Domestic Disputes

Other research (for a review see Hilton 1993a) suggests that some officers blame women for provoking the violence. We used a set of attitudinal items to assess officers' general beliefs about

---

intervention from the likelihood with intervention with higher positive numbers, indicating that arrest will be more effective at reducing further violence.

[11] The mean of three items formed a reliable scale of husband's dangerousness (alpha = .71; M = 5.01; SD = 1.37): dangerous to family, dangerous to other people, and aggressive. Ratings were made on a 7-point scale with 1 = "not at all" and 7 = "completely." The mean of the same three items and the ratings on how likely it is that the wife will inflict severe harm on her husband if she remains in the home formed a reliable scale of the wife's dangerousness (alpha = .81; M = 3.00; SD = 1.42).

[12] Officers separately rated each disputant on several adjectives using a 1–7 scale with 1 = "not at all" and 7 = "completely." The mean ratings of two adjectives (believable, truthful) formed a reliable scales of credibility (for ratings of husband, Cronbach's alpha = .84; M = 3.12; SD = 1.44, and for ratings of wife, alpha = .80; M = 4.81; SD = 1.40). Because the husband's and wife's credibility were negatively correlated (r = –.37) and the legal statute requires an assessment of relative credibility, we created a scale of relative believability by subtracting the husband's perceived credibility from the wife's perceived credibility; the scale ranged from –4.5 to 6 with positive numbers indicating that the wife was more credible and negative numbers indicating that the husband was more credible (M = 1.68; SD = 2.35). Cronbach's alpha indicates the amount of consistency between the items, with values of .70 or greater indicating that the measurement of credibility is reliable (consistent) across the items.

[13] Correlations were performed within each level of experience. For untrained novice officers, the open-ended measure of substantiating claims was related to closed-ended measures of the wife's credibility (r = .37, p < .05), the wife's dangerousness (r = –.37, p < .04), and the wife's control over her actions (r = .45, p < .01). For experienced officers, the open-ended measure was related to closed-ended measures of relative credibility (r = .37, p < .01), the dangerousness of the wife (r = –.50, p < .001), and her responsibility for the occurrence of the violence (r = –.44, p < .001). Credibility, dangerousness, and responsibility for the violence are all moderately correlated. For trained novice officers, the open-ended measure did not correlate with the closed-ended measure; this suggests that trained novice officers have not thought about the closed-ended measures before the questions were posed, and are using simple heuristics such as "when injuries are present, arrest."

whether battered wives provoked their husbands.[14] We also assessed officers' beliefs about the amount of habitual violence within social class.[15] Because direct questions about officers' views of persons with mental illness have social desirability problems, we assessed officers' views of types of mental illness indirectly by examining how they interpret situations involving wives with mental illness compared with wives without signs of mental illness.

IV. Results and Discussion

Our research examines why officers interpret and respond differently to wife assault situations involving victims who fit societal norms of appropriate conduct and those who deviate from them. We first present data suggesting that irrespective of their experience, officers perceive wives who abuse alcohol or hallucinate as more untruthful and dangerous than normal wives or wives who show signs of battered spouse syndrome. We then show how these perceptions of wives' actions affect officers' referral and arrest decisions, and use a comparison between the normal wife and the hallucinating wife to test whether experienced officers make decisions based on efficiency considerations more than blame, whereas novice officers are more inclined to consider blameworthiness.

A. How Officers Perceive Wives' Actions

Table 3 reports the mean ratings for inferences about normative and efficiency considerations within each of the four mental state conditions.[16] People have acquired stereotyped images of

---

[14] Respondents were told: "Below are several possible explanations for why women are physically injured in domestic disputes. Based on your experiences and what you know about domestic violence situations, please indicate how much you agree with each statement using the scale below." Respondents rated each item using a 1–7 scale where 1 is "strongly disagree" and 7 is "strongly agree." Four items formed a reliable scale (alpha = .70; $M = 3.03$; SD = 1.15) of knowledge that wives provoke violence: (*a*) wives are beaten because they have personality problems; (*b*) wives are beaten because they often point out the husband's weaknesses; (*c*) wives are beaten because they are mentally disturbed; and (*d*) wives are beaten because they provoke anger from their husbands.

[15] Respondents were asked, "What percentage of domestic violence calls in poverty areas are: __ situations where disputants have resorted to physical violence for the first time and __ situations where disputants habitually resort to physical violence." They were told to assign percentages so that they added to 100%. The same question was asked for middle-class neighborhoods.

[16] Separate multivariate analysis of variances (MANOVAs) were employed for correlated and conceptually related inferences. Each MANOVA tested the direct and two-way interactive effects of three factors: (*a*) officers' experience (untrained novice, trained novice, experienced); (*b*) couple's social class; and (*c*) wife's mental state. No direct or interactive effects for officers' experience or couple's social class were significant. The mental illness variable significantly affected perceptions of all variables listed in Table 1. One MANOVA tested the effects of three inferences about the wife (MANOVA Wilks $F(9, 229) = 17.41$, $p < .001$): (*a*) mental illness contributed to violence (ANOVA $F(3, 96) = 64.46$, $p < .001$); (*b*) control over actions (ANOVA $F(3, 96) = 8.23$, $p < .001$); and (*c*)

mentally ill persons as dangerous, unpredictable, and untruthful (Desforges et al. 1993; Scheff 1984). Consistent with these stereotyped images, officers indicated that compared with normal wives, wives with hallucinations or alcoholism were less credible and more dangerous. Officers also believed husbands were less dangerous when wives were hallucinating or had alcoholism than when they were normal.

Table 3. Officers' Perceptions of Victims with and without Mental Illness

	Normal	Perceptual Disorder	Alcoholism	Unusual Startled Response
Efficiency Considerations				
Wife is more credible than husband	2.78	−.14****	1.26*	3.01
Wife is more responsible	2.63	3.40****	3.23	2.12
Wife is more dangerous	2.44	4.35****	3.20**	2.05
Husband is more dangerous	5.35	4.31****	4.71*	5.42
Normatiave Considerations				
Wife has more control over actions	4.02	2.35****	3.29	4.18
Wife's mental illness[a] contributed more to the violence	2.03	5.49****	2.03	1.97
Wife has more ability to understand violence is wrong	5.04	3.03****	5.06	4.98
Husband has more ability to understand violence is wrong	3.74	5.37****	4.53	3.39

[a] The row label indicates the direction of the variable has the value of the mean increases. For example, a higher positive mean indicates that wife is more credible than the husband.
One-tailed probability: * $p < .05$; ** $p < .025$; *** $p < .01$; **** $p < .001$.

The ability to control one's own actions and to understand that violence is wrong is crucial in assessing blameworthiness. Officers perceived wives who were hallucinating as having less ability to control their actions and to understand that violence is wrong than wives who were normal, showed signs of alcoholism, or unusual startled responses. Officers also were more likely to infer that the wife had hit her husband before when she had hallucinations (75.5% of those with hallucinations) than when she had alcoholism (35.5%), unusual startled responses (21.9%), or was normal (24.1%), $\chi^2(3) = 25.26$, $p < .001$. Officers believed the wife's mental illness contributed more to the violence when she

---

ability to understand violence is wrong (ANOVA $F(3, 96) = 11.99$, $p < .001$). Another MANOVA tested the effects of four correlated inferences about credibility, dangerousness, and responsibility (MANOVA $F(12, 249) = 5.99$, $p < .001$): (a) scale of wife's dangerousness (ANOVA $F(3, 97) = 20.94$, $p < .001$); (b) scale of relative credibility (ANOVA $F(3, 97) = 13.70$, $p < .001$); (c) wife's responsibility for violence (ANOVA $F(3, 97) = 3.54$, $p < .02$); and (d) scale of husband's dangerousness (ANOVA $F(3, 97) = 3.95$, $p < .02$). The last MANOVA tested effects of three inferences about the husband (MANOVA $F(9, 231) = 3.95$, $p < .001$): (a) perception of husband's mental state (ANOVA $F(3, 97) = 7.98$, $p < .001$); (b) ability to understand violence is wrong (ANOVA $F(3, 97) = 5.17$, $p < .001$); and (c) ability to control action (ANOVA for mental state is not significant, $p > .29$).

was hallucinating (due to her perceived propensity toward violence) than when she was not.

While situations involving alcohol abuse and perceptual disorders are interpreted differently from those without these signs, officers perceive situations involving unusual startled responses to be like normal situations. This overall lack of difference is due in part to the fact that 59% of the officers failed to associate this sign with repeat abuse. When officers who recognized the signs as indicators of repeat abuse were compared with officers who did not, differences in perceptions did occur. Officers who inferred repeat abuse indicated that the wife was more in control of her actions (M = 5.38) than did officers who did not infer repeat abuse (M = 3.18), t (28) = 4.30, $p < .001$); this finding supports prior findings from observational research which suggest that officers have stereotypes of battered women as being in control of their actions (Ferraro & Pope 1993). Officers who inferred repeat abuse indicated that wives were less dangerous (M = 1.58), more credible (M = 3.92), and less responsible for the occurrence of the violence (M = 1.62) than did officers who failed to recognize signs of repeat abuse (M for dangerous = 2.61; M for credibility = 1.31; M for responsibility = 2.69) ($t(30)$ = 28.15, 19.56, 21.50, $p < .01$). When officers recognized signs of repeat abuse, wives with battered spouse syndrome were seen as having more control over their actions, as less dangerous, and as less responsible.

B. How Officers' Perceptions Determine Their Referral Decisions

Given that officers have more negative perceptions of women who suffer from hallucinations and alcoholism, how do officers' beliefs affect their decisions to make referrals to shelters and outpatient mental health treatment programs?[17] We first examine what beliefs led officers to recommend outpatient mental health treatment. Officers recommended such treatment when wives were perceived as dangerous (change in odds = 1.64, $p < .01$) and as less able to understand that violence is wrong (change in odds = .57, $p < .01$). Officers also were more likely to recommend outpatient services for wives when they believed that husbands understood that violence is wrong (change in odds = 1.65, $p < .01$), perhaps because officers believed mental health treatment for wives would be more effective when husbands already understood the wrongfulness of their violence.

Because novice officers often do not know when to recommend mental health treatment, we expected that these inferences would predict experienced officers' decisions better than

---

[17] Dichotomous measures represented decisions about referrals to outpatient mental health treatment (28.9% referred, coded as 1) and decisions about referrals to shelters (50.0% referred victim to shelter, coded as 1).

novice officers' decisions. An analysis indicates that this is in fact the case.[18] The model for experienced officers has substantial accuracy at predicting decisions to not recommend (91.43% accuracy) and decisions to recommend (100% accuracy), monte carlo $p < .001$. These estimates are stable in that UniODA only misclassifies 3 people and the LOO analysis misclassifies 5 people. In contrast, these same beliefs are less predictive of novice officers' decisions to recommend treatment. The UniODA misclassifies 20 of the 76 novice officers, which is not a significant improvement over chance (monte carlo $p < .07$). Moreover, the model for novices is quite inaccurate when it predicts recommended treatment (31.58% accuracy). Consistent with prior research (Bittner 1990; Teplin 1984b), these findings suggest that experienced officers may develop common frames in which they reserve referrals for those who are obviously mentally ill and are seen as dangerous and incapable of understanding the wrongfulness of violence.

In addition to making decisions about referrals to mental health treatment, officers must decide whether to refer a wife to a battered spouse shelter (Belknap & McCall 1994). Consistent with prior observational field research (Ferraro 1989a), we find that officers who noticed a pattern of repeat abuse or perceived that the husband as dangerous were more likely to refer victims to shelters than officers who did not infer repeat abuse or perceived less danger (for repeat abuse change in odds = 2.90, for husband's dangerousness change in odds = 1.28, one-tailed $p < .05$). Officers who perceived a wife as more credible than the husband were more likely to recommend shelters (change in odds = 1.28, one-tailed $p < .008$).[19]

---

18 Predictive accuracy provides an index of how well a set of interpretations applies to the sample and can predict the responses of new samples. Because logistic regression employs suboptimal heuristics to classify cases, we used univariate optimal discriminant analysis (UniODA) to find the theoretical maximum possible level of percentage accuracy in classification because it makes no assumptions about the underlying configuration of the data. UniODA classifies cases based on the response function scores from the logistic regression equation (for more detailed information, see Soltysik & Yarnold 1993; Yarnold & Soltysik 1991). Based on a meta-analysis of 15 data sets, Yarnold, Hart, & Soltysik (1994) found that UniODA obtained a mean increase of 5.8% in overall percentage of accurate classification compared to the suboptimal procedures of logistic regression and Fisher's discriminant analysis. In addition, using Optimal Data Analysis Software (Soltysik & Yarnold 1993), a leave-one-out (LOO) validity jackknife analysis was performed to evaluate the stability of the optimized logistic regression model. In this analysis, each observation is classified using a model created on the basis of the entire sample except for the observation being classified. The results serve as an upper-bound estimate of the classification performance that is expected were the optimized model to be used to classify an independent sample of observations. Separate analyses were performed for novice and experienced officers.

19 These beliefs had similar predictive accuracy for novice and experienced officers' decisions, though the model was more stable for experienced officers than for novice officers. The UniODA analysis for the overall sample correctly classified 76.67% of the nonreferrals and 56.45% of the referrals and correctly predicted 63.01% of the nonreferrals and 71.43% of the referrals (monte carlo $p < .01$).

By using these beliefs to guide their decisions, officers deny some women knowledge about these services. Table 4 shows that officers primarily recommended mental health treatment for wives with hallucinations or with alcoholism, which are associated with danger and an inability to understand that violence is wrong.[20] Officers, however, rarely refer women with unusual startled responses (6.3% were referred) because they perceive them as not dangerous and as understanding that violence is wrong.

Table 4. Relationship between Wife's Mental State and Officers' Recommendations about Mental Health Treatment and Shelters

	Wife's Mental State			
	Normal	Perceptual Disorder	Alcoholism	Unusual Startled Response
% recommended to outpatient[a] mental health treatment	3.1%[b]	65.6%	21.9%	6.3%
Standardized residual	−2.4[c]	4.8	−0.3	−2.1
% recommended to battered[d] spouse shelters	59.4%	21.9%	43.8%	75.0%
Standardized residual	0.8	−2.3	−0.5	2.0

[a] The relationship between wife's mental state and referrals to outpatient mental health treatment is significant, χ^2 (3; N = 128) = 43.38, p < .001.

[b] These numbers represent the percentage of wives with this mental state who were referred to outpatient treatment or were referred to battered spouse shelters.

[c] These numbers are standardized residuals. Negative and positive numbers that are greater than 1.0 indicate that the cell is significantly different from the other cells.

[d] The relationship between wife's mental state and referrals to battered spouse shelters is significant, χ^2 (3; N = 128) = 19.75, p < .001.

While officers often recommend battered spouse shelters for women displaying unusual startled responses (75% were referred), they refer fewer women with alcoholism or hallucinations to shelters. These disparate decisions occur because officers perceive men as less dangerous when they beat women who have hallucinations and alcoholism (see Table 3).

C. Officers' Use of Prior Knowledge in Their Decisions to Arrest

Prior studies examining broad attitudinal statements about officers' role orientations find that these attitudes are weakly related to their arrest decisions (Worden 1989). Our findings suggest that a more promising approach is to examine specific knowledge about the domain. Our findings, moreover, emphasize that officers do not interpret every situation based on their general beliefs about typical domestic disputes or about the wife's provocation. The application of beliefs, as suggested by

---

[20] Social class and officers' experience did not have either significant direct or interactive effects with mental illness on officers' recommendations about shelters or mental health treatment.

schema theory, is contingent on the situation. We tested whether officers categorized wives as typical battered wives when they abused alcohol or had unusual startled responses, and based decisions on prior beliefs about provocation in these situations. We also tested whether experienced officers place more importance on efficiency considerations than do novice officers.[21] Table 5 shows that the situation defined whether officers use their general beliefs about wives' provocation of violence to form their decisions. Only when wives showed signs of alcoholism did officers' beliefs about provocation in a typical domestic dispute guide their decisions about arrest. In situations where wives were abusing alcohol, officers who believed that wives usually provoke their husbands were less likely to arrest than were officers who did not believe that wives provoke their husbands. Alcohol abuse may have served as a cue that allowed officers to classify the case as a typical domestic dispute and to use their content specific knowledge about wife assaults.[22]

In situations where officers cannot easily categorize the dispute into their prior content knowledge about wife assaults, they must use frames to organize and interpret the conflicting stories and use these interpretations to form decisions.[23] Table 5 also supports the hypothesis that experience partly determines the importance of normative and efficiency framing. Both novice and experienced officers considered efficiency concerns about

---

[21] Because few officers chose mediation as the only response to handling the situation (11.7%), we employed a dichotomous measure of how the wife assault was handled: 0 = informal mediation or ask one disputant to leave (41.4%); 1 = arrest the husband or arrest both (59.4%). Only five respondents decided to arrest both spouses; we included these respondents with "arrest the husband" to assess when officers use formal intervention methods.

We created two dummy-coded variables for officers' experience and training with untrained novice officers serving as the baseline: (*a*) 1 = experienced officers and 0 = novice; and (*b*) 1 = trained novice officers and 0 = other. To create interaction term for officers' experience and substantiating claims, we assigned a value of 1 to experienced officers who mentioned evidence to substantiate claims and a value of 0 to all other officers. We treated wife's mental state as a grouping variable and tested the overall effect of officers' general beliefs across situations, the effect within the normal condition, the unusual started response condition, and the alcoholism condition. We tested the effect within the normal condition because officers may have developed a category for situations where wives' actions are consistent with societal norms. We did not test the effect within the hallucinating condition because officers have fewer experiences from which to create a category of this type of battered wife.

[22] Some research suggests wives who are drinking are held more responsible for the violence (Ferraro 1989a; Richardson & Campbell 1980; Waaland & Keeley 1985). Officers more often spontaneously attributed the cause of the violence to the wife's behavior when she showed signs of alcoholism (53.3%) than when she was normal (20.0%), hallucinating (20.0%), or had unusual startled responses (3.1%) ($\chi^2(3) = 8.62$, $p < .03$). Women with alcoholism were seen as provoking the violence perhaps because officers believe they were more dangerous and often hit their husbands.

[23] Based on these predictors, UniODA was correct 68.63% of the time when it predicted informal measures and 84.29% of the time when it predicted arrest. It correctly classified 76.09% of the informal responses and 78.67% of the arrest responses. LOO analysis showed no shrinkage in classification or predictive accuracy, indicating that the model should generalize to other samples.

308   **How Novice and Experienced Officers Interpret Wife Assaults**

Table 5. Inferences Related to Officers' Decision to Arrest: Logistic
Coefficients and Change in Odds

Predictors	b	Change in Odds
Constant	−2.35*	
Officers' experience		
Trained novice officers	1.38**	3.98**
Experienced officers	−.24	.786
Officers' beliefs about wives provoke		
Overall wives provoke beating	−.14	.87
Effect within normal condition	−.21	.81
Effect within unusual startled	−.16	.85
Effect within alcoholism	−.38*	.68*
Officers' inferences		
Husband is blamed	1.38**	4.00**
Substantiating claims	.16	1.17
Husband is dangerous	.51***	1.67***
Effectiveness of arrest	.44**	1.56**
Effect of substantiating claims for experienced officers	1.98**	7.25**
−2 log likelihood		112.45
Model χ^2		48.27***

NOTE: Numbers in the "*b*" column are unstandardized logistic estimates. Numbers under the "Odds" column are the change in odds of choosing arrest. Higher odds indicate that as the predictor variable increases the odds of arresting the man or both disputants increases. For example, when the man is seen as more dangerous, officers are 1.67 times more likely to arrest compared with when the man is seen as less dangerous.
One-tailed probability: * $p < .05$; ** $p < .025$; *** $p < .01$; **** $p < .001$.

the effectiveness of arrest at reducing violence and about the perceived dangerousness of the husband. Novice and experienced officers, however, placed a different emphasis on substantiating claims for successful prosecution. As expected, experienced officers with their pragmatic and self-interested concerns were 7.25 times more likely to arrest if they mentioned evidence to substantiate claims than if they did not. Experienced officers then spontaneously framed decisions in terms of whether claims could be supported and successfully prosecuted—when the woman was seen as more dangerous or as causing the violence to occur, officers were less likely to take formal action. In contrast, novice officers did not frame the decision based on evidence to substantiate claims (change in odds = 1.17, $p < .34$).[24]

Table 5 provides support that officers also use blameworthiness to frame situations. Officers who blamed the husband were four times more likely to arrest than were officers who did not blame the husband. Novice and experienced officers, as expected, also differ on their propensity to frame situations in terms of blame. Novice officers more often spontaneously mentioned that the husband should have acted otherwise (23.7%)

---

[24] Untrained novice officers did not differ from trained novice officers as supported by the zero-ordered correlations between substantiating claims and arrest (for untrained novice officers, $r = .21$, $p < .28$; for trained novices, $r = .14$, $p < .34$).

than did experienced officers (10.4%;, χ^2 (1; $N = 128$) = 3.66, one-tailed $p < .03$).[25]

Novice officers place more priority on normative framing, whereas experienced officers place more importance on efficiency framing. This differential framing shapes how they define the effectiveness of arrest at reducing future violence. Table 6, which supports this conclusion, presents the correlations between inferences about the husband's ability to understand the wrongfulness of violence and inferences about the effectiveness of arrest within the officers' experience.

Table 6. Novice and Experienced Officers' Definitions of Effectivenss of Arrest (Correlations Within Experience/Training)

	Officers' Experience and Training		
Correlations of Husband's Ability to Understand Wrongfulness with:[a]	Untrained Novice (*N*=32)	Trained Novice (*N*=42)	Trained Experienced (*N*=45)
Arrest reduces likelihood husband†† will severely harm wife again	.41**	.28*	−.30**
Husband will inflict severe harm on†† wife if he remains in the home	.34*	−.10	−.47***
Believes husband should have† acted otherwise	.30*	−.29*	−.14

NOTE: The negative sign by a correlation indicates that as the value of the row variable increases, the perceived dangerousness of the husband decreases. E.g., experienced officers believe that arrest is less effective if husbands have more ability to understand that violence is wrong ($r = -.30$).

One-tailed probability: $*p < .05$; $** p < .025$; $*** p < .01$.

[a] Z-tests for differences between correlations from independent samples were performed to assess differences between untrained novice officers and expereinced officers.

Two-tailed probability that correlation for untrained novice officers differs from that for experienced officers: † $p < .05$; †† $p < .01$.

Novice officers with their normative perspective define the effectiveness of arrest based on their belief that individuals who understand right from wrong choose whether to commit wrongful acts such as violence, and arrest serves as punishment or an opportunity to correct their choice to commit violence either through deterrence or rehabilitation. Untrained novice officers ($r = .41$) and trained novice officers ($r = .29$) believed that arrest

---

25 When an interaction term between untrained novice officers and their perceptions of the husband's ability to understand wrongfulness is substituted for overtly blaming the husband in the equation on arrest decisions, it is significant and in the expected direction. As the ability to understand wrongfulness increases, untrained novice officers are more likely to arrest (change in odds = 1.69, $p < .05$). We found, however, that when we controlled for the other inferences, trained novice officers and experienced officers do not consider husband's ability to understand wrongfulness. Further supporting the idea that untrained novice officers think about blame, untrained novice officers are more likely to blame the husband when he understands the wrongfulness of violence ($r = .30$, $p < .05$). Such novices do not consider a pattern of repeat abuse in placing blame, whereas trained novice officers do; this may explain why untrained officers are more likely to blame the husband when the husband has less understanding of the wrongfulness of his actions ($r = -.30$, $p < .05$).

would be more effective when the husband understood that violence is wrong. Recent formal training then appears to have little effect on shifting novice officers' focus away from normative considerations toward efficiency considerations; this is consistent with ethnographic research that indicates that experience is more important than formal academy training (Van Maanen 1974).

Conversely, experienced officers define the effectiveness of arrest for reducing future violence based on the current situational contingencies and such practical considerations as time and limited resources (e.g., Berk & Loseke 1981; Bittner 1967; Ferraro & Pope 1993) rather than the personality style of the disputants. With this efficiency framing, experienced officers believed husbands who understood that violence is wrong were *less* likely to harm the wife if they remained in the home than were husband who lacked this understanding ($r = -.47$). Experienced officers, then, believed that arrest was unnecessary for those who understood that violence was wrong because informal mediation or a "cooling-off" period could remove the environmental stress that caused the violence, but that arrest became necessary to protect a wife when a husband was less able to understand the wrongfulness of his actions.

C. Consequences of Different Frames

When injured wives violate behavioral norms and cannot control their actions, normative framing suggests that the husband acted unjustifiably and should be arrested, whereas efficiency framing suggests that these wives will be seen as less credible and more dangerous than the husband, characteristics which make arrest a less effective technique. Both novice and experienced officers perceive wives who are hallucinating as less able to control their actions and understand that violence is wrong. Because novice officers more often use normative framing, they will be more likely to arrest the husband when a wife is hallucinating than will experienced officers. Table 7 supports this hypothesis: Novice officers were 3.10 times more likely to arrest a husband when he injured a hallucinating wife than were experienced officers (one-tailed $p < .01$). Some research suggests that women are blamed because officers see them as choosing to violate norms (e.g., Ferraro 1989b; Hatty 1989; Hilton 1993a; Saunders & Size 1986). Experienced officers with an efficiency frame offer less protection to wives who violate norms about appropriate thoughts and behavior, irrespective of whether the officers perceive these wives as being able to control their actions. This finding suggests that broader concerns such as substantiating claims for successful prosecution and conserving time for other cases may be more central to officers' decisions than whether wives have control over their actions.

Table 7. Novice and Experienced Officers' Decisions to Arrest When the Wife is Hallucinating

Predictors	b	Change in Odds
Constant	−.64	
Couple's social class	−.17	.84
Trained, novice officers	1.17***	3.22
Experienced officers	.99*	2.68
Hallucinating wife	.12	1.13
Alcoholism	.28	1.32
Unusual startled response	.60	1.81
Response to hallucinating wife:		
Increase for novice officers compared with that for experienced officers	1.13***	3.10
−2 log likelihood		160.28***
Model χ^2		12.62*

NOTE: Numbers in the "*b*" column are unstandardized logistic estimates. Numbers under the "Odds" column are the change in odds of choosing arrest. Higher odds indicate that as the predictor variable increases the odds of arresting the man or both disputants increases.

One-tailed probability levels: * $p < .05$; ** $p < .025$; *** $p < .01$; **** $p < .001$.

Moreover, the significant direct effect of trained novice officers compared with other officers suggests that trained novice officers are more likely to arrest than either untrained novice or trained experienced officers because their recent training sensitizes them to do something. The difference between trained novice officers and trained experienced officers suggests that the sensitizing effects of formal training fade with time.

Prior observational studies find that officers are less likely to arrest in wife assault situations involving lower-income couples than in those involving middle-income couples because they infer habitual violence among lower-income couples (Black 1980; Ferraro 1989a; Smith 1987). Officers, irrespective of experience, believed 71.30% of couples in poverty habitually resort to violence compared with 57.45% of middle-income couples (pairwise *t*-test (116) = 8.03, $p < .003$). Social class of the couple, contrary to prior observational studies, did not have direct effects on officers' decisions to arrest as shown in Table 6. Social class, however, did have indirect effects through officers' assessment of the husband's dangerousness. Officers relied on their prior knowledge about social class differences to assess dangerousness. Because of these different schemata for low-income and middle-income couples, officers perceived low-income husbands as dangerous irrespective of their perceptions about whether a wife had hit her husband in the past ($M = 5.4$). Conversely, middle-income husbands are seen as more dangerous when officers infer that a wife has not hit her husband in the past ($M = 5.46$) than when they infer she has hit him (M = 3.91; p < .05). This finding suggests that inferences about wives' past actions may have more influence on officers' judgments of dangerousness in situations with middle-income couples than in situations with lower-income couples.

V. Conclusions

Prior research has produced mixed claims about how much officers frame situations in terms of blameworthiness and how wives' actions shape their interpretations. Some feminist scholars make the strongest argument that officers focus on blameworthiness but provide weak systematic data on how officers interpret situations. For example, Hanmer et al. (1989a:6) have asserted:

> The police are making a distinction between attacks they deem to be justifiable and those that are not—that is, those that require police attention. This decision-making process demonstrates that police do not offer unconditional protection to all women against forms of men's violence. Rather any protection they offer is conditional upon women meeting police notions of "deservedness" and the circumstances of the attack meeting their definition of "crime." These notions are inevitably informed by the misogyny, racism, classism, and heterosexism of dominant social ideologies.

Feminists criticize police use of the victim's deservedness because they believe that it determines officers' reluctance to use formal arrest and to listen to victims' preferences. Conversely, other researchers find that officers often remain neutral (Black 1980) and base arrest on efficiency considerations of time needed to process an arrest, the likelihood of severe harm in the future, and substantiating claims for successful prosecution (Ferraro & Pope 1993).

Prior research derives claims about the decisionmaking process from retrospective data and from weak indirect observational data without asking officers follow-up summary questions (Mastrofski & Parks 1990). We collected data on officers' spontaneous inferences to address more directly whether officers frame situations more in terms of blameworthiness or of efficiency concerns about substantiating claims and devoting time to those situations which may result in severe harm in the future. Our findings address two important theoretical issues: (*a*) how officers make decisions when women's actions deviate from societal norms due to mental illness; and (*b*) the priority novice and experienced officers place on normative and efficiency considerations when women conform to or deviate from societal norms.

Hallucinating wives who have moderately severe injuries present dilemmas for officers. On the one hand, officers perceive difficulty in successfully prosecuting husbands because they believe

these wives are less credible and more dangerous than their husbands. On the other hand, they see hallucinating wives compared with normal wives as less able to control their provoking
actions and as less able to understand that violence is wrong,
which suggests that the husbands acted unjustifiably even if their
hallucinating wives provoked them. Novice officers, consistent
with using blameworthiness as a decision criteria, more often
blamed the husband and arrested him when the wives were hallucinating than when they were normal. By contrast, when experienced officers must assign different importance to normative
and efficiency considerations because the situation creates conflict between these concerns, they place priority on efficiency
considerations. Experienced officers arrested husbands less often
when wives were hallucinating than when they were normal because they perceived the hallucinating wives as relatively less
credible and more dangerous than the husbands. Indeed, when
the wives were normal, experienced officers were more likely to
arrest the husbands than were novice officers. These findings
suggest that experienced officers do not use informal methods
because they see women as capable of controlling their actions
but because they perceive women who conform to societal norms
as more believable, less dangerous, and more able to facilitate
successful prosecution. In doing so, experienced officers think
more about irreparable harm and substantiated claims, which
supports much prior research on police decisionmaking (e.g.,
Berk & Loseke 1981; Ferraro & Pope 1993; Kerstetter & Van Winkle 1990; Manning 1977; Van Maanen 1974) but challenges
claims that officers often blame women (Ferraro 1989b; Hanmer
et al. 1989a; Hawkins 1992; Hilton 1993a; Jaffe et al. 1993). Experienced officers base decisions on the appropriateness of a
wife's action primarily when it is pragmatically feasible—when
they can defend their decision based on disinterested objectivity,
and such decisions will not increase their time on undervalued
tasks or threaten their job status.

Though officers try in good faith to be disinterested and im-
partial decisionmakers, categorical knowledge systems often
shape their interpretations and lead them to use informal methods when wives violate societal norms. Our findings, consistent
with schema theory (Fiske & Taylor 1991; Stalans & Lurigio
1990), indicate that content knowledge about mental illness and
wife assaults shapes interpretations when a specific case shares
features with the exemplar or typical member. Stereotyped
images of mentally ill persons, for example, informed officers'
neutral assessments and produced a systematic bias toward a reluctance to use arrest and shelters for injured hallucinating
wives. Our findings also suggest that officers have and use prior
beliefs about whether wives typically provoke their husbands' violence when wives are abusing alcohol. Alcohol abuse is a salient

cue within our society (e.g., Kantor & Straus 1987; Waaland & Keeley 1985) and is seen as a common occurrence in domestic violence situations (Ferraro 1989a); this feature allows officers to conclude that the situation exemplifies a typical case. Thus, strong claims about police officers making decisions based on the victim's deservedness or blameworthiness should be softened and reframed to highlight how prior categorical knowledge such as mental illness and social class shapes neutral assessments.

Similarly, officers use their prior knowledge to interpret situations, and these interpretations determine which battered wives will receive information about shelters and mental health treatment. We found that officers referred very few women with unusual startled responses and alcoholism to outpatient mental health treatment centers. Because officers serve as primary referral sources (Gilboy & Schmidt 1971; Sheridan & Teplin 1981) and are less likely to provide these women with information about the availability of outpatient mental health treatment, these women have less opportunity to seek possibly beneficial outpatient mental health treatment. Although some research suggests that mental health treatment can benefit women who suffer from battered spouse syndrome (for a review see Barnett & LaViolette 1993), additional research could determine the benefits and costs associated with officers' selective referrals to outpatient mental health treatment. We also found that officers refer very few women who have alcoholism or hallucinations to battered spouse shelters, even though officers regard these situations as highly prone to violence. Several possible consequences of withholding information about battered spouse shelters could be explored in future research. For example, does lack of knowledge about battered spouse shelters perpetuate violence against women who suffer from mental illnesses such as alcoholism or perceptual disorders?

Schema theory predicts that people can more easily recall and may automatically use frames that are often employed in other decisionmaking tasks or have been recently employed. This prediction and our research findings imply that organizations can influence the priority officers place on normative framing compared with efficiency framing. We, however, do not provide direct empirical support for this implication. Based on the assumed connection between organizational socialization and framing, our findings for experienced officers should generalize to departments that emphasize efficiency considerations of time and quantity of service but should not generalize to departments that emphasize the normative basis of criminal law and the enforcement of laws for the sake of reinforcing societal and individual understanding of the wrongfulness associated with violations of these laws. While prior research makes clear that individual officers may find ways to avoid organizational policies that require certain response styles (Brown 1981), research needs to examine how organizational culture relates to how officers think about situations. We suggest that officers within an organization after similar socialization may think more like each other than would a randomly selected group of officers from different organizations.[26] To examine this proposition, future studies should employ additional measures of the nature of officers' prior experience with domestic violence cases, measures of the departmental policies for handling wife assaults, and measures of the incentives to either arrest or not arrest in wife assault situations. Future studies also should compare novice officers' decisionmaking with laypersons' decisionmaking to assess whether the propensity to use normative framing derives from common earlier socialization or from conservative political philosophies.

Our approach highlights the pitfalls of preferred and mandatory arrest policies. These policies attempt to constrain officers' responses to situations without considering how officers make decisions. Given the complexity and inherent ambiguity in most domestic violence situations, telling officers what to do without understanding how they do their job opens the door to resentment and to decisions that provide unequal protection. Officers may respond better to a cooperative and collaborative effort at improving a grave social problem. To take this approach with officers requires an understanding that many officers often do not employ biased attitudes that blame women for their abuse but operate based on self-interest and job demands. On an organizational level, departments can increase personal incentives for arresting husbands when wives have moderately severe injuries, which sends a normative message that violence in the home is wrong; of course, research should examine whether this policy leaves women at more risk of future physical harm and creates more community support for the wrongfulness of wife assaults. Without changes in how prosecutors and courts handle these cases, however, such departmental policies may not lead to greater numbers of arrests of batterers or greater protection of battered victims. In addition, officers must be made aware of the fallacies in the categories that they use to interpret credibility and dangerousness; without such instructions, efficiency framing will still lead to unequal application of arrest to handle wife as-

---

26 This statement, however, should not be taken to mean complete homogeneity among officers in the same office; it implies that organizational culture does influence how officers frame situations. The same frame, as our results clearly demonstrate, can lead to quite divergent responses depending on the situation. Individuality, moreover, can occur due to differences in the kinds of domestic disputes experienced, the nature of the beat, and the nature of informal socialization. Muir (1977) provides a clear example of how an officer who always had to work the third shift had little contact with fellow officers and developed inadequate skills to handle domestic violence situations. Brown (1981) also suggests that police officers' attitudes about bureaucratic control may determine in part their susceptibility to organizational incentives and policies.

saults involving women who deviate from societal norms, which leaves departments open to civil liability suits based on unequal protection claims. Some research shows that instructions about how beliefs about certain categories should be ignored reduces the biasing nature of these categories (see Fiske & Taylor 1991) and may reduce disparity in officers' decisions about wife assault situations involving similar evidence of harm but dissimilar victims.

Appendix

Scripts Using Normal, Low-Income Couple

The script begins with the dispatcher reporting that a caller reports hearing shouting and screaming coming from the dwelling. Officers go to the scene. After informing the husband why they are there and receiving permission to enter, the officers begin with simple questions they were taught in academy training. They ask for his name, whether he lives alone, whether the couple is legally married, and whether they have any children. Bob and Sally Jones, the disputants, are legally married and have no children. The officers note Bob's height and weight (5 feet 7 inches tall, weighing about 150 pounds) and then ask to see Mrs. Jones.

Bob, like many batterers, tries to convince the police officers that everything is fine before they see the wife: "Where is your wife, Mr. Jones?" asks Officer Kelley. "She's layin' in the livingroom. She ain't feelin' too good," says Mr. Jones. "Do you mind if we speak to her?" asks Officer Kelly. "Well, she ain't feeling good, like I told ya. I don't think she wants to see nobody," replies Mr. Jones. "I must insist that we see her, Mr. Jones," replies the officer. "Okay, she's in the first room on the left," pointing down the hall. "Why don't we all go to the livingroom?" replies Officer Kelly, motioning with his arm.

The officers enter the livingroom and see Mrs. Jones sitting in a chair. "She looks to be about 5 feet 4 inches tall and weighing about 120 pounds. Her right eye and neck are bruised and swollen. The right sleeve of her shirt is torn and the shirt is twisted across her chest. She looks at the officers, her eyes are red and swollen, and her lip is cut and bleeding." The two officers decide to split up and interview each disputant separately. The respondent first reads the exchange between Officer Kelley and the husband, Bob Jones.

Officer Jones begins with a less threatening question: "Have you lived here long, Mr. Jones?" (Here Mr. Jones provides information about the couple's social class.) He replies, "We moved into this dump about six months ago after Sal and I lost our cleanin' jobs at the hotel down the street. Place just up and closed like that. Left us with nothin' out there." Officer Kelly asks, "We heard the two of you yelling as we came to the door, what was that all about?" "Oh, was no big deal. My wife didn't pick me up at the welfare office and it took me an extra hour to get home cuz the bus is so slow." [For the middle-income disputants, Mr. Jones replies, "We moved in here about six months ago after Sally and I got our teaching jobs. I teach at the high school and she teaches at the middle school." Officer Kelly asks, "We heard the two of you yelling as we came to the door, what was that all about?" Mr. Jones replies, "Oh, it was no big deal. My wife didn't pick me up at school and it took me an extra hour to get home because the bus is so slow."]

When Officer Kelly suggests that the noise sounded like a big deal, Mr. Jones volunteers to tell him the whole story: "Like I said, Sal didn't pick me up from welfare. I told her to be there at 3:30, but today she didn't show. So I decided I would take the bus and I hate taking the bus. . . ." Officer Kelly interjects, "What happened when you got home, Mr. Jones?" "Well, I open the door and Sal starts yellin' at me about somethin'. I didn't even get the door closed before she attacked me. All she wants to do is pick fights for somethin' minor. I think she's really mad cuz I went out last night with some friends. We argued yesterday morning about something . . . When she starts yellin' I stay clear of her. I usually ignore her hopin' she will quiet down, but usually, she keeps rantin' until finally I lost it. I tell her to shut up, that I had a long day and that she didn't pick me up and I'm really mad. She started hittin' me. I shoved her off me. I think she fell pretty hard. Man, she can't even fall right," says Mr. Jones, shaking his head." [Batterers often blame the victim as Mr. Jones does here (Barnett & LaViolette 1993).] Officer Kelly then asks, "Do your arguments often come to blows?" Mr Jones replies, "I usually ignore her by walking away when she starts yelling. This time, when I walked away, I had to push her off me."

The script then turns to Officer Johnson's interview with Mrs. Jones. After introducing himself and the purpose of his visit, Officer Johnson asks, "Are you okay, Mrs. Jones?" She responds, "These bruises and cuts will heal, I guess." Officer Johnson asks, "How did this happen to you?" Mrs. Jones states, "Oh, there's ain't much I remember. It's been a long day and I ain't thinkin' too good. I guess my husband was mad cuz I didn't pick him up at the welfare office. Damn car ran out of gas and I had to walk about a mile to get some. It took me about half an hour or so, so I was late gettin' to welfare. Bob wasn't there on the corner, so I figured he found another way to get home. The minute he got home we started yellin' back and forth at each other." Officer Johnson asks, "You said we started yelling, were you also angry about something?" Mrs. Jones replies, "No, I wasn't angry 'til he screamed at me as soon as he came through the door. It didn't kill him to take the bus. He is so lazy. I told him two days ago we were out of milk and cigarettes and he ain't picked that stuff up yet. Tonight when I asked him about it, he flew off the handle. . . . Things got so bad, I decided to leave and let him cool off, but before I could make it out the door, he jumped me." Officer Johnson asks, "Has this ever happened before?" Mrs. Jones replies, "Every now and then, I guess."

When Officer Johnson finishes interviewing Mrs. Jones, the two disputants are brought together and begin to argue. The script ends with their argument: Mr. Jones asks his wife, "What did you tell him?" Sally remains silent. Mr. Jones continues, "Did you tell him that you started this fight by yellin at me after you didn't pick me up from welfare when you were supposed to? No, I suppose you told him it was all my fault." Mrs. Jones states, "I told him the truth, Bob. That you came in the door angry and we started yellin'. You wouldn't let me go over to Carol's place and I . . ." Mr. Jones interrupts, "That's a lie. I ain't never stopped you from visitin' your friends. I only asked you to tell me where you

318   **How Novice and Experienced Officers Interpret Wife Assaults**

were goin' and when you'd be back. I don't mind when you visit your
friends. Actually, I wish you had gone over to Carol's place when you
first got home, maybe talking to her would have cooled you off some.
I'd rather you complain to her than bite my head off when I come in
the door." Mrs. Jones replies, "You're always sayin' I'm attackin' you. I
don't like to argue. I'm stinkin' tired of it. I'm tired of your constant
nagging. I'm tired of being angry." Mr. Jones replies in a sharp tone,
"I'm tired of your demands. I'm tired of you puttin' me down and
shovin' me around."

References

American Psychiatric Association (1987) *Diagnostic and Statistical Manual of
    Mental Disorders.* 3d ed. rev. Washington, DC: American Psychiatric Associa-
    tion.
Barnett, Ola W., & Alyce D. LaViolette (1993) *It Could Happen to Anyone: Why
    Battered Women Stay.* Newbury Park, CA: Sage Publications.
Barnett, Ola W., & R. W. Fagan (1993) "Alcohol Use in Male Spouse Abusers
    and Their Female Partners," 8 *J. of Family Violence* 1.
Baumgartner, M. P. (1992) "The Myth of Discretion," in Hawkins 1992b.
Bell, D. J., & S. L. Bell (1991) "The Victim Offender Relationship as a Determi-
    nant Factor in Police Dispositions of Family Violence Incidents: A Replica-
    tion Study," 1 *Policing & Society* 225.
Belknap, Joanne, & K. Douglas McCall (1994) "Woman Battering and Police
    Referrals," 22(3) *J. of Criminal Justice* 223.
Berk, Sarah Fenstermaker, & Donileen R. Loseke (1981) " 'Handling' Family
    Violence: Situational Determinants of Police Arrest in Domestic Distur-
    bances," 15 *Law & Society Rev.* 317.
Bittner, Egon (1967) "Police Discretion in Emergency Apprehension of Men-
    tally Ill Persons," 14 *Social Problems* 278.
———— (1990) *Aspects of Police Work.* Boston: Northeastern Univ. Press.
Black, Donald J. (1980) *The Manners and Customs of the Police.* New York: Aca-
    demic Press.
Black, John B., James A. Galambos & Stephen J. Read (1984) "Comprehending
    Stories and Social Situations," in R. S. Wyer & T. K. Srull, eds., 3 *Handbook
    of Social Cognition* 45. Hillsdale, NJ: Lawrence Erlbaum Associates.
Brown, Michael K. (1981) *Working the Street: Police Discretion and the Dilemmas of
    Reform.* New York: Russell Sage Foundation.
Carlile, J. B. (1991) "Spouse Assault on Mentally Disordered Wives," 36(4) *Ca-
    nadian J. of Psychiatry* 265.
Carroll, John S., Richard L. Wiener, Dan Coates, Jolene Galegher, & James
    Alibrio (1982) "Evaluation, Diagnosis, and Prediction in Parole Decision-
    making," 17 *Law & Society Rev.* 199.
Chi, M. T. H., R. Glaser, & M. J. Farr (1988) *The Nature of Expertise.* Hillsdale, NJ:
    Lawrence Erlbaum Associates.
Desforges, D. M., C. G. Lord, S. L. Ramsey, J. A. Mason, M. D. Van Leeuwen, S.
    C. West, & M. R. Lepper (1993) "Effects of Structured Cooperative Contact
    on Changing Negative Attitudes toward Stigmatized Social Groups," 60 *J. of
    Personality & Social Psychology* 531.
Dobash, R. Emerson, & Russell Dobash (1979) *Violence against Wives: A Case
    against the Patriarchy.* New York: Free Press.
Drass, Kriss A., & J. William Spencer (1987) "Accounting for Pre-sentencing
    Recommendations: Typologies and Probation Officers' Theory of Office,"
    34(7) *Social Problems* 277.
Emerson, Robert M. (1969) *Judging Delinquents: Context and Process in Juvenile
    Court.* Chicago: Aldine Publishing Co.

—— (1983) "Holistic Effects in Social Control Decision-making," 17 *Law & Society Rev.* 425.

Feldman, Martha S. (1992) "Social Limits to Discretion: An Organizational Perspective," in Hawkins 1992b.

Ferraro, K. J. (1989a) "Policing Woman Battering," 36(1) *Social Problems* 61.

Ferraro, Kathleen J. (1989b) "The Legal Response to Woman Battering in the United States," in Hanmer et al. 1989b.

—— (1993) "Cops, Courts, and Woman Battering," in P. B. Bart & E. G. Moran, eds., *Violence against Women: The Bloody Footprints*. Newbury Park, CA: Sage Publications.

Ferraro, Kathleen J., & Lucille Pope (1993) "Irreconcilable Differences: Battered Women, Police and the Law," in Hilton 1993b.

Fielding, Nigel G. (1986) "Evaluating the Role of Training in Police Socialization: A British Example," 14 *J. of Community Psychology* 319.

—— (1988) *Joining Forces: Police Training, Socialization, and Occupational Competence*. New York: Routledge.

Fielding, Nigel G., & J. Fielding (1991) "Police Attitudes to Crime and Punishment: Certainties and Dilemmas," 31 *British J. of Criminology* 39.

Fiske, Susan T., & Steven L. Neuberg (1990) "A Continuum of Impression Formation from Category-based to Individuating Processes: Influences of Information and Motivation on Attention and Interpretation," in M. P. Zanna, ed., 23 *Advances in Experimental Social Psychology*. San Diego, CA: Academic Press.

Fiske, Susan T., & Shelley E. Taylor (1991) *Social Cognition*. New York: McGraw-Hill.

Gilboy, Janet A. (1991) "Deciding Who Gets in: Decisionmaking by Immigration Inspectors," 25 *Law & Society Rev.* 571.

Gilboy, Janet A., & John R. Schmidt (1971) " 'Voluntary' Hospitalization of the Mentally Ill," 66 *Northwestern Univ. Law Rev.* 429.

Hanmer, Jalna, Jill Radford, & Elizabeth A. Stanko (1989a) "Policing, Men's Violence: An Introduction," in Hanmer et al. 1989b.

Hanmer, Jalna, Jill Radford & Elizabeth A. Stanko, eds. (1989b) *Women, Policing, and Male Violence: International Perspectives*. New York: Routledge.

Hatty, Suzanne E. (1989) "Policing and Male Violence in Australia," in Hanmer et al. 1989b.

Hawkins, Keith (1992a) "The Use of Legal Discretion: Perspectives from Law and Social Science," in Hawkins 1992b.

——, ed. (1992b) *The Uses of Discretion*. Oxford: Clarendon Press.

Hilton, Zoe N. (1993a) "Police Intervention and Public Opinion," in Hilton 1993b.

——, ed. (1993b) *Legal Responses to Wife Assault: Current Trends and Evaluation*. Newbury Park, CA: Sage Publications.

Hirschel, J. David, & Ira Hutchinson (1991) "Police-preferred Arrest Policies," in M. Steinman, ed., *Woman Battering: Policy Responses*. Cincinnati, OH: Anderson Publishing Co.

Jaffe, Peter G., Elaine Hastings, Deborah Reitzel, & Gary W. Austin (1993) "The Impact of Police Laying Charges," in Hilton 1993b.

Kantor, Glenda Kaufman, & Murray A. Straus (1987) "The 'Drunken Bum' Theory of Wife Beating," 34(3) *Social Problems* 213.

Kerstetter, Wayne A., & Barrick Van Winkle (1990) "Who Decides? A Study of the Complainant's Decision to Prosecute in Rape Cases," 17(3) *Criminal Justice & Behavior* 268.

Law Enforcement News (1987) "Roughening Up: Spouse Abuse Arrest Grow," *Law Enforcement News*, p. 1 (10 March 10).

Lurigio, Arthur J., & John S. Carroll (1985) "Probation Officers' Schemata of Offenders: Content, Development, and Impact of Treatment Decisions," 48 *J. of Personality & Social Psychology* 1112.

320   **How Novice and Experienced Officers Interpret Wife Assaults**

Lurigio, Arthur J., & Loretta J. Stalans (1990) "Thinking More about How Criminal Justice Decision Makers Think," 17(3) *Criminal Justice & Behavior* 260.

Manning, Peter (1977) *Police Work*. Cambridge, MA: MIT Press.

Manning, Peter, & Keith Hawkins (1989) "Police Decision-Making," in M. Weatheritt, ed., *Police Research: Where Now?* Brookfield, VT: Gower.

—— (1990) "Legal Decisions: A Frame Analytic Perspective," in S. Riggins, ed., *Beyond Goffman*. Berlin: Mouton de Gruyter.

Martin, Del (1976) *Battered Wives*. San Francisco, CA: Glide Publications.

Mastrofski, Stephen, & Roger B. Parks (1990) "Improving Observational Studies of Police," 28 *Criminology* 475.

Mastrofski, Stephen D., R. Richard Ritti, & Jeffrey B. Snipes (1994) "Expectancy Theory and Police Productivity in DUI Enforcement," 28 *Law & Society Rev.* 113.

Muir, William Ker, Jr., (1977) *Police: Streetcorner Politicians*. Chicago: Univ. of Chicago Press.

Reiss, Albert J., Jr. (1971) *The Police and the Public*. New Haven, CT: Yale Univ. Press.

Richardson, D. C. & Campbell, J. L. (1980) "Alcohol and Wife Abuse: The Effect of Alcohol on Attributions of Blame for Wife Abuse," 6(1) *Personality & Social Psychology Bull.* 51.

Riksheim, Eric C., & Steven M. Chermak (1993) "Causes of Police Behavior Revisited," 21 *J. of Criminal Justice* 353.

Roy, M. (1988) *Children in the Crossfire*. Deerfield Beach, FL: Health Communications.

Rumlehart, David E. (1984) "Schemata and the Cognitive System," in R. S. Wyer & T. K. Srull, eds., 1 *Handbook of Social Cognition*. Hillsdale, NJ: Lawrence Erlbaum Associates.

Saunders, D. G., & P. B. Size (1986) "Attitudes about Woman Abuse among Police Officers, Victims, and Victim Advocates," 1 *J. of Interpersonal Violence* 25.

Scheff, T. J. (1984) *Being Mentally Ill*. New York: Aldine Publishing Co.

Shaver, K. G. (1985) *The Attribution of Blame: Causality, Responsibility, and Blameworthiness*. New York: Springer-Verlag.

Sheridan, E., & Linda Teplin (1981) "Police-referred Psychiatric Emergencies: Advantages of Community Treatment," 9 *J. of Community Psychology* 140.

Sherman, Lawrence W., & Richard A. Berk (1984) "The Specific Deterrent Effects of Arrest for Domestic Assault," 49 *American Sociological Rev.* 261.

Simon, Herbert A. (1976) *Administrative Behavior*. New York: Free Press.

Smith, Douglas A. (1987) "Police Response to Interpersonal Violence: Defining the Parameters of Legal Control," 65 *Social Forces* 767.

Smith, Douglas A., & Klein, J. R. (1984) "Police Control of Interpersonal Disputes," 31 *Social Problems* 468.

Soltysik, Robert C., & Paul R. Yarnold (1993) *ODA 1.0: Optimal Data Analysis for DOS*. Chicago: Optimal Data Analysis, Inc.

Stalans, Loretta J. (1988) "Sentencing in Ambiguous Cases: Prototypes, Perceived Similarity and Anchoring." Master's thesis, Department of Psychology, University of Illinois at Chicago.

Stalans, Loretta J., & Arthur J. Lurigio (1990) "Lay and Professionals' Beliefs about Crime and Criminal Sentencing: A Need for Theory, Perhaps Schema Theory," 17 *Criminal Justice & Behavior* 333.

Stith, S. M. (1990) "Police Response to Domestic Violence: The Influence of Individual and Familial Factors," 5 *Violence & Victims* 37.

Sudnow, David (1965) "Normal Crimes: Sociological Features of the Penal Code in a Public Defender Office," 12 *Social Problems* 255.

Teplin, Linda A. (1984a) "Criminalizing Mental Disorder: The Comparative Arrest Rate of the Mentally Ill," 39 *American Psychologist* 794.

—— (1984b) "Managing Disorder: Police Handling of the Mentally Ill," in L. A. Teplin, ed., *Mental Health and Criminal Justice*. Beverly Hills, CA: Sage Publications.

Teplin, Linda A., & N. S. Pruett (1992) "Police as Streetcorner Psychiatrist: Managing the Mentally Ill," 15 *International J. of Law & Psychiatry* 139.

Tuohy, Alan P., Michael J. Wrennall, Ronald A. McQueen, & Stephen G. Stradling (1993) "Effect of Socialization Factors on Decisions to Prosecute: The Organizational Adaptation of Scottish Police Recruits," 17 *Law & Human Behavior* 167.

Van Maanen, John (1974) "Working The Street: A Developmental View of Police Behavior," in H. Jacob, ed., *The Potential for Reform of Criminal Justice*. Beverly Hills, CA: Sage Publications.

—— (1975) "Police Socialization: A Longitudinal Examination of Job Attitudes in an Urban Police Department," 20 *Administrative Science Q.* 207.

Waaland, Pam, & Stuart Keeley (1985) "Police Decisionmaking in Wife Abuse: The Impact of Legal and Extralegal Factors," 9 *Law & Human Behavior* 355.

Walker, Lenore E. (1984) *The Battered Woman Syndrome*. New York: Springer Publishing Co.

White, Susan O. (1972) "A Perspective on Police Professionalization," 7 *Law & Society Rev.* 61.

Worden, Robert E. (1989) "Situational and Attitudinal Explanations of Police Behavior: A Theoretical Reappraisal and Empirical Assessment," 23 *Law & Society Rev.* 667.

Worden, Robert E., & Alissa A. Pollitz (1984) "Police Arrests in Domestic Disturbances: A Further Look," 18 *Law & Society Rev.* 105.

Yarnold, Paul R., & Robert C. Soltysik (1991) "Refining Two-Group Multivariable Classification Models Using Univariate Optimal Discriminant Analysis," 22 *Decision Sciences* 1158.

Yarnold, Paul R., L. A. Hart, & Robert C. Soltysik (1994) "Optimizing the Classification Performance of Logistic Regression and Fisher's Discriminant Analysis," 54 *Educational & Psychological Measurement* 73.

Yellowlees, P. M., & A. V. Kaushik (1992) "The Broken Hill Psychopathology Project," 26(2) *Australian & New Zealand J. of Psychiatry* 197.

Statute

Family Violence Act of Georgia, 1991 Ga. Laws sec. 17-4-21.

[15]

DIFFERENTIAL POLICE TREATMENT OF MALE-ON-FEMALE SPOUSAL VIOLENCE*

James J. Fyfe
Temple University

David A. Klinger
University of Houston

Jeanne M. Flavin
Fordham University

Recent studies of police response to violence in which men attack women with whom they have a history of shared intimacy have not addressed the issue that inspired research in the first place: the "leniency thesis" that police treat men who beat their spouses less punitively than other violent offenders. In addition, research examining the deterrent effects of various police treatments of misdemeanor domestic violence is not responsive to complaints that abused women are denied protection of law when they have been victims of serious, felony-grade, abuse by their spouses. This research analyzes the response of the Chester, Pennsylvania, police to 392 consecutively reported felony-grade assaults by persons whose identities were known to victims and police. Results confirm the leniency thesis. Tabular analysis demonstrates that arrests occurred in 13% of male-on-female spousal assaults and 28% of other assaults. Logit analysis indicates that this difference in police response is not attributable to other variables that might be expected to result in differential treatment. We conclude that the practices and results reported by research conducted in progressive police jurisdictions that volunteer to participate in studies of police response to violence against women may not be generalizable to the great majority of U.S. police agencies that have not welcomed such study.

Social scientists have devoted considerable attention to developing knowledge about how and why police officers intervene in the lives of citizens. Among the many issues examined in this research program is the role that gender plays in police decisions to arrest. Some scholars (e.g., Visher, 1983) have studied how the gender of criminal suspects affects the odds that they will be arrested, but the dominant line of inquiry in gender-focused arrest research concerns police handling of cases in which men

---

* The authors wish to thank Joan McCord and four anonymous *Criminology* reviewers for their comments and assistance in preparing this article.

FYFE ET AL.

physically assault their wives or girlfriends. In the 1970s several writers (e.g., Dobash and Dobash, 1979; Martin, 1976) posited that police officers typically viewed such attacks as private matters best handled outside the domain of the justice system and, hence, that officers were less likely to arrest in assault cases in which men batter current or former female partners—henceforth called *male-on-female spousal violence*—as compared to other types of assaults.

EVIDENCE FROM RESEARCH

This line of argument led to two distinct lines of research in the 1980s. The primary one, animated by assertions that the police should adopt a harsher stance against male-on-female spousal violence (e.g., Dobash and Dobash, 1979; Martin, 1976), sought to establish whether arresting men who attack their female partners would deter future assaults. The first study to examine this question—The Minneapolis Domestic Violence Experiment (e.g., Sherman and Berk, 1984)—compared the frequency of subsequent violence following arrest with two other police responses (mediation and separation) to misdemeanor assaults by men against their mates. The major conclusion of the Minneapolis study was that arrest apparently did reduce the likelihood of future violence. This conclusion, coupled with its suggestion that police officers should treat male-on-female spousal violence as criminal activity that warrants arrest, led to a series of replications, some of which yielded findings generally consistent with the Minneapolis study (e.g., Berk et al., 1992; Pate and Hamilton, 1992), and some that did not (e.g., Dunford et al., 1990; Hirschel et al., 1992; Sherman et al., 1992).

The second line of inquiry sought to test the proposition that officers were less likely to arrest for male-on-female spousal violence, which we will henceforth call the *leniency thesis*. Five studies—four published in the early 1980s (Berk and Loseke, 1981; Oppenlander, 1982; Smith and Klein, 1984; Worden and Pollitz, 1984) and one in the mid-1990s (Klinger, 1995)—examined the leniency thesis. None, however, produced results supporting that thesis. This does not mean, however, that there is strong evidence against the leniency thesis. Klinger (1995:311-312) has identified three reasons why none of the studies published during the 1980s can be considered valid tests of the leniency thesis. First, Berk and Loseke (1981) and Worden and Pollitz (1984) studied only conflict between male-female couples. Consequently, they offer no evidence on the comparative probability of arrest in such cases vis-à-vis other types of violence. Second, Oppenlander (1982) and Smith and Klein (1984) did conduct comparative analyses, but neither study compared the probability of arrest in male-on-female spousal cases versus other types of violence. Oppenlander

POLICE TREATMENT OF VIOLENCE 457

(p. 451) compared the likelihood of arrest in disputes between "relatives, ex-spouses, and cohabitants" with that for other types of disputes, and Smith and Klein compared arrest rates in disputes between people who lived together with those involving people who did not. Because many relatives and people who live together (e.g., siblings and roommates) do not constitute male-female couples, and some people who live apart (e.g., boy- and girlfriends) do, neither Oppenlander's nor Smith and Klein's analysis speaks to the issue of whether officers are less likely to arrest men who batter their mates. Third, the majority of the conflicts examined by Berk and Loseke (1981), Smith and Klein (1984), and Worden and Pollitz (1984) involved no apparent unlawful physical contact or criminal violence. Such cases are irrelevant to the leniency thesis, which by definition, pertains only to cases in which arrest is an option because crimes, rather than simple arguments, have taken place.

Klinger's (1995) research has different limitations. Because he restricted his sample to disputes that involved criminal violence and compared the odds of arrest in cases in which men attacked their current, former, or estranged female partners with all other cases, he did test the leniency thesis. Therefore, his finding of no difference in the odds of arrest in male-on-female spousal assault and other types of violence does offer evidence that speaks directly against the thesis. The negative result of Klinger's test, however, by no means is the last word on the matter for his study was conducted in a single jurisdiction and involved a rather modest number of cases ($N = 77$), the vast majority of which involved minor, misdemeanor-level, assaults. The misdemeanor nature of violence in Klinger's sample is particularly salient because there is some evidence from outside the realm of academic research that suggests that the leniency thesis may hold for the serious sorts of assaults that are scarce in the data he examined.

EVIDENCE FROM CIVIL LITIGATION

During the years between the initial research on the leniency thesis and Klinger's recent study, testing the thesis took a backseat to econometric modeling of the consequences of arresting men who attacked their mates. In the same period, attorneys representing battered women in civil litigation against police departments asserted before judges and juries that police officers were indeed less likely to arrest for male-on-female spousal violence. In these cases, the issue raised by plaintiffs was, in effect, whether alleged police adherence to the leniency thesis violated abused women's constitutional right to equal protection of law.

One way that plaintiffs' attorneys have attempted to prove these cases is to present statistical evidence that officers have arrested less often when

FYFE ET AL.

women are assaulted by current or former male partners as compared to other sorts of violence. In *Watson v. City of Kansas City, Kansas*, 857 F.2d 690 (10th Cir. 1988), plaintiffs introduced such evidence from a study of assault cases that the police themselves defined as sufficiently serious to warrant documentation in crime reports. As the Tenth Circuit U.S. Court of Appeals wrote,

> The plaintiff has presented evidence showing that out of 608 non-domestic assault cases in Kansas City, Kansas, from January 1, 1983, to September 8, 1983, where there was a known perpetrator, there were 186 arrests for an arrest rate of 31%. Out of 369 domestic assaults, there were only 69 arrests for a rate of 16% (p. 695).

While this pattern suggests that claims of differential policing in cases in which women are attacked by their male partners may accurately describe officers' response to serious violence (at least in Kansas City), it is by no means compelling evidence for the leniency thesis. First, the court's opinion includes no indication of the criteria plaintiffs used to differentiate between domestic and nondomestic assaults. Consequently, it is not possible to ascertain if the lower arrest rate for domestic cases means that Kansas City officers less often arrest in cases in which males attacked their current or former female partners. Second, other variables that might account for the differences—for example, the seriousness of assaults; whether offenders had attacked the police rather than, or as well as, private citizens; and the number of suspects—were not taken into account. It is thus possible that the reported "domestic" effect, whatever it represents vis-à-vis spousal violence, is spurious.

Three points, therefore, summarize extant evidence bearing on the thesis that police officers are less likely to arrest for assaults in which males batter their female partners:

1. There is little social scientific evidence that bears directly on the leniency thesis.
2. The sparse social scientific evidence against the thesis is limited primarily to minor violence.
3. Less than compelling evidence from America's courtrooms suggests that the thesis may hold for more serious types of violence.

The remainder of this article attempts to add more substance to the sketchy nature of knowledge about how officers police male-on-female spousal violence by testing the leniency thesis in a sample of cases that involve serious, felony-grade, violence.

DATA

As was the case with the evidence from Kansas City, the data used in this study are drawn from police department records obtained during the course of a lawsuit alleging police failure to protect a woman who was repeatedly assaulted by a male partner (*Hynson v. City of Chester*, 731 F. Supp. 1236 [E.D. Pa. 1990]. On October 15, 1984, after a long series of attacks and threats against her, Alesia Hynson's estranged common-law husband, Jamil Gandy, shot and killed her in Chester, Pennsylvania. Prior to her death, Ms. Hynson had repeatedly notified police in Chester and at least one other nearby jurisdiction of these attacks. Despite these pleas for help, police took no action against Gandy. Two days before she was killed, Hynson had successfully sought renewal of a court order of protection against Gandy. Late the following night, she returned to her home after Gandy had threatened her with a gun at a local bar. She learned then from her teenaged babysitter that Gandy had also attempted to break into her apartment. Hynson, who had not yet obtained physical possession of the order, then called Chester police and asked them to go to the bar to arrest Gandy. They refused to do so, reportedly because Hynson had declined to leave her home and infant daughter in order to accompany them and identify Gandy. A day later, and several hours after he was scheduled to begin a prison sentence for an unrelated matter, Gandy went to Hynson's place of work, where he shot and killed her.

The *Hynson* plaintiffs subsequently sought to analyze and introduce into the trial statistical evidence similar to that used in the *Watson* case. If a similar pattern could be demonstrated in *Hynson*, plaintiffs reasoned, jurors could conclude that the wrongful police behavior alleged was the result of a Chester Police Department (CPD) custom and practice that authorized or encouraged officers to give differential treatment to victims in circumstances like those that eventually culminated in Hynson's death. If this could be proven, plaintiffs would be able to recover damages against the City of Chester, as well as any officer who had failed to provide Alesia Hynson with equal protection of law.

To determine whether such a pattern existed in Chester, Hynson's attorney obtained data on assault complaints and processing under discovery proceedings. The data covered all CPD reports of assaults for approximately 15 months immediately prior to Ms. Hynson's death (July 18, 1983–October 14, 1984) and included 994 cases. The case files were collected in the fall of 1986, which allowed ample time—some two years from the time of the last assaults—for officers to have cleared cases by making arrests. These 994 cases form the basis of the data in this study.

We took several steps to refine these data. First, because the possibility of arrest is remote in cases in which unknown assailants have fled before arrival of the police, we culled from the data 272 cases in which victims had no idea who had attacked them. This left 722 cases in which either assailants were still on the scene when police arrived or there was substantial evidence of the offenders' identity (e.g., offense reports either named

FYFE ET AL.

suspects or included information that would likely lead to the identification of suspects, such as nicknames, addresses or other reasonably specific
areas of residence or work, and description and vehicle license numbers).[1]

A review of the assault reports made it apparent that CPD officers followed a nonarrest policy in cases with juvenile offenders; they typically
referred such cases to other authorities. Because the police treated juvenile cases in a unique fashion, we excluded from analysis the 197 cases
involving a known juvenile suspect. Of the 525 cases that remained, we
deleted 7 cases in which offenders were arrested under the authority of
court orders issued prior to the assaults in question, on the grounds that
the arrests involved were results of court mandates rather than officers'
discretion. Next, to ensure that this study would examine unambiguously
serious crimes, the 115 misdemeanor assaults that remained after the
aforementioned culling process were also dropped from analysis. Among
the 403 cases that remained after dropping the misdemeanor assaults were
11 in which the sex of the victim and/or the suspect could not be determined from the police report. Given the research question at hand, we
also eliminated these cases from analysis.

Thus pared to consider the role that male-female spousal relationships
play in police arrest decisions, the data we examined included 392 non-
stranger, felony-grade assaults and other violent crimes (most notably,
rape, robbery, and attempted murder) committed by adults who, for all
intents and purposes, had been identified and who were not arrested pursuant to existing court orders.

ANALYSIS AND FINDINGS

The first analytic step we took was to compare arrest rates in the 82
male-on-female spousal cases (i.e., those in which a male assaulted a
woman with whom he had or previously shared an intimate relationship)
with the 310 *other* cases, which involved persons in a wide variety of relationships. The *other* cases included, for example, violence between siblings, parents and children, neighbors, friends, barroom and street-corner
acquaintances, as well as 27 cases in which women attacked their male
partners. Again, these were counted in our *other* category because the
leniency thesis addresses violence against, rather than by, women.

---

1. We took this step knowing that it would understate any differences between
arrest probability in male-on-female spousal cases and other cases. The male-on-female
spousal cases we analyzed were all placed in that category on the basis of very specific
identifications of suspects (e.g. "Robert Jones, address, the victim's former live-in boyfriend and the father of her child"). It generally is far easier to make arrests in such
cases than is true in many of the *other* cases in which assailants' identities were less
precise (e.g., "Victim indicates that he was assaulted by a male he knows as 'Reggie'
and who frequents the bar at the northeast corner of Main St. and First Ave.").

POLICE TREATMENT OF VIOLENCE 461

Table 1, which cross-tabulates arrest and victim-offender relationship, indicates that the probability of arrest is significantly lower in male-on-female spousal cases than in others: Officers made arrests in 13% of the male-on-female spousal felonies and 28% of other cases ($\chi^2 = 7.7$ with 1 d.f., $p < .05$). Thus, an initial look at the data offers strong support for the leniency thesis: CPD officers were less than half as likely to arrest for male-on-female spousal violence as for other violence.[2]

Table 1. Cross-Classification of Victim-Offender Relationship and Arrest ($N = 392$)

Arrest	Violence Type		Row Total
	Non-Spousal	Male-on-Female Spousal	
No Arrest	222	71	293
	72%	87%	75%
Arrest	88	11	99
	28%	13%	25%
Column Total	310	82	
	79%	21%	

$\chi^2 = 7.7, p < .05$.

We then utilized logistic regression to assess whether the bivariate association between spousal status and arrest could be attributable to some uncontrolled factor(s). The first three factors we controlled for in the logit modeling relate to the legal character of assault cases: the use of weapons by assailants (0 = unarmed, 1 = weapon used), the degree of injury sustained by victims (0 = none/minor, 1 = major; split on whether hospitalization was required), and whether incidents involved attacks on responding officers as well as civilian assault victims (0 = no attack, 1 = officer attacked).

We also controlled for four extralegal factors that could affect the likelihood that assault cases would culminate in arrest. Since the prospect of arrest presumably increases with the number of attackers, the first controlled factor is the number of assailants (0 = one assailant; 1 = multiple

---

2. We conducted two other tabular analyses. First, we split the *other* category into domestic cases (e.g., parent/child, siblings) and nondomestic cases and found significant differences among the resulting three categories. Arrests occurred in 33% of the nondomestic cases, in 20% of the domestic cases, and 13% of the male-on-female spousal cases ($\chi^2 = 13.5$; $p < .05$). Second, we compared arrest rates between the 82 male-on-female spousal assaults and the 27 cases in which women attacked their intimate male partners. Two of the 27 female-on-male cases—7%—resulted in arrest. While the 7% figure is just over half the size of the 13% arrest rate observed among the male-on-female spousal cases, the difference between arrest rates for the two types of cases is not statistically significant.

assailants) for, as the number of assailants increases, so too does the prospect of arrest. This is particularly important in this research, because the
male-on-female spousal cases are almost invariably one-on-one attacks. If
other sorts of assaults more frequently include multiple offenders, the
lower arrest rate observed in male-on-female spousal cases could be due
to the fact that there are fewer offenders per case. The second extralegal
variable we measured concerns the gender structure of the violent epi-
sodes we examined. It is possible that the arrest rate is lower in male-on-
female spousal assaults because officers are less likely to arrest when
women are victimized by men, regardless of the nature of the victim-
offender relationship. To examine this possibility, we crafted a set of four
dummy variables (male-on-female attack = 1, other = 0; female-on-male
attack = 1, other = 0; male-on-male = 1, other = 0; and female-on-female =
1, other = 0). This measure also enables us to examine the independent
effect of sex on arrest.

A good deal of literature suggests that the race of suspects and victims
may influence police arrest decisions (e.g., Chevigny, 1969; Smith et al.,
1984). In order to assess this possibility, we developed a set of four
dummy variables (white-on-white attack = 1, other = 0; black-on-black
attack = 1, other = 0; white-on-black attack = 1, other = 0; and black-on-
white attack = 1, other = 0). Other literature suggests that social class may
affect how officers intervene in the lives of citizens (e.g., Chambliss, 1973;
Lundman, 1974). Unfortunately, police reports do not include information on the social class of victims and suspects. Consequently, we could
not measure the class of the suspects and victims in our data. We therefore turned to an area-level proxy indicator that measures the poverty
level of the neighborhoods where attacks occurred to operationalize social
class.

Chester, which lies just south of Philadelphia on the western bank of the
Delaware River, is a declining northeastern blue-collar city that includes
numerous areas that are particularly blighted. A good deal of recent
research on the spatial distribution of urban poverty in the United States
has sought to establish satisfactory criteria to distinguish neighborhoods
that are truly impoverished from other sorts of neighborhoods. In their
influential work, *Ghetto Poverty in the United States, 1970-1980*, Jargowsky
and Bane (1991) use a three-step measure of the percentage of population
in census tracts living in poverty to distinguish among three types of neighborhoods. They identify census tracts where greater than 40% of the population lives in poverty as "ghetto" neighborhoods, those with 20%-40%
poverty as "mixed income" neighborhoods, and those below the 20% poverty threshold as "nonpoor" neighborhoods. The 1980 census data indicate that four of Chester's 19 census tracts have poverty rates above 40%,
9 lie in the 20%-40% range, and the remaining 6 fall below the 20% figure.

POLICE TREATMENT OF VIOLENCE 463

One "mixed income" tract had a poverty rate of 39.48%. After moving this tract into the "ghetto" category, we used Jargowsky and Bane's three-level scheme to measure area social class, assigning a score of 3 to those cases that occurred in "ghetto" tracts, 2 to those that occurred in "mixed income" tracts, and 1 to those that occurred in "nonpoor" tracts.

Several cases were missing data on one or more of these control variables, most often the race of victims and suspects, one or both of which could not be determined in 34 cases. Thirteen of these cases occurred in census tracts where the racial composition of the population was more than 90% black. In order to maximize our *N*, we counted the race of the missing parties in each of these 13 cases as black, eliminating from analysis the 21 other cases with missing data on race. We were also forced to drop 8 cases in which we could not determine the location of the attack from the police reports, along with 7 other cases that were missing data on one or more of the other predictors.

Frequency distributions for arrest and the several predictors in the 356 cases that remain for multivariate analysis are displayed in Table 2. There were 80 male-on-female spousal assaults and 276 other cases. Officers were attacked in 13 cases; suspects used weapons in 206; and victims received injuries requiring medical treatment in 255. One hundred thirty of the assaults involved male suspects and female victims, and 45 involved female assaults on males; 153 were male-on-male assaults; and 28 were female-on-female assaults. Three hundred sixteen of the assaults were committed by lone assailants. Whites attacked whites in 70 cases; blacks attacked blacks in 251; whites attacked blacks in 10; and blacks attacked whites in 25. Sixty-one cases occurred in low-, 183 in medium-, and 112 in high-poverty areas. The final column of Table 2 lists the percentage of cases resulting in arrest for each category of the independent variables. Zero-order correlations between all variables are displayed in the appendix.

464   FYFE ET AL.

Table 2.   Distribution of Variables (N = 356)

Variable	Code	Number	Percent	Percent Arrested
Arrest	0 = no arrest	264	74%	—
	1 = arrest made	92	26%	—
Spousal Status	0 = non-spousal	276	79%	29%
	1 = spousal	80	21%	14%
Officer Attacked	0 = no	343	96%	24%
	1 = yes	13	4%	85%
Weapon Used	0 = no	150	42%	19%
	1 = yes	206	58%	31%
Degree of Injury	0 = none/minor	101	28%	25%
	1 = major	255	72%	26%
Number of Suspects	0 = single	316	89%	26%
	1 = multiple	40	11%	25%
Male Attacker/	0 = no	226	63%	28%
Female Victim	1 = yes	130	37%	22%
Female Attacker/	0 = no	311	87%	28%
Male Victim	1 = yes	45	13%	11%
Male Attacker/	0 = no	203	57%	19%
Male Victim	1 = yes	153	43%	35%
Female Attacker/	0 = no	328	92%	27%
Female Victim	1 = yes	28	8%	14%
White Victim/	0 = no	286	80%	26%
White Suspect	1 = yes	70	20%	27%
Black Victim/	0 = no	105	29%	29%
Black Suspect	1 = yes	251	71%	25%
White Victim/	0 = no	346	97%	25%
Black Suspect	1 = yes	10	3%	40%
Black Victim/	0 = no	331	93%	26%
White Suspect	1 = yes	25	7%	28%
Area Poverty	1 = low	61	17%	30%
	2 = medium	183	51%	23%
	3 = high	112	32%	29%

With these several measures in hand, we regressed arrest on the predictors (using black-on-black crimes as the suppressed racial category and male-on-male crime as the suppressed sex category). We then calculated semistandardized logit coefficients—which allow for comparison of the relative strength of the net effect of independent variables—by multiplying the unstandardized coefficients (i.e., the Bs) for each predictor by its standard deviation (see Kaufman, 1996, for details on calculating standardized logit coefficients). Table 3 displays the results of our logit modeling.

POLICE TREATMENT OF VIOLENCE 465

Table 3. Logit Estimates of Determinants of Arrest ($N = 356$)

	B	S.E.	Semistandardized Coefficients
Male/Female Spousal	−.87*	.44	−.37
Officer Attacked	3.00*	.82	.57
Weapon Use	.87*	.30	.43
Degree of Injury	.10	.31	.04
Number of Suspects	−.22	.43	−.07
Male-on-Female Attack	.07	.35	.03
Female-on-Male Attack	−1.55*	.53	−.51
Female-on-Female Attack	−.91	.58	−.24
White Victim/White Suspect	.08	.34	.03
White Suspect/Black Victim	.43	.69	.07
Black Suspect/White Victim	.17	.54	.04
Area Poverty	.10	.20	.07
Constant	−1.68	.57	
−2 Log Likelihood	357.07		
Pseudo R^2	.51		

* $p < .05$.

The primary point of interest in Table 3 is that male-on-female spousal status exerts a significant negative effect on arrest. Thus, the negative bivariate relationship between male-on-female spousal status and arrest shown in Table 1 holds after taking into account the effects of the several controls. The logit modeling also discloses that officers were significantly more likely to arrest when assailants used weapons and when officers were themselves attacked, and that they were significantly less likely to arrest when females attacked males. A third point of interest is that the semistandardized coefficients indicate that all three of the other significant variables had a larger net effect on the odds of arrest than did spousal status. Finally, the logit modeling discloses that the likelihood of arrest was not affected by the degree of injury, the number of suspects, the race of the involved parties, whether the attack was male on female or female on female, or the level of poverty in the area in which the attacks occurred.

DISCUSSION

The foregoing analysis shows that Chester police officers were less likely to arrest male felony assailants who had attacked current or former female partners than to arrest other persons who had committed similarly serious violence. Thus, the answer to the question that prompted this study, *Do officers treat male-on-female spousal violence differently from other forms*

466   FYFE ET AL.

of violence? is affirmative. Our test supports the leniency thesis.[3]

Beyond the central issue of how officers treat male-on-female spousal violence, this study offers evidence that bears on other matters pertinent to police behavior. The results of the logit analysis indicate that two legal factors—using a weapon and attacking responding officers—significantly increase the odds of arrest in felony assault cases. These findings are consistent with other research on the determinants of arrest—for example, Klinger's (1994) report that officers arrested all six of the people who attacked them during interpersonal disputes in Dade County, and Smith's (1987) finding that weapon use increased the odds of arrest in his study of police response to interpersonal violence. Our finding that the degree of injury did not affect the odds of arrest is also consistent with Smith's 1987 study wherein he reported that officers were no more likely to arrest in cases that involved injuries.

Where extralegal factors are concerned, most did not affect Chester officers' arrest decisions. The finding of no difference in the odds of arrest for attacks that involved single as compared to multiple assailants indicates that more attackers did not mean a higher probability of arrest in Chester. The nonsignificant logit coefficients for the race dummies indicate that the race of the involved parties did not affect Chester officers' response to interpersonal violence, and they run counter to arguments that race is a critical determinant of arrest. Similarly, the nonsignificant area-poverty coefficient speaks against assertions that the social class composition of areas where police encounter citizens affects their decisions, at least in Chester, Pennsylvania.

The single significant extralegal finding concerned the gender composition of the parties to violence. The logit model indicates that Chester officers less often arrested in cases in which females attacked males, as compared to cases of male-on-male violence. The nonsignificant coefficient for the female-on-female dummy indicates that the leniency Chester officers extend to female assailants holds only when the target of violence is male. These findings suggest that the Chester police adopt a somewhat nuanced approach to female attackers, treating them differently according to the sex of their victim.

We advise caution regarding this issue, however. Because we used an area-level measure to assign the race of citizens in 13 cases with missing data on race (see above) we reestimated the logit model in Table 3 (as well as the other models discussed below) with these 13 cases excluded from

---

3. We also estimated a logit model in which we substituted the three-level measure presented in note 2 (i.e., nondomestic, domestic, and male-on-female spousal) for the spousal/other dichotomy. This produced no change in the direction or significance of results.

analysis. The only notable difference among the control variables between models with 356 and 343 cases is that the coefficient for the female attacker/male victim dummy is nonsignificant in the models with 343 cases. That the coefficient is no longer significant when 13 cases are deleted from the sample indicates that the initial finding of a female-on-male effect lacks robustness and, hence, should be viewed with suspicion.

The fact that the male-on-female spousal effect held up in light of control for the sex dummies indicates that the observed differential leniency in such cases is not due to a broader tendency among Chester police to downplay (comparatively) male attacks on females. A closer look at the data suggests that the observed male-on-female spousal effect *could be* due to another aspect of the nature of this violence, however. Black (1976, 1980), among others, has asserted that the likelihood of arrest varies inversely with the degree of intimacy between parties to conflict. This proposition points to the possibility that the observed male-on-female spousal effect may be part of a broader tendency among Chester officers to be more lenient as the relational distance between victims and suspects decreases.

To gain some empirical purchase on this possibility, we created a new variable by combining the 27 cases in which women attacked their male partners (which had been in the *other* category) with male-on-female spousal assaults to form a single *couples* category. We then split the remaining *other* cases into two groups: those involving relatives (e.g., parent/child, siblings) and those involving nonfamily members. We then calculated arrest rates for these three groups and found that the arrest rate for acquaintance violence was 33%; for family violence, 24%; and for couple violence, 12%. This pattern is consistent with the notion that intimacy may be driving the male-on-female spousal finding.

To explore further the possibility that the observed male-on-female spousal effect could be due to the highly intimate nature of such assaults, we conducted additional logit analysis. We first reestimated the equation in Table 3 with the three-step intimacy variable (1 = acquaintance; 2 = family; 3 = male-female couple; identified as *intimacy* in the appendix) in place of the spousal measure. The intimacy indicator is a significant correlate of arrest in this model ($B = -.37$; S.E. $= .199$; one-tailed $p < .05$). We then estimated the model again, this time including both the dichotomous male-on-female spousal/other and intimacy measures as predictors. Both of the coefficients produced by this model are nonsignificant correlates of arrest (spousal $B = -.65$; S.E. $= .68$; one-tailed $p > .05$; intimacy $B = .14$; S.E. $= .313$; one-tailed $p > .05$).

Consideration of the matter indicates that these results are due to a strong correlation between the dichotomous male-on-female spousal/other and intimacy measures ($r = .77$). In comparatively small samples such as is the case here (356 cases in the multivariate models), a high degree of collinearity between two predictors can inflate the standard errors of regression coefficients. In this analysis, then, the observed nonsignificant effects for the dichotomous male-on-female spousal/other and intimacy measures when both are included in a single logit model are statistical artifacts rather than true reflections of the net effect of either spousal status or intimacy on arrest. Because we cannot disentangle the independent effects of the two measures, we cannot be sure that spousal status independently lowers the odds of arrest for felony violence in our data.

CONCLUSION

While we cannot establish whether the differential leniency observed in our data for cases in which women are attacked by their male partners is due to the spousal nature of the violence or the more general tendency for increased leniency as the relational distance between parties to violence decreases, the fact remains that Chester officers were less likely to jail men who attacked their female partners. This finding, presented in bivariate form, was included in plaintiffs' evidence in *Hynson v. City of Chester*, and the case eventually settled before trial. The finding is especially remarkable in light of the extreme violence of many of the male-on-female spousal assault cases. Included among the cases in which Chester officers did not arrest men who attacked their mates were 4 in which batterers used guns; 38 involving knives or other cutting instruments, including axes; and 27 in which clubs or other similar weapons (usually baseball bats or hammers) were used against current or former female spouses. In addition, several women were thrown down stairs, some were raped, and one was held by her feet over a second floor landing and dropped to the floor below, where she landed on her head. No case in the data could be classified as involving minor violence.

The severity of violence extends beyond the male-on-female spousal cases we studied, and we were surprised that the department's arrest rate for *other* violence was only 28%, despite the fact that all such offenders had been identified. These data from the declining blue-collar city of Chester suggest that the subprofessional, highly personalized, and discretionary "watchman" variety of policing James Q. Wilson (1968) found in similar places a generation ago still prevails.

This is important because while Wilson's pioneering research was among the very first empirical studies of police at work, it was also among the very last studies of police in such an environment. Since 1968, police research—particularly that involving male-on-female spousal violence—typically has been conducted in a few progressive jurisdictions that have closely regulated officers' conduct and that, presumably, have had little to

POLICE TREATMENT OF VIOLENCE 469

fear from publication of what researchers might find in their observations and archival searches. As a consequence, and regardless of the sophistication of the methodologies they have employed, police researchers generally have provided information concerning the operations of a small, self-selected, and therefore, nonrepresentative sample of American police agencies that probably most closely approximate Wilson's more professional "legalistic" and "service" styles of policing. Klinger's spousal violence research (1995), for example, was conducted in an agency in which he has reported in other works that officers' arrest decisions are relatively unaffected by extralegal considerations (Klinger, 1994, 1996). Chester is different; unlike the jurisdictions that welcomed researchers to study their officers (e.g., Minneapolis, Charlotte, Metro-Dade, Omaha), Chester did not embrace this research. Instead, Chester released the data used in it only under court order. In that sense, the Chester Police Department is far more representative of this country's 17,000 or so municipal police agencies than are the very few that have hosted research. Chester's experience and efforts in responding to serious interpersonal violence, therefore, may also tell more than most research about the type of protection that victims of male-on-female spousal violence—and other violent crime—can expect from police in most places.

At the same time, inferences about the generalizability of our Chester data are only that: This study does not speak directly to questions of whether and to what extent differential police response to male-on-female spousal assault may exist beyond Chester's borders. Clearly, additional evidence is needed from other places about the comparative probability of arrest for male-on-female assault relative to other forms of felonious violence. Because it is unlikely that police departments that may be practicing discriminatory leniency would willingly open their doors to researchers, such evidence may become available during collaboration between researchers and attorneys who seek official records in order to test and support their allegations of improper police action.

Police records seem a likely data source for another reason, as well. In the aggregate, felonious violence in which offenders are identified is all too common. For individual patrol officers and the researchers assigned to observe them, however, such criminality is a comparatively infrequent event. Consequently, the costs of observational research designed to capture data related to how officers handle such cases—waiting, in effect, for domestic pots to boil—generally is prohibitive. While archival research has built-in biases (a criticism that may be applied with equal force to observational research), additional studies of records of police encounters with serious violence seem a cost-effective method of developing a more complete picture of police response to spousal assault.

The examination of the relationship between our three-level intimacy

FYFE ET AL.

variable and arrest probability suggests that future researchers may also wish to measure the full range of human relationships in a more fine-grained manner than was possible with our data. This might be accomplished by devising an indicator that categorizes victim-offender relationships along a continuum ranging from a "total stranger" value through various degrees of acquaintanceship, kinship, and intimacy to "long-term intact married couples" (Black, 1976:42-47). Such a measure would be less strongly associated with the spousal dichotomy and would thus allow researchers to tease out the independent effects of intimacy and spousal status on arrest. By developing and analyzing more refined data sources, future researchers may be able to increase knowledge of the role of gender and other situational factors in police arrest decisions. Moreover, by studying these decisions in other places, they will be able to explore the effects of such situational factors in different settings.

REFERENCES

Berk, Sarah F. and Donileen R. Loseke
  1981   Handling family violence: Situational determinants of police arrest in domestic disturbances. Law & Society Review 15:317-346.

Berk, Richard A., Alec Campbell, Ruth Klap, and Bruce Western
  1992   The deterrent effect of arrest in domestic violence: A Bayesian analysis of four field experiments. American Sociological Review 57:598-708.

Black, Donald
  1976   The Behavior of Law. New York: Academic Press.
  1980   The Manners and Customs of the Police. New York: Academic Press.

Chambliss, William J.
  1973   The saints and the roughnecks. Society 11:24.

Chevigny, Paul
  1969   Police Power: Police Abuse in New York City. New York: Pantheon.

Dobash, R. Emerson and Russell Dobash
  1979   Violence Against Wives: A Case Against Patriarchy. New York: Free Press.

Dunford, Franklyn W., David Huizinga, and Delbert S. Elliot
  1990   The role of arrest in domestic assault: The Omaha police experiment. Criminology 28:183-206.

Hirschel, J. David, Ira W. Hutchison, and Charles W. Dean
  1990   The failure of arrest to deter spouse abuse. Journal of Research in Crime and Delinquency 20:7-33.

Jargowsky, Paul A. and Mary Jo Bane
  1991   Ghetto poverty in the United States, 1970-1980. In Christopher Jencks and Paul E. Peterson (eds.), The Urban Underclass. Washington, D.C.: The Brookings Institution.

POLICE TREATMENT OF VIOLENCE 471

Kaufman, Robert L.
1996   Comparing effects in dichotomous logistic regression: A variety of standardized coefficients. Social Science Quarterly 77:91-109.

Klinger, David A.
1994   Demeanor or crime? Why "hostile" citizens are more likely to be arrested. Criminology 32:475-493.
1995   Policing spousal assault. Journal of Research in Crime and Delinquency 32:308-324.
1996   More on demeanor and arrest in Dade County. Criminology 34:301-323.

Lundman, Richard J.
1974   Routine police practices: A commonweal perspective. Social Problems 22:127-141.

Martin, Del
1976   Battered Wives. San Francisco: Glide Publications.

Oppenlander, Nan
1982   Coping or copping out: Police service delivery in domestic disputes. Criminology 20:449-465.

Pate, Anthony M. and Edwin E. Hamilton
1992   Formal and informal deterrents to domestic violence: The Dade County spouse assault experiment. American Sociological Review 57:691-697.

Sherman, Lawrence W. and Richard A. Berk
1984   The specific deterrent effects of arrest for domestic assault. American Sociological Review 49:261-272.

Sherman, Lawrence W., with Janell D. Schmidt and Dennis P. Rogan
1992   Policing Domestic Violence: Experiments and Dilemmas. New York: Free Press.

Smith, Douglas A.
1987   Police response to interpersonal violence: Defining the parameters of legal control. Social Forces 65:767-782.

Smith, Douglas A. and Jody R. Klein
1984   Police control of interpersonal disputes. Social Problems 31:468-481.

Smith, Douglas A., Christy A. Visher, and Laura Davidson
1984   Equity and discretionary justice: The influence of race on police arrest decisions. Journal of Criminal Law and Criminology 75:234-249.

Visher, Christy A.
1983   Gender, police arrest decisions, and notions of chivalry. Criminology 21:5-28.

Wilson, James Q.
1968   Varieties of Police Behavior. Cambridge, Mass.: Harvard University Press.

Worden, Robert E. and Alissa A. Pollitz
1984   Police arrests in domestic disturbances: A further look. Law & Society Review 18:105-119.

Appendix. Zero-Order Correlations ($N = 356$)

	1	2	3	4	5	6	7	8	9	10	11	12	13	14	15	16
1. Arrest	—															
2. M/F Spousal	-.15*	—														
3. Off. Attacked	.26*	-.10	—													
4. Weapon Use	.14*	-.21*	-.08	—												
5. Injury	.02	-.05	-.14*	.11*	—											
6. No. Suspects	-.01	-.15*	.03	.02	-.03	—										
7. Male/Female	-.06	.61*	-.05	-.27*	-.01	-.14*	—									
8. Female/Male	-.13*	-.16*	-.03	.17*	-.08	.05	-.29*	—								
9. Female/Female	-.08	-.08	-.06	-.00	-.00	.06	-.22*	-.11*	—							
10. Male/Male	.19*	-.44*	.10	.15*	.07	.07	-.66*	-.33*	-.25*	—						
11. Both White	.01	.00	.02	-.05	.01	-.02	.01	-.08	-.07	.08	—					
12. Both Black	-.04	.05	-.01	-.05	-.01	-.06	.04	.04	.01	-.07	-.76*	—				
13. White/Black	.06	-.09	-.03	.08	-.04	-.01	-.06	-.01	-.05	.09	-.08	-.26*	—			
14. Black/White	.01	-.04	.01	.12*	.03	.15*	-.05	.06	.12*	-.06	-.14*	-.42*	-.05	—		
15. Area Poverty	.01	.02	-.02	.00	.01	.00	.05	.04	-.00	-.08	-.22*	.24*	.01	-.11*	—	
16. Intimacy	-.20*	.77*	-.14*	-.16*	.05	-.19*	.44*	.21*	-.12*	-.50*	-.01	.12*	-.11*	-.13*	.03	—

* $p < .05$.

POLICE TREATMENT OF VIOLENCE 473

James J. Fyfe is Professor of Criminal Justice and Senior Public Policy Research Fellow at Temple University. His research has focused on police field behavior and control of police discretion. His most recent publication is the fifth edition of O.W. Wilson's *Police Administration* (McGraw-Hill, 1997).

David A. Klinger is Assistant Professor of Sociology at the University of Houston. His current research includes the determinants of police behavior, the community context of social control, and the measurement of crime.

Jeanne M. Flavin is Assistant Professor in the Department of Sociology and Anthropology at Fordham University. She earned her Ph.D. in sociology and justice at The American University in 1995, and has conducted research on gender bias among attorneys and police officers, racial bias among South African schoolchildren, and the effects of cultural setting on the fear of crime.

[16]

DECIDING WHEN HATE IS A CRIME: THE FIRST AMENDMENT, POLICE DETECTIVES, AND THE IDENTIFICATION OF HATE CRIME

Jeannine Bell*

INTRODUCTION

A cartoon that appeared in a major United States newspaper several years ago aptly illustrates many of the fears that have been expressed regarding the enforcement of hate crime laws. The cartoon shows a man in a suit standing in front of a judge.[1] The caption reads, "I had no idea I was violating his civil rights, your honor. I only intended to punch him in the nose."[2] The man has been charged with some type of hate crime. A hate crime is a crime motivated by prejudice toward the "victim's race, color, ethnicity, religion, or national origin."[3] Hate crime laws typically require proof of the individual's motivation for the crime in order to convict the defendant.[4] In the cartoon, the judge appears to have been saddled with the responsibility of determining the individual's true motivation.[5] The cartoon seems to cast aspersions on the judge's ability to evaluate whether a hate crime has been committed. This is precisely what worries many who are concerned about enforcement of hate crime laws.[6]

---

* Associate Professor of Law, Indiana University (Bloomington). A.B., Harvard College; J.D., University of Michigan Law School; Ph.D. (Political Science) University of Michigan. I would like to thank the editors of the RUTGERS RACE & THE LAW REVIEW. I would also like to extend special thanks to Craig Bradley, Kevin Brown, Ken Dau-Schmidt, Rob Fischman, Dawn Johnsen, Lisa Farnsworth, and Susan Williams for their valuable comments on earlier versions of this Article.

1. Cartoon on file with author.
2. *Id.*
3. BLACK'S LAW DICTIONARY 378 (7th ed. 1999).
4. *See* LU-IN WANG, HATE CRIMES LAW § 10:4 (2001).
5. Cartoon on file with author.
6. *See* Phyllis B. Gerstenfeld, *Smile When You Call Me That!: The Problems With Punishing Hate Motivated Behavior*, 10 BEHAV. SCI. & L. 259, 270 (1992).

For example, critics see the task of proving and judging motivation in this context complex, if not impossible.[7] They find the task not only difficult, but one fraught with grave First Amendment difficulties.[8]

Critics' concerns contribute to the impassioned decade-long debate concerning hate crime legislation.[9] This debate has only intensified and grown more polarized in the past few years as legislatures around the country have considered passing hate crime legislation, frequently in response to dramatic hate crimes like the dragging death of James Byrd in Texas,[10] the murder of Matthew Shepard in Wyoming,[11] and the murder of a Filipino-American letter carrier, Joseph Ileto, by Burford Furrow in Los Angeles.[12] Critics do not believe that hate crime legislation is an appropriate response to such crimes.[13] They assail hate crime legislation for a variety of reasons,[14] one of the most serious being the problem of controlling hateful behavior without offending the First Amendment by silencing speech.[15] Critics are concerned that people will be convicted for hate crimes in cases in which the crime is not motivated by bias and the only evidence of the defendant's motivation is hate speech.

Unfortunately, the current debate over hate crime is predicated mainly on doctrinal, historical, and emotional arguments as neither supporters nor critics ground their arguments in empirical evidence of how hate crime laws actually work in practice. Scholars have questioned whether hate crime legislation can be enforced by those charged with enforcement, many of

---

7. *See id.* at 271.

8. *See id.* at 278.

9. *See id.* at 266.

10. Patty Reinert & Allan Turner, *Jasper killer gets death penalty: A smirking King shows no remorse*, HOUS. CHRON., Feb. 26, 1999, at 1A.

11. Elaine Herscher, *Wyoming Death Echoes Rising Anti-Gay Attacks*, S. F. CHRON., Oct. 13, 1998, at A-7.

12. James Sterngold, *Suspect Targeted Letter Carrier: He Asked a Favor, then Shot 9 Times*, NEW ORLEANS TIMES-PICAYUNE, Aug. 13, 1999, at A1.

13. *Cf.* Murad Kalam, *Hate Crime Prevention*, 37 HARV. J. ON LEGIS. 593, 597 (2000).

14. *See generally* Gerstenfeld, *supra* note 6, at 269-84 (reviewing critics' opinions).

15. *See id.* at 278-80.

whom are unschooled in the vagaries of First Amendment law.[16] This Article argues that ultimately, whether hate crime laws can be enforced constitutionally is an empirical question that raises important concerns regarding the behavior of those charged with their enforcement. Without some sense of whether hate crime laws can be enforced constitutionally, it is hard to accept the arguments of supporters that the benefits of passing hate crime legislation outweigh the significant harm that critics argue such legislation may cause.

Based on interviews with and observations of those responsible for hate crime law enforcement in a metropolitan city, this Article provides much-needed empirical data to illuminate the contentious debates over the constitutional and practical dimensions of using hate crime law to punish bias crime. This Article adds a story of how hate crime law is enforced to the debate, based on the experiences of the police detectives who are required to enforce hate crime law. Part I of this Article provides a brief description of hate crime laws and argues that the police play an important role in the determination of how hate crime law is enforced and ultimately, whether defendants' First Amendment rights will be respected. Part II describes critics' concerns about defendants' First Amendment rights and the narrow constitutional line that enforcers of hate crime law must walk between enforcing hate crime and policing free speech. In Part III, I describe how enforcers decide that incidents are hate crimes and argue that they are able to avoid the pitfalls identified by critics. The Article concludes in Part IV with a discussion of the disconnect between hate crimes and hate speech and an exploration of new justifications for hate crime law.

---

16. *See* Jeannine Bell, Policing Hatred: Law Enforcement, Civil Rights, and Hate Crime (forthcoming 2002) (manuscript at 14-22, on file with author).

36   *RUTGERS RACE AND THE LAW REVIEW*   [Vol. 4

PART I: THE POLICE ROLE IN HATE CRIMES LAW

A. *Hate Crimes Law*

The best way to distinguish hate crimes is to highlight how they are different from non-bias-motivated incidents. Hate or bias crimes[17] are not committed because of animosity towards the victim as an individual, but rather because of hostility toward the group to which the victim belongs.[18] The prejudice which motivates the commission of a hate crime may be based on the victim's actual or perceived race, religion, ethnicity, or sexual orientation. Though usually the vast majority of incidents investigated as hate crimes are assaults and vandalism, if they show evidence of biased motivation the following type of incidents can be hate crimes: murder, non-negligent manslaughter, forcible rape, intimidation, and arson.[19]

The distinction between "hate crime" and "hate speech" is important. Hate speech, sometimes called "assaultive speech"[20] is "[s]peech that carries no meaning other than the expression of hatred for some [particular] group, . . . especially in circumstances where the communication is likely to provoke violence."[21] Examples of hate speech include, for instance, anti-religious and anti-gay slurs and racial epithets.[22] Though universities and public institutions have attempted to regulate this type of offensive speech,[23] courts have agreed the First

---

17. In this Article, the terms "hate crime" and "bias crime" are used interchangeably.

18. Troy A. Scotting, *Hate Crimes and the Need for Stronger Federal Legislation*, 34 AKRON. L. REV. 853, 856-57 (2001).

19. FBI, U.S. DEP'T OF JUSTICE, CRIMES IN THE UNITED STATES UNIFORM CRIME REP. 1999 59 (1999) (collecting hate crime statistics for murder, non-negligent manslaughter, forcible rape, aggravated assault, simple assault, intimidation, robbery, burglary, etc.).

20. *See* MARI J. MATSUDA ET AL., WORDS THAT WOUND: CRITICAL RACE THEORY, ASSAULTIVE SPEECH, AND THE FIRST AMENDMENT 1 (Robert W. Gordon & Margaret Jane Radin eds., Westview Press, Inc. 1993).

21. BLACK'S LAW DICTIONARY 1407-1408, (7th ed. 1999).

22. MATSUDA ET AL., *supra* note 20, at 67.

23. *Id.* at 1.

Amendment protects hate speech in these contexts and thus, defendants may not be prosecuted just for using it.[24]

Hate crime, by contrast, can be prosecuted under a variety of federal[25] and state laws. The vast majority of criminal acts that are prosecuted as hate crimes are prosecuted under state law specifically punishing hate crime, which is not surprising since states have jurisdiction over most criminal matters.[26] Nearly every state has some type of legislation that criminalizes bias-motivated conduct.[27] Prosecutors may charge individuals who have committed hate crimes under a variety of types of legislation including ethnic intimidation statutes, statutes that prohibit cross burning,[28] institutional vandalism statutes that prohibit the vandalism and defacement of a variety of locations, including public monuments and institutions;[29] and anti-mask statutes that penalize wearing a mask, hood, or disguise while in public.[30]

When commentators refer to hate crime laws however, they are generally referring to bias-motivated violence or ethnic intimidation statutes. Such statutes are found in many states.[31]

---

24. See R.A.V. v. City of St. Paul, 505 U.S. 377, 381 (1992) (striking down city ordinance which prohibited symbols which arouse alarm on the basis on race, color, creed, religion or gender); Doe v. Univ. of Mich., 721 F. Supp. 852, 868 (E.D. Mich. 1989) and UWM Post v. Bd. of Regents of the Univ. of Wis., 774 F. Supp. 1163, 1181 (E.D. Wis. 1991) (striking down campus speech codes).

25. WANG, supra note 4, § 2.1 (discussing the federal legislation under which hate crimes may be prosecuted).

26. Id. at app. B.

27. Id. (noting that only Wyoming had no legislation specially related to bias crime).

28. Id. (delineating state cross burning statutes; most states also prohibit the burning of any other religious symbol).

29. Id. (delineating state institutional vandalism statutes); see e.g., WASH. REV. CODE ANN. § 9A.36.080(2)(b) (West 1998), § 9.61.160-.180 (West 1998) ("dealing with threats to bomb or injure property."); WIS. STAT. ANN. § 943.012 (West 1996) (criminalizing the destruction of religious or other public institutional structures).

30. WANG, supra note 4, at App. B (delineating state anti-mask statutes); id. at § 11:1 (generally statutes have exemptions for innocent activities such as wearing a mask as part of a holiday costume, "by persons under sixteen years of age," or safety reasons); see, e.g. N.C. GEN. STAT. §§ 14-12.7 to 14-12.10. (1999).

31. WANG, supra note 4, § 10:2.

Though state hate crime statutes take slightly different approaches, most statutes do one of the following: (1) make bias-motivated intimidation a separate crime; (2) "automatically enhance the penalty" for crimes motivated by forbidden prejudices; or (3) give a judge discretion to increase penalties when the crime is motivated by a forbidden prejudice.[32] The majority of bias-motivated violence and intimidation statutes bar threats, harassment, assaults, and trespassing on account of a person's "race, color, religion, or national origin."[33] Some state statutes of this type prohibit crimes committed because of an individual's disability status,[34] because of his or her sexual orientation,[35] or because of one's gender.[36] Less commonly proscribed motivations include political affiliation[37] and age.[38]

A frequently misunderstood characteristic of bias-motivated violence and intimidation statutes is that they proscribe particular types of motivation, rather than protecting only individuals who belong to particular groups. Many critics of hate crime legislation assert that such laws constitute special protection for racial and ethnic minorities.[39] This confuses both the structure of most hate crime legislation and the empirical realities of hate crime in most jurisdictions. Hate crime law protects people of every background. Attacks against anyone who is victimized because of his or her race, religion, or sexual

---

32. *Id.* at § 10:3; *see, e.g.,* D.C. CODE ANN. § 22-4003 (1981) (enhancing fine and imprisonment penalties for bias-related crimes).

33. WANG, *supra* note 4, at §§ 10:2-10:3.

34. *See, e.g.,* IOWA CODE § 729A.1, 716.6A (1993). *See generally* WANG, *supra* note 4, at app. B (delineating intimidation statutes which proscribe disability as motivation).

35. *See, e.g.,* DEL. CODE ANN. Tit. 11, § 1304(a)(2) (Supp. 2000); *see generally* WANG, *supra* note 4, at app. B (delineating state intimidation statutes which proscribe anti-gay and lesbian bias as motivation).

36. *See, e.g.,* ARIZ. REV. STAT. ANN § 13-702.C.14 (2001). *See generally* WANG, *supra* note 4, app. B (delineating state intimidation statues which include gender as a proscribed motivation).

37. *See, e.g.,* D.C. CODE ANN. § 22-4001(1) (1981). *See generally* WANG, *supra* note 4, app. B (delineating state intimidation statutes which include political affiliation as a proscribed motivation).

38. *Id.*

39. *See, e.g.,* JAMES B. JACOBS & KIMBERLY POTTER, HATE CRIMES: CRIMINAL LAW & IDENTITY POLITICS 77 (1998).

orientation—depending on the categories listed under the ju-risdiction's statute—can be prosecuted under hate crime laws. Moreover, both national and state statistics show that individ-uals of a variety of races, religions and other backgrounds are victimized by hate crimes.[40]

B. *The Centrality of the Police Role*

The police play a crucial, though largely ignored, role in in-terpreting hate crime law and ultimately in determining whether the dictates of the First Amendment will be fol-lowed.[41] The importance of the police role stems in part from their place as gatekeepers in the criminal justice system.[42] Before most incidents are ever sent to the District Attorney's office, they are reported to the police, who are responsible for investigating the crime and in many jurisdictions, for seeking the initial criminal complaint.[43] As the first organization re-sponsible for deciding whether an individual's actions consti-tute a hate crime, the police become very important criminal justice gatekeepers and interpreters of motivation. If the po-lice believe that the suspect's actions constitute a hate crime, they investigate.[44] If the investigation confirms their suspi-cions, they may suggest that the suspect be charged with a hate crime.[45] Once the police finish investigating the crime, there is unlikely to be time to gather further evidence of bias motiva-tion. The small amount of time that most district attorney's offices allocate to the investigation of low-level crimes, the cat-egory into which most hate crimes fall, allows few if any cases

---

40. FBI, U.S. Dep't of Justice, *supra* note 19, at 59.

41. *See generally* James Garofalo & Susan E. Martin, Ctr. for the Study of Crime, Delinq. and Corr., S. Ill. Univ., Bias-Motivated Crimes: Their Characteristics and the Law Enforcement Response (1993) (not formally published report by the Center for the Study of Crime, Delinquency, and Corrections at Southern Illinois University at Carbondale).

42. *See* Brian Levin, *Bias Crimes: A Theoretical & Practical Overview*, 4 Stan. L. & Pol'y Rev. 165, 173 (1992-93).

43. *See* Jack Levin & Jack McDevitt, Hate Crimes: The Rising Tide of Bigotry and Bloodshed 165-67 (1993).

44. *See id.* at 166.

45. *See id.* at 166-67.

to receive further investigation. If police decide that the case does not warrant hate crime charges, or they do not include some type of evidence of bias motivation in their reports, it is very unlikely the defendant will be charged with a hate crime.

While the police examination of the perpetrator's motive is crucial in hate crime cases, the requirement to discern motivation is rare for detectives. Though other types of crimes may require a particular *mens rea*, police detectives are not ordinarily required to investigate why a person committed a crime.[46] As one detective responsible for investigating hate crime said:

> In hate crime cases you have to investigate the crime, who the perpetrator was and what was their motivation. In other crimes, you have the first two, but evidence of motivation is not required. Even though they say it all the time on TV that you're looking for motivation in an ordinary crime, you aren't.[47]

In addition to having to perform tasks to which they are unaccustomed, detectives' work enforcing bias crimes legislation is made more difficult by the absence of statutory guidelines regarding what constitutes evidence of bias motivation.[48] Few statutes describe what may be used as evidence of bias-motivation. The lack of statutorily defined procedures and criteria for selecting permissible evidence of bias motivation would not be as much of a problem were bias motivation not so difficult to identify.[49] Bias motivation may assume very different

---

46. *See id.* at 171.

47. *See* BELL, *supra* note 16 (manuscript at 52-53).

48. *See* Linda Bean, *Prosecuting Bias Cases: A Delicate Balancing Act*, N.J. L.J., Sept. 27, 1993, at 4; *see generally* LEVIN & McDEVITT, *supra* note 43, at 166-171 (describing hate crime policy and procedures); Susan E. Martin, *A Cross-Burning Is Not Just An Arson: Police Social Construction Of Hate Crimes In Baltimore County*, 33 CRIMINOLOGY 303 (1995) (reviewing special bias crime procedures in Baltimore County, MD); Chuck Wexler & Gary J. Marx, *When Law and Order Works: Boston's Innovative Approach to the Problem of Racial Violence*, 32 CRIME & DELINQ. 205, 206-16 (1986) (describing Boston's Community Disorders Unit).

49. *See* Garofalo & Martin, *supra* note 41, at 49-51 (describing ambiguity inherent in those cases in which bias is a motivation); Alison Mitchell, *Police Find Bias Crimes Are Often Wrapped in Ambiguity*, N.Y. TIMES, Jan. 27, 1992, at B2; *Revision to hate crimes law is offered; But debate over gays might kill movement to clarify statute*, AUSTIN AM-STATESMEN, Apr. 2, 1995, at B1 (describing law enforcement officers' reluctance to use a "loosely defined"

forms.[50] Frequently, bias-motivated incidents reported to police do not involve organized hate groups and are not characterized by graphic racist or anti-religious acts such as cross-burnings. Consequently, police are not able to rely on traditional signs of bias motivation.[51]

C. Murky Constitutional Waters

Police difficulty is compounded by the fact that they must grapple with the fine constitutional line between hate crime and hate speech. The Supreme Court cases in this area are confusing, and as some argue, contradictory.[52] The Court's decision in a 1992 case, *R.A.V. v. City of St. Paul*,[53] suggested that hate crimes are difficult to identify because they are so closely linked to politically protected speech.[54] That case examined the conviction of Robert Viktora, who burned a cross on the front lawn of the Jones, a Black family who had recently moved to an all-White neighborhood.[55] Viktora was

---

Texas hate crime law and fear of having a conviction overturned on constitutional grounds); Rhonda Smith & Larry Murphy, *Protection from hate crimes on gay agenda*, AUSTIN AM. STATESMAN, Jan. 18, 1995, at B3 (describing a year old hate crime law that does not mention specific racial or minority groups and the difficulty in enforcing such an ambiguous law).

50. *See generally* LEVIN & McDEVITT, *supra* note 43 (describing crimes motivated by resentment, mission crimes, thrill-seekers and reactive hate crimes).

51. *See* Elizabeth A. Boyd, et al, *"Motivated by Hatred or Prejudice": Categorization of Hate Crimes in Two Police Divisions*, 30 L. & SOC'Y. REV. 819, 822 (1996).

52. *See* Craig Peyton Gaumer, *Punishment for Prejudice: A Commentary on the Constitutionality and Utility of State Statutory Responses to the Problem of Hate Crimes*, 39 S. D. L. REV. 1, 24-6 (1994); Susan Gellman, *Transcript: Hate Crime Laws After Wisconsin v. Mitchell*, 21 OHIO N.U.L. REV. 863, 865 (1995); Steven G. Gey, *What if Wisconsin v. Mitchell Had Involved Martin Luther King, Jr.? The Constitutional Flaws of Hate Crime Sentence Enhancement Statutes*, 65 GEO. WASH. L. REV. 1014 , 1019-20 (1997) (arguing that *Mitchell* was incorrectly decided); Robert R. Riggs, *Punishing the Politically Incorrect Offender Through "Bias Motive" Enhancements: Compelling Necessity or First Amendment Folly?*, 21 OHIO N.U.L. REV. 945, 950 (1995); Terrance Sandalow, *Transcript: Opening Address Equality and Freedom of Speech*, 21 OHIO N.U.L. REV. 831, 843 (1995).

53. 505 U.S. 377 (1992).

54. *Id.* at 396 .

55. *See id.* at 379.

convicted under the St. Paul Bias Motivated Crime Ordinance, which prohibited the placement of any object, such as a burning cross or a swastika, that one has reason to know arouses anger or alarm in others on the basis of race, color, creed or gender.[56] He challenged his conviction on First Amendment grounds, arguing the statute was "substantially overbroad and impermissibly content-based."[57] On appeal, the Minnesota Supreme Court rejected the defendant's claim,[58] but limited the ordinance to expressions of fighting words within the meaning of *Chaplinsky v. New Hampshire.*[59] In *Chaplinsky*, the Supreme Court declined to extend First Amendment protection to "fighting words" or those "[words] which by their very utterance inflict injury or tend to incite an immediate breach of the peace."[60]

The Supreme Court reversed the Minnesota Supreme Court's decision.[61] Justice Scalia, who wrote the majority opinion, argued that by not criminalizing all fighting words, the Minnesota statute was clearly attempting to isolate certain words based on their political content.[62] Calling the singling out of fighting words based on race, color, creed, religion and gender, "viewpoint discrimination,"[63] Scalia insisted, "St. Paul has no such authority to license one side of a debate to fight freestyle, while requiring the other to follow Marquis of Queensberry rules."[64] The Court also held that the city's desire to communicate to the minority population its condemna-

---

56. *Id.* at 380. The ordinance provided:
   Whoever places on public or private property a symbol, object, appellation, characterization or graffiti, including, but not limited to, a burning cross or Nazi swastika, which one knows or has reasonable grounds to know arouses anger, alarm or resentment in others on the basis of race, color, creed, religion or gender commits disorderly conduct and shall be guilty of a misdemeanor.
Id.
57. *Id.*
58. *See.* In re Welfare of R.A.V., 464 N.W.2d 507, 510–11 (Minn. 1991).
59. 315 U.S. 568 (1942).
60. *Id.* at 572.
61. *Id.* at 391.
62. *See R.A.V.* 505 U.S. at 396.
63. *Id.*
64. *Id.* at 392.

tion of the message in bias-motivated speech was insufficient to justify a content-based ordinance.[65] Although the Court found St. Paul's interests compelling,[66] it deemed the ordinance not reasonably necessary, maintaining that "[a]n ordinance not limited to the favored topics . . . would have precisely the same beneficial effect."[67]

Less than one year later, apparently in light of much confusion among the states' high courts on the constitutionality of penalty enhancement statutes,[68] the Court elected to rule on another bias crime case, *Wisconsin v. Mitchell*.[69] In this case, after viewing the movie "Mississippi Burning," the defendant Todd Mitchell, who was Black, incited a group of Black men and boys to attack a 14-year-old White youth.[70] Mitchell was convicted under Wisconsin's bias crime statute which provided that the penalty for crimes be increased if the victim was selected because of the actor's belief or perception regarding the victim's "race, religion, color, disability, sexual orientation, national origin or ancestry."[71] Because the jury found that the victim had been selected because of his race, Mitchell's sentence was increased to the maximum penalty—seven years.[72]

Mitchell challenged his conviction on Fourteenth Amendment grounds, arguing that the Wisconsin statute violated the equal protection clause and was vague.[73] He also argued that providing enhanced penalties whenever a defendant intention-

---

65. *Id.*

66. *Id.* at 395.

67. *Id.* at 395-96.

68. *See, e.g.*, State v. Wyant, 597 N.E.2d 450, 459 (Ohio 1992) (striking down Ohio's ethnic intimidation statute); State v. Plowman, 838 P.2d 558, 565-566 (Or. 1992) (upholding Oregon's criminal intimidation statute); State v. Mitchell, 485 N.W.2d 807, 817 (Wis. 1992) (striking down Wisconsin's hate crime statute), *rev'd*, 508 U.S. 476 (1993). There is some evidence that there was police confusion in this area as well. *See* Katia Hetter, *Enforcers of Hate-Crime Laws Wary After High Court Ruling*, WALL ST. J., Aug. 13, 1992, at B1 (describing law enforcement officials as wary of enforcing hate crime laws after Supreme Court's decision in *R.A.V.*).

69. 508 U.S. 476 (1993).

70. *Id.* at 479–80.

71. *Id.* at 480 n.1.

72. *Id.* at 480.

73. *Id.* at 481 n.2.

ally selects a victim on the basis of race violates an individual's First Amendment rights.[74] On appeal, relying on *R.A.V.*, the Wisconsin Supreme Court held that the statute violated the First Amendment by punishing offensive thought and by chilling speech.[75] It also found the statute to be unconstitutionally overbroad.[76]

In *Mitchell*, the Supreme Court surprised many by reversing the Wisconsin Supreme Court's decision, insisting that both the punishment of Mitchell's discriminatory conduct and use of Mitchell's speech as evidence of discriminatory motive was permissible.[77] The Court held out as examples two other contexts where the motive was considered—the sentencing of aggravated crimes and state and federal anti-discrimination law.[78] The Court held that to assign a harsher penalty when the defendant selected his victims for discriminatory reasons is consistent with these other contexts and does not violate the First Amendment.[79] The Court insisted that Wisconsin's desire to prohibit retaliation by the community that was victimized by the bias-motivated conduct provides sufficient evidence that the penalty enhancement is not based on disagreement with the offender's constitutionally protected beliefs.[80]

D.   *The First Amendment Standard for Hate Speech*

It seems clear that in deciding to uphold the use of speech as evidence of motivation, the Court did not intend to allow jurisdictions to criminalize pure hate speech.[81] In *Mitchell*, there are two signs that pure hate speech remains protected.[82] First,

---

74. *Id.* at 481.
75. *Id.* at 481-82.
76. *Id.*
77. *See id.* at 485-90.
78. *Id.* at 485-87.
79. *See id.* at 487-88.
80. *Id.* at 488.
81. *See generally id.*; *R.A.V.* 505 U.S. at 382. (governments disagreeing with ideas expressed are prevented by the First Amendment from prohibiting speech).
82. *See generally Mitchell*, 508 U.S. at 476 (1993) (holding that penalty enhancement is not prohibited by the First and Fourteenth Amendments).

the Court explicitly declined to overrule two of its earlier cases that provided protection for hate speech,[83] *R.A.V.* and *Dawson v. Delaware*.[84] The Court declined to overrule *R.A.V.*, insisting that the ordinance at issue in *R.A.V.* "was explicitly directed at the expression (i.e., "speech" or "messages")."[85] Here, the Court draws a line between punishing speech and punishing an act when the nature of the act is in part a product of biased motive.[86] Second, the Court suggests that First Amendment protection exists for hate speech or, at least for the expression of biased ideas. The Court stated that a sentencing judge may not take into consideration a "defendant's abstract beliefs, however obnoxious to most people."[87] The Court supported this proposition with *Dawson*, a case decided the previous term, in which the Court held that the introduction of evidence that the defendant was a member of a White supremacist gang violated his First Amendment rights.[88]

R.A.V. and *Mitchell* provide an idea of the constitutional limits established by the Supreme Court for the regulation of hate speech and for the regulation of bias-motivated conduct. First, from *R.A.V.*, we learn that states may not single out bias-motivated speech or expressive acts for special regulation, even when such are defined as fighting words. Protected speech and association may not be made a crime, nor may it, as it was in *Dawson*, be used to increase the penalty for a crime for which it is not connected.[89] In *Mitchell*, the Court emphasized that violent conduct associated with hate crimes is neither speech nor expressive conduct protected by the First Amendment.[90] Thus, jurisdictions may punish hate crime without violating the First Amendment. Jurisdictions that have penalty enhancement statutes can use speech as evidence of motivation that a hate crime was committed so long as it is

---

83. *Id.* at 585-87.
84. 503 U.S. 159 (1992).
85. *Mitchell*, 508 U.S. at 487 (internal quotations omitted).
86. *See id.*
87. *Id.* at 485 (citing *Dawson*, 503 U.S. at 167).
88. *Id.* at 486 (citing *Dawson*, 503 U.S. at 167).
89. *Dawson*, 503 U.S. at 166-67.
90. *See Mitchell*, 508 U.S. at 484.

discriminatory *conduct* and not just speech that is being punished.

PART II.   PRACTICAL CONCERNS
IMPACTING ENFORCEMENT

A.   *Critics' First Amendment Concerns*

The narrow standard created by the Supreme Court in *Mitchell* requiring that the police search for motivation heightens the salience of critical arguments regarding enforcement. First Amendment critics of hate crime legislation, both before and after *Mitchell*, have made both doctrinal and practical arguments questioning these statutes' constitutionality.[91] Below I discuss several of the practical arguments addressing whether hate crime legislation can be enforced constitutionally. The critics' disagreements with hate crime legislation revolve around the issue of motivation, and the likelihood that enforcers will interfere with protected speech and association.

While speech can be used as evidence in hate crime cases, *Dawson* and *Mitchell* seem to limit the use of speech to evidence of motivation for the crime.[92] Critics are concerned that those enforcing hate crime laws will be unable to uncover perpetrators' motivation and thus, will use protected speech as evidence of the crime's motivation. Part of this stems from the nature of motivation. Several of these scholars suggest that bias motivation is something hidden, difficult to disentangle, or otherwise impossible to discern.[93] One critic writes, "[A]ssessing motive presents more than the problem of somehow reading the defendant's mind, for the defendant himself may not know his true motive. Social psychology is full of research that demonstrates people often are unaware of what is

---

91. *See supra* note 52. Though scholars criticize hate crime legislation on several fronts, this Article only addresses critics' arguments regarding enforcement.

92. *See generally* Dawson v. Delaware, 503 U.S. 159 (1992); Wisconsin v. Mitchell, 508 U.S. 476 (1993) (noting that defendant's motive is an important factor when sentencing for crimes).

93. *See supra* note 53.

truly influencing their behavior."[94] In critics' eyes, the slippery nature of bias motivation means that law enforcers will be forced to search for evidence of the crime's motivation by looking to cues from words, thoughts or associations that are protected by the First Amendment.[95]

Critics are also concerned that an offender's hate speech will be used as evidence when hate crime legislation is enforced.[96] Many critics assume that what was said during the crime serves as the starting point in the search for evidence of bias motivation in hate crimes.[97] Critics are fearful that once enforcers have slurs, epithets or other speech evidence, they will never really get beyond this point.[98] Enforcers will use the defendant's biased utterances (or symbols, in the case of property crimes) during the commission of the crime as the only evidence of bias motivation.[99] From a First Amendment perspective there are two worries here. The first is that the defendant would be punished for saying the words, thereby obviating the First Amendment protection for bigoted beliefs.[100]

Critics of hate crime legislation raise an important issue here. For example, *Mitchell* is silent on the question of whether, in situations in which words are the *only* evidence of motivation, it is acceptable to charge persons with violating hate crime laws.[101] Given the Court's explanation of these issues in *Mitchell*, it is possible that even in instances in which hate speech serves as the only evidence of bias motivation, hate crime charges are constitutional. Allowing an additional

---

94. Gerstenfeld, *supra* note 6, at 270; *see, e.g.* Robert I. Corry, Jr., *Burn This Article: It is Evidence in Your Thought Crime Prosecution,* 4 Tex. Rev. L. & Pol. 461 (2000).

95. *See, e.g.,* Susan Gellman, *Sticks and Stones Can Put You in Jail, but Can Words Increase Your Sentence? Constitutional and Policy Dilemmas of Ethnic Intimidation Laws,* 39 UCLA L. REV. 333, 359 (1991); Martin H. Redish, *Freedom of Thought as Freedom of Expression: Hate Crime Sentencing Enhancement and First Amendment Theory,* 11 Crim. Just. Ethics 29, 30 (1992).

96. *See* Jacobs & Potter, *supra* note 39, at 109-10.

97. *Id.* at 103.

98. *See id.*

99. *See id.*

100. *See id.*; Gellman, *supra* note 95, at 363.

101. *See id.*

punishment under hate crime law in instances when there is hate speech *and* evidence that the crime was committed for other reasons, however, seems inconsistent with the protection for hate speech the Court granted in *R.A.V.* and *Dawson*.

The second concern stemming from enforcers scrutinizing the words uttered during the incident as evidence of bias motivation, is that individuals with constitutionally benign motives will be penalized under hate crime laws because enforcers are unable to disentangle criminal action from protected expression of speech or thought.[102] Critics' articles are replete with "hard cases" that seem clearly unintended by the law but have been allegedly punished as hate crimes. Susan Gellman provides an example that she insists will fall within the ambit of the bias crime statutes, even though the alleged perpetrator had benign motives. Her hard case involves a "racial champion," White woman A, who, hearing another White woman B, calling C, an African American child, a racist name, threatens B in an attempt to protect C.[103] Gellman suggests that under many hate crime statutes, both A and B, two individuals with wholly different motives could be prosecuted.[104] One real case, widely cited by critics, involved an African American man in Florida who was charged with a hate crime after he called a White policeman trying to break-up a domestic disturbance a "cracker."[105] That defendant, one critic writes, "clearly was not motivated to commit his crime because of the policeman's race . . . His name-calling is not being used as evidence that he was hate motivated. Instead, he is being prosecuted for evidencing prejudice by calling the officer a racial epithet."[106] Hate crime charges against the man were later dropped.[107]

---

102. Gellman, *supra* note 95, at 364-65.

103. *See id.* at 356.

104. *Id.* at 355-56.

105. *Id.* at 361 n.134; Gerstenfeld, *supra* note 6, at 279; Barbara Dority, *The Criminalization of Hatred,* 54 HUMANIST 38 May/June 1994, *available at* http://ehostvgw11.epnet.com.

106. Gerstenfeld, *supra* note 6, at 279.

107. Gellman, *supra* note 95, at 361 n.134.

As the frequent use of the example of the police officer in Florida suggests, some scholars are particularly worried because it is police officers that are given discretion to enforce hate crime law.[108] Their assumption is that police will transform incidents that are obviously not bias-motivated into hate crimes. One critic who acknowledges that police generally have discretion to deal with crime bemoans police discretion in hate crime cases. He writes:

> If some sort of word was said, some sort of slur was used, does not that make what is otherwise a generic crime into a hate crime as well? I think that it is extremely problematic. And though law enforcement officers exercise a fair amount of discretion with every law at the crime scene, certainly these decisions will be even more sensitive and difficult with hate crime laws.[109]

The broad inquiry into words, thought, and association that critics assume will occur as enforcers investigate hate crime leads to yet another First Amendment problem: one of overbreadth leading to the chilling of speech, thought, and association. Although the *Mitchell* Court rejected this argument as too attenuated, scholars have expressed the concern that enforcers will not just investigate the defendant's words or actions during the crime, but also "all of his or her remarks upon earlier occasions, any books ever read, speakers ever listened to, or associations ever held."[110] In a similar vein, another scholar describes a very intrusive inquiry required in all "competent" hate crime prosecutions. He asserts that evidence would have to be collected regarding, among other things, the past expressions of hatred or tolerance of the individuals, the beliefs and thought patterns of persons with whom the defendant associated.[111] One scholar worries that racist jokes will be used as evidence of guilt.[112] Gerstenfeld writes: "Unless the defendant is an avowed member of the Ku Klux Klan, or

---

108. *See* Richard Cordray, *Free Speech and the Thought We Hate*, 21 OHIO N.U.L. REV. 871, 880 (1995); JACOBS & POTTER, *supra* note 39, at 92-100 (expressing skepticism regarding police enforcement).

109. Cordray, *supra* note 108, at 880.

110. *See* Gellman, *supra* note 95, at 360.

111. Riggs, *supra* note 52 at 953.

112. Gerstenfeld, *supra* note 6, at 270.

another hate group, it might be difficult to determine his motive. One can imagine prosecutors canvassing the defendant's neighbors and coworkers to discover how many times he made racist comments or told an ethnic joke."[113]

The worry about the scope of law enforcers' inquiry is a good one, for the Court did not specify in *Mitchell* how far back one might go in seeking evidence of motivation, or what might count as evidence of motivation in bias crime cases. Leaving this discretion up to those enforcing the law creates questions about whether defendants' privacy will be protected. While this is not a First Amendment concern, it is important. In addition, depending on how enforcers behave, it creates the possibility, particularly in cases where there is no other evidence of bias motivation, that enforcers will use the defendant's abstract beliefs, wholly unconnected to the crime, as evidence of bias motivation. The use of such evidence is a clear violation of the standard established by the Court in *Dawson.*

B. *Empirical Evidence and Further Concerns*

The evidence from the field gives cause for further concern regarding how enforcers are behaving with respect to the First Amendment. One study of detectives classifying hate crime in a large police department revealed that police resist enforcing hate crime law.[114] According to this study, the general perception among the majority of officers was that "only a few crimes [could] . . . 'really' be called hate motivated, such as a cross burning on the lawn of an African American family or the organized activities of the KKK or Aryan Nation."[115] The authors of the study found that police at all levels—patrol officers, detectives and commanding officers—expressed resentment over the departmental policy giving priority to hate crimes.[116] Officers dismissed hate crimes as "'overkill,' 'mostly bull,' 'a pain in the ass,' 'media hype,' 'a giant cluster

---

113. *Id.*
114. *See* Boyd et al., *supra* note 51, at 827.
115. *Id.*
116. *Id.*

fuck.'"[117] Even those who thought that hate crimes were a problem did not feel they deserved priority over what they considered "real" crime—burglary, theft, and rape.[118] The detectives' belief that hate crimes were not a problem in the city translated into different, though equally disturbing types of behavior.[119] Detectives affiliated with one precinct, police "Division A" categorized only cases marked by the clearest signs of bias as "normal hate crimes"—cases with racial epithets, those with symbols of hate, and those involving hate groups.[120] The detectives in Division A rejected all cases that did not have those features.[121] By only viewing as hate crimes the cases with the clearest signs of bias, the detectives in Division A were, strictly from a First Amendment perspective, enforcing the law in the proper cases—those cases that appear unambiguously motivated by bias. Adopting the normal crime/hate crime typification most likely led them to under-enforce the law, however. The routines used by the detectives in Division A may have caused them to miss crimes that did not contain extreme manifestations of bias, but were nonetheless bias-motivated.

In the alternative, the behavior of the police detectives in the other police precinct, "Division B," was, from a constitutional perspective, even more troubling. The detectives in Division B ignored the issue of motivation altogether.[122] They behaved as critics expected them to, classifying incidents as hate crimes without inquiry into whether they were actually motivated by bias.[123] Thus, cases that were not bias-motivated could have been identified as hate crimes.[124] The Detectives in Division B left it up to the district attorney (DA) to determine the perpetrator's motivation.[125] If the detective has conducted little or no inquiry in this area, however, the DA may

---

117. *Id.*
118. *Id.* 827-28.
119. *Id.* at 827.
120. *Id.* at 839.
121. *Id.* at 832-40.
122. *Id.* at 845.
123. *Id.* at 840.
124. *Id.*
125. *Id.* at 845.

have little evidence from which to draw conclusions regarding the perpetrator's motivation.

Another study, this time of bias units in New York City and Baltimore, raises different questions about the enforcement of hate crime law.[126] The authors of the study indicate that in a number of cases "the primacy of the element of bias was ambiguous . . . [and that] . . . [o]ften the police have to deal with cases that seem to contain bias as a secondary motivation . . . [or] an additional motivation."[127] Another issue that effects the classification of an incident "include[s] the weight to be accorded [to] the victim's perception relative to other factors . . . [and] . . . whom to believe . . . when there are conflicting statements about an incident"[128] These questions are important. Unfortunately, the study does not describe in detail how police address these issues.

News reports from around the country seem to support the idea that officers find the situations in which hate crimes occur ambiguous.[129] One detective from the New York City Police Department is quoted as saying, "I hate these cases because they become real mysteries . . . [E]verybody jumps on the bandwagon but nobody has the facts."[130] In cases that are ambiguous, officers may question whether the perpetrator was motivated by bias or whether the incident was a prank and not aimed at a particular victim. From these news stories it is unclear whether ambiguous cases are the exceptions or, as many critics of bias crime legislation would have us believe, the rule. The news stories also fail to provide evidence regarding whether police officers are equipped to sort through these interpretive difficulties systematically. The worries that First

---

126. Garofalo & Martin, *supra* note 41, at 33-45 (comparing responses of law enforcement officers to bias crimes).

127. *Id.* at 49-50.

128. *Id.* at 50.

129. *See* Leslie Berger, *Police Seek Motive in Shop Fire*, L.A. TIMES, April 21, 1992, at 3; Meg McSherry Breslin, *Vandals Leave Trail of Racist Graffiti Homes, Cars Damaged in Joliet Neighborhood*, CHI. TRIB., September 6, 1999, at 1; David Birkland, *Lake Forest Park Hit with Racist Graffiti, Police Unsure Whether Vandalism Was Hate Crime or Prank*, THE SEATTLE TIMES, May 12, 2001 at B2.

130. JACOBS & POTTER, *supra* note 39, at 91.

Amendment critics of hate crime legislation and others concerned with their enforcement have raised creates three main implications for enforcement. First, many critics argue that enforcers of hate crime laws are unable to discern the defendant's motive and thus will seize on the defendant's speech during the crime as evidence that the crime was bias-motivated.[131] Other critics worry not about the narrowness of the inquiry into motivation, but its breadth, worrying the enforcers of hate crime legislation will reach into areas of protected thought and association as they hunt for bias.[132] Finally, critics' charge that bias motivation is so difficult to discern, and there are so many ambiguous cases that many individuals with wholly benign motives will be charged with violating hate crime laws.[133]

PART III.   ARE THE CRITICS RIGHT? —THE POSSIBILITY OF CONSTITUTIONALLY ENFORCING HATE CRIME LAW

Examining the reality of bias crime law enforcement is one method of empirically testing concerns about the First Amendment dangers created by bias crime legislation. Using data collected in "Center City," a metropolitan city, this section will evaluate whether individuals are charged with hate crime violations based on the use of biased language, or words alone; and whether the enforcement of bias crime legislation reaches into areas of protected speech. This section focuses on the behavior of officers in the "Center City" police hate crime unit, appraising police officers' ability to enforce vague statutes, and evaluates their treatment of hate speech, beliefs, and conduct protected by the First Amendment.

A.   *The Anti-Bias Task Force*

Between September of 1997 and May of 1998, I conducted a study that focused on the detectives in a hate crime unit in

---

131. *See supra* p. 46.
132. *See supra* pp. 42-45.
133. *See supra* pp. 42-47.

"Center City,"[134] a large city in the United States. During this time period, I was granted access to observe the detectives, and was also allowed access to their case files spanning two decades, and to most of their other records.[135] The Center City "Anti-Bias Task Force" (ABTF), the unit I studied, was formed in the late 1970's, two years before the state's hate crime statute was passed.[136] The unit was created to address the violence many minorities experienced after they moved into all-White neighborhoods.[137] The unit was supposed to respond to three types of situations: 1) crimes where there was evidence that victim(s) were selected on account of race, or incidents and situations occurred that were precipitated by racial motives; 2) incidents of group activity and demonstrations where there was a potential for inciting group conflict and violence; and 3) incidents where there were concerted efforts by a person or a group of persons to deprive minorities of free access to any neighborhood or community within the city.[138] After the state civil rights law—which served as the jurisdiction's hate crime statute—was passed, the unit became responsible for investigating and preparing hate crime charges.[139]

As a detective unit, the ABTF received case files after the officers who reported to the scene of a crime determined that an incident was possibly bias-motivated. Police department policy required those on the scene to forward the cases to the ABTF if they believed a case to be bias-motivated.

---

134. The city's actual name and some of its identifying details have been changed to protect the identity of the respondents.

135. The study, its methodology, and its conclusions are described in much greater detail in BELL, *supra* note 16.

136. *Id.* (manuscript at 29).

137. *Id.*

138. Special Order 78-28 from "Center City" to ABTF (unpublished document on file with the author).

139. To preserve the confidentiality of respondents, the statute is not cited.

B. *Determining Bias: Detectives' systematic search for motivation*

Bias crime legislation is not, as critics suggest, so vague that police officers have no means of enforcing it systematically.[140] My observation of detectives' practices revealed the classification of bias crime to be quite systematic. Far from random, the identification of bias crime is a multifaceted process, in which detectives weighed the facts and circumstances of the crime as well as the characteristics of the case against their experience. The decision that officers had to make was twofold: officers first identified the bias-motivation and then made strategic decisions about whether to actually seek charges. Below are the rules of thumb that officers used to identify and select cases appropriate for hate crime charges.[141]

Detectives developed filtering mechanisms and employed rules of thumb to isolate bias motivation in part because many of the cases referred to the unit were not bias-motivated. The unit received a high percentage of non-bias-motivated cases because the ABTF encouraged patrol officers to send any case to the unit that could possibly be bias-motivated. This resulted in large numbers of cases being sent to the unit in which the perpetrator had used slurs and epithets while committing a crime. The unit encouraged patrol officers to be over inclusive rather than under inclusive in their forwarding of incidents because as detectives, they were trained in investigation and wished to take filtering power out of the hands of less well-trained patrol officers. In addition, as a check on patrol, the ABTF also had the Reports Bureau forward any cases with the possibility of bias to the unit. In keeping with the unit's

---

140. *See generally* Jeannine Bell, *Policing Hatred: Police Bias Units and the Construction of Hate Crime*, 2 Mich. J. Race & L. 421, 443 (1997) ("While there may be no inherent difficulty in identifying bias crimes, as free speech absolutists suggest, separating bias crimes from free speech may at the very least require police officers to make extremely fine legal distinctions, a job that may require a clear understanding of the vagaries of First Amendment jurisprudence. In addition, police officers' jobs are often complicated by the lack of public understanding about what bias crime laws prohibit.").

141. The following discussion of the routines that the detectives in Center City use to identify hate crime is drawn from BELL, *supra* note 16 (manuscript at 141-152).

request, the Reports Bureau forwarded all reports that had slurs or epithets and a difference in race between the victim and the perpetrator. This drastically increased the unit's caseload, since vulgarity, especially slurs and epithets, were common in acts of violence. For instance, one officer estimated that slurs and epithets were used in 70% of incidents with injuries and 90% of traffic accidents.[142]

C. Basic Requirements for Hate Crimes

Detectives' practices reveal that hate crimes had two basic requirements. The perpetrator and victim had to have different identities—race, gender, sexual orientation, etc.—and the context in which the crime occurred needed to be one that suggested that it had been motivated by bias, rather than some other emotion—anger, revenge, jealousy, etc.

1. Different Identities

The first and most important requirement was that the victim and perpetrator have different identities or backgrounds. In the vast majority of cases if detectives accepted that the victim had been attacked because of his or her race, the victim and perpetrator had to have different racial backgrounds. Detectives did not believe that bias-motivated incidents happened within the same identity group; incidents in which the victim and the perpetrator had the same race were routinely dismissed as having other origins.

The heavy presumption against bias-motivation among individuals of the same race applied to cases involving anti-gay bias as well. It was assumed that gays could not commit hate crimes against other gays. In one case involving one Black gay man who was attacked by another and called a "faggot," two detectives called the man "a victim of no crime," since the other man was also gay.

There were two important exceptions to the practice of dismissing same-group attacks. The first involved heterosexual men who were attacked by other heterosexuals because their

---

142. *Id.* (manuscript at 141).

attackers believed that they were gay. The unit had investigated several cases that fit this scenario. For example, in one case the victims, who were not gay, were in a taxicab and approached by a group of men who said, "Get out of the car, faggots." After one man exited the car and ran, the perpetrator gave chase. When he caught the victim, he began to kick him, screaming, "Fucking homos." The unit sought hate crime charges in this case because the victim had been attacked because he was *presumed* to be gay. In this case, the two defendants pled guilty to both criminal charges and hate crime charges.[143]

The second important exception to the practice of dismissing same-group attacks concerned attacks against one member of an interracial couple. ABTF detectives accepted that same race attacks against a member of an interracial couple were frequently bias-motivated. The unit had seen particularly dramatic examples of this, especially involving Whites attacked by other Whites for dating minorities.

The practice of dismissing cases when individuals had similar identities meant that detectives were often unable to appreciate the fact that victims and perpetrators had multiple identities and myriad perspectives on these identities. In the case involving the gay victim who the detectives decided was not a victim of a hate crime, the detective did not even explore the possibility that the hate crime could be a race-based crime, or that the perpetrator was a "self-hating gay" and the attack occurred because of the victim's sexual orientation.[144]

Automatic dismissal of all cases in which both the perpetrator and the victim are gay means that detectives may miss cases that should be treated as hate crimes. Center City had cases involving so-called self-hating gays who targeted and killed other gay men. Detectives told of several homicides that occurred in a public area where many gay men had sex. The killer selected sex partners and clubbed each to death while the two were engaged in intercourse. The detectives said that when they caught the man, he claimed that he committed the

143. *Id.* (manuscript at 142).
144. *Id.* (manuscript at 142-43).

crimes because he hated gays.[145] In 1991, a similar case occurred in Minneapolis: a gay man committed two anti-gay murders on the eastern banks of the Mississippi in a secluded area frequented by gay men. The perpetrator discussed his self-hatred and hatred of other gay men in Arthur Dong's documentary film, *Licensed to Kill* (1997).[146]

2. *Looking to the Crime's Context*

Rather than just using speech as evidence of bias motivation, as several critics assume that enforcers of bias crime legislation will do, detectives used mechanisms that helped them look beyond the defendant's speech for clues to his or her motivation. Looking widely for evidence of the motive for the crime did not, as critics argue, mean that detectives scrutinized the defendant's beliefs or association. Detectives looked to the setting and other situational aspects of the crime in order to shed light on why the incident occurred. The setting of the crime included the crime's precise location, whether the crime occurred in or outdoors, and what the perpetrator and the victim were doing immediately before the crime. In exploring these situational aspects of the crime, the detectives were looking for evidence that the crime was *not* motivated by bias, but rather by anger, jealousy, or revenge. These are a few of the motivations that ABTF detectives wish to rule out when deciding whether a bias crime has occurred. If a crime were motivated by jealousy over a woman, to use an example that detectives sometimes mentioned, it was not a hate crime.[147]

As part of evaluating context, detectives were trained to ask whether the incident could have happened or would have escalated if the perpetrator and the victim were the same race. If the incident would still have occurred and would have unfolded in the same manner even if the perpetrator and victim had the same identity, then the detectives assumed that the incident was not a hate crime.

---

145. *Id.*

146. Videotape: License to Kill (Arthur Dong 1997), *available at* http://www.deepfocusproduction.com.

147. Bell, *supra* note 16 (manuscript at 143).

a.   *"The Typical Non-Hate Crime"*

Detectives did not examine the setting of every crime and weigh whether the perpetrator was motivated by anger, jealousy, or revenge. Instead, they used shortcuts to filter out non-bias-motivated cases. These shortcuts were based on incidents that were repeatedly referred to the unit that had been determined to be non- bias-motivated. I call these the "typical non-hate crime." The typical non-hate crime involved five scenarios—cases involving drugs, fights, retaliation for earlier fights, traffic accidents, and neighbor disputes. These cases were among the ones in which detectives were able to identify the perpetrators' motivation. Detectives were frequently not able to determine what motivated an incident (and no hate crime charges were sought). Typical non-hate crimes were the types of cases in which the detectives decided that the incident was not motivated by bias. One detective explained these types of cases as incidents that were "less than 51% bias-motivated."[148] When asked for an example he replied, "[a] traffic accident between someone Asian and someone White. Racial epithets, slurs are exchanged."[149]

Typical non-hate crimes were not characterized by a specific set of events. As long as incidents that were really about "traffic" involved cars, and neighbor disputes involved individuals who lived near each other, a non-hate crime could occur in many ways. Any and every case involving a car could really be over traffic. Any situation involving a drug transaction could really be about drugs. One example of such cases involved a young White man who had been shot in the buttocks. He claimed that he had been shot by a group of Black men and that the crime was racially motivated. ABTF detectives investigated and determined that the victim had placed a gun in his back pocket for protection during a drug transaction. During the meeting the gun discharged accidentally.[150]

For the detectives, deciding that something is bias-motivated began with the process of ruling out alternate explanations.

---

148. *Id.* (manuscript at 144).
149. *Id.*
150. *Id.* (manuscript at 13).

Since every incident involving traffic, or drugs, or neighbors, for example, could be non-bias-motivated, incidents were first evaluated against typical non-hate crime. Real hate crimes then became defined, in part, in opposition to the typical non-hate crime. In this way, ABTF practices were distinct from those other detectives investigating hate crime. Instead of creating archetypal hate crimes with particular characteristics—cases with extreme violence, those involving members of organized hate groups, and other significant outward manifestations of bias—and calling these the "normal hate crimes," detectives identified classes of crimes frequently referred to the unit that should *not* be considered hate crimes.

b. *Weeding out False Reports*

In trying to discern whether an incident was a typical non-hate crime, the detective's initial task involved the ordinary detective work of trying to "figure out what happened." Part of figuring out what happened required sorting the conflicting stories that emerged from interviewing suspects and victims and often figuring out who was telling the truth and who was lying. Though a sample of the case files revealed less than one manufactured hate crime a year, the specter of false reports—incidents individuals manufactured to extract some type of benefit—loomed large. Nearly every detective mentioned that sometimes individuals made things up to manipulate the system. When asked for examples, detectives generally gave the same ones: prominent cases in which individuals had deliberately claimed to be a victim when he or she was not, either for attention or in order to receive some tangible benefit.

Detectives were well aware that some individuals might be lying in order to attract attention or sympathy. One such incident involved a Jewish college student who reported that swastikas and anti-Semitic threats had been drawn on her door. After several incidents, the college installed a hidden camera that captured the woman calmly stepping over a page with a swastika on it that had been slid under the door. The note was not reported to the police until the next day when the woman's roommate discovered it. The victim's cavalier attitude toward the note when she believed herself unobserved signaled to the police that she was the person who left the note. The detectives surmised that the victim's reporting of the earlier notes had been a plea for attention.[151]

Another situation that detectives in the unit encountered on several occasions involved individuals living in public housing who faked hate crimes so that the housing office would move them to another housing development or give them a Section 8 certificate allowing them to move into private housing. One detective explained:

> There is money to be made in false civil rights reports. If someone wants a Section 8 certificate, right now they are not taking applications unless one is a victim of a hate crime. We had an incident when a guy who was gay knew that he could get a Section 8 certificate if he said that his civil rights were violated. He said that he was being harassed, that he had no entrance to certain courtyards, and [that] he could not park his car in certain areas. Sometimes people will say they are being harassed and that they want a transfer to a certain housing development. Then you find out they have a mother or sister in that development.[152]

One downside to the unusual degree of service that the unit provided to victims was that it attracted the attention of those who wanted the police to investigate crimes that had happened to them. A variation on the false report was the victim who deliberately misrepresented what happened to him or her in order to get the system to pay attention to the crime. Officers were forced to weed out cases in which the victim had added slurs and epithets in order to get the police—any police—to investigate the crime. One detective remarked:

> People realized that they were getting more attention. They were aware of our success rate, also aware of other steps. Other things were done to protect you. People started wising up, if you say it's racial you get personal attention—round-the-clock protection, nail the guy to the wall [when we catch him] high bail or no bail. That's what we started asking for in civil rights cases. They started to think, "I want to really slam this guy who hurt me so I'm

---

151. *Id.* (manuscript at 145).
152. *Id.* (manuscript at 145-46).

going to say it's racial and I'm going to get attention." Like when people want someone to come right away and they report an OT, officer in trouble.[153]

D. *Policing crime, not speech*

When asked about the importance of slurs and epithets, or as they called it, "language," detectives denied that language used by the perpetrator automatically signaled the necessary bias to establish motive. Language alone, detectives insisted, was not enough to prove the crime was motivated by bias.[154] One had to look to the suspect's actions and the crime's context to evaluate whether the suspect would still have committed the crime if the victim were of another background. If for instance a detective were investigating an assault that was reported as a racially motivated crime and the victim of the crime was Asian American and the perpetrator was White, the detective would evaluate whether the crime would have still happened if the victim were White. If the detective came to the conclusion that the crime would still have occurred if the races of the perpetrator and the victim were the same, then the crime would not be considered bias-motivated. One detective explained:

> It's not language alone. You investigate actions. Words are the secondary buttress of actions. They prove the history of the action; prove that they went after someone because of race. You have to put the blinders on. Is this something the perpetrator would have done if the victim were Black or White? You have to consider both sides, walk the line.[155]

Critics worry that hate crimes statutes are overbroad and will have a chilling effect on protected speech. It is unclear whether individuals in Center City felt "chilled" and were less reluctant to use hate speech, or other speech that may be construed as evidence of motivation after hate crime statutes were enacted.[156] Some individuals were clearly not deterred by hate

---

153. *Id.* (manuscript at 146).
154. *Id.* (manuscript at 147).
155. *Id.*
156. Between 1990 and 1998, the number of possible hate crimes the unit investigated increased. In light of this, some might contend that an increase

crime legislation. The unit had had several cases with repeat offenders, individuals who had committed a number of similar bias-motivated incidents, frequently against members of the same victim group. For these individuals, their behavior in similar cases sometimes served as an important contextual variable. One detective explained:

> We look to the totality of the circumstances, criminal action and the words and also at the incident . . . Language alerts us to the possibility of bias, but it's just the possibility.

It's not clear-cut. It's easier for us when you have, as we've . . . had, the same defendant for two crimes. It's hard because of the totality of the circumstances. None of us are in the minds of the perpetrators. They may have acted because they're ticked off because someone is hitting on their girlfriend or because the person is of a different race and is hitting on the girlfriend.[157]

The comments of the two detectives quoted above are representative of the views of most ABTF detectives. In cases in which slurs or epithets had been used detectives were very receptive to the possibility that bias had not motivated the incident. The typical non-hate crime and their use of context are indicative of their desire to look beyond language for other indications of bias motivation.

E. *Relationship and Bias*

Further evidence of the importance situational factors to detectives' determination that a crime has been motivated by

---

in the number of cases indicates that the community was not "chilled" by hate crime legislation. I think that this explanation is far too simplistic. First, as other scholars have recognized an increased number of hate crimes can be attributed to a variety of factors, such as increased reporting. See, e.g., JACOBS & POTTER, *supra* note 39, at 58-59. Second, chilling effects on speech address the effect on speech not formally covered by the restriction. EUGENE VOLOKH, THE FIRST AMENDMENT: PROBLEMS, CASES, AND POLICY ARGUMENTS 337-40 (2001). In the case of hate crime, critics worry about the chilling effect on protected speech. Unless one were to actually conduct a survey of the community, one could not evaluate whether the community felt chilled and neglected to speak or otherwise express themselves because of hate crime legislation.

157. Bell, *supra* note 16 (manuscript at 147).

bias can be seen in the detectives' evaluation of the relationship between the victim and the suspects. ABTF detectives identified the relationship between people as an important part of the context of the crime. Language was discounted as a factor indicating motivation in exchanges between people who knew each other. As other research has found,[158] a pre-existing relationship, good or bad, between the victim and the suspect is a sign to the police that an incident is not bias-motivated.[159] One former detective complained about a case, saying, "it was . . . a gay guy complaining about his boyfriend. It was not a legitimate case."[160] In another case, a gay man repeatedly tried to get civil rights (hate crime) charges against someone with whom he had had consensual sex in the past. Like prosecutors who refuse to bring charges in rape cases in which the victim may have had previous consensual sex with the perpetrator,[161] ABTF detectives refused to consider the gay victim's case for civil rights charges.[162] They insisted that because the victim and the perpetrator had consensual sex on a previous occasion, what had happened to the victim was not a hate crime.[163]

Cases involving people who had some other relationship, such as friends or neighbors, were considered problematic by those enforcing the law in Center City. ABTF detectives were not alone in assuming that racial or anti-gay bias was less likely

---

158. *See* Martin, *supra* note 48, at 314. Martin's study of verified and unverified racial, religious, and ethnic incidents by police in Baltimore County, Maryland found that unverified incidents more often than not had a history of conflict between the parties.

159. *Cf.* FREDERICK M. LAWRENCE, PUNISHING HATE: BIAS CRIMES UNDER AMERICAN LAW 15 (1999). "Particularly in cases of acquaintance rape and domestic violence, the prior personal relationship between victim and assailant makes it difficult to prove that gender animus, and not some other component of the relationship, is the motivation for the crime." *Id.*

160. BELL, *supra* note 16 (manuscript at 148).

161. Lisa Frohmann, *Convictability and Discordant Locales: Reproducing Race, Class, and Gender Ideologies in Prosecutorial Decisionmaking,* 31 LAW. & SOC'Y REV. 531, 535-43 (1997) (discussing the impact of race and class on prosecutor's decision to reject rape cases).

162. BELL, *supra* note 16 (manuscript at 148).

163. *Id.*

to be the reason for the crime if the individuals involved the incident were acquainted. Lawyers responsible for seeking injunctive relief under the civil rights law also discounted bias as an explanation in cases in which the victim and suspect knew each other.[164] A previous relationship and sustained contact over time can afford myriad opportunities for one to develop reasons, aside from issues of bias, to attack the victim. Cases between those who knew each other could have multiple motives, any of which could be the reason for the attack. One lawyer explained why cases between friends and neighbors did not make good cases for injunctive relief and why she discounted the use of slurs and epithets in such cases:

> Often you have cases with dual motives. Maybe they used slurs, but they knew each other. They were neighbors and the incident could have been because the dog was barking. Even though a racial slur was used, we may have cut them [the perpetrator] some slack. We all have biases and we have different ways of negotiating the fact that [different] people are in our community.[165]

In a similar vein, a different Assistant Attorney General replied, in response to a question about the additional evidence she wants when she is not sure about a case:

> I want to find more evidence of bias, more evidence in general. They should ask, is there a history between these two individuals? If they've never encountered each other before that suggests two things, first that it is bias-motivated and second, that it's likely to be repeated.[166]

Most of the cases the unit investigated involved attacks committed by perpetrators unknown to the victims, something that made finding the person who committed the crime more challenging. It makes intuitive sense that strangers, who are unlikely to know the victim personally, are less likely to have reason other than bias—anger or revenge, for instance—to serve as the motivation for the attack. Perhaps the police and those prosecuting bias crimes favored cases with strangers as perpetrators rather than neighbors or friends because bias

---

164. *Id.*
165. *Id.* (manuscript at 148-49).
166. *Id.* (manuscript at 149).

crimes committed by stranger-perpetrators make for simpler and more believable stories.

A related worry is that detectives will uncritically accept the victim's view of what happened and identify cases as hate crimes that are really only hate speech. This is of particular concern when police are given open-ended criteria and not told exactly what weight to ascribe to a victim's story.

ABTF detectives were especially careful to weigh the victim's perception of whether a hate crime had occurred. Distinguishing between hate speech and hate crimes, detectives insisted that although words of hate may hurt or inflame, they were not in and of themselves criminal. Detectives in the unit regularly acknowledged that a line exists between hate speech and hate crime. Their conversations suggest that hate speech was wholly legal, while hate crime, which involves criminal action, was what the law criminalized. This conversation took place in the office, while one detective was looking at an incident report and talking with another.

> Detective 1: A White teacher, the victim, has asked a Black student to leave the room. Evidently, the perpetrator, the student, said to the victim teacher, "What are you looking at you fucking honkey?" [Reading directly from the crime report] "The victim thinks his constitutional rights are violated." [Looking up from the sheet] Names is not a crime.
>
> Detective 2: No.
>
> Detective 1: I'll screen this one out.[167]

Another detective described how he weighed victims' stories with hate speech.

> Hate crimes are a challenge. Take an offensive term. The victim hears the term and also the offensive history. You have to remain objective. Take the swastika. That has meaning to people. The "n-word," too. Sometimes words alone don't rise to the level of a hate crime.[168]

The detective continued, giving an example:

---

167. *Id.* (manuscript at 150).
168. *Id.*

A gay man is walking down the street. He hears the words, "Hey, faggot." Those are just words. Or hears, "Hey, White honkey." We have to look to see if he feels intimidated. It's not a crime to just use words. It's words alone in that context in a manner that may make it a hate crime. Did they threaten? Did they have intent? Someone can yell, "Faggot!," but to have intent, you need action.[169]

F. *Questioning the Suspect about Motivation*

As mentioned earlier, critics worry that enforcers will inquire into a defendant's beliefs and protected expression—the defendant's thoughts and associations—as they investigate hate crimes.[170] The vast majority of the detectives' questioning of suspects occurred during police interrogations. The interrogations of suspects in Center City reveal that detectives were not concerned with the perpetrator's abstract beliefs, but rather, like other criminal investigations, focused on marshalling evidence of who committed the crime. Unlike other crimes, however, even after the perpetrator had confessed, the detectives often spent a large amount of time clarifying the perpetrator's motivation. In this regard, the detectives used the interrogation to gather facts regarding the context of the crime. Suspects were frequently questioned about particular situational aspects of the crime such as what the suspect and the victim had been doing before the crime occurred and the prior relationship between the victim and the suspect. A prior altercation in which the victim had been the aggressor suggested that the second incident may not have been a hate crime, but rather connected to the earlier incident.

In the interrogation below, the detective is trying to find out why a Puerto Rican man was maced on public transportation by two young White men:

---

169. *Id.*

170. Lisa M. Stozek, *Wisconsin v. Mitchell: The End of Hate Crimes or Just the End of the First Amendment?*, 14 N. ILL. U. L. REV. 861, 887 (1994) (concluding that hate crimes statutes impinge on the First Amendment "by punishing motive, thought and speech. Even though bigotry and racism are deplorable to most people, it is a strongly ingrained principle that the government may not regulate expression because of its message, ideas, subject matter or content").

Detective:	I think . . . he was sprayed because he was a Puerto Rican, right?
Suspect:	Because he bothered my friend.
Detective:	You don't even know for sure whether he was the one who bothered your friend. So there were two reasons, he was Puerto Rican and he bothered your friend?
Suspect:	MMM.
Detective:	Is that a yes?
Suspect:	Yes.
Detective:	And he was a Puerto Rican and he was in [names the White neighborhood in which the crime occurred], is that a yes?
Suspect:	Yes.
Detective:	And neither Puerto Ricans or Blacks should be in [the White neighborhood] at night, is that a golden rule? If he was Black and he was walking down that street and that girl yelled, "Hey nigger," he would have got the same treatment as the Puerto Rican?
Suspect:	So wouldn't have a White walking through [a Black neighborhood]?
Detective:	I'm not saying, but he would have got the same treatment, right?
Suspect:	I don't know.
Detective:	And you went over and you sprayed him like you said for two reasons. He was a Puerto Rican in [the neighborhood in which the attack occurred] and he beat up your friend?
Suspect:	He was a Puerto Rican and he beat up my friend.[171]

Before the interrogation, the detective had several reasons to believe that the crime was bias-motivated. The crime occurred in a White neighborhood in which a large percentage of the city's hate crimes had occurred. Many of the White residents in that particular neighborhood showed open dislike for minorities who were moving to the neighborhood. In other hate crime cases, White perpetrators preceded attacks with language indicating that they were attacking the victim because he or she did not belong in the neighborhood. In this case, the victim said that prior to the attack, the suspect said,

---

171. *Id.* (manuscript at 79-80).

"Hey, spic, you shouldn't be around here." The detective tried to get the suspect to admit that the defendant was attacked because of his race. Eventually, the defendants pled guilty to hate crime charges.[172]

1. *The First Amendment*

ABTF detectives were neither lawyers nor legal scholars. They received little or no training in what the First Amendment demands. Few detectives in the unit had even gone to college. What knowledge they had of the First Amendment came mainly from high school civics or popular culture. Despite a lack of formal training in jurisprudence, many of the detectives' responses to questions about the First Amendment implications of their job were rather sophisticated. Like critical race theorists who argue for protections against hate speech,[173] detectives recognized the pain of racial words to hate crime victims. At the same time, detectives seemed to clearly understand that words—taunts, threats, and epithets— were protected.[174] One detective insisted: "Racial words are very violent. Racial words may be hate incidents, but words aren't a crime. He called her a nigger? It's not a crime to say that—the First Amendment right may be violated."[175]

Even when pressured, ABTF detectives resisted seeking civil rights charges in cases that reached the outer limits of acceptability under the Supreme Court's standard in *Mitchell*— cases in which there was only speech and no other evidence that the crime was motivated by bias. In one such case, a group of heterosexual men went to a gay bar and began making anti-gay jokes and remarks. According to one witness, after the group of men was told that it had no right to be in a gay bar, the men hurled a beer at the bar, and a fight ensued. Gay and lesbian organizations were quite vocal in the case, and pressured the unit to seek civil rights charges against two of

---

172. *Id.*

173. *See* Dana Moon Dorsett, *Hate Speech Debate and Free Expression,* 5 S. CAL. INTERDIS. L.J. 259, 262-73. (1997).

174. *See* Toni M. Massaro, *Equality and Freedom of Expression: The Hate Speech Dilemma,* 32 WM. & MARY L. REV. 211, 222-30 (1991).

175. BELL, *supra* note 16 (manuscript at 151).

the straight men. The unit refused and sought criminal charges instead. As the detective on the case noted in his report, the case did not merit charges, in part for First Amendment reasons:

> [M]y evaluation of the evidence to this point reveals neither of these defendants was in violation of the civil rights statutes. While both admit that they were telling anti-gay jokes and making inflammatory comments, they state those comments and jokes were directed to each other. This behavior is verified by [two other defendants], as well as other witnesses. While this behavior may be inflammatory in nature, it is within the First Amendment right to speak in this manner.[176]

Detectives did not view their actions as depriving defendants of their rights to free speech. Consistently, the response to the question about the difference between their actions and behavior that infringed on a defendant's free speech rights was that a hate crime involved violence and action. When asked whether perpetrators were really being punished just for saying something, one detective responded: "That's not really the case. We normally had them for something else, not just for saying something. The perp said something, then beat someone up with their fists."[177]

Another detective evinced an appreciation of the difference between hate crime and hate speech. When asked about the free speech implications of hate crime enforcement, he responded, "People can call you a name, as long as there's no overt act, you're on firm constitutional ground. It's a very fine line."[178] One detective, who manifested deep dislike for hate speech was clear about the protection that the Constitution gives it:

> If you call someone a nigger . . . I don't think that language should be used. But if it's used in a context where the words aren't directed at anybody. . . . [Hesitating]. It's not OK to use it at all. You can never call anybody a nigger. You can't use it when directed at someone or in a park in a crowd. Both are a problem. You say that, you might be

---

176. *Id.*
177. *Id.*
178. *Id.* (manuscript at 151-52).

looking for trouble. You might intimidate people, a little
kid. I don't think it's OK but the Constitution allows it.[179]

Critics' fears have not been realized in Center City. Their
assumption that enforcers cannot accurately identify perpetrators' motivations, the worry that enforcers will not carefully
search for what motivated the crime, and the worry that inquiries into motivation will be too intrusive, have not come to
pass in Center City. ABTF detectives were surprisingly conservative in their use of hate crime law. In Center City, detectives adopted a complex series of routines that helped them
identify bias motivation. The process involved an initial
screening, followed by a series of filtering mechanisms that required detectives to remove whole categories of cases likely
motivated by a variety of other emotions—anger, resentment
and jealousy—before conducting a detailed examination of the
perpetrator's motivation.[180] Rather than focusing on the defendant's abstract beliefs and association, the detectives' inquiry was generally restricted to contextual clues regarding the
crimes.

Critics also worry that those with benign motives who use
slurs or epithets during some type of crime will be punished
under hate crime legislation. Both the screening processes and
the detectives' own reluctance to take cases which lacked evidence of bias motivation aside from language helped to safeguard against the punishment of those with benign motives.
Not every case in which detectives found the perpetrator to
have been motivated by bias resulted in hate crime charges.
Detectives preferred cases with injured victims and disliked
cases with very young perpetrators.[181] While detectives' decisions not to enforce the law against very young perpetrators
raises the specter of under-enforcement of hate crime law, the
failure to enforce the law in this context suggests that detectives may have eliminated cases that were problematic from a
First Amendment perspective.

---

179. *Id.* (manuscript at 152).
180. *See generally* BELL, *supra* note 16.
181. *See id.* (for more on the cases in which detectives chose not to invoke
the law).

PART IV.   CONCLUSION: THE HATE CRIME HATE SPEECH DISCONNECT

This Article maintains that critics are incorrect when they insist that enforcers are unable to separate instances of pure hate speech from hate crime and that they take language alone as evidence of motivation. In contrast to what critics of hate crime legislation assume, the detectives in Center City did not use language as the sole indication of whether perpetrators committed a hate crime. Because many cases that were clearly not hate crimes were referred to the unit in which the perpetrators used slurs or epithets, ABTF detectives developed procedures focused on the context in which language was used to discern motivation. Their use of the law was judicious and as a result, the detectives did not consider every case with bias-motivation appropriate for charges.

It is not my intention to argue that that the police officers enforcing bias crime legislation in every city behave as they do in Center City. Indeed there is evidence to the contrary.[182] However, the Article suggests that with the proper procedures, enforcers of hate crime laws can provide the protection for hate speech that the First Amendment demands. Protecting perpetrators' First Amendment rights involves a searching examination into the context of the crime, detailed investigation, and as a consequence, an extraordinary commitment of resources by the police department to the investigation of these incidents. It may be possible to explain the difference in outcomes, and as a result, First Amendment protection, by looking to the resources that a department commits to the investigation of a hate crime.[183] Whether such a commitment of resources is appropriate for what is arguably a tiny percentage of crime is a policy question that is beyond the scope of this Article. Nevertheless, the experience of Center City suggests

---

182. *See, e.g.,* Boyd, *supra* note 51.

183. For instance, the police department studied by Boyd, discussed in Part II was not a hate crime unit, but rather consisted of individual detectives placed in each police precinct around the city. This arrangement, while more economical, does not allow detectives sufficient frequency in dealing with hate crimes to develop procedures protective of First Amendment rights.

that hate crime legislation can be enforced without violating the First Amendment, and supporters' arguments regarding the value of this legislation should not be ignored on First Amendment grounds.

This research from Center City raises broader issues that may apply in other jurisdictions in which police enforce hate crime law. In preparing cases for hate crime prosecution, detectives may be given an enormous amount of discretion to decide the circumstances in which the law will be invoked. Giving detectives broad discretion to decide when to enforce hate crime law means that judges and lawyers are not the only actors in the criminal justice system with powers of definitive interpretation of the First Amendment.[184] Police officers' interpretations in this area matter, not only in the critical role they play in screening the disputes that come to court, but also in their ability to decide when hate is a crime.[185]

Detectives' conservative use of the law and the elaborate system they created for identifying bias indicates that critics' predictions that protected speech will be punished, or that people whose actual motive is not biased will face hate crime charges, have not come to fruition in Center City. Evidence from Center City and research in other jurisdictions suggests that this may be true in part because the types of cases the critics imagine—cases involving pure hate speech, conversations, remarks, racist jokes—are rarely reported to the police; and when they do get reported, are quickly discarded.[186] The actual hard cases from a First Amendment perspective are cases in which slurs or epithets are used during the commission of a crime. The rigorous system of inquiry into motivation that

---

184. *Cf.* R. Alex Morgan, *Jury Nullification Should Be Made a Routine Part of the Criminal Justice System, But It Won't Be*, 29 ARIZ. ST. L.J. 1127, 1140 (1997) (stating that "the other participants in the criminal judicial system are granted a significant amount of discretion. Police use discretion in deciding whether to make an arrest; prosecutors exercise discretion in deciding whether to charge a defendant and with what crime") (footnotes omitted)).

185. *See id.*

186. *See, e.g.*, Donald Green, et al., *Defended Neighborhoods, Integration, and Racially Motivated Crime*, 104 AM. J. OF SOC. 372, 383 (1998).

detectives practice makes it highly unlikely that cases of protected speech will survive until the charging process.

Casting hate crime as an issue connected to hate speech is a
mischaracterization that ignores the empirical basis of many of
the incidents investigated by the police. The cases that the
ABTF investigated suggest that hate crimes arise as White residents try to protect "their" neighborhoods from outsiders.[187]
This is clear from the language used in these crimes. "Go back
to where you belong," "Go back to China," "No niggers in
'Hillsdale'" are common taunts that accompany the assaults
and other harassment in many of the ABTF's cases. The vast
majority of the unit's cases did not involve mere name-calling,
or even garden-variety bigots airing their views. Hate crimes
were not ordinary muggings with slurs attached. The hundreds
of cases investigated by the ABTF were the stories of perpetrators whose intention was not to express views but, rather, to
drive people out of their neighborhood or off the streets because the perpetrator did not like their victim's race, religion,
or sexual orientation. In Center City, the detectives and defendants knew that hate crimes are not about hate speech. Enforcers of the hate crime law rarely saw their jobs as
implicating the First Amendment, and defendants almost
never asserted their First Amendment right to use slurs or epithets. Thus, enforcers and perpetrators realized that although
defendants' criminal actions were not protected, defendants
retained their right to hate.

A.   *New Justifications for Hate Crime Legislation*

At both the national level and in states without bias-motivated violence and intimidation statutes, activists recently
have demanded hate crime legislation as the appropriate response to well-publicized hate murders, such as that of James
Byrd and Matthew Shepard.[188] In calling for hate crime legislation, supporters see three primary goals served by this legis-

---

187. BELL, *supra* note 16 (manuscript at 189).

188. *See, e.g.,* Roxanne Roberts, *Voices of Reason: At the HRC Dinner,
Coming Out Against Hate*, WASH. POST, Oct. 11, 1999, at C1 (describing
activism by the parents of James Byrd and Matthew Shepard).

lation. The first is that such legislation will deter perpetrators of hate crimes.[189] They also believe that hate crime legislation will serve as a tool for law enforcement in fighting this type of violence.[190] Finally, they insist that it will provide punishment appropriate to the crime.[191]

As many critics of the legislation are quick to note, such arguments are weak, particularly when supporters hold out hate murders as evidence that hate crime legislation is needed.[192] As a class of crime, homicides are usually quite aggressively investigated by specialized detective units. Though there are no figures for how aggressively hate murders are prosecuted, *vis à vis* other murders, if the intense public scrutiny focused on the Shepard, Byrd, and Ileto killings occurs in other cases, prosecutors will be unable to push hate murders under the rug. Finally, with respect to adequately punishing hate crimes, perpetrators of graphic bias-motivated murders are likely to be eligible for the death penalty, provided this remedy is available under state law. If a hate crime is punishable by death, a more serious penalty is scarcely needed.

Though hate murders have served as a clarion call for activists, a far better justification for passing hate crime legislation is that it is needed in order to deal with the vast majority of hate crime—low-level criminal assaults, intimidation, and property damage.[193] Most hate crimes are not homicides. According to the FBI's Hate Crime Report, law enforcement agencies identified only sixteen hate murders out of 8,063 offenses in 2000.[194] Most of the crimes identified as hate crimes

---

189. Dan M. Kahan, *The Secret Ambition of Deterrence*, 113 HARV. L. REV. 413, 465 (1999).

190. *Id.*

191. *Id.* at 467-68.

192. *Id.* at 472 ("I don't think an enhancement statute provides a deterrent effect . . . [but] . . . it sends a message about how the people of the state feel.") (quoting Nevada's hate crime statute sponsor).

193. *See* FBI, U.S. DEP'T OF JUSTICE, HATE CRIME STATISTICS 2000 8 (2000), *available at* http//www.fbi.gov/ucr/cius 00/hate.pdf (discussing that in 2000, the latest year for which figures are available, the FBI Hate Crime Statistics reported 8,063 incidents nationwide, only 16 of which were murders).

194. *Id.* at 59

were low-level crimes—simple assault, harassment, threats, and vandalism—crimes normally given the lowest priority.[195] In stark contrast to hate murders, low-level hate crimes are largely invisible. Moreover, if the state makes no particular effort to designate low-level bias crimes as eligible for special treatment, the police may not take them seriously.[196] That police do not take low-level crime seriously is not new; studies of the police suggest that low-level crimes get little or no investigation.[197] The decreased priority given to low-level bias-motivated assaults might be acceptable were it not for the fact that studies suggest that victims of bias-motivated crimes suffer more severe psychological effects than victims of similar non-bias-motivated crimes.[198] In addition, unlike non-bias-motivated violence, as a general matter, bias crime tends to be repetitive, cumulative, and frequently interfere with other hate crime victims' rights, particularly their rights under Fair Housing laws to live in the neighborhood of their choice.[199] The importance of such rights and the damage caused by bias-motivated violence provides a compelling justification for hate crime legislation.

---

195. *Id.* at 60.

196. *See* Boyd, *supra* note 51, at 821

> Issues of 'linguistic ambiguity' are anything but theoretical for police personnel; on the contrary, these issues are of immediate, practical concern. Decisions, interpretations, and categorization must be—and are—made as a matter of course in the routine work of police officers. Theoretical problems aside then, the question remains: How do police personnel recognize, identify, and categorize certain crimes as hate motivated?) (footnotes omitted).

Id.

197. Nat'l Inst. of Law Enforcement and Crim. Justice Law Enforcement Assistance Admin., U. S. Dep't of Justice, part IV The Crim. Investigation Process: A Summary Report The Rand Paper Series *in* The Crim. Investigation Process: A Dialogue on Research Findings, 5-20 (1977); Richard v. Ericson, Making Crime: A Study of Detective Work 81 (1981) (reporting that detectives devote very little investigative time to cases).

198. *See* Jack McDevitt Et Al., *Consequences for Victims: A Comparison of Bias- and Non-Bias Motivated Assaults*, 45 Am. Behav. Scientist 697, 708-10 (2001).

199. *See* Green, *supra* note 186, at 397.

[17]

EXAMINING THE INFLUENCE OF DRIVERS' CHARACTERISTICS DURING TRAFFIC STOPS WITH POLICE: RESULTS FROM A NATIONAL SURVEY*

ROBIN SHEPARD ENGEL**
University of Cincinnati

JENNIFER M. CALNON***
Pennsylvania State University

The factors that influence officer decision making after a traffic stop is initiated are examined using the Police-Public Contact Survey data collected in 1999. This investigation of police behavior is framed with an understanding of the organizational roots of racial profiling tactics and policies. The findings show that young black and Hispanic males are at increased risk for citations, searches, arrests, and uses of force after other extralegal and legal characteristics are controlled. Additional analyses show that minority drivers are not, however, more likely to be carrying contraband than are white drivers. The implications for policy and future research are discussed.

The perceived phenomenon of racial profiling is well known in American society. Researchers and the media have repeatedly documented individual cases of prominent minority citizens being stopped, detained, and often harassed by police solely or partially

---

* Direct all correspondence to Robin S. Engel, Division of Criminal Justice, University of Cincinnati, P.O. Box 210389, Cincinnati, OH 45221-0389, e-mail: robin.engel@uc.edu. The authors thank Jim Lynch, Chris Dunn, Tom Zelenock, and all the participants in the BJS-sponsored 2001 summer ICPSR workshop, Quantitative Analysis of Crime and Criminal Justice, for their help and support with the quantitative analyses.

** Robin Shepard Engel, Ph.D., is an associate professor of criminal justice at the University of Cincinnati. Her current research involves theoretical and empirical explorations of police supervision, patrol officers' behavior, police response toward problem citizens, and criminal justice theory. She is currently engaged in the collection and analysis of police-citizen contact data during all traffic stops for the Pennsylvania State Police. Recent articles have appeared in *Criminology*, *Justice Quarterly*, and the *Journal of Criminal Justice*.

*** Jennifer M. Calnon, MA, is a doctoral candidate in crime, law, and justice at Pennsylvania State University. Her research interests include patrol officers' decision making, the role of race and gender in the criminal justice system, and intimate partner violence. She recently finished her tenure as the project manager for the Project on Police Citizen Contacts with the Pennsylvania State Police. She is currently working on her dissertation research, examining drivers' speeding behavior in Pennsylvania.

50   INFLUENCE OF DRIVERS' CHARACTERISTICS

on the basis, they believe, of their race and/or ethnicity (e.g., Harris, 1999b; Reilly, 2002; West, 1993). The phenomenon has been so widespread that the term "DWB" (driving while black/brown) has become part of the American lexicon (Harris, 1999a, 1999b). Likewise, a 1999 Gallup poll reported that the vast majority of Americans (77% of blacks and 56% of whites) believed that racial profiling is widespread and that 81% reported disapproval for this practice (Newport, 1999).[1]

The practice of targeting racial minorities for routine traffic and pedestrian stops can be traced back to the war on drugs, which promoted profiling as an effective policing tactic to detect drug offenders (Harris, 2002; Tonry, 1995). The legitimacy of this tactic, however, has recently come under increased scrutiny, and a debate regarding the effectiveness of profiling strategies has ensued. Some scholars and activist groups argue that targeting individuals solely on the basis of their race and/or ethnicity is an ineffective and discriminatory police practice (Harris, 2002; Kennedy, 1997), while other scholars and police officials argue that since minorities are more likely to commit crimes, profiling strategies represent a rational policing response (Herszenhorn, 2000; J. Taylor & Whitney, 1999). This debate has brought to light the realization that, until recently, most police departments did not collect information that is necessary to examine the problem (and possible effectiveness) of racial profiling strategies (Harris, 2002). Scholars have also noted the weaknesses of much of these official data, including the lack of important legal and extralegal variables and the limited statistical rigor applied in the analyses (Engel, Calnon, & Bernard, 2002).

In this article, we document the inextricable relationship between racial profiling policing strategies and the nationwide war on drugs through an understanding of profiling strategies generated from Scheingold's (1984, 1991) theory of the politics of law and order and Crank and Langworthy's (1992) institutional perspective of policing. This framework, which describes the organizational roots of racial profiling tactics and policies, serves as a guide for the empirical examination of individual police behavior. Past research on the influence of drivers' race-ethnicity on police behavior during traffic stops is reviewed, and its associated strengths and weaknesses are noted. The Police-Public Contact Survey (PPCS), a nationwide survey of citizens conducted in 1999 that explores police-citizen interactions, is examined to determine the relative influence

---

[1] *Racial profiling* was defined as the practice of "police officers stopping motorists of certain racial and ethnic groups because the officers believe that these groups are more likely than others to commit certain types of crimes" (Newport, 1999, p. 1).

of drivers' characteristics over officers' behavior during traffic stops after controlling for other extralegal and legal factors. In addition, the likelihood of discovering contraband during searches of citizens and vehicles for different racial, ethnic, and gender groups is assessed. Finally, the research and policy implications of the findings are discussed.

THE WAR ON DRUGS AND RACIAL PROFILING

The 1980s witnessed a combination of citizens' increased fear of street crime, increased violent crime, and more punitive responses from policy makers. Scheingold (1984, 1991) described the interaction effects among citizens' fear, media coverage, and the political environment as the *myth of crime and punishment*. According to Scheingold (1984, p. 60), the myth of crime and punishment is "a simple morality play that dramatizes the conflict between good and evil: because of bad people, this is a dangerous and violent world." The media and politicians exploit and perpetuate this myth as a way to simplify the dangers of street crime and, more important, the solutions to these problems. Quite simply, criminals, who are portrayed as predatory strangers, are to be controlled through punishment, which is depicted as "both morally justified and practically effective" (Scheingold, 1984, p. 60). Scheingold suggested that based on the increased rates of violent crime, greater fear of victimization, and heightened media attention to crime, these predatory strangers were represented as young minority males, particularly young black males (see also Chambliss, 1995; Cooper, 2002; Tonry, 1995). Society's response to the myth of crime and punishment was what Scheingold described as the "politicization" of crime, or the *politics of law and order*—increasingly harsher penalties and the widening of the punishment net.

The myth of crime and punishment and the resulting politics of law and order had a significant impact on policy making in the 1980s as the war on drugs was waged. As Kennedy (1997, p. 351) noted, the war on drugs sparked policies that were devised "to reduce the supply, distribution, and use of illicit narcotics," and these policies disproportionately focused on criminal justice enforcement and punishment of drug offenses. The federal government's expenditure on resources for criminal justice agencies' war on drugs increased dramatically throughout the 1980s and into the early 1990s, as the annual budget of $2.9 billion in 1976 grew to $18.8 billion in 2002 (Office of National Drug Control Policy, 2002; Walker, 2001). The federal government's expenditure on the war on drugs topped $140 billion from 1991 to 1999 alone (General Accounting Office, GAO, 1999). Financial resources for law enforcement were also shifted from the federal to the local level through the creation of joint task forces of the Drug Enforcement Administration and local police, and other cooperative policing strategies (Cooper, 2002).

The outcome of the war on drugs has been a dramatic change in policing strategies nationally, including the aggressive targeting of drug offenders at the street level, and the profiling of drug traffickers. These aggressive policing strategies were used in conjunction with increased rates of incarceration and lengths of sentences for a significant portion of the American population (Harris, 1999a; Scalia, 2001). For example, in 1980, 25% of federal prisoners were drug offenders, compared to 52% in 1990 and 57% in 1999 (Maguire & Pastore, 2000).

The burden of the war on drugs was especially heavy for young minority males, who were disproportionately subject to police surveillance and imprisonment for drug offenses (Harris, 1999a, 2002; Kennedy, 1997; Walker, 2001). At the height of the war on drugs in 1988, drug arrest rates were five times higher for blacks than for whites, despite consistent evidence from the annual National Household Survey on Drug Abuse of similar rates of drug usage by the two racial groups (Substance Abuse & Mental Health Services Administration, 2001; Tonry, 1995; but see National Institute of Justice, 2003, for evidence of higher rates of drug use by minority arrestees). Similarly, according to statistics from the Bureau of Justice Statistics (BJS), compared to whites, blacks were disproportionately represented in the percentage of drug traffickers who were convicted (57% versus 42%) and in the percentage of drug offenders who were convicted overall (53% versus 46%) (Maguire & Pastore, 2000). Finally, the increasing number of drug offenses accounted for different percentages in the growth in racial groups' state prison populations. That is, drug offenses explained 27% of the growth in the black prison population, compared to only 14% of the growth in the white prison population (Beck & Harrison, 2001). As Tonry (1995, p. 82) dramatically stated, the war on drugs "foreseeably and unnecessarily blighted the lives of hundreds of thousands of young disadvantaged black Americans and undermined decades of effort to improve the life chances of members of the urban black underclass."

The infiltration of aggressive police targeting strategies that produced these disparities in arrests and convictions can best be explained by Crank and Langworthy's (1992) institutional perspective. These authors argued that the incorporation of powerful myths into the activities and structure of police organizations provides legitimacy, stability, and protection from powers outside the institutional environment. However, legitimacy problems that result from conflicting institutional myths can lead to organizational crises that are eventually handled through "ceremonial rituals" that publicly degrade the police department and legitimate a new administration. This institutional perspective of policing has been used to explain police appearances and uniforms, specialized law enforcement units, preventive patrol and rapid response systems, and community policing (Crank, 1994; Crank & Langworthy, 1992, 1996).

Combining Crank and Langworthy's (1992) institutional perspective of conflicting myths and organizational crisis with Scheingold's (1984, 1991) propositions regarding the politics of law and order clearly indicates that the incorporation of aggressive profiling strategies into the activities and structure of police organizations (resulting from the politicization of the war on drugs) provided police departments with stability, legitimacy, and additional resources. According to Crank and Langworthy, institutional myth building occurs because leading police departments and strong individual leaders actively engage in the construction and shaping of myths within their institutional environment. This seems to be especially true with profiling policies because as departments and officers were initially rewarded for being "tough on crime," or waging "the war on drugs," the activities associated with tactics of targeting minorities became institutionalized in many police departments across the country (Cole, 1999; Harris, 1999a; Skolnick & Caplovitz, 2001). The outcome of these aggressive policing strategies was initially celebrated in the media through the frequent and positive reporting of major drug arrests and the seizure of millions of dollars in drugs, property, and cash. Russell (1999) suggested that profiling had become so entrenched in U.S. society that its legitimacy extended beyond police agencies to the general public.

DISCRIMINATION OR GOOD POLICING?

Crank and Langworthy (1992) suggested that a "legitimation conflict" occurs when entities outside the police organization begin to question the legitimacy of existing police tactics and policies. In the past few years, police agencies have witnessed such a conflict with respect to profiling activities. Specifically, the myth that police are equally enforcing the laws has come into direct conflict with profiling activities. The current pressure from powerful outside groups who have questioned the legitimacy of profiling strategies

54   INFLUENCE OF DRIVERS' CHARACTERISTICS

has led to the conflicting institutional myths regarding the effectiveness of these strategies. That is, the effectiveness of racial profiles in controlling serious crime and drug trafficking that were incorporated into the structures and activities of police departments is now being questioned.

Legislators at the state and national levels have proposed, and in some cases passed, formal prohibitions of racial profiling and departmental data collection initiatives on drivers' race and ethnicity for traffic stops (National Conference of State Legislatures, 2001; Police Foundation, 2001; Strom, Brien, & Smith, 2001). In addition, civil rights groups, such as the American Civil Liberties Union (ACLU) and the National Association for the Advancement of Colored People, are actively engaged in informing citizens of their rights during traffic stops and battling the abuses that have resulted from aggressive police stops (Beck & Daly, 1999; Russell, 1999). Some academic scholars have also expressed opinions against profiling (Cole, 1999; Harris, 2002; Kennedy, 1997; Lamberth, 1996), and many others have conducted studies in police departments across the nation, trying to improve the quality of the data that speak to the questions of racially disparate policing. Likewise, many police administrators and minority officer groups themselves have criticized profiling as a valid police tactic (Beck & Daly, 1999; Fridell, Lunney, Diamond, & Kubu, 2001). The mass media have also played an important role in bringing racial profiling to the public's attention by reporting police stops of well-known minority celebrities (Russell, 1999; Trende, 2000). As a result, the public has grown somewhat dissatisfied with the criminal justice focus of the war on drugs generally and racial profiling as one of its tactics more specifically, calling into question the legitimacy and effectiveness of these practices (Lock, Timberlake, & Rasinski, 2002; Newport, 1999).

Despite this growing crisis of legitimacy, some scholars and police officials still embrace the informal use of profiles as an effective and efficient policing strategy. Advocates of profiling practices argue that given the distribution of criminal behavior in this country, it is reasonable and efficient for police to consider race in their decision making (Herszenhorn, 2000; MacDonald, 2001, 2002; J. Taylor, 2002; J. Taylor & Whitney, 1999). For example, MacDonald (2001, p. 18) argued that "if the police are now to be accused of racism every time that they go where the crime is, that's the end of public safety." Others, however, have challenged this argument by citing self-report statistics that suggest similar levels of drug usage across racial groups and by further contending that official statistics that show disproportionately high black arrests, convictions, and imprisonments do not represent the actual criminal behavior of individuals of different racial groups but, rather, reflect the activities of criminal justice agents like police officers, judges, and prosecutors (Harris, 1997, 1999a; Kennedy, 1997).

Most research on police profiling, however, has generally failed to adequately address the "profiling as good policing" controversy. These studies have strictly examined whether or not the rates of minority stops, citations, searches, and arrests differ for minority compared to white drivers and pedestrians. Much of this research has concluded that disparities in these rates are due to the racism and discrimination of individual police officers (for a review, see Engel et al., 2002). As we discuss in the next section, few of these studies have theoretically and empirically explored why differences in these rates exist and whether or not profiling policies are "effective" policing strategies.

PRIOR RESEARCH

Research on Police Behavior

The crisis of legitimacy associated with racial profiling strategies has prompted an overwhelming move toward the collection of official data on traffic and pedestrian stops in state and local police departments across the country (Fridell et al., 2001; Police Foundation, 2001; Strom et al., 2001). Nearly all of the publicly available reports and studies that we are aware of reveal disparities in the percentages of minority citizens who are stopped, cited, searched, or arrested as compared to selected benchmarks.[2]

Although the amount of data on police-citizen encounters has grown significantly, understanding of the factors that influence police behavior in these encounters is still limited partly because of two contributing factors. First, researchers have been relatively unsuccessful in determining the characteristics of drivers who are not stopped by police. While this is an important research question, it is not directly addressed in this article, since the empirical analyses to follow are based on officer decision making that occurs *after* a stop

---

[2] See, for example, ACLU (2000); Carter, Katz-Bannister, & Schafer (2001); Cordner, Williams, & Zuniga (2001); Cox, Pease, Miller, & Tyson (2001); Criminal Justice Training Commission (2001); Decker, Rosenfeld, & Rojek (2002); Fagan & Davies (2000); Farrell, McDevitt, & Ramirez (2002); Greenwald (2001); Harris (1999b); Institute on Race & Poverty (2001); Lamberth (1996); Lansdowne (2000); Michigan State Police (2001); Moose (2002); Morgan (2002); Novak (in press); M. R. Smith & Petrocelli (2001); Spitzer (1999); Texas Department of Public Safety, TDPS (2001); Thomas & Carlson (2001); Verniero & Zoubek (1999); Zingraff et al. (2000); cf. Helmick (2000). Benchmark comparisons for these studies include the percentage of the population, the percentage of the driving-age population, and the percentage of the law-violating driving population (see Engel & Calnon, in press).

has been made. Second, statistical analyses of poststop outcomes often do not control for relevant legal and extra legal factors that may explain racial differences. The lack of multivariate statistical models is particularly problematic, given that much of the recent empirical research that has been based on systematic observational data has concluded that citizens' race has substantively small or no statistically significant influences on police behaviors, such as arrest and use of force (see, e.g., Engel & Silver, 2001; Mastrofski, Worden, & Snipes, 1995; Novak, Frank, Smith, & Engel, 2002; Riksheim & Chermak, 1993; Terrill & Mastrofski, 2002). It is on this second question that our empirical analyses are based.

Some recent racial profiling studies that have used official data have gone beyond basic comparisons and cross tabulations by applying multivariate statistical techniques to explain officer behavior toward motorists and pedestrians (e.g., Cox et al., 2001; Fagan & Davies, 2000; Novak, in press; Smith & Petrocelli, 2001; Spitzer, 1999). These studies have examined a number of legal and extralegal variables that previous research has shown can influence officer behavior, including individual officer variables (e.g., age, gender, race, and experience), legal variables (e.g., reason for the stop), situational variables (e.g., drivers' race, gender, age, and residence and time of day), and community variables (e.g., percent minority population, crime rate, poverty rate, and social and physical signs of disorder). Collectively, the findings from these studies suggest that at least some of the racial disparity detected at the bivariate level can be explained by other factors.

Research on the "Effectiveness" of Profiling Strategies

Several of the reports on police encounters with motorists and pedestrians also have included official data relevant to the question of whether racial profiling is simply "nothing more than rational law enforcement" (Harris, 2002, p. 11). One of the most direct ways to address the debate of whether racial profiling is ineffective and discriminatory or good policing is to examine differences in law-violating behavior by racial and ethnic groups. For example, racial differences in the severity of speeding behavior have been examined on the New Jersey Turnpike (Lange, Blackman, & Johnson, 2001), roadways in North Carolina (Smith et al., 2000), and interstate and state highways in Pennsylvania (Engel & Calnon, in press; Engel, Calnon, Liu, & Johnson, 2004). Each of these studies has reported racial differences in speeding behaviors that may at least partially explain racial disparities in traffic stops for speeding.

Studies that explore differences in driving behavior, however, do not get at the heart of the profiling controversy, which is justified by police officials on the basis that minorities are more likely to be carrying and/or transporting contraband (e.g., illicit drugs and weapons). To examine this issue, one must consider the discovery of evidence during searches of citizens, often referred to as search success rates, or "hit rates" (i.e., the percentage of searches conducted that produced contraband and/or resulted in arrest). Some scholars and police officials have argued that searches of minorities are likely to produce more contraband than are searches of whites (Herszenhorn, 2000; Knowles, Persico, & Todd, 2001). Others have argued that minority citizens are not more likely to being carrying illegal substances and that a comparison of hit rates will show that racial profiling policies are ineffective (Cole, 1999; Harris, 2002). As Ayres (2001, p. 134) summarized:

> A finding that the search success rate (i.e., the probability of finding evidence of illegality) is systematically lower for searched minorities than for searched whites suggests that minorities less deserved (that is, were less qualified) to be searched. A defense that police searching decisions were driven by the underlying criminality of those searched—and that minorities make up a larger proportion of those deserving to be searched—would be contradicted by systematically lower success rates when such searches were in fact completed.

Several studies have examined differences in the percentage of searches that produce contraband for minority and white citizens. Table 1 presents a review of 16 studies that examined search success rates in traffic, pedestrian, and airport stops. These studies, all conducted and published in the past decade, have reported findings based on data collected from local police departments, state agencies, and the U.S. Customs Service. Table 1 summarizes the overall success rate for searches, as well as comparisons of success rates for racial and ethnic groups. Although Harris (2002) noted in his review of the research that there was no evidence of higher hit rates for minorities, the most recent evidence is not supportive of this claim. Several studies did find that searches of white citizens produced similar and often higher search success rates than did searches of minorities (e.g., Criminal Justice Training Commission, 2001; Decker et al., 2002; Lamberth, 1996; Moose, 2002; Spitzer, 1999; TDPS, 2001; Zingraff et al., 2000). Eight other studies, however, reported that black and/or Hispanic citizens had higher success rates than did whites (Carter et al., 2001; Cordner et al., 2001; Farrell et al., 2002; Greenwald, 2001; Knowles et al., 2001; Morgan, 2002; Thomas & Carlson, 2001; Verniero & Zoubek, 1999). In addition, the findings from the U.S. Customs study offer mixed evidence

Table 1. Studies of Search Hit Rates in Traffic and Pedestrian Stops

Author and Year Published	Data Collection Site	Data Collection Period	Number of Stops	Number of Searches	Dependent Variable	Overall Hit Rates[a]	White Hit Rates	Black Hit Rates	Hispanic Hit Rates
Lamberth (1996)	Maryland	Jan. 1995–Sept. 1996	2,372[b]	2,372	Contraband	28.1%	28.8%	28.4%	NA
Spitzer (1999)	New York City	Jan. 1998–Mar 1999	174,919	69.1% frisk	Arrest	9.0:1[c]	7.9:1	9.5:1	8.8:1
Verniero & Zoubek (1999)	New Jersey	1994–99	87,489[d]	1,193	Arrest and/or contraband	19.2%	10.5%	13.5%	38.1%
General Accounting Office (2000)	Nationwide airports U.S. Customs	1997–98	140,000,000	3,872 strip[e]	Contraband	23% strip	25.1% (WM) 19.5% (WF)	61.6% (BM) 27.6% (BF)	58.8% (HM) 45.7% (HF)
				1,419 x-ray		31% x-ray	58.7% (WM) 58.7% (WF)	58.7% (BM) 28.2% (BF)	34.1% (HM) 34.1% (HF)
				96,769 frisk		3% frisk	NA	NA	NA
Zingraff et al. (2000)	North Carolina	Jan.–Dec. 1998	906,758	826	Contraband	30.8%	33.0%	26.3%	NA
Carter et al. (2001)	Lansing, MI	Feb.–Aug. 2001	15,509	1,418	Contraband	17.3%	17.2%	16.7%	19.2%
Cordner et al. (2001)	San Diego, CA	Jan.–Dec. 2000	168,901	10,754	Contraband (C) and/or property (P)	12.5%	13.1% (C) 12.7% (P)	13.9% (C) 13.0% (P)	5.1% (C) 7.0% (P)
Criminal Justice Training Commission (2001)	Washington	May–Oct. 2000	338,885	7,727	Contraband	30.0%	32.6%	25.0%	19.0%
Greenwald (2001)	Sacramento, CA	July 2000–June 2001	36,854	5,832	Contraband	22.0%	22.2%	23.3%	20.5%
Knowles, Persico, & Todd (2001)	Maryland	Jan. 1995–Jan.1999	NA	1,590	Drugs	NA	32.0%	34.0%	11.0%

Author and Year Published	Data Collection Site	Data Collection Period	Number of Stops	Number of Searches	Dependent Variable	Overall Hit Rates[a]	White Hit Rates	Black Hit Rates	Hispanic Hit Rates[a]
Texas Department of Public Safety (2001)	Texas	Jan.–Dec. 2001	1,873,960	65,916	Drug charge	22.0%	14.6%	3.6%	3.9%
Thomas & Carlson (2001)	Denver	June–Aug 2001	55,524 Traf (T) & Ped (P)	12,945	Contraband	14.6% (T) 28.4% (P)	17.6% (T) 26.9% (P)	19.6% (T) 30.1% (P)	10.4% (T) 28.9% (P)
Decker et al. (2002)	Missouri	Jan.–Dec. 2001	1,389,947	99,860	Contraband	20.0%	22.0%	15.0%	11.0%
Moose (2002)	Montgomery Co., MD	Oct. 2001–Mar. 2002	31,752	383 (consent only)	Contraband	27.7%	40.6%	39.6%	11.3%
Morgan (2002)	Tennessee	Jan.–Dec. 2001	450,366	Approximately 7% of stops	Contraband	1.4%	1.2%	1.6%	1.8%
Farrell et al. (2003)	Rhode Island	Jan. 2001–Dec. 2002	445,593	14,660	Contraband	NA	23.5% (White)	17.8% (Nonwhites)[f]	

[a] Unless otherwise noted, the hit rate measures the percentage of searches conducted during traffic stops that produced contraband or resulted in arrest.
[b] The Maryland study did not analyze traffic stops without searches.
[c] The New York City study reported hit rates as a ratio of the number of stops per arrest.
[d] The New Jersey study examined searches over a longer period (1994–99) than traffic stops (1997–98).
[e] The Tennessee study measured hit rates as the percentage of all stops (rather than searches) that produced contraband
[f] Note, however, that these percentages are based on statewide statistics. Looking at individual police agencies, the authors found variation in the hit-rate patterns. Of the 45 agencies, two thirds had higher hit rates for whites, and the other third had higher hit rates for nonwhites.

60   INFLUENCE OF DRIVERS' CHARACTERISTICS

regarding the search success rates of different racial groups. Combined, the research findings on the success of searches conducted during traffic and pedestrian stops for different racial groups have been mixed.

Some researchers have used the "outcome test" to identify racial and ethnic discrimination by examining differential outcomes in search success rates. Originally applied by Becker (1957) to examine the economically disparate treatment of minorities, the basic notion of the outcome test is to analyze whether outcomes are systematically different across groups. Ayres (2001, 2002) has argued that the "outcome test" can be used to examine racial disparities in police practices, including searches. According to Ayres, one of the advantages of the outcome test is that unlike multivariate regression models, it does not suffer from specification errors that are due to bias from omitted variables. Furthermore, the "qualified pool" problem is not an issue for the outcome test because "the decision maker in the outcome test defines by her own decisions what she thinks the qualified pool to be, and the outcome test then directly assesses whether the minorities and non-minorities so chosen are in fact equally qualified" (Ayres, 2001, p. 407; for more information on the underlying assumptions and limitations of the outcome test, see Ayres, 2001, 2002; Knowles et al. 2001). The outcome test has been used in a wide array of inquiries to examine racially disparate impacts—for example, in bail decisions (Ayres, 2001), mortgage lending (Becker, 1993), and the publication of academic articles (Ayres & Vars, 2000).

When applied to police searches, the outcome test is essentially a comparison of the success of these searches—or a statistical comparison of hit rates. For example, using the outcome test, Knowles et al. (2001) reported that although 63% of the searches conducted by the Maryland State Police from 1995 to 1999 were of black drivers, there were no statistically significant differences in the success rates of these searches across racial groups. These authors concluded that the racial groups' similar search success rates were "consistent with the hypothesis of no racial prejudice against African-American motorists" (2001, p. 203). Note, however, that this interpretation was criticized by Fagan (2002, p. 121), who suggested that despite the assumptions of the outcome test, Knowles et al.'s failure to take into account officers' decisions of who to stop initially renders their "race-neutral assumption inherently implausible."

RESEARCH ISSUES

If the propositions regarding the influence of policing strategies resulting from the war on drugs are accurate, one would expect that police officers disproportionately target young minority males, in part because of formal and informal organizational policies. Therefore, one would also expect to find racial, ethnic, age, and gender disparities in the rates of police behavior after stops are made (e.g., citations, searches, arrests, and use of force). Prior research on these propositions has been based nearly exclusively on official police data collected at the local and state levels (cf. GAO, 2000; Langan, Greenfeld, Smith, Durose, & Levin, 2001; Schmitt, Langan, & Durose, 2002). The robustness of previous research findings that police inappropriately cite, search, and arrest minority motorists remains an open question because of the lack of statistical controls for other relevant factors. Furthermore, the evidence is mixed on the effectiveness of targeting particular types of citizens for further police scrutiny (e.g., through searches for contraband).

The purpose of the current study is to examine these questions using data from a national survey of citizens in 1999—the PPCS— that captured police behavior during police-citizen interactions, including traffic stops, as self-reported by citizens. The national scope and citizen reporting of police behavior in the PPCS offers a unique opportunity to examine police behavior during traffic stops with appropriate statistical controls. Following previous research on racial profiling during traffic stops, we focus on police decisions to cite, search, and arrest drivers. In addition, we examine police use of force during these encounters. We also explore racial, ethnic, and gender differences in the likelihood of discovering contraband during searches of vehicles and persons using multivariate statistical models.

METHOD

Data

The PPCS was a BJS-sponsored national survey of citizens that was designed to examine citizens' interactions with police. After a pilot test was fielded in 1996, a revised version of the survey was administered to citizens as a supplemental questionnaire to the National Crime Victimization Survey (NCVS) during the last six months of 1999 (Langan et al., 2001). As a supplement to the NCVS, the PPCS was a complex survey design that used a cluster sampling method. The sampling frame consisted of "approximately 50,000 sample housing units selected with a stratified multi-stage cluster design" (U.S. Department of Justice, 2001, p. 3). Specifically, the NCVS sample included 94,717 respondents aged 16 or older. Of these respondents, 85.0% (80,543) completed questions that were included in the PPCS.[3] After adjustments for nonresponse, this sample weights to a national estimate of 209,350,600 persons aged 16 or older (U.S. Department of Justice, 2001).

The analyses reported here are based on respondents who indicated that they were the drivers during traffic stops with police in the past year. Of the 80,543 respondents, 17,720 (22.0%) reported that they had some type of contact with police during the past year, and of those who had contact with police, 7,054 (39.8%) reported they were the drivers during traffic stops.[4] The descriptive statistics reported below are based on weighted data; this sample of 7,054 drivers who were stopped by police (8.7% of all valid interviews) weights to a national estimate of 19,277,001.[5]

Analyses reported by the BJS used the percentage of the driving population by race, as measured by the 1995 National Personal Transportation Survey, to construct baseline comparisons. Langan et al. (2001, p. 13) reported significant differences in the rates of traffic stops for black compared to white citizens:

> There was some indication that black drivers were more likely than white drivers to be stopped at least once in 1999: 12.3% of blacks versus 10.4% of whites. There was also some indication that black drivers were more likely than whites to be stopped more than once that year: 3.0% of blacks versus 2.1% of whites. Put another way, blacks were 9.8% of licensed drivers but 11.6% of drivers stopped at least once and 13.7% of drivers stopped more than once. . . . In short, the survey results indicate that in 1999 blacks had higher chances than whites of being stopped at

---

[3] Of the 15% of respondents who were not interviewed, 73% were NCVS noninterviews (someone else in the household was interviewed), 4.5% refused to answer questions for the PPCS, 0.9% were not available for the PPCS portion of the interview, 19.5% were ineligible because the respondent was giving a proxy interview for the NCVS, and for 1.6% the reason is unknown. The overall response rate for the PPCS was 85%, compared to an overall response rate of 89% for the NCVS. For more information, see U.S. Department of Justice (2001).

[4] Approximately 15% ($n = 1,232$) of the respondents who reported contact with police indicated that they were passengers in vehicles during traffic stops. These respondents were eliminated from the analyses because only drivers were asked specific questions regarding the stops and police behavior.

[5] Academics have debated the use of weighted data in regression analyses. As described by Lohr (1999), two approaches have been adopted: design based and model based (see also Brewer & Mellor, 1973; DuMouchel & Duncan, 1983). In the design-based approach, "inferences are based on repeated sampling from the finite population, and the probability structure used for inference is that defined by the random variables indicating inclusion in the sample" (Lohr, 1999, p. 363). This approach does not rely on a theoretical model and uses weighted data. In contrast, the model-based approach describes the relation between the variables that holds for every observation in the population. This approach does rely on a theoretical model and assumes that the observations in the population follow that model (Lohr, 1999, p. 363). For our purposes, the design-based approach is more appropriate; therefore, the analyses reported in the text are based on the weighted data. However, as noted in the Analysis and Findings section, the differences between weighted and unweighted analyses are minimal for logistic regression models.

least once and higher chances than whites of being stopped more than once.

While the official report produced by the BJS also documented differences in the rates for other police behaviors (e.g., arrest and use of force), it did not examine any explanatory factors for police officers' decision making.

The current study furthers previous research that has used the PPCS by examining explanatory factors for police officers' dispositions of traffic stops. While the BJS-sponsored reports clearly show bivariate differences in officers' behavior on the basis of drivers' race (see also Schmitt et al., 2002), it is unknown if these findings hold in the face of controls for other legal and extralegal factors that have been shown in prior research to have a significant influence over officers' behavior. Of particular importance is the influence of legal variables (e.g., the initial or primary reason for the traffic stop, any evidence of wrongdoing) that could reasonably be expected to influence officers' decision making. In addition, we explore the hit rate debate by estimating multivariate models predicting the discovery of evidence.

Measures

Officers' Actions. As is shown in Table 2, we examined four coercive police behaviors for all traffic stops: issuing citations, searching individuals and/or their property, making arrests, and using threatened or actual physical force. Each of these police actions is captured as a dichotomous variable. Of the respondents who were stopped by police, 52.1% indicated they had received a citation. Vehicle and citizen searches were combined into an "any search" dichotomous variable, with 6.6% of respondents indicating that officers searched their vehicles, their person, or both.[6] In addition, 3.0% of the drivers who were stopped by police reported being arrested, and 3.4% indicated that they had force threatened or used against them by police.[7]

---

6 Of the respondents who were stopped by police for traffic offenses, 4.3% reported that police officers searched, frisked, or patted them down and 5.3% indicated that police officers searched their vehicles. Given the similar invasive nature of these police actions, personal and vehicle searches were combined into one dichotomous measure.

7 Police use of force was also measured on a 5-point coercion scale, similar to that used by Terrill and Mastrofski (2002). However, given the infrequency of the use of force by officers during traffic stops, there were too few cases to examine on a 5-point scale. Therefore, the information was collapsed into a dichotomous (no force–force) variable. The use of force includes officers' threats or actual use of the following tactics: (1) push or grab that did not cause pain, (2) handcuffing (3) push or grab that did cause pain, (4) kick or hit with officer's hand or something held in officer's hand, (5) bite from an unleashed police dog, (6) spray with chemical or pepper spray, (7) pointed a gun but did not shoot, (8) fired a gun at the citizen, or (9) any other form of physical force.

Table 2. Police-Public Contact Survey, 1999: Drivers stopped by police ($N = 19,277,002$ weighted cases).

Variables	Minimum	Maximum	Mean	SD
Officers' Behavior				
Citation	0	1	.52	.50
Any search (vehicle or citizen)	0	1	.07	.25
Arrest	0	1	.03	.17
Any use of force (including handcuffed)	0	1	.03	.18
Drivers' Characteristics				
Male	0	1	.61	.49
Age	16	88	35.96	14.20
White	0	1	.77	.42
Black	0	1	.12	.32
Hispanic	0	1	.08	.28
Other race	0	1	.03	.17
Employed	0	1	.80	.40
Income less than $20,000	0	1	.28	.45
Income $20,000–$49,999	0	1	.35	.48
Income greater than $50,000	0	1	.37	.48
Characteristics of the Traffic Stop				
White officer	0	1	.82	.39
Number of traffic stops (past year)	1	10	1.36	.99
Number of people in the vehicle	1	8	1.38	.77
Any evidence (in vehicle or on citizen)	0	1	.01	.09
Reason for the Stop				
Speeding	0	1	.49	.50
DUI roadside check	0	1	.02	.14
Other traffic offense	0	1	.22	.42
Vehicle defect	0	1	.11	.31
License/registration check	0	1	.09	.28
Driver suspected of something	0	1	.02	.15
Other reason /unknown	0	1	.05	.22
Community/Control Characteristics				
MSA central city	0	1	.26	.44
MSA non-central city	0	1	.53	.50
Non-MSA	0	1	.21	.41
CATI survey	0	1	.24	.43

Predictor variables are also reported in Table 2 and described in detail below. These variables are grouped as citizens' characteristics, characteristics of the traffic stop, the primary reason for the stop, and community/control variables.

Citizens' Characteristics. As we previously described, prior research has shown a mixed effect regarding the influence of citizens' characteristics (e.g., sex, race, age, and social class) on officers' behavior. To test the proposition that officers' actions are based, at least partially, on citizens' characteristics, we created several dichotomous variables. Specifically, citizens' sex is captured as male or female, while citizens' race is captured through four dichotomous variables: non-Hispanic white, non-Hispanic black, Hispanic, and other (including American Indian, Eskimo, Asian, Pacific Islander, and other nonspecified). For the multivariate models that follow,

non-Hispanic white is the excluded comparison category. A dichotomous variable also measures respondents' employment status, and
three separate dichotomous variables capture respondents' annual
income levels: less than $20,000, $20,000–$49,999, and greater
than $50,000.[8] In the multivariate analyses that follow, income
greater than $50,000 is the excluded comparison category. Finally,
citizens' age is measured as a continuous variable, ranging from 16
to 88 years. As Table 2 indicates, the majority of citizens who were
stopped by police were male (60.8%), white (77.0%), and employed
(79.5%). Furthermore, about 37% of the citizens who were stopped
reported annual incomes of more than $50,000, and the average age
of the drivers who were stopped was 36.

Characteristics of the Traffic Stop. We created additional measures
to examine the influence of specific situational extralegal and legal
factors. For example, it is plausible that officers of different races
may behave differently. The underlying assumption of many discussions of racial profiling is that white officers act in a discriminatory and racist manner when interacting with drivers. Therefore, to
examine the relationship between officers' race and behavior during
traffic encounters further, we capture officers' race as a dichotomous (nonwhite-white) variable.[9] Other characteristics of the situation may also be expected to have an influence on officers' behavior
during traffic stops with police. For example, the number of passengers in the vehicle may influence an officer's decision to issue a citation, search the vehicle or driver, arrest the driver, and/or use force
against the driver. To examine this proposition, we measured the
number of people in the vehicle as a continuous variable (range =
1–8). The number of prior stops, also included in the analyses, is
likely to be correlated with other unmeasured legal and extralegal
factors. For example, it is possible that drivers are stopped more
frequently for reasons related to the quality of their driving (e.g.,
the general condition of the vehicle, drivers' skill and/or aggressiveness) that we were unable to measure and that may have an impact
on officers' decision making once the stop is made. Alternatively,
the frequency of the prior number of stops can also reflect the use of
"profiles" by law enforcement. Therefore, it is expected that drivers
who report more prior stops are more likely to receive some type of
coercive action by police than are drivers who report having been

---

8 Income is measured as three dichotomous variables because a continuous
measure was not included in the publicly available data set.

9 An interaction term examining officers' race and suspects' race was initially
created and included in the multivariate analyses that follow. This interaction term
was not statistically significant, and its inclusion in the models with the main effects
of officers' and drivers' race added collinearity to the models. Therefore, the interaction term is not included in the results reported here.

66   INFLUENCE OF DRIVERS' CHARACTERISTICS

stopped less frequently. The number of prior stops in the past year is measured as a continuous variable, ranging from 1 to 10. Finally, a dichotomous variable captures whether or not any evidence of criminal wrongdoing was found during searches of a vehicle or person. It is expected that the presence of contraband will be one of the strongest predictors of police actions (citation, arrest, and use of force).[10]

Reason for the Stop. The primary reason for a traffic stop is an important variable to consider for several reasons. First, the "severity" of different types of offenses that are associated with types of traffic stops is likely to vary. For example, the likelihood of arrest during a stop for driving under the influence (DUI) is probably higher than the likelihood of arrest for a vehicle defect. Therefore, the reason for the stop represents an important legal variable that should be examined. In addition, one of the most common complaints among minority citizens is that police officers stop them for minor or invalid reasons (Browning, Cullen, Cao, Kopache, & Stevenson, 1994). To examine this concern, we used a series of dichotomous variables to capture the primary reason why citizens were stopped. Respondents were initially asked if the police indicated to them the reason why they were stopped—97.6% reported that the police had informed them why they were stopped. The percentages reported in Table 2 indicate the primary reason for the stop: 2.1% of the respondents were stopped for a DUI check, 49.2% for speeding, 22.2% for a traffic offense other than speeding, 10.7% for a problem or defect with the vehicle, 8.7% for a license or registration check, 2.2% for a suspicious driver, and 5.0% for some other or unknown offense.[11] In

---

[10] It is likely that at least some discovery of contraband occurs *after* an arrest is made because all drivers who are arrested may be legally subjected to search (see *Chimel v. California,* 1969). Unfortunately, temporal ordering cannot be established with the PPCS data. Therefore, the predictive power of the discovery of evidence on the decision to arrest must be interpreted with caution.

[11] If the respondent indicated that the officer had notified him or her about the reason for the stop, the respondent was asked a series of questions to indicate the specific reason for the stop. As initially captured in the survey, these categories were not mutually exclusive (e.g., 10.7% of the respondents indicated they were stopped for multiple reasons). For the multivariate models that follow, a series of dichotomous variables were created to measure the categories as mutually exclusive. These variables were created by initially ranking the reasons for the stop: from those that involved the *least* discretion by an individual officer to those that involved the *most* discretion. On the basis of this criterion, the following ranking structure was used: (1) DUI checkpoint, (2) speeding, (3) traffic offense other than speeding, (4) problem or defect with the vehicle, (5) license or registration check, (6) suspicious driver, and (7) other. The dichotomous variables measuring the primary reason for the stop were created using the *least* discretionary reason. For example, if a respondent indicated that he or she was stopped for speeding and for a license and registration check, we assumed that speeding was the primary reason for the stop. Thus, the speeding variable would be coded 1, and the license-and-registration check variable would be coded 0.

the multivariate models that follow, the speeding offense category is the excluded comparison category.

Community and Control Characteristics. Prior research has suggested that community context plays an important role in explaining police behavior (see, e.g., Klinger, 1997). Unfortunately, only crude community-level measures can be created with the PPCS data. Specifically, community context is measured with three dichotomous variables: central city metropolitan statistical area (MSA), non-central city MSA, and non-MSA.[12] The majority of respondents (53.4%) resided in a non-central city MSA location. In the multivariate analyses that follow, central city is the excluded comparison category. Finally, a dichotomous variable was created that measures whether or not the citizen was responding to a computer- assisted telephone interview (CATI). This variable was included in the analyses to control for the possibility that the manner in which the survey was administered might have influenced the citizens' responses (Lohr, 1999).

Data Limitations

As with all quantitative analyses, the analyses that follow are limited because of the structure and measures included in the data. First, some theoretically relevant variables simply were not measured in the PPCS data. The use of skip patterns in the survey design produced unacceptable levels of missing data on some variables of interest (e.g., citizens' actions toward officers, citizens' use of drugs or alcohol), that are not included in the analyses.[13] Second, the community measures are only crude indicators of the type of areas in which the respondents resided. Therefore, a comprehensive test of the proposition that neighborhood characteristics supercede the influences of drivers' race and ethnicity cannot be adequately examined with these data.

Third, because the PPCS data were collected as a supplement to the NCVS, they have many of the same potentially problematic

---

[12] An MSA is defined by the U.S. Census Bureau as either an area that includes a city with a population of at least 50,000 people or an urbanized area that has a population of at least 50,000 people with a total metropolitan-area population of at least 100,000 people.

[13] The respondents were asked the following questions *only* if they indicated that police had used force against them: At any time during this incident did you (1) argue with or disobey the police officer(s); 2) curse at, insult, or call the police officer(s) a name; (3) say something threatening to the police officer(s); (4) resist being handcuffed or arrested; (5) resist being searched or having the vehicle searched; or 6) try to escape by hiding, running away, or being in a high-speed chase? Likewise, only respondents who had force used against them were asked if they thought any of their actions might have provoked the officers, if they were using drugs at the time of the incident, or if they were using alcohol.

methodological issues as the NCVS (for reviews, see Biderman, Lynch, & Petersen, 1991; Lynch, 2002). Fourth, and most important, the reliability and validity of self-report data are not well understood. This becomes a major limitation if there are systematic biases in responses—that is, if particular types of citizens have differential reporting patterns on some variables. For example, Smith et al. (2000) reported that in follow-up surveys with citizens who had received traffic citations, black respondents were significantly less likely to self-report that they had received tickets than were white respondents (see also Hindelang, Hirschi, & Weis, 1979). It is unknown if this trend of systematic underreporting by citizens' race that was found in the North Carolina data is also a problem with the PPCS. If black citizens systematically underreport being stopped by police or receiving traffic citations, then our analyses of citations and arrests may represent more conservative tests of hypotheses of the influence of drivers' race on police coercive behavior. If however, black citizens also underreport criminal wrongdoing, then the analyses on hit rates may be of questionable validity. Nevertheless, as other scholars have argued, the use of self-report data is still an important addition to research on racial profiling (Lundman & Kaufman, 2003; Weitzer & Tuch, 2002).

ANALYSES AND FINDINGS

In complex survey designs, such as that used for the PPCS, the observations have different probabilities of selection. That is, because of nonresponse and undercoverage in the population, certain groups (e.g., young black males in urban areas) may be underrepresented in the sample. Therefore, analyses based on these data must account for these potential differences. The failure to do so could lead to biased regression parameters and inflated standard errors (Lohr, 1999). With logistic regression, if the model estimated is a good fit to the data, "the only difference between weighted and unweighted analyses would appear in the intercept terms" (Lohr, 1999, p. 372). Nevertheless, the PPCS has a cluster sample design that must be accounted for in the logistic regression models. That is, "the dependence of the data induced by clustering will need to be considered in the logistic regression model for variance estimation" (Lohr, 1999, p. 372). Therefore, we generated the analyses using the WesVar statistical software package, with the jackknife replication method used to generate estimate variances. After weighting the sample, the jackknife procedure produces degrees of freedom that are equal to the number of sampled primary sampling units minus the number of strata. The WesVar software takes into account the inflation factor and clustering when computing standard errors.

Therefore, the jackknife replication estimator produces standard errors that are less likely to be inflated (for a full description of the jackknife procedure, see Lohr, 1999). Thus, the use of weighted data in the analyses that follow is more appropriate than is the use of nonweighted data because of the need for poststratification adjustments. The standard errors that are generated through these procedures are not inflated, and therefore the tests of significance are reliable.

Bivariate Results

To examine differences in drivers' race and ethnicity, we initially explore bivariate relationships using chi-square tests for dichotomous independent variables and f-tests (one-way analyses of variance, ANOVAs) for continuous-level independent variables. As is shown in Table 3, for the bivariate comparisons, driver's race was measured as a four-category nominal variable. The results indicate significant differences across driver's race and ethnicity for all types of officer behavior (citation, arrest, use of force, and searches). Specifically, 49.9% of white drivers reported receiving traffic citations, compared to 57.3% of black drivers, 62.6% of Hispanic drivers, and 61.4% of drivers of other races and ethnicities ($\chi^2 = 53.30$, $p = .000$). The percentage of minority drivers who reported having their person or vehicle searched was double that of white drivers: 5.4% of white drivers were searched, compared to 10.9% of blacks, 11.2% of Hispanics, and 6.5% of others ($\chi^2 = 57.25$, $p = .000$). Likewise, only 2.6% of white drivers reported being arrested, compared to 5.2% of black drivers, 4.2% of Hispanic drivers, and 2.1% of drivers of other races and ethnicities ($\chi^2 = 19.73$, $p = .000$). Similar patterns were also found for the use of force: 2.7% of whites reported having force used against them, compared to 6.7% of blacks, 5.4% of Hispanics, and 1.7% of drivers of other races and ethnicities ($\chi^2 = 44.68$, $p = .000$).

Significant differences in other characteristics of drivers were also found by drivers' race and ethnicity. White drivers who were stopped by police were more likely to be female ($\chi^2 = 14.21$, $p = .003$), older (f-test $= 24.48$, $p = .000$), and have higher incomes ($\chi^2 = 98.70$, 15.55, 158.20; $p = .000$, for incomes less than $20,000, $20,000–$49,999, and greater than $50,000, respectively) than were black and Hispanic drivers. Likewise, white drivers were more likely to be stopped by white police officers ($\chi^2 = 73.11$, $p = .000$), stopped less frequently (f-test $= 5.79$, $p = .001$), and have fewer passengers in their vehicles (f-test $= 7.98$, $p = .000$) than were minority drivers.

Table 3.   Police-Public Contact Survey, 1999 (N = 19,277,002 weighted cases): Officers' Behavior, Drivers' Characteristics, Stop Characteristics, Community, and Control Variables, by Drivers' Race

Variables	Drivers' Race / Ethnicity			
	White	Black	Hispanic	Other
Officers' Behavior				
Citation***	.50	.57	.63	.61
Any search***	.05	.11	.11	.07
Arrest***	.03	.05	.04	.02
Any use of force***	.03	.07	.05	.02
Drivers' Characteristics				
Male**	.60	.60	.68	.63
Age***	36.60	35.30	32.19	32.90
Employed	.80	.79	.81	.79
Income less than $20,000***	.25	.40	.37	.27
Income $20,000–$49,999***	.34	.37	.41	.31
Income greater than $50,000***	.41	.23	.22	.43
Characteristics of the Traffic Stop				
White officer or officers***	.84	.72	.81	.75
Number of traffic stops***	1.33	1.52	1.39	1.24
Number of people in the vehicle***	1.35	1.43	1.48	1.46
Any evidence	.01	.01	.01	.00
Reason for the Stop				
Speeding***	.52	.41	.40	.44
DUI roadside check	.02	.01	.01	.01
Other traffic offense***	.21	.27	.27	.29
Vehicle defect***	.10	.13	.15	.15
License/registration check*	.09	.10	.09	.04
Driver suspected of something	.02	.02	.03	.02
Other reason/unknown	.05	.07	.05	.05
Community/Control Characteristics				
MSA central city***	.21	.45	.40	.30
MSA non-central city***	.55	.43	.49	.67
Non-MSA***	.24	.12	.11	.03
CATI survey***	.26	.23	.14	.19

Note: Entries are percentages for dichotomous and continuous variables. Asterisks represent statistically significant differences between racial-ethnic groups as measured by chi-square tests for dichotomous variables and f-tests (one-way ANOVA) for continuous variables.
* $p < .05$, ** $p < .01$, *** $p < .001$.

There were also significant differences by race and ethnicity for the primary reason of the traffic stop. Among all drivers who indicated that they were involved in a traffic stop, a higher proportion of white drivers than of minority drivers were stopped for speeding ($\chi^2 = 57.77$, $p = .000$), while higher proportions of black and Hispanic drivers compared to whites drivers were stopped for other traffic offenses ($\chi^2 = 30.61$, $p = .000$), vehicle defects ($\chi^2 = 19.92$, $p = .000$), and license/registration checks ($\chi^2 = 8.72$, $p = .033$). Finally, white drivers who were stopped by police were more likely to reside in suburban ($\chi^2 = 60.52$, $p = .000$) and rural areas ($\chi^2 = 148.74$, $p =$

.000), than were black and Hispanic drivers, who disproportionately resided in central city areas ($\chi^2 = 285.30, p = .000$). More rigorous testing of the influence of drivers' race and ethnicity on officer
behavior is provided in the multivariate analyses that are
presented next.

Multivariate Results

Using dichotomous variables measuring officers' behaviors, we
estimated four binary logistic regression models to predict the
probabilities of response categories compared to an excluded category of no police action (see Liao, 1994). The findings from these
analyses are presented in Table 4 (citations and searches) and Table 5 (arrests and uses of force). For each logistic regression model,
the first column displays the regression coefficients and statistical
significance, the second column reports the standard errors, and
the third column shows the odds ratios for each predictor.

Model 1 in Table 4 estimates the issuance of citations by police.
The results show that men, younger drivers, blacks, Hispanics,
drivers of other races, drivers with fewer previous traffic stops, and
drivers traveling with fewer passengers were significantly *more*
likely to receive citations than were women, older drivers, whites,
drivers with more previous traffic stops, and drivers traveling with
more passengers. Specifically, after controlling for other relevant
factors, the odds that black drivers would receive a citation were
47% greater compared to the odds for white drivers, and the odds
for Hispanic drivers were 82% higher. In addition, compared to
drivers who were stopped for speeding, drivers who were stopped
for any other reason were significantly *less* likely to receive citations. Finally, drivers who reside in suburban and rural areas were
significantly *less* likely to receive citations than were drivers who
reside in central-city areas. Collectively, this model explains 18.2%
of the variance in the dependent variable.

Model 2 in Table 4 displays the estimates of vehicle and/or citizen searches by police. Of the 6.6% of drivers who were searched,
52% were also arrested. It is unknown whether the search preceded
or occurred after the arrest; therefore, it is possible that any racial
and ethnic disparities in the rate of searches may be due to the disproportionate number of minorities who were arrested and
searched subsequent to their arrest. Thus, arrest is included as a
control variable in the model.[14] The results indicate that males,

---

14 To examine the potential problem of multicollinearity by including arrest in
this model, we estimated a separate model excluding arrest as a predictor variable.
The statistical and substantive significance of drivers' race and ethnicity remain
similar, but the overall predictive power of the model is substantially reduced

72 INFLUENCE OF DRIVERS' CHARACTERISTICS

Table 4. Logistic Regressions of Officers' Actions: Citation and Search ($N = 19,277,002$ weighted cases)

Variables	Model 1: Citation			Model 2: Search		
	Coeff.	SE	Odds Ratio	Coeff.	SE	Odds Ratio
Intercept	1.54***	.17		-3.75***	.39	
Drivers' Characteristics						
Male	.20***	.06	1.23	1.37***	.19	3.94
Age	-.01***	.00	.99	-.04***	.01	.96
Black	.39***	.11	1.47	.41*	.21	1.50
Hispanic	.60***	.11	1.82	.35*	.18	1.42
Other race	.39**	.15	1.47	.08	.36	1.08
Employed	-.01	.07	.99	-.08	.17	.93
Income less than $20,000	.10	.07	1.11	.62***	.18	1.86
Income $20,000–$49,999	.06	.07	1.06	.27	.18	1.31
Characteristics of the Stop						
White officer	-.01	.09	.99	-.31	.17	.74
Number of traffic stops	-.11***	.04	.89	.22***	.04	1.25
Number of people in vehicle	-.10**	.04	.90	.09	.07	1.10
Any evidence	-.41	.38	.66	—	—	—
Arrest	—	—	—	4.40***	.22	81.64
Reason for the Stop						
DUI roadside check	3.98***	.48	.02	.40	.56	1.49
Nonspeeding traffic offense	-.72***	.07	.49	.61***	.16	1.84
Vehicle defect	1.70***	.10	.18	1.08***	.21	2.94
License/registration check	2.07***	.16	.13	.86**	.28	2.37
Driver suspect	3.13***	.28	.04	1.99***	.36	7.32
Other reason/unknown	2.09***	.16	.12	1.45***	.27	4.25
Community/Control Variables						
MSA non-central city	-.24***	.07	.79	-.16	.15	.85
Non-MSA	-.87***	.11	.42	-.47	.26	.63
CATI survey	.05	.07	1.05	-.08	.17	.92
Overall Fit (f-value)	37.39***			30.08***		
Pseudo R^2	.18			.55		

* $p < .05$, ** $p < .01$, *** $p < .001$.

younger drivers, blacks, Hispanics, and drivers with lower and middle incomes were significantly *more* likely to report being searched than were females, older drivers, whites, and drivers with higher incomes. After controlling for arrest, the odds of being searched were 50% higher for black drivers and 42% higher for Hispanic drivers than for white drivers. In addition, drivers who reported being stopped more frequently were *more* likely to be searched. So too were drivers who were stopped for nonspeeding traffic offenses, vehicle defects, license/registration checks, suspicion, and other/unknown reasons compared to drivers who were stopped for speeding. Collectively, the predictors in this model explain 55% of the variance in the dependent variable.

The estimates predicting arrest are displayed in Table 5, Model 3. Once again, the results show that after other factors are controlled, males, younger drivers, blacks, and drivers with lower and

(pseudo $R^2 = 0.21$). These analyses are not displayed in tabular form, but are available from the authors on request.

middle incomes were significantly *more* likely to be arrested. Although Hispanic and other drivers were not significantly more likely to be arrested, the odds of arrest for black drivers were 79% higher than the odds for white drivers. Not surprisingly, one of the strongest predictors of arrest is the discovery of any evidence during the search of a person or vehicle. In addition, compared to drivers stopped for speeding, drivers stopped for nonspeeding traffic offenses, vehicle defects, suspicion, and other/unknown reasons were significantly *more* likely to be arrested. Together, the variables in this model explain 23.4% of the variance.

Table 5. Logistic Regressions of Officers' Actions: Arrest and Use of Force (N = 19,277,002 weighted cases)

Variables	Model 3: Arrest			Model 4: Force		
	Coeff.	SE	Odds Ratio	Coeff.	SE	Odds Ratio
Intercept	4.74***	.06		−4.86***	.50	
Drivers' Characteristics						
Male	1.03***	.22	2.80	1.20***	.20	3.32
Age	−.02***	.01	.98	−.03***	.01	.97
Black	.58*	.27	1.79	.73**	.25	2.08
Hispanic	.11	.25	1.11	.27	.22	1.31
Other race	−.28	.63	.75	−.53	.72	.59
Employed	−.28	.21	.75	−.16	.21	.85
Income less than $20,000	.82***	.22	2.28	.67**	.23	1.96
Income $20,000–$49,999	.74***	.22	2.09	.62**	.23	1.86
Characteristics of the Stop						
White officer	.17	.22	1.19	−.18	.19	.83
Number of traffic stops	−.20	.14	.82	.06	.08	1.06
Number of people in the vehicle	.08	.10	1.08	.18*	.09	1.20
Any evidence	3.59***	.37	36.18	3.42***	.40	30.51
Reason for the Stop						
DUI roadside check	.24	.66	1.27	.72	.60	2.06
Nonspeeding traffic offense	1.14***	.28	3.13	1.27***	.27	3.55
Vehicle defect	.99**	.36	2.70	.98**	.33	2.67
License/registration check	.30	.49	1.35	.52	.44	1.69
Driver suspect	1.76***	.40	5.84	1.73***	.40	5.64
Other reason/unknown	1.91***	.35	6.76	2.14***	.33	8.49
Community/Control Variables						
MSA non-central city	−.14	.22	.87	.20	.18	.82
Non-MSA	−.20	.26	.82	.19	.23	.83
CATI survey	−.05	.21	.95	−.04	.20	.96
Overall fit (f-value)	11.72***			16.05***		
Pseudo R^2	.23			.27		

* $p < .05$, ** $p < .01$, *** $p < .001$.

Finally, estimates of the use of force are presented in Table 5, Model 4. Similar patterns as those for arrest were found.[15] Specifically, males, younger drivers, blacks, lower and middle income

---

15 The use-of-force and arrest models are similar because the measure of use of force includes handcuffing, which is a standard procedure for arrests in most jurisdictions. Thus, the use-of-force measure including handcuffing is highly correlated with arrest (Pearson's $r = 0.78$). Specifically, of the 3.4% of drivers who had any force used against them, 78.6% were only handcuffed. Given the relative infrequency of the use of force excluding handcuffing during traffic stops (0.7% of all the drivers),

drivers, and drivers who reported that evidence was found were significantly *more* likely to report having force used against them by police. Again, although Hispanics and drivers of other races were not more likely to report having force used against them, the odds for black drivers were 2.1 times greater than the odds for white drivers. Compared to drivers stopped for speeding, drivers stopped for nonspeeding traffic offenses, vehicle defects, suspicion, and other/unknown reasons were also significantly *more* likely to have force used against them. This model explains 27.0% of the variance in officers' use of force.

Additive Probabilities

In addition to the independent influence of drivers' race-ethnicity on officer behavior, it is also hypothesized that some additive combinations of drivers' characteristics may put particular types of people at increased risk. For example, some scholars have speculated that while citizens' race alone may influence police behavior, some groups (e.g., young, minority males) are disproportionately targeted by law enforcement (Kennedy, 1997; Walker, 1999). To illustrate the joint effects of drivers' gender, age, and race-ethnicity, the additive probabilities of these characteristics are displayed in Table 6. For each action by an officer (i.e., citation, search, arrest, and force), the probabilities of individual and combined driver characteristics are reported when all other variables in the equations (listed in Tables 4 and 5) are held constant at their means. As Table 6 indicates, the predicted likelihood of citations, searches, arrests, and use of force was dramatically increased when drivers' age, sex, and race were combined. For example, the predicted percentage of drivers issued citations when all variables are at their means is 51.9%, compared to 53.8% for men, 56.3% for young drivers, 60.3% for black drivers, 65.1% for Hispanic drivers, 66.3% for young black men, and 70.7% for young Hispanic males. Even more dramatic patterns were reported for the likelihood of searches, arrests, and use of force for young black and young Hispanic males.

Although the logistic regression models in Table 5 revealed that Hispanic drivers were not significantly more likely to be arrested or have force used against them, as shown in Table 6, the combined influence of sex, age, and ethnicity does put young Hispanic male drivers at increased risk for police action. Specifically, young Hispanic male drivers were 3.6, 2.3, and 3.4 times more likely to report being searched, arrested, and have force used against them, respectively, than was the average driver (i.e., when

---

the multivariate model used to predict this behavior is inappropriate, producing artificially inflated standard errors and unstable coefficients.

all other variables are at their means). Likewise, young black male drivers were 3.7, 3.4, and 5.0 times more likely to report being searched, arrested, and have force used against them, respectively, compared to the base model.

Table 6. Predicted Probabilities (%) of Police Actions, by Drivers' Gender, Age, and Race[a]

Variable	Model 1: Citation	Model 2: Search[b]	Model 3: Arrest	Model 4: Force
Base model	51.85	8.81	1.64	1.47
Male	53.80	14.18	2.43	2.36
Young (average age = 18)	56.31	16.54	2.33	2.52
Black	60.32	12.19	2.71	2.80
Hispanic	65.11	11.75	1.81	1.89
Young, black, male	66.30	32.76	5.63	7.32
Young, Hispanic, male	70.72	31.84	3.80	5.04

[a] Other citizen characteristics, characteristics of the traffic stop, reason for the stop, and community/control characteristics were held constant at their means.
[b] Predicted probabilities for the search model were calculated on the basis of the statistical model that included arrest as a predictor variable. Predicted probabilities that are based on the search model that excluded arrest have substantively similar additive effects.

Estimating Search Success Rates

One of the most common rationales for targeting minority drivers is the perception among law enforcement officials that minority drivers—specifically, young black and Hispanic males—are more likely to be transporting drugs, unregistered weapons, or other contraband (Harris, 2002; Ramirez, McDevitt, & Farrell, 2000). As we previously reported, some crime statistics support this proposition. For example, the NCVS has consistently found that blacks have higher rates of violent offending than do whites (Lauritsen & Sampson, 1998). In addition, research that is based on official arrest statistics has consistently shown that young minority males are significantly more likely to be arrested for drug offenses and violent crime (for reviews, see LaFree, 1995; Lockwood, Pottieger, & Inciardi, 1995). It has been argued, however, that minorities are disproportionately represented in official crime statistics (e.g., Uniform Crime Reports, National Incident-Based Reporting System) because these data are measured through arrests. If officers are more likely to stop, question, and search young minority males, then arrest statistics may become what Harris (1999a) described as a "self-fulfilling prophecy." Thus, it is important to examine the "good policing" argument in support of profiling techniques through other data sources.

One way to explore this controversy further is to measure the self-reported success rates of police searches. For the PPCS, the success rates of discovering evidence on drivers or in vehicles searched by police for each racial category are measured by examining only drivers who were searched (6.6% of the drivers who were stopped, $n = 1,263,141$ weighted cases). Contrary to the argument made by many law enforcement officials that minorities are more likely to be carrying drugs and/or weapons, contraband was discovered on fewer minority drivers than on white drivers. Specifically, 16.6% of the white drivers who were searched reported the discovery of contraband, compared to only 9.4% of Hispanic drivers, 7.1% of black drivers, and no drivers of other races/ethnicities. While a cross-tabulation analysis conducted using WesVar revealed that these differences between racial ethnic groups are not statistically significant using a two-tailed test, the differences do approach the conventional .05 p-value ($\chi^2 = 5.16$, $p = .076$). Furthermore, when black, Hispanic, and other ethnicities are collapsed into a Caucasian/non-Caucasian dichotomy, there are significant differences in search success rates between groups. Specifically, 16.6% of the Caucasian drivers who were searched were found to be in possession of contraband, compared to only 7.5% of non-Caucasian drivers ($\chi_2 = 7.26$, $p = .007$). Thus, strictly on the basis of the outcome test, the results suggest that racial disparities do exist in police searching practices.

Additional analyses revealed other differences based on drivers' race-ethnicity. Of the drivers who were stopped by police, officers asked 2.9% if they could search their person and/or their vehicle. Of these 2.9% of drivers, nearly all (97.7%) gave consent to be searched. Officers' requests to search, however, differed significantly by drivers' race-ethnicity. Officers asked for consent to search 2.5% of white drivers, compared to 3.9% of black drivers, 4.1% of Hispanic drivers, and 3.9% of drivers of other races ($\chi^2 = 9.83$, $p = .020$). Contraband was discovered on 12.5% of those who gave consent to be searched.

The outcome test can also be used to examine differences between male and female drivers. Of the male drivers who were stopped by police, 9.3% were searched, compared to only 2.3% of female drivers. Furthermore, of all the searches that were conducted, 86.4% were of male drivers. The success of these searches, however, is relatively equivalent across groups. Specifically, 11.6% of the searched female drivers reported being in possession of contraband, compared to 13.5% of the searched male drivers ($\chi^2 = 0.16$, $p = .69$). Thus, although male drivers were more likely to be searched, these searches were proportionally as productive as the searches of female drivers.

Although the outcome test is considered an appropriate test by some academics for determining racial disparities in police search practices (e.g., Ayres, 2001, 2002; Knowles et al., 2001), it is still informative to identify other factors that may be related to search success rates. One of the underlying assumptions of the outcome test is that no additional factors (i.e., the decision to stop) are relevant. As Fagan (2002) noted, however, these assumptions may not be plausible. Fagan's criticism of this approach cannot be directly addressed with the current data because information is not available on who is not stopped by police. What can be examined with these data are the factors that are correlated with search success rates.

To investigate further the likelihood of discovering evidence during a search, we estimated a multivariate logistic regression model. It is expected that driver characteristics, characteristics of the stop (including consent to search), the primary reason for the stop, and community characteristics may also influence the likelihood of discovering contraband. Table 7 reports the unstandardized regression coefficients, statistical significance, standard errors, and odds ratios for a logistic regression model predicting the discovery of evidence.[16] The results show that the full model is *not* statistically significant and that together, the variables explain less than 1% of the variance. In addition, no individual variables are significant predictors of the discovery of evidence. These null findings suggest that the success rates of vehicle and person searches that are based on any of these predictors cannot be accurately determined.

DISCUSSION

Analyses of officers' coercive actions toward drivers during traffic stops (i.e., citation, search, arrest, and use of force) show consistent and substantial differences that are based, in part, on drivers' characteristics. For example, controlling for other relevant extralegal and legal factors, the odds of citation, search, arrest, and use of force for black drivers are 1.5, 1.5, 1.8, and 2.1 times higher, respectively, than for white drivers. Furthermore, the additive influence of age, race, and gender places young black male drivers at an even greater risk for coercive action by police. Compared to the base model, in which all the characteristics are held constant at their mean, young black male drivers are 1.3, 3.7, 3.4, and 5.0 times more

---

16 No drivers of "other" race and no drivers who were stopped for license or registration checks reported the discovery of evidence after a search. Therefore, these variables were eliminated from the multivariate model.

78   INFLUENCE OF DRIVERS' CHARACTERISTICS

Table 7.   Logistic Regression of Evidence Found on
           Drivers or in Vehicles Searched by Police
           (N = 1,263,141 weighted cases)

Variables	Coefficient	SE	Odds Ratio
Intercept	−1.75	1.06	
Drivers' Characteristics			
Male	0.14	0.47	1.15
Age	−0.01	0.02	0.99
Black	−0.89	0.53	0.41
Hispanic	−0.54	0.52	0.58
Employed	0.02	0.48	1.02
Income less than $20,000	−0.53	0.51	0.59
Income $20,000–$49,999	−0.09	0.45	0.91
Characteristics of the Stop			
White officer	−0.01	0.39	0.99
Number of traffic stops	−0.00	0.10	1.00
Number of people in the vehicle	0.10	0.18	1.11
Consent given for search	−0.20	1.39	0.82
Reason for the Stop			
DUI roadside check	2.08	0.56	8.01
Nonspeeding traffic offense	0.81	0.63	2.24
Vehicle defect	0.78	0.61	2.19
Driver suspect	1.14	0.82	3.13
Other reason/unknown	0.09	0.32	1.10
Community/Control Variables			
MSA non-central city	−0.10	0.50	0.91
Non-MSA	0.53	0.71	1.70
CATI survey	−0.87	0.35	0.42
Overall fit (f-value)	0.95		
Pseudo R^2	0.07		

likely to be issued a citation, searched, arrested, and have force used against them by police, respectively. Hispanic drivers are also significantly more likely to receive a citation and be searched compared to white drivers, but ethnicity alone does *not* place drivers at a greater risk for arrest or use of force by police. Nevertheless, the additive influence of age, ethnicity, and gender does place young Hispanic male drivers at a higher risk for these more coercive actions. Specifically, compared to the base model, young Hispanic males are 1.4, 3.6, 2.3, and 3.4 times more likely to report being issued a citation, searched, arrested, and have force used by police, respectively.

The results also show that other characteristics of drivers have important independent influences on officers' behavior. Male drivers, younger drivers, and lower- and middle-class drivers are all significantly more likely to be the recipients of coercive police actions. In addition, the findings suggest that situational and legal characteristics have a mixed influence on officer behavior. An important finding is that officers' race does not have a statistically significant influence on the use of coercive actions toward drivers. Additional analyses (not displayed in tabular form) indicated that officers' and drivers' racial interaction terms are also not significant predictors of officers' behavior. This finding suggests that the elevated rates of coercive behaviors toward minority drivers are not strictly a problem of white officers targeting nonwhite drivers, but, rather, that all officers (regardless of race) cite, search, arrest, and use force against black drivers at higher rates.

Contrary to expectations, the number of prior traffic stops reported by drivers has a significant and positive influence only on being searched. If the number of prior stops was related to legal considerations, such as reckless or aggressive driving behavior, one would expect that drivers with more prior stops would be more likely to receive a citation or be arrested. However, the lack of influence of this variable on arrest and its significant—but negative—influence on being issued a citation suggests that the number of prior stops may be better interpreted as a proxy measure for particular "profiles" to conduct searches, rather than the result of legal factors that are based on the drivers' behavior. Although the exact "profile" related to the frequency of traffic stops is unknown, it is suggestive that drivers who are male, younger, black, unemployed, and have incomes lower than $20,000 all report significantly higher frequencies of prior traffic stops.[17]

As expected, the discovery of evidence had the strongest influence on police decision making for the most coercive actions (i.e., arrest and use of force). This finding is consistent with the larger literature on police behavior that has found legal variables to be the strongest predictors of police behaviors (Klinger, 1997; Mastrofski et al., 1995; Riksheim & Chermak, 1993). As we previously noted, however, the PPCS data did not capture the sequencing of events during police-citizen encounters. Therefore, it is unclear if the discovery of contraband preceded or followed officers' actions. As a result, the coefficients for evidence generated in the multivariate analyses cannot be interpreted in a causal sense because temporal ordering has not been established. Future data collection efforts should attempt to measure the discovery of evidence as it unfolds in time.

In these data, the primary reason for the traffic stop also had a strong and consistent influence on the eventual disposition of that police-citizen encounter. Drivers who were stopped for speeding

---

17   One-way ANOVAs indicated that male (f-test $= 48.20$, $p = .000$), younger (f-test $= 4.169$; $p = .000$), black (f-test $= 14.44$, $p = .000$), unemployed (f-test $= 3.67$, $p = .055$), and low-income (f-test $= 9.58$, $p = .002$) drivers report significantly higher frequencies of prior traffic stops.

80   INFLUENCE OF DRIVERS' CHARACTERISTICS

were significantly more likely to receive citations, while drivers who were stopped for other reasons (e.g., nonspeeding traffic offenses, vehicle defects, suspicion, and other/unknown reasons) were significantly more likely to be searched, arrested, and have force use against them. These findings are particularly important because minority drivers are significantly more likely than are white drivers to report being stopped for reasons other than speeding (e.g., nonspeeding traffic offenses, vehicle defects, and license/registration checks), which result in the most coercive actions taken by police. Note, however, that it is unknown if police are inappropriately stopping minorities for minor offenses. It is possible that racial and ethnic minorities, who are overrepresented in low-income groups, may be more likely to drive vehicles with equipment violations. Although the analyses reported here controlled for differences in income, they did not include measures of the quality of vehicles. Thus, the findings do not address the larger question of *why* minorities are more likely to be stopped for nonspeeding offenses. Rather, they demonstrate that minority drivers are more likely to be stopped for offenses other than speeding and that drivers who are stopped for reasons other than speeding are more likely to be the recipients of coercive police actions.

The analyses of hit rates of searches have clear and important results, demonstrating the potential inappropriate use of profiling strategies. One of the most frequently cited justifications for the higher rates of stops, searches, and arrests of minorities is the perception by law enforcement officials that minorities are more likely than are whites to be carrying or transporting contraband. Results from this national survey of drivers who were stopped by police suggest that this perception is not accurate. Over twice as many white drivers as black drivers reported the discovery of contraband during a person or vehicle search. One explanation for the racial disparity reported in search success rates is that black citizens are simply less likely to be in possession of contraband than are other racial-ethnic groups. The "carrying rates" of different racial and ethnic groups in the overall population, however, are unknown. The PPCS provides information only on citizens who were stopped and subsequently searched. Thus, results from these data cannot be used to determine behavior in the population as a whole.

Another explanation for the racial disparity reported in search success rates is that officers may impose a lower threshold for black drivers than for white drivers when they determine whether to conduct a search. If police do impose a lower threshold for black drivers (either consciously or unconsciously), the result would likely be a

widening of law enforcement's net to include a larger pool of innocent black drivers (Harris, 2002; Russell, 1999; Skolnick &
Caplovitz, 2001). Analyses based on the outcome test found that
searched black drivers were significantly less likely than were
searched white drivers to report being in possession of contraband.
Ayres (2001, p. 133) concluded that such evidence "would suggest
that if police require the same level of probable cause when searching minorities as when searching whites, there would be fewer minorities searched (or proportionally more whites searched)."

Still another possible explanation that cannot be ruled out with
these data is that black drivers are less likely to self-report carrying
contraband than are drivers of other racial-ethnic groups. As we
previously noted, research in North Carolina indicated that black
motorists who had been ticketed were significantly less likely than
were white drivers who had been ticketed to report that they had
received citations when they were subsequently asked on self-report surveys (Smith et al., 2000). And, as is evident in Table 1, research that has used official police data to examine hit rates has
resulted in mixed findings. Although the validity of self-report data
cannot be directly assessed, these data can be used in combination
with other official data sources to triangulate. As Lundman and
Kaufman (2003, p. 214) noted, "there is a pressing need and ample
scholarly room for additional research on Driving While Black using triangulated police-reported, citizen-reported, and observer-re-
ported data."

The multivariate model for the discovery of contraband during
the search of a person or vehicle indicated that no measured factor
accurately predicted who was in possession of contraband. On the
basis of the legal and extralegal predictor variables used in this
study, what types of drivers and/or traffic stops are more likely to
result in the discovery of contraband after the search of a person or
vehicle is conducted by police simply cannot be determined. These
findings, which suggest that racial, ethnic, gender, and social-class
"profiles" are not likely to be effective, are counter to many of the
prevailing "myths" in policing. It is unknown, however, if other verbal and nonverbal "suspicion" cues can effectively predict the discovery of contraband. Future research must explore other factors
that may be related to both drivers' characteristics (e.g., race,
ethnicity, gender, and age) and reasons to conduct a search. For
example, officers are often trained to look for "suspicious behavior"
that would lead to reasonable suspicion and/or probable cause to
conduct a search. It is possible that some of these "suspicious" behaviors (e.g., the failure to maintain eye contact, aggressive hand
gestures, particular verbal cues, and general nervousness) may be

more prevalent for young, male, and/or minority drivers (Blubaugh & Pennington, 1976; Fugita, Wexley, & Hillery, 1974; Garratt, Baxter, & Rozelle, 1981; Pennington, 1979; Vrij & Winkel, 1991, 1992). Future research should explore whether verbal and nonverbal cues, which may differ by race, age and gender, influence officers' perceptions of suspicion and ultimately whether or not these cues are effective predictors.

These findings suggest that targeting drivers solely or even partially on the basis of their race/ethnicity is not an effective, efficient, or responsible policing strategy at the national level. The results of this study, however, cannot address the effectiveness of targeting particular types of citizens in particular neighborhoods for more specialized purposes (e.g., policing hot spots, localized gun interdiction programs). Prior research that has examined these types of localized aggressive policing tactics has generally reported positive, although short-term, results (for a review, see Eck & Maguire, 2000). The findings from our study suggest, however, that more generalized policing strategies that are geared toward disrupting the flow of drug trafficking on interstate highways by focusing on searches of particular types of drivers are not likely to be effective. At the national level, the "good policing" argument in support of racial profiling is simply not supported.

In addition to the ineffectiveness of targeting minority drivers for pedestrian and vehicle searches as a policing strategy, this technique often leads to poor police-minority relations. Results from the PPCS data show that drivers' perceptions of the legitimacy of police searches differ significantly by drivers' race-ethnicity. Specifically, 77.8% of the black drivers who were searched perceived that the search was not legitimate, compared to 58.2% of the white drivers, 61.0% of the Hispanic drivers, and 30.9% of the drivers of other races-ethnicities ($\chi^2 = 15.54$, $p = .001$). Numerous studies have also demonstrated that compared to white citizens, minority citizens have more negative attitudes toward police, perceive that they are treated unjustly, and are more likely to question the legitimacy of the police (see, e.g., Albrecht & Green, 1977; Bayley & Mendelsohn, 1969; Browning et al., 1994; Carter, 1983; Decker, 1981; Dunham & Alpert, 1988; Jacob, 1971; Lasley, 1994; Scaglion & Condon, 1980; T. J. Taylor, Turner, Esbensen, & Winfree, 2001; Tuch & Weitzer, 1997; Webb & Marshall, 1995; Weitzer, 2000; Weitzer & Tuch, 1999, 2002).

Despite the strengths of using the PPCS to examine police behavior during traffic stops, there are clear limitations as well. First, several potential predictors of police coercive behavior simply cannot be measured with these citizen survey data. For example, the results suggest that community characteristics have a weak and inconsistent influence on officers' behavior. Unfortunately, these somewhat crude measures of MSAs do not allow for the adequate examination of the influence on officers' behaviors of the location of the traffic stop, characteristics of the drivers' neighborhood residence, or the type of roadway where the stop was made. Therefore, the effectiveness of policing strategies that target particular individuals at specific locations cannot be assessed. Future research should attempt to gather more information about the time and location of police contacts, along with more detailed information on the characteristics of drivers' residential neighborhoods.

In addition, future research should measure more specific details regarding the interaction between citizens and police after stops have been made. For example, some scholars have suggested that nonwhite suspects, particularly young black males, are more likely to display some form of disrespect and/or noncompliance toward police (for a review, see Engel, 2003). The perceived relationship between demeanor and race has been used to explain higher arrest rates for young black males (see Walker, 1999). Engel et al. (2002) have argued that studies of racial profiling could be greatly enhanced if they included more information about the interaction between officers and citizens, along with relevant legal characteristics prior to and during traffic and field interrogation stops (e.g., the seriousness of the offense, the amount/strength of the evidence regarding that offense). Unfortunately, the PPCS does not include measures of offense seriousness or self-assessments of guilt. Thus, the testing of these and other theoretical propositions must await future research.

As we previously noted, this research was also limited by its inability to measure variables that may be likely to have an influence on officers' decision making. That is, the statistical models we estimated are likely to suffer from specification error. For example, although the reason for the stop was examined, there are no direct measures of the seriousness of the violation (e.g., a speeding violation does not capture total speed over the limit). In addition, aggressive driving patterns that may have led to the stop were not ascertained. Social scientists and police officials have explored the possibility that particular types of citizens (e.g., young black males) may drive more aggressively and therefore may be more likely to violate traffic laws and/or commit more serious violations (Engel & Calnon, in press; Lange et al., 2001; MacDonald, 2002; Smith et al., 2000). A national survey by the National Highway Traffic Safety Administration observed both gender and age differences in the frequency of driving, speeding, and other unsafe driving behavior

84   INFLUENCE OF DRIVERS' CHARACTERISTICS

(Boyle, Dienstfrey, & Sothoron, 1998). Additional studies have shown that black and Hispanic drivers have slightly higher rates of involvement in both accidents and alcohol-related accidents than do white drivers (Royal, 2000; Voas, Tippetts, & Fisher, 2000). The PPCS data, however, do not capture information on the quality of driving patterns by racial, ethnic, gender, and age groups. Once again, the most prudent course of action for researchers who explore police behavior during traffic stops is to triangulate data and research methodologies (Lundman & Kaufman, 2003).

CONCLUSION

The perpetuation of the crime-focused policies of the war on drugs has produced lasting effects on minorities' perceptions of the criminal justice system, in general, and on minorities' interactions with the police in particular. The findings presented here are likely one result of the disproportionate focus on minority offenders as the target of the enforcement and punishment of the war on drugs. As has been shown in this and other criminal justice research, the burden associated with being young, minority, and male is particularly high (Miller, 1996; Spohn & Holleran, 2000). These findings show that even after relevant legal and extralegal factors are controlled, reports from young minority males indicate they are at the highest risk for citations, searches, arrests, and use of force during traffic stops. Yet, these drivers are not more likely to report carrying contraband, which, it has been suggested, is one of officers' primary motivations for conducting disproportionate stops and searches of minority citizens.

Combining Scheingold's (1984) theory of the politics of law and order with Crank and Langworthy's (1992) institutional perspective, it is likely that profiling strategies have become institutionalized in police organizations because of the war on drugs. As a result, the "good policing" argument to justify the use of targeting strategies was well received by police officers, whose daily experiences confirmed their expectations (MacDonald, 2001). Thus, it is not surprising that both white and minority police officers engage in these behaviors (see Novak, in press; Smith & Petrocelli, 2001).

If profiling strategies have become institutionalized, racial sensitivity training along with other types of police training that are designed to reduce the prejudice of individual officers, is not likely to address the core issue of why officers target minority citizens. To be effective in changing officers' behavior, police administrators need to address the informal policies and organizational cultures that perpetuate the "myth" of the effectiveness of profiling strategies. For example, police administrators should demonstrate to their officers the factual outcomes of their behavior. That is, officers should be given information on their hit rates for different racial, gender, and age groups. Likewise, departmental training on searches and seizures should include findings from empirical studies that have demonstrated that the generalized targeting of minority drivers, in an effort to disrupt the flow of drug trafficking and/or to confiscate weapons, is an ineffective and inefficient use of police resources that leads to poor police-community relations.

The "legitimation conflict" that Crank and Langworthy (1992) described has been occurring in police departments across the country, as entities outside the police organization have begun to question the legitimacy of police profiling tactics and policies. It is only when police officers begin to question the legitimacy of these tactics themselves, however, that true reform may occur.

REFERENCES

Albrecht, S. L., & Green, M. (1977). Attitudes toward the police and the larger attitude complex: Implications for police-community relationships. *Criminology, 15*, 67-86.

American Civil Liberties Union. (2000). *Plaintiff's fifth monitoring report: Pedestrian and car stop audit.* [On-line]. Available: http://www.aclupa.org/report.htm

Ayres, I. (2001). *Pervasive prejudice? Unconventional evidence of racial and gender discrimination.* Chicago: University of Chicago Press.

Ayres, I. (2002). Outcome tests of racial disparities in police practices. *Justice research and Policy, 4*, 131-143.

Ayres, I., & Vars, F. E. (2000). Determinants of citations to articles in elite law review. *Journal of Legal Studies, 29*, 427.

Bayley, D. H., & Mendelsohn, H. (1969). *Minorities and the police.* New York: Free Press.

Beck, D. A., & Daly, A. (1999). State constitutional analysis of pretext stops: Racial profiling and public policy concerns. *Temple Law Review, 72*, 597-618.

Beck, A. J., & Harrison, P. M. (2001). *Prisoners in 2000.* Washington DC: U.S. Department of Justice.

Becker, G. S. (1957). *The economics of discrimination.* Chicago: University of Chicago Press.

Becker, G. S. (1993). Nobel lecture: The economic way of looking at behavior. *Journal of Political Economy, 101*, 385-389.

Biderman, A. D., Lynch, J. P., & Petersen, J. (1991). *Understanding crime incidence statistics: Why the UCR diverges from the NCS.* New York: Springer-Verlag.

Blubaugh, J. A., & Pennington, D. L. (1976). *Crossing differences . . . Interracial communication.* Columbus, OH: Merrill.

Boyle, J. Dienstfrey, S., & Sothoron, A. (1998). *National survey of speeding and other Unsafe driving actions: Driver attitudes and behavior* (Vol 2.). Washington, DC: National Highway Traffic Safety Administration.

Brewer, K. R. W., & Mellor, R. W. (1973). The effect of sample structure on analytical surveys. *Australian Journal of Statistics, 15*, 145-152.

Browning, S., Cullen, F. T., Cao, L., Kopache, R., & Stevenson, T. J. (1994). Race and getting hassled by the police: A research note. *Police Studies, 17*, 1-11.

Carter, D. L. (1983). Hispanic interaction with the criminal justice system in Texas: Experiences, attitudes and perceptions. *Journal of Criminal Justice, 11*, 213-227.

86   INFLUENCE OF DRIVERS' CHARACTERISTICS

Carter, D. L., Katz-Bannister, A., & Schafer, J. (2001). *Lansing Police Department MATS data: Six month analysis* [On-line]. Available: http://www.lansingpolice.com/site/profile/mats%206%20month%20Report.pdf

Chambliss, W. J. (1995). Another lost war: The costs and consequences of drug prohibition. *Social Justice, 22,* 101-124.

Cole, D. (1999). *No equal justice: Race and class in the American criminal justice system.* New York: New Press.

Cooper, F. R. (2002). The un-balanced Fourth Amendment: A cultural study of the drug war, racial profiling and *Arvizu. Villanova Law Review, 47,* 851-894.

Cordner, G., Williams, B., & Zuniga, M. (2001). *Vehicle stop study: Year end report.* San Diego, CA: San Diego Police Department.

Cox, S. M., Pease S. E., Miller D. S., & Tyson C. B. (2001). *Interim report of traffic stops Statistics for the state of Connecticut.* Rocky Hill, CT: Division of Criminal Justice.

Crank, J. P. (1994). Watchman and community: Myth and institutionalization in policing. *Law & Society Review, 28,* 325-351.

Crank, J. P., & Langworthy, R. (1992). An institutional perspective of policing. *Journal of Criminal Law and Criminology, 83,* 338-363.

Crank, J. P., & Langworthy, R. (1996). Fragmented centralization and the organization of the police. *Policing and Society, 6,* 213-229.

Criminal Justice Training Commission. (2001). *Report to the legislature on routine traffic stop data.* Seattle: Washington State Patrol and Criminal Justice Training Commission.

Decker, S. H. (1981). Citizen attitudes toward the police: A review of past findings and suggestions for future policy. *Journal of Police Science and Administration, 9,* 80-87.

Decker, S. H., Rosenfeld, R., & Rojek, J. (2002). *Annual report on 2001 Missouri traffic stops* [On-line]. Available: http://www.ago.state.mo.us/rpexecsummary2001.htm

DuMouchel, W., & Duncan, G. (1983). Using sample survey weights in multiple regression analyses of stratified samples. *Journal of the American Statistical Associations, 383,* 535-543.

Dunham, R. C., & Alpert, G. P. (1988). Neighborhood differences in attitudes toward policing: Evidence for a mixed-strategy model of policing in a multi-ethnic setting. *Journal of Criminal Law and Criminology, 79,* 504-523.

Eck, J., & Maguire, E. (2000). Have changes in policing reduced violent crime? An assessment of the evidence. In A. Blumstein & J. Wallman (Eds.) *The crime drop in America* (pp. 207-265). Cambridge, England: Cambridge University Press.

Engel, R. S. (2003). Explaining suspects' resistance and disrespect toward police. *Journal of Criminal Justice, 31:* 475-492.

Engel, R. S., & Calnon, J. M. (In press). Comparing benchmark methodologies for police-citizen contacts: Traffic stop data collection for the Pennsylvania State Police. *Police Quarterly.*

Engel, R. S., Calnon, J. M., & Bernard, T. J. (2002). Theory and racial profiling: Shortcomings and directions in future research. *Justice Quarterly, 19,* 249-273.

Engel, R. S., Calnon, J. M., Liu, L., & Johnson, R. (2004). *Project on Police-Citizen Contacts: Year 1, Final report.* Report submitted to the Pennsylvania State Police, Harrisburg.

Engel, R. S., & Silver, E. (2001). Policing mentally disordered suspects: A reexamination of the criminalization hypothesis. *Criminology, 39,* 225-252.

Fagan, J. (2002). Law, social science, and racial profiling. *Justice Research and Policy, 4,* 103-129.

Fagan, J., & Davies, G. (2000). Street stops and broken windows: *Terry,* race, and disorder in New York City. *Fordham Urban Law Journal, 28,* 457-504.

Farrell, A., McDevitt, J., & Ramirez, D. (2002). *Rhode Island Traffic Stop Statistics Act Quarterly report on data collection* [On-line]. Available: http://www.riag.state.ri.us/Reports%20and%20Publications/Default.htm

Fridell, L., Lunney, R., Diamond, D., & Kubu, B. (2001). *Racially biased policing: A principled response.* Washington, DC: Police Executive Research Form.

Fugita, S. S., Wexley, K. N., & Hillery, J. M. (1974). Black-white differences in nonverbal behavior in an interview setting. *Journal of Applies Social Psychology 4,* 343-350.

Garratt, G. A., Baxter, J. C., & Rozelle, R. M. (1981). Training university police in black-American nonverbal behaviors. *Journal of Social Psychology, 113*, 217-229.

General Accounting Office. (1999). *DEA operations in the 1990s*. Washington, DC: Author.

General Accounting Office. (2000). *U.S. Customs Service: Better targeting of airline passengers for personal searches could produce better results*. Washington, DC: Author.

Greenwald, H. P. (2001). *Final report: Police vehicle stops in Sacramento, California* [On-line]. Available: http://www.sacpolice.com/report.pdf

Harris, D. A. (1997). "Driving while black" and all other traffic offenses: The Supreme Court and pretextual traffic stops. *Journal of Criminal Law & Criminology, 87*, 544-582.

Harris, D. A. (1999a). *Driving while black: Racial profiling on our nation's highways* [On-line]. Available: http://www.aclu.org/profiling/report/index.html

Harris, D. A. (1999b). The stories, the statistics, and the law: Why "driving while black" matters. *Minnesota Law Review, 84*, 265-326.

Harris, D. A. (2002). *Profiles in injustice: Why racial profiling cannot work*. New York: New Press.

Helmick, D. O. (2000). *Public contact demographic data summary*. Sacramento, CA: California Highway Patrol.

Herszenhorn, D. M. (2000, October 22). Police and union chiefs meet to address racial profiling. *New York Times*, Sec.1, p. 41.

Hindelang, M. J., Hirschi, T., & Weiss, J. G. (1979). Correlates of delinquency: The illusion of discrepancy between self-report and official measures. *American Sociological Review, 44*, 995-1014.

Institute on Race and Poverty. (2001). *Saint Paul traffic stops data analysis*. Minneapolis: University of Minnesota.

Jacob, H. (1971). Black and white perceptions of justice in the city. *Law and Society Review, 6*, 69-89.

Kennedy, R. (1997). *Race, crime, and the law*. New York: Vintage Books.

Klinger, D. A. (1997). Negotiating order in patrol work: An ecological theory of police response to deviance. *Criminology, 35*, 277-306.

Knowles, J., Persico, N., & Todd, P. (2001). Racial bias in motor vehicle searches: Theory and evidence. *Journal of Political Economy, 109*, 203-229.

LaFree, G. 1995. Race and crime trends in the United States, 1946–1990. In D. F. Hawkins (Ed.), *Ethnicity, race, and crime: Perspectives across time and place* (pp. 169-193). Albany: State University of New York Press.

Lamberth, J. (1996). *A report to the ACLU*. New York: America Civil Liberties Union.

Langan, P. A., Greenfeld, L. A., Smith, S. K., Durose, M. R., & Levin, D. J. (2001). *Contacts between police and the public: Findings from the 1999 national survey*. Washington, DC: U.S. Department of Justice.

Lange, J. E., Blackman, K. O., & Johnson, M. B. (2001). *Speed Violation Survey of the New Jersey Turnpike: Final report*. Trenton, NJ: Office of the Attorney General.

Lansdowne, W. M. (2000). *Vehicle Stop Demographic Study*. San Jose, CA: San Jose Police Department.

Lasley, J. R. (1994). The impact of the Rodney King incident on citizen attitudes toward police. *Policing and Society, 3*, 245-255.

Lauritsen, J. & Sampson, R. J. (1998). Minorities, crime, and criminal justice. In M. Tonry (Ed.), *The handbook of crime and punishment* (pp. 58-84). New York: Oxford University Press.

Liao, T. F. (1994). *Interpreting probability models: Logit, probit, and other generalized linear models*. Thousand Oaks, CA: Sage.

Lock, E. D., Timberlake, J. M., & Rasinski, K. A. (2002) Battle fatigue: Is public support waning for "war"-centered drug control strategies? *Crime and Delinquency, 48*, 380-398.

Lockwood, D., Pottieger, A. E. & Inciardi, J. A. (1995). Crack use, crime by crack users, and ethnicity. In D. F. Hawkins (Ed.), *Ethnicity, race, and crime: Perspectives across time and place* (pp. 213-234). Albany: State University of New York Press.

Lohr, S. L. (1999). *Sampling design and analysis*. Pacific Grove, CA: Brooks/Cole.

88   INFLUENCE OF DRIVERS' CHARACTERISTICS

Lundman, R. J., & Kaufman, R. L. (2003). Driving While Black: Effects of race, ethnicity, and gender on citizen self-reports of traffic stops and police actions. *Criminology, 41,* 195-220.

Lynch, J. P. (2002). Using citizen surveys to produce information on the police: The present and potential uses of the national crime victimization survey. *Justice Research and Policy, 4,* 61-72.

MacDonald, H. (2001). The myth of racial profiling. *City Journal, 11,* 14-27.

MacDonald, H. (2002). The racial profiling myth debunked. *City Journal, 12,* 63-73.

Maguire, K., & Pastore, A. L. (2000). *Sourcebook of criminal justice statistics.* Washington, DC: U.S. Government Printing Office.

Mastrofski, S. D., Worden, R. E., & Snipes, J. B. (1995). Law enforcement in a time of community policing. *Criminology, 33,* 539-563.

Michigan State Police. (2001). *Traffic enforcement summary year end report* [Online]. Available: http://www.msp.state.mi.us/REPORTS/Trafsum_Year_End/trafsum_yr_end.htm

Miller, J. G. (1996). *Search and destroy: African American males in the criminal justice system.* New York: Cambridge University Press.

Moose, C. A. (2002). *Traffic stop data collection analysis: Third report.* Montgomery County, [no city provided] MD: Department of Police. Available: www.montgomerycountymd.gov/mc/services/police/media/report/ts0102.pdf

Morgan, J. G. (2002). *Vehicle stops and race: A study and report in response to Public Chapter 910 of 2000.* Nashville: State of Tennessee Comptroller of the Treasury.

National Conference of State Legislatures. (2001). *State laws address "racial profiling."* Washington, DC: Author.

National Institute of Justice. (2003). *2000 arrestee drug abuse monitoring: Annual report.* Washington, DC: Author.

Newport, F. (1999). Racial profiling seen as widespread, particularly among young black men. *The Gallup poll.* Available: www.gallup.com/poll/releases/pr991209.asp

Novak, K. J. (In press). Disparity and racial profiling in traffic enforcement. *Police Quarterly.*

Novak, K. J., Frank, J., Smith, B. W., & Engel, R. S. (2002). Revisiting the decision to arrest: Comparing beat and community officers. *Crime and Delinquency, 48,* 70-98.

Office of National Drug Control Policy. (2002). *National drug control strategy: FY 2003 Budget summary* [On-line]. Available: http://www.whitehousedrugpolicy.gov/publications/pdf/budget2002.pdf

Pennington, D. L. (1979). Black-white communication: An assessment of research. In M. E. Asante, E. Newmark, & C. A. Blake (Eds.), *Handbook of intercultural communication* (pp. 383-402). Beverly Hills, CA: Sage.

Police Foundation. (2001). *Racial profiling: The state of the law.* Washington, DC: Author.

Ramirez, D., McDevitt, J., & Farrell, A. (2000). *A resource guide on racial profiling data collection systems: Promising practices and lessons learned.* Washington, DC: U.S. Department of Justice.

Reilly, R. (2002, August 12). Color scheme. *Sports Illustrated, 97,* 160.

Riksheim, E., & Chermak. S. M. (1993). Causes of police behavior revisited. *Journal of Criminal Justice, 21,* 353-382.

Royal, D. (2000). *Racial and ethnic group comparisons, National surveys of drinking and driving attitudes and behavior—1993, 1995, and 1997* [On-line]. Available: http://www.nhtsa.dot.gov//people/injury/alcohol/ethnicity/racialethnic/summary.html.

Russell, K. K. (1999) "Driving while black": Corollary phenomena and collateral consequence. *Boston College Law Review, 40,* 717-731.

Scaglion, R., & Condon, R. G. (1980). The structure of black and white attitudes toward police. *Human Organization, 39,* 280-283.

Scalia, J. (2001). *Federal drug offenders, 1999, with trends 1984-1999.* Washington, DC: U.S. Department of Justice.

Scheingold, S. A. (1984). *The politics of law and order: Street crime and public policy.* New York: Longman.

Scheingold, S. A. (1991). *The politics of street crime: Criminal process and cultural obsession.* Philadelphia: Temple University Press.

Schmitt, E. L., Langan, P. A., & Durose, M. R. (2002). *Characteristics of drivers stopped by police.* Washington, DC: U.S. Department of Justice.

Skolnick, J. H., & Caplovitz, A. (2001). Guns, drugs, and profiling: Ways to target guns and minimize racial profiling. *Arizona Law Review, 43*, 413-437.

Smith, M. R., & Petrocelli, M. (2001). Racial profiling? A multivariate analysis of police traffic stop data. *Police Quarterly, 4*, 4-27.

Smith, W. R., Tomaskovic-Devey, D., Mason, M., Zingraff, M. T., Chambers, C., Warren, P., et al. (2000). *"Driving while black:" Establishing a baseline of driver behavior by measuring driving speed and demographic characteristics*. Unpublished manuscript, North Carolina State University, Raleigh.

Spitzer, E. (1999). *The New York City Police Department's "stop and frisk" practices: A report to the people of the state of New York from the Office of the Attorney General*. Albany: New York Attorney General's Office.

Spohn, C., & Holleran, D. (2000). The imprisonment penalty paid by young, unemployed black and Hispanic male offenders. *Criminology, 38*, 281-306.

Strom, K., Brien, P., & Smith, S. (2001). *Traffic stop data collection policies for state police 2001*. Washington, DC: U.S. Department of Justice.

Substance Abuse and Mental Health Services Administration. (2001). *Summary of findings from the 2000 National Household Survey on Drug Abuse*. Rockville, MD: Author.

Taylor, J. (2002). Reply to Professor Lynch. *Mankind Quarterly, 42*, 331-342.

Taylor, J., & Whitney, G. (1999). Crime and racial profiling by U.S. police: Is there an empirical basis? *Journal of Social, Political and Economic Studies, 24*, 485-510.

Taylor, T. J., Turner, K. B., Esbensen, F., & Winfree, L. T. (2001). Coppin' an attitude: Attitudinal differences among juveniles toward police. *Journal of Criminal Justice, 29*, 295-305.

Terrill, W., & Mastrofski, S. D. (2002). Situational and officer-based determinants of police coercion. *Justice Quarterly, 19*, 215-248.

Texas Department of Public Safety. (2001). *Traffic stop data report* [On-line]. Available: http://www.txdps.state.tx.us/director_staff/public_information/trafrep2001 totals.pdf

Thomas, D., & Carlson, R. (2001). *Preliminary summary report Denver Police Department contact card data: June 1, 2001 through August 31, 2001* [On-line]. Available: http://www.denvergov.com/admin/template3/forms/DPD%20BP%20 Preliminary%20Report.pdf

Tonry, M. (1995). *Malign neglect*. New York: Oxford University Press.

Trende, S. P. (2000). Why modest proposals offer the best solution for combating racial profiling. *Duke Law Journal, 50*, 331-380.

Tuch, S. A., & Weitzer, R. (1997). The polls—trends: Racial differences in attitudes toward the police. *Public Opinion Quarterly, 61*, 642-663.

U.S. Department of Justice. (2001). *Police-Public Contact Survey, 1999: United States*. Ann Arbor, MI: Inter-university Consortium for Political and Social Research.

Verniero, P., & Zoubek, P. H. (1999). *Interim report of the state police review team regarding allegations of racial profiling*. Trenton: New Jersey Attorney General's Office.

Voas, R. B., Tippetts, A. S., and Fisher, D. A. (2000). *Ethnicity and alcohol-related fatalities: 1990 to 1994* [On-line]. Available: http://www.nhtsa.dot.gov//people// injury//alcohol/ethnicity/ethnicity.html

Vrij, A., & Winkel, F. W. (1991). Cultural patterns in Dutch and Surinam nonverbal behavior: An analysis of simulated police/citizen encounters. *Journal of Nonverbal Behavior, 15*,169-183.

Vrij, A., & Winkel, F. W. (1992). Cross-cultural police-citizen interactions: The influence of race, beliefs, and nonverbal communication on impression formation. *Journal of Applied Social Psychology, 22*, 1546-1559.

Walker, S. (1999). *The police in America* (3rd ed.). Boston: McGraw-Hill College.

Walker, S. (2001). *Sense and nonsense about crime and drugs*. Belmont, CA: Wadsworth.

Webb, V. J., & Marshall, C. E. (1995). The relative importance of race and ethnicity on citizen attitudes toward the police. *American Journal of Police, 14*, 45-66.

Weitzer, R. (2000). Racialized policing: Residents' perceptions in three neighborhoods. *Law and Society Review, 34*, 129-155.

Weitzer, R., & Tuch, S. A. (1999). Race, class, and perceptions of discrimination by the police. *Crime and Delinquency, 45*, 494-507.

90   INFLUENCE OF DRIVERS' CHARACTERISTICS

Weitzer, R. & Tuch, S. A. (2002). Perceptions of racial profiling: Race, class, and
    personal experience. *Criminology, 40*, 435-456.
West, C. (1993). *Race matters*. Boston: Beacon Press.
Zingraff, M. T., Mason, H. M., Smith, W. R., Tomaskovic-Devey, D., Warren, P., Mc-
    Murray, H. L., et al. (2000). *Evaluating North Carolina State Highway Patrol
    data: Citations, warnings, and searches in 1998* [On-line]. Available: http://
    www.nccrimecontrol.org/shp/ncshpreport.htm

CASE CITED

Chimel v. California, 395 U.S. 752 (1969).

[18]

ATTRITION IN RAPE CASES

Developing a Profile and Identifying Relevant Factors

SUSAN J. LEA, URSULA LANVERS and STEVE SHAW*

This study sought to develop a profile of rape cases within a Constabulary in the South West of England, and identity factors associated with attrition. All cases of rape or attempted rape of a female or male over the age of 16 from 1996 to 2000 were identified. Quantitative and qualitative data on 379 cases was collected using the CIS and questionnaires sent to the relevant Chief Investigating Officer. The profile of attrition differed in several respects from previous research. Analysis of the extensive written comments provided by the officers afforded insight into the police perspective on rape. The findings are discussed with reference to future research and practice.

The attrition of rape cases within the criminal justice system has been of concern to academics and practitioners across a range of disciplines for at least the last 20 years. Crime statistics reveal an increase in the number of reported rapes (Adler 1991), yet Home Office research has shown that the number of convictions secured in rape cases has fallen from 24 per cent in 1985 in England and Wales to just under 9 per cent in 1997 (Home Office Research Study 196). Thus, despite radical reform within the administration of the Criminal Justice System (CJS) in respect of rape and sexual assault cases, attrition remains a serious problem (Gregory and Lees 1996; Temkin 1997).

Attrition refers to the process whereby cases drop out of the criminal justice system at one of a number of potential points of exit from that system. Such points of exit could be located within the police service, Crown Prosecution Service or in court. Although all crimes have some attrition due to a number of factors (such as the victim not wishing to press charges or insufficient evidence), the rate of attrition for cases of rape is above that of other crimes. In a study conducted by Roberts (1996) the attrition rate for sexual assault offences was compared with those of 15 other offences and found to be the highest. Indeed, Phillips and Brown (1998) report that this offence has the lowest conviction rate of all serious crime. In practice, therefore, 'the average citizen may suppose that when a serious crime occurs the victim reports it to the police, who verify the report, try to identify and arrest the perpetrator and turn the case over to a prosecutor . . . In practice, the system does not work that way. The justice system has been likened to a giant sieve, filtering out cases at every stage of the process' (Bryden and Lengnick 1997: 1208).

Four major points of attrition in dealing with rape cases have been identified (Lees and Gregory 1996). First, the police must decide whether to record the case as an offence

* Susan J. Lea and Ursula Lanvers, Department of Psychology, University of Plymouth, Steve Shaw, Department of Mathematics and Statistics, University of Plymouth. Correspondence should be addressed to: Dr Susan J. Lea, Department of Psychology, University of Plymouth, Drake Circus, Plymouth, PL4 8AA, Devon, UK; e-mail: slea@plymouth.ac.uk.

We are extremely grateful to the Chief Constable who provided his support for this project, to the staff of the Victim Centred Crime Unit who assisted us tirelessly with setting up the research and collecting the data, and the police officers who filled in the questionnaires so fully and frankly. This research was supported by a small internal grant from the University of Plymouth.

or to 'no-crime' it. Second, the police must decide whether to refer the case to the Crown Prosecution Service or to take no further action (NFA, police). Third, the Crown Prosecution Service must decide whether to prosecute the defendant or to take no further action (NFA, CPS). Fourth, the jury must decide whether to convict the defendant or not. Three issues arise in relation to this process. First, how many cases exit the system at each potential point of attrition? Second, what factors are associated with those cases? And third, what impact have changes to policy and practice within the criminal justice system had upon the process of attrition?

One of the earliest studies into attrition examined incidents recorded as rape or attempted rape[1] between 1972 and 1976 in six English counties involving solitary offenders (Wright 1984). Wright's findings revealed a pattern of attrition that has subsequently been found in a number of other studies (e.g. Chambers and Miller 1986; Grace et al. 1992; Harris and Grace 1999). This pattern involved a high percentage of cases being no-crimed (25 per cent) and a very small percentage of cases returning a verdict of guilty of rape (11 per cent) or guilty of attempted rape (6 per cent). The majority of the remaining cases dropped out of the criminal justice system along the way, while in a minority the defendant was found guilty of a lesser offence. The research led Wright to conclude, 'given the attrition of rape cases at every stage from the attack onwards, the rapist who receives a stiff fine must consider himself extremely unlucky. And the rapist who goes to gaol must believe that he was doubly unfortunate-the odds weigh heavily against that happening' (1984: 400).

Reforms introduced in the 1980s, particularly in respect of the police service, were anticipated to have an impact on the attrition of rape cases. The catalyst for these reforms was a television documentary aired in 1982 (Temkin 1987), which led to a public outcry regarding the treatment of rape victims. Consequently, the Sexual Offences Steering Committee was established in 1983. The recommendations of this committee and those of the Women's National Commission (1985) led to the introduction of changes of style and procedure in handling rape cases by the Metropolitan Police Service and other forces in England and Wales (i.e. Circular 25/1983, 69/1986; Smith 1989; Temkin 1999). However, relatively little research has systematically evaluated the effectiveness of these changes with regard to the attrition of rape cases (Temkin 1997) and the few studies that have been conducted do not indicate consistently positive results.

Grace et al. (1992) conducted research into the process of attrition during the second half of 1985, which aimed to provide a benchmark against which to assess changes post 1985. The sample was comprised of just over 300 rapes recorded by the police in all police forces in England and Wales, with the exception of the Metropolitan Police District, and included in the monthly returns to the Home Office. Grace et al., like Wright (1984), found a no-criming rate of 24 per cent, although cases no-crimed within a month were excluded from the study and therefore the true figure would be expected to be higher. Twelve per cent of cases were no-crimed on the basis of insufficient evidence. Grace et al. reported a conviction rate for rape or attempted rape of 25 per cent, somewhat higher than Wright's and possibly due to some of the changes to policy and practice. However, cases in which a conviction was secured were more likely to involve young single women attacked by a stranger and physically injured during the attack.

---

[1] In England and Wales rape was not actually defined by statute until 1976 in the Sexual Offences (Amendment) Act (Smith and Hogan 1996, in Tang 1998).

ATTRITION IN RAPE CASES

Around the same time, a further study was conducted by Smith (1989) that allowed greater consideration of the impact of changes to policy and procedure upon practice. The research examined attrition between reporting and recording during the three-year period of 1984–86 within two London Boroughs. About this time the Home Office had issued two important circulars to all Chief Officers of Police in England and Wales. Circular 25/1983 concerned the treatment of rape victims while circular 69/1986 informed police practice in respect of criming. The latter advised that rape cases could only be no-crimed where the complaint was retracted or the complainant admitted making a false allegation. Cases could not be no-crimed on the basis of insufficient evidence. During the period of Smith's study (1989) the number of rapes reported to the police decreased, while the number of cases crimed between 1984 and 1986 increased by 50 per cent. Despite this increase, which would be anticipated in line with circular 69/1986, Smith found that in 1986 'insufficient evidence was the major reason for no-criming' (p. 25). Hence, some police officers were not complying with the advice on no-criming and Smith concluded that no-criming practices in operation needed to be the subject of further research. Finally, and supporting Grace et al. (1992), Smith also found that different types of rape case were differentially subjected to the process of attrition. While the majority of rapes in Smith's sample were committed by men known to the victim, indoors and often in the victim's home, it was the classic stereotypical rape (violent rape by a stranger) that was more likely to be officially recorded as a crime.

The slight improvements in terms of no-criming suggested by Smith's (1989) research are unfortunately not borne out in subsequent studies. Lees and Gregory (1993) examined the crime report forms of cases of rape, attempted rape, indecent assault and attempted indecent assault over a two-year period (1988-90) at three London police stations. For cases of rape and attempted rape, the authors report an alarming no-criming rate of 43 per cent, one that is substantially higher than the rates reported by Grace et al. (1992) and Smith (1989). Unlike the latter Home Office studies, Lees and Gregory's (1993) figure includes cases no-crimed in the first month and therefore offers a more realistic assessment of this point of attrition. However, in common with the Home Office studies, Lees and Gregory found that contrary to the directives of the Home Office circular (69/1986), many cases were no-crimed for reasons other than the retraction of the complaint by the victim or an admission of false allegation. Interviews with a number of police officers led the authors to suggest that 'old attitudes die hard' (e.g. scepticism about why women report rape) and that this 'helps to explain why the service has been so slow to respond to the new policy guidelines on "no-criming"' (p. 6).

Apart from the problems with no-criming, Lees and Gregory (1993) report a conviction rate for cases of rape and attempted rape of approximately only 10 per cent. Between not recording the offence as a crime and conviction, a number of other significant points of attrition were identified. The reclassification of offences accounted for just under 10 per cent of cases recorded as crimes. In the majority of cases reclassification resulted in the original offence being downgraded and in some instances the sexual classification being entirely removed. Just over 20 per cent of cases were subject to a decision to take no further action by the Crown Prosecution Service. Although Lees and Gregory report that just over half of the cases with which the CPS did proceed resulted in a conviction, they suggest that this figure is misleading in terms of the number of offenders actually convicted. This is because in some cases suspects were sentenced for a number of offences simultaneously. Moreover, convictions were often for a lesser charge.

Concerns about rape (Smith 1989) and subsequent reforms, therefore, appear not to have had the anticipated impact. Indeed, a recent Home Office study (Harris and Grace 1999) suggests that the passage of time has done little to improve attrition rates. The research investigated nearly 500 cases of reported rape in 1996 and followed their progress through the criminal justice system. With respect to attrition, the significant points of drop out were no-criming (25 per cent of cases) and the police taking no further action (31 per cent of cases). Harris and Grace note (1999) that any reduction in no-criming has been offset by an increase in NFA-ing. Of those cases that were crimed only 9 per cent led to a conviction, a much lower rate than was found in the previous Home Office report but in line with the figure recorded in the national statistics. Despite an increase in the reporting of acquaintance and intimate rapes, cases involving acquaintances were most likely to be no-crimed by the police while those involving intimates were most likely to be NFA-ed or discontinued by the CPS. In line with previous research, in three-quarters of cases reaching court, the defendant pleaded guilty to lesser charges and was convicted of those charges only. Factors that were pertinent to the process of attrition were the age of the victim, the relationship between the complainant and the suspect and the degree of violence used.

Despite the consistently depressing statistics with respect to rape cases and the criminal justice system, some improvements in women's experiences of reporting rape have been documented. Hence the greater numbers of women reporting rape have indicated increased satisfaction with the service they have received, in particular from the police. For example, Adler (1991) assessed how women who had reported rape or a serious sexual offence to the Metropolitan Police felt about the treatment they had received. The majority of women spoke favourably of their experience and many found the police to be caring and sympathetic. The main criticism the women had was to do with lack of information. Respondents felt that they were not kept adequately informed of the progress of their case or of the rationale behind the way things were done, were not given up to date information and were not informed of support organizations. Despite these criticisms, which of course warrant attention, Adler's (1991) research indicates that some things have improved for women who report rape cases. Unfortunately improvements remain somewhat confined to the realms of '*police* policy and procedure, rather than permeating through to the courts and members of the judiciary who sometimes appear to be operating from a position of considerable ignorance and social isolation' (Mezey 1997: 241, author's emphasis). Indeed, research involving the observation of rape trials at the Old Bailey has led to stern criticism of the current adversarial system of justice (Lees 1993).

To date then, a handful of studies have established a sustained and high rate of attrition for rape cases and have found some evidence for a number of factors being associated with that attrition. Recently, a change in the pattern of attrition has been observed in response to reforms within the criminal justice system; that is, a decrease in no-criming as a consequence of key Home Office Circulars in the 1980s. However, Harris and Grace's (1999) study suggests that any gains made in respect of no-criming appear to have been lost later in the process in terms of NFA-ing. Moreover, while improvements may be witnessed within the police service, similar reforms have not occurred within other key areas of the criminal justice system.

One of the problems in interpreting existing research is that it is limited and that the few studies that have been conducted are characterized by a number of biases. First, the

ATTRITION IN RAPE CASES

research is dominated by London samples. Even where data have been gathered on other areas in the UK using Home Office information, interviews with victims and professionals have been confined to this particular region. It is, therefore, important to redress this imbalance and to establish whether similar patterns of attrition are evident in other areas of the United Kingdom. Second, the plight of male rape victims has been almost totally ignored (Rumney 2001). Moreover, the taboos and stigma surrounding male rape are enormous (Kramer 1998) suggesting that male rape victims will have no better time of it within the criminal justice system than female victims. Again, this is an imbalance that needs to be redressed. Third, while a number of studies were conducted during the 1980s, very little has been done in the 1990s. More research is needed to establish the current situation especially in the light of important changes within the realms of sexual offending (e.g. legislation pertaining to sex offenders) and the decrease in conviction rates. The way rape cases move through both the police and the legal system continues to be a matter of grave concern (Phillips et al. 1998) and further research is needed to both elucidate the process of attrition (Temkin 1997) and to point the way to improving practice.

The aim of this research was to examine the attrition of cases of rape or attempted rape as they progress through the criminal justice system outside of the London area and over a full five-year period. The study aimed specifically to: develop a profile of attrition which could be compared to the profiles found in previous research, and to explore further the factors associated with the attrition of cases at each point of exit within the criminal justice system.

Method

Case identification

All cases of rape or attempted rape upon a person of either gender reported to a Constabulary in the South West of England within the five-year period from 1 January 1996 to 31 December 2000 formed the data for this investigation. This period was selected as it was hoped to generate a large corpus of recent cases. Cases were identified using the Forces' Central Intelligence System (CIS) upon which both the first and second researchers were trained. In terms of this data system, all cases within the following categories were selected: female rape, female attempted rape, male rape, and male attempted rape. Cases within the categories rape of female under 16 years of age, attempted rape of female under 16 years of age, rape of male under 16 years of age and attempted rape of male under 16 years of age were excluded from this study for the following reasons. First, this study was concerned with adult rape, and second the procedures for dealing with cases where the victim is below 16 years of age differ markedly from those used in cases where the victim is 16 or older.

A total of 471 cases were identified through the CIS database as occurring within the 5-year period specified. These comprised 410 female rape cases, 19 male rape cases, 40 attempted female rape cases and two attempted male rape cases.

Data collection

It was originally hoped that once cases had been identified using the CIS database, the information that was required for this study could also be acquired from the database itself. However, this proved not to be the case. Consequently, senior officers in the

Constabulary recommended that the data be collected via a questionnaire, which was sent to the senior investigating officer who had dealt with each identified case. It was felt that this method would provide the most accurate data, as cases of rape and attempted rape are very serious crimes and most officers would be able to recall and readily look up the information required. In addition, officers were able to provide a more comprehensive picture of each case than would have been achieved through accessing the database, which provides minimal information that has not always been updated.

Details associated with each identified case were transcribed off the CIS computer screen using a pro-forma. Such details included the crime reference number and the name and number of the reporting and investigating officers. This information was passed to an Inspector within the Constabulary who checked the current whereabouts of each investigating officer in order to forward the questionnaire.

The questionnaire was drawn up in consultation with members of the Constabulary and was informed by and extended questionnaires used in previous studies of a similar nature (e.g. Grace et al. 1992; Harris and Grace 1999). Headed 'Data Collection Template', the questionnaire asked for the provision of information about the alleged crime, the victim, and the alleged offender using closed ended questions. Each questionnaire was clearly marked with the name and number of the reporting officer, the investigating officer and the crime number of the case to which the questionnaire was referring. A large space for additional comments or information about the case was provided at the end of the questionnaire. A formal letter written on Constabulary letterhead by the head of a specialist unit requested that the recipient complete and return the questionnaire within two weeks. After four weeks, a further letter was sent out reminding officers who had failed to return the questionnaire that they should do as a matter of urgency.

Three hundred and seventy-nine questionnaires were finally returned, a response rate of 80 per cent. The majority of questionnaires were extremely comprehensively filled in with many officers (80 per cent of returns) taking the opportunity to write comments and provide further information. The quantitative data from the questionnaires was put into a spreadsheet for analysis. Univariate statistical analyses included chi-squared (X^2) tests and Spearman's correlation coefficients to assess associations for nominal and ordinal data, respectively. Logistic regression was used to investigate the relationship between a range of variables, relating to the victim and the case, on the current status of the case and the reasons for the current status. The qualitative data (the police officers' comments) was transcribed and analysed using thematic content analysis in order to elucidate and enrich the quantitative data.

Findings

Three hundred and seventy-nine cases of rape and attempted rape reported within the Constabulary, during the five-year period from 1 January 1996 to 31 December 2000 form the basis of the findings. A profile of the cases is provided and, where applicable, statistical analyses have been performed. The analysis thereby aims to establish a recent and comprehensive picture of cases of rape and attempted rape in the South West of England and to assess the influence of various factors upon the attrition of rape cases as they progress through the criminal justice system.

ATTRITION IN RAPE CASES

A five-year profile of rape in the South West of England

Of the 379 cases, the overwhelming majority (84.7 per cent) constituted a reported rape of a female over the age of 16 years. Attempted rape of a female over the age of 16 accounted for 10 per cent of the cases, rape of a male over the age of 16 comprised just under 5 per cent and attempted rape of a male over the age of 16 comprised a mere 0.5 per cent (only two cases in the five-year period). In 14 per cent of cases, additional charges were involved although the main offence in each case remained rape or attempted rape. In two cases the charge was buggery and in 11 cases the charge was buggery and rape. A third of cases were linked to other crimes (e.g. GBH, threats of violence, threat to kill).

The majority of victims were female (95 per cent). Only 5 per cent of cases involved a male victim. Most victims were younger, with 78 per cent being less than 35 years of age. However 16 per cent of rapes or attempted rapes were perpetrated against a person of 35–50 years of age and 6 per cent were perpetrated against a person over 50. Almost all of the victims were 'white', quite possibly because the population of the South West of England is predominantly 'white'. Two-thirds (66 per cent) of the victims were single at the time of the rape or attempted rape, 23 per cent were married or cohabiting, and 11 per cent were divorced or separated. One victim was a widow. Victims represented a range of occupations. Approximately 18 per cent were professionals or skilled workers, 11 per cent were semi-skilled and 4 per cent were unskilled. Fourteen per cent were housewives and/or mothers and 19 per cent were students or still at school. Thirty-three per cent had no current occupation and were unemployed, dependent or claiming some form of benefit/allowance.

Offenders ranged in age from under 20 (9 per cent) to over 50 (8 per cent). The majority of offenders were aged between 26 and 35 (33 per cent), with 22 per cent being between 20 and 25 years of age and 29 per cent being between 36 and 50 years of age. Somewhat unexpectedly, a significant positive correlation was found between the age of the victim and the age of the offender (Spearman's rho = .364, p < .01, n = 320). Thus, as the age of the victim increased, so too did the age of the offender. The vast majority of offenders were white, again mirroring the population distribution in the South West of England. In terms of marital status, 58 per cent of offenders were single, 31 per cent were married or cohabiting, and 11 per cent were divorced or separated. One offender was a widower. As with the victims, offenders represented a range of occupations. Just over a quarter were professionals or skilled workers (26 per cent), 20 per cent were semi-skilled and 4 per cent were unskilled. Four per cent of offenders were students while 41 per cent had no current occupation and were unemployed, dependent or claiming some form of benefit/allowance.

Fifty per cent of all cases were reported equally to police stations in urban and rural areas. Urban areas were loosely defined as cities and large towns while rural areas were defined as small towns and villages.[2] Most rapes or attempted rapes (whether intimate, acquaintance or stranger rapes) were committed at the weekend, with Saturday being the most frequently reported day. An interesting profile emerged (see Figure 1) revealing a stepped progression whereby the frequency of rape is lowest on Mondays, increasing each day through to being highest on Saturday. Sunday was the second most

---

[2] Defining urban and rural populations is problematic and, therefore, this figure should be interpreted with caution.

LEA ET AL.

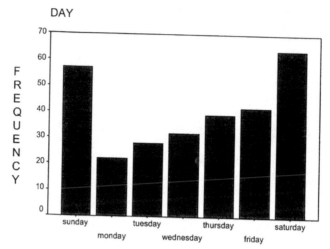

FIG. 1   Frequency of reported rapes perpetrated by day of the week on which committed

frequently reported day for the alleged crime to have been committed. The time of day at which such crimes were committed was most frequently between midnight and 6 am but also commonly between 6 pm and midnight. These two time periods accounted for 76 per cent of cases. Hence, almost a quarter of cases of rape and attempted rape took place during the day. In terms of the length of time over which the crime was reported to have taken place, 90 per cent of cases lasted up to one day, with roughly a quarter of cases each lasting less than 30 minutes, up to two hours, between two and 12 hours and between 12 and 24 hours. The remaining 10 per cent of cases involved lengthy periods of abuse, 3 per cent of which stretched over many years.

Sixty-six per cent of cases were reported within a day of the alleged crime being perpetrated. Thirteen per cent were reported within two weeks, with the remaining 21 per cent being reported some time after the crime. In 6 per cent of cases, the crime was reported more than six months after the crime, sometimes many years later. A significant, though small correlation was found between the relationship between victim and perpetrator and time elapsed between the offence and its reporting (Spearman's rho = −.237, p < .01, n = 365): the closer the relationship between the victim and the perpetrator, the longer the time taken to report the crime. Victims of stranger and acquaintance rapes, therefore, were more likely to report the crime within one to two days of its occurrence, while victims of rape by a male relative or partner sometimes did not report the case for years.

A quarter of cases in this sample involved intimate rapes, nearly one half could be described as acquaintance rapes and a further quarter involved stranger rapes. Hence 24 per cent of cases involved allegations against a current husband, partner or boyfriend (14 per cent) or an estranged husband, partner or boyfriend (10 per cent). A further 6 per cent of cases involved an accused who was a male relative, such as an uncle. Forty-four per cent of cases revealed that the perpetrator was an acquaintance or friend (30 per cent and 14 per cent respectively), while 26 per cent of cases involved a stranger.

ATTRITION IN RAPE CASES

The majority of rapes or attempted rapes (62 per cent) took place within the home of either the complainant (30 per cent) or the accused (17 per cent) or the home in which they lived together (15 per cent). Approximately 4 per cent of cases took place in either the complainant or the accused's car (most frequently that of the accused). Six per cent of rapes or attempted rapes took place in an indoor private place such as a friend's house while 28 per cent occurred in a public place (indoors such as nightclub: 7 per cent; outdoors such as in an alleyway: 20 per cent). In nine cases a second or further rapes took place in other locations. A significant association ($X^2 = 175.9$, DF = 24, $p < 0.01$) was found between location of rape and the relationship between the victim and the perpetrator. Not surprisingly, more intimate and male relation rapes took place in the home of the victim, the suspect or the home they both occupied (90 per cent and 83 per cent respectively) than was the case with either acquaintance or stranger rapes (65 per cent and 26 per cent respectively). A further significant relationship ($X^2 = 54.33$, DF = 16, $p < 0.01$) was found between the age of the victim and the initial place of contact. Younger victims tended to have encountered the perpetrator for the first time in a public place (such as a club, disco or hotel) than older victims who were more likely to encounter the perpetrator in a private place (their own home or someone else's).

In 37 per cent of cases, the victim reported having no prior contact with the accused. Nineteen per cent reported having full sexual intercourse with the accused prior to the alleged rape or attempted rape. Twenty-four per cent of victims had some physical contact with the accused, in most cases kissing the accused or allowing an arm to be put around him or her. In 10 per cent of cases the victim accepted a lift home from the accused (3 per cent) or accepted an invitation to his house (7 per cent). The victim went for a walk with the accused in 8 per cent of cases and in a further 2 per cent they danced with the accused or allowed him to buy him/her a drink. Not surprisingly, a significant association was found between the relationship between the victim and the perpetrator and degree of contact between them ($X^2 = 127.4$, DF = 24, $p < 0.01$). Thus, the closer the relationship between the victim and perpetrator, the closer the degree of contact prior to the rape.

Most cases (98 per cent) of rape or attempted rape involved a single victim and a single offender (95 per cent). Usually, a single act of sexual violence was perpetrated or attempted. In the majority of cases this act comprised vaginal intercourse. Anal intercourse was involved in 5 per cent of cases, while oral intercourse on or by the offender was involved in 1 per cent of cases. In a minority of cases (4 per cent) other acts of sexual violence such as digital penetration or penetration of the victim with an object were committed, sometimes in conjunction with the rape or attempted rape of the victim.

In the majority of cases (71 per cent) the victim reported no threats of additional violence (that is, beyond the obviously violent act of rape or attempted rape). In 13 per cent of cases, vague threats were made. In the remaining 16 per cent of cases, the perpetrator verbally threatened to kill the victim, threatened manual violence, threatened to use a weapon or used some combination of these threats. With respect to the actual use of violence in these cases, 46 per cent were characterized by no violence being exerted. However, in 38 per cent of cases the victim was treated roughly. Mirroring the findings in respect of threats of violence, in the remaining 16 per cent of cases a range of violent measures were used. These involved beating, punching and kicking the victim, using a weapon, using an object to penetrate the victim or some combination of these

LEA ET AL.

violent acts. A significant positive correlation was found between threat of violence and actual use of violence (Spearman's rho = .266, p < 0.01, n = 316). Thus, in cases where violence was threatened, it was more likely to be used. Since the use of further violence was relatively low, in the majority of cases (64 per cent) the victim did not sustain additional injuries (beyond those sustained through the rape or attempted rape). In the remaining 36 per cent of cases, slight injuries were sustained in 33 per cent, moderate injuries were sustained in 1 per cent, and severe injuries in 2 per cent. Not surprisingly, there was a significant positive correlation between the amount of violence used and the victim's sustaining additional injuries (Spearman's rho = .454, p < 0.01, n = 317).

The current status of the 379 crimes of rape or attempted rape is illustrated in Figure 2 below. As can be seen, the largest category of cases was comprised of those that were NFA-ed. Taken together, 61 per cent of cases were NFA-ed by the police (detected NFA: 26 per cent; undetected NFA: 7 per cent) or the CPS (14 per cent). In 14 per cent of cases it was unclear whether the police or the CPS had NFA-ed the case, and whether it was detected or not, despite further work by police personnel. Of the remaining 39 per cent of cases 10 per cent were pending 11 per cent were no-crimed, in 7 per cent the victim refused to assist with the inquiry or retracted the allegation, and 11 per cent resulted in a conviction of some kind.

With respect to conviction, however, only 5 per cent (19 cases) of the 379 cases resulted in a conviction of rape, none of which involved the rape of a male. In 1 per cent of cases the accused was cautioned while in a further 5 per cent of cases (including two cases where the victim was male), the accused was convicted of a lesser crime. These crimes incorporated a sexual component in 2.9 per cent of cases, were non-sexual in nature in 1.6 per cent of cases and were for attempted rape in 0.5 per cent of cases. The rationale behind this plea-bargaining, according to police officers, was that in some cases the defendant was willing to plead guilty to a lesser offence. In the remaining cases, it was

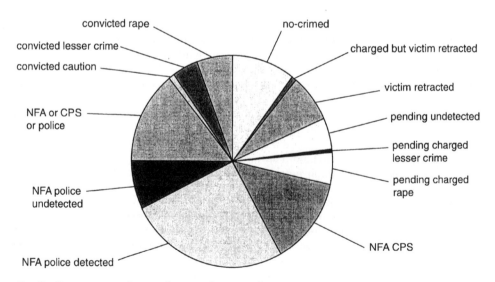

FIG. 2   Current status of cases of rape and attempted rape

claimed that the CPS charged the defendant with a lesser crime in order to spare the victim the ordeal of court.

Reasons for the current status of the crime (i.e. that it was no-crimed, NFA-ed etc.) were provided for 191 cases. The main reason for crimes not progressing through the criminal justice system was lack of evidence, this reason constituting 39 per cent of cases where reasons were proffered. In most cases this led to the decision to NFA the case; however, some cases were no-crimed on the basis of insufficient evidence, in contravention of the recommendations of Circular 69/1986. For example, one officer wrote 'there was no evidence, therefore the case was no-crimed'. In many cases where insufficient evidence led to the attrition of the case, the police felt that a rape had been committed. The following statement made by another officer is exemplary: 'although the crime was NFA-ed, I have strong suspicions that this was rape by a family friend.'

A significant proportion of the 191 cases (38 per cent) dropped out of the criminal justice system as a consequence of the victim retracting her allegation or refusing to assist with the case. Alarmingly in 50 per cent of these cases police officers suspected that the victim had been intimidated and that her action was a consequence of this intimidation. These cases invariably involved intimate rapes. In many cases police officers stated that the reason for the retraction or refusal to assist was that the victim was too afraid to continue due to fear of further violence. This was often the case in situations where the police were aware of or suspected a history of abuse. In other cases the victim was said to have retracted or refused to cooperate because she had been reunited with the accused or because she wanted to 'spare him the ordeal of court'. Pressure from the victim's family not to proceed with the case also accounted for a proportion of retractions or refusals to assist. With respect to these cases, many police officers wrote poignant comments on the questionnaires which demonstrated a great deal of understanding of the pressures victims of intimate rapes endure, and expressed their frustration at not being able to do more in such cases.

Police officers quite often claimed that a false allegation of rape had been made. Indeed, this constituted the main reason for cases being no-crimed (although, as noted, there was evidence that some cases were no-crimed on the basis of insufficient evidence). In just under 10 per cent of cases the police claimed that a false allegation had been made and in a further 10 per cent of cases the police claimed that the victim had admitted to making a false allegation or to the 'rape' being consensual. Despite this, the victim was charged with wasting police time in very few cases. Thus, in 20 per cent of cases where a reason was offered for the current status of the crime, that reason was that the allegation was false. Police officers claimed that such allegations were made either when the complainant was an 'an unstable female' or when the complaint was 'malicious'. The grounds for deeming a complainant as 'unstable' seemed entirely dependent upon the investigating officer's personal judgment. Malicious complaints were suspected on a number of grounds. These included that the complainant's partner had called off their engagement, that the complainant 'wanted to force her lover to marry her', or that the complainant suspected her partner of having sex with someone else or that she herself had had sex with someone else. While many officers did seem to be able to empathize with rape victims, there was also evidence of officers who still held traditional views about rape and rape victims. These officers appeared to be less sympathetic to rape victims and more likely to doubt their reporting of rape. Indeed, they still seemed to believe that many women cry rape in order to seek attention.

In 3 per cent of cases the case did not progress on the grounds that the victim was deemed inconsistent. It appeared that this judgment was more likely to be made in cases where the victim was 'vulnerable'. Thus, in cases where the alleged rape or attempted rape involved a victim with learning disabilities, psychiatric problems or physical disabilities, the attrition rate appeared very high. A number of these cases were no-crimed as police felt that the allegation was false or that consensual sex had probably taken place. Problems in communicating with the victim and the possibility that the victim would not be a credible witness led to the remainder being NFA-ed.

Inconsistency on the part of the victim was also an issue where alcohol and/or drugs were involved, particularly in respect of the victim. If the victim could not be clear about what happened due to substance effects, the chances of the case getting to court, as rape, were very small. In a couple of cases of 'date' rape police officers suspected that the drug Rohypnol had been used and were convinced that the incident had taken place. However, due to lack of evidence these cases were NFA-ed.

Apart from illuminating some of the patterns found in the data, in particular in respect of the reasons for the attrition of rape cases, the comments offered by police officers on the questionnaires raised a number of other issues with respect to the processing of rape cases. First, many officers took the opportunity to express their own frustration and disillusionment with the system. This revolved around the relationship between the CPS and the police being unsatisfactory, in terms of information and communication, and the attitudes and perceptions of barristers and judges in terms of rape victims specifically and the crime of rape generally. Thus officers complained that they were uncertain as to what the CPS needed in order to proceed with a rape case. Consequently, some officers felt very aggrieved at having worked long hours on cases in which they were convinced that the accused was guilty, only to have the case NFA-ed by the CPS. With respect to the conduct of legal professionals, officers felt that the views held by some professionals had influenced the outcome of cases. For example, in one case, the officer felt that the barrister did not use the victim's injuries sufficiently to incriminate the offender. As a consequence the court returned a non-guilty verdict. The police officer involved was convinced that the defendant was guilty and felt very upset that he had walked free. In another case, an angry police officer felt that the prosecution barrister handled the case very badly, as he was unable to relate to the victim who was shy, frightened, poorly educated and sexually naive. Again, the defendant was found not guilty.

Toward an Understanding of Attrition

In an attempt to understand further the attrition of rape cases as they progress through the criminal justice system, factors that may affect the current status of cases of rape or attempted rape were examined, individually and together. Chi-squared tests of association were performed between the current status of the case and a range of variables relating to the victim, the perpetrator and to features of the case itself. Only two significant associations were found. If pending cases were excluded from the analysis, a significant association was found between current status and the degree of contact between the victim and the perpetrator ($X^2 = 36.58$, DF = 24, $p < 0.05$). Although this association was difficult to unravel, the most interesting aspect was that if the victim and the perpetrator had engaged in sexual intercourse previously, retraction was more likely than expected. Further, a significant association was found between current status and the relationship between the victim and the perpetrator, if the relationship was defined in bivariate terms; that is, as close or known as opposed to unknown. If the relationship between victim and perpetrator was close or they knew one another, the case was more likely than would be expected to be NFA-ed by the police, or to secure a conviction. Cases where the victim did not know the perpetrator were more likely than expected to fall into the category of cases where it could not be distinguished whether the police or CPS had NFA-ed the case.

Chi-squared tests of association were similarly performed between the variable 'reasons for current status of the case' and the range of variables relating to the victim, the perpetrator and to features of the case itself. Only one variable, the degree of initial contact between the victim and the perpetrator, was significantly associated ($X^2 = 33.05$, $DF = 16$, $p < 0.01$) with reasons for current status. The reason 'lack of evidence' was more likely if initial contact between victim and perpetrator occurred within a private place and the reason 'false allegation' was more likely if the victim had been willingly within the home of the perpetrator.

The chi-squared tests look at each possible explanatory variable independently ignoring any associations between them. Hence logistic regression was used to investigate simultaneously the effect of the above range of variables on the current status of the case and the reasons for the current status. The relationship between the victim and the perpetrator was the only variable significantly associated with the current status of the case ($p = 0.046$), although the way in which relationship was associated was not particularly clear. The significant predictors of the reasons for the current status are place of initial contact ($p < 0.01$) and location of the offence ($p = 0.01$) together with current status itself ($p < 0.01$).

Discussion

This research set out to examine the attrition of rape cases as they progress through the criminal justice system over a five-year period within a Constabulary in the South West of England. The aim of the research was to develop a profile of attrition and to identify factors that may be associated with this process. With respect to the profile, a number of trends or patterns could be identified in the data. However, as the vast majority of reported rapes or attempted rapes were perpetrated by men against women, the profile is unfortunately largely restricted to this type of rape.

The findings of this study suggest that the attrition of rape cases is still extremely high, with just under 10 per cent leading to some sort of conviction and only 5 per cent resulting in a conviction for rape. These figures support those of Lees and Gregory (1993) and Harris and Grace (1999) whose studies of attrition revealed conviction rates of 10 per cent and 9 per cent respectively. Similar to Harris and Grace's findings, this study also found that the pattern of attrition has changed from that found in previous research. A decrease in no-criming has been offset by an increase in NFA-ing. However, the rate of no-criming was considerably lower in this study (10 per cent) than that in Harris's which reported a rate of around 25 per cent, very similar to earlier studies (e.g. Grace et al. 1992). This suggests that in the Constabulary in which this research took place at least, the Home Office guidelines on no-criming may finally be having an impact.

A further difference between the findings of this study and those of previous research is the rate of NFA-ing cases. While Harris and Grace (1999) also report a decrease in no-criming and an increase in NFA-ing, the differences in rates in this study are considerably greater than those of Harris and Grace. Thus while Harris and Grace reports that a total of 39 per cent of cases were NFA-ed, 31 per cent by the police and 8 per cent by the CPS, this study found that 61 per cent of cases were NFA-ed, 33 per cent by the police 14 per cent by the police and 14 per cent by the CPS or police. It would seem that the trend picked up in Harris and Grace's study has, therefore, become more exaggerated in recent years.

The high rate of NFA-ing seems to be driven by a number of factors. In the first instance, many cases are NFA-ed due to lack of evidence. In cases of rape, attaining sufficient evidence is notoriously difficult due to the very nature of the crime. Indeed, the majority of rape cases NFA-ed by the police were detected. In many of these the chief investigating officer knew who had committed the crime but was unable to pursue the case against the perpetrator, often due to insufficient evidence-particularly in cases where the victim and perpetrator were known to one another. Despite these difficulties, many officers felt that there was room for improvement. One of the issues they raised in respect of evidence was what they perceived to be an inadequate relationship between the police force and the Crown Prosecution Service. Hence police officers felt that what the Crown Prosecution Service required in terms of evidence was not made explicit enough. On the whole, officers desired a closer working relationship with the CPS, with an increased flow of information and more open channels of communication.

A second factor that accounted for a considerable number of cases being NFA-ed involved intimidation of the victim, particularly where the victim and perpetrator were currently or had in the past been involved in an intimate relationship with one another. In many instances the police officers involved in these cases expressed frustration and sadness at not being able to do more for the victim. This facet of rape highlights the need to examine this crime within a theoretical framework that takes account of social, political and economic factors. Many of the victims in this study appeared to be trapped within an abusive relationship due to their economic dependence upon their partner, especially when children were involved. For these women, pursuing the conviction of their partner through the courts is perceived not to be an option. For this reason, rape needs to be understood as more than an act of violence perpetrated against an individual woman. Rather, it needs to be seen as part of a set of violences that maintain abused women within particular relations of power. As Tang (1998: 266) has noted the law tends to frame issues in terms of individual pathology and fails to attend to 'the institutions and practices that are at the root of women's subordination'.

Echoing previous research (e.g. Lees and Gregory 1993), concern for the victim and the consequences of proceeding with the case for her, given the low probability of achieving a conviction, constituted the third factor involved in cases being NFA-ed, or reduced to a lesser crime. Protecting the victim in this way is undoubtedly a humane response, given the circumstances. However, it does raise questions about the criminal justice system. Where it appears that a rape has been committed and there is a strong case to answer, it should not be necessary to protect the victim by NFA-ing the case or by plea-bargaining if all components of the criminal justice system are functioning optimally. However, while reforms in respect of dealing with rape cases have been introduced within the police force, similar levels of reform do not appear to have been implemented within the CPS and the courts (cf. Lees 1993; Mezey 1997; Hinchcliffe 2000). Furthermore, while some studies have been conducted which focus on the treatment of rape cases within the police force, very few have examined this within the CPS and the courts and those that have, have not revealed overwhelmingly positive findings. In this study, a number of police officers were of the opinion that barristers and judges were informed by conservative and traditional attitudes toward rape victims that made them less than sympathetic to their cause. The perception that these attitudes exist and that they impact upon the victim partly accounts for the need to protect the victim. Further research is needed into this much-neglected area of rape.

Finally, despite the decrease in the rate of no-criming, there was still evidence that a significant minority of police officers were no-criming for reasons other than those recommended by Circular 69/1986. Furthermore, there were officers who deemed allegations of rape to be false on less than solid grounds, most frequently their personal judgment that the victim was 'unstable'. In the majority of these cases, no action was taken against the victim for wasting police time. Although there are undoubtedly cases where a false allegation might be made, there is no evidence to suggest that the crime of rape has a higher rate of false allegations than any other crime. This study, like others before it (e.g. Lees and Gregory 1993), therefore suggests that within the police force there are still officers, albeit now probably a minority, for whom stereotyped attitudes about women who report rape remain in tact and that further training in dealing with rape cases is indicated.

The findings of this study therefore mirror previous findings in revealing a high rate of attrition for rape, but suggest that the pattern of attrition has changed in recent years in line with reforms introduced, particularly within the police force. In terms of the factors associated with the attrition of cases, this research found that only the relationship between the victim and the perpetrator was related to attrition, as indicated by the current status of the case. However, this finding must be interpreted with caution as despite the relatively large sample size and the application of an appropriate statistical test, closer inspection of the results did not reveal a coherent pattern. Thus while previous research (e.g. Grace et al. 1992) has suggested that rapes of single young women by a stranger and involving physical injury were the most likely to secure a conviction, this pattern did not emerge clearly in this research. Indeed, a higher than expected rate of conviction was achieved for rapes involving a partner or male relative. Consequently, it would appear that while the relationship between the victim and the perpetrator is implicated in attrition, further research is needed in order to clarify precisely how it is so implicated.

While attempts to identify factors involved in attrition using advanced statistical techniques were not particularly successful, this study has still been able to identify trends in the data that illuminate the attrition process. Specifically, some groups remain under-represented in and possibly disadvantaged by current practice within the criminal justice system. The first of these is male rape victims. In this study so few rapes were reported by men that it was impossible to draw any conclusions about male rape, except to confirm that there is almost undoubtedly a serious under-reporting of this crime (cf. Rumney 2001) and to argue that the issue of male rape warrants attention. As Mezey (1997) has pointed out in a review of Lees' (1996) recent book, many researchers investigating rape, including Lees herself, have little to say on the subject of male rape. Research methods based on survey data, such as used in this study and others before it, are probably inadequate for exploring the issue of male rape due to the very small sample sizes which reflect the differences in reporting behaviour for male and female victims (Pino and Meier 1999). Future research should probably adopt a qualitative approach or at least a combination of qualitative and quantitative approaches if much needed progress is to be made in this sphere.

The second group, which is particularly disadvantaged by the criminal justice system, is comprised of victims who are considered to be vulnerable in some way. Victims with learning disabilities or psychiatric problems continue to be over-represented in terms of cases that drop out of the system. While it undoubtedly difficult to deal with the complex issues that these cases throw up, it is apparent that greater expertise is required in the handling of these cases. In addition, more research is needed which focuses exclusively upon this group, which has been largely neglected by research into attrition. Furthermore, specialist training for those dealing with such cases may be appropriate.

While attrition remains high and some groups appear to be disadvantaged by the criminal justice system, this research did find a relatively high level of commitment and concern among the police officers that participated. In line with Adler's (1991) findings, it was obvious that many officers had gone out of their way to support victims of rape. Indeed, many of the police officers were themselves very concerned about the progress of rape cases. They too suggested that further improvements within their own organization should be coupled with reforms within the CPS and the courts. Closer collaboration with the CPS and a greater understanding of rape victims, particularly by barristers and judges, were the two main areas they highlighted for further reform. With respect to the latter, a substantial body of work has shown that observers attribute both characterological and behavioural blame to rape survivors and that some differences in blaming the victim were found between men and women observers (e.g. Anderson 1999). Such research could usefully inform future changes.

In conclusion, this research aimed to update research on the attrition of rape cases as they progress through the criminal justice system by examining a large sample of recent cases. Despite the gloomy finding that attrition remains high and the observation that identifying factors associated with attrition is difficult, there are grounds for some optimism. Reforms aimed at reducing no-criming seem, generally speaking, to have had the required effect and many police officers participating in this study were clearly committed to supporting rape victims. However, perhaps one of the clearest findings of this research is that not enough is being done within the criminal justice system for victims of rape. More research into various facets of attrition, highlighted by this study, is needed urgently. Such research should facilitate the planning and development of further reform, within the police, the CPS and the courts. Without strategic reform, we will continue to fail victims of rape and sustain a culture in which getting away with rape is a sine qua non.

REFERENCES

ADLER, Z. (1991), 'Picking up the Pieces', *Police Review*, 31 May: 1114–15.

ANDERSON, I. (1999), 'Characterological and Behaviour Blame in Conversations about Male and Female Rape', *Journal of Language and Social Psychology*, 18/4: 377–94.

BRYDEN, D. P. and LENGNICK, S. (1997), 'Rape and the Criminal Justice System', *Journal of Criminal Law and Criminology*, 87/4: 1194–384.

ATTRITION IN RAPE CASES

CHAMBERS, G. and MILLER, A. (1986), *Prosecuting Sexual Assault.* Edinburgh: HMSO.

GRACE, S., LLOYD, C. and SMITH, L. (1992), *Rape: From Recording to Conviction*, Research and Planning Unit Paper 71. London: Home Office.

GREGORY, J. and LEES, S. (1996), 'Attrition of Rape and Sexual Assault Cases', *British Journal of Criminology*, 36: 1–17.

HARRIS, J. and GRACE, S. (1999), *A Question of Evidence? Investigating and Prosecuting Rape in the 1990s*, Home Office Research Study 196. London: Home Office.

HINCHCLIFFE, S. (2000), 'Rape Law Reform in Britain', *Society*, 37: 57–62.

KRAMER, E. J. (1998), 'When Men are Victims: Applying Rape Shield Laws to Male Same–Sex Rape', *New York University Law Review*, 73/1: 293–331.

LEES, S. (1993), 'Judicial Rape', *Women's Studies International Forum*, 16/1: 11–36.

——(1996), *Carnal Knowledge: Rape on Trial.* London: Hamish Hamilton.

LEES, S. and GREGORY, J. (1996), 'Attrition in Rape and Sexual Assault Cases in England and Wales', *British Journal of Criminology*, 36: 1–17.

——(1993), *Rape and Sexual Assault: A Study of Attrition.* Islington Council.

MEZEY, G. (1997), 'Review of Carnal Knowledge: Rape on Trial by Sue Lees', *Journal of Forensic Psychiatry*, 8/1: 240–3.

PHILIPS, C. and BROWN, D. (1998), *Entry Into the Criminal Justice System: A Survey of Police Arrests and Their Outcome.* London: Home Office.

PINO, N. W. and MEIER, R. F. (1999), 'Gender Differences in Rape Reporting', *Sex Roles*, 40: 979–90.

ROBERTS, J. V. (1996), 'Sexual Assaults in Canada: Recent Statistical Trends', *Queens Law Journal*, 21: 395–421.

RUMNEY, P. (2001), 'Male Rape in the Courtroom: Issues and Concerns', *Criminal Law Review*, 1: 205–13.

SMITH, L. J. F. (1989), *'Concerns about Rape'*, A Home Office Research and Planning Unit Report. London: Home Office.

TANG, K. (1998), 'Rape Law Reform in Canada: The Success and Limits of Legislation', *International Journal of Offender Therapy and Comparative Criminology*, 42/3: 258–70.

TEMKIN, J. (1999), 'Reporting Rape in London: A Qualitative Study', *The Howard Journal*, 38: 17–41.

——(1997), 'Plus ça change: Reporting Rape in the 90s', *British Journal of Criminology*, 37: 507–28.

——(1987), *Rape and the Legal Process.* Sweet and Maxwell: London.

WRIGHT, R. (1984), 'A Note on the Attrition of Rape', *British Journal of Criminology*, 24: 399–400.

Name Index